Handbook of
ASIAN AMERICAN
PSYCHOLOGY

Handbook of
ASIAN AMERICAN
PSYCHOLOGY

Lee C. Lee
Nolan W. S. Zane
Editors

SAGE Publications
International Educational and Professional Publisher
Thousand Oaks London New Delhi

For information:

SAGE Publications, Inc.
2455 Teller Road
Thousand Oaks, California 91320
E-mail: order@sagepub.com

SAGE Publications Ltd.
6 Bonhill Street
London EC2A 4PU
United Kingdom

SAGE Publications India Pvt. Ltd.
M-32 Market
Greater Kailash I
New Delhi 110 048 India

Printed in the United States of America

Library of Congress Cataloging-in-Publication Data

Main entry under title:

Handbook of Asian American psychology / edited by Lee C. Lee and
Nolan W. S. Zane.
    p. cm.
   Includes bibliographical references and index.
    ISBN 0-8039-4963-4 (alk. paper)
    1. Asian Americans—Psychology. 2. Asian Americans—Social
conditions. I. Lee, Lee C. II. Zane, Nolan W. S.
    E184.O6 H36 1998
    155.8'4951073—ddc21
                                              98-8967

This book is printed on acid-free paper.

99 00 01 02 03 10 9 8 7 6 5 4 3 2

Acquiring Editor:	Jim Nageotte
Editorial Assistant:	Heidi Van Middlesworth
Production Editor:	Sherrise M. Purdum
Editorial Assistant:	Denise Santoyo
Typesetter/Designer:	Danielle Dillahunt
Indexer:	Juniee Oneida
Cover Designer:	Candice Harman

TABLE OF CONTENTS

FOREWORD

I t is a pleasure to call attention to this volume by some brief comments. Research on ethnic minority issues might be said to have an initial start with an article by Dr. George I. Sanchez, in the *Journal of Applied Psychology*, in 1932 which challenged the research conclusions regarding the intelligence of Mexican American children. It was many years later before journals devoted to research on ethnic groups were established: the *Hispanic Journal of Behavioral Science* and the *Journal of Asian American Psychological Association* in 1979. In 1985, in recognition of the major role of scientific research, NIMH establishes funding mechanisms for support of ethnic minority focused research and ethnic minority investigators.

Today, ethnic minority psychology has visibility and acceptance both as a scholarly area, and an area of relevance to practitioners. As a scholarly area, ethnic minority psychology is now based on a foundation of scientific research findings. As a practitioner area, ethnic minority psychology provides the substance meeting the needs of those who would provide quality services to this population—a population which is rapidly becoming the majority. By the year 2000 more than one third of the population is expected to be ethnic minorities. A large segment of this population are the Asian Americans; over the ten year period from 1980 to 1990, while the White population has slowed to a 6.01% rate of growth, while in contrast the Asian American/Pacific Islander population has increased 107.71%.

With this expansion, Asian Americans are rapidly becoming a visible group in everyday encounters: they are our students, our neighbors, our colleagues, our customers, our employers, our clients. Traditional European structures must accept the urgent need to adjust in relevant ways the way in which education is delivered, the policies utilized in employment settings, the ways in which community and regional policies are developed,the ways in which our science is applied, and the attitudes and values which form the foundation for all aspects of our existing environments. The need has never been more urgent than today for our society to respond to the challenges from the changing demography of the United States. The *Handbook of Asian American Psychology* seeks to offer an understanding of Asian Americans through the lens of Asian American professionals.

Westerners have easily misunderstood and readily stereotyped Asian Americans, ranging from that of being handy gardeners, to computer geniuses, or from being the dangerous "yellow peril" to being the "model minority." Asian Americans themselves have been coping with their own personal identities, partly reflecting the Asian sub-group to which they belong, partly reflecting generational issues, and the challenges of assimilation or biculturalism. In some regards, there is no typical Asian American. Instead there are individuals from various Asian sub-groups, individuals from different generations, individuals who have become Westernized, individuals who have rejected their Asian backgrounds, and individuals who have embraced their ancestral cultural characteristics. Complexity is also added when Asian American characteristics can be understood as made up of at least three potentially independent components: attitudes or values, overt behavioral actions, and personal self-identity. The *Handbook of Asian American Psychology* discusses ways of conceptualizing Asian Americans in a way that takes into account these many variables and forces and complexities and in a way to avoid creating further stereotypes.

The Handbook recognizes the diversity within the term "Asian-American" while still attending to models for understanding and working with the individual sub-groups. Research, theoretical issues, and implications for applications are covered along with recognition of both stereotypes and the changing characteristics of existing ethnic sub-groups. The challenge to reach the editors' goal of designing a volume which avoids simple answers based on stereotypes, while still integrating research findings on Asian Americans, has been accepted by Asian American authors drawing from their personal and professional expertise. This volume is another milestone in the evolving history of ethnic minority psychology, and a major one for Asian American Psychology.

Dick Suinn,
President-elect 1998,
American Psychological Association
Colorado State University,
Fort Collins, CO

PREFACE

This book has been a long time in the making. The idea of having such a handbook was conceived back in the late 1980s when it was apparent that the Asian American population was exploding not only in size but also in diversity. The popular press was increasingly portraying Asian Americans as a homogeneous group, and much of that presented was within the context of many Asian stereotypes. The scientific inquiry into the psychological state of Asian America also grew, but the research often was narrowly confined within certain ethnic subgroups on disparate topics and was published in varied disciplinary journals. The mass of new material in various journals on different Asian American subgroups appeared incomprehensible, and it was believed that a secondary digest would be useful to assess the state of psychological research on Asian Americans. Other specialized handbooks on Asian Americans are appearing in recent years, but none in which the purpose, as in the current handbook, is to make available in a single source concrete integrative descriptions and evaluations of current research on all ethnic subgroups of Asian Americans. Although the objective was a comprehensive presentation of research on Asian Americans, it obviously is impossible to encompass all that has been done; thus, we have focused on topics that are particularly germane to the understanding of Asian America.

The volume begins with an overview of Asian America to provide a historical and contemporary context of U.S. societal treatment of Asians. It provides a basis for understanding the research findings presented in the subsequent chapters.

There is no greater requirement in psychological research than that of construct validity. The complex nature of doing research with Asian Americans amplifies this task. Chapter 2 examines construct validity by using Asian American ethnic identity as a base on which to build an argument concerning its importance when doing research with this population.

The understanding of family socialization; the states of children, youths, and the elderly; and the role of women all are critical issues essential to our understanding of Asian Americans. These are presented in Chapters 3, 4, 5, and 6, in which the authors integrate past research findings and identify gaps in knowledge. In some cases, models are generated for future research in the area. The diversity of familial patterns of the various ethnic subgroups is made apparent.

In recent years, interracial marriages have been on the rise in the United States. Chapter 7 presents data showing that the rise in interracial marriages also is the case for Asian Americans. Asian women are reported to have greater rates of out-marriages than those of men. Of course, with this rise in interracial marriage, multiracial Asian Americans are on the rise as well. Chapter 8 delineates issues central to the multiracial group and proposes that this demographic change in the Asian American population will have a lasting sociopolitical impact on the nation.

In many of the chapters of this volume, the issue of Asian American identity is discussed. Intertwined with this is the issue of ethnic identity. Chapter 9 examines the various identity models relevant for Asian American perspectives and proposes how cultural variables might affect these constructions.

There is no greater stereotype of Asian Americans than that of their superior academic achievement. Chapter 10 provides some hard data on these achievements and performance and raises the issue of validity of assessment. Given these early academic "successes" of Asian American youths, what are their later career interests and choices? Chapter 11 answers that question and examines how personality, familial, and societal variables affect work adjustment and career advancement.

Institutional racism has been present throughout recorded U.S. history, and when such racism has been sanctioned by the government in the form of laws, it also affects moral guidelines for behavior. The impact of early patterns of discrimination and racism and how they are alive and well as we prepare to enter the 21st century are delineated in Chapter 12. In Chapter 13, a concrete example of institutional racism, the internment of Japanese Americans during World War II, is presented. The chapter also examines how such acts have had long-term effects that affect the intergenerational relations of Japanese Americans.

There is a general belief that Asian Americans experience few mental health problems and do not need or use mental health services. There appears, however, to be little support for this notion. Chapter 14 examines issues of vulnerability, experience, manifestation, and prevalence of mental illness. Chapter 15 examines the problems of treatment and mental health services available to the diverse Asian American populations. Chapter 16 addresses issues of domestic violence focusing centrally on wife abuse, and Chapter 17 deals with issues of addictive behaviors. A recurrent theme in these chapters speaks to the issue of culture and its impact on diagnosis, availability and use of services, and treatment. The problem of construct validity is illustrated by many examples here as well.

This volume should provide insights into the diverse and varied nature of Asian American cultures and communities. It also should provide an auspicious opportunity for psychologists and others interested in the welfare of Asian America. As the Asian American population further multiplies, so will the need for understanding. It is imperative that scholars undertaking research to further this understanding do so with culturally appropriate measures so that the knowledge gained is valid. It is our hope that this volume will encourage more scholars and students to undertake the many tasks that are needed and forge new inroads toward a greater understanding of the full spectrum of the various Asian American communities.

This handbook is truly the product of a collaborative effort between the editors, who shared equally in the responsibilities of this work. More important, this work reflects the collective effort of each chapter's contributors, who demonstrated exceptional scholarship as well as persistence and patience in helping us bring this handbook to completion. We are greatly indebted to them and thank them for their willingness to write, rewrite, and update their chapters. Many thanks go to the reviewers of chapters: Peter Chi, Eunice Dong, John Doris, Katrina Greene, Margaret Lay-Dopyra, Sarah Johnson, Cybelle Raver, Rajiv Rawat, Henry Ricciuti, and Michael Thornton. Special thanks are due to Denise Saludares, who did all the essential support work for the editors. Special thanks also are due to our editor, Jim Nageotte, whose patience and gentle prodding finally helped bring the book to production. Lastly, we appreciate the support and continued faith that our publisher, Sage Publications, has shown in this long but, in the end, immensely rewarding process.

Lee C. Lee
Nolan W. S. Zane

AN OVERVIEW

LEE C. LEE

*People must realize that there really isn't such a thing as an
Asian American. There are Chinese, Koreans, Japanese,
Vietnamese, Indians, and so forth. So many different cultures.
So many different experiences. We need to understand their
differences and complexities, their successes and failures. The
first priority for Americans is to learn more about Asia.*

I. M. Pei, Chinese American architect

During the decade between 1980 and 1990, the Asian American population increased by more than 95%, from 3,726,440 to 7,273,662. According to mid-census estimates, more than 9 million Americans consider themselves of Asian descent. That figure will pass 12 million by the year 2000, boosted in large measure by the continuing strength of Asian immigration through the 1990s. By 2050, the Asian American population will swell to more than 40 million, constituting more than 10% of the total U.S. population. Despite its relatively small size, it already is playing a large and visible role in American society (Day, 1993).

The vast ethnic, racial, economic, and social diversity of Asians living in the United States renders any exhaustive survey of their history, culture, and socioeconomic status extremely difficult. But in spite of these difficulties, this chapter attempts to present a brief historical overview that might assist the reader's effort to contextualize the Asian American experience. Furthermore, it highlights selected current events and recent demographic data that can help clarify the present status of Asian Americans. Although far from complete and exhaustive, it endeavors to introduce some important aspects of Asian American life that should provide a context or working framework for exploring topics in subsequent chapters.

"A STORY IN SEVERAL ACTS": THE LONG HISTORY OF ASIANS IN AMERICA[1]

Asian American history can be divided into three distinct periods for Chinese, Japanese, Koreans, Filipinos, and Asian Indians: the early years of labor migration, the interim period of settlement and consolidation of communities, and the post-1965 immigration surge. Although diverse in timing, numbers, and level of entrenchment in American society, these groups' migration patterns remained somewhat parallel for each of these nationalities, particularly in the early years of labor migration. By contrast, most Indochinese arrivals date from 1975 and America's involvement in the Vietnam war, whereas other Asian immigrants such as Thais, Malaysians, Sri Lankans, Pakistanis, and Bangladeshis have reached the United States even more recently. As yet, little research on these newly arrived immigrants has been undertaken.

Antecedents

The first Asians to reach North America in the modern era might have been galley slaves on Spanish, Portuguese, Dutch, and English vessels that plied the ocean waters in search of trade. In the 1760s, Chinese and Filipino sailors founded settlements in Louisiana and came to be called Manilamen. South Asians and Malaysians arrived on English ships, served as indentured servants on the American East Coast, and joined African American communities in the 1780s and 1790s (Okihiro, 1994).

By the mid-1800s, Asian laborers were being brought over to work plantations scattered throughout the Americas and Pacific Islands. "Coolie" trade flourished after the British ban on slavery in 1833. The slave trade also had declined with the advent of the abolitionist movement in the northern United States. Coolie servitude, although less permanent than slavery, incorporated many similar practices and served the same purposes. Coolie transport ships were overcrowded and filthy. Mortality rates often exceeded 30% on long sea voyages. Sickness, brutality, and suicide stalked the workers. Treated like nothing more than human chattel, coolies sought liberation at the earliest possible opportunity, although chances of escaping bonded labor often remained slim. To this day, the descendants of these Asian populations live in the Caribbean and Latin America; thus, one half of Trinidad's and Guyana's population remains Indian. Chinese populations are found in several Latin American countries, and most remarkably, the president of Peru is of Japanese descent.

Labor and Immigration

The first large contingents of modern Asians to arrive on U.S. soil proper sought their fortunes on *Gam San* or Gold Mountain. During the 1849 California Gold Rush, impoverished Chinese miners from present-day Guangdong and Fujian provinces crossed the Pacific, leaving their wives and families behind. Although intending to return to China, many decided to remain because southern China at the time was wracked with famine, pestilence, overcrowding, natural calamities, political turmoil, and Western penetration.

In the 1860s, railroad companies found in the Chinese a cheap and skilled supply of labor that could help finish the transcontinental lines at minimum cost. In 1868, the United States concluded a treaty with China that allowed for the unlimited movement of labor. Chinese workers proved themselves to be especially adept at blasting and tunneling. More than 1,000 Chinese railroad workers lost their lives building the transcontinental railroad lines. The exact number never will be known. Many more suffered hardship on termination of their contracts. Unemployed and without the fare to travel back west, hundreds starved to death trekking along the tracks in search of work. Some found work as tenant farmers, yet most streamed back into the Chinatowns on the West Coast. Driven out of most other industries, a significant number founded laundries across the West. By the 1870s, the American public was clamoring for restrictions on Chinese immigration. In response, the 1875 Page Law prohibited so-called coolie labor from entry to the mainland.

Unlike the Chinese, whose national government was disintegrating, Japanese immigrants benefited from a strong state that looked after their affairs. Following the Meiji Restoration of 1868, Japanese migrants began settling in Hawaii. Although a few ventured over to the continental United States, their numbers were small until the passage of the Chinese Exclusion Act in 1882. With the effective end of Chinese immigration, demand for Japanese labor increased dramatically and large-scale immigration began in earnest. The passage of the 1900 Organic Law that abolished contract labor in Hawaii prompted further increases in Japanese immigration to the mainland United States. Although initially forming bachelor societies of male laborers similar to those of the Chinese, Japanese American communities benefited greatly from the Gentlemen's Agreement of 1907. This U.S.-Japan accord restricted Japanese and Korean labor yet permitted unlimited immigration of wives and family members. As a consequence, fully functional communities were formed and laid the groundwork for integration into mainstream American society.

Missionaries played an instrumental role in the early years of Korean immigration. Fully 40% of these early immigrants were Christian, and many more converted on settling in Hawaii or the West Coast. The time frame of Korean immigration was short as Japan officially annexed Korea in 1910, and thus Korea was bound by the Gentlemen's Agreement between Japan and the United States. Among early Korean Americans, the Japanese occupation of their mother country would dominate their experience and political life. Korean families sacrificed a great deal for the cause of Korean independence. The first president of South Korea drew much of his early support from Korean Americans.

Although Spain ceded the Philippines to the United States during the Spanish-American war, bitter fighting continued for several years between American forces and Filipino guerrillas. By the time the hostilities subsided, thousands of people had died and the Philippines were annexed to the United States. As new American nationals, Filipinos did not face the same legal barriers to immigration as did other Asians. Plantation owners began procuring Filipino labor for that other American Pacific possession, Hawaii, to fill the workforce vacuum created by the Chinese Exclusion Act and the Gentlemen's Agreement. In time, Filipinos supplanted Japanese as the largest ethnic group in the Hawaiian islands.

Early Asian Indians had to travel farther and wider to settle in America. No direct steamship service existed between Indian ports and the American West. As such, Asian Indians tended to migrate to Canada, although this movement was terminated in 1908 through a series of legislative actions. Although Canada could not easily deprive fellow subjects of the British Empire of their rights, Canada could actively discourage and prevent their landing on Canadian shores. Many Asian Indians moved south to the United States from 1907 to 1910 because the Gentlemen's Agreement had opened a small window of opportunity for labor. These laborers/settlers were primarily Sikhs from the Punjab region of India. As police and soldiers employed by the British all over its empire—in Hong Kong and Shanghai as well as at trade missions, embassies, and military posts—these former peasants learned of the opportunities available in the Americas. A large portion of them eventually found work as lumberjacks and farmworkers.

The great San Francisco earthquake of 1906 had the fortuitous effect of opening California's doors to immigration of family members. Because fire gutted practically all of the city's municipal archives, authorities lost all birth records and thus the citizenship status of Chinese residents. Consequently, Chinese men could declare themselves citizens without fear of contradictory evidence. Furthermore, they could bring over relatives, long denied entry by immigration policy.

By 1917, pressure again was mounting to curtail immigration. In 1924, the National Origins Act established guidelines that effectively barred all Asians except Filipino nationals from immigration. Ten years later, Congress enacted the Tydings-McDuffie Act, which established a timetable for the Philippines' independence while, in the meantime, reducing Filipino immigration to a trickle.

Societal values, as expressed in legislative activities, often have profound impacts on members of society. Figure 1.1 traces the impacts of U.S. legislation on the immigration of Asians from 1820 to 1990, and it is quite evident that the ebb and flow of Asian immigration to the United States closely followed historic legislative events.

Reaction and Strife

As is apparent, Asian immigration to the United States was fraught with difficulties. The first American immigration law of 1790 ascribed citizenship and

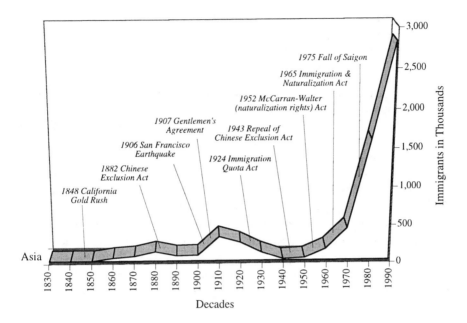

Figure 1.1. Significant U.S. Events and Asian Immigration, 1820-1990
SOURCE: U.S. Immigration and Naturalization Service (1991, pp. 28-31).

naturalization rights only to "free White males." As early as 1853, California imposed the Foreign Miner's Tax as a punitive fine on Chinese and Mexican miners. This resentment toward gold prospecting and extraction by non-White foreigners would manifest itself in countless subsequent clashes between Whites and Asians.

That same year, San Francisco's Chinatown population swelled to more than 25,000. Although the Chinese initially were greeted warmly by town officials, the growing aggregate prompted outcries from city newspapers throughout the West over the apparent tide. Two years later, the White residents in the Puget Sound area of Washington conducted the first of several forced expulsions of Asians from Tacoma and Seattle. In later years, concerns over unfair economic competition would prompt much unrest among the White working class. With the completion of the transcontinental railroad lines and economic depression of the 1870s, public anger over the railroad barons' policies and greed boiled over in scapegoating. In a series of violent nativist reactions, anti-Asian agitators inspired reprisals against Asians throughout the West. In 1871, White mobs rampaged through Los Angeles's Chinatown, lynching 23 Chinese or more than 10% of the city's 200 Chinese inhabitants. During a bitter labor dispute in 1885, White immigrant miners in Rock Springs, Wyoming, killed 28 Chinese and drove the rest out of town. So severe was the violence that federal troops intervened to restore order. In the same year, race riots erupted in Tacoma and Seattle, killing at least 5 more people and forcing the beleaguered Chinese residents out in a repeat of the 1855 expulsions. Mark Twain commented on the consequences of this national hate directed against the Chinese:

He [the Chinese] is a great convenience to everybody, even to the worst class of White men, for he bears the most of their sins, suffering fines for their petty thefts, imprisonment for their robberies, and death for their murders. Any White man can swear a Chinaman's life away in the courts, but no Chinaman can testify against a White man. Ours is the "land of the free"—nobody denies that, nobody challenges it. . . . As I write, news comes that in broad daylight in San Francisco, some boys have stoned an inoffensive Chinaman to death, and that although a large crowd witnessed the shameful deed, no one interfered. (Twain, 1872, pp. 391-393)

Such scapegoating likewise dogged all the Asian groups through the early 20th century. In 1907 and 1908, White mobs drove hundreds of Asian Indian farmworkers from their communities in Bellingham, Washington, and Live Oak, California, respectively. In 1913, Whites threatened Korean laborers with violence if they did not leave Riverside County, California. Attempts also were made in the 1920s and 1930s to drive Filipinos from parts of the West. In 1930, a 4-day riot in Watsonville, California, ended in the murder of a Filipino worker by enraged Whites. Violent anti-Asian sentiment expressed itself in similar incidents throughout the West and eventually culminated in the deportation or incarceration of the entire West Coast Japanese American population during World War II.

In the early years of Asian immigration, women were rare. Although skewed sex ratios prevailed throughout most migrant labor groups in the "wild West," cultural, geographic, and political factors were particularly effective in discouraging Asian women from joining their menfolk. From the 1850s to 1870s, bars and brothels served the Chinese laborer bachelor societies. During these rough-and-tumble times, the majority of women transported to America served as prostitutes. Mostly children of impoverished families, these poor women were tricked or sold into prostitution and were transported overseas by unscrupulous and deceitful traders.

Fully 61% of Chinese women in the American West were engaged in prostitution by 1870. Venereal diseases, violence, suicide, debasement, and humiliation deepened the desperate and wretched status of these women. Eventually, the authorities came to see all Chinese women as possible prostitutes and barred their entry in 1875. Prostitution declined as more women became engaged in domestic work and as more entered the country as wives of merchants exempt from previous exclusion laws.

By the 1900 census, the ratio of Chinese men to women dropped to 26:1. However, Chinese American communities remained primarily bachelor societies for a long time. By the 1930s, Chinatown populations began to decline as older men passed away. Their abandoned wives in China grieved as few men were able to return to China owing to reentry difficulties and the onerous steamship fares. For Sikh men, sex ratios were even more skewed. Many married Mexican women as only a small handful brought their wives from India. Some Filipino laborers skirted anti-miscegenation laws and married European women, but many more remained single and alone.

With the passage of the Gentlemen's Agreement of 1907, Japanese and Korean women arrived in America in increasing numbers through the 1920s. Although further male migration was halted, wives and picture brides joined their husbands, stabilizing the sex ratio at more balanced levels. Many of these women found employment outside of the home in the agricultural sector. Others worked in the fishery industry. Some worked alongside their husbands. As a result, more traditional communities flourished and a new generation, the Nisei, came into its own.

The War Brides Act of 1945 brought new vitality to some Asian communities. Chinese and Filipino servicemen took particular advantage of the law and rejuvenated male-dominated communities with new families.

Responses

As the 20th century dawned, the Chinese population became increasingly urbanized in response to anti-Asian agitation and the resulting displacement from rural, resource-driven communities. Ghettoization began in major cities such as San Francisco, Los Angeles, and New York. Former prospectors eventually were driven out of most other industries yet found a niche in the laundry business. Merchants serving communities with food stocks and textiles from China provided a measure of familiar comforts in a strange land.

Legislative limitations on Asian business opportunities came in the form of restrictive land laws. In 1913, the state of California enacted the Alien Land Act that prohibited land ownership by noncitizens. Similar legislation was passed throughout most of the western states. This forced Asian farmers to circumvent the law to hold onto their land.

Although a handful of Asian immigrants gained citizenship through regular channels, naturalization was, for the most part, prohibited. Even after the Civil War, when American males of African descent gained some rights of citizenship, Asians remained noncitizens. Court decisions in 1878, 1922, and 1923 barred in swift succession Chinese, Japanese, and Asian Indian immigrants, respectively, from gaining citizenship and full equal rights in the United States. Such policies posed serious questions about racial justice throughout the country. Immigration, religious freedom, school segregation, the franchise, interracial marriage, equal representation before the law, and discriminatory taxes and fees all were major concerns for Asian American groups. Asian Americans actively challenged unjust or odious laws and did not stand idly by as mere passive victims.

The Chinese formed mutual aid societies within their concentrated Chinatown communities. The most powerful of these was established in 1862 as the Chinese Consolidated Benevolent Association. Initially intended to look after the affairs of Chinese residents in Chinatowns, it was later organized throughout North America. Other groups contending for space were the *Tongs*, secret fraternal organizations that were, unfortunately, often caught up in illicit and illegal activities.

Japanese Americans drew on their communities' considerable strength to form the Japanese American Citizens League. Composed mostly of *Nisei* (second-generation Japanese Americans), the members were well educated and politically articulate. However, the strength of the Japanese American community was shattered and members were dispersed across America by their traumatic internment experience during World War II.

NEW BEGINNINGS

World War II proved to be a watershed moment in Asian American history. Not only was the Chinese Exclusion Act repealed, but long withheld naturalization rights were conferred to all Asian groups through the 1952 McCarran-Walter Act. However, tiny quotas remained, allowing only a select few to enter the country. Therefore, between 1945 and 1965, many of the Asians arriving in America were highly educated skilled professionals, academics, and students.

As the United States took center stage in world affairs, it no longer could afford a parochial, exclusionary immigration policy. At the height of the civil rights era, Congress finally abolished national origins quotas. The Immigration and Naturalization Act of 1965 came to represent the first effectively nonracist immigration act in American history.

The Asian American population skyrocketed over the following decades as communities were reconstituted and new ones were born (see Figures 1.1 and 1.2). Figure 1.2 presents U.S. census data from 1980 and 1990. It not only shows the tremendous population growth but also demonstrates that this growth was fed differentially by the various ethnic subgroups. Few Japanese arrived during these years as the robustness of the Japanese economy retained its people. Many more Koreans and Asian Indians immigrated in the same period, boosting their respective communities' populations from negligible before 1965 to practically the same as that of the Japanese by 1990. Chinese and Filipino immigration figures remained considerably higher.

The post-World War II era also had dramatically increased American involvement in Asia. With the occupation of Japan, the cold war with the People's Republic of China, the onset of the Korean and Vietnam conflicts, and the continued military presence in the Philippines and Taiwan, Asia loomed large in the American psyche. The fate of Asia was thus intertwined with the fate of Asian Americans.

Many Asian newcomers were fleeing increasing turmoil in Asia. The Korean conflict created enormous dislocation in that country, and the reconstruction of South Korea involved an ongoing American presence. Japanese, Korean, Vietnamese, and Filipino wives of American GIs began following their husbands to the United States. In addition, American families accepted war orphans into their homes, a precursor to the contemporary trend of childless American couples adopting Asian children. By 1975, refugees from war-torn Southeast Asia began arriving in significant numbers for the first time in American history.

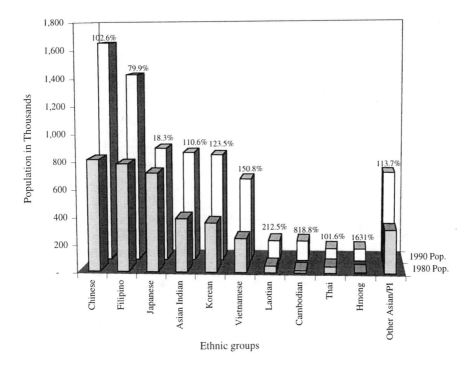

Figure 1.2. Asian American Population: Changes Between 1980 and 1990
SOURCE: U.S. Bureau of the Census (1980, 1990).
NOTE: PI = Pacific Islander.

The Vietnam war had an enormous impact on all of Indochina. Indeed, the war spanned three decades. In the end, those who had sided with the United States, feared the Communist government, or sought a better life elsewhere fled their devastated homeland. Seeking refuge in surrounding countries and Western nations, the flow continued unabated well into the 1980s.

By 1979, the refugee situation had reached a crisis point. The United Nations and the Vietnamese government established the Orderly Departure Program for the systematic processing of refugees and settlement of safe havens around the world. American assistance encouraged sponsorship by volunteer agencies that largely consisted of church service committees. These groups helped settle Vietnamese, Cambodian, Laotian, and Hmong refugees in cities and towns across America. Their work was indispensable in aiding this group of immigrants to adapt to U.S. society. As a group, the Southeast Asians had the largest percentage of population increase between 1980 and 1990, as can be seen in Figure 1.2—from the low of a 150% increase of Vietnamese to the high of a 1,631% increase of Hmong ethnicity.

Given the rapid growth and high immigration rate of the Asian and Pacific Islander population in the past decade, it is not surprising that this fastest-growing

TABLE 1.1.   Selected Economic Characteristics of Asian American Households in 1993

Group	Per Capita Median Income		Per Household Median Income		Percentage of Three or More Earners in Household	
	National	West	National	West	National	West
Asian	15,691	14,609	38,346 (1,981)	37,083 (2,733)	12.70	13.50
White	17,204	19,739	34,172 (200)	37,045 (446)	9.80	9.40
All groups	15,777	16,441	31,240 (146)	33,737 (392)	9.90	10.40

SOURCE: U.S. Bureau of the Census (1995).
NOTE: Standard errors are in parentheses.

group in the United States is 66% foreign born or that a little over 38% of this group are naturalized citizens (U.S. Bureau of the Census, 1997). Members of this group reside mostly in the western region of the United States (57.6%), with almost equal proportions living in the Northeast (17.5%) and the South (16.7%); only 8.2% live in the Midwest. A majority of Asian Americans (94.7%), regardless of region of residence, live in metropolitan areas, with 42% living in central cities. The size of Asian American households tends to be larger than the national norm, with 18.3% of households having five or more persons compared to the national norm of 10%. Asian American households also have a lower (16%) incidence of one-person households compared to the national norm of 23%. Approximately 57% of Asian Americans own homes compared to 73% of White Americans who own homes (U.S. Bureau of the Census, 1995). Their per capita income is lower than the national norm and substantially lower than that of White Americans, as seen in Table 1.1. It is interesting to note that although the median per capita income increases substantially for the national and White samples of Americans residing in the West, this is not the case for Asian Americans. In fact, their per capita median income is less for residents who live in the West than for those who live in the East. Much has been made of the fact that Asian Americans' median household income is the highest in the nation. Indeed, Table 1.1 supports this assertion. However, it is important to ascertain the number of individuals who contribute to this household income. As can be seen, Asian Americans have the highest percentage of three or more earners per household when compared to the national and White samples. Furthermore, households in the West have higher median income for the national and White samples; however, Asian American households in the West have lower median household income than does the national Asian American sample. Because almost 60% of Asian Americans live in the West and more than 94% live in metropolitan areas where the cost of living is highest, it is thus important to place income data within the context of their residence. These basic descriptors of Asian American households have ramifications when general statistics are used to describe and verify the successes of Asian Americans.

CONTEMPORARY ISSUES

Asian Americans have been hailed as the "model minority" by the media for more than three decades. This national conception has created images of Asian Americans within U.S. society that have significant implications for the social and psychological well-being of Asian Americans. Unlike the portrayal of Whites, which is diverse enough to allow audiences to recognize stereotypes for the stock characterizations that they are, the portrayal of Asians tends to be limited in range and depth. This feeds into the ignorance of those audiences where stereotypes become truths that are viewed as universally applicable to all Asians and Asian Americans alike, regardless of individual circumstances.

It was no coincidence that the birth of the model minority stereotype occurred at the height of the civil rights movement, a time when the Black citizens of this nation were making headway with their demands for equal rights and equal opportunity. In this context, the "uncomplaining Chinese" were used as a model for other "more recalcitrant minorities." Given the fact that the achievements of Asian Americans had not changed for many years preceding this period, one must ask whether the image of the model minority was conceived in celebration of Asian Americans' achievements or as a means of undermining the civil rights movement.

Like other visible minorities, Asian Americans face the danger of always being perceived within the narrow confines of stereotypes. The repercussions resonate through the way in which society deals with Asian Americans as minorities and as individuals. The current seemingly innocuous success images suggest that a comparable change in Asian Americans' social and political status ought to have occurred. This has not happened. In fact, the mid-census estimate of the U.S. Bureau of Census report on the relationship of 1993 earnings and educational attainment shows that Asian Americans have not been able to reap benefits from education comparable to those reaped by most Americans. Table 1.2 indicates that in three of the four educational attainment categories, Asian Americans have lower earnings than the national and White samples. The one category in which Asian Americans have slightly higher earnings is that of "some college or associate degree." However, in examining this table, it is important to note that in every category, the Asian American population's standard error is extremely large. In fact, this is the case for almost all statistics presented by the U.S. Bureau of the Census and is particularly evident in comparisons with other ethnic groups (see Table 1.1). This is one indicator of the diversity of the Asian American population. It is clear that there are some Asian Americans that might fit the model minority image, but many do not.

Curiously enough, one consequence of these positive images is that Asian Americans are now excluded from many entitlement programs such as affirmative action programs and social services designed specifically to meet the needs of Asian Americans. Another much grimmer consequence has been the increase in anti-Asian violence in U.S. society today (U.S. Commission on Civil Rights, 1992).

TABLE 1.2. Earnings by Educational Attainment, Region, and Race

Group	Not a High School Graduate		High School Graduate		Some College or Associate Degree		Bachelor's Degree or More	
	National	West	National	West	National	West	National	West
Asian	14,459 (1,940)	15,526 (3,136)	21,076 (792)	22,893 (1,679)	29,481 (1,556)	30,815 (1,679)	36,844 (1,323)	35,750 (2,040)
White	19,022 (431)	20,767 (1,174)	24,124 (212)	25,579 (380)	27,932 (325)	29,878 (621)	41,094 (184)	42,649 (907)
All groups	17,020 (180)	16,352 (335)	22,719 (198)	24,323 (480)	27,003 (143)	28,836 (654)	40,240 (174)	41,418 (378)

SOURCE: U.S. Bureau of the Census (1995).
NOTE: Standard errors are in parentheses.

Resurgence of Anti-Asian Violence

With the advent of the 1990s, Asian Americans have rapidly emerged as an important minority in the United States, yet not all have accepted their growing presence with tolerance and accommodation. Racism and anti-Asian violence, once the purview of yesterday's bitter labor disputes, have resurfaced in recent years in various guises. With the mass immigration of thousands of newcomers since 1965, America's racial dynamics have changed fundamentally. Readily identifiable scapegoats for periodic economic recessions and intensifying labor competition have once more fueled anti-immigration sentiment. Resentment of economic gains made by newcomers also has added to the mix, further troubling communities coping with cultural friction and social adjustment. This state of affairs has prompted intolerance and hate crimes over the past two decades. Several Asian Americans have been murdered and countless more have been harassed, intimidated, or assaulted (U.S. Commission on Civil Rights, 1992). In 1982, two unemployed auto workers in Detroit, Michigan, killed Vincent Chin, a Chinese American. Ironically, they assumed he was Japanese and blamed him for their lost jobs. An assailant in Raleigh, North Carolina, attempted to avenge his brother's death in Vietnam by murdering Jim Ming Hai Loo in 1989. After a campaign of violent intimidation directed at Asian Indians in Jersey City, New Jersey, a gang killed Navroze Mody in 1987. In 1990, skinheads murdered Hung Truong in Houston, Texas. In 1992, a Japanese American was stabbed to death by another unemployed White. In Stockton, California, a deranged gunman opened fire with an assault rifle, killing five Indochinese children and wounding 30 others.

Apart from these spectacular cases, Asian Americans have encountered neighborhood conflicts in which the lines between victim and victimizer have blurred. The infamous Flatbush grocery store boycotts and Los Angeles riots are seared into the American psyche. More than 2,000 Korean-owned businesses were looted and torched in the days following the Rodney King verdict. Ironically, a majority of these stores served inner-city clientele that most other small business owners had abandoned. Nevertheless, they became the primary targets of rampaging mobs, seething with resentment and rage at the economic and legal injustices they had experienced.

Vandalism to houses of worship, selective enforcement of regulations, and harassment by the authorities also have alarmed Asian American communities. The recent scrutiny of Asian American campaign donations has adversely affected Asian Americans in that much of the general public has again failed to discern the difference between citizens and foreigners. This long-standing confusion has been at the heart of several discriminatory practices over the years. As succinctly noted by the U.S. Commission on Civil Rights (1992), "The perception of Asian Americans as foreigners may also impede their acceptance in all areas of their lives and contribute to subtle as well as overt forms of discrimination against them in education, employment, and other areas" (p. 20). From restrictive immigration laws to Japanese American internment, early perceptions of Asian Americans as transient residents effectively rendered them second-class citizens. Although

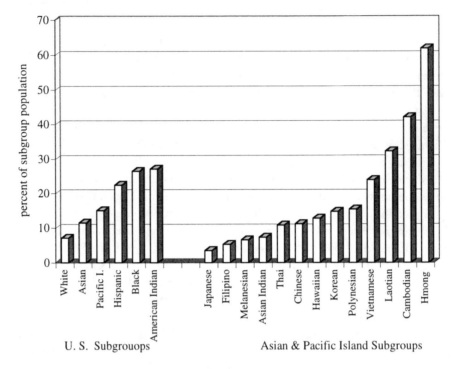

Figure 1.3. Percentage of Families Living in Poverty by Ethnicity in 1990
SOURCE: U.S. Bureau of the Census (1990).
NOTE: Pacific I. = Pacific Islander.

less severe and less brazenly prejudiced than reactions of the past, today's perceptions have led to discrimination and violence. Recent events suggest that such tenacious views will continue to affect Asian Americans well into the future.

Social and Economic Issues

By the mid-1990s, much discussion had ensued over affirmative action policies in place across the country. Asian Americans were caught in the middle, some arguing that Asians would benefit from dropping race as a factor in university admissions. Indeed, on University of California campuses alone, Asian Americans make up 36% of the student bodies, far above and beyond their proportion of the state's population (9.5%) ("The Ruling Class," 1994). This apparent overabundance in academia has prompted universities and businesses alike to narrow affirmative action objectives to supporting "underrepresented minorities" only, a deliberate move to exclude Asian Americans from intended remedies to institutional racism in hiring and admission processes.

Unfortunately, this debate has overshadowed the harsh realities of many Asian American families' lives. In 1990, the U.S. census recorded the poverty rate of Asian Americans to be almost twice that of White Americans but far less than those of other minority groups. However, when the Asian American population is separated into the various ethnic groups, an enormous disparity becomes readily apparent. Figure 1.3 shows that in 1990, the poverty rates across the various ethnic groups that make up Asian America were very disparate. On the low end are the Japanese and Filipino American ethnic groups with poverty rates far lower than those of other American subgroups, whereas the Southeast Asians have poverty rates above 30%, 40%, and 60% for Laotians, Cambodians, and Hmongs, respectively. The high percentages of these ethnic groups living in poverty are far above those of most Americans.

Looking at the breakdown of poverty rates for the different ethnic groups only gives a broad brushstroke picture of the overall economic condition in the various Asian American communities. It does not present the total picture of the diversity within each community. In large cities, where the largest concentrations of Asian Americans are clustered, poverty is endemic. For example, the Chinese ethnic group's poverty rate is well below that of other minorities, as can be seen in Figure 1.3. But the diversity of earnings for this ethnic group is great. In fact, most Chinatowns have wards just as poor as African American ghettos or Hispanic barrios. Unfortunately, these pockets of poverty have escaped the notice of the general American public. In San Francisco, 33% of all families living in poverty are Asian Pacific Islander Americans (Guillermo, 1996). Although this is just slightly higher than their proportion (30%) of the city's overall population, these figures do reflect a level of impoverishment that upends many model minority myths. Yip (1996) reported that in 1990, more than 11% of California's Asian American and Pacific Islander children lived in poverty. That year, more than 200,000 Asian American children relied on funding from Aid to Families with Dependent Children (U.S. General Accounting Office, 1990). Just 3 years later, in 1993, the percentage jumped to 17%. This represents approximately 358,000 Asian American children living in poverty throughout the United States (U.S. Bureau of the Census, 1995).

Language barriers and inadequate political representation only perpetuate these conditions. Approximately 22.4% of Asian and Pacific Islander Americans between 18 and 64 years of age cannot communicate in English. More than half of the elderly (53.5% of those age 65 years or over), who have the greatest need for social services, cannot converse in English (Yoon & Chien, 1995). In San Francisco, 39% of Asian American children do not feel comfortable enough with English to succeed academically (Guillermo, 1996).

Very few Americans beyond the Asian American communities are aware of the extraordinary problems confronting several Asian American ethnic groups. For most Southeast Asians, their journeys to America were marked by fear and trepidation. Their hurried departures from war zones—the leaving of families, homes, and belongings to their unknown fates—have caused enormous psychological dislocation. Thousands experienced terrifying ordeals during the war years, and many now suffer along with Vietnam veterans from various forms of posttraumatic stress disorder. The Hmong, perhaps affected the most by their wholesale relocation from tribal life in Laos to modernity in America, have suffered greatly.

In addition, the highly variable and almost bimodal occupational status of Asian American populations disguises the real hardship of many who struggle at the bottom of the economic ladder. Model minority identities such as the jet-set investment firm banker, engineer, or doctor dominate media stereotypes of Asian Americans. A high percentage of Asian American professionals do indeed fulfill these roles. For many Asian American women, however, such perceptions are particularly misleading. Although most Americans have accepted the ubiquity and high visibility of Asian American anchorwomen on the nightly news, few have noticed the thousands of women who struggle every day to provide for their families. Although Chinese restaurants, long a fixture of American cultural life, employ many Chinese men and women as cooks, waiters, and waitresses, the *dim sum* that many Americans enjoy are prepared by women who are mostly paid below minimum wage. Most work 12-hour days, 6 days a week, with low wages and without benefits or paid leave. Similar conditions prevail in Korean, Vietnamese, and Indian restaurants as well. In New York City alone, only 10 out of 1,400 Chinese restaurants are unionized (Asian American/Pacific Islander in Philanthropy, 1992).

Asian American women have worked as low-wage garment workers and assembly line factory workers for decades. In recent years, sweatshops have proliferated throughout major urban centers. In the United States, most are concentrated in New York City's Chinatown, where cheap, exploitable, nonunionized labor always has been widely available (Asian Women United of California [AWUC], 1989). Although a relic of the early 20th century, sweatshops have been revived in the 1990s with the emergence of new global economic forces. In isolated Third World pockets in the United States, Asian and Hispanic American women have borne the brunt of plummeting working conditions. New immigrants, many illegal and indebted to their smugglers, have gravitated to these employment centers, locking them into a cycle of poverty akin to indentured labor.

These hardships have taken their tolls on families. Work-related stress among the Asian American working class and underclass has exacerbated domestic tensions. Adjustment difficulties and challenges to traditional relations have troubled many marriages. Indeed, domestic violence afflicts all classes of Asian American families. Shelters for battered Asian women and Asian women's community centers have opened in a few cities across North America to address the particular needs of Asian victims. Children have borne a particularly heavy burden of mediating for their families and at the same time coping with their own traumas (AWUC, 1989).

Likewise, interracial marriages have their share of problems. Issues of dependency, subservience, inequality, abuse, and cultural conflict have plagued many such relationships. For women accompanying U.S. servicemen to America, adjustment was difficult. These war brides often were alienated from the broader Asian American community. Settling in the vicinity of military bases scattered throughout the country, such women remain to this day an invisible minority. Some "mail-order brides" endure similar conditions. Because men relying on these services ordinarily seek docile, submissive, and compliant women from the

Far East, these marriages encourage traditionally restrictive gender roles. Distressingly, their relative obscurity has contributed to sparse support services that are available to them. Such services are necessary to stem the high domestic violence rates among these types of marriages.

Many Identities

Awareness of Asian American issues was inspired in part by the struggle of college students in the 1960s and early 1970s. At a time of democratic renewal and self-discovery for Americans in general, Asian Americans rediscovered their roots and challenged long-held practices and beliefs in their respective communities. As the racial overtones of the Vietnam war became glaringly apparent, radicalized Asian Americans no longer could resign themselves to another destructive war in Asia. Their participation in the antiwar movement signaled their newfound understanding. Consequently, activists pursued the ideals of self-determination, an end to institutional racism, and the establishment of ethnic studies programs for all minorities. Asian Americans gained a sense of themselves as proud Americans with their own culture and history. Indeed, they defined themselves as Asian Americans for the first time, reaching out and allying with other Asian ethnic groups who shared their experiences. This political awakening translated into very real and effective efforts to address pressing issues in their own communities. Activists established health and welfare projects, English language training programs, and youth centers (Wei, 1993). Although wary of traditional conservative organizations such as the Consolidated Benevolent Associations and the Japanese American Citizens League, the new generation nevertheless proved instrumental in reinvigorating Asian American life. Just as many American Indians, Chicano Americans, and African Americans demonstrated their commitment to helping their communities, so did Asian American students as they strove for a sense of place in America. The dedication and idealism of the movement eventually led to the founding of Asian American studies programs throughout the country. In recent years, students have gone to the ramparts again for ethnic studies programs and represent a new generation striving for self-realization (Wei, 1993).

Today's generation of young Asian Americans represents a wide spectrum of experiences and social classes. The Asian American identity of the 1960s and 1970s has been supplanted by a diverse collage of dramatically different philosophies and approaches to American life. With new ethnic groups and communities joining the fray, the Asian American narrative has become much more rich and complicated than ever before.

Lee (1996), in a Philadelphia high school study, found at least four attitudes among Asian American students. Only a small segment held values similar to those of the 1960s generation of Asian American activists that contributed so much to modern Asian American studies. Many more represented themselves as hard-working, self-reliant immigrants who maintained a strong sense of identity but were willing and ready to uphold model minority stereotypes as a key to success in America. Recent East Asian arrivals also tended to cling strongly to Confucian gender roles in which liberties traditionally were bestowed on boys and limited for girls.

Many Southeast Asian students whose parents, some on public assistance, worked at restaurants, factories, farms, or small start-up businesses struggled through school. Tensions and privation at home undermined their educational attainment. Some of these students drifted toward gang-related activity as a way in which to survive the tough inner-city streets. Others became vocal advocates for their community, forging a dynamic street-wise consciousness to cope with the difficulties of urban life.

For all students, academic pressures were exacerbated by the model minority stereotype. Asian American students still were expected to be well behaved, quiet, polite, passive, yielding, academically gifted, and diligent. Those who failed to meet such expectations frequently suffered psychological consequences. Few were encouraged to study the social sciences by parents and teachers alike. A significant portion stopped caring about school altogether, preferring to drift through their studies and live for the day.

Furthermore, Lee (1996) discovered that a culture of competition exacerbated racial tensions. Some Whites were resentful of the praise lavished on Asian American students. Many Asian Americans also adopted prevailing stereotypes of African Americans and acted accordingly. Their consumption of stridently negative views of racial minorities allowed Asian Americans to be pitted against African Americans. In recent affirmative action debates and battles in California, Governor Pete Wilson went out of his way to enlist Asian support for Proposition 209, which would have rescinded affirmative action policies in the University of California system. Asian Americans were held up as an example for African Americans, in an echo of the model minority divisive tactics of the past three decades. The message—that without government intervention or programs of social redress, a minority can raise itself by its own bootstraps—resonated with many Asian Americans. The argument that affirmative action discriminated against deserving Asians also was introduced. For Asian Americans struggling at the bottom of the economic ladder, this charge was particularly disturbing because it pitted the poor of different minority groups against each other in a bitter contest for jobs, resources, and opportunities. Asian American voters, however, rejected these efforts, with a majority voting against the California civil rights initiative that passed in 1996.

CONCLUSION

With the dawn of the 21st century, Asian Americans undoubtedly will play an increasingly important and complex role in American society. With the growth and expansion of Asia's economy, some Asian Americans are positioning themselves as intermediaries between the two continents, whereas others are continuing the fight for freedom and democracy in their homelands. Some are achieving high office as governors of states or managers in corporations, whereas others are barely surviving on poverty wages or hiding from the Immigration and Naturalization Service. All are grappling with the age-old issues of place and identity that inhabit the boundaries between disparate cultures. Coming to understand the forces and conditions that have created such diversity requires far-reaching and diligent efforts. The task will continue to challenge scholars in the years ahead.

NOTE

1. Sources for this section were primarily from Chan (1991) and Takaki (1990).

REFERENCES

Asian American/Pacific Islander in Philanthropy. (1992). *Invisible and in need: Philanthropic giving to Asian Americans and Pacific Islanders.* San Francisco: Author.

Asian Women United of California. (1989). *Making waves: An anthology of writings by and about Asian American women.* Boston: Beacon.

Chan, S. (1991). *Asian Americans: An interpretive history.* Boston: Twayne.

Day, J. C. (1993). *Asian/Pacific Islander percentage of total U.S. population (1990-2050).* Washington, DC: U.S. Bureau of the Census.

Guillermo, E. (1996, October 4). Pearls of wisdom: On model minorities and immigrant makeovers. *Asian Week,* p. 5.

Lee, S. J. (1996). *Unraveling the "model minority" stereotype: Listening to Asian American youth.* New York: Columbia University, Teachers College Press.

Okihiro, G. (1994). *Margins and mainstreams: Asians in history and culture.* Seattle: University of Washington Press.

The ruling class. (1994, September 17). *The Economist,* p. 28.

Takaki, R. (1990). *Strangers from a different shore: A history of Asian Americans.* New York: Penguin Books.

Twain, M. (1872). *Roughing it.* Hartford, CT: American Publishing.

U.S. Bureau of the Census. (various years). *Statistical abstract of the United States: 19_.* Washington, DC: Government Printing Office.

U.S. Bureau of the Census. (1995). *Selected social characteristics of the population, by region and race: March, 1994.* (Internet: http://www.census.gov/population/socdemo/race/api)

U.S. Bureau of the Census. (1997). *Selected characteristics of the population by citizenship: 1996.* (Internet: http://www.census.gov/population/socdemo/race/api)

U.S. Commission on Civil Rights. (1992). *Civil rights issues facing Asian Americans in the 1990s.* Washington, DC: Government Printing Office.

U.S. General Accounting Office. (1990). *Asian Americans: A status report 1990.* Washington, DC: Government Printing Office.

U.S. Immigration and Naturalization Service. (1991). *1991 statistical yearbook of Immigration and Naturalization Service.* Washington, DC: Government Printing Office.

Wei, W. (1993). *The Asian American movement.* Philadelphia: Temple University Press.

Yip, A. (1996, August 9). The Asian American mosaic: APAs emerge as a leading force on many fronts. *Asian Week,* pp. 14-16.

Yoon, E., & Chien, F. (1995). Asian American and Pacific Islander health: A paradigm for minority health. *Journal of American Medical Association, 275,* (9) 736-737.

CHAPTER

2

RESEARCH METHODS

*The Construct Validity of Self-Identity
and Its Psychological Implications*

JEFFREY S. TANAKA
ANGELA EBREO
NANCY LINN
OSVALDO F. MORERA

Appropriate research methods form the heart of any scientific inquiry. Without appropriate methods with which to investigate hypotheses, research data cannot be summarized in a comprehensible form. These same research methodologies also allow investigators to assess the phenomena in which they are interested in reliable and valid ways. Investigators develop questions about phenomena, design studies to answer these questions, and employ research methods and statistics to provide empirical support for the answers. Although the actual process of research might not necessarily follow this type of

AUTHORS' NOTE: The listing of the final three authors' names is alphabetical; all authors contributed equally to the conceptualization and presentation of the ideas contained within this chapter. The authors thank Michael E. Walker for his insightful comments on earlier drafts of this chapter and thank Lawrence Hubert and the Department of Psychology at the University of Illinois, Urbana-Champaign, for their support. This chapter was supported, in part, by funds made available to Jeffrey S. Tanaka by the University of Illinois University Scholars program, by a training grant awarded to Nancy Linn by the National Institute of Mental Health, National Service Award (MH 14257-17) to the University of Illinois, and by a postdoctoral fellowship awarded to Osvaldo F. Morera by the National Cancer Institute (CA42760, principal investigator: Richard B. Warnecke) to the University of Illinois, Chicago. The chapter is dedicated to the memory of our colleague, Jeffrey S. Tanaka—teacher, researcher, and mentor.

a linear progression (and, in fact, might better be thought of as a spiral [e.g., Cattell, 1988]), this model gives us a framework in which to understand the interconnections between research questions and research methods.

In writing this chapter, we have chosen not to recapitulate much of the standard discussions of research methodology that would be applicable in any psychological research. There are a number of excellent texts that summarize this material (e.g., Rosenthal & Rosnow, 1991). Our goal in this chapter is to ask a slightly more refined question. Specifically, we are interested in determining what some appropriate research methods might be for inquiry about Asian Americans. To accomplish this task, we draw on the ideas that exist within general research methodological frameworks and adapt them to explore the unique psychology of Asian Americans. As we began to formulate our initial thoughts on this topic, we found that we could develop this chapter around a core idea that will elucidate our ideas about research methodologies applicable to the study of Asian Americans: What is an Asian American, and what are the behavioral implications of membership in this social category? We might further delineate this question into two subcomponents: What does the researcher assume when he or she sets out to study Asian American populations, and what do Asian American research participants believe about the extent to which their "Asian Americanness" serves as a guide to their behavior?

A desired outcome in any discussion of research methodology is the ability to parse a research question into its fundamental components. If we do this with the present example with Asian American scholastic achievement, we see that a number of implicit assumptions are involved. The first assumption is that membership in the social category "Asian American" has a particular behavioral correlate (i.e., success on standardized tests of school achievement). Interpreted as a causal statement, the implication is that ethnicity is a determining agent of the behavior (academic achievement). If we pursue this logic a little further, we may attribute such an association to a biological substrate because sociocultural factors do not qualify this hypothesis as stated. Furthermore, whatever biological substrate that is likely to be implicated must reflect a common mechanism across all Asian Americans because of the absence of any discussion of heterogeneity among different Asian American groups. Even if such a biological substrate is not presumed, membership in the class of individuals labeled "Asian American" is thought to be a sufficient cause of some behavioral outcome. Thus, after the release of national test score results, one of us had the experience of fielding telephone calls from the news media inquiring about the "factors that make Asian Americans do well on the SAT [Scholastic Aptitude Test]."

A reasonable question to ask is the extent to which similarities and differences among different Asian American groups can be thought of as forming a common core experience. In the context of this model, research would be interested in testing the aggregation assumption made in cross-ethnic comparisons. Thus, we can develop the question of, for example, why Asian Americans do so well on the SAT into component elements. Do all Asian American groups (e.g., Japanese

Americans, Chinese Americans, Korean Americans) perform at an above-average level on these tests? If so, what set of core experiences might explain this phenomenon (e.g., emphasis on academic achievement among Asian Americans)? Are these experiences unique to Asian Americans and thus uniquely attributable to Asian Americanness, or might we see similar outcomes in other groups (e.g., would an emphasis on academic achievement within Latino or European American groups lead to the same outcome)? Alternatively, in the extent to which differences exist among different Asian American groups or within the same Asian American group, what type of validity is there in aggregating the information to the umbrella group-level designator "Asian American"? For example, on a test of English achievement, we would expect that recently arrived Asian American immigrants would be less fluent in English than third- or fourth-generation Asian Americans.[1]

If similarities among different Asian American groups are assumed, then there exist a wealth of possibilities that would contribute to similarities such as common immigration experiences, patterns, and other sociocultural influences in trying to adjust to majority American society. It is likely that similar encounters with racism exist across all Asian groups due to the failure of society to make differentiations among Asian American subpopulations. Asian Americans may share undifferentiated perceptions as "gooks" and "slant eyes" as negative characterizations or "smart" and "intelligent" as positive attributes. The salience and persistence of these types of stereotypes can be seen in terms of incidents of racially motivated violence against Asian Americans (e.g., Chinese Americans mistaken for Japanese Americans or native Japanese) as well as (perhaps) more benign manifestations of the same phenomenon (e.g., "Boy, you speak English well" or "All of you Asians are so good in math").

Although it is undeniable that some social forces tend to homogenize the experiences of Asian Americans, countervailing forces also exist. For example, the unique cultural heritages that each Asian American subpopulation draws on should serve as a buffer against the homogenization of Asian Americans. Other types of buffers are perhaps more structural in nature. For example, the existence of "Little Tokyos" and "Little Seouls" in major urban U.S. cities suggests the presence of a social structure that is more firmly centered around particular Asian American subpopulations and the unique ethnic identities that can be found therein.

It is important to explore what it means to be Asian American. The development of Asian American identity is guided by social structures and individual-level processes. If there are to be individual-level behavioral consequences of "being an Asian American," then such individuals must be guided by standards associated with Asian American self-identity. If this "self-labeling" does not occur, then it is unlikely that an individual's behavior can be thought to be guided by Asian American identity.

We see as our goal in this chapter the articulation of the various levels at which research questions can be asked in Asian American psychology. As can be seen from the brief examples already given, it is likely that a comprehensive research model will have to embrace paradigms that include both individuals and their social ecology. We view these as interconnected systems in which a unique Asian American psychology emerges.

Given the central focus of this chapter on research methodology, we embed this discussion in the context of construct validity (e.g., Campbell & Fiske, 1959; Cronbach & Meehl, 1955; Loevinger, 1957) as well as more recent perspectives on this topic (e.g., Houts, Cook, & Shadish, 1986). We feel that many research designs in Asian American psychology have been relatively insensitive to the types of classic concerns raised in methodological literatures. Our goal in this chapter is to highlight the relevance of these concerns to an Asian American psychology.

The structure of the chapter is as follows. First, a very brief summary of Asian American history and social demographics is presented. We then develop the core of our construct validity perspective and its relevance for Asian American psychology. We subsequently apply the ideas from this core to comparisons of Asian Americans with other populations, comparisons within different Asian American populations, and the role of individual differences (and, more specifically, Asian self-identity) in Asian American psychology. We review both the strengths of past research (and the underlying implicit assumptions that have guided this research) and suggestions for how future research might be better directed given our construct validity perspective. In conclusion, we emphasize how attention to construct validity in Asian American psychology will improve the quality of inferences made about Asian Americans.

Who Are Asian Americans?

The identification of a group (or groups) of people as Asian Americans is central to the arguments for the existence of Asian American psychology. This issue is more complex than when one first perceives it. It is easier to define Asian Americans in historical and sociological terms than to define them in psychological terms. Although this chapter focuses on psychology, the social-historical-political contexts in which contemporary Asian Americans are situated are important to understand because these contexts influence the perceptions of Asian Americans by others and by themselves. Our purpose here is to summarize facts about Asian Americans for the reader who is less familiar with these communities. The reader interested in general histories of Asian Americans is referred to Chan (1991), Kitano and Daniels (1995), Min (1995), and Takaki (1989).

▨ Historical Influences on Asian American Communities

Chan (1991) described how the five largest groups of Asian immigrants came to the United States under three different sets of circumstances. The first group to arrive, the Chinese, were attracted by jobs created by expansion into the American West. Japanese, Korean, and Filipino immigrants initially traveled to Hawaii to work in the sugar cane plantations; in time, persons of these ethnicities traveled to the mainland. Asian Indian immigrants also came to the United States in search of work but did so in smaller numbers than the other groups.

In adjusting to American society, Asian immigrants of the late 19th and early 20th centuries faced problems different from those experienced by European immigrants. Unlike European immigrants who found jobs in regions of the country dependent on manufacturing and industry, Asian immigrants found jobs in agricultural and service sectors in the West. Workers in these occupations did not benefit from unionization as did workers in industrial occupations. Chan (1991) argued, however, that economic factors alone do not fully account for the past and current experiences of Asian Americans. Social, political, and legal barriers, created and enforced according to race, served to limit the aspirations of Asian immigrants.

Faced with obstacles due to differences in culture and language, and targeted with racially discriminatory policies and practices, each Asian immigrant group developed social means, in the form of community groups, to ensure the survival of its members. These groups included those based on structural ties (e.g., groups based on kinship, common locality of origin, or religion) and those based on pragmatic ties (e.g., business or political organizations). The development of the pragmatic organizations is important because they played a role in reshaping the immigrants' identification.

During World War II and the years immediately following, the lives of Asian Americans were tied to the relations between their countries of origin and the United States. During the war, Japan and Japanese Americans were perceived as enemies, whereas Chinese were perceived as friends because China was an ally. Japanese Americans were relocated from the West Coast to internment centers located in desolate parts of the United States. Sentiments toward Japanese Americans and Chinese Americans switched, however, as China became communist and Japan became democratic.

The Immigration and Naturalization Act of 1965 drastically changed the pattern of immigration to the United States from that of the previous century and the first half of the 20th century. Before the passage of this legislation, the majority of immigrants to the United States were from Europe; now, more than half are from Asia. The Immigration and Naturalization Act specifies seven preferences for immigrants; four deal with family relationships, two deal with occupational and labor preferences, and one deals with refugee status. Currently, many immigrants file for residency under the familial preferences portion of the law.

▨ Social Demographics of Asian Americans

According to the 1990 census, the Asian American population in the United States doubled in size from 1980 to 1990, from approximately 3.7 million to 7.3 million people (U.S. Bureau of the Census, 1993). As of 1990, Asian Americans constituted 2.9% of the total U.S. population. As in the previous decade, immigration was the major factor accounting for the increase in the size of the communities. Larger numbers of Asian Americans have entered the United States from China, India, Korea, the Philippines, and other Asian Pacific areas as a result of the Immigration and Naturalization Act of 1965. Another sizable number entered this country in the late 1970s from Southeast Asia under the Refugee Resettlement Program.

According to the 1990 census, the largest Asian American groups (ranked by size) were Chinese, Filipino, Japanese, Asian Indian, Korean, Vietnamese, and Loatian, whereas the largest Pacific American groups were Hawaiians, Samoans, and Guamanians (U.S. Bureau of the Census, 1993). The majority of Asian Americans are recent immigrants; fully 59% (1980) and 63% (1990) indicated that they were born in foreign countries. Although Asian Americans live in every area of the country, the majority live in the West. This does not represent a change from 1980 to 1990. Nearly 40% live in the state of California. Other states with high concentrations of Asian Americans include New York, Hawaii, Texas, Illinois, New Jersey, and Washington. In terms of the 1990 percentage of the population within each state, Asian Americans make up 61.3% of the population of the state of Hawaii and 9.6% of the population of California. The concentration of Asian Americans differs by Asian and Pacific ethnic group. For instance, the majority of Pacific Americans reside in Hawaii and California. The majority of Asian Americans live in metropolitan areas, equally divided between central cities and their suburbs. In 1980, about half of the Asian American population lived in one of six metropolitan areas: Honolulu, Los Angeles-Long Beach, San Francisco-Oakland, New York, Chicago, and San Jose.

According to 1990 (and 1980) census figures, Asian Pacific Americans differ from the general U.S. population on several sociodemographic characteristics. Similar to other immigrants, Asian Pacific Americans are younger; their median age is 30.1 years (28.4 years in 1980) compared to 33.0 years (30.0 years in 1980) for the nation. The average family size for Asian Pacific Americans, 3.8 persons in 1990 (and in 1980), was somewhat larger than that for the average U.S. family, 3.2 persons (3.3 persons in 1980). The nature of the extended family among Asian Pacific Americans accounted for this; a larger number of children under 18 years of age (82% vs. 72% for the general U.S. population) and relatives other than spouse and children (39% vs. 13%) were part of the household.

The educational attainment of Asian Pacific Americans as a whole is higher than that of the general U.S. population, but ethnic groups within the Asian Pacific American population vary widely. A greater proportion of Asian Pacific Americans, 78% (75% in 1980), graduated from high school than did the general U.S. population, 75% (66% in 1980). Hmong Americans (31%) and Samoan Americans (71%) had smaller proportions of high school graduates compared to national norms. A greater proportion of Asian Pacific Americans also obtained at least a bachelor's degree than did the general population (37% vs. 20%), with 58% of Asian Indian Americans obtaining at least a bachelor's degree.

The economic and occupational status of Asian Pacific Americans presents a complex picture. The 1990 census figures indicated that a larger proportion of Asian Pacific Americans (68%) than of the general U.S. population (65%) is in the labor force. Laotian Americans (58%), Cambodian Americans (47%), and

Hmong Americans (29%) were below the national norms for labor force participation; these are among the most recent immigrant groups. In terms of occupation, Asian Pacific Americans were more likely than the general U.S. population to be in a managerial/professional specialty, 31% versus 26% (18% vs. 12% in 1980) or service occupations, 15% versus 13% (14% vs. 11% in 1980) and thus is another indicator of the diversity among Asian Americans.

The median family income of Asian Pacific Americans, $41,300 ($22,700 in 1980), also was higher than the national median, $35,200 ($19,900 in 1980). Family income, however, is affected by educational attainment and the number of employed household members. The proportion of Asian Pacific American families with three or more workers was 20% (17% in 1980) compared to 13% (in 1980 and 1990) for the nation as a whole. The range of family incomes among Asian Pacific Americans is large, with the most established groups having higher median incomes than the groups who have immigrated more recently. In addition, all Pacific American groups had incomes lower than the national average. The poverty rate among Asian Pacific Americans was slightly higher, 14% (13% in 1980), than in the nation as a whole, 13% (12% in 1980). Poverty rates for Hmong Americans (62%), Cambodian Americans (42%), and Laotian Americans (32%) were even higher, in contrast to those for Japanese Americans (3%) and Filipino Americans (5%).

This brief historical overview provides some minimal background context for factors that might be important to take into account in studying Asian American populations but are ignored due to interests in more psychological processes. We provide this information to acknowledge that such historical factors will necessarily shape the psychology of the Asian American experience. With this backdrop, we go on to discuss the development of Asian American psychology from a construct validity perspective.

The Construct Validity of Asian American Psychology

In what are now classic works in research methodology, a number of authors in the 1950s pointed to problems in the operationalization of research constructs in psychology (e.g., Campbell & Fiske, 1959; Cronbach & Meehl, 1955; Loevinger, 1957; Torgerson, 1958/1985). These authors suggested that the level of discussion about psychological constructs should be at least one level of abstraction beyond the particular measured variable operationalization of that construct. So, for example, if one is interested in a psychological construct such as "test anxiety," then it would be fallacious to equate a specific measure of test anxiety with the underlying psychological construct of interest.

These core methodological ideas about assessments and their relations to underlying psychological constructs have been articulated in a number of different ways in the psychological literature. For example, Campbell and Fiske (1959) referred to the convergent and discriminant validity of psychological assessments. From this perspective, a specific measure of test anxiety should correlate highly with other, alternative measures of test anxiety (convergent validity) but should not correlate highly with a measure of some other psychological construct where the correlation might be due to, for example, common method variance (discriminant validity).

Torgerson (1958/1985) spoke of the nomological net in which psychological constructs are embedded. In this discussion, a distinction was made between interrelations that can be observed among measures and the hypothesized, theoretically guided interrelations that might be expected at an unobserved level among psychological constructs. It is interesting that the conceptual perspective outlined by Torgerson (1958/1985) subsequently has been operationalized in a formal manner in the literature on latent variable structural equation modeling (e.g., Bentler, 1978; Tanaka, Panter, Winborne, & Huba, 1990).

Finally, in a more recent discussion of construct validity, Cook and his colleagues (e.g., Houts et al., 1986), advancing the perspectives initially developed by Donald Campbell, discussed a "multiplist" perspective on psychological research and theory. The multiplist perspective emphasizes multiple operationalizations of psychological constructs obtained from multiple agents (reporters) over multiple time points to obtain convergent information about a psychological construct of interest. Two empirical examples of the utility of this perspective are presented in diverse areas of psychological inquiry such as personality consistency by Houts et al. (1986) and family processes (Bank, Dishion, Skinner, & Patterson, 1990).

The most typical way of assessing whether or not an individual respondent is a member of an Asian American category is a single-item, self-report assessment in which a respondent is asked to differentiate among multiple presented nominal categories (e.g., Black/African American, European American, Hispanic/Latino, Asian/Pacific Islander). Sometimes this classification is not self-generated but instead reflects a categorization made by an investigator (e.g., on the basis of surnames). Although this fundamental information sometimes is supplemented by other measures taken on an individual (e.g., generational status), it typically is the case that an individual is classified as an Asian American on the basis of this single-item response.

Consider what we believe to be a not too atypical example of this that occurs in research settings. An Asian American respondent is presented with an item asking for a response to this "ethnicity" question. From the researcher's perspective, this should allow a reliable classification into a category that will allow for a discussion of similarities among respondents who check off the same alternative and differences among groups of respondents who choose different alternatives. From the respondent's phenomenology, a response to this question might mean something entirely different. In answering this question, the respondent might adopt a "rule out" strategy (i.e., "I'm not Black/African American, I'm not European American, I'm not Hispanic/Latino . . .") and simply check off the one response that remains after having exhausted all other possible alternatives. This respondent might have no other "common" characteristics with other Asian Americans and, in fact, might not spontaneously self-generate ethnicity as a salient self-characteristic.

This leads to an obvious construct validity problem and a conundrum for research on Asian American populations. As noted recently by Funder (1991), one precondition that the researcher might wish to establish for construct validity is congruence between self- and other-judgments. In the example we have just presented, Asian Americanness clearly means something different to the research investigator from what it means to the respondent.

A more sensitive assessment of Asian American self-identification also can help to clarify differences that may exist among Asian American subpopulations. Behavioral and psychological implications are different for individuals who spontaneously self-identify as "Asian American" and for those individuals who refer to themselves as "Korean American." Work on the spontaneous self-concept by McGuire and his colleagues (e.g., McGuire, 1984; McGuire, McGuire, & Cheever, 1986) can be applied to the study of ethnic self-identity. The behavioral consequences of self-identification as a member of a specific ethnic group or nationality (e.g., Korean) versus self-identification as a member of the broader category "Asian American" versus dual self-identification can be examined by isolating subsets of Asian American respondents who view their attitudes, values, and actions as being guided by internalized standards of Asian Americanness or Korean Americanness.

When Should Ethnicity Guide Behavior?

Discussions of ethnic psychology have greatly oversimplified the complexity of the ethnic minority experience and the implications of that experience for behavior. In many ways, we feel that this reflects the ease with which the researcher can address issues of differences among different subpopulations through crude classifications based on single-item probes. A more elaborated view of the role of ethnicity in guiding behaviors and attitudes might establish some conditions for when we might expect effects of ethnic self-identity to be salient. We offer some of these conditions as a mechanism to move us beyond simple characterizations of ethnicity. We view these conditions not as operating in isolation of each other but rather as working together in complementary and dynamic ways.

> *Postulate 1:* The psychological implications of being Asian American should be apparent in an individual to the extent that the individual views ethnic group membership as being a relevant and salient guide for behavior.

A clear counterexample to this postulate is given by the respondent who employs the "rule out" strategy to complete a demographic item probe related to ethnicity. Although this respondent is providing descriptively correct information to the investigator, it is unlikely that this individual has any internalized standard relating to Asian American self-identity. Thus, classifying this individual into a category of "Asian American" and then studying the extent to which such a descriptive variable might explain between-group differences simply adds noise to the phenomenon being studied.

The previous example demonstrates the invalidity of the single-item probe and suggests that multiple assessments need to be made to make this classification and the subsequent between-group comparison more valid. Such additional assessments might include the extent to which individuals view themselves as Asian American or the accessibility of ethnic status as a salient aspect of the self-concept. These other measures should help to clarify the extent to which respondents view themselves as Asian American and, by implication, the extent to which they might use Asian Americanness as a self-guide for behavior. With regard to this postulate, it is interesting to note the observation made by Steele (1991), who stated, "Identity is not the same thing as the fact of membership in a collective; it is, rather, a form of self-definition, facilitated by images of what we wish our membership in the collective to mean" (p. 96).

> *Postulate 2:* The psychological implications of being Asian American should be more apparent in the extent to which social forces make ethnic group membership salient for an individual.

Our second postulate addresses two different issues that occur among ethnic minority populations in general and among Asian American populations more specifically. One way for group membership to become salient is for there to be a large degree of homogeneity within a group. The implication of this group homogeneity within a more heterogeneous context should be to foster in-group/out-group perceptions. Within a relatively more homogeneous social context, we believe that an individual is more likely to make stronger differentiations among out-groups, which, in turn, should make in-group ethnic identity more salient. We expand on these ideas in a later section of this chapter.

The second social context in which ethnic self-identity should become salient is the converse of the homogeneous social context. In this situation, a small number of ethnic minorities within a social context become a clearly defined out-group relative to a majority (nonethnic) in-group. There are two possible countervailing forces that might occur in this social structure. First, social forces might work to move an individual closer to the majority in-group, thus decreasing the likelihood of ethnic minority self-identity for this individual. Alternatively, the clearly defined out-group might create its own social links, establish within-group heterogeneity, and create a stronger sense of ethnic self-identity. These alternative scenarios suggest that social cohesion of an individual to a group might be an important predictor of ethnic self-identity in this case. However, even in the extent to which this or other salient predictors might be identified, this suggests that the process by which ethnic self-identity may be thought to guide behavior and attitudes is more complex than can be assessed in a single-item probe.

We examine the implications of each of these two postulates for research conducted at each of the three levels mentioned at the outset of this chapter (i.e.,

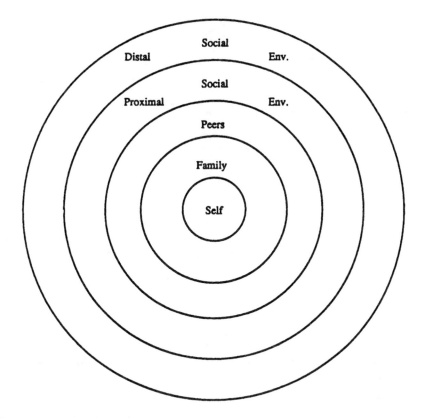

Figure 2.1. Embedded Contexts

research comparing Asian Americans to other groups, research among different Asian American subpopulations, and research within a specific Asian American subpopulation). We feel that Asian American psychology can benefit by more closely articulating the level and specificity with which research questions are addressed.

Emerging Perspectives on the Nature of Asian American Self-Identity

In defining research methodologies appropriate for Asian American psychology, we propose that two different perspectives can be advanced. These are presented schematically in Figures 2.1 and 2.2. We refer to Figure 2.1 as representing a contextual paradigm on the issue of Asian American self-identity and to Figure 2.2 as a social consensus paradigm.

▨ *A Contextual Paradigm*
   for Asian American Ethnicity

The contextual paradigm examines research elements derived from a consideration of psychological phenomena manifested by the individual's position

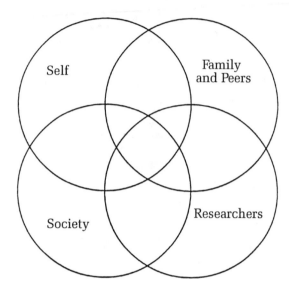

Figure 2.2. "True Score" Model

within different social systems (i.e., the research participant's family, friends and peers, ethnic group, or neighborhood). It is assumed that ethnic identity is affected by the degree to which the different social systems present positive and negative reinforcements for the development, maintenance, and transmission of behavioral patterns characteristic of Asian culture. The paradigm focuses on the social influences inherent in the individual's environment and the individual's response to these social factors.

An example of the influence that social contexts have on the behavior of ethnic persons was provided by Trimble (1990). He stated,

> A number of American Indian groups rely on a nested hierarchy to define their identity that begins with identifying the nation, the tribe, followed subsequently by identifying with a band, a camp, and finally a family. The degree to which one moves through the nested layers depends on whom one is talking to. (p. 161)

This example clearly illustrates how ethnic self-identification can be manifested differently in one realm of behavior (conversation) depending on the context of the behavior (the relationship of the person with whom one is conversing).

It is important to note that the paradigm proposes the individual as the unit of analysis; that is, research conducted within this paradigm still would examine individual-level phenomena. The contextual paradigm does not refer to the level at which the researcher would perform his or her analysis. For example, a study using this paradigm would not focus on families or neighborhoods as the units of analysis. Instead, the behavior of individual persons is examined within specific social contexts. Rather than viewing the individual as acting in isolation from other persons and social institutions, this paradigm takes into account the social forces that act on the individual.

The contextual paradigm proposes that research elements be studied as the participants move within different social contexts. In this paradigm, the researcher collects information about ethnic group members at different points in time or about ethnic group members with different "social ecologies" and searches so for similarities and differences. The paradigm presents a complex picture of the influence of the various social environments within which individuals act. Contexts are embedded within each other such that environmental forces operating in more distal contexts, although weaker in direct influence, interact with those present in more proximal contexts. Individual differences, for example, might be manifested differently when a person interacts with his or her peer group from when the person interacts with his or her family. Due to the time and expense involved, most researchers do not consider all of the possible contexts presented by the participant's ecology; only a limited set of contexts usually are scrutinized in any single study.

Figure 2.1 depicts the different embedded contexts in which the Asian American identity construct can be investigated. The outermost ring represents the most typical representation of Asian Americans in research, members of an ethnic group living within the dominant society. Individuals are seen as bonded to other members of the broad category "Asian American" for comparisons between the category and members of other broad categories (e.g., African Americans, Latinos/Latinas, European Americans) to be made. Although not often explicitly stated, such comparisons are indirectly tied to intergroup relations in that Asian Americans are contrasted with members of other groups, all of whom differ in status within American society. Although this perspective dominates much of the research done on Asian Americans (particularly when this research is conducted by non-Asian Americans), we feel that this is the least interesting approach to studying Asian Americans due to the aggregation issue raised earlier.

The next inner layers (ethnic group, community, and neighborhood) represent more proximal social contexts. At this level, the researcher may distinguish between subgroups of Asian American participants (e.g., Japanese Americans, Indonesian Americans). Obtained differences among these subgroups might be due to social structural factors or barriers (e.g., Asian American enclaves in urban areas [such as Chinatown, Manilatown, or Little Seoul], the internment of Japanese Americans during World War II) or more informal social ties that develop around notions related to a sense of community (Fugita & O'Brien, 1991).

The innermost circles of Figure 2.1 suggest other forces that might be operating to determine appropriate research methodologies and questions for Asian American psychology. At these levels, the researcher can consider the influence of intimate social ties such as peer and family relations and the role of individual differences, particularly those related to self-perception. The paradigm proposes that more proximal and intimate social relationships exert greater influences on ethnic identification than do more distal social contexts, which is a testable proposal.

Ethnic identity might not guide behavior in some social situations because it is considered to be irrelevant to the task at hand or because an individual assumes that the persons with whom he or she is interacting implicitly understand the role of ethnicity (i.e., ethnic identification is an automatic categorization process). In the interpersonal domain, Suinn (1992) provided an anecdote regarding how ethnicity became salient to him in regard to his experiences as a psychologist. Formerly, he had not thought a great deal about his own ethnicity because most of his colleagues did not mention it and it did not seem to be relevant to evaluations of his job performance. After he was confronted with a racist colleague, Suinn became quite aware of the fact that he is an Asian American in addition to being a psychologist. Shortly thereafter, he became involved in the Asian American Psychological Association. This is just one example of how the behavior of one's peers can make ethnicity accessible in memory and affect overt behavior.

Other variables, in addition to experiences of discrimination and racism, might operate as moderators of the ethnicity-behavior relationship. For example, the greater levels of interpersonal sensitivity demonstrated by women in a number of domains (see Tanaka, Panter, & Winborne, 1988, for a possible explanation of this gender difference) might lead to differences in the degree to which men and women facilitate cohesive ties. The greater cohesiveness in relationships among women and their peers and family would, in turn, facilitate greater interaction and, following Postulate 2, possibly greater ethnic self-identification. Evidence for women as facilitators of network maintenance is provided by Yamagisako (1977).

Finally, at the level of self-perception, one can use the notion of ethnic identification as developed in Reitz (1980; see also Fugita & O'Brien, 1991), where the relevant standard of reference is the extent to which individuals view themselves as members of a particular ethnic group in the conceivable absence of direct social contact with fellow ethnic group members. Mura (1991) recounted the potential difficulties of maintaining such an ethnic self-identity in the absence of specific social reinforcement of an ethnic self-identity (and, perhaps, in the presence of social forces that would serve to minimize in-group/out-group perceptions, a type of behavior we observe on a daily basis among many ethnic students on our predominantly European American university campus located in rural Illinois).

Research conducted within the contextual paradigm would attempt to delineate those social conditions that affirm and foster ethnic identity from those conditions that deny its expression or even its existence. A person's identity as an Asian American is seen as a result of the interaction of these social conditions and individual differences. The paradigm does not assume that aspects of Asian Americanness can be demonstrated (at least on a conscious level) by all individuals of Asian descent to the same degree. Differences between persons who are very Asian identified and those who are less Asian identified exist in part because of forces within societies that influence people's willingness to be identified as members of an ethnic group and because of personality characteristics that make them more or less immune to these social forces.

The contextual paradigm is, then, more a model of psychological divergence than of psychological convergence. The model assumes that aspects of Asian American self-identity exist but that outer markers of this identity (behavior and self-reports of attitudes and values) are mutable depending on existing social supports and reinforcers. Operationally, it is difficult to define the construct validity of ethnicity in this paradigm because the researcher would not expect participants' self-reports of behavior to match their inner experiences. There would likely be little cross-situational consistency of ethnicity defined as in this paradigm. Despite this complication, we believe that research guided by this paradigm would be useful in developing an understanding of the issues relevant to Postulate 2, which was described in the previous section. A fruitful avenue for future research would be in understanding the processes that underlie the effects of both distal and proximal social contexts on ethnic self-identification.

Another neglected issue in Asian American psychology is raised by the embedded contexts proposed within the contextual paradigm. We know of no psychological research that addresses the notion that social contexts exert mutual influences on the behavior of individuals. Suppose that a psychologist has decided to study the influence of peer and family relationships on the educational achievement of Asian American children. The psychologist collects data pertaining to the children's school friendships as well as data pertaining to their relationships with their parents. The researcher fails to consider, however, the influence of the parents over the choice of friends and the amount of time spent with friends. He or she also does not recognize the influence of the children's friendships on the family environment. In this case, the researcher has lost an important perspective and, more important, information about the interdependence of social systems for an individual.

▨ *A Social Consensus Paradigm
for Asian American Ethnicity*

In the social consensus paradigm, the researcher's definition of Asian American ethnic identity is insufficient. The research participants, members of the participants' ethnic peer group or in-group, and members of the participants' ethnic out-groups also must agree on a definition of Asian American identity. When a consensus cannot be reached among the researcher, participants, and other relevant groups on elements of ethnic identity of the participants, the following hierarchy of definitions should be used: (a) the participants, (b) the participants' ethnic in-group, and then (c) the researcher's or participants' ethnic out-groups.

Research findings and interpretations of these findings are considered valid when the perspectives of the different groups coincide. It is assumed that there exists some common aspect of Asian American identity that can be identified across all of these perspectives and that is indicated by the intersection of the four circles in Figure 2.2. Drawing from psychometric terminology (e.g., Lord & Novick, 1968), the intersection of the circles represents a "true score" model of Asian American identity.

As with all true score theories (Lord & Novick, 1968), the accuracy of this representation rests on how well the true score is assessed (Lumsden, 1976). In the case of research on Asian American populations, we think it can be safely argued that many research efforts have failed to take into account convergent validity information in calibrating this particular true score. This failure leads to inevitable problems in terms of being able to specify the psychological and behavioral consequences of Asian American identity. Consider, for example, research that looks at between-group comparisons on mathematics performance among different ethnic groups. A reasonable point of departure for such research would be to draw from the existing literature that suggests that Asian Americans demonstrate higher performance on such tests than do other groups of individuals. If a study were then to be designed from this point, it might be reasonable to look for, at a minimum, a replication of this finding. The information relevant to calibration of the true score of Asian American identity is derived from only two perspectives: prior research (or what we have labeled "society" in Figure 2.2) and the researcher's current set of assumptions ("researchers" in Figure 2.2). There might be no motivation to move beyond this relatively simple conceptualization toward a more complete specification of the underlying process that might be shared across the different perspectives depicted in Figure 2.2. To accomplish this, the researcher might have to go on to isolate those specific within-group conditions that might contribute to the observed performance differences.

The social consensus paradigm poses some issues for Asian American psychology. Suppose that a psychologist has decided to include Asian Americans as one of several targeted ethnic groups in a survey of preventive health behaviors. The researcher chooses to define Asian Americans as any persons who are of Asian ancestry or origin and who currently are residing in the United States, in effect choosing to ignore any differences among Asian subgroups. The psychologist decides to develop a sampling frame for the study by examining the U.S. census records, which define Asian Americans in a similar manner. During the data collection phase of the study, some persons refuse to participate in the study, stating that they are not Asian American and that the questions do not apply to them. A problem arises because the definition of the term "Asian American" has different meanings for the researcher and other members of society from those it has for the participants. The researcher had used the term to apply to the racial/ancestry characteristics of the participants, whereas the persons who chose not to participate had applied the term to their ethnic self-identification. In this case, the problem might have been averted if, during the planning stages of the study, the researcher had consulted with selected Asian American informants about their perceptions of the survey and its purpose.

Some researchers might argue that the perspective of researchers and that of ethnic out-groups should have smaller roles than self-reported ethnic identity in defining research aimed at building an information base about ethnic groups. This argument is not about the quality of the research per se; rather, it is about its meaning for the research participants and its potential implications. One basis for this argument stems from a concern for the ethnic group to determine what concepts are valuable and useful, what problems need to be addressed, what methods are most appropriate, and what possible interpretations exist. In this sense, the community works toward developing research that is applicable to its needs. Another advantage of exclusion of the researcher and out-groups is that stereotypes held by these groups are less likely to be directly incorporated into the research process. This is not to say that the researcher no longer is involved in the process; rather, the researcher acts in a consultative role rather than a supervisory one.

Another issue arises when one tries to understand the validity of consensus as it operates within this paradigmatic framework. Stereotypical beliefs about Asian Americans can be held by both in-group and out-group members. However, this shared consensus or a social stereotype probably should not be taken as indicative of being Asian American. We cannot empirically bootstrap results in the context of this model and assume that agreements or aspects of Asian American identity imply an underlying truth.

We offer our two figures as points of departure for a discussion of the different ways in which ethnic status might be conceptualized when conducting research on ethnic groups or, more specifically for our current purposes, on Asian American populations. Using these models, we next describe how past, current, and future research efforts in Asian American populations might be informed by these models.

WHAT METHODOLOGIES ARE APPROPRIATE FOR ASIAN AMERICAN PSYCHOLOGY?

A scientific paradigm, as Kuhn (1970) stated, defines the boundaries of what questions can be asked and what methods can be used to answer these questions. Thus, a paradigm presents a model that can be applied by various persons conducting research at a specific point in time. In this section, we examine the appropriateness of the Euro-American research paradigm for the study of Asian Americans and other racial/ethnic groups. We then examine some issues that have been raised by researchers who have used methods based on the Euro-American paradigm.

The Euro-American Research Paradigm

The dominant paradigm in psychology has been the Euro-American or Western model (Akbar, 1991). The basic ideology behind this model was the ascription of psychological normality to Euro-American males and abnormality to all persons who were not Euro-American males (i.e., females, members of racial/ethnic minority groups). As Akbar (1991) mentions, the paradigm defines the psychologically healthy person as being individualistic, competitive, materialistic, and masculine.

The methodological result of following such a paradigm is seen in the accumulation of studies of psychological difference, that is, studies that have compared groups on these characteristics to determine deviance from what is considered normal. This presentation of psychological reality encourages deficit model interpretations of comparative research, regardless of whether the research findings are approached from a sociobiological, cultural, or individual differences point of view. Even when interpretations are not made from a deficit perspective as is the case with Asian American scholastic achievement, no suggestion is made that additional merit-based resources be made available to this group or that changes in the White majority group culture be considered. Although Akbar's (1991) discussion of the Euro-American paradigm was developed in reference to African Americans, the ideas are applicable to all racial/ethnic minority groups. We focus on the three problematic characteristics of methodologies based on this paradigm and their implications for research on Asian Americans. First, good research inevitably is comparative in nature. In this manner, the Euro-American male is treated as the standard for behavior. Research that does not involve comparisons with the normative group is not considered to be valuable or significant. Several issues arise as a result. Gender differences are ignored, even though the experiences of females can result in worldviews, attitudes, and behaviors that are quite different from those of males. Comparative research of this nature results in the attachment of value to any differences that are obtained (i.e., the behavior of one group [usually the majority] is "healthy," whereas the behavior of the other group is "unhealthy").

Second, focus on psychological differences can influence the selection of research participants. Members of minority groups might be included in a study precisely because they are expected to deviate the most from the normative model. When differences between the majority and minority groups are found, they are explained in terms of group membership (i.e., in terms of race).

Lastly, methods used in the Euro-American paradigm assess only those psychological phenomena that are defined to be within the realm of the paradigm; other phenomena are ignored or misunderstood. Phenomena that are unique to the experiences of the minority group might never be uncovered as the group is studied using the normative standard of Euro-American males. In fact, differences due to the sociohistorical experiences of members of minority groups are not seen as being relevant to an understanding of human behavior. Akbar (1991) mentioned the fallacy of objectivity as an example. Objectivity involves the labeling of some sources of information (e.g., introspection) as being "unscientific." Similar critiques of Eurocentric social science have been proposed by feminist (e.g., Jayaratne & Stewart, 1991; Lott, 1991; Mies, 1991; Westkott, 1979) and Asian American (e.g., see Chapter 9, this volume; Uba, 1994) researchers.

Eurocentric researchers often rely on questionnaires and other methods that are developed for use in Euro-American research samples. Psychologists interested in generating useful information about Asian Americans would use assessment instruments and methods that are ideally derived from Asian American cultures and experiences. The methods would be culturally sensitive and subjective in that they incorporate information about cultural patterns of responding to the research process. The researcher might, for example, use information concerning interracial relations to govern whether or not he or she would include non-Asian American interviewers as part of the research team.

"Traditional" Methodological Issues

In this subsection, we summarize two methodological areas (measurement and data interpretation) that have been critiqued by psychologists interested in ethnic and feminist psychology. The reader is referred to other sources (e.g., Brislin, 1986; Landrine, 1995; Takeuchi & Young, 1994) for more detailed discussion of these issues.

▓ *Measurement Issues*

Although the following three measurement issues are of concern to researchers conducting studies of other ethnic minority groups, they are particularly important to researchers working with Asian Americans: the cultural appropriateness of the assessment instruments, use of standardized instruments, and the measurement equivalence of translations of these instruments.

The need for assessing culturally appropriate constructs has been noted by cross-cultural and Asian American psychologists (e.g., Sue, Chun, & Gee, 1995) for some time. These psychologists have contributed to ethnic psychology by explicitly distinguishing between constructs that are universal (*etic*) and those that are specific to a particular culture (*emic*). Triandis and Marin (1983) and others argued that measurement instruments should include both emic and etic items to provide a clearer picture of the cultural groups under study. One example of this approach can be found in a cross-cultural study of job satisfaction by de Vera (1986).

A second issue concerns the use of instruments normed on non-Asian or non-Asian American populations. Earlier we mentioned that bias can be introduced into noncomparative research when such instruments are administered to different ethnic minority groups. The researcher might find that such instruments measure different constructs in these groups from those they measured in the normed sample. In addition to this problem, the psychometric properties of the instrument might change (e.g., the reliability of the measure might decrease). The researcher who decides on using standardized instruments should assess their comparability across the different racial/ethnic groups sampled beforehand.

A third measurement issue concerns the use of translated instruments. Use of translations often is necessary when research participants are unable to read or understand English versions. The major goal of translation is the development of a version of the standardized instrument that is culturally equivalent (i.e., has the same connotative meaning) to the original. Marin and Marin (1991) mentioned translation techniques that are acceptable for achieving cultural equivalence: translation by committee (two or more bilingual/bicultural individuals independently translate the instrument and the versions are compared), double (back) translation (one bilingual/bicultural translator translates the measure from English into the Asian language, the second translates this version back into English, and the English versions are compared), and decentering (a version of double translation in which both languages are considered important [i.e., the original English language version of the instrument also can be modified]). Translation to achieve cultural equivalence is illustrated in the development of a Korean version of the Myers-Briggs Type Indicator (Sim & Kim, 1993).

▨ Data Interpretation Problems

Another set of issues (response styles, inaccurate responses, and misinterpretation of responses) was raised by Marin and Marin (1991) in their discussion of threats to the validity of researchers' interpretation of their findings. To date, few studies have documented these problems in relation to Asian Americans.

Research with African Americans and Hispanics (e.g., Hui & Triandis, 1989; Marin & Marin, 1991) has indicated that members of ethnic minority groups tend to exhibit extreme response styles in answering scaled items. Other research (e.g., Ross & Mirowsky, 1984, as cited in Marin & Marin, 1991) has shown that ethnic group members also tend to exhibit an acquiescent response style (i.e., agreement with items regardless of their content). Hui and Triandis propose that these response sets are moderated by the cultural values of the respondents, whereas research by Marin, Gamba, and Marin (1992) indicated that the response sets are culturally determined but moderated by the educational and acculturation levels of the research participants. The latter finding also has been suggested in research on Asian Americans (e.g., Smith, 1990).

The tendency for respondents to behave in socially desirable ways is another way in which bias enters the research process. Depending on the degree to which they have maintained certain cultural values related to interpersonal relations and behavioral appropriateness, Asian American respondents might invalidate reports of their behavior and attitudes by selecting the socially/culturally desirable responses over the less desirable ones. Response bias also is evident in tendencies to overreport or underreport the frequency of certain behaviors (e.g., drug consumption, sexual behavior). Such inaccuracies in self-report might occur because respondents feel a need to present a favorable view of themselves to the researcher. In addition, concern for one's self-image might lead a respondent to avoid answering particular items. A study of responses to health items by East Asians (Park, Upshaw, & Koh, 1988) illustrates issues related to social desirability. Although these issues have not been investigated to a great extent in the general Asian American population, the researcher might want to consider them as interfering with the integrity of their data, particularly when studying sensitive or personal issues.

Even when research participants respond accurately, their behaviors are subject to possible misinterpretation. These misinterpretations might be due to the investigator's stereotypes or lack of cultural sensitivity or knowledge. For example, suppose that the researcher is interested in social interactions between schoolteachers and their pupils. This researcher obtains videotapes of classroom behavior and develops a coding scheme that includes the amount of time a pupil has direct eye contact with the teacher when being addressed. This might be a problematic measure in populations in which looking directly at the teacher is indicative of disrespect and gaze aversion is a dominant behavioral response in dealing with a dominant other. In this example, the researcher's assumption about the meaning of gaze aversion is not consistent with the meaning of this behavior for the respondent. Additional examples pertaining to children can be found in Gibbs, Huang, and Associates (1990), whereas a counseling process example can be found in research by Pearce (1994).

COMPARISONS OF ASIAN AMERICANS WITH OTHER RACIAL/ETHNIC GROUPS

Although comparative studies of different racial and ethnic minority groups are prone to the problems of interpretation, this type of research continues. Rather than debate the merit of these comparisons based on their substantive content, we analyze the implications of conducting research that assumes that Asian Americans can be defined as a broad social group of persons (as depicted in Figure 2.1). We pay particular attention to the consequences of the labeling of individuals as "Asian American."

Asian Americans in the Context of Intergroup Relations

As the ecological paradigm (Figure 2.1) states, Asian American identity at the broadest conceptual level consists of the aggregation of members from all Asian ethnicities into one conglomeration. At this level, the researcher might attempt to understand the psychological characteristics of Asian Americans in contrast to those characteristics present in other social groups. Research based on this paradigm likely involves racial/ethnic group comparisons. Most often, interpretation of findings from these comparisons hinges on racial and, therefore, sociobiological explanations.

The use of racial typologies in social science research has been defended by some researchers (e.g., Rushton, 1989) and questioned by others (e.g., Fairchild, 1991; Tucker, 1994; Zuckerman, 1990). When the term "Asian American" is used to designate race, the researcher has assumed that physical and psychological differences between different racial groups are a result of natural selection occurring during the process of human evolution. Classification of members of the human species into racial categories based on the uniqueness of group phenotypes ignores the similarities in genetic composition across these categories and the wide variance in characteristics that is present within each category. Race and ethnicity also often are confounded with other factors, such as gender and social class, introducing additional complexity into a paradigm in which racial/ethnic groups most often are characterized as being homogeneous.

Oyama (1991) stated that sociobiological explanations are inadequate insofar as "they retain the dualistic idea that genes and environment constitute alternative sources of organic form rather than parts of complex, integrated systems" (p. 32). She argued further that human natures are the result of developmental histories and that these histories are as much a product of environmental factors and genetics. Fairchild (1991) argued that racial classifications are tied to specific social and political contexts, echoing the need to understand the sociohistorical relations among members of different racial/ethnic groups.

Given the complex social, historical, and political context in which members of different racial/ethnic groups have lived in American society, it is important for the researcher to understand intergroup phenomena, in particular, issues that concern intergroup relations. Research in the area of intergroup relations can help the researcher understand how minority group status can influence the psychological characteristics of members of racial/ethnic groups. Particular studies in this area can give the researcher some insight into the reasons why groups perceive themselves to be different in status (often of lower status) from members of the majority. Research using interracial comparisons can thus reflect some understanding of the roles and perspectives of ethnic minority groups in society. We particularly urge researchers to become aware of stereotyping that might occur during the interpretation stage of their projects. An awareness of the processes by which stereotypes form within the minds of the persons we study can serve to remind us that we, as researchers, are not immune to these phenomena.

The social consensus paradigm (Figure 2.2) states that the convergence of many different perspectives may serve as a guide for the study of Asian American psychology. When studying any categorized group of people, the perspective of the researcher is of importance. For example, the researcher might be unfamiliar with members of an ethnic group and enter the experimental session with stereotypes of the research participants. If this is indeed the case, then the perspective of an unfamiliar researcher will diverge from the participants' perspective.

In the next few paragraphs, we explore topics in intergroup relations that can inform the researcher of the complexities involved in conducting research using interracial/interethnic comparisons. The reader requiring more detail on these issues is referred to comprehensive reviews of the intergroup relations literature that are available in the *Annual Review of Psychology* (e.g., Brewer & Kramer, 1985; Messick & Mackie, 1989).

▦ *Social Contact Between In-Groups and Out-Groups*

In societies in which racial/ethnic minority groups exist alongside a more dominant group (or groups), both majority and minority groups tend to form stereotypes about each other. Stereotypes about one's out-groups (groups to which one does not belong) often contain negative traits. Whereas stereotypes of social groups can develop and even be maintained in the absence of actual experience with the out-groups, perceptions might change when one is exposed to individual out-group members. The contact hypothesis, developed over several years of field research on desegregation, states that contact with individual representatives of a social out-group leads to more positive intergroup attitudes.

Brewer and Kramer (1985) reported that empirical research gives mixed support for the contact hypothesis. Findings indicate that several structural features of the situation affect intergroup differentiation and intergroup attitudes. Some of these structural features are the proportion of persons in the minority, the number of out-groups, the total group size, the cooperativeness of the interaction between the groups, and the relative status of the groups.

Differences in status among groups have been shown to moderate the effect of increased intergroup contact (Schwarzwald & Cohen, 1982). Unequal status inhibits the formation of positive intergroup attitudes. Interestingly, other research indicates that, although equal status can be promoted and produced within a single contact situation, historical differences in status also affect opinions of the out-group (Norvell & Worchel, 1981; Riordan & Ruggerio, 1980).

More recent discussions of the effects of contact with out-groups have indicated the importance of distinguishing between effects on evaluations of individuals versus evalutions of the group as a whole (e.g., Hamburger, 1994), the effect of ethnic identity on out-group preferences (e.g., Masson & Verkuyten, 1993), and the influence of typicality of the group representative on the contact effect (e.g., Desforges et al., 1991; Werth & Lord, 1992).

▨ *Perceptions of Similarity and Variability
in Out-Groups and In-Groups*

A second finding in intergroup relations concerns the differences in perception of in-groups and out-groups. In general, individuals tend to perceive a greater degree of variability among in-group members than among out-group members (Brewer & Kramer, 1985). For instance, people are better able to discriminate between pictures of own-race faces than between those of other-race faces. It may be easier for Asian Americans than non-Asian Americans to distinguish between a Laotian American and a Thai American. Similar results have been found with respect to personality traits (Park & Rothbart, 1982). Other research indicates that group base rate information more often is applied to the behavior of out-group members than to that of in-group members (Higgins & Bryant, 1982). Linville and her colleagues (Linville, 1982; Linville & Jones, 1980) propose that the difference in the perceived variability of in-groups and out-groups is due to differences in the complexity of the cognitive representations of these groups. Lesser degrees of complexity imply greater polarization of intergroup attitudes.

More recent research has indicated that the perceived variability is related to perceptions of the degree of similarity between in-groups and out-groups (e.g.,

Kashima & Kashima, 1993), the importance of the rated dimensions to the in-group's identity (e.g., Brown & Wooton, 1993), and motivations to differentiate one's in-group from other groups (e.g., Brewer, 1993).

Social identity theory, proposed by Tajfel and his colleagues (Tajfel & Turner, 1979), explains differences in in-group/out-group perception using both cognitive and motivational factors. This theory in part was developed to account for in-group bias; that is, out-group characteristics are evaluated more negatively than are in-group characteristics. The theory states that settings that promote the categorization of individuals into social categories also promote the inclusion of category membership as part of one's social identity in those settings. Due to social comparisons among these social categories and the motivation to maintain and enhance social identity, people seek ways in which to distinguish between their own group and out-groups. One test of social identity theory has shown that, given cooperative tasks, groups equal in social status or social roles exhibited increased in-group favoritism (Deschamps & Brown, 1983).

▧ Use of Individuating Information in Perception of In-Groups and Out-Groups

Cognitive heuristics are used in forming judgments under conditions of uncertainty or unavailability or indeterminacy of important information (Tversky & Kahneman, 1974). Heuristics are likely strategies for making social judgments as well as nonsocial ones (Taylor, 1982). Information about people is more ambiguous, less reliable, and more unstable than is information about objects or nonsocial events. People also have intentions, and Taylor (1982) suggested that, because most significant social actions can be committed for a variety of reasons and will produce a variety of consequences, the meaning of social interaction is fundamentally ambiguous. Stereotyping people is a heuristic. It is easier to give a label to a group of people than to remember information about individuals who belong in that group. For example, Asian Americans are commonly stereotyped as mathematically inclined, successful, and nearsighted.

To use individuating information is to use variability judgments in forming impressions of people instead of placing group members into a homogeneous mass. The accumulated research reported in Messick and Mackie (1989) supports the idea that *subtypes,* which in our discussion correspond to differentiations among the Asian American ethnic groups, would lead to individualization of the groups subsumed by the Asian American label. Eventually, one would expect to see changes in the perceptions of out-group members and improved relations between the in-group and the out-group.

Individuating information that can be used in making several social judgments reduces the representativeness of the individual group member, thus decreasing the role of the group stereotype (e.g., Fein & Hilton, 1992). Such a result can be positive for individual group members. In a study of group persuasiveness, Wilder (1990) found that individuating information increased the persuasive capability of out-group members such that they were as influential as in-group members.

There are instances, however, when the beneficial effects of individuation are moderated by other variables (as in the case of group status) or when use of individuating information is inappropriately generalized to the group as a whole. Work by Brewer, Weber, and Carini (1995), for instance, indicated that minority group members are individuated less than are majority group members. Other studies have found that people differ in the relative emphasis they place on their individual and social identities. Simon, Pantaleo, and Mummendey (1995), for example, found that awareness of special treatment of the in-group by society can influence self-identification.

Asian American groups are not homogeneous in terms of their historical experiences. Some experiences are etic (e.g., discrimination), whereas others are emic (e.g., Japanese American internment during World War II). Emic concepts of a particular ethnic group might generalize to form a stereotype of the broad category of Asian Americans. For example, Vincent Chin was murdered in 1980 because two men who blamed Japan for the United States' failing auto industry mistakenly identified him as being of Japanese ancestry.

Individuating information might alter the perception of Asian American ethnic groups, but there is a limit to the amount of information a person can reasonably attend to at a given time. Although the contact hypothesis may suggest that meeting additional group members leads to the use of individuating information, atypical behavior or attributes of these members can be discounted or discarded in favor of the group stereotype (e.g., Bar-Tal, Raviv, & Arad, 1989). A personal example is given by one of the authors, who was consistently questioned as to her native language. She was assumed, falsely, to be a foreign student and was offended because her verbal Graduate Record Examination (GRE) score was higher than her quantitative GRE score.

Asian Americans as an Out-Group

The preceding findings concerning stereotyping of group members are relevant to research methods in the sense that research design, implementation, and interpretation can be performed by researchers who are not members of the Asian American group(s) being studied. We are not stating that research on Asian Americans should be conducted only by Asian American researchers, but we are advocating that research studies be carried out in consultation with Asian Americans who are familiar with and understand the unique social contexts surrounding the group(s). We also need to acknowledge that membership in the Asian American community does not automatically guarantee that researchers are knowledgeable about all aspects of the Asian American experience. Membership does provide for a means to compare stereotypes both within and without the Asian ethnic groups.

People perceive their own groups as exhibiting a greater degree of variability in personality traits than exists in out-groups. Psychologists are prone to the same sort of cognitive bias. Thus, an Asian American social psychologist might provide a very different interpretation of findings involving Asian Americans from that provided by a non-Asian American psychologist. The Asian American psychologist might attribute the research participants' behaviors to some individual difference variable or to some situational variable, whereas an out-group psychologist might be more likely to attribute the same behaviors to a group-level variable (e.g., race). Out-group bias occurs when group members evaluate the characteristics of nonmembers more negatively than they do the characteristics of their own group. One example of out-group bias would be when a Euro-American researcher obtains a difference between Asian American and Euro-American groups in his or her research and then places a pejorative label on the responses of the Asian Americans.

A similar result is obtained when results are interpreted in an ethnocentric manner by non-Asian American researchers. Interpretations based on an ethnocentric view of what is appropriate behavior can have detrimental effects on ethnic communities. As Akbar (1991) pointed out, findings from Eurocentric research often are used to maintain the dominant social relations between members of the majority culture and members of ethnic groups. The construction of findings as evidence for what the ethnic group lacks (i.e., differences imply deficiencies) leads to a focus on altering the characteristics of the minority group. Eurocentric researchers do not often consider the possibility that the responses exhibited by minorities are typical reactions to the situations to which they are exposed, nor do these researchers continue to search for culturally defined strengths that characterize healthy adjustment for ethnic groups. Asian American psychology can contribute to the well-being of Asian Americans by (a) challenging the assumption that characteristics of Euro-Americans can be used to typify the healthy responses of Asian Americans, (b) identifying the unique strengths of each culture, and (c) reinforcing cognitive and behavioral systems that are beneficial to Asian Americans.

The impact of in-group/out-group phenomena on the interpretation of research on Asian Americans varies depending on the conceptual level at which Asian Americans are identified. The phenomena certainly exist at the level of the aggregate category "Asian American." We assume that categorization effects are evident at the level of subtypes (i.e., Asian American ethnic groups). As noted earlier, subtypes are important because they have been proposed as a basic level of categorization and their use leads to individualization of the target persons (Messick & Mackie, 1989). In the case of people, in comparison to objects, it is generally agreed that individuals initially activate primary categories such as race and gender (e.g., Brewer, 1988; Fiske & Neuberg, 1988) rather than subtypes. In this way, ethnic group members always may be perceived as members of a minority rather than as individuals.

Research also can be affected in circumstances where the research participants' self-reference is not congruent with the researcher's definition. For example, research participants might not consider themselves as members of the category "Asian American," choosing to identify with the majority group instead. For whatever reason, such individuals choose *not* to incorporate themselves into the category "Asian American" and view members of the category as out-group members.

We do not discuss the psychological aspects of this choice here, but we do assert that these individuals will exhibit cognitive biases that are similar to those exhibited by non-Asian American out-group members.

Research participants also may prefer to identify themselves as members of a more specific Asian ethnic group (e.g., Indonesian American) rather than as members of the broader category "Asian American." The consequences of this self-identification depend on whether the individuals' cognitive structuring of Asian ethnic groups is or is not hierarchical (e.g., Indonesian American is a sub-category of Asian American). In their review, Messick and Mackie (1989) provided some evidence that cognitive representations of dominant and minority groups are not organized hierarchically. In recent research with Latino ethnic groups, Huddy and Virtanen (1995) found that subgroup differentiation was related to the desire to make positive distinctions between one's own group and others. It remains to be seen whether a similar result would hold for Asian American ethnic groups. The researcher's lack of distinctions among members of Asian American ethnic groups leads to erroneous conclusions, particularly in cases where the groups are considered to be the same when in fact they are not. It is erroneous, for instance, to assume that all Asian Americans have a similar religious background; many Asian Americans are Christians, whereas others practice Hinduism, Taoism, Buddhism, or Islam, and still others might have no particular belief system.

Biases due to in-group/out-group phenomena need not occur only in cases where Asian Americans are research participants; they also can occur when Asian Americans are used as research stimuli (e.g., as target persons in studies of social perception). Stereotypical views of the majority culture can be reinforced through inclusion of characteristics that are regarded, by non-Asian Americans, as being descriptively accurate. Given a limited information base, these stereotypes can crystallize into the undifferentiated majority view of Asian Americans. The most prolific of these myths is that of the "model minority." The model minority myth presents Asian Americans as a standard for other minority groups to emulate because they have better jobs, higher incomes, and more education than does the rest of the American population. Evidence exists (e.g., Lee, 1994; Toupin & Son, 1991) to support the notion that the model minority is a stereotype, that it does not apply to all groups, and that it ignores social-historical information about the immigration experiences and social institutions of each group that account for the differences.

Perceptions of Asian Americans as a Cultural Group

As we have argued thus far, the use of the term "Asian American" as a racial categorization is inadequate in explaining group differences, primarily because racial interpretations ignore the influence of cultural factors. In this subsection, we examine the term's use in designating persons assumed to have some cultural similarities. This is similar to the use of the term "Hispanic" in relation to studies of Latinos in the United States. Marin and Marin (1991) noted that, despite disparate sociodemographic characteristics, Latinos "share some basic cultural values that make them members of a clearly identifiable group" (p. 1). They cited familialism and *simpatia* as values that Latino ethnic groups share.

A purely cultural definition of the term "Asian American" seems to be useful at first, at least in comparative research. Clearly, Asian American groups are culturally different from Euro-Americans and from members of other ethnic minority groups. Two problems, related to the degree of cultural similarity among ethnic groups, arise with use of the cultural definition. First, Asian ethnic groups differ widely in some aspects of culture. Although some foods, family centeredness, and filial piety may be common to many Asian groups, other aspects of culture are less common. Recall our earlier illustration of religious differences. Variability in culture may be so great that aggregation across Asian ethnic groups obscures any differences between the broader category "Asian American" and the other groups to which it is compared.

Second, even if ethnicity is accounted for, Asian American individuals differ in the extent to which they acknowledge, express, and act on common cultural values. This difference is partially due to the level of acculturation each person has achieved. Persons who are bicultural (i.e., those who maintain a sense of cultural identity and value relationships with the majority culture) and persons who are separated (i.e., those who maintain their identity and do not relate to majority culture) adhere to ethnic cultural values more than do assimilated or marginalized individuals. The consequences of acculturation include shifts in behaviors, cognitions, and personality characteristics (Berry, Trimble, & Olmedo, 1986).

Crucial to obtaining a sample of research participants representative of a particular group is the identification of possible differences of psychological or behavioral importance within the group. Examples of such group-level parameters that are commonly used in psychological research are gender, age, and educational level. Of specific interest to us is the identification of those parameters that help us define the ethnicity of the respondents. Ethnicity refers to the degree to which an individual maintains some tie to an ethnic group; an ethnic group is defined as a category of persons who share a common socio-cultural history. We note in passing that race is not always synonymous with the term "ethnicity."

Traditional Operationalizations of Ethnicity

Marin and Marin (1991) presented three general ways in which Hispanic ethnicity can be operationalized: ancestry/national origin, cultural characteristics, and self-identification (ethnic identity). These three operationalizations of ethnicity are examined here for their usefulness with Asian American populations. Operationalized in the first manner, ethnicity refers to characteristics of persons living in the United States who trace their ancestry to one of the nations of Asia or the Pacific Rim. Classification of individuals as "Asian American" proceeds by asking the research participants questions pertaining to their national origins or birthplaces or the national origins of their family members. If family members are from more than one Asian/Pacific Rim country, then participants indicate the country from which most family members come or the country to which they feel the closest. Misclassifications can occur in cases where the participants' families have resided in the United States for several generations. One flaw with this method is that it does not adequately address mixed ancestry or instances of long-term residence in countries outside of the United States, Asia, or the Pacific Rim.

Although respondents may be accurate in their reports of their ancestry/ national origin, its use as the sole indicator of ethnicity is not recommended. Knowledge of one's ancestry is not necessarily correlated with knowledge of, or adherence to, the customs, values, beliefs, and attitudes governing the behavior of persons raised within that ethnic culture. Transmission of these aspects of culture may or may not have occurred because of the level of acculturation evident in the respondents' families, the research participants' age cohort, and other factors.

A second operationalization of ethnicity involves the use of sociocultural characteristics such as surname, language, and religion. Ethnic identification by Asian surname is more problematic for some Asian ethnic groups than for others. Filipinos, for instance, may have Spanish surnames (due to the Spanish colonization of the Philippines). Misidentification also occurs as a result of out-marriages; a non-Asian spouse acquires an Asian surname, or an Asian spouse loses one. As mentioned earlier, it is difficult to assess the ethnicity of children of mixed heritage. This problem will continue to arise in the future as the rate of interracial marriages increases. A possible alternative to reliance on surnames involves questioning individuals about their middle names because many first-generation Asian parents give their children Asian middle names.

Asian language use, proficiency, and/or preference as measures of ethnicity also are problematic. Use of an Asian language may affirm the interpersonal ties within the ethnic social network. Proficiency in an Asian language is more common for recent immigrants; it is less common for later generation individuals. Preference denotes one aspect of a person's motivation to affirm ethnic self-identity. Language as an index of Asian American ethnicity is fallible because members of some ethnic communities may be more or less bilingual on their entrance to the United States (e.g., Asian Indians, Filipinos).

A direct means of assessing Asian American ethnicity is to query the respondents about their self-identification. As mentioned earlier, individuals might prefer the more narrowly defined ethnic subgroup label to the broad category label, or they might perceive the meaning of these categories differently from the researcher. Research by Giachello, Bell, Aday, and Anderson (1983, as cited in Marin & Marin, 1991) provided evidence for differences in self-identification as a function of place of birth.

Each of these approaches depends on single-item probes and, for reasons argued in the introduction to this chapter, will be inherently unreliable markers of Asian American ethnicity. Consistent with a multiple indicator approach to the identification of Asian American ethnicity, an investigator who wanted to employ markers such as language or self-reported identification might employ them in combination to define the ethnicity construct. These markers might be employed as measured indicators of a latent variable of Asian American ethnicity, consistent with the true score perspective given in Figure 2.2. Alternatively, one might think of each of these indicators as accounting for an independent component of Asian American ethnicity that jointly predicts the degree of expressed ethnicity (as in the "cause indicator" models discussed by Bollen & Lennox, 1991). In any case, we believe that a careful consideration of a psychological construct of Asian American identity requires a multiple indicator perspective.

ASIAN AMERICAN ETHNIC IDENTITY

In this section, we illustrate the complexities of the construct of ethnic identity through discussion of some practical and theoretical issues. We do not consider models of the development and maintenance of Asian American ethnic identity because this is presented elsewhere (cf. this volume, Chapter 9). In our view, understanding the nature of ethnic identity is crucial insofar as identity serves to guide overt behavior and psychological responses in various settings.

Domains of Ethnicity

Trimble (1990) posited that ethnicity, a latent variable, can be measured in three domains: *natal*, where typical questions might ask respondents to indicate their place of birth as well as the places of birth of their parents, grandparents, and great-grandparents; *behavioral*, which indicates language usage and the settings in which different languages are used, media usage, patterns of friendship, membership in various organizations, and food and musical preferences; and *subjective*, in which respondents indicate their values, assess their own ethnicity, and state their attitudes toward out-groups. These three domains of ethnicity have been postulated elsewhere (Smith, 1980; Weinreich, 1986). Employment of such a framework of ethnic identification enables the researcher to classify respondents along an ethnic identification continuum. Several problems might arise, however, when ethnicity is construed as a unidimensional construct. For example, a biculturalism construct might be difficult to account for in a continuous, unidimensional framework. An implicit assumption in the categorization of an individual as a Tibetan American, for instance, is that this person exhibits attributes that are explained to some extent by "Tibetanness" and by "Americanness." Unidimensional frameworks cannot account for persons who exhibit both Tibetanness and Americanness.

Unidimensional frameworks also are problematic in handling differences in the degree to which individuals identify themselves with particular ethnicity domains. It certainly is possible for a person to self-identify with one ethnicity domain but not with others. For example, although a Tongan American might easily be able to state where he or she was born and what languages he or she speaks, the individual might not be able to articulate any beliefs he or she holds as being specifically American or Tongan. The incorporation of ethnicity into one's self-identification depends on several factors including the degree to which one has been socialized as a member of an ethnic group, one's generation, the social environment in which the research takes place, and one's acculturative status. We describe each of these in turn.

▩ Ethnic Socialization

To a large degree, ethnic self-identification results from a socialization process that is dependent on the person's parents, extended family, the presence or absence of other members of the same ethnic groups, and other ethnic groups (including the majority group). As mentioned earlier, social identity theory explains how interactions with members of other groups can result in the motivation to consider social group membership as an aspect of one's identity.

In a recent review article on the family ecologies of ethnic minorities, Harrison, Wilson, Pine, Chan, and Buriel (1990) discussed how adaptive strategies develop in response to the challenges brought about by ethnic status. The goal of socialization, for both the majority and minorities, is the development of children into functioning members of society. Ethnicity directs the course of socialization in minority families in different directions from those of the majority; ethnic group behavioral patterns, values, beliefs, customs, and the like are ingrained in the lives of minority children (Phinney & Rotheram, 1987).

Harrison et al. (1990) described two socialization goals that have been adopted by minority families. The first, positive orientation toward one's ethnic group, promotes "biculturalism and acceptance of the orientations of the ancestral worldview" (p. 355). In one of the few studies of family socialization of ethnic attitudes, Bowman and Howard (1985) demonstrated how the success of African American children is related to what their parents had taught them about racial barriers in society.

The second goal, interdependence, promotes connection to the extended family and the ancestral worldview of collectivism. Parents encourage the development of personality traits that are consistent with interdependence (e.g., cooperation, obligation, sharing). The developmental literature contains studies of this aspect of socialization in African American, American Indian, and Hispanic families (Kagan & Madsen, 1971; Osborne, 1985; Sims, 1978), but Harrison et al. (1990) reported that no comparable studies exist for Asian American families.

The role of nonsociodemographic factors such as parental and school influences on racial identification is increasingly mentioned in the literature. Unfortunately, many of the existing studies that have examined the role of parental influence on racial identification have been criticized because they rely on the doll preference methodology (Clark & Clark, 1947). Some researchers have begun to consider intergroup and intragroup interaction as necessary parameters in theories of racial identification. Helms (1990) proposed a model of racial identity development in African Americans that includes such factors. White and Parham

(1990) also hypothesized that the level of interaction within one's racial group influences the degree to which identification with the in-group is exhibited.

Sanders Thompson (1991) noted that few studies have examined the effects of sociodemographic variables and experiences with intergroup relations at the same time. One study (Sanders Thompson, 1990) showed that racial attitudes and perceived experiences with racism were more important influences than were sociodemographic variables on ethnic identification. In a more recent study, Sanders Thompson (1991) found that both intergroup and intragroup variables predicted racial identification. One intergroup variable, age at which racism was first experienced, predicted the physical and sociocultural factors of racial identification, whereas experiences with discrimination predicted the psychological dimensions.

▨ Generational Differences

Two types of generational influences can be considered when studying Asian American ethnic identity. The first deals with intrafamily dynamics (e.g., parent-child relations), whereas the second is concerned with the influence of the immigration experience and, more specifically, with the number of generations an Asian American has resided in the United States (e.g., the Issei, Nisei, Sansei, and Yonsei distinctions made among Japanese Americans). In a discussion of generational influences, it is important to ascertain the unique roles played by the number of generations a target individual is removed from the immigrant experience and the role of family dynamics. Generational processes were investigated by Masuda, Matsumoto, and Meredith (1970) and by Pierce, Clark, and Kaufman (1978-1979), who found differences among three generations of Japanese Americans with distinct successive attentuation of ethnic identity with increasing acculturation. The generational differences among members of a particular Asian American group occur because of cultural and developmental influences, especially between parents or elders who were raised in a more traditional Asian culture and children who were greatly influenced by the prevailing American culture. Differences in dietary preferences are more easily accommodated than are differences in values between the ethnic culture and American culture. Gradual changes in food habits of Asian Indian immigrants from vegetarianism to meat eating occurred with increased residency in the United States (Gupta, 1975). The children of these Asian Indian immigrants are Americanized in their associations with the opposite sex, attitudes toward dating, and marriage practices despite familial influences. Traditional Chinese cultural norms and social roles have less of an influence in Chinese American families, especially in the case of adolescent females (Fong, 1973).

Generational differences are confounded with differences due to one's pattern of acculturation, which also depends on the time period during which the individual immigrated to the United States. Earlier immigrants (pre-Immigration

Act of 1965) tended to be less educated, came from poor rural villages, and were primarily sojourners. Wong-Rieger and Quintana (1987), in a comparative study of Southeast Asian (Vietnamese, Malaysian, Thai, Singaporean, and Indonesian) and Hispanic immigrants and sojourners, found that immigrants and intended sojourners have different attitudes toward acculturation and the acceptance of American values. The researchers found biculturalism to be the most satisfactory form of acculturation in both immigrants and sojourners. Certain recent immigrants such as Asian Indians, Chinese from Taiwan, and Vietnamese who came immediately after the fall of Saigon are well educated, have English language skills, and emigrated for economic and educational reasons.

The importance of acculturation and ethnic identity rises and diminishes during various stages of development such as those found by Phinney (1989), Phinney and Alipuria (1990), and Rotheram-Borus (1990) in studies of Asian Americans, African Americans, Latinos, and European Americans. During adolescence, depending on one's peers and family relationships, the individual might feel pressure to become either more or less ethnic. Individuals who were raised in the United States might feel the need to reaffirm their ethnic identity when they have children of their own (e.g., Spencer & Markstrom-Adams, 1990). Phinney and Chavira (1992) also showed that the need to affirm one's ethnic identity takes place in minority youths.

There also are acute differences between recent immigrants and each succeeding generation that is raised in the United States. The further away an individual is from the ancestors who immigrated, the closer that individual is to the American norm in terms of frequently measured social and developmental variables such as achievement in mathematical and verbal skills, delinquency, and dating behavior. Acculturation and ethnic self-identity always will be an issue for all Asian Americans simply because of physiognomy. Each succeeding generation is faced with the retention or reacquisition of traditional ethnic values as a consequence of parental, peer, ethnic group, and societal pressures.

The American myth of a melting pot society cannot be fully realized with Asian Americans because of their obvious and salient physical features. Because of their physiognomy, it is difficult to speak of Asian assimilation into the prevailing European American society even by way of plastic surgery or intermarriage. Acculturation must be addressed instead of assimilation, as would be the case with European Americans. Even these strategies do not guarantee unconditional acceptance by the dominant society.

The acculturation process is accelerated by social contacts and by social and economic mobility. Prior to World War II, Asian immigrants and sojourners were legally restricted to certain areas, enclaves, or ghettos. Recent immigrants tend to cluster together because of language and other barriers, not because of restrictive laws. Increasing competency in the English language, increasing education, and higher socioeconomic status allow Asian Americans greater structural social mobility and status but not greater social acceptance.

▮ Situated Identity

Trimble (1990) pointed out that "one's identification with an ethnic group is not static or immutable. It can and does change over time as a function of varied circumstances and social contexts" (p. 161). In other words, ethnic self-identity is situated, at least partially, on the basis of the social environment in which individuals are placed.

The social environment can be defined in terms of geographic location. There are differences between individuals who are in an atmosphere where ethnicity is not salient or where it is so pervasive that they do not commonly think of themselves as belonging to an ethnic group and those persons who are constantly reminded of their ethnicity through overt or covert racism.

A striking comparison can be made between Asian Americans living in Hawaii and those living on the mainland United States. A totally different, almost insurmountable, set of circumstances exists for these Asian Americans. Japanese Americans form the largest Asian American group in Hawaii, comprising about 23% of the population. Together, all Asian American groups make up 43% of the population of Hawaii. Although European Americans make up 32% of the population, most of them live on military bases, away from the indigenous population of which the vast majority are Asian or Pacific Americans. Because the social environment in Hawaii is so dissimilar to that on the mainland, the inclusion or exclusion of Asian Americans from that state as research participants must be indicated.

A different type of geographic comparison can be made between Asian Americans living in enclaves (e.g., Chinatown, Little Tokyo) and those living among European Americans in cities and in suburbia. Differences between these two groups of Asian Americans are likely to be affected by social demographic factors, especially in the case of newly arrived immigrants who prefer, want, and need resources provided by the ethnic community. Different types of ethnic social networks and systems of social support have evolved due to different concentrations of Asian Americans living in various locations. Indeed, the influences exerted by family and peer groups through social norms, roles, and modeling result in varying degrees of ethnic self-identification; social support for maintaining one's ethnicity is more easily found within ethnic enclaves and in communities where there is a significant percentage of one's own ethnic group.

▮ Acculturative Status

To distinguish among ethnic groups identified as Asian American on a target set of questions (particularly those that assess ethnicity on the basis of natality), one might well consider the individual's level of acculturation. Acculturation has been of primary interest to cross-cultural psychologists. For example, acculturation has been shown to be associated with mental health (Szapocznik & Kurtines, 1980), social deviance (Graves, 1967), health-related behaviors (Marin, Perez-Stable, & Marin, 1989), levels of social support (Griffith & Villavicencio, 1985), and political participation (Lien, 1994). We believe that the concept is useful in ethnic psychology as well because consideration of differing levels can yield finer distinctions among Asian Americans. We now turn to some of the problems that investigators have confronted in operationalizing and measuring acculturation.

Mendoza and Martinez (1981) defined acculturation as "the process of accumulating and incorporating the beliefs and customs of an alternate culture" (p. 71). Acculturation thus involves changes in the behavioral and subjective domains of ethnicity. Among first- and second-generation individuals, degree of acculturation may be influenced by the reasons for their immigration to the United States. Chinese who left their country for political reasons may be more likely to accept Western lifestyles than will individuals who left China for economic reasons and want to return.

Many researchers have expressed ideas concerning the process of acculturation. Triandis (1985) posited that individuals can (a) *accommodate* or move in the direction of the mainstream culture, (b) *overshoot* or move beyond the level of the mainstream, or (c) undergo *ethnic affirmation* in which the individual's behavior moves away from the mainstream. Padilla (1980) proposed a model of acculturation that has two aspects: cultural awareness and ethnic loyalty. According to Keefe and Padilla (1987), cultural awareness "refers to an individual's knowledge of cultural traits (for example, language, history, culture heroes) of the traditional and host cultures" (p. 46). Ethnic loyalty is defined as the preference for one's own culture over other cultures. Padilla (1980) hypothesized that less-acculturated persons will be more likely to prefer ethnic-related activities. Most important, Padilla believed that acculturation is multidimensional. His model posits five dimensions: (a) language familiarity and usage, (b) cultural heritage, (c) ethnic pride, (d) ethnicity, and (e) interethnic distance. Moreover, this definition of acculturation indicates that acculturation is not a unidimensional process that ultimately assesses whether the individual can "pass" as a member of the host society. Berry (1980) stated that people have mistakenly referred to such a unidimensional process as acculturative when in fact it is an assimilation hypothesis. As mentioned throughout this chapter, the physiognomy of Asian Americans does not make such an assimilation hypothesis conducive for measuring the acculturation of Asian Americans. As research has shown with Latinos (Felix-Ortiz, Newcomb, & Myers, 1994), the construction of Asian American ethnic identity is a multidimensional process, and research methodologies must take multidimensional approaches to this problem.

A second multidimensional model of acculturation was offered by Mendoza and Martinez (1981). The first dimension of their model distinguishes among the affective, cognitive, and behavioral components. Certain aspects of behavior are more susceptible or amenable to change than are others (e.g., a newly immigrated Asian Indian woman might readily discard her sari for Western attire but still prefer vegetarian cuisine). In addition, a person can exhibit varying degrees of acculturation within each of these aspects. For instance, a Japanese American might speak Japanese but, at the same time, follow more American norms of politeness.

The second dimension of the Mendoza and Martinez (1981) model classifies people based on their degree of assimilation of the dominant culture's behavioral patterns and the extinction of indigenous patterns. The authors propose four possible profiles:

1. Cultural resistance indicates the lack of assimilation as individuals actively or passively resist the host culture.
2. Cultural shift denotes assimilation without extinction as tendencies of one's own culture are replaced with those of the host culture.
3. Cultural incorporation also indicates assimilation without extinction because individuals retain patterns representative of both cultures.
4. Cultural transmutation indicates the transformation of patterns from both cultures into a third culture.

Mendoza and Martinez note three advantages of a multidimensional approach to acculturation. First, the level of acculturation can be assessed on any or all of the modalities (affective, cognitive, and behavioral). An example is the assessment of cognitive acculturation through language usage. Cultural resistance would be evidenced by sole use of one's native language, cultural incorporation would be assessed through bilingualism, cultural transmutation would consist of the simultaneous use of both languages (e.g., the use of Taglish, Tagalog, and English by Filipino Americans), and cultural shift would be indexed by adoption of the host culture's language. Second, a multidimensional perspective also provides for the classification of individuals on the different modalities. Third, one can view the inclusive approach as an inventory of acculturation.

Whereas there is a general understanding of the definition of acculturation, a variety of research issues need to be addressed before concluding that acculturative processes can be easily and adequately assessed. First, there is a host of acculturation scales and ethnic identity scales that have taken different approaches to measuring acculturation. Results from studies using different measures of acculturation are not directly comparable. We know that there is a fair degree of factorial validity between the Suinn-Lew Asian Self-Identity Acculturation Scale (SL-ASIA) (Suinn, Rickard-Figueroa, Lew, & Vigil, 1987) and the Acculturation Rating Scale for Mexican Americans (Cuellar, Harris, & Jasso, 1980), but this finding appears to be the exception rather than the rule. Phinney (1992), on the other hand, developed a multigroup ethnic identity scale for comparative purposes across groups.

Marin (1992) also pointed to a number of general problems with the assessment of acculturation. We feel that these problems are worth mentioning as they pertain to the research undertakings using acculturation as an explanatory variable. First, Marin pointed out that previous efforts to measure acculturation are not psychometrically grounded. For example, analyses of internal consistency and validity are not given their due attention. Moreover, sociodemographic characteristics such as generational status are treated not as correlates of acculturation but rather as direct measures of acculturation. Such a procedure will lead to spuriously high correlations. The Hispanic Health and Nutrition Survey, for example, combines criterion and measurement variables in its assessment of acculturation.

Marin (1992) stated that the researcher must guard against overemphasizing variables such as educational level and language usage as measures of acculturation. Marin pointed out that when he used language as an approximate measure of acculturation, 12% of his respondents would be misclassified when compared to their scores on a psychometrically sound acculturation scale. Moreover, recent immigrants might have high educational levels and low levels of acculturation, so educational status is not an adequate proxy variable for acculturation.

Marin (1992) also pointed to the need to develop multidimensional scales of acculturation. For example, he argued that unidimensional frameworks of acculturation often assume that the usage of one's native language decreases as acculturation increases. Moreover, this framework assumes that bilingualism falls in quite nicely between being monolingual in the native and host languages. Such a framework does not reflect the multidimensional aspects of acculturation. In fact, these language assessments can easily be performed separately to circumvent simplifying unidimensional approaches.

STATISTICAL AND METHODOLOGICAL APPROACHES FOR THE INVESTIGATION OF ASIAN AMERICAN IDENTITY

Ethnic Identification

In addition to assessing Asian American ethnicity by self-reporting ancestry/national origin, cultural characteristics, and ethnic self-identification, we suggest a method that involves collecting information on an individual from persons in the respondent's perceived in-group. The proposed alter/ego method rests on the proposition that a person belongs to a group only if the group accepts the person as a member; in this regard, it is related to the contextual approach mentioned earlier. The alter/ego method is similar to social network techniques (Breiger, 1981) used in the study of corporate structure (Galaskiewicz & Wasserman, 1981), group problem solving (Bavelas, 1950), social perception (Krackhardt, 1987), and social support (Wellman & Wortley, 1990).

In the proposed alter/ego method, a person names the ethnic group with which he or she identifies and then lists other persons in this group who know the person. The researcher asks the named others (alters) to identify the ethnic group to which the target respondent (ego) belongs. If the ego and the alters all agree on the ego's ethnicity, then there is no ambiguity in assigning the ego to an ethnic group. If the alters do not all agree among themselves, then the researcher could assign the ego to the ethnic group to which the preponderance of alters assign him or her; the researcher could obtain a "percentage agreement" measure based on the proportion of alters who identified the ego as belonging to the assigned ethnic group.

The researcher may wish to use a degree measure of ethnicity (rather than an "either/or" measure) such as is obtained with most acculturation scales. The percentage agreement measure just mentioned could be used as it is. As another possibility, the researcher may ask the alters to rate, on a Likert-type scale, the degree to which the ego exhibits important or distinguishing characteristics of the ethnic group in question. The researchers could average these ratings across the alters to obtain the desired measure. Identity structure analysis (ISA) is another method of determining ethnicity. ISA defines and operationalizes a number of superordinate concepts pertaining to sociophysical processes of identity development and change within specific sociohistorical contexts (Weinreich, 1991). As in all research of this type, the researcher should take care to avoid eliciting stereotypes or employing ethnic glosses. These issues should be of little importance so long as the alters, rather than the researcher or other outside members, define the characteristics they feel are important.

Several issues deserve consideration with regard to the suggested method of identifying ethnicity. One set of concerns focuses on the group from which one selects the alters. Another treats the issue of how to handle disagreements in classification among the ego and the alters. These two sets of issues can be discussed in terms of the contextual and consensus models mentioned earlier.

▨ Issues of Context

The researcher defines the context of the ethnic identification by selecting the pool from which alters are drawn. At the very narrowest, the researcher would question only the ego about ethnicity, yielding the one-item measure discussed previously. The researcher also could question the family, other relatives, friends, co-workers, members of the ethnic community, or the community at large.

With family and close friends or other small communities, the researcher could easily obtain information from every member in the pool. Every person in the group could conceivably rate every other person, possibly using the Likert format mentioned previously. A degree measure of ethnicity could be obtained for every person. The researcher could use the ethnicity ratings for the alters to weight their respective ratings of the ego, under the assumption that those individuals most immersed in the culture would be best able to judge the cultural identification of others.

When the researcher focuses on a large community, only a subset of all possible alters can be sampled. The researcher should be careful to elicit the names of those in the community who are ethnically identified and who are in a position to assess the characteristics of the ego rather than just eliciting the names of the ego's friends. On the other hand, the researcher might want to assess how well or in what contexts the alters know the ego so that the researcher may judge for himself or herself how much stock to place in the alters' ratings of the ego. Indeed, the perceptions of alters who know the ego well might be qualitatively (and not just quantitatively) different from the perceptions of alters who know the ego only by reputation or hearsay.

▦ *Issues of Consensus*

Another set of issues deals with consensus. If everyone agrees on the ethnicity of the ego, then there is no problem. If the ego and alters disagree, however, then the researcher must decide how to resolve the conflict. We argue that in this situation, the researcher should emphasize the judgments of the alters over that of the ego. The members of the group of which the ego claims to be a part should determine whether or not the ego actually exhibits the characteristics of that group. It is important that research with an ethnic group include respondents who have shared the core experiences that define the group.

Problems could arise even when the ego and the alters all agree. Suppose that a certain clique of individuals claims to be a part of an ethnic group, which in turn does not recognize the clique as being part of the ethnic group. (If this scenario sounds unrealistic, then consider a recent musical group called Young Black Teens, of which none of the members is African American.) Suppose that the ego is drawn from this clique and that the ego names as alters only (or primarily) members of the clique. In this case, the ego and alters all would reach consensus on the ego's ethnicity, although the larger ethnic community would disagree. We do not imagine that this situation would occur often; however, the researcher should be aware of it and try to guard against it. The researcher can do so by judiciously wording the name generator or the probe that elicits names of alters.

The proposed alter/ego method of identifying ethnicity differs from the consensus model in Figure 2.2 in another important respect. Here we focus exclusively on the ethnic group in which the ego claims membership. We pay no attention to the views of the out-groups or even to those of the researcher. We already have stated that people tend to employ superficial characteristics to classify those not in their own group and use these classifications to generate stereotypes about individual behaviors. Insofar as research on ethnicity should focus on how an individual's particular cultural characteristics and experiences shape his or her interactions with the environment, the researcher should question only those in a position to accurately identify those characteristics and experiences.

Ethnic Glosses

Trimble (1990) referred to the use of labels such as "Asian American" and "Latino" as "ethnic glosses." Using these ethnic glosses leads one to homogenize very distinct Asian American (or other ethnic) populations that may differ in cultural origins, religion, immigration history, foreign/domestic upbringing, generational upbringing, gender, and other characteristics. Wong (1982) indicated that at least 32 ethnic and cultural populations may be considered as Asian American and Pacific Islander. The 1980 census provides information on only eight distinct subgroups of Asian Americans and Pacific Islanders with a ninth category for "others." The 1990 census gives information for 15 ethnic subgroups of Asian Pacific Americans; the 13 distinct subgroups are Chinese, Filipino, Japanese, Asian

Indian (not in 1980 census), Korean, Vietnamese, Cambodian (not in 1980 census), Laotian (not in 1980 census), Thai (not in 1980 census), Hmong (not in 1980 census), Hawaiian, Guamanian, and Samoan, with 2 separate categories for other Asian and other Pacific Islander (not in 1980 census). These added Asian and Pacific Islander ethnic subgroups in the 1990 census are an improvement, but ethnic glosses certainly are not an accurate method of identifying ethnic subgroups.

To illustrate our point, consider the findings of Marin and Marin (1982) on ethnic glosses. A total of 500 medical patients in East Los Angeles, an area that is densely populated with Latinos, were asked to indicate their ethnicity from a list containing various ethnic glosses. A number of respondents with Spanish surnames indicated that they were "White" or "other." Interestingly, those who checked the "other" category specified it with the term "Mexican American" or "Chicano." Acuña (1988) and Barrera (1979) found that people have these terms as well as others, such as "Hispano" or "Raza," to identify themselves as Mexican. Obviously, the use of categories such as "Asian American" instead of "Oriental," or "African American" instead of "Negro," conveys different connotations to the individual. As an example, it has been shown that more positive characteristics are associated with the label "Mexican American" compared to the label "Chicano" (Lampe, 1977). Furthermore, as times change, some terms may become unacceptable.

A number of studies show differences among subgroups of Asian Americans. Barringer, Takeuchi, and Xenos (1990) used the 1980 census to examine differences in education, occupation, and personal income among several subgroups of Asian Americans. They found that each of the Asian American subgroups (except Vietnamese) was more educated than European Americans, African Americans, and Latinos; that Asian American men (except Filipinos) had more formal education than did the women in their respective subgroups; and that Vietnamese Americans had the lowest income of all ethnic groups including Latinos and African Americans. Japanese Americans were found to be more similar to European Americans in socioeconomic terms than were the other subgroups of Asian Americans. Barringer et al. note that the Japanese "have a long history of immigration but few recent immigrants." These authors hypothesize that Chinese Americans, Korean Americans, and Asian Indian Americans have varied income levels due to their different times of immigration.

Two studies cited by Sue and Okazaki (1990) also showed differences among various Asian American subgroups. Sue and Abe (1988) found that educational performance significantly differed across some Asian American subgroups. Acculturation differences among high school Asian American subgroups were found by Dornsbuch, Prescott, and Ritter (1987).

As an illustration of the argument against using ethnic glosses, consider a typical study in which the researcher is interested in studying differences in scholastic achievement between Asian Americans and European Americans. Let us assume that the Asian American sample comes from an educational setting on the West Coast of the United States; furthermore, assume that the majority of the Asian Americans are Vietnamese American. In Orange County in Southern California, these are very reasonable assumptions. Sampling another group of Asian Americans, say Japanese Americans, would lead to very different results. External validity is severely damaged by use of ethnic glosses.

Trimble (1990) suggested that relying on ethnic glosses provides little information on the cultural framework of the groups and, more important, provides no means for replicating the study. We also argue that the findings of studies using the rubrics of ethnic glosses are relevant only to the samples used in the study and that there exists little, if any, generalizability of results. Instead of ethnic glosses, Trimble encouraged researchers to provide detailed information that yields measures of (a) ethnic identification, (b) situated identity, and (c) acculturative status. Acquiring information on these measures should satisfy Postulates 1 and 2 presented earlier in the chapter.

Convergent Ethnic Identity:
Self-Identification Versus Classification by the Researcher

Depending on the way in which questions about ethnic identity are phrased, the individual may answer differently. The individual could answer with the family name, the region of the country from which his or her ancestors emigrated, the particular Asian ethnic group, Asian American, or American. In addition to this ethnic self-label, the individual forms differing cognitive representations of ethnic self-identity within varying social contexts. The degree of Asian Americanness reported by an individual at a particular point in time also depends on the self-identified image perceived through interaction with the researcher and with the immediate social environment.

An individual could assert that he or she is Laotian to one person and a few minutes later assert that he or she is an American. There need not be any conflict in the individual's psyche; the statements could be based on the perceived social support for, and the perceived persecution based on, one's ethnicity. The plasticity of ethnic self-identification makes it imperative that the researcher be extremely careful in wording questions about ethnicity if a single ethnic term is used to describe the individual. Use of an ethnic self-identification index would be a better way in which to ascertain the degree of Asian Americanness of a research participant.

The idea that the definition of the category "Asian American" has similar meaning for the research participants as it does for the researcher often is only an untested assumption. Although on the exterior it might appear that the participants understand the meaning of the category label, researchers do not often ask their respondents whether the label has any psychological meaning beyond categorization; it is not clear whether identifying oneself with a category necessarily implies that belonging to the category has other behavioral consequences.

In the case where the researcher is using a label to apply to a group of persons with a common social-historical experience, it is important to determine whether or not the study participants view themselves as having these experiences. Due to a lack of information about their cultural and national backgrounds and the social, political, and economic histories of their ethnic groups, some individuals might not identify with the label because they do not consider themselves as having anything in common with others in the group. This might be particularly true of those persons who have not had the opportunity to meet or socialize with other Asian Americans (e.g., persons who live in areas far removed from other Asian Americans). This would be consistent with our Postulate 2 because the existing social context would not support (and might even extinguish) attempts to self-identify as an Asian American.

A contrast can be made with those persons who do not classify themselves as Asian American because they identify specifically with their ethnic group rather than with the broader social category. Again, this is consistent with our Postulate 2; the existing social context in this case supports a more differentiated and specific view of ethnic identity. A dramatic example is found in the types of inter-Asian gang violence in which clear social demarcations among different Asian groups exist. Gang members might see themselves as having more similar experiences with persons of their own ethnic group than with persons of other Asian ethnicities. In addition, participants who label themselves in this manner probably are more likely to believe that their ethnic group maintains a culture that is different from that of other Asians. Clearly, the self-identities of these persons are more narrowly defined than a global (and externally provided) characterization of Asian Americans (as might be provided by the researcher).

The model of egocentric social categorization (ESC model) predicts an asymmetry in the cognitive construal of in-groups and out-groups as social categories (Simon, 1993). First, there is a differentiation between *me* and *not me*. Second, there is an asymmetry in the cognitive construal of in-groups and out-groups in which the in-group is construed as a heterogeneous aggregate of separate entities and the out-group is construed as a homogeneous social category. The ESC model differs from ethnic glosses in that it is the out-group that is homogenized. A study by Crocker and Luhtanen (1990) showed that people who are high in collective self-esteem rated their own in-group higher on test scores than did those low in collective self-esteem. Analyses based on personal esteem did not show an interaction.

Differences in the acculturation patterns of research participants might be related to differences in the attachment to the "Asian American" label. On the one hand, individuals of Asian ancestry and heritage may identify themselves solely as being American and not as Asian American or as members of a particular ethnic group. This would be more likely to occur for those individuals who have acculturated with the majority culture. In some instances, individuals may deny their ethnic heritage completely, even neglecting their physical attributes. On the other hand, individuals may identify themselves as being Asian, not Asian American. This would be more likely to occur for first-generation immigrants, foreign nationals, sojourners, and others who are less acculturated. In both instances, the term is viewed as being inappropriate to the participants.

Lastly, differences in attachment to the "Asian American" label might be a response to the political climate rather than a feeling of ethnic identity. Depending on the context in which the research is conducted, an individual who chooses to identify himself or herself by using a more narrowly defined ethnic label (e.g., Cambodian, Thai, Indian) also may identify at some other level as Asian American. One example might be when the participants perceive that the research involves comparisons between Asian Americans and persons of other racial/ethnic groups. Again, this illustrates how social context may affect the salience of specific features of ethnic self-identity.

Assessment of Ethnic Identity

▓ *Domains of Ethnicity*

There are a variety of statistical techniques that can be employed to better understand ethnic identification. Trimble (1990) suggested the use of a hierarchical nesting procedure in which respondents first provide information on birthplace (their own as well as that of their parents, grandparents, great-grandparents, etc.), and next on their preference for ethnic composition of their neighborhood. The third level of this nesting procedure would consist of information on friends, acquaintances, and so forth.

Another method that may be used to determine the strength of ethnic identification was developed by Bogardus (1925), who measured attitudes of different ethnic groups. He developed a scale that ranged from asking people to indicate whether they "would marry" a person from another ethnic group to asking whether they "would live outside [their] country." Bogardus' social distance procedure is similar to one of the levels of the nesting procedure suggested by Trimble (1990).

Factor analysis is a popular method of obtaining scores on multiple scales to reflect levels of ethnic identity. Phinney (1992) proposed the Multigroup Measure of Ethnic Identity, to be used with diverse groups, which assesses three aspects of ethnic identity: positive ethnic attitudes and sense of belonging, ethnic identity achievement, and ethnic behaviors. The SL-ASIA was developed specifically for Asian Americans and identified five factors: reading/writing/cultural preference, ethnic interaction, affinity for ethnic identity and pride, generational identity, and food preference (Suinn, Ahuna, & Khoo, 1992).

A fourth possible strategy would be to employ multidimensional techniques to investigate ethnic identity. Earlier, we strongly discouraged viewing ethnic identity as a unidimensional continuum. Multidimensional scaling (MDS) (Kruskal & Wish, 1978) could be used to determine the perceived psychological distances among groups of stimuli, which in our case would be among the various Asian American ethnic groups. Multidimensional scaling of Latino ethnic groups was studied by Morera and Bolt (1996).

A hypothetical Asian American MDS research strategy follows. Respondents are first asked to rate the similarity of various Asian American ethnic groups to each other. Assuming that all Asian American ethnic groups are the same (an assumption we believe to be false), the stimulus spaces for each ethnic group should be the same. If these stimulus spaces are different for each ethnic group, then the Asian American ethnic groups are perceived to be different from each other. From each stimulus space, a number of dimensions are extracted. If one dimension is extracted, then similarities among different groups are based on a single dimension. If more than one dimension is extracted, then similarity judgments are more complex. If various strategies yield similar results with respect to ethnic identification, then Postulate 1 has been satisfied.

▨ Situated Identity

According to Trimble (1990), specific situations must be taken into consideration when determining ethnic identity, thereby obtaining situated identity. Identity structure analysis (ISA) is a method developed by Weinreich (1986, 1991) to assist in ethnic self-identification in various situations. ISA is a method of determining "a person's conflicted identification with another, so that the relative magnitudes of self's various identification conflicts may be estimated" (Weinreich, 1986, p. 300). Trimble (1990) considered ISA to be a "complex array of measurement items, and therefore could be time-consuming" (p. 161), but a shortened version of ISA could be used.

▨ Acculturative Status

A factor analytic approach may be used to determine acculturative status. Factor analysis of a large number of items that purport to measure cultural awareness and ethnic loyalty, among other central constructs, may yield fewer factors than constructs. A decision rule, based on interitem correlations and frequency distributions, to determine which items to delete also would shorten the questionnaire.

The SL-ASIA (Suinn et al., 1987) is an acculturation scale modeled after Cuellar et al.'s (1980) acculturation scale for Chicanos. The 21 items of the SL-ASIA cover language, identity, friendship patterns, generational level, behaviors, and attitudes. The scale allows for the assessment of preferences as well as behavior. Reliability estimates for the SL-ASIA were more than adequate. Concurrent validity results showed that the SL-ASIA scores were correlated with demographic information hypothesized to reflect levels of Asian American identity (Suinn et al., 1992). Factorial validity was determined by comparing factors obtained for the SL-ASIA with factors reported for a similar scale measuring ethnic identity of Hispanics.

There are many advantages in using the SL-ASIA. First, the SL-ASIA addresses the issue of acculturative multidimensionality by attempting to account for biculturalism as well as for cognitive, behavioral, and attitudinal modalities. Second, each of the 21 questions is worded such that it indicates specific Asian American ethnic group membership (e.g., Thai, Burmese).

A possible problem with the SL-ASIA is the determination of an acculturation score. Participants respond to 21 multiple choice questions, and a total value is found by summing across the responses for these items. The summed score is divided by 21 to obtain an average acculturation score, which may range from 1 to 5. A problem arises in the arbitrary weighting of each of the dimensions because there are four questions that deal with language and therefore approximately 19% (4/21) of the acculturation score has a language component.

Another problem that needs to be addressed is the implicit assumption that one acculturation scale is adequate for all Asian American ethnic groups. Among Latinos, acculturation scales have been designed for Cubans (Garcia & Lega, 1979) and Chicanos (Cuellar et al., 1980; Olmedo & Padilla, 1978). Considering that Wong (1982) identified 32 distinct Asian American ethnic groups, it might be a bit tedious to construct 32 acculturation scales. However, one acculturation scale for all Asian American ethnic groups may be inadequate.

One possible alternative to numerous acculturation scales is to form focus groups (H. C. Triandis, personal communication, 1992). We may assume that there is an etic or universal construct of acculturation that a given scale such as the SL-ASIA may tap. In a focus group, a few members of various Asian American ethnic groups are interviewed to discover possible emic or culture-specific items that members of a particular Asian American ethnic group think are important to their respective group. Such a procedure will add items to the general acculturation scale, and the additional items should form a new factor that might enable the researcher to differentiate among various Asian American ethnic groups. For example, speaking the Nepalese language among the third- and fourth-generation Nepalese Americans might not be a dimension that these individuals take into consideration when identifying themselves as Nepalese.

Having presented paradigms for how investigators might more informatively ask questions about Asian American populations that have emphasized clear articulation of the research questions to be addressed and the development of an index of Asian American ethnicity based on multiple indicators, we next go on to present ways in which statistical methods can be employed to test these research hypotheses. We do not intend this as an all-exhaustive review of the types of methodological and statistical techniques that can be brought to bear in studies of Asian American populations, nor can we anticipate the types of research questions that might arise in any particular study. We offer this review as a way of introducing some basic concepts and directing readers to additional readings.

Analysis of Between-Group Designs

In research involving the comparison of Asian Americans with other ethnic groups, questions often are framed in terms of hypotheses of mean differences or the degree to which some outcome assessed in Asian Americans exceeds or falls short of performance in other groups. Research questions involving the comparative academic performance of Asian Americans versus that of other groups imply mean differences among the groups ("Do Asian Americans score higher on the SAT than other ethnic groups?"). These mean level differences are analyzed by a between-group analysis of variance, which is discussed in a number of standard psychological statistics texts (e.g., Keppel, 1973; Neter, Wasserman, & Kutner, 1994).

After determining that such between-group differences exist, slightly more elaborate hypotheses about the nature of these differences might be entertained. The researcher could attribute the apparent main effect of ethnicity to the amount of time parents spend with their children. In this case, the operating assumption is that of a closed system in which all factors that might influence an outcome are taken into account within a particular study; in other words, no spurious relations among factors exist. Cook and Campbell (1979) framed this discussion in terms of the internal validity of a study. As it relates to this particular example, the research question being posed is the extent to which ethnic group differences decrease if child-parent interaction time is assessed.

We can generalize examination of these between-group differences in two ways. Besides main effect hypotheses, we can examine nonlinearities between predictors and an outcome. In our example, it might be the case that, even among families with high levels of child-parent interaction, Asian American academic performance is even greater than that of other ethnic groups. Such a finding would represent the presence of a statistical interaction between ethnic group membership and child-parent interaction in the prediction of academic performance or what is referred to as a moderator effect (Aiken & West, 1991; Baron & Kenny, 1986; Cohen & Cohen, 1983). By taking into account the joint multiplicative effects of ethnic group membership and child-parent interaction, we can reliably improve the prediction of academic performance over considering their joint additive effects. Ethnic/cultural background also is critical for understanding personal development and family interactions (Hines, Garcia-Preto, McGoldrick, Almeida, & Weltman, 1992).

A second method of extending this basic result is to consider studies with more than one outcome variable. The benefit of a multivariate approach to outcomes is that the intercorrelations among study outcomes are accounted for simultaneously. Among multivariate techniques, the multivariate analysis of variance can be employed to determine where between-group level differences exist on multiple outcome variables, whereas discriminant analysis can be used to determine what combination of variables maximally discriminates among ethnic groups.

We see two problems in focusing on statistical methods that highlight between-group comparisons. The first is what is referred to as a mixture problem in statistics (Stuart & Ord, 1987). Interpretation of simple between-group differences will be complicated to the extent that intragroup (within Asian American) heterogeneity exists. Factors such as acculturation level and sociodemographic status may contribute to such heterogeneity, as may the differences that exist among the ethnic groups classified as being Asian American.

A second problem in employing these comparative statistical models to evaluate between-group differences is their emphasis on description; observed differences between the groups in cognitions, behaviors, personality, attitudes, and other psychological phenomena are merely recorded and documented. If any explanations are developed for these differences, they often emerge post hoc in response to research findings. What is missing from this perspective is an emphasis on the process by which these between-group differences emerged (McLoyd, 1991). Methods that explore only mean differences among groups will be less interesting than a process-oriented approach that attempts to understand the culturally and ethnically specific (emic) factors that contribute to a psychological outcome.

Research Methods Directed Toward a Process Orientation in Asian American Psychology

We develop an example to show how an initial hypothesis that would appear to implicate simple between-group differences can be stated in terms of a more interesting model of psychological process. Take the superior performance of Asian Americans in computationally and mathematically oriented professions. As a level hypothesis, this can be simply stated as "Asian Americans do better in mathematics." This explanation focuses on the extent to which category membership predicts success in particular professions.

A process-oriented strategy might instead focus on those factors that mediate the relation between ethnic group membership and the outcome. Suppose that societal norms on the career aspirations of ethnic group members create perceived barriers to entry into and achievement in other, nontechnical fields. In this context, success in technical occupations is the end point of a set of background factors that are ignored when drawing simple conclusions based on between-group differences.

The multiple factors that contribute to psychological outcomes in Asian American populations require more complex statistical models. The embeddedness of Asian American identity within a social structure will likely serve as mediators of a simple characterization of an Asian American research participant as a member of a particular group. As more interrelated constructs are added to models in Asian American psychology, statistical methods involving multivariate methods will become increasingly appropriate. Among these multivariate techniques, latent variable structural equation modeling (e.g., Tanaka et al., 1990) provides one comprehensive statistical model that allows us to address in a simultaneous fashion within-group questions about mediators as well as the between-group comparisons that have typified research with Asian American participants to date. Tanaka et al. (1990) provided a nontechnical introduction to this area as well as a list of references that will guide the appropriate use of this statistical method.

The strength in Asian American psychology will come from the replicability of findings across multiple studies. This simply echoes our earlier concerns with construct validity and planned multiplism. Phinney (1990) reviewed 70 studies published since 1972 on ethnic identity and suggested focusing on common elements that apply across groups. Given that any single study of an Asian American population will be insufficient to draw more general conclusions, a more productive strategy for advancing knowledge in Asian American psychology would be to develop collaborations across research sites and populations that focus on comparable assessment techniques. This suggestion is conceptually similar to work in meta-analysis that focuses on the aggregated relations among psychological constructs across multiple studies. By approaching the study of Asian American psychology in this manner, the researcher will be able to better understand both the extent to which findings do generalize across diverse Asian American sub-populations and the conditions that limit such generalizations.

CONCLUSION

So far, we have attempted to mention pertinent issues in the enhancement of Asian American psychology. In studying any racial/ethnic group, the researcher may either compare his or her findings to another group of individuals (e.g., the dominant culture) or investigate research findings solely within the realm of the particular racial/ethnic group under consideration. This section outlines issues to consider when studying racial/ethnic groups in a comparative and noncomparative fashion. Following a discussion on comparative and noncomparative research, we mention a paradigm for research methods in the study of Asian American psychology.

Comparative Research

In comparative studies, the researcher investigates the similarities and differences between Asian Americans and members of other broad ethnic/racial categories. Asian Americans frequently are compared to members of other racial/ethnic groups. The classic research design consists of the introduction of race/ethnicity as a predictor or control variable. In studies where the researcher reports differences between ethnic groups, data typically are analyzed using some form of the general linear model (e.g., analysis of variance, multiple regression) (Tidwell, 1980).

The stated goal of comparative research often is descriptive; that is, observed differences between the groups in their cognitions, behaviors, personality, and other psychological phenomena are merely recorded and documented. Explanations for the differences are derived after the fact; they are developed in response to research findings. We argue that hypotheses and explanations for differences should be developed before the research is conducted; they are developed to guide the research strategy and methodology.

The absence of a priori theoretical approaches to guide the development of research questions in this context leads to several problems. We argued earlier that the researcher's and research participants' definition of the category "Asian American" may result in interpretations of the findings that are psychologically meaningless, inaccurate, unreliable, or ambiguous. Faulty interpretations are especially likely to occur when the label is used to designate a racial category.

Other problems pertaining to comparative research have been noted elsewhere by McLoyd (1991) in regard to research about African Americans. Comparisons of different ethnic/racial groups may result in interpretations that have negative consequences for the minority groups, especially in those instances where the researcher does not have an understanding of the unique cultural and social-historical experiences of the members of those groups. When Asian Americans or other minority groups are compared to Euro-American groups, the psychology of the latter often is held as the standard. Consequently, findings are presented in ways that describe how minority members *do not* behave rather than how they *do* behave, thus neglecting any culturally or ethnically specific (emic) factors that contribute to their psychological well-being. This situation also encourages interpretation of psychological and behavioral differences between the groups as deficiencies or abnormalities rather than as unique responses to the environments encountered by minorities. As McLoyd states, we need to "understand the processes of transmission and acquisition of required competencies in the context of cultural and survival tasks presented by the environment" (p. 431).

In this sense, comparisons of racial groups are incomplete in that they focus primarily on categorizations based on physical attributes or personal characteristics that are associated with race and disregard characteristics of the social ecology that contribute to the individual's psychology. For example, inattention to the effects of racism and discrimination (a situational and systematic factor) on the aspirations of minorities (a psychological phenomenon) may result in concluding that Asian Americans have a particular aptitude (a second psychological phenomenon) for computationally based occupations because they enroll and succeed (the observed behavioral phenomenon) in these fields. An alternative interpretation for their observed success in technical fields is that Asian Americans perceive and experience a wide variety of barriers to entry and achievement in other, nontechnical fields. This is one example in which a person-blame/person-centered explanation was derived in lieu of a person-environment one. We argue that there is nothing inherently risky about comparative research conducted within a cultural framework. However, such characterizations are more fruitful when couched in terms of the psychological processes that contribute to between-group differences.

As noted previously, comparison of Asian Americans with other racial/ethnic groups is difficult to interpret due to intragroup heterogeneity introduced by level of acculturation and social-demographic variables. Thus, the researcher who decides on doing such comparisons should deal with them in some way, either methodologically or statistically. Depending on the researcher's resources, theoretical orientation, and personal preferences, several avenues are available to deal with these third variables.

One acceptable means of dealing with acculturation and social-demographic characteristics is to gather information about these variables beforehand and use this information in the sampling and research design of the study. Within each racial/ethnic group, a sample of research participants stratified according to the values on these variables could be obtained. For instance, the researcher may stratify according to level of acculturation. In a different instance, persons of each racial/ethnic group can be matched according to the information gathered about the third variables.

Another means of dealing with third variables is to design a study in which the variable is held constant. For example, the researcher may decide to study only those individuals in each racial/ethnic group who are recent immigrants to the United States. This can happen only in those instances where the researcher had access to information about these variables before the research sample is drawn. In most cases, particularly in terms of level of acculturation, the researcher does not have access to this information beforehand. Finally, the influence of these third variables can be investigated by measuring them within the context of other aspects of the study. For example, the researcher assesses the generational level of his or her research participants by asking them whether they were born and raised in the United States or in some other country.

The effects of these third variables can be treated statistically in several different ways. The researcher can analyze their effects by including these variables as additional predictors, covariates, or mediators within different linear models based on psychological theory or the researcher's hypotheses concerning the relationship between these variables. There is, however, one instance in which the use of acculturation as a predictor is not always meaningful; that is when one of the racial/ethnic groups is composed of Euro-Americans. Because Euro-Americans are members of the dominant culture in the United States, it is fallacious to consider adaptation to their own culture as being comparable to the adjustment of racially distinct ethnic groups to the same culture.

So far, we have dealt primarily with the issues that traditionally have been addressed in discussions of internal validity, the degree to which "we infer that a relationship between two variables is causal or that the absence of a relationship implies the absence of a cause" (Cook & Campbell, 1979, p. 37). We now devote some space to issues concerning external validity, the degree to which "we can infer that the presumed causal relationship can be generalized to and across different types of persons, settings, and times" (p. 37). Cook and Campbell (1979) made explicit the distinction between generalization to target populations (ascertaining whether or not results hold for target populations) and generalization across populations (ascertaining whether or not the results hold in specific subpopulations).

Cook and Campbell (1979) advanced three threats to external validity that are described in terms of statistical interaction effects: selection by treatment, setting by treatment, and history by treatment. Selection by treatment involves consideration of the categories of persons to which cause-and-effect relationships can be generalized. Setting by treatment involves consideration of the context in which research is conducted. History by treatment involves consideration of replicability of results at different time points.

In our discussion of comparative research, we are concerned with the use of race/ethnicity as a "treatment" and the interaction of race/ethnicity with selection, setting, and history. As mentioned previously, Asian American subpopulations vary greatly in terms of acculturation, language, and social-demographic characteristics. It would be erroneous for the researcher to conclude, on the basis of a single comparative study in which only a few Asian American ethnic subgroups were sampled, that his or her findings were generalizable to Asian Americans as a whole. The last two threats to external validity, setting by racial/ethnic group and history by racial/ethnic group, often are evident in comparative studies, the first due to differences between ethnic groups in the willingness to cooperate with researchers coupled with differences in social ecologies of these groups and the second due to differences in these groups' social ecologies.

Other than the fact that these threats exist, we return to the question of whether or not cross-racial/ethnic comparisons yield information that is useful to the advancement of Asian American psychology. We repeat that if the purpose of research is to understand "universal" aspects of human behavior, then comparisons of this nature are useful. If the purpose of the research is to understand how the behavior of Asian Americans differs from that of Asians, then such a comparison would yield a wealth of information about cultural transmission and maintenance as well as information about ecological influences. In other instances, comparisons with other groups might be unnecessary. Hence, we turn to an ethnic discussion of noncomparative research.

Noncomparative Research

In contrast to comparative research, research in this context avoids comparisons across racial/ethnic groups and focuses on the psychology of a single group as a whole. The goal of this research also might be descriptive, but in this case the research findings pertain only to Asian Americans. Thus, the psychology of members of the category "Asian American" would not be judged relative to that of any other racial/ethnic group. In this type of research, the validity of research findings is judged in terms of their applicability to Asian Americans.

Many of the threats to internal and external validity mentioned in the previous subsection describing comparative research are applicable here as well. Inferences made about the relationship between genetic or biological factors/race and various psychological phenomena still will be confounded by the interaction of these factors with cultural and environmental factors, which indicates that variables such as level of acculturation, self-identification as a member of an ethnic group, and social-demographics should be included in research. In addition, researchers who want to make generalizations about the psychology of Asian Americans as a group should be concerned about the representativeness of the research samples they have obtained or should at least know something about the particulars of the Asian ethnic subgroups they have sampled to determine the samples' representativeness.

We perceive other difficulties that are inherent in noncomparative approaches to research on Asian Americans. First, even if no overt comparisons with the majority are being made, inadvertent comparisons might be operating because the researcher has selected culturally insensitive measurement instruments. This occurs when the instruments have been developed and normed on European American samples. Second, nonverbal assessment instruments (e.g., behavioral observations) also can exhibit Eurocentric bias in that persons who are unfamiliar with Asian Americans might not recognize cultural responses. In other instances, non-Asian American research assistants might elicit reactions different from those of ethnically similar research assistants. Lastly, noncomparative research suffers from the same lack of cultural specificity that occurs in comparative research when Asian ethnic groups are combined into the broader category. Aggregation conceals the variance in psychological and behavioral pehenomena within the Asian American population. Interpretations based on aggregation may apply to no single Asian American individual or even to one specific Asian American ethnic group.

A Paradigm for Asian American Research Methods

We began this chapter with the assumption that rigorous research methods are imperative for any investigation within an Asian American psychology. Our conclusions about this point relate around a central theme of Asian American self-identity. In the absence of this psychological construct, we feel it is difficult to draw conclusions about the way in which ethnicity should serve to predict or guide behavior. In the service of this theme, we believe that investigators need to consider process-oriented models that explain both the antecedents of Asian American self-identity and its subsequent behavioral consequences.

What types of efforts of individual investigators interested in Asian American psychology would contribute to achieving this goal? In any single investigation, sampling pragmatics will minimize the generalizabilty of study findings. In our midwestern setting, we clearly would be unable to identify as many Asian respondents as we might if we were located along the Pacific Rim. It also seems intuitively clear to us that the characteristics of respondents in our setting would likely not be comparable to those found in other settings, again limiting the types of conclusions and generalizations that we would like to make.

We will not be able to understand the complex processes in Asian American psychology without a better comprehension of the nature of our study populations. This suggests to us that a fruitful Asian American psychology that focuses on process-oriented research might begin with a better understanding of sampling. Rather than relying on convenience samples, we might need to understand the characteristics of our Asian American respondents in a more complete way. The two-stage sampling strategy in prevention research by Kellam (1990) might successfully be adapted in the study of Asian Americans. After obtaining an initial population-based sample of Asian Americans, we might subsequently draw a subsample of those individuals who either strongly or weakly identify as being Asian American. Such a sampling strategy might provide great insight into how Asian American self-identity serves as a guide for behavior.

After this first step, we believe that a critical second step is the development of methods that ensure construct comparability in defining Asian American self-identity. Again, any single study will be limited in the extent to which generalizable conclusions can be drawn. The extent to which investigators interested in Asian American issues can work in a collaborative atmosphere to provide both conceptual and empirical links across studies will be highly useful. Although this does not mean that all investigators need to run replications of each other's work, the extent to which links can be made will strengthen unifying themes in Asian American psychology.

NOTE

1. This does raise an interesting question to which we do not have an answer. If, in fact, the scores of recently arrived Asian American immigrants are included in the aggregated reported scores on, for example, the Verbal subtest of the SAT and our speculation is correct, then a more closely focused comparison looking at native English-speaking Asian Americans and other groups defined by ethnicity would likely yield even larger differences.

REFERENCES

Acuña, R. (1988). *Occupied America: A history of Chicanos* (3rd ed.). New York: Harper & Row.

Aiken, L. R., & West, S. G. (1991). *Multiple regression: Testing and interpreting interactions.* Newbury Park, CA: Sage.

Akbar, N. (1991). Paradigms of African American research. In R. L. Jones (Ed.), *Black psychology* (pp. 709-725). Berkeley, CA: Cobb & Henry.

Bank, L., Dishion, T., Skinner, M., & Patterson, G. R. (1990). Method variance in structural equation modeling: Living with "glop." In G. R. Patterson (Ed.), *Depression and aggression in family interaction* (pp. 247-279). Hillsdale, NJ: Lawrence Erlbaum.

Baron, R. M., & Kenny, D. A. (1986). The moderator-mediator distinction in social psychological research: Conceptual, strategic, and statistical considerations. *Journal of Personality and Social Psychology, 51,* 1173-1182.

Barrera, M. (1979). *Race and class in the Southwest.* Notre Dame, IN: University of Notre Dame Press.

Barringer, H. R., Takeuchi, D. T., & Xenos, P. (1990). Education, occupational prestige, and income of Asian Americans. *Sociology of Education, 63,* 27-43.

Bar-Tal, D., Raviv, A., & Arad, M. (1989). Effects of information on student-teachers' stereotypic perceptions of pupils. *British Journal of Educational Psychology, 59,* 143-154.

Bavelas, A. (1950). Communication patterns in task-oriented groups. *Journal of the Acoustical Society of America, 22,* 271-282.

Bentler, P. M. (1978). The interdependence of theory, methodology, and empirical data: Causal modeling as an approach to construct validation. In D. B. Kandel (Ed.), *Longitudinal research on drug use: Empirical findings and methodological issues* (pp. 267-302). Washington, DC: Hemisphere.

Berry, J. W. (1980). Acculturation as varieties of adaptation. In A. Padilla (Ed.), *Acculturation: Theory, models and some new findings.* Boulder, CO: Westview.

Berry, J. W., Trimble, J. E., & Olmedo, E. L. (1986). Assessment of acculturation. In W. J. Lonner & J. W. Berry (Eds.), *Field methods in cross-cultural research* (pp. 291-324). Beverly Hills, CA: Sage.

Bogardus, E. S. (1925). Measuring social distance. *Journal of Applied Psychology, 11,* 299-308.

Bollen, K., & Lennox, R. (1991). Conventional wisdom on measurement: A structural equation perspective. *Psychological Bulletin, 110,* 305-314.

Bowman, P. J., & Howard, C. (1985). Race-related socialization, motivation, and academic achievement: A study of Black youth in three-generation families. *Journal of the American Academy of Child Psychiatry, 24,* 134-141.

Breiger, R. L. (1981). The social class structure of occupational mobility. *American Journal of Sociology, 87,* 578-611.

Brewer, M. B. (1988). A dual process model of impression formation. *Advances in Social Cognition, 1,* 1-36.

Brewer, M. B. (1993). Social identity, distinctiveness, and in-group homogeneity. *Social Cognition, 11,* 150-164.

Brewer, M. B., & Kramer, R. M. (1985). The psychology of intergroup attitudes and behavior. *Annual Review of Psychology, 36,* 219-243.

Brewer, M. B., Weber, J. G., & Carini, B. (1995). Person memory in intergroup contexts: Categorization versus individuation. *Journal of Personality and Social Psychology, 69,* 29-40.

Brislin, R. W. (1986). The wording and translation of research instruments. In W. J. Lonner & J. W. Berry (Eds.), *Field methods in cross-cultural research* (pp. 137-164). Beverly Hills, CA: Sage.

Brown, R., & Wooton, M. L. (1993). Perceptions of group homogeneity during group formation and change. *Social Cognition, 11,* 126-149.

Campbell, D. T., & Fiske, D. W. (1959). Convergent and discriminant validation by the multitrait-multimethod matrix. *Psychological Bulletin, 56,* 81-105.

Cattell, R. B. (1988). Psychological theory and psychological method. In J. R. Nesselroade & R. B. Cattell (Eds.), *Handbook of multivariate experimental psychology* (pp. 3-20). New York: Plenum.

Chan, S. (1991). *Asian Americans: An interpretive history.* Boston: Twayne.

Clark, K. B., & Clark, M. P. (1947). Racial identification in Negro children. In T. M. Newcomb & E. L. Hartley (Eds.), *Readings in social psychology* (pp. 169-178). New York: Holt.

Cohen, J., & Cohen, P. (1983). *Applied multiple regression/correlation analysis for the behavioral sciences* (2nd ed.). Hillsdale, NJ: Lawrence Erlbaum.

Cook, T. D., & Campbell, D. T. (1979). *Quasi-experimentation: Design and analysis issues for field settings.* Boston: Houghton Mifflin.

Crocker, J., & Luhtanen, R. (1990). Collective self-esteem and ingroup bias. *Journal of Personality and Social Psychology, 58,* 60-67.

Cronbach, L. J., & Meehl, P. E. (1955). Construct validity in psychological tests. *Psychological Bulletin, 52,* 281-302.

Cuellar, I., Harris, L. C., & Jasso, R. (1980). An acculturation scale for Mexican American normal and clinical populations. *Hispanic Journal of Behavioral Sciences, 2,* 199-217.

Deschamps, J. C., & Brown, R. J. (1983). Superordinate goals and intergroup conflict. *British Journal of Social Psychology, 22,* 195-198.

Desforges, D. M., Lord, C. G., Ramsey, S. L., Mason, J. A., van Leeuwen, M. D., West, S. C., & Lepper, M. R. (1991). Effects of structured cooperative contact on changing negative attitudes toward stigmatized social groups. *Journal of Personality and Social Psychology, 60,* 531-544.

de Vera, M. (1986). *Establishing cultural relevance and measurement equivalence using emic and etic items.* Unpublished doctoral dissertation, University of Illinois, Urbana-Champaign.

Dornsbuch, S. M., Prescott, P. L., & Ritter, P. L. (1987, April). *The relation of high school academic performance and student effort to language use and recency of migration among Asian- and Pacific-Americans.* Paper presented at the annual meeting of the American Educational Research Association, Washington, DC.

Fairchild, H. H. (1991). Scientific racism: The cloak of objectivity. *Journal of Social Issues, 47,* 101-115.

Fein, S., & Hilton, J. L. (1992). Attitudes toward groups and behavioral intentions toward individual group members: The impact of nondiagnostic information. *Journal of Experimental Social Psychology, 28,* 101-124.

Felix-Ortiz, M., Newcomb, M. D., & Myers, H. (1994). A multidimensional measure of cultural identity for Latino and Latina adolescents. *Hispanic Journal of Behavioral Sciences, 16*(2), 99-115.

Fiske, S. T., & Neuberg, S. L. (1988). A continuum model of impression formation: From category based to individuating processes as a function of information, motivation, and attention. *Advances in Experimental Social Psychology, 23,* 1-74.

Fong, S. L. M. (1973). Assimilation and changing social roles in Chinese Americans. *Journal of Social Issues, 29,* 115-127.

Fugita, S. S., & O'Brien, D. J. (1991). *Japanese American ethnicity: The persistence of community.* Seattle: University of Washington Press.

Funder, D. C. (1991). Global traits: A neo-Allportian approach to personality. *Psychological Science, 2,* 31-39.

Galaskiewicz, J., & Wasserman, S. (1981). A dynamic study of change in a regional corporate network. *American Sociological Review, 46,* 475-484.

Garcia, M., & Lega, L. (1979). Development of a Cuban ethnic identity questionnaire. *Hispanic Journal of the Behavioral Sciences, 1,* 247-261.

Giachello, A. L., Bell, R., Aday, L. A., & Anderson, R. M. (1983). Uses of the 1980 census for Hispanic health service research. *American Journal of Public Health, 73,* 266-274.

Gibbs, J. T., Huang, L. N., & Associates. (1990). *Children of color: Psychological interventions with minority youth.* San Francisco: Jossey-Bass.

Graves, D. T. (1967). Acculturation, access and alcohol in a tri-ethnic community. *American Anthropologist, 69,* 306-321.

Griffith, J., & Villavicencio, S. (1985). Relationships among acculturation, sociodemographic characteristics and social support in Mexican American adults. *Hispanic Journal of Behavioral Sciences, 7,* 75-92.

Gupta, S. P. (1975). Changes in the food habits of Asian Indians in the United States: A case study. *Sociology and Social Research, 60,* 87-99.

Hamburger, Y. (1994). The contact hypothesis reconsidered: Effects of the atypical outgroup member of the outgroup stereotype. *Basic and Applied Social Psychology, 15,* 339-358.

Harrison, A. O., Wilson, M. N., Pine, C. J., Chan, S. Q., & Buriel, R. (1990). Family ecologies of ethnic minority children. *Child Development, 61,* 347-362.

Helms, J. E. (1990). The beginnings of a diagnostic model of racial identity. In J. E. Helms (Ed.), *Black and White racial identity: Theory, research, and practice* (pp. 83-104). Westport, CT: Greenwood.

Higgins, E. T., & Bryant, S. L. (1982). Consensus information and the fundamental attribution error: The role of development and in-group versus out-group knowledge. *Journal of Personality and Social Psychology, 43,* 889-900.

Hines, P. M., Garcia-Preto, N., McGoldrick, M., Almeida, R., & Weltman, S. (1992). Intergenerational relationships across cultures. *Families in Society: The Journal of Contemporary Human Services, 73,* 323-338.

Houts, A. C., Cook, T. D., & Shadish, W. R., Jr. (1986). The person-situation debate: A critical multiplist perspective. *Journal of Personality, 54,* 52-105.

Huddy, L., & Virtanen, S. (1995). Subgroup differentiation and subgroup bias among Latinos as a function of familiarity and positive distinctiveness. *Journal of Personality and Social Psychology, 68,* 97-108.

Hui, C. H., & Triandis, H. C. (1989). Effects of culture and response format on extreme response style. *Journal of Cross-Cultural Psychology, 20,* 296-309.

Jayaratne, T. E., & Stewart, A. J. (1991). Quantitative and qualitative methods in the social sciences: Current feminist issues and practical strategies. In M. M. Fonow & J. A. Cook (Eds.), *Beyond methodology: Feminist scholarship as lived research* (pp. 85-106). Bloomington: Indiana University Press.

Kagan, S., & Madsen, M. C. (1971). Cooperation and competition of Mexican, Mexican-American, and Anglo-American children of two ages under four instructional sets. *Developmental Psychology, 5,* 32-39.

Kashima, E. S., & Kashima, Y. (1993). Perceptions of general variability of social groups. *Social Cognition, 11,* 1-21.

Keefe, S. E., & Padilla, A. (1987). *Chicano ethnicity.* Albuquerque: University of New Mexico Press.

Kellam, S. (1990). Developmental epidemiological framework for family research on depression and aggression. In G. R. Patterson (Ed.), *Depression and aggression in family interaction* (pp. 11-48). Hillsdale, NJ: Lawrence Erlbaum.

Keppel, G. (1973). *Design and analysis: A researcher's handbook* (2nd ed.). Englewood Cliffs, NJ: Prentice Hall.

Kitano, H. H. L., & Daniels, R. (1995). *Asian Americans: Emerging minorities* (2nd ed.). Englewood Cliffs, NJ: Prentice Hall.

Krackhardt, D. (1987). Cognitive social structures. *Social Networks, 9,* 109-134.

Kruskal, J. B., & Wish, M. (1978). *Multidimensional scaling.* Beverly Hills, CA: Sage.

Kuhn, T. (1970). *The structure of scientific revolution* (2nd ed.). Chicago: University of Chicago Press.

Lampe, P. (1977). Ethnic identification among minority groups in public and parochial school. *Ethnic Groups, 1,* 337-352.

Landrine, H. (1995). *Bringing cultural diversity to feminist psychology: Theory research and practice.* Washington, DC: American Psychological Association.

Lee, S. J. (1994). Behind the model-minority stereotype: Voices of high- and low-achieving Asian American students. *Anthropology and Education Quarterly, 25,* 413-429.

Lien, P. (1994). Ethnicity and political participation: A comparison between Asian and Mexican Americans. *Political Behavior, 16,* 237-264.

Linville, P. W. (1982). The complexity-extremity effect and age-based stereotyping. *Journal of Personality and Social Psychology, 42,* 193-211.

Linville, P. W., & Jones, E. E. (1980). Polarized appraisals of out-group members. *Journal of Personality and Social Psychology, 38,* 689-703.

Loevinger, J. (1957). Objective tests as instruments of psychological theory. *Psychological Reports, 3,* 635-694.

Lord, F. M., & Novick, M. R. (1968). *Statistical theories of mental test scores.* Reading, MA: Addison-Wesley.

Lott, B. (1991). Social psychology: Humanist roots and feminist future. *Psychology of Women Quarterly, 15,* 537-548.

Lumsden, J. (1976). Test theory. *Annual Review of Psychology, 27,* 251-280.

Marin, G. (1992). Issues in the measurement of acculturation among Hispanics. In K. F. Geisinger (Ed.), *Psychological testing of Hispanics* (pp. 235-252). Washington, DC: American Psychological Association.

Marin, G., Gamba, R. J., & Marin, B. V. (1992). Acquiescence and extreme response sets among Hispanics: The role of acculturation and education. *Journal of Cross-Cultural Psychology, 23,* 498-509.

Marin, G., & Marin, B. V. (1982). Methodological fallacies when studying Hispanics. In L. Brickman (Ed.), *Applied social psychology annual* (Vol. 3, pp. 99-117). Beverly Hills, CA: Sage.

Marin, G., & Marin, B. V. (1991). *Research with Hispanic populations.* Newbury Park, CA: Sage.

Marin, G., Perez-Stable, E. J., & Marin, B. V. (1989). Cigarette smoking among San Francisco Hispanics: The role of acculturation and gender. *American Journal of Public Health, 79,* 196-198.

Masson, C. N., & Verkuyten, M. (1993). Prejudice, ethnic identity, contact and ethnic group preferences among Dutch young adolescents. *Journal of Applied Social Psychology, 23,* 156-168.

Masuda, M., Matsumoto, G. H., & Meredith, G. M. (1970). Ethnic identity in three generations of Japanese Americans. *Journal of Social Psychology, 81,* 199-207.

McGuire, W. J. (1984). Search for the self: Going beyond self-esteem and the reactive self. In R. A. Zucker, J. Aronoff, & A. I. Rabin (Eds.), *Personality and the prediction of behavior* (pp. 73-120). New York: Academic Press.

McGuire, W. J., McGuire, C. V., & Cheever, J. (1986). The self in society: Effects of social contexts on the sense of self. *British Journal of Social Psychology, 25,* 259-270.

McLoyd, V. C. (1991). What is the study of African American children the study of? In R. L. Jones (Ed.), *Black psychology* (pp. 414-440). Berkeley, CA: Cobb & Henry.

Mendoza, R. H., & Martinez, J. L. (1981). The measurement of acculturation. In A. Baron (Ed.), *Explorations in Chicano psychology* (pp. 71-82). New York: Praeger.

Messick, D. M., & Mackie, D. M. (1989). Intergroup relations. *Annual Review of Psychology, 40,* 45-81.

Mies, M. (1991). Women's research or feminist research? The debate surrounding feminist science and methodology. In M. M. Fonow & J. A. Cook (Eds.), *Beyond methodology: Feminist scholarship as lived research* (pp. 60-84). Bloomington: Indiana University Press.

Min, P. G. (1995). *Asian Americans: Contemporary trends and issues.* Thousand Oaks, CA: Sage.

Morera, O. F., & Bolt, D. (1996, May). *Is social distance influenced by social contact and context?* Paper presented at the annual meeting of the Midwestern Psychological Association, Chicago.

Mura, D. (1991). *Turning Japanese: Memoirs of a Sansei.* New York: Atlantic Monthly Press.

Neter, J., Wasserman, W., & Kutner, M. H. (1994). *Applied linear statistical models: Regression, analysis of variance, and experimental designs* (3rd ed). Homewood, IL: Irwin.

Norvell, N., & Worchel, S. (1981). A reexamination of the relation between equal status contact and intergroup attraction. *Journal of Personality and Social Psychology, 41,* 902-908.

Olmedo, E., & Padilla, A. (1978). Empirical and construct validation of a measure of acculturation for Mexican Americans. *Journal of Social Psychology, 105,* 179-187.

Osborne, B. (1985). Research into Native North Americans' cognition: 1973-1982. *Journal of American Indian Education, 24,* 9-25.

Oyama, S. (1991). Bodies and minds: Dualism in evolutionary theory. *Journal of Social Issues, 47,* 27-42.

Padilla, A. (1980). The role of cultural awareness and ethnic loyalty in acculturation. In A. Padilla (Ed.), *Acculturation: Theory, models, and some new findings* (pp. 74-84). Boulder, CO: Westview.

Park, B., & Rothbart, M. (1982). Perception of out-group homogeneity and levels of social categorization: Memory for the subordinate attributes of in-group and out-group members. *Journal of Personality and Social Psychology, 42,* 1051-1068.

Park, K. B., Upshaw, H. S., & Koh, S. D. (1988). East Asians' responses to Western health items. *Journal of Cross-Cultural Psychology, 19,* 51-64.

Pearce, A. (1994). Investigating biases in trainee counsellors' attitudes for clients from different cultures. *British Journal of Guidance and Counselling, 22,* 417-428.

Phinney, J. S. (1989). Stages of ethnic identity development in minority group adolescents. *Journal of Early Adolescence, 9,* 34-49.

Phinney, J. S. (1990). Ethnic identity in adolescents and adults: Review of research. *Psychological Bulletin, 108,* 499-514.

Phinney, J. S. (1992). The Multigroup Ethnic Identity Measure: A new scale for use with diverse groups. *Journal of Adolescent Research, 7,* 156-176.

Phinney, J. S., & Alipuria, L. L. (1990). Ethnic identity in college students from four ethnic groups. *Journal of Adolescence, 13,* 171-183.

Phinney, J. S., & Chavira, V. (1992). Ethnic identity and self-esteem: An exploratory longitudinal study. *Journal of Adolescence, 15,* 271-281.

Phinney, J. S., & Rotheram, M. J. (1987). *Children's ethnic socialization: Pluralism and development.* Newbury Park, CA: Sage.

Pierce, J. S., Clark, M., & Kaufman, S. (1978-1979). Generation and ethnic identity: A typological analysis. *International Journal of Aging and Human Development, 9,* 19-29.

Reitz, J. G. (1980). *The survival of ethnic groups.* New York: McGraw-Hill.

Riordan, C., & Ruggerio, J. (1980). Producing equal-status interracial interaction: A replication. *Social Psychology Quarterly, 43,* 131-136.

Rosenthal, R., & Rosnow, R. L. (1991). *Essentials of behavioral research: Methods and data analysis* (2nd ed.). New York: McGraw-Hill.

Ross, C. E., & Mirowsky, J. (1984). Socially-desirable response and acquiescence in a cross-cultural survey of mental health. *Journal of Health and Social Behavior, 25,* 189-197.

Rotheram-Borus, M. J. (1990). Adolescents' reference-group choices, self-esteem, and adjustment. *Journal of Personality and Social Psychology, 59,* 1075-1081.

Rushton, J. P. (1989). Genetic similarity, human altruism, and group selection. *Behavioral and Brain Sciences, 12,* 503-559.

Sanders Thompson, V. L. (1990). Factors affecting the level of African American identification. *Journal of Black Psychology, 17,* 14-23.

Sanders Thompson, V. L. (1991). Perceptions of race and race relations which affect African American identification. *Journal of Applied Social Psychology, 21,* 1502-1516.

Schwarzwald, J., & Cohen, S. (1982). Relationship between academic tracking and the degree of interethnic acceptance. *Journal of Educational Psychology, 74,* 588-597.

Sim, H. S., & Kim, J. T. (1993). The development and validation of the Korean version of the MBTI. *Journal of Psychological Type, 26,* 18-27.

Simon, B. (1993). On the asymmetry in the cognitive construal of ingroup and outgroup: A model of egocentric social categorization. *European Journal of Social Psychology, 23,* 131-147.

Simon, B., Pantaleo, G., & Mummendey, A. (1995). Unique individual or interchangeable group member? The accentuation of intragroup differences versus similarities as an indicator of the individual self versus the collective self. *Journal of Personality and Social Psychology, 69,* 106-119.

Sims, S. A. (1978).. Effects of modeling processes and resources on sharing among Black children. *Psychological Reports, 43,* 463-473.

Smith, B. M. (1990). The measurement of narcissim in Asian, Caucasian, and Hispanic American women. *Psychological Reports, 67,* 779-785.

Smith, T. W. (1980). Ethnic measurement and identification. *Ethnicity, 7,* 78-95.

Spencer, M. B., & Markstrom-Adams, C. (1990). Identity processes among racial and ethnic minority children in America. *Child Development, 61,* 290-310.

Steele, S. (1991). *The content of our character.* New York: Harper Perennial.

Stuart, A., & Ord, J. K. (1987). *Kendall's advanced theory of statistics* (Vol. 1). New York: Oxford University Press.

Sue, S., & Abe, J. (1988). *Predictors of academic achievement among Asian American and White students* (Report No. 88-11). New York: College Entrance Examination Board.

Sue, S., Chun, C., & Gee, K. (1995). Ethnic minority intervention and treatment research. In J. F. Aponte, R. Y. Rivers, & J. Wohl (Eds.), *Psychological interventions and cultural diversity* (pp. 266-282). Boston: Allyn & Bacon.

Sue, S., & Okazaki, S. (1990). Asian-American educational achievements: A phenomenon in search of an explanation. *American Psychologist, 45,* 913-920.

Suinn, R. M. (1992). Reflections on minority developments: An Asian-American perspective. *Professional Psychology: Research and Practice, 23,* 14-17.

Suinn, R. M., Ahuna, C., & Khoo, G. (1992). The Suinn-Lew Self-Identity Acculturation Scale: Concurrent and factorial validation. *Educational and Psychological Measurement, 52,* 1041-1046.

Suinn, R. M., Rickard-Figueroa, K., Lew, S., & Vigil, P. (1987). The Suinn-Lew Asian American Self-Identity Acculturation Scale: An initial report. *Educational and Psychological Measurement, 47,* 401-407.

Szapocznik, J., & Kurtines, W. (1980). Acculturation, biculturalism, and adjustment among Cuban Americans. In A. M. Padilla (Ed.), *Acculturation: Theory, models and some new findings* (pp. 139-159). Boulder, CO: Westview.

Tajfel, H., & Turner, J. C. (1979). An integrative theory of intergroup conflict. In W. Austin & S. Worchel (Eds.), *The social psychology of intergroup relations* (pp. 113-140). New York: Academic Press.

Takaki, R. (1989). *Strangers from a different shore.* New York: Penguin.

Takeuchi, D. T., & Young, K. N. J. (1994). Overview of Asian and Pacific Islander Americans. In N. W. S. Zane, D. T. Takeuchi, & K. N. J. Young (Eds.), *Confronting critical health issues of Asian and Pacific Islander Americans* (pp. 3-50). Thousand Oaks, CA: Sage.

Tanaka, J. S., Panter, A. T., & Winborne, W. C. (1988). Dimensions of the need for cognition: Subscales and gender differences. *Multivariate Behavioral Research, 23,* 35-50.

Tanaka, J. S., Panter, A. T., Winborne, W. C., & Huba, G. J. (1990). Theory testing in personality and social psychology with latent variable models: A primer in 20 questions. *Review of Personality and Social Psychology, 11,* 217-242.

Taylor, S. E. (1982). The availability bias in social perception and interaction. In D. Kahneman, P. Slovic, and A. Tversky (Eds.), *Judgement under uncertainty: Heuristics and biases* (pp. 190-208). New York: Cambridge University Press.

Tidwell, R. (1980). Gifted students' self-images as a function of identification procedure, race, and sex. *Journal of Pediatric Psychology, 5,* 57-69.

Torgerson, W. S. (1985). *Theory and methods of scaling.* Malabar, FL: Krieger. (Originally published in 1958)

Toupin, E. A., & Son, L. (1991). Preliminary findings on Asian Americans: "The model minority" in a small private East Coast college. *Journal of Cross-Cultural Psychology, 22,* 403-417.

Triandis, H. C. (1985). Acculturation indices as a means of confirming cultural differences. In R. Diaz-Guerrero (Ed.), *Cross-cultural and national studies in social psychology* (pp. 143-156). Amsterdam: Elsevier Science.

Triandis, H. C., & Marin, G. (1983). Etic plus emic versus pseudoetic: A test of basic assumption of contemporary cross-cultural psychology. *Journal of Cross-Cultural Psychology, 14,* 489-500.

Trimble, J. E. (1990). Ethnic specification, validation prospects and the future of drug use research. *International Journal of Addictions, 25,* 149-170.

Tucker, L. (1994). *The science and politics of racial research.* Champaign: University of Illinois Press.

Tversky, A., & Kahneman, D. (1974). Judgment under uncertainty: Heuristics and biases. *Science, 185,* 1124-1131.

Uba, L. (1994). *Asian Americans: Personality patterns, identity, and mental health.* New York: Guilford.

U.S. Bureau of the Census. (1993). *Social and economic characteristics of the United States* (1990 census of the population). Washington, DC: U.S. Department of Commerce, Economics and Statistics Administration.

Weinreich, P. (1986). The operationalisation of identity theory in racial and ethnic relations. In J. Rex & D. Mason (Eds.), *Theories of race and ethnic relations* (pp. 299-320). Cambridge, UK: Cambridge University Press.

Weinreich, P. (1991). Ethnic identities and indigenous psychologies in pluralist societies. *Psychology and Developing Societies, 3,* 73-92.

Wellman, B., & Wortley, S. (1990). Different strokes from different folks: Community ties and social support. *American Journal of Sociology, 96,* 558-588.

Werth, J. L., & Lord, C. G. (1992). Previous conceptions of the typical group member and the contact hypothesis. *Basic & Applied Social Psychology, 13,* 351-369.

Westkott, M. (1979). Feminist criticism of the social sciences. *Harvard Educational Review, 49,* 422-430.

White, J. L., & Parham, T. (1990). *The psychology of Blacks: An African American perspective.* Englewood Cliffs, NJ: Prentice Hall.

Wilder, D. A. (1990). Some determinants of the persuasive power of in-groups and out-groups: Organization of information and attribution of independence. *Journal of Personality and Social Psychology, 59,* 1202-1213.

Wong, H. Z. (1982). Asian and Pacific Americans. In L. Snowden (Ed.), *Researching the unobserved: Mental health needs of neglected populations* (pp. 185-204). Beverly Hills, CA: Sage.

Wong-Rieger, D., & Quintana, D. (1987). Comparative acculturation of Southeast Asian and Hispanic immigrants and sojourners. *Journal of Cross-Cultural Psychology, 18,* 345-362.

Yamagisako, S. J. (1977). Women-centered kin networks in urban bilateral kinship. *American Ethnologist, 4,* 207-266.

Zuckerman, M. (1990). Some dubious premises in research and theory on racial differences: Scientific, social and ethical issues. *American Psychologist, 45,* 1297-1303.

PART I

LIFE COURSE DEVELOPMENT

3

FAMILIES

Life-Span Socialization in a Cultural Context

BARBARA W. K. YEE
LARKE N. HUANG
ANGELA LEW

A critical strength of Asian and Pacific Islander (API) communities is strong family and social ties that buffer many API individuals from the devastating consequences of life crises. Despite the critical role that families play in API communities, there is a scarcity of psychological research on how socialization and life-span developmental processes produce resiliency or nonadaptiveness among API families living in the United States. This chapter highlights our current knowledge about API families.

A basic function of families across human cultures is to nurture adaptive life skills and positive emotional attachment for support of family members over the life course. This is a series of complex processes in one cultural context but becomes even more challenging when families must bridge two sometimes conflicting cultures. Culture is not homogeneous or static but rather is tempered by what exists in a given historical time in which it is learned and by whom it is learned; varied by the family socialization of these attitudes, values, and behaviors; and incorporated by the individual's perception of this cultural training that changes with life experiences, social context, and developmental challenges. In other words, a person's cultural schema is a slice of an individual's interpretation of a family's perception and socialization of culture within a given historical moment that is subject to continual revision over a lifetime.

Research on API families living in the United States must examine interactional socialization processes as intentional socialization or unintentional processes of *enculturation* (Kagitcibasi, 1989) within the context of acculturation. To enhance socialization goals, family elders must first nurture emotional bonds between family members to establish and maintain cohesiveness, expressions of love, and positive emotions that support adaptation over a lifetime. To fulfill this basic function, cultures shape characteristics of the family such as its composition, power structure, division of labor, privileges and responsibilities, and inculcation of cultural values with their accompanying behavioral patterns to be adaptive for particular environmental niches such as living in the United States.

Family socialization is a reciprocal process flowing from older to younger family members and with younger family members also socializing their elders (Basic Behavioral Science Task Force of the National Advisory Mental Health Council, 1996). Enculturation, socialization, and acculturation are ongoing processes that exert their influences by generation, age and developmental tasks, gender, ethnicity, and social class across behavioral and situational domains. Acculturation refers to the process of accommodation and acceptance of certain elements from two distinct cultures through contact, conflict, and adaptation.

Kagitcibasi (1989) argued that even when contextual conditions change from agrarian to industrial societies, the maintenance of interdependence as a family value must be explained as more than a function of environmental conditions. Findings across Japan, China, Hong Kong, Singapore, Taiwan, and India, as well as among ethnic minorities and working-class families in the United States, suggest that across these varied contextual environments, expectations of interdependency and close-knit family relations might not have direct survival value but might have psychological, emotional, social, and economic benefits in urban environments.

Data suggest that important API cultures persist beyond more superficial cultural habits, often used as indicators of acculturation due to ease of measurement (e.g., language, arts and crafts, dress habits). A closer examination of the patterns of social relationships, such as family problem-solving skills, role of culturally shaped emotional responses, and communication patterns in API families, may reveal maintenance of important cultural features due to adaptive value in the new sociocultural context. What appears as complete Americanization over one or two generations may, in fact, be acculturation for more superficial American behaviors such as in food preferences, dress, language, and communication patterns than for more deep-seated values, social support practices, and emotional responses to life crises (Nishi, 1995). These deep API cultural roots might be evident two generations past the American-born generation of APIs. Moreover, American-born generations of APIs behave in a more situation-specific manner in response to the specific demands of the social context. For example, Nisei Japanese Americans might behave more American at work while among American co-workers, whereas they might behave more Japanese at home or while visiting more traditional family members (Miyamoto, 1986-1987).

This chapter takes an ecological approach to examining life-span developmental challenges for API families living in the United States. These issues change as API family members make transitions throughout each stage of the life cycle.

Although the focal developmental tasks for each family member are specific to his or her developmental stage, the whole family unit has influenced and is influenced and transformed by these developmental transitions undertaken by other family members. We then discuss developmental challenges and tasks confronted by API families acculturating to life in the United States by their efforts to teach adaptive life skills (e.g., intellectual, emotional, social, worldviews) and to maintain kin-keeping functions over the life course. By examining these processes, we learn how resilient API families model and socialize their family members toward healthy identities with life and social skills to enable them to be adaptive in dealing with normative life-span developmental hurdles or when confronted by more devastating challenges that life may present. This chapter concludes by highlighting key research initiatives that must be undertaken to more fully understand API families in the American cultural context.

ECOLOGICAL APPROACH AND CHALLENGES FOR ASIAN AND PACIFIC ISLANDER FAMILIES

An ecological approach views persons as active agents in a series of interlocking systems that pose both risks and opportunities. Interaction with the immediate social environment in the context of the larger society propels development. Development is viewed as the individual's evolving understanding of the ecological environment, one's relation to it, and the capacity to discover, explore, and change its properties (Bronfenbrenner, 1979). As families encounter ecological challenges, they develop adaptive strategies reflective of the cultural and family system (DeVos, 1982). These strategies may be viewed as maladaptive by society, yet they serve some functional value within the immediate social environment. There is increasing consensus that the individual must be understood in the context of the family and sociocultural environment (Basic Behavioral Science Task Force of the National Advisory Mental Health Council, 1996; Kaslow, 1987; Sampson, 1988; Sue & Zane, 1987; Szapocznik & Kurtines, 1993).

Ecological Challenges

The ecological challenges and their resulting adaptive strategies can lead to differential outcomes for ethnic minorities (Harrison, Wilson, Pine, Chan, & Buriel, 1990). Two ecological challenges commonly faced by API families are minority status and acculturation.

Minority status, often associated with physical and linguistic differences from the mainstream society, confers a subordinate position, a restricted range of options, and reduced opportunities for mobility and success. In addition to the normative tasks of development, APIs must master the stress of "being different" and overcome the labels of "inferior" and "not belonging." Minority youths often suffer from early traumas, such as personalized taunts of racial prejudice on the playground and discrimination in the classroom, that can be attributed to the dynamics of race and minority status (Phinney & Rotheram, 1987; Stiffman & Davis, 1990). Although many young minority children enter school with strong, positive self-concepts, the stigma of racism, ethnocentrism, and restricted resources can negatively affect children's positive self-images (Cross, 1987).

A family and social ecology that is adaptive for minority children will generate support systems to minimize the destructiveness of minority status. Children are taught to selectively internalize "reflected appraisals" (Rosenberg, 1979) from their surroundings to establish strong self-concepts and healthy self-esteem. Spencer (1987) found that parental interventions to increase awareness of unique ethnic strengths provided resilience in the face of racial insults and produced highly developed social skills among African American children. The salience of a child's minority status will vary according to the ethnic composition of the daily contexts. As Asian American children negotiate these various contexts, coping with hostility or acceptance becomes entwined with the developmental tasks at hand.

Another ecological challenge for API families is the tensions felt by the varying acculturation levels of family members. For API Americans, the meaning of being API is complex and often associated with mixed valence. Although Asian American groups have resided in the United States for several generations, the majority of the current API population are foreign born and still in the process of acculturating to the host society.

Varying degrees of acculturation in API families is an ever present intervening variable that produces different ecological challenges as these families attempt to master developmental tasks. For example, if the parents are monolingual Chinese, then the bilingual child's entry into the school system and the associated tasks might be quite different from those of a child from a third-generation, English-speaking Chinese American family. The task of language acquisition might be confounded by different language priorities. Immigrant parents emphasize the native language, whereas children prefer to speak the language of their mainstream peer group.

The influence of culture might not always be so apparent. Each successive generation of Japanese Americans was more acculturated than the previous generation, yet studies indicate that significant differences remain between Japanese American and Caucasian American families such as "behaves well" versus "self-directed" as developmental goals (O'Reilly, Tokuno, & Ebata, 1986) and maintenance of Japanese rearing patterns among third-generation Japanese Americans (Caudill & Frost, 1972).

Family Characteristics and Socialization Strategies

An effective strategy might involve an integration of the dominant culture's values with those of the minority group such as recognition of minority status and its implications for the social hierarchy (DeVos, 1982). Ethnic minority parents use socializing and learning strategies found to be effective and passed down by family elders to inculcate types of competencies that they believe will enhance success of younger family members. Although the salience of specific strategies varies across ethnic minority groups, the similarities across family ecologies in the United States are notable—biculturalism, collectivism, and ancestral worldviews (Harrison et al., 1990; Ogbu, 1981).

In a classic API family study, Johnson (1977) examined how interdependence, reciprocity, and indebtedness helped maintain family solidarity among third-generation Japanese Americans in Hawaii. She argued that maintenance of kinship relations among second- and third-generation Japanese Americans was based on an obligatory system rather than on an optional one as in the Caucasian American kinship system. Lifelong and ongoing exchange of services, advice, reciprocity, and indebtedness increased the level of social contact and sociability among Japanese families. Johnson noted that the Japanese values of interdependence, reciprocity, and indebtedness were present three generations past the first American-born generations and served to preserve adaptive family strengths while strengthening Japanese families in Hawaii. Grandparents cared for grandchildren because both adult children worked to afford the high cost of living in Hawaii. In turn, grandparents were provided care when they became frail or during episodic health crises. Johnson suggested that traditional cultural family patterns are maintained, although somewhat changed, but remain adaptive long after acculturation to more superficial American lifestyles has occurred.

Collectivism is another adaptive family pattern among API Americans. Global studies of non-Western cultures and minority groups in Western countries have suggested that the boundary of self versus nonself is less rigidly drawn and that significant others are important components of the self (Hsu, 1981; Sampson, 1988). This suggests that there are multiple dimensions of identity.

In this model, the individual is embedded in a network of social relationships and obligations that play a primary role in determining behavior. For example, Asian individuals make more "collective" self-statements than "private" statements about themselves in comparison to European and North American individuals (Higgins & King, 1981). Triandis (1989) noted that the Asian self depends more on the situation and the values of the group than does the Caucasian self. Asian Americans tend to respond strongly to the judgments and demands of the social environment, taking into consideration external influences more than self-assessments and individual motives (Yeh & Huang, 1994). This collectivist approach to development and its resulting behavior is an important cultural contribution to adaptation by Asian American families.

Harrison et al. (1990) regarded ancestral worldviews, rooted in spirituality/religiosity and philosophical orientation, as another adaptive strategy used by ethnic minority families. These worldviews provide a framework for coping with contemporary life situations. For API Americans, traditions offer a prescription for living and adherence to codes of behavior. These comfortable cultural traditions offer stability in a new country that often is confusing and difficult to understand.

FAMILY SOCIALIZATION OF
IDENTITY FORMATION AND LIFE SKILLS

Identity

A critical family function is its role in identity formation and development of critical life skills to produce successful family members. The formation and reworking of certain parts of identity is an ongoing task from birth to death within a familial and sociocultural context (Erikson, 1968). The critical period in which humans form a solid, enduring identity typically is during adolescence into early adulthood (Erikson, 1950). The development of a coherent self-identity is more complex for API adolescents, as visible racial/ethnic minorities, who must resolve conflicts among competing cultural values (Ross-Sheriff, 1992) as well as cope with prejudice and discrimination that affect their identity and self-esteem (Canino & Spurlock, 1994).

Commitment to an ethnic identity is considered an important factor contributing to positive adjustment, ego identity, and self-esteem among adolescents and college students of minority status in the United States (Phinney, 1992; Phinney & Alipuria, 1990; Phinney & Chavira, 1992; Phinney, Lochner, & Murphy, 1990). API families have a significant role in teaching children and adolescents about the strengths of their cultural heritage. Findings by Rosenthal and Feldman (1992) suggested that a warm family environment consisting of explicit rules, control, and encouragement of autonomy predicted ethnic pride but not ethnic knowledge. Ethnic behavior and knowledge were thought to be influenced by specific parental practices. Okano and Spilka (1971) showed that parents serving as ethnic role models for adolescents did not adequately account for ethnic identification of second- and third-generation Japanese Americans. Aside from these studies, there is little research examining how familial or parental interactions affect the formation of the ethnic identity of API adolescents (Serafica, 1990). Hence, more research is needed to further elucidate how parents can promote ethnic identification in API adolescents.

Autonomy and Family Dependence

Rapid physical growth and sexual maturation during puberty propel the identity formation process as well as increased autonomy from the family during adolescence (Preto, 1988). The developmental task for Asian American adolescents is to develop a sense of autonomy and competence within the context of maintaining close relationships with the family. The available literature indicates that Asian American parents tend to be more restrictive of their children's independence in social activities and occupational choices (Yao, 1985a) but foster early independence in the academic area (Lin & Fu, 1990) compared to Caucasian American parents. Uba (1994) noted that acculturated Chinese and Japanese

American parents were less restrictive and encouraged greater behavioral auton-omy than did their nonacculturated Asian American counterparts. Thus, adoles-cents from immigrant or traditional Asian families appear to be more interdependent.

Many API adolescents experience an increased awareness of their racial/ethnic group status (Sata, 1983) with poorer body image and self-image that can intensify self-consciousness in the presence of the opposite sex (Chen & Yang, 1986). The authors interpret this finding as suggestive of a negative impact of racial stereo-typing on self-concept. The impact of families in soliciting positive self-concepts and body images for APIs must be investigated.

The empirical literature (e.g., Han, 1985; Nguyen & Williams, 1989) has identified larger emotional and communicational gaps between API adolescents and parents as compared to their Caucasian American counterparts. These in-tergenerational gaps are attributed to differential acculturation rates and limited proficiency in the Asian language. McDermott et al. (1983) reported that Japanese American parents in Hawaii endorsed the value of the family as a reference group for decision making, fulfillment of family obligations, clear lines of authority, and open sharing among members, whereas adolescents emphasized the need for privacy of thoughts and feelings except to express anger. Immigrant and second-generation Chinese, Filipino, and Vietnamese American adolescents reported greater reliance on the family as a source of support, advice, and guidance than did their Euro-American counterparts (Cooper, Baker, Polichar, & Welsh, 1993). These adolescents turned to siblings and age peers in discussing sexuality, dating, and marriage. Likewise, Han (1985) noted that Korean American adolescents dis-closed the most to their same-sex peers, whereas Caucasian American adolescents disclosed the most to their mothers.

The process of immigration or resettlement during adolescence can exacer-bate normal developmental struggles with identity, self-concept, and generational conflicts with parents (Ho, 1992). Not only do API adolescents encounter highly disparate social norms in the United States, but they are vulnerable to changing social norms within their own families (Uba, 1994). They are actively exploring roles and behaviors of the American culture, redefining their values and self-concepts, and renegotiating social roles and family relationships (Huang, 1989). The de-velopmental task of forging their own identity and acquiring a sense of autonomy can be particularly challenging in the context of Asian family norms of filial obe-dience and family interdependence coupled with American societal goals of verbal assertiveness, individualism, and independence (Nagata, 1989). Immigrant par-ents commonly instill a desire for maintenance of language and traditions in their adolescent children (Huang, 1989). Adolescent-parent conflicts in immigrant families are further exacerbated by disruption of roles associated with hierarchical family structure including parent-child role reversal (Ho, 1987). Out of helpless-ness and frustration, parents might increase discipline as a reaction to restore traditional family roles. Internal and intergenerational conflict might manifest in its most extreme forms as gang involvement, substance use, and delinquency (Furuto & Murase, 1992).

Language Acquisition

It is generally believed that language acquisition occurs through the socialization process, resulting primarily from social interaction. One's primary language derives from interactions with significant others in a child's earliest social interactions (usually the parents). In extended family situations, multiple adult caretakers might influence language development. For example, in households of multiple generations, grandparents might be the primary caretakers and interact with the child in their native language. In preschool years, the child might be non-English speaking and then acquire English with the emergence from the home setting. Language is an implicit vehicle of cultural transmission and cultural identity.

Research on children's acquisition of bilingualism indicates that children associate languages with the people who commonly speak to them and situations in which they are used (McClure, 1981). In a study of bilingual socialization, Kuo (1974) found that children tended to be more proficient in Chinese than in English when the general language orientation of the family was Chinese (i.e., when parents used Chinese in conversation and when reading stories to children). The children tended to be more proficient in English when parents were naturalized citizens, when parents had resided longer in the United States, and when more American food was served in the family. Kuo's study suggested that the family had a strong impact on the Chinese language competence of children rather than inhibiting children's English proficiency. The age of the children was correlated with English proficiency, suggesting that as a child gets older and extra familial contacts become more important, the relative impact of the family on language socialization tends to decline.

Family extendedness also plays a role in language acquisition in that different generations in the household may exert different language preferences. Unfortunately, the literature has not systematically investigated the relationship of multigenerational, multilingual families and language proficiency outcomes. Anecdotally, the combination of monolingual parents or grandparents and bilingual children may upset the traditional role configuration within the family as children more easily communicate with the outside world and become spokepersons for their families. A child's language preference might reflect cultural identification or more normative developmental issues such as compliance with or rejection of parental expectations.

Schooling and Achievement

With entry into school, children are confronted by a myriad of new challenges and opportunities. Much of children's earlier dependence on the family and home environment needs to be relinquished, and attention must be redirected to unfamiliar adults. Successful transition to the school environment and academic achievement experiences is linked to the adaptive strategies of Asian American families that either enhance or impede API children's performance.

Depending on the ethnic composition of their neighborhood or preschool experiences, entry into schooling might be children's first formal contact with a culture different from the home. As such, it presents one of the earliest occasions for possible cultural clash and for emergence of biculturalism as an adaptive strategy. A discontinuity between home and school might result in differing contextual demands, requiring children to develop new modes of interacting and behaving. Holliday (1985) observed that the discontinuity between home and school facilitated the development of situational problem solving among these children. Young Asian American children negotiate between the sometimes conflicting and sometimes compatible expectations or cultural styles required in the two settings (Huang & Ying, 1989). Ethnic minority families are bicultural in terms of different culturally determined patterns for dealing with the public versus private domains of family life. In a comparison of child-rearing practices among Chinese, immigrant Chinese, and Caucasian American parents, Lin and Fu (1990) found that the Chinese groups adapted to necessary changes while maintaining certain traditional family values. For example, these parents had higher ratings on parental control and more of an emphasis on achievement, consistent with traditional Confucian values, than did Caucasian American parents. However, contrary to expectations and previous research, these parents had higher ratings on encouragement of independence in school and achievement domains. This combination of values facilitated a bicultural socialization that enabled these immigrant children to function effectively in both cultures. Degree of acculturation, adherence to ancestral world values, and balancing of American individuality with Asian collectivity each contributed to strategies developed by these children.

Much of the research on academic achievement by Asian American children has focused on Asian cultural values that promote educational endeavors (Sue & Okazaki, 1990). Asian families teach children the importance of repaying parents for their sacrifices, and one highly valued path is through high educational achievement. The achievement success of Japanese Americans is attributed to the compatibility of Japanese and American cultural/familial values. Lee (1987), Mordkowitz and Ginsburg (1987), and Yao (1985b) all attempted to delineate specific family characteristics associated with successfully achieving Asian American students. They concluded that a strong home environment with strict monitoring of children's free time, investment in educational opportunities, and parental emphasis on respect for education and expectation of achievement were correlated with high academic achievement.

In a study of Japanese, Chinese, and Korean American 6th and 7th graders, Lee (1987) found that Asian American parents held higher educational expectations for their children than did White parents and were reinforced by teacher and peer perceptions. Campbell and Mandel (1990) concluded that ethnicity directly influenced parental behavior, which in turn influenced achievement. In contrast to Caucasian parents, who provided less pressure but more psychological support to increase achievement, Asian American parents pressured and monitored their children more while offering little help.

A large, comprehensive survey study of 536 school-age children from low-income Southeast Asian refugee families examined factors that contribute to school achievement (Caplan, Choy, & Whitmore, 1992). A factor analysis of a values rating scale indicated that parents and children honor mutual collective obligation to each other and to the extended family and strive to attain respect, cooperation, and harmony within the family. One of the most powerful predictors of academic performance is adherence to the belief that the "past is as important as the future." This supports the notion that ancestral worldviews may be an adaptive strategy used by ethnic minority families in dealing with contemporary life challenges (Harrison et al., 1990). In this study of Vietnamese refugees, the value of studying and learning was reinforced at home and in school.

In a further analysis, Dornbusch, Prescott, and Ritter (1987) used Baumrind's (1971) typology of parental authority to attempt to explain different achievement outcomes. Results from students of African American, Mexican American, and White families confirmed the hypothesis that high authoritarian (or permissive) parenting was related to lower grades and that authoritative parenting was associated with higher grades. Parental authority type did not appear to play a role in predicting academic achievement among Asian American children; rather, ancestral worldviews such as reciprocating parents' sacrifices by doing well in school, positive teacher expectations (Wong, 1980), and cultural attributions of effort as the primary factor responsible for successful learning (Stevenson & Stigler, 1992) were more important predictors.

Asian American children are socialized to the value that their performance, whether laudable or disappointing, reflects family upbringing and brings pride or disgrace to the family name. This socialization process has transcended American generations in the United States. Asian and Asian American families emphasize educational achievement to a greater extent, have higher educational and occupational aspirations, and exert much more parental control and supervision over youths' academic and social affairs than do Caucasian American families (Lin & Fu, 1990; Sata, 1983; Sollenberger, 1968; Sung, 1990; Uba, 1994; Yao, 1985b). One developmental task of API adolescents is to fulfill their filial responsibility of academic excellence to enhance family honor (Serafica, 1990) and to take advantage of occupational opportunities to further enhance the social standing and economic well-being of the entire family (Uba, 1994).

For Asian immigrant and refugee children, the pressure to succeed academically is intense because families assume that academic achievement ultimately will bring success and upward mobility to the family. Interestingly, the intensity of this value appears to diminish through acculturation. Studies indicate that more recent immigrants or less acculturated Asian American students do better on academic measures than do their more acculturated peers (Dornbusch et al., 1987).

Slaughter-Defoe, Nakagawa, Takanishi, and Johnson (1990) noted a model minority myth that emphasized only academic and educational successes of Asian

American youths versus other minority children. Stereotypical cultural characteristics, such as respect for authority, are typically highlighted in the literature.
A more important characteristic of Asian parental beliefs is attributing academic
success to effort and practice rather than ability. However, these traditional Asian
parental attributions for success can be a two-edged sword. For example, Taiwanese mothers tended to attribute poor math performance of 6th-grade children
to lack of effort, but they gave inadequate personal credit to their children for
successes as compared to that given by Caucasian American mothers to their
children (Stevenson & Stigler, 1992). The pattern for Chinese American mothers
appeared to fall between the two groups. Not providing appropriate amounts of
credit for successes might have negative implications for self-esteem and identity
such as "never feeling good enough" and producing academic burnout (Uba,
1994). We see a darker side of this trend among Japanese children in Japan who
develop ulcers or commit suicide if they do not make straight A's in elementary school
or junior high. Being singled out as the hope and savior of the family can be a
very heavy burden for Asian youth. It might be the last stressor; when accompanied by low self-esteem and poor identity, it might make the Asian youth feel like
a failure and push him or her to experiment and cope by abusing substances, to
be depressed, and perhaps to contemplate suicide (Gleason & Sasao, 1992).

A cultural ecological approach has identified variables significantly associated
with academic achievement among Asian Americans: individual, family and parent, and teacher and school variables. What is lacking in the research is identification of academic risk factors among API American children. In current literature,
there is strong support for biculturalism, rather than assimilation, as an adaptive
strategy prerequisite for success and academic achievement in this society.

Occupational Achievement

Preparing for and launching one's career is an important developmental task
for API adolescents and young adults. Adequate preparation and launching a
career successfully help API young adults fulfill their filial obligations (Uba, 1994).
Although it is a critical life task, Leong (1991) noted few studies on career development of Asian and Pacific Americans.

The enculturation of certain intellectual and behavioral skills, valued by families and reinforced by Asian culture through the educational system, can produce
the occupational segregation found among APIs in the United States. The pattern
of occupational segregation of Asian American males into scientific or technical
fields, and the avoidance of vocations requiring strong verbal skills or social interaction, can be understood within the framework of the API's ethnic identity
and Asian cultural values emphasizing formality in relationships, restraint and
inhibition of strong feelings, and obedience to authority (Sue, 1973) as well as
differential rates of acculturation and historical and political factors (Sue & Kirk,
1973). "Glass ceilings" (Leong & Hayes, 1990), culturally preferred leadership
styles (James, Chen, & Cropanzano, 1996), and occupational segregation have
serious implications for financial success and API family roles into the next century

(Hing & Lee, 1996; LEAP Asian Pacific American Public Policy Institute and UCLA Asian American Studies Center, 1993; Leong & Chow, 1994).

Asian Americans have a preference for a collectivistic rather than an individualistic orientation in career decision making and in problem-solving approach (Leong, 1991). API families, especially immigrant families, exercise authority in supervising and making unilateral decisions concerning the API's academic and career goals, with a preference for occupations in medicine, physical science, and business (Uba, 1994). Data on Asian American college students reveal that an individualistic achievement style is related to endorsement of both Asian and Anglo values, whereas collectivistic achievement orientation is marginally associated with endorsement of Asian values (Lew, 1994).

Across many Asian ethnic groups, families continue to retain important influence and decision-making power over college selection and career decisions for young adults. Second-generation Korean Americans, for example, exhibit career choices involving prestigious professional occupations consistent with parental values of success (Kim, 1993). We can anticipate that Asian American families will continue to expect high career aspirations for young adults but that more acculturated families may permit greater input by young adults in career selection in an expanded range of acceptable career choices.

SOCIAL AND KIN-KEEPING TASKS OF ASIAN AND PACIFIC ISLANDER FAMILIES

Another critical family function is development of social skills and fulfillment of kin-keeping tasks for survival, maintenance, and socialization of API family members. This section describes how API families socialize their youngest members to engage in critical social and kin-keeping tasks throughout the life course.

Adaptive Function of Emotions in Asian and Pacific Islander Family Life

Within nurturant family environments, socialization can most effectively enhance survival of family members and facilitate coping with normative and nonnormative life transitions by providing possible scripts for behaviors among younger generations that have proved to be adaptive in cultural, family, and personal history. Cultures vary in use of specific motivational strategies to maintain family solidarity. Nydegger (1983) found that use of emotional tenor in the family might not be a very good predictor of family cohesion. Americans use positive emotions to cement familial bonds. Feelings are very powerful in motivating people's behaviors. The inherent difficulty in using this motivational strategy is that emotions are volatile and can be switched off or reassigned more quickly. Relying solely on positive emotions as the glue to hold families together can create fragile and unstable family relations during bad times. Resilient families have strong emotional bonds that work synergistically with a sense of lifelong responsibility, obligations, and duty that works to enable families to mobilize resources and face almost any crisis.

Emotions are a critical basis for all social relationships and have special implications for maintenance of lifelong family relationships. Emotions and their expression are critical moderators of stress behavioral reactions. Expression of emotions, communication patterns, and cultural use of confessionals and disclosure have clear implications for API families. Kitayama and Markus (1994b) described the impact of culture on the expression of emotion and social relationships. How emotions are formulated, are expressed, and moderate behaviors has significant implications for API families because these cultural features temper the modes of relating to other family members and the environment (Frijda & Mesquita, 1994). For instance, the suppression of negative emotional expression might actually enhance the stability and socially supportive nature of API families. However, suppression of positive emotional expression, such as verbal praise for successes, might produce APIs who lack confidence in abilities or produce lowered self-esteem (Stevenson & Stigler, 1992).

The work of Kitayama and Markus (1994a) suggested that culture might not be static; rather, it might be dynamic and responsive to a rapidly changing environment, as within the same generation or across one generation. Accordingly, culture and its tenets are customized and personalized by the individual to make social situations and the world meaningful within a particular time and place and, hence, may change over the life cycle. The work of Nagata (1993) demonstrated that internment during World War II systematically and profoundly changed Japanese American families, particularly the Issei and Nisei generation. Many Issei never recovered economically or spiritually after their release from camps. Even third-generation Japanese Americans, who had not directly experienced internment, nevertheless had been transformed by their families' perceptions regarding the values of life, liberty, and justice. There has been a conspiracy of silence concerning this trauma among Issei in the Japanese American community. Nagata (1993) identifies this conspiracy of silence as a coping mechanism to avoid additional racism, avoid the appearance of being un-American, avoid traumatic memories, or protect their children. In fact, during congressional redress hearings, internment victims often spoke of their experiences for the first time in 40 years.

Several Pacific Islander groups—*Kwara'ae* and *A'ara* speakers among Solomon Islanders in Melanesia, Hawaiians, and Nukulaelae Islanders of Polynesia (White & Watson-Gegeo, 1990)—believe that illness or misfortune may be brought about by engaging in unpleasant or troubling thoughts and feelings. By contrast, the Ifaluk of Micronesia believe that by engaging in direct verbal expression of emotions, one can avoid illness (Lutz, 1988). The expression of emotions and its relationship to social processes or health is by no means homogeneous among Pacific Islanders. The use of confession and disclosure as a mechanism for symbolic healing or the expression of feelings varies by family and API culture and has significant influences on how family members relate to each other.

In an anthropological analysis of *ho'oponopono*, Shook (1985) found that this traditional Hawaiian family problem-solving process had universal relevance yet particular efficacy with native Hawaiian families. This Hawaiian conflict resolution process was led by a family elder or respected outsider such as a healer. A prayer asked God for assistance, and a blessing started this process. During the problem identification phase, the leader was responsible for reaching resistant family members and fully engaging them in the process. A review of the ho'oponopono procedures and sequence was outlined. There was a discussion of thoughts and feelings by all members of the family in a calm manner so that all members could be heard. There was a pooling of family strengths to solve the family problem. During the resolution phase, exchanges of confession and forgiveness and release of the family problem were made. During the closing session, a summary of transpired events and spiritual and individual thanks were made. This traditional family conflict resolution process had fallen into disuse with the acculturation of Hawaiians. It currently is experiencing a cultural resurgence.

Family Extendedness

Types of family structures, developed in particular environmental niches around the world, appear to be maintained in a new culture if it serves a useful function. Various types of family structures exist in ethnic minority communities, but a common form is the extended family system.

Traditional Asian families have been characterized by a system of hierarchical roles based on age, birth position, and gender. Within this extended family system, the privileges, obligations, and responsibilities of each role are clearly delineated according to a vertical structure. In many instances, multiple generations and multiple caretakers reside within one household. For some immigrant families, a significant family member might remain in the country of origin. Although not physically present, this member might exert a psychological presence and contribute to family decision-making processes in absentia. With increasing acculturation, the form of the extended family has evolved. Shared households may be replaced by individual family units. However, decision-making, resource allocation, and role relationships still may be determined by the hierarchical structure in the extended family. Although members of the family might leave the family and kinship group for specific purposes, they often are expected to return to this innermost family circle. The primary importance of the kinship relationship supersedes development of ties to other groups, organizations, or individuals. Even with marriage, it is assumed that the spouse and the spouse's family will be incorporated within this family boundary (Hsu, 1981). Thus, familial and social behaviors are governed by respect for the hierarchy of roles and the value of filial piety (Tseng, 1973). API family interactional patterns and socializing principles support avoidance of personal confrontations to produce smooth interpersonal relationships (Agbayani-Siewert & Revilla, 1995; Yee & Hennessey, 1982).

Ching, McDermott, Fukunaga, and Yanagida (1995) found that Japanese American families, as measured by the Thematic Apperception Test and California Personal Inventory, were more likely to adopt the hierarchical family status with role differentiation that focused on the male. Japanese American families in Hawaii emphasized collective harmony, cooperation, interpersonal acceptance, and positive mutual social interactions to a greater extent than did Caucasian Americans. These data suggest that there is maintenance of some traditional Japanese values and behavior among second- and third-generation Japanese American families in Hawaii.

Pacific Islanders share many similar family values with Asian families, but the specific manner in which these values manifest varies across Pacific Islander families. Although nurturance of Hawaiian children and food preparation were primarily the responsibility of women, grandparents frequently raised children. The custom of *hanai,* giving one or more children to members of the older generation or to a female relative who could not have children, was common. This custom developed from the belief that the grandparent or adult role would be incomplete and would create loneliness if grandparents or adults were unable to raise children as a significant part of their family function. The oldest woman in the Hawaiian family (*ohana*) presided over the family. This family matriarch was responsible for preservation of tradition and for maintaining harmony in the family. If a family conflict arose, then the matriarch and patriarch presided over a Hawaiian family problem-solving process called ho'oponopono (Ogawa, in press). It is a method for restoring harmony and maintenance of good relationships between family members and the family with supernatural powers (Pukui & Elbert, 1971).

The Hawaiian extended family is central to Hawaiian culture; children are highly desired, are indulged, and often are the center of attention. Toddlers are expected to begin assuming family responsibilities, and older siblings care for younger children. These child-rearing strategies foster interdependence and increased opportunities for children to exercise adult roles as part of their family duties. According to Shook (1985), the Hawaiian family can be described as "benevolent authoritarianism" with the elders (*kupunas*) acting as teachers of the children. Learning is gained by observation and through experience. Sibling cooperation and conflict avoidance with adults are encouraged as primary coping strategies (Gallimore, Boggs, & Jordan, 1974). All socialization practices reinforce the value of affiliation. Cooperation (*laulima*) and help (*kokua*) reflect this cultural value of interdependence. A mature Hawaiian person is achieved when he or she can accurately perceive and attend to another person's needs, often without being asked (Shook, 1985).

The affiliative nature of interpersonal relations is a central theme in the Hawaiian identity and socialization (Ito, 1985). The generous giving of the self is viewed as an altruistic exchange to maintain affiliative bonds. According to Ito (1985), this is not a reciprocal exchange; rather, it is a generalized exchange in which *aloha* and goodwill can be extended by one family member and could be returned through a number of affiliative ties with others in that family. Exchanges of material goods are only metaphors for the obligation that perpetuates a cycle of reciprocity in emotional exchanges. In other words, the exchanges of people, food, service, or ceremony are not viewed as materialistic exchange but rather help to maintain old social relationships and consolidate new ones. Past relationships are emotional conduits to affective exchange in the absence of current communication because they are resident in emotional memories (Howard, 1974). Emotional exchange links might include hostile and hurtful feelings as well as altruistic indebtedness (Pukui & Elbert, 1971). Children younger than 6 or 7 years of age are considered the "weak link" because they have not had the time to build up their network of protectors. Therefore, older family members must shield children from hostilities that might have been generated by other family members or spirits.

As an adaptive strategy, reliance on the Hawaiian extended family has led to a greater sense of interdependence, a greater focus on group goals, and less emphasis on individuality and individual needs. With increased acculturation, however, the extended family may be experienced as a strength for some members but as a restriction in autonomy.

Certain features of the Samoan kinship system have been retained in the United States such as the temporary financial and material support to new immigrants from the homeland. In a study of the largest overseas community of Samoans living in Southern California (Shu, 1985-1986), nearly 88% of interviewed Samoans wanted their elderly parents or relatives to live with them under all circumstances. However, because only 3.8% of all respondents were age 60 years or older, very few Samoans actually had elderly relatives living in the household.

Chain migration of young relatives was very high, with 42% of respondents acknowledging the presence of kin living in the household. Kin provided living accommodations after migration from Samoa and helped with employment referral. It appears that the presence of kin is a source of social support but can lead to both financial and social stress for Samoans. Janes (1990) found that two types of life events cause Samoans concern: life events that upset daily routines of life and demand extraordinary attention or monetary expenses and life events that affect relationships within the immediate or extended family. Samoans lacked the economic resources to cope with economic crises because nearly one third of those in Janes's sample were below the poverty level.

Fujita and O'Brien (1991) found a persistence of traditional social relationships across Japanese American generations. In a survey of 490 second- and third-generation Japanese Americans in California from 1979 to 1990, Fujita and O'Brien found that involvement with Japanese voluntary associations, such as *tanomoshi* or rotating credit associations, served to reinforce *iemoto* or cultural origin of the household. This reinforcement of the mutually dependent hierarchical relationships in the Japanese community and family served to buffer against assaults coming from outside this community and strengthened ethnic solidarity. Tamura (1994) argued that Nisei Japanese Americans may be more direct, aggressive, and individualistic in public or among Caucasian Americans but very traditional, group consensus-focused, and subtle in communication style at home or among Japanese friends. In other words, the context determines the behavior among API individuals. Johnson and Marsella (1978) found traditional Japanese attitudes and verbal behavior evident among third-generation Japanese Americans in Hawaii who did not speak Japanese. The maintenance of traditional social and verbal behavior suggests that these cultural characteristics might have some adaptive function beyond those in the Japanese language. These traditional cultural beliefs and their behavioral outcomes have persisted. The question is what adaptive value they have in American culture. One may speculate that these cultural values contribute to ethnic solidarity within the family and across the Japanese community to cope with a foreign, hostile, or racist society.

Sibling Relationships

Another critical socialization function of families is to enhance social and kin-keeping skills among younger family members. These social skills enhance their ability to adapt and function in important social spheres while traversing developmental transitions over the life course. Sibling relationships are learning and testing grounds for practicing and sharpening social skills. Siblings also provide a source of conflict, as seen in studies of sibling rivalry during childhood, but can be a great source of support and comfort over a lifetime. The source of its power is poorly understood, but the impact of negative sibling interaction might have a more dramatic impact on the family than does the impact of any other social relationship (Basic Behavioral Science Task Force of the National Advisory Mental Health Council, 1996).

Cicirelli (1994) suggested that the nature of sibling relationships cross-culturally and among minority groups in the United States is notably distinct from the Caucasian American pattern. He argued that these differences are reflected in the way in which siblings are defined, cultural norms regulating sibling role responsibilities and behaviors, the nature and extent of sibling caregiving and socialization, the specific nature of sibling relationships, and variability of sibling behaviors. For instance, Seymour (1993) found sibling caretaking typical of South Asian societies, where older siblings care for younger siblings and teach them survival skills such as personal self-care and domestic or occupational skills. Older siblings were provided parent training skills and served as insurance against early parental death. Sibling caretaking also may have adaptive value in single-parent or dual-career households, in families that cannot afford babysitting expenses, and in families that do not have adult extended family members to provide these services. Sibling caregiving has been transplanted by API families in the United States but has not been examined systematically.

Cicirelli (1994) found that sibling relationships were discretionary among industrialized societies, whereas they were obligatory in nonindustrialized societies or among more traditional minority groups in the United States. Maintenance of sibling relationships in industrialized societies is largely volitional, with a weak norm for close contact with siblings. The majority of adult siblings keep in touch during adulthood, but this contact varies across times of the life cycle, proximity, and closeness of the relationship with competing commitments and responsibilities. In general, sister-sister relationships are particularly close, with brother-sister relationships somewhat intermediate in closeness and brother-brother relationships the least close sibling relationships (Gold, 1989).

API sibling relationships must be examined because they are one of the longest types of family relationships that humans may have. Research among older adults shows that positive sibling relationships can be a tremendous source of support during later life. More research must be done to examine the impact of sibling relationships over the life course in API communities.

Peer Interaction

During the elementary school years, children's interactions with peers become increasingly important and broaden the range of interpersonal relationships beyond the family. From these interactions, API children develop new perceptions of themselves, different social skills, and varied coping strategies for dealing with social stressors. The social skills, role relationships, patterns of communication, and language usage as established in the home might require modification to be effective with these children's peer group. Children receive feedback from their peers as to the success or failure of their social interventions.

The level and type of discontinuity between family and peer values offers opportunities and challenges for the child. Adopting a bicultural adaptive strategy enables the child to move fluidly between the cultures of the family and the peer group by using the cultural behaviors most appropriate to the situation. Whereas dutiful, attentive, respectful behavior is practiced in the home, the Asian child might join in more noisy, playful, boisterous behavior with his or her peers. The competent bicultural child is able to assess the situation and select behaviors appropriate to the context.

For some children, there might be little discontinuity between values of the family culture extending to the peer culture. A study of the Hawaiian culture found that noncompetitive, affiliative patterns of interrelationships among Hawaiians were pervasive (Howard, 1974; Howard & Associates, 1971). The family socialization patterns deemphasized individual competitive behavior and stressed the social values of peer group affiliation and cooperation across generations in the family and in peer groups. Developmentally, the peer group served to reinforce the cultural value of collectivity. However, more studies must examine how discouragement of individually competitive behavior in academic performance by Hawaiian children relates to their lifelong achievements and development of resiliencies. Unlike their Asian peers, who may be more academically assertive at school, many Hawaiian children have not adapted their behaviors to these Westernized academic settings. Both familial and social support networks must reinforce the idea that education is an effective adaptive tool for life, but they also must use culturally competent motivational strategies, such as the strong Hawaiian cultural value of peer group affiliation with cooperation, to increase academic performance of these Pacific Islander children.

Hirayama (1985) looked at teachers' and students' assessments of Hmong, Vietnamese, and Korean students' relationships with American peers. More than half of the teachers thought that Asian students were well accepted by their American peers; the remainder thought that they were accepted with some distance. However, 63% of the students reported that "American students are mean to me," and of the 18% who disliked school, two of the main reasons were "being insulted or laughed at by classmates" and "not having friends in school." When interviewed about leisure time, 91% of the Asian students reported having friends among their own nationality; 50% of the Korean and Vietnamese students and 10% of the Hmong students had close American friends whom they spent time with outside of school. These parents have much control over whom their children spend time with and how much time the children spend with peers. Inclusion of school classmates in leisure activities appears to lessen school isolation and ostracism felt by many API children.

Managing peer interactions is a critical developmental task. Peers serve as an important reference group and contribute to a child's development of social competence and self-esteem. For the Asian American child, the discontinuities between family and peer group may result in different developmental outcomes. A bicultural adaptive strategy juxtaposes two cultures by enhancing flexibility in choices across values, identity, and behavioral domains as in coping strategies used to negotiate peer stressors and relationships (Huang, Leong, & Wagner, 1994).

Intimacy

Salient developmental tasks for API young adults include intimacy and commitment to a love relationship that establishes an individual's path toward greater financial and emotional independence from his or her family of origin. Commitment to a love relationship can lead to a traditional Asian adult goal of marriage and children to ensure survival of the family.

Families with strong ethnic identification may encourage dating and commitment to individuals within one's ethnic group, emphasizing continuing the family line (especially for males) and saving face. Immigrant families might perceive interracial dating and marriage as a loss of culture and going against filial piety. The flexibility and particular style of problem solving in the family will exert a powerful influence on the individual's management of this developmental phase (Serafica, 1990).

One area of frequent cultural conflicts between API adolescents and foreign-born parents pertains to dating (Yu & Kim, 1983). Asian immigrant parents tend to be more restrictive about allowing adolescents, and especially females, to date (Ho, 1992). One study (Feldman & Rosenthal, 1990) reports significantly older age expectations for heterosexual contacts (i.e., dating or participating in an overnight trip with mixed-sex friends) among first- and second-generation Chinese

American and Chinese Australian 10th- and 11th-grade students, but attitudes toward dating and sexual behavior of Asian American adolescents became more similar to American behavioral norms with acculturation (Chen & Yang, 1986). The trend of increased interracial or interethnic dating and intermarriages has become more prominent, particularly for third-generation API individuals. Tinker (1982) reported intermarriage rates for Japanese Americans in three California cities to be around 50%. Third-generation Chinese American and Japanese American females tend to out-marry at a higher rate than do their male counterparts (Kitano, Yeung, Chai, & Hatanaka, 1984).

Mok (1995) found that the likelihood of dating Caucasians by Asian American college students was higher with acculturation, perceiving Caucasians as more attractive than Asians, and interracial dating experiences. The likelihood of dating other Asian American college students was higher when related to higher Asian ethnic identity, percentage of Asian friends, parental influences, and growing up in high Asian ethnically dense neighborhoods. Her study suggests that the family, likelihood of past and current proximity, and dating experiences have affected dating patterns.

Fujino (1992) modified the exchange theory to examine the impact of ethnicity and gender on Asian American heterosexual relationships. She found that the motives for interracial dating mirror those found for interracial marriages. In her college student sample of Americans of Chinese, Japanese, and Caucasian descent, Japanese out-dated more than did Chinese Americans, Caucasians exhibited low rates of interracial dating, and women out-dated more than did men. Physical attractiveness was valued more highly by men and Caucasian Americans. Caucasians were considered more physically attractive, and Asians were regarded as more caring. Critical variables were used in a predictive model for Asian Americans, but the same model was not significant for Caucasians. The variable that was unique for Asian Americans appeared to be propinquity, the availability of possible API persons to date in their current lives. Limited support was found for exchange interactions on interracial attraction. These studies suggest that the influence of culture, gender, and social characteristics of the past and current environments (i.e., availability of API dating and marital partners) has important implications for dating, marriage, and patterns of API families.

Gender Role Socialization

Gender role socialization is another critical task of families. Gender roles are influenced by traditional beliefs concerning the roles of men versus women in the family. A Canadian study of South Asian women found that the impact of acculturation on gender roles was multidimensional. Naidoo and Davis (1988) found that South Asian Indian women were traditional in domains of home, family, children, religion, and marriage but were contemporary with regard to success, achievement, education, and aspirations for women and their daughters. Acculturation was clearly domain and situation specific for South Asian women. This study clearly suggests that multidimensional measurement tools are war-

ranted to disentangle the influence of life domains or context on API and multicultural populations (Yee, 1992).

Maintenance of familial continuity through the millennium is a traditional
Asian imperative and sometimes gets translated into a very strong sanction against
gay young adults because there is less likelihood of producing grandchildren as
the next generation. In addition, having a homosexual family member also might
bring shame to the family because this sexual orientation is very stigmatizing in
API communities (Hom, 1994). Interviews with Asian American parents of gay
children revealed that parental attitudes regarding homosexuality before disclosure or discovery of their children's sexual orientation can influence parents'
reactions. If Asian parents were aware of homosexuality in their native countries,
then this prior knowledge decreased the blaming of Westernization for this sexual
orientation. Many Asian American parents of gay adult children successfully
coped with this disclosure by viewing sexual orientation as a singular aspect of
their children, having open lines of communication, and believing that their relationships remained the same in spite of the shame that can be induced by disclosure in their ethnic communities.

Lesbian and bisexual South Asian women feel alienation and isolated from
their own families while fearing and feeling anxious about their ethnic communities' detection of their sexual orientation (National Asian Women's Health Organization, 1996). These lesbian and bisexual South Asian women feel frustrated
that non-South Asian therapists lack cultural competence to understand the stigmatization in South Asian cultures and fear lack of confidentiality with South
Asian therapists.

Marriage

Marriage is a critical decision in the lives of many APIs because it has direct
implications for the maintenance of the family and culture across generations.
Within the traditional Asian framework, marriage does not mark the creation of
a new family; rather, it marks the continuation of the husband's family line (Ho,
1987). In traditional API families, other family members have a central role in
mate selection in contrast to the secondary role found in Western societies. This
central role has diminished with acculturation, but API families still yield strong
but indirect influence over selection of mates. Culture exerts its influence in the
process of mate selection, marital rituals, marital satisfaction, and the manner in
which spousal or parental roles are negotiated and enacted (Ho, 1987). Marriage
based on love and mutual interests or compatibility has increasingly become a
norm for API young adults (Ho, 1987).

One clear example of how culture affects marrriage is found in the relative
timing of marriage among Hmong living in St. Paul, Minnesota. Hutchinson and
McNall (1994) found that half of the female Hmong students were married by
their senior year in high school but that the majority remained in school. The
results indicated that early marriage had no significant negative effects because
few differences were found between married and unmarried Hmong females in

overall educational expectations and indexes of depression, psychological well-being, self-esteem, self-derogation, and mastery. They also indicated that at least half of this sample of high school females had not chosen to adopt the traditional Hmong ways and marry by 15 or 16 years of age, indicating some acculturation to American marital patterns.

Despite the importance of intimacy and commitment to love relationships in young adulthood, there are few empirical studies of APIs. Traditional Asian marital and parental roles are clearly defined by Confucian role definitions that are patriarchal, with females at the bottom of the hierarchy (del Carmen, 1990). API women from immigrant, working-class backgrounds tend to be less educated and are reported to be more tradition bound in terms of their sex role orientation (True, 1981). Disruptions in the family hierarchy, such as higher employment status of the wife, might be perceived by the husband as a threat to his patriarchal authority (Ho, 1987). Changes in social roles found among Southeast Asian families were reported to result in more frequent marital conflicts, family violence (wife or child abuse), depression, or alcoholism (Lin, Masuda, & Tazuma, 1982). Renegotiation of roles and expectations in a new social context is particularly difficult when some family members rigidly cling to traditional Asian roles, communication patterns of indirectness, and prohibition in the expression of emotions (Ho, 1987). Adaptive family development requires modifications of roles, expectations, and behaviors to adjust to new and changing environmental conditions.

API women with higher education and middle-class backgrounds might be exposed to feminist ideas, egalitarian marital role attitudes, and expectations for greater occupational mobility (Chow, 1985). Japanese American males were found to be high on male-dominant, patriarchal attitudes pertaining to marital roles (Arkoff, Meredith, & Iwahara, 1964), whereas Japanese American females scored higher on egalitarian conceptions of marriage and not significantly different from Caucasian American females. There often is a gap between expression of egalitarian attitudes or values and actual behavior. Even among Caucasian American families who express egalitarian attitudes, women still have a disproportionate share of the child and household responsibilities relative to time spent by the husbands engaged in those tasks (see review in Schellenberger & Hoffman, 1995).

A standard family studies mantra is that selection of marital partners is based on similarity of key characteristics such as education, social class, religion, ethnicity, cultural background, and values. It appears that choosing a marital partner from one's own ethnic group might be less important after the first immigrant generation; however, understanding various factors that lead to selection of a marital partner is far from simple. Shinagawa (1996) reported that 31.2% of API husbands (19.0% interethnic and 12.3% interracial, with 9.9% to non-Hispanic Whites) and 40.4% of API wives (16.6% interethnic and 24.2% interracial, with 20.0% to non-Hispanic Whites) intermarried, according to the 1990 U.S. census. Japanese Americans, with a significant number of wives married to U.S. servicemen (51.9%), and Filipino American wives (40.2%) account for the highest proportion of intermarriages among APIs. Marriage patterns among California APIs in 1990 suggested that a large number of intermarriages were among other API ethnicities, with small increases of interracial marriages. These demographic trends suggest a decrease in racial barriers to intermarriage and an increasing similarity between marital partners on other characteristics that are important in selection of marital partners.

Fong and Yung (1995-1996) interviewed Chinese and Japanese Americans born in the 1940s to 1950s cohort who had married Caucasian Americans. These authors suggested that although decreasing racial barriers and acculturation can facilitate intermarriage to Caucasian Americans, other factors also must be considered. Aversion to Asian patriarchy, overbearing Asian mothers, cultural and economic compatibility, upward mobility, and media representations of beauty and power contribute to the increasing intermarriages between Asian and Caucasian Americans. Proximity in school or work was a precondition to marrying on the basis of compatibility, love, and trust. Timing and availability of Asian American partners of the same ethnicity are critical when the individual feels ready to be married. For API women, the childbearing clock often is a factor. Geographic area has an impact on availability of potential Asian American marital partners. Cultural affinity—whether one's cultural/family background values strong family ties, ethnic traditions, and educational achievement—could lay a strong foundation for marriage and family. In Fong and Yung's sample, Jewish partners and the Hawaiian connection facilitated interracial marriages. An aversion for marrying within the same ethnicity, such as disliking some aspects of one's own culture, contributed to marrying a White spouse. Some of the same factors that impinged on selection of marital partners among the general population also affected APIs, such as similarity of core values and proximity. Yet, there are some unique API differences such as wanting to avoid traditional marriages of their parents and being repelled from others of the same culture because of a dislike for Asian patriarchy.

As in other API family research areas, there are both push and pull factors for marrying from within one's ethnic group or selecting a marital partner from outside one's ethnic community. For example, a surprising number of mates are selected by advertisements, visits to India, and referrals from family, friends, and marriage brokers among South Indian immigrants (Sheth, 1995) and South Indians born in America, although for the latter group this is a less commonly used mechanism to meet potential mates. Eligibility for permanent residency can be an important reason for mate advertisements. Matrimonial candidates are screened by relatives, and the engagement processes are supervised by parents or relatives. It appears that caste and dowry considerations still are issues for South Asian Indian immigrants and their families (Durvasulas & Mylvaganam, 1994). This is a potential source of intergenerational conflict surrounding marriage and the family.

The quality of marriages is influenced by the rules or norms of giving and receiving benefits in marital relationships. For instance, providing benefits without the expectation of repayment (i.e., for love and caring about the recipient of benefits) as in communal relationships produced long-term improvements in marital harmony (Basic Behavioral Science Task Force of the National Advisory Mental Health Council, 1996). Promotion of an exchange orientation provided short-term marital harmony (i.e., contingency-reward system for desired behavior) within a marital relationship but suggested detrimental results over the long term. These are suggested findings within a cultural environment where love and romance drive marital relationships. However, within a different cultural framework for marriage, marriage based on continuity of the family or on other factors in addition to love, marital harmony might not be related to either communal or exchange relationships in precisely the same manner (Yanagisako, 1985).

Ramola (1992) found changes in the division of labor and decision-making power among immigrant South Indian Americans living in Chicago, but husbands and wives did not want to give up their traditional gender roles. South Indian wives were found to be more satisfied with their marriages than were their husbands, and Ramola attributed this finding to the increased freedom of wives with lessening of social control and authority of elders in the extended family.

Family adaptation often is dependent on the sociocultural context that has different implications for each family member. Kim and Kim (1995) examined Korean immigrant families and work roles in Chicago. They found that three fourths of Korean immigrant wives were employed in contrast to traditional Korean norms of married women as full-time homemakers. More than two thirds of the dual-earner families did not accept the wives' work role. Nonacceptance of working wives was even greater among single-earner families. In the dual-earner Korean families, spouses of both genders agreed that it was the wives' responsibility to do the housework. In effect, Korean immigrant wives had a culturally sanctioned "double shift" of paid work and unpaid work in the family. The wives' voluntary obligation to take a double shift can be an adaptational strategy for API families in which the husbands might have limited employment opportunities and the wives work to produce or maintain high family incomes. This Korean immigrant family pattern could be stress ridden and particularly burdensome for wives.

Determinants of marital satisfaction can vary across cultures and the specific ways in which marital satisfaction is expressed. Noda, Noda, and Clark (1990) found that communication with a housewife's spouse was the primary determinant of marital satisfaction and adjustment among Japanese immigrant housewives living in Canada. Gender differences can be found in what determines marital satisfaction, happiness, and well-being. For instance, according to Sasao and Chun (1994), subjective well-being on psychological and physical dimensions is higher if Korean women are married than if they are not. The frequency of contact and support by their families was correlated to physical health for Korean women. Happiness was related to how often Korean women saw their friends. These findings are mirrored in the Caucasian family literature, but the impact of culture and language might determine how often Korean women see their friends and the composition of their friendship networks.

Similar to marriages among the general population, marital adjustment among Koreans living in the United States is dependent on value congruence between marital partners. Education and social status issues are factors in marital conflicts for White Americans. These relationships are not straightforward among immigrant Korean marriages. For example, Min (1993) found that local community factors such as availability of potential spouses and acculturation affected marriage and divorce among Korean immigrants. In the Los Angeles community, the sex imbalance in favor of females made it more difficult for these females to find Korean spouses. Therefore, Korean females either remained single, went to Korea to seek potential spouses, or intermarried. The second choice put Korean American women at higher risk for divorce. Typically, 1 month of prenuptial engagement in Korea might not be sufficient time or ideal conditions in which to determine whether the marriage should proceed. Immigration stress and marital adaptation with an Americanized wife put stress on the marriage. The scenario is similar for Korean American males finding more educated brides in Korea. Social status and educational hypergamy (i.e., higher status of the male partner) are predictors of marital conflict in American marriages. It appears that Americanization among the 1.5-generation Korean Americans (i.e., born in Korea but raised in America) is sufficient to generate marital conflicts if they are married to spouses from Korea and especially if the wives desire egalitarian marriages.

Chan and Wethington (1995) argued that few studies have examined the marital relationships among interracial couples, yet the literature has presumed negative well-being and instability of such marriages. The presumption commonly made about interracial couples or raising biracial and multiracial children is that these families would be prone to difficulties. This negative attribution can be linked to the inappropriate generalization of studies that typically examined interracial marriages among newly arrived and less acculturated foreign-born individuals who are less educated and have poor English-speaking abilities (Jeong & Schumm, 1990). These authors suggested that unique cultural resources and strengths that are not available to other families might be mobilized by multicultural families. Very little is known about these issues because current sampling of ethnic identification often precludes identification of biracial and multiracial status in marriage and divorce statistics.

Studies have suggested that spouses in interracial marriages tend to be older, be more educated, and have higher incomes (Sung, 1990). These three factors are demonstrated to contribute to higher marital stability in the general population (White, 1990). Challenges faced by interracial couples are family opposition, especially among immigrant generations (Lee & Yamanaka, 1990), gender role expectations (Chan, 1990), and difficulties that might arise from cultural conflicts in parenting biracial children (Johnson & Nagoshi, 1986). The more compatible gender role expectations between marital partners, the more stability and satisfaction is likely to occur in the marriage.

In traditional families, Asian males have the responsibility for continuing the family lineage. Therefore, the impetus for traditional families is to encourage the eldest males to marry within the cultural group to maintain family lineage. Because daughters do not have this responsibility, their out-marriages might not be opposed as readily (Chan, 1992). Family opposition toward a disliked in-law could be expressed as strong support for a child's divorce as the only solution to marital problems. Or a family's attribution for marital difficulties to a large cultural gap that is not amenable to negotiation could be expressed as well.

In an effort to disentangle the effects of socioeconomic status (SES) on selectivity of interracially married Asians, Hwang, Saenz, and Aguirre (1995) used 1980 U.S. census 5% public use microdata samples limited to Chinese, Filipino, Japanese, Korean, Asian Indians, and Vietnamese. They found that Asian women married to White men in this sample tended to have lower SES when compared to their in-married counterparts. Asians with lower SES also were more likely to marry members of other minority groups such as Blacks. Having higher SES did not affect these Asians' tendency to out-marry interethnically, but it affected rates of interracial marriages as opposed to marrying within their own groups. Asian persons who married interracially tended to marry persons with an SES inferior to their own. The authors argued that this tendency could be attributable to Asian immigrants marrying lower SES minority persons as a convenient way in which to obtain their green cards.

Agbayani-Siewert (1994) noted that Filipino marital relationships differ in two ways from those of other Asian couples. Filipino families are based on egalitarian rather than patrilineal principles, and that ancestry is traced across both sides of the family in accordance with Spanish traditions. More consistent marital expectations pose less variant marital roles and cultural shock for Filipino couples in Western countries than for other Asian families. Another difference between Filipino and other Asian families is Filipinos' strong Catholic beliefs regarding male and female family roles. "Machismo" mannerisms and behaviors by Filipino males or submissive behavior by females outside the family might be mere public display, but behind family doors a more egalitarian relationship exists. This paradoxical description must be examined more closely among Filipino marriages. Similar to other Asian ethnicities, Filipino couples are described as "noncommunicative" by not confronting each other, and marital difficulties are considered private matters not to be disclosed in public. Public versus private discussions and behaviors might be notably different in API families in contrast to Caucasian American, middle-class families. We currently do not know the extent of this discrepancy and how this issue might affect API family research.

Parenting

API cultures, families, and individuals have different definitions of what it means to be a parent, mother, father, or surrogate parent. In Western societies, the focus on parenting revolves around the role of mothers. In other countries, parenting and socialization of children might be the responsibility of a whole village rather than focus solely on mothers (Ambert, 1994). API families have a broader range of adults and older children who might have responsibility for what Americans define as parenting responsibilities. These varied parental definitions, roles, and responsibilities systematically shape family processes. For example, the mother role is the most important role for women in traditional Japan, and the mother's adult status is contingent on transition to this role (Lebra, 1984). Certain socioeconomic conditions and cultural contexts force other family members, such as grandparents, to engage in traditional parenting roles as demanded by the sociocultural environment.

According to Serafica (1990), counseling API parents about their parenting roles is a critical gap in our society. On the one hand, API parental doggedness concerning education as a means of achieving success is adaptive, but not at the cost of parents alienating their child or pushing the child to suicide because he or she received a B in one academic subject. On the other hand, some of the extreme rigidity concerning absolute parental authority until marriage may be softened to gradual loosening of authority through adolescence to avoid adolescent rebellion to extreme authoritarian parenting. This need is particularly critical for immigrant parents who are coping with the rapid acculturation of their children, with age and gender role shifts, while also coping with a sometimes hostile American environment (Chan & Leong, 1994; Yee, in press).

In a study of Vietnamese immigrant parent and college-age child relationships, Dinh, Sarason, and Sarason (1994) found that Vietnamese-born college students felt they had lower quality of parental relationships and were less socially integrated than were American-born students. Vietnamese-born male college students were at high risk for poor relationships with their fathers. Vietnamese mothers perceived less social support than did their American counterparts. However, social support was measured by the average number of potential providers of support and might be problematic because it did not assess types of support or the level of support provided. The conflict between parents and college-age children centered around the view of the parents as being overprotective and controlling. The quality of the Vietnamese father-son relationship appeared to be negatively affected by acculturation.

Fathers can make a unique contribution in the lives of their children. Traditional API culture has placed fathers as the family patriarchs, yet we know little about how that traditional role has changed with acculturation in America (Mirande, 1991). For example, in an agrarian society, property was passed along the male line to ensure integrity of land to grow crops. When these economic issues no longer press Asian families, lineage, inheritance, and filial piety can change with demands of the new sociocultural context. We currently see variations in how fathers carry out their role in API families. An economic push requires mothers to work outside the home. Two family incomes are an economic requirement for most API families, but whether fathers take on more child caretaking and household tasks as a result of mothers working outside the home is yet to be determined.

Marsella, Oliveira, Plummer, and Crabbe (1995) reported that Native Hawaiians had the highest rate of pregnancy and births to unmarried mothers. Sufficient attention to the impact of this single-parent status on family processes and socialization of these Hawaiian children was examined by Thompson, McCubbin, Thompson, and Elver (1995). These authors stated that the accumulation of family life events or pressures that occurred in the preceding 12 months was the most important predictor of family distress. The second predictor of family distress for Hawaiian families was the presence of an incendiary problem-solving communication style such as yelling or screaming at each other. The last predictor of family distress for Native Hawaiian families was level of social support. The only significant difference between the single-parent and two-parent families occurred in the pileup of family pressures. This study suggested that being the only parent in the household to handle family pressures concentrated these responsibilities on one person and made these families more vulnerable to family distress over and above the impact of problem-solving communication and level of social support. The specific risk mechanism for single-parent Hawaiian American families is yet to be determined.

We see changes in who takes responsibility for children and households as well as changes in child socialization goals that are adaptations to new sociocultural environments faced by API families in Western countries. Schneider, Hieshima, Lee, and Plank (1994) found a retention of East Asian traditions such as high educational expectations, respect for authority, and reliance on tacit understandings between children and parents to monitor and motivate improvement of educational performance by the children. In a high-context culture such as traditional Japanese culture, shared meanings do not have to be explicitly expressed. Japanese parents nurture empathy as the most important of moral values in Japanese culture (Lebra, 1994). Socialization of children focuses on how well the children demonstrate sensitivity to the needs, desires, and feelings of others (Schneider et al., 1994). These characteristics are not verbally instilled but are socialized by appropriate behavioral modeling demonstrated across family routines and life domains by older family members. The focus of socialization comes from example and behavior rather than being socialized through verbal commands. Life's lessons are taught by living an exemplary life rather than by talking about what exemplary living should be.

Extended family members have taken on traditional parenting roles for API families in America. Tam and Detzner (1995) found that Chinese immigrant grandparents provided critical child care services for families. After visiting, grandmothers often would take their grandchildren back to Hong Kong. Grandparents acted as surrogate parents, family historians, cultural gurus, mentors, and role models in families, but geographic proximity and belief in the socializing ability of family elders determined the extent of this grandparent role in Asian families. A barrier to using grandparents as family resources stemmed from acculturated middle-generation parents who did not want to impose parenting responsibilities on their elderly parents. Other respondents believed that their elderly parents could not provide the type of socialization that had relevance in this society or disagreed with the child-rearing strategy. Differences in preferred socialization and social control strategies can be a source of conflict between generations in the family.

Another adaptational strategy found among API families is inclusion of close family friends to provide a protective supportive network typically provided by large extended families. For example, compadre systems from the Spanish colonial Catholic system have been incorporated into the Filipino family system as fictive relatives. This family structure adaptation expands the number of adults who children may depend on to support them through religious rites of passage and over the life cycle (Agbayani-Siewert & Revilla, 1995) considering that immigration barriers produced incomplete extended family systems in America. We see the inclusion of close family friends into the family network as an adaptational strategy among Native Hawaiians, Samoans, and other API groups.

Divorce

Divorce makes the family situation more complicated because family lines become blurred and discontinuous. Divorce is not very common except among younger and acculturated APIs. Lind (1964) did a cohort analysis of interracial marriage and divorce rates in Hawaii between 1958 and 1962. He found that out-marriage divorce rates for Hawaiian, Korean, Puerto Rican, Filipino, and Caucasian Americans were lower than those for individuals married to individuals from their own ethnic group. Sanborn (1977) analyzed this same database and found an increased divorce risk for Caucasian women married to Chinese or Japanese American men. Blood (1969) attributed an increased divorced risk to the gender role incompatibility between traditional Asian husbands and emancipated Caucasian wives as a chief culprit for marital strife. The least divorce-prone marriages in Hawaii were between Caucasian men and Puerto Rican or Filipino American women. Lu (1982) found that traditional Chinese women had a lessened risk for divorce because divorce was not considered a viable option for an unhappy marriage.

In a longitudinal study of divorce in Northern California, 333 persons who recently had filed for divorce were interviewed and followed over 3.5 years (Chiriboga & Catron, 1991). This data set contained 18 Asian American divorcees (8 Chinese, 4 Japanese, and 6 Filipino Americans); of these, two thirds were female and one third were male. Yee, Chiriboga, and Catron (1991) collapsed these Asian American respondents into one group because samples were too small to conduct analyses for each Asian group. These authors found that half of the sample exhibited high symptomatology measured by the California Symptoms Checklist-42 at baseline, with the symptomatology decreasing 3.5 years later for Asian males only, from 9.0 to 5.4 symptoms. The number of symptoms reported for Asian females remained about the same, changing only from 12.7 to 12.8 symptoms at follow-up. The long-term divorce adaptation implications for Asian females appear to be much bleaker, and the study should be replicated with a larger sample.

In a detailed analysis of childhood stressors among this sample of Asian divorcees, Yee et al. (1991) found that they experienced higher stress in being required to work during their younger years, had more parents who were divorced, and experienced absence from their parents to a greater extent than did the Caucasian divorcees. Asian divorcees experienced fewer arguments among family members, specifically arguments between parents or arguments with a parent, than did Caucasian divorcees. The outstanding question to be answered is whether these Asian divorcees experienced more family discord than did APIs who were not divorced. Family discord in childhood can be a risk mechanism for divorce and appeared to have negative implications for API divorcees at much lower levels of discord. This makes sense if the normative set for traditional Asians is maintenance of harmony; even the slightest discord can have dramatically negative implications.

Parental identification has been found to play a critical role in divorce adjustment among Caucasian divorcees. More than one half of the Asian divorcees saw dissimilarity between either parent and themselves. According to Yee et al. (1991), this might be due to a wide generation gap in ethnic and self-identification between immigrant and American generations in API families. This wide generation gap ultimately might contribute to poorer adaptation among Asian divorcees, but it is unclear whether poor identification with parents or some other factor directly caused poorer divorce adaptation.

Sheth (1995) found that South Indian Americans have the lowest divorce rates in comparison to Chinese, Filipino, and Korean couples, according to U.S. census data from 1993. The author attributed this lower rate of divorce among South Indian Americans to stronger emphasis on marriage and family, divorce stigma, and high socioeconomic background of these couples.

Fujita and O'Brien (1991) found that association with Japanese organizations served to be a resource to the family during times of crisis and that these ethnic affiliations were associated with a decreased incidence of divorce among Japanese Americans. What must be examined more closely is whether close ties with Japanese culture, as well as cultural variables, might be implicated as the critical factors or whether some other moderating variable is accounting for the lower divorce rate among more traditional Japanese couples. Having a good support system that promotes marriage and is available during times of crises, such as marital difficulties, is one of many moderating factors contributing to marriage outcomes.

Intergenerational Relationships

One critical role that older generations play in the lives of API families is social support and transmission of culture to younger members of the family. The spirits of dead relatives were believed to dwell at the heart of the family and to guide the behavior of each of its members. Each family member formed a link with past and future generations. Family solidarity was the goal of maintaining this historical continuity. Filial piety was paid to older members of the family because they gave life to younger members and would join the family's ancestors after death. In Asian American families, filial piety might no longer be the driving force that binds families together, but reciprocity between generations such as exchanges of emotional, financial, and child care support has been adaptive in the United States.

The cultural clashes come not so much from the basic family values to provide social support and transmission of culture as from the behavioral expressions of those values. Common family disagreements arise from rapid shifts in family roles and expectations surrounding fulfillment of the roles in a new cultural context (Yee, 1997). Yee (1992) found that some elderly Vietnamese had difficulty coping with their younger grandchildren's lack of socialization in expressing respect and filial piety in the traditional manner. Traditional ways in which to address respected family elders might not be used by younger Asians, and this is taken as a lack of respect. Rather, the values of filial piety often are present, but the manner in which it is demonstrated changes with acculturation. This synchrony between cultural values and the behavioral expressions of those values becomes less harmonious with acculturation, blending of families (i.e., marriages) across generations, and time. Social status of Asian elderly remains long after the social and contextual situation has shifted away from supporting traditional demonstrations of filial piety. For example, contributions of Vietnamese elders might be critical to family survival soon after immigration to the United Status because they provide needed services such as child care and household maintenance while adult children hold paying jobs or go on to further schooling (Yee, 1997), but they might erode when family elders no longer can make these contributions or when services no longer are needed.

Asian elders traditionally were authority figures who kept younger members in line by threatening shame to the family if they were indiscreet. Elders were looked up to, had control over the family purse, and had authority to make decisions for each younger family member (Yee & Hennessey, 1982). Asian elders living in the United States often find themselves with less control, experience role reversal, and, instead of controlling financial resources, might find themselves to be totally dependent on their adult children for support.

The nature of intergenerational relationships and its cultural transmission can be illustrated by the 60th birthday rituals celebrated among Japanese families. Doi (1991) contended that the *Kanreki,* a traditional rite of passage to old age at 60 years of age, had been adopted by the Nisei (second-generation, first American-born Japanese) as a cultural response to the dilemmas of growing older in urban America. Doi argued that this rite of passage has not been directly observed by Sansei (third-generation Japanese American) adults but rather has been transmitted to this generation symbolically. Nisei parents could not celebrate their grandparents' 60th birthdays due to logistical barriers such as World War II and their internment. Having to recover economically after being interned also prevented the enactment of these celebrations. Issei (first-generation immigrant Japanese American) could not be used as role models to help Nisei adjust to their old age because life situations and circumstances were so different. Younger Nisei looked to older Nisei for adaptational strategies used successfully during their elderly years. Doi suggested that this rite of passage for Japanese American elders demonstrated the importance of family ties and ethnic solidarity across Japanese community. These 60th birthday rituals reinforced the idea that ethnicity was a resource during old age by enlisting and reaffirming the support of younger generations to help during the frail years ahead.

Cultural transmissions and maintenance of family bonds can be seen in Hmong American New Year rituals. Lynch, Detzner, and Eicher (1995) found that older Hmongs living in the United States use clothing attire during New Year rituals as a medium in which to express their vision of the Hmong culture as expressed in the past and its relevance for American culture. While engaging in the rituals, formalized linkages between family elders occur as they teach younger generations Hmong traditions. This formalized role has reinforced and raised the status of Hmong elders as cultural historians in contrast to the American context in which younger, highly educated members are esteemed and rewarded.

Caring for Elders

A major challenge faced by families is caring for elderly, frail, and chronically ill relatives. The cultural values regarding social relationships within the API family show evidence of strong cultural clashes in the area of caregiving and end of life decisions for frail family members. There have been few studies on caregiving for frail family members among API communities. Role modeling of the traditional caregiving roles might not be direct observations. First, many API middle-aged individuals have not directly observed their parents caring for frail grandparents because these grandparents might never have lived to a very old age in the home country or because these caregiving responsibilities were left to siblings caring for these elderly relatives back in the homeland. Learning about filial piety from a distance, through stories, or in the abstract produces greater diversity in expressions of filial beliefs and behaviors than if these API individuals directly observed their parents taking care of their elderly grandparents. The resulting filial piety beliefs and behaviors may be romanticized and take idealized forms in practice, show differences between values and behaviors, or show variance from behaviors actually exhibited by an earlier cohort.

Because only a handful of empirical studies have examined caregiving for API elders, living arrangement patterns, such as three-generational families, may reveal whether relatives might be available to help during a health crisis. The 1980 census revealed that situational or contextual variables such as SES or availability of adult children, as well as cultural values of filial piety or the practice of primogeniture (i.e., agricultural practice of oldest son living with parents after he gets married and identified as the unquestionable heir), contributed to the pattern of living arrangements found among Asian elderly. Burr and Mutchler (1993) found that single women (i.e., widowed, never married, divorced) who were age 55 years or older and of Japanese, Chinese, Filipino, or Korean descent varied in their living arrangements. These authors found that older, single Chinese and Filipino women who were less acculturated were more likely to live with others (i.e., relatives, nonrelatives, group quarters) than were those who were acculturated. Although the rate of coresidence of Japanese American single older women was lower than those of other groups of Asian women, Japanese American elderly women still were significantly more likely to coreside with others than were non-Hispanic White women. Recent immigration after 1965 increased the likelihood of coresidence among these single Asian elderly women. Higher English language proficiency and incomes decreased coresidence. In other words, there are separate predictors of coresidence contributed by ethnic group and culture; health, age, and disability; and situational/demographic circumstances such as number of children, SES, and availability of cultural competence services for these older single Asian women. At least according to relationships found among variables in the 1980 census, health and demographic characteristics might be more important, as compared to ethnicity or economics, in predicting institutionalization for Asian elderly single women (Burr & Mutchler, 1993).

A different living arrangement pattern emerges for Asian Indian elderly women. Burr (1992) examined the 1980 census and found that unmarried elderly Asian Indian women were much more likely to live alone than were other Asian elderly groups and lived alone at higher rates than did their Caucasian counterparts. Higher income levels were associated with greater independent living among Asian Indian unmarried elderly women. Lower income levels and difficulty with using public transportation were associated with living in complex households (i.e., with relatives or nonrelatives). What could not be answered from this study of census data is whether this independent living is preferred by the Asian Indian elderly women themselves or desired by their relatives. Availability of children and other Asian Indians in close proximity reduces the odds of unmarried Asian Indian living alone. This suggested that perhaps multiple factors (e.g., higher income levels, unavailability of Asian Indian relatives and friends) contributed to a higher proportion of Asian Indian elderly women living alone.

Kamo and Zhou (1994) suggested that once key predictor variables (e.g., marital status, state of residence, gender) are controlled, the probability of elderly coresiding in extended family households is very similar for Japanese and Chinese elderly, as reflected in the 1980 census. Living in extended family settings is adaptive for API elderly. The impact of cultural values and filial piety can be maintained across as many as four API generations. Other variables may work to increase or decrease the impact of culture but may do so in a nonlinear fashion. This study suggested that the multivariate impact of key predictors is no simple matter. Coresidence makes caregiving more convenient but does not ensure it. What we now need to know is how API families make decisions about living arrangements, what contextual factors influence these decisional processes, and how caregiving is provided to vulnerable elderly relatives in API families.

Changes in caregiving expectations and the practice of filial piety among Asians can be seen cross-culturally and within Asian Americans living in Western countries. For example, Ikels (1983) did an extensive ethnographic study examining adaptation and aging among Chinese in Hong Kong and Boston. What she discovered was a wide variation among the Chinese families in their behavioral expressions of filial piety.

Ikels (1983) found that most older people made major contributions to running the household so that other household members were free to engage in money-making activities. Problems arose most acutely during times of incapacitating illnesses. Ikels suggested that the major difference between Hong Kong and Boston was the degree to which an older person could function independently and the level of sociocultural supports for elders in the immediate environment in which the elderly person lived. Hong Kong elders appeared to manage most activities without assistance. Hong Kong elders had ready access to shopping and medical treatment of choice and were surrounded by people who shared the same language. Yet, Hong Kong Chinese elders' independence was limited by financial constraints and availability of alternatives that created higher coresidence. By contrast, Chinese elders living in Boston acknowledged the notion that coresidence was less culturally accepted, but when the elderly became frail, coresidence was an acceptable alternative to institutionalization. The majority of middle-aged residents in Boston recognized that their parents could enjoy life to a greater extent in Hong Kong or Taiwan rather than in the United States. Elders who were becoming frail and could not manage on their own then moved permanently to the United States to be with or near their children.

Yu, Kim, Liu, and Wong (1993) found an inverse relationship between health status of Chinese elders and the likelihood of recommending a nursing home as the best living arrangement. Nearly 90% of healthy Chinese elders selected the nursing home; 84% of chronically ill elders, 76% of disabled elders, and 60% of incontinent elders felt this same way. Living in the home of one's children or having other living arrangements increased as the health condition of the Chinese elder declined. By contrast, only 6% of Korean elders recommended a nursing home for elders who had children living in the same city. Korean elders strongly desired living independently if healthy, but with chronic illness, the desire to turn to a nursing home increased to 31%. In addition, 60% of Chinese elders in this sample thought that children should support their parents, even when the parents were financially self-supportive. By contrast, only 46% of Korean elders felt that children should support their parents. According to Yu et al. (1993), Chinese dependence on children went beyond mere economics. The large majorities of Chinese (76%) and Korean (81%) elders felt that if they could not care for themselves, then their children would take care of them in the short and long term.

The scant caregiving literature suggests that multiple patterns of caregiving exist among API families today. Yu (1983) surveyed four age cohorts (18-25 years, 26-35 years, 36-55 years, and 56 years or older) totaling 510 Chinese residents in a midwestern university town concerning how filial obligations are met. She did not find a positive correlation between filial beliefs and age cohorts. The 26-to 35-year age cohort held the highest filial beliefs; however, these beliefs had no correspondence to their filial behaviors such as contributing money and meeting housing needs of their parents. It appears that acculturation interacts with proximity when expected filial behaviors might actually be solicited.

Yu and Wu (1985) examined the impact of length of residency on filial beliefs and behaviors. The sample was divided into newcomers (1-5 years in the United States), new-old residents (6-15 years), old-old residents (longer than 16 years), and American-born Chinese. They found that longer residency in the United States resulted in less distress felt when giving financial support to parents. The newcomers were very distressed at giving financial support to parents. This might be due to multiple acculturation stressors and strains experienced by new Chinese immigrants in the United States. U.S.-born Chinese females were distressed in meeting financial needs of parents-in-law. Old residents and females experienced significantly higher distress levels than did males in meeting housing needs of parents-in-law. Old residents and U.S.-born respondents felt more comfortable in meeting filial responsibilities.

In an unpublished study of 4,029 Hawaii government employees, Takamura, Nitz, and Haruki (1991) found that 20% were assisting older adults with one or more of the activities of daily living or providing direct financial help to persons age 60 years or over. Fully 68% of caregivers were women, with an average age of 44 years. In addition, 70% of care recipients in Hawaii were female, with an average age of 76 years and with 58% of the sample suffering from health-related problems. Asian Americans (i.e., Japanese, Chinese, Filipino, and Korean Americans) were overrepresented in the caregiver group relative to their proportions in the sample as compared to Caucasians in the sample. Cultural values, longevity, and low family mobility led to the presence of API elders living in close proximity and contributed to higher Asian American caregivers in this Hawaiian sample.

Takamura et al. (1991) also found ethnic group differences in the use of caregiver services and materials. Caucasian caregivers used written materials, caregiver workshops, and counseling to a higher degree than did API caregivers in this sample. They proposed that this low level of caregiver service use might relate to language difficulties, feelings of alienation, distrust of health professions, limited financial resources, and the desire to provide caregiving within the family. They also found differences in the effects of caregiving responsibilities. API caregivers mentioned being overwhelmed, feeling confined, and paying back family obligations more frequently than did Caucasian caregivers. This stressful life experience was balanced by the opportunity to fulfill family obligations and demonstrate filial piety among API caregivers.

Interviews with an immigrant Chinese wife, immigrant Chinese daughter, and Japanese American daughter-in-law revealed that providing care was considered a required and necessary family function (Goodman, 1990). English-only services were not a viable option for a demented relative who either never had or lost his or her English skills due to dementia. Osako and Liu (1986) found that among Nisei and Sansei (second- and third-generation Japanese Americans, respectively), only 12.6% of parents and 7.6% of daughters felt that they should share a household, although almost 50% of the elderly lived with one of their children. This implied that although independent living was the goal, when the elderly parents needed assistance, Japanese American children moved them into their homes. These circumstances might differ for future generations of elderly and their families.

The caregiving literature suggests that women bear a disproportionate amount of the burden in caregiving for both children and elderly relatives in their families (Chiriboga, Yee, & Weiler, 1992). The job of caregiver for elderly relatives usually is based on ritualized patterns of inheritance, proximity, emotional closeness, and gender roles (Caffrey, 1992). Caregiving for elderly relatives facilitated their kin-keeping role by maintaining the emotional interdependence of families and ensured that obligations to elders, who were soon to be ancestors, had been met. Although Asian American families in general have become more accepting of institutionalization of their elderly relatives, they still are more reluctant than the general population to do so. This reluctance is broken by behaviors such as wandering, incontinence, or secondary illnesses that overwhelm families' ability to manage everyday functions (Goodman, 1990; Morton, Stanford, Happersett, & Molgaard, 1992).

Our current notions about caregiving in a handful of studies on Chinese and Japanese American families might not be found in other API ethnic groups; generalizations might be limited by the cohort, generational, social class, and acculturative characteristics of API families such as those found among recent immigrant segments of these populations or refugee families. Critical issues expressed by a focus group of Asian Indian elderly women (National Asian Women's Health Organization, 1996) were financial and physical dependence. After years of caring for their grandchildren, these elderly women found it difficult to ask for care and help in dealing with chronic illness or disability. These sentiments were expressed as fears by these Asian Indian elderly women, who experienced loneliness because they lacked mobility and could not speak English. The high incidence of independent living among this group suggests that appropriate aging services must be accessed because, at least for this Asian elderly group, families might not be willing or able to provide these services. As API families care for elderly relatives in frail physical or mental health, the likelihood of elder abuse can increase. API traditional beliefs about caring for elderly relatives as the family's sole responsibility make these API families less likely to seek outside caregiver respite and support services.

Elder Abuse

Elder abuse can occur when the family's resources, in the context of acculturative stressors by new immigrants, are stretched beyond the family's capacity to care for frail and vulnerable family elders. In a rare study of elder abuse, Moon and Williams (1993) found that Korean American elders perceived less abuse and defined it more narrowly than did either African or Caucasian American samples. The Korean American elders were the least educated, had the lowest income, were more likely to live alone, and had the least number of children living in the same state as compared to African and Caucasian American elders in the sample. These elderly were presented with 13 hypothetical scenarios, and the authors found Korean American elders to be least likely to perceive situations as abusive or were more tolerant of these potentially abusive situations. Moon and Williams suggested that these Korean American elders were significantly less likely to seek help than were the other two groups. The authors concluded that Korean American elders were reluctant to reveal "family shame" to others and feared creating family conflict as a consequence of divulging an abusive family situation to outsiders.

API elders see the enormous stress and burden that their caregiver must shoulder and might seek to lessen their burden by not asking for help when needed or by committing suicide to get rid of the family burden. Investigators (Liu & Yu, 1985; McIntosh & Santos, 1981; Yu, 1991) have noted higher rates of suicide among elderly Asian women and in particular among Chinese elderly women. Contextual precursors for high rates of suicide among elderly Asian women must be examined more closely.

Death and Dying

Another stressful challenge for API families is the family processes in dealing with a dying family member, grieving, and death. Issues that revolve around death and dying are not so complex in developing countries. However, in our technologically advanced and litigious society, these issues are brought to our attention every day. There is a dramatic effect of culture on advanced directives and life-support decisions in America. Withdrawing life support always is a difficult decision for families, and the idea of terminating life support can be offensive, wrong, and not consistent with their worldview.

Klessig (1992) examined life-support decisions for terminal situations among African American, Chinese, Jewish, Iranian, Filipino, Mexican American, and Korean young or middle-aged patients. Caucasian Americans were less willing to start life support and strongly agreed to stop life support. There were wide variations among Asian patients; Chinese patients were equivocal about starting life support and generally agreed to stop life support, Koreans wanted to start life support and disagreed to stop, and Filipinos strongly agreed to start and strongly disagreed to stop. This study suggested that life-support decisions can be influenced by cultural and religious beliefs regarding active and human interventions to prolonging or ending life. The cultural barriers lay in different acculturation levels within the family, which gets translated into different beliefs about the use of extraordinary means (e.g., high-technology medicine that keeps organs alive although the brain is dead) to keep dying patients alive. There might be differences between the generations regarding the older or dying patient's wishes to turn off artificial means of living versus the family wanting to keep the patient alive as long as possible to fulfill its filial responsibility.

Cultural values concerning disclosure of health diagnosis and prognosis, the role of the family in making medical decisions, and the withholding or withdrawing of treatment for terminally ill patients are complicated by linguistic and communication difficulties that can have significant impacts on the interactions between

API families and medical personnel. Muller and Desmond (1992) provided an example of how these cultural issues provide ethical dilemmas for health care workers and API families. If a patient does not speak English, then health care professionals often must communicate with the patient through an interpreter but more often through an English-speaking family member. This family spokesperson becomes the conduit through which information flows from health care provider to patient and other family members. Both the content (or lack thereof) and the manner in which it is communicated are culturally translated by this family spokesperson. Cultural differences shape the family communication of "bad news" (i.e., that the diagnosis is terminal and cannot be healed or that nothing more can be done) and set the stage for what news, if any, is given to the dying patient. API families are faced with our legal system, which believes in primacy of self-determination and privacy regarding requesting or refusing medical treatment. Traditional Chinese and many other Asian groups believe in a different treatment of dying people and the role of truth telling between physician and patient, as contrasted by health care practices in our American legal system. Many traditional Chinese believe that a sick person should be treated as someone to be protected (Krantzler, 1982). Telling the sick person about his or her illness and its severity should not be done because this information might only increase suffering. With increases in severity of illness, tandem increases in protection of the sick person might be seen. Many Asian groups believe that telling someone he or she is dying is not only rude but actually dangerous to the patient (Hospice of the Valley, n.d.; Orona, Koenig, & Davis, 1994; Tung, 1990). Openly acknowledging an impending death is similar to casting a death curse on the dying person, making the person despair and hastening his or her death. Any discussions regarding the patient's resuscitation status or advanced directives or whether hospice care might be the next step could be perceived as an act of inviting bad luck and giving up hope and as a preparation for death. Truth telling by physicians to patients communicates that physicians have given up hope and so the patient should succumb to his or her fate as well. Traditional Asian expectations are to not acknowledge and discuss the situation openly with the patient; rather, it should be discussed outside hearing distance of the patient. The Asian family imperative and filial obligation is to protect the patient by decreasing worry and stress and by maintaining the highest quality of life as long as possible (Orona et al., 1994). The family's obligation is to maintain hope and ensure a "good death" (i.e., dying peacefully in old age surrounded by family) because a "bad death" (i.e., short life with high emotional outbursts of the dying patient and perhaps negative accusations directed at family members) creates shame for the entire family. With acculturation, Nisei and Sansei have expressed a desire to have control over their own health care decisions (Nishimura & Yeo, 1992).

Recent literature suggests a more complex picture expressed in the notion that traditional APIs cannot be told about fatal illnesses. Der-McLeod (1995) at On Lok, a community-based agency serving mostly Chinese frail elderly in Northern California, found under culturally competent conditions that Chinese elderly would discuss and make decisions concerning end of life interventions such as cardiac pulmonary resuscitation, nasogastric tube feeding, and death and dying. These authors suggest that discussions of advanced directives can be conducted in a culturally competent manner within the context of an established trusting relationship prior to development of a health crisis.

Procedures for cardiac pulmonary resuscitation or nasogastric tube feeding were described in detail. The majority of Chinese frail elderly did not want someone pounding on their chest to resuscitate them or putting a respirator tube down their throat to help them breathe. Most said that they wanted to go peacefully because they lived a long time and had outlived family and friends. A smaller group would not answer or did not want to discuss the question. In response to a second advance directive, use of a nasogastric tube to maintain nutritional status, the majority of Chinese elders preferred to make this decision when the situation was more imminent. After determination of the Chinese elder's health wishes, a social worker followed up with family members and presented these health wishes. Der-McLeod (1995) found that family members often were relieved that their elderly relative had made the decision so that they no longer had that responsibility. On Lok encouraged family members to discuss this issue with their elderly relative. Der-McLeod contended that carrying out contracts and obligations is based on building correct relationships (i.e., family, friendships, professional relationships) and not based on law. Decisions are not based on what an individual decides; rather, they are based on what is best for the common good. It appears that if an appropriate cultural context is provided, then end of life decisions and advanced directives can be discussed with the majority of Asian patients and their families.

Death rituals and the expression of grief vary by culture, acculturation, and API ethnicities. The API family must cope with feelings of grief and deal with the aftermath of these events (Kagawa-Singer, 1994). Death and dying is a universal human experience, but culture provides practices to enable the grieving family to better cope with the loss of a loved one and provides ritual proscriptions for supportive activities during a stressful and often confusing time (Janes, 1990).

The Cult of the Ancestors is maintained for Asians who are Buddhists; they believe that ancestors who are not properly respected and prayed to after death will come back to haunt the family. Family shrines and proper rituals on death anniversaries still are maintained today. According to Buddhist beliefs, the state of mind of the dying person at the moment of death is thought to influence the rebirth process. Being calm and having a positive state of mind improves the chances of a favorable rebirth (Truitner & Truitner, 1993). According to Bliatout (1993), the Hmong believe that proper burial and ancestor worship directly influence the health, safety, and prosperity of the family. As the time of death grows nearer, family members gather around the sickbed of the dying elder and talk about family history. Funeral rituals and exchange of labor during this grieving process provide needed social support that strengthen Hmong communities. Proper displays of grief by the surviving spouse and children demonstrate family loyalty. Kind thoughts and expressions about the deceased relative are proper protocol. Family members reciprocate by describing how calm and good-humored the deceased was just before death. This suggests that Buddhist beliefs about dying, death, and rebirth would significantly affect how an Asian family copes with the loss of a family member.

ASIAN AND PACIFIC ISLANDER FAMILY RESEARCH GAPS AND CHALLENGES

The empirical work on API families has just begun and is a relatively unexplored area of psychology. Conducting research on API families offers many challenges to psychology. The first research challenge is to highlight typical life-span developmental hurdles and life crises that expend resources of even the most resilient API families. We need to better understand how acculturation to the American cultural context, through socialization and enculturation processes, produces adaptive strategies that enable API individuals to traverse life-span developmental dilemmas for immigrant API families as well as examine how these same processes operate across second, third, and fourth generations of API families. Development of resiliencies and family difficulties relates to how acculturative and socialization processes blend and shape API families to produce a wider variety of adaptive strategies to deal with a multicultural world. The resiliency model reinforces the notion that a sole focus on the negative repercussions of trauma loses sight of the tremendous resilience demonstrated by some humans under the most deplorable of conditions. Adversity can be an insurmountable barrier or a worthy challenge to spite the odds. Many API families take this challenge to heart, yet psychologists must not lose sight of those API families who might need a little support to deal most effectively with these critical life events. Rutter (1994) suggested that we must differentiate between risk indicators and those mechanisms that put individuals at risk. For instance, poverty makes good family functioning more difficult, but poverty alone is not a sufficient precursor of conduct disorder (Shawtaylor & Benokratis, 1995). A consideration of risk mechanisms for family discord, such as witnessing strong negative interactions between parents or between parents and children, and poor parental modeling or maladaptive parenting practices can lead to failure to learn effective coping or social problem-solving skills during key developmental periods and can lead to lifelong chaining of deviance or psychopathology from childhood into adulthood. We know little about the risk mechanisms for API families because culture and minority experiences complicate our study of these issues. A closer examination of acculturation mechanisms to determine what aspects of traditional cultures are maintained and what aspects of the new culture are adopted should be explored.

Although there has been a steady increase of API family research initiatives, better conceptual models are needed to explain the impact of family and its socialization practices on the development of API children. These conceptual models should take into account the cultural context of API children and heterogeneity of these API populations rather than being devoid of many cultural underpinnings of their behavior or producing stereotypical formulations of API children. A closer examination of how collectivism and multiple cultural resources create adaptive coping strategies to navigate developmental tasks for API children and their families is warranted.

API research initiatives in adolescence and young adulthood should explore questions such as the following. How do families encourage development of positive ethnic identities and adaptive life skills in the context of American culture? How do families influence occupational achievement and choices? How do occupational stereotypes and societal barriers such as glass ceiling issues affect API individuals and their families? How do families exert their influence over dating, marital choices, and sexual behavior among API youths in the context of acculturation factors?

Research initiatives on API families during the second half of life is only beginning as an empirical science. There is much research to be done regarding family relationships, family coping processes, and family decision making revolving around issues of later life, disability, and caregiving in API communities. We know almost nothing about API family decision-making processes in dealing with the needs of older family members, critical predictors of caregiving, and institutionalization among the variety of API communities across the United States. API families are called on to advocate on behalf of their non-English-speaking and frail elderly relatives to access services and effectively manage affairs during health care crises.

An often overlooked and understudied function of the family (Yee, in press) is the enculturation and socialization in the face of acculturative factors of certain cultural and lifestyle habits that promote health such as nutritional patterns, physical activities, use of medicinal and other substances, coping strategies (Marsella & Dash-Scheuer, 1988), stress reduction, adaptive strategies such as use of confession as symbolic healing (Georges, 1995; Wellenkamp, 1995), and other worldviews that can affect physical and mental health. Socialization of traditional lifestyle habits may or may not promote health under significantly different environmental conditions from which these lifestyle habits evolved or at different developmental stages.

Many questions need to be answered, such as the following. How does acculturation of younger family members affect middle age and elderly life-span transitions of older family members? How does this vary by gender and API ethnic group? How does acculturation interact with socialization in the process of child care by family elders who hold more traditional cultural beliefs? What is the impact of acculturative and enculturative processes on identity, social roles, and life skills among middle-aged and elderly API family members in later life? What is the nature of supportive family relationships across generations such as grandparents, parents, and children as well as within generations such as among spouses, siblings, or cousins over the life span? How have family supportive relationships been influenced by acculturation over the life span? How do API families cope with the incomplete social support systems during times of crises?

How do API families make decisions when faced with chronic or debilitating health conditions of older family members?

A second research challenge involves developing measurement, instrumentation, and research methodologies for API families residing in the United States. McCubbin, Thompson, and McCubbin (1996) summarized the literature on families within a theoretical framework and presented some family assessment instruments that should enhance the API family research efforts. What is clear from this review is that there is very little research on API families. The majority of psychological research on API families is descriptive, is of secondary or ancillary nature, and often is derived from clinical observations or study of individual family members rather than from examination of the family as the focal unit of analysis (Jackson & Hatchett, 1986; Kagitcibasi, 1989). The ways in which APIs perceive family function, family roles, and social relationships might be significantly different from how Caucasian Americans perceive them. What is lacking is an examination of API family functioning and adaptation from different generational perspectives within their particular social and cultural contexts and followed longitudinally. Cross-sectional research designs allow a small glimpse of family processes within a given historical moment and give us microscopic insight into family adaptational processes over time. These are critical research gaps. Standard methodological problems of reliability and validity must be addressed with regard to specific age, gender, social class, and ethnicities that comprise the diverse API community. Even definitions of what constitutes a "family" and how families are counted must be considered in family methodology because they vary across cultures and studies (Fitisemanu et al., 1994).

The development of psychosocial instruments and research methodologies that are culturally valid to ensure reliability and validity with API populations has just begun (Munet-Vilaro & Egan, 1990; Zane, Park, & Aoki, in press). Because development of culturally appropriate API research methodologies and instruments is in its infancy, the empirical literature on API families cannot move forward until these crucial steps are taken (Yee, Mokuau, & Kim, in press). Psychology has made significant advancement in the measurement of acculturation that has good psychometric properties for the API young adult population. However, these are tested mostly on college student samples and some API ethnic groups but are untested on other API ethnicities, socioeconomic classes, or a broader age range than that of college samples. The basic instrumentation and research methodologies in API family development have lagged far behind.

Key methodological strategies that may be considered "gold standards" in family research are triangulation of standardized family instruments, physiological measures such as heart rate and blood pressure, and observations of family interaction (Gorall & Olson, 1995). Culture has been shown to significantly influence the validity and reliability of questionnaire instrumentation and observational methodology (McCubbin et al., 1996). After this methodological foundation is built, API families must be studied using family system methodologies such as an examination of marital relationships from the perspective of both marital partners or discussion of key developmental transitions from a multiple generational perspective followed over time. Challenges in selection of self-report measures of family functioning are abundant (del Carmen, 1990; McCubbin et al., 1996; Yee, in press). Yet, gold standard family methodology of videotaping family interactions can be inherently problematic because this situation brings public (i.e., saving face and shame in public) versus privacy issues as a confound into our research design, and one can call into question the validity of these data for API families. For instance, the presentation of self in public versus private settings has significance for API individuals (Lebra, 1992; Uba, 1994). Cultural features such as face/shame mechanisms, differences in what APIs consider family versus public arenas, and the social constraints that strangers might have on family interaction should be examined carefully. For instance, observed API family interactions (e.g., videotaped, audiotaped, physiological monitoring) can be significantly altered for API families who are very self-conscious and worried about being shamed (Uba, 1994; Yee, 1997). The very act of observing API families in our family research might systematically change the very behavior we are studying. This standard family observational methodology must be examined, its validity must be established, or alternative methodologies must be proposed for API families. Cultural family norms for API populations have not been established, so it is difficult to examine a particular family's interactions without the appropriate normative data from each API population of interest.

Another research challenge is to solicit a greater number of longitudinal studies of family processes in API communities. We discuss how socialization, enculturation, and acculturation typically measured over an annual time frame affect API family processes. Yet, we know very little about how these processes exert their influence over decades of API generations living in the United States. The problem is that much of our research on adaptation and family processes is examined over microscopic time segments of behavior, as in cross-sectional designs (e.g., 1-2 hours of behavioral samples), and might produce a vastly different empirical picture to one generated by examining these processes over a longer period of time (e.g., 1-10 years or longer) (Rosenbaum, 1990; Werner & Smith, 1982). This suggests that one must examine adaptational and family processes that occur over a more lengthy but natural time frame in which they evolve, as in months, years, or decades rather than in an hour or a week, as is typically measured. Hypotheses could be generated and tested cross-sectionally but rigorously tested longitudinally in the specific API population for which it will be generalized.

With more research methodologies that integrate heterogeneity of API families into their conceptual frameworks, we might be able to ascertain key strengths of resilient API families while addressing the needs of API families struggling to cope with life in America. The key to the next century lies in what family psychology can uncover about the dynamic and multidimensional interactions between API family processes and the larger sociocultural environment. We have only begun this journal of many thousand steps to understand API families throughout the life course.

REFERENCES

Agbayani-Siewert, P. (1994). Filipino American culture and family: Guidelines for practitioners. *Families in Society: The Journal of Contemporary Human Services, 75,* 429-438.

Agbayani-Siewert, P., & Revilla, L. (1995). Filipino Americans. In P. G. Min (Ed.), *Asian Americans: Contemporary trends and issues* (pp. 134-167). Thousand Oaks, CA: Sage.

Ambert, A. (1994). An international perspective on parenting: Social change and social constructs. *Journal of Marriage and the Family, 56,* 529-543.

Arkoff, A., Meredith, G., & Iwahara, S. (1964). Male-dominant and egalitarian attitudes in Japanese, Japanese-American, and Caucasian-American students. *Journal of Social Psychology, 64,* 225-229.

Basic Behavioral Science Task Force of the National Advisory Mental Health Council. (1996). Basic behavioral science research for mental health: Family processes and social networks. *American Psychologist, 51,* 622-630.

Baumrind, D. (1971). Current patterns of parental authority. *Developmental Psychology Monograph, 4,* 1-103.

Bliatout, B. T. (1993). Hmong death customs: Traditional and acculturated. In D. P. Irish, K. F. Lundquist, & V. J. Nelsen (Eds.), *Ethnic variations in dying, death, and grief: Diversity in universality* (pp. 79-100). Washington, DC: Taylor & Francis.

Blood, R. O. (1969). *Marriage.* New York: Free Press.

Bronfenbrenner, U. (1979). *The ecology of human development: Experiments by nature and design.* Cambridge, MA: Harvard University Press.

Burr, J. A. (1992). Household status and headship among unmarried Asian Indian women in later life: Availability, feasibility and desirability factors. *Research on Aging, 14,* 199-225.

Burr, J. A., & Mutchler, J. E. (1993). Nativity, acculturation, and economic status: Explanations of Asian American living arrangements in later life. *Journal of Gerontology: Social Sciences, 48,* S55-S68.

Caffrey, R. A. (1992). Caregiving to the elderly in northeast Thailand. *Journal of Cross-Cultural Gerontology, 7,* 117-134.

Campbell, J., & Mandel, F. (1990). Connecting math achievement to parental influences: Annual meeting of the National Association for Research in Science Teaching. *Contemporary Educational Psychology, 15*(1), 64-74.

Canino, I. A., & Spurlock, J. (1994). *Culturally diverse children and adolescents: Assessment, diagnosis, and treatment.* New York: Guilford.

Caplan, N., Choy, M., & Whitmore, J. (1992, February). Indochinese refugee families and academic achievement. *Scientific American,* pp. 36-42.

Caudill, W., & Frost, L. (1972). A comparison of maternal care and infant behavior in Japanese-American, American and Japanese families. In U. Bronfenbrenner (Ed.), *Influences on development* (pp. 3-15). Hinsdale, IL: Dryden.

Chan, A. Y. (1992). *Marital satisfaction and marital stability of interracial/interethnic couples.* Unpublished master's thesis, University of Utah.

Chan, A. Y., & Wethington, E. (1995). Factors promoting marital resilience among interracial couples. In H. I. McCubbin, E. A. Thompson, A. I. Thompson, & J. E. Fromer (Eds.), *Resiliency in ethnic minority families: Native and immigrant American families* (Vol. 1, pp. 71-85). Madison: University of Wisconsin Press.

Chan, D. (1990). Sex knowledge, attitudes, and experiences of Chinese medical students in Hong Kong. *Archives of Sexual Behavior, 19,* 73-93.

Chan, S., & Leong, C. W. (1994). Chinese families in transition: Cultural conflicts and adjustment problems. *Journal of Social Distress and the Homeless, 3,* 263-281.

Chen, C. L., & Yang, D. C. Y. (1986). The self image of Chinese-American adolescents: A cross-cultural comparison. *International Journal of Social Psychiatry, 32,* 19-26.

Ching, J. W. J., McDermott, J. F., Fukunaga, C., & Yanagida, E. (1995). Perception of family values and roles among Japanese Americans: Clinical considerations. *American Journal of Orthopsychiatry, 65,* 216-224.

Chiriboga, D. A., & Catron, L. (1991). *Divorce: Crisis, challenge or relief?* New York: New York University Press.

Chiriboga, D. A., Yee, B. W. K., & Weiler, P. G. (1992). Stress in the context of caring. In L. Montada, S.-H. Filipp, & M. Lerner (Eds.), *Life crises and experiences of loss in adulthood* (pp. 95-118). New York: Plenum.

Chow, E. N. L. (1985). The acculturation experience of Asian American women. In A. G. Sargent (Ed.), *Beyond sex roles* (2nd ed., pp. 238-251). St. Paul, MN: West.

Cicirelli, V. G. (1994). Sibling relationships in cross-cultural perspective. *Journal of Marriage and the Family, 56,* 7-20.

Cooper, C. R., Baker, H., Polichar, D., & Welsh, M. (1993). Values and communication of Chinese, Filipino, European, Mexican, and Vietnamese American adolescents with their families and friends. *New Directions for Child Development, 62,* 73-89.

Cross, W. (1987). A two-factor theory of Black identity: Implications for the study of identity development in minority children. In J. Phinney & M. Rotheram (Eds.), *Children's ethnic socialization: Pluralism and development* (pp. 117-133). Newbury Park, CA: Sage.

del Carmen, R. (1990). Assessment of Asian-Americans for family therapy. In F. C. Serafica, A. I. Schwebel, R. K. Russell, P. D. Isaac, & L. B. Myers (Eds.), *Mental health of ethnic minorities* (pp. 139-166). New York: Praeger.

Der-McLeod, D. (1995, November). *Alternative ways of talking with elderly Chinese concerning end-of-life choices.* Paper presented at the annual meeting of the Gerontological Society of America, Los Angeles.

DeVos, G. (1982). Adaptive strategies in U.S. minorities. In E. Jones & S. Korchin (Eds.), *Minority mental health* (pp. 74-117). New York: Praeger.

Dinh, K. T., Sarason, B. R., & Sarason, I. G. (1994). Parent-child relationships in Vietnamese immigrant families. *Journal of Family Psychology, 8,* 471-488.

Doi, M. L. (1991). A transformation of ritual: The Nisei 60th birthday. *Journal of Cross-Cultural Gerontology, 6,* 153-163.

Dornbusch, S., Prescott, B., & Ritter, P. (1987, April). *The relation of high school academic performance and student effort to language use and recency of migration among Asian—and Pacific—Americans.* Paper presented at the annual meeting of the American Educational Research Association, Washington, DC.

Durvasulas, R. S., & Mylvaganam, G. A. (1994). Mental health of Asian Indians: Relevant issues and community implications. *Journal of Community Psychology, 22*(2), 97-108.

Erikson, E. H. (1950). *Childhood and society.* New York: Norton.

Erikson, E. H. (1968). *Identity: Youth and crisis.* New York: Norton.

Feldman, S. S., & Rosenthal, D. A. (1990). The acculturation of autonomy expectations in Chinese high schoolers residing in two Western nations. *International Journal of Psychology, 25,* 259-281.

Fitisemanu, D., Green, K. K., Hall, D., Wright, D. H., MacKenzie, B., Nautu, D., & Spickard, P. (1994). Family dynamics among Pacific Islander Americans. *Social Process in Hawaii, 36,* 26-40.

Fong, C., & Yung, J. (1995-1996). In search of the right spouse: Interracial marriage among Chinese and Japanese Americans. *Amerasia Journal, 21,* 77-98.

Frijda, N. H., & Mesquita, B. (1994). The social roles and functions of emotions. In S. Kitayama & H. R. Markus (Eds.), *Emotion and culture: Empirical studies of mutual influence* (pp. 51-87). Washington, DC: American Psychological Association.

Fujino, D. (1992). Extending exchange theory: Effects of ethnicity and gender on Asian American heterosexual relationships. *Dissertation Abstracts International, 53*(9), 4932-B. (University Microfilm No. DA9301528)

Fujita, S. S., & O'Brien, D. J. (1991). *Japanese American ethnicity: The persistence of community.* Seattle: University of Washington Press.

Furuto, S. M., & Murase, K. (1992). Asian Americans in the future. In S. M. Furuto, R. Biswas, D. K. Chung, K. Murase, & F. Ross-Sheriff (Eds.), *Social work practice with Asian Americans* (pp. 240-253). Newbury Park, CA: Sage.

Gallimore, R., Boggs, J., & Jordan, C. (1974). *Culture, behavior and education: A study of Hawaiian Americans*. Beverly Hills, CA: Sage.

Georges, E. (1995). A cultural and historical perspective on confession. In J. W. Pennebaker (Ed.), *Emotion, disclosure, and health* (pp. 11-22). Washington, DC: American Psychological Association.

Gleason, A. E., & Sasao, T. (1992, August). *Substance abuse in Asian Pacific communities: A qualitative approach*. Paper presented at the annual meeting of the American Psychological Association, Washington, DC.

Gold, D. T. (1989). Generational solidarity. *American Behavioral Scientist, 33,* 19-32.

Goodman, C. C. (1990). The caregiving roles of Asian American women. *Journal of Women and Aging, 2,* 109-120.

Gorall, D. M., & Olson, D. H. (1995). Circumplex model of family systems: Integrating ethnic diversity and other social systems. In R. H. Mikesell, D. Lusterman, & S. H. McDaniel (Eds.), *Integrating family therapy: Handbook of family psychology and systems theory* (pp. 217-233). Washington, DC: American Psychological Association.

Han, Y. K. (1985). Discriminant analysis of self- disclosing behavior and locus of control among Korean American and Caucasian American adolescents. *Pacific/Asian Mental Health Research Review, 4,* 20-21.

Harrison, A., Wilson, M., Pine, C., Chan, S., & Buriel, R. (1990). Family ecologies of ethnic minority children. *Child Development, 61,* 347-362.

Higgins, E., & King, G. (1981). Accessibility of social constructs: Information-processing consequences of individual and contextual variability. In N. Cantor & J. Kihlstrom (Eds.), *Personality, cognition and social interaction* (pp. 69-121). Hillsdale, NJ: Lawrence Erlbaum.

Hing, B. O., & Lee, R. (Eds.). (1996). *The state of Asian Pacific America: Reframing the immigration debate*. Los Angeles: LEAP Asian Pacific American Public Policy Institute and UCLA Asian American Studies Center.

Hirayama, K. (1985). Asian children's adaptation to public schools. *Social Work in Education, 7*(4), 213-230.

Ho, M. K. (1987). *Family therapy with ethnic minorities*. Newbury Park, CA: Sage.

Ho, M. K. (1992). *Minority children and adolescents in therapy*. Newbury Park, CA: Sage.

Holliday, B. (1985). Developmental imperative of social ecologies: Lessons learned from Black children. In H. McAdoo & J. McAdoo (Eds.), *Black children* (pp. 53-71). Beverly Hills, CA: Sage.

Hom, A. Y. (1994). Stories from the homefront: Perspectives of Asian American parents with lesbian daughters and gay sons. *Amerasia Journal, 20,* 19-32.

Hospice of the Valley. (n.d.). *Ethnic diversity and the care of the terminally ill in Santa Clara County: A handbook*. San Jose, CA: Author.

Howard, A. (1974). *Ain't no big thing*. Honolulu: University of Hawaii Press.

Howard, A., & Associates. (1971). Households, families and friends in a Hawaiian American community (Working Paper 19). Honolulu, HI: East-West Population Institute.

Hsu, F. (1981). *Americans and Chinese: Passage to differences*. Honolulu: University of Hawaii Press.

Huang, K., Leong, F., & Wagner, N. (1994). Coping with peer stressors and associated dysphoria: Acculturation differences among Chinese-American children. *Counseling Psychology Quarterly, 7*(1), 53-68.

Huang, L. N. (1989). Southeast Asian refugee children and adolescents. In J. T. Gibbs & L. N. Huang (Eds.), *Children of color: Psychological interventions with minority youth* (pp. 278-321). San Francisco: Jossey-Bass.

Huang, L., & Ying, Y. (1989). Chinese American children and adolescents. In J. Gibbs & L. Huang (Eds.), *Children of color: Psychological interventions with minority youth* (pp. 30-66). San Francisco: Jossey-Bass.

Hutchinson, R., & McNall, M. (1994). Early marriage in a Hmong cohort. *Journal of Marriage and the Family, 56,* 579-590.

Hwang, S., Saenz, R., & Aguirre, B. E. (1995). The SES selectivity of interracially married Asians. *International Migration Review, 29,* 469-491.

Ikels, C. (1983). *Aging and adaptation: Chinese in Hong Kong and the United States.* Hamden, CO: Archon Books.

Ito, K. L. (1985). Affective bonds: Hawaiian interrelationships of self. In G. M. White & J. Kirkpatrick (Eds.), *Person, self, and experience* (pp. 301-327). Berkeley: University of California Press.

Iu, C. R. (1982). Ethnic and economic correlates of marital satisfaction and attitudes towards divorce of Chinese American women. *Dissertation Abstracts International, 43*(4A), 1293.

Jackson, J. S., & Hatchett, S. J. (1986). Intergenerational research: Methodological considerations. In N. Datan, A. L. Greene, & H. W. Reese (Eds.), *Life-span developmental psychology: Intergenerational relations* (pp. 51-76). Hillsdale, NJ: Lawrence Erlbaum.

James, K., Chen, C., & Cropanzano, R. (1996). Culture and leadership among Taiwanese and U.S. workers: Do values influence leadership ideals? In M. N. Ruderman, M. W. Hughes-James, & S. E. Jackson (Eds.), *Selected research on work team diversity* (pp. 33-52). Washington, DC: American Psychological Association and Center for Creative Leadership.

Janes, C. R. (1990). *Migration, social changes, and health.* Stanford, CA: Stanford University Press.

Jeong, G. J., & Schumm, W. (1990). Family satisfaction in Korean American marriages: An exploratory study of the perception of Korean wives. *Journal of Comparative Family Studies, 21*, 325-333.

Johnson, C. L. (1977). Interdependence, reciprocity and indebtedness: An analysis of Japanese American kinship relations. *Journal of Marriage and the Family, 39*, 351-363.

Johnson, F. A., & Marsella, A. J. (1978). Differential attitudes toward verbal behavior in students of Japanese and European ancestry. *Genetic Psychology Monographs, 97*, 43-76.

Johnson, R. C., & Nagoshi, C. (1986). The adjustment of offspring of within group and interracial/intercultural marriages. *Journal of Marriage and the Family, 48*, 279-284.

Kagawa-Singer, M. (1994). Diverse cultural beliefs and practices about death and dying in the elderly. *Gerontology and Geriatrics Education, 15*, 101-116.

Kagitcibasi, C. (1989). Family and socialization in cross-cultural perspective: A model of change. In R. Dienstbier (Ed.), *Nebraska Symposium on Motivation, Vol. 37: Cross-cultural perspectives* (pp. 135-200). Lincoln: University of Nebraska Press.

Kamo, Y., & Zhou, M. (1994). Living arrangements of elderly Chinese and Japanese in the United States. *Journal of Marriage and the Family, 56*, 544-558.

Kaslow, F. (1987). Trends in family psychology. *Journal of Family Psychology, 1*, 77-90.

Kim, K. C., & Kim, S. (1995). Family and work roles of Korean immigrants in the United States. In H. I. McCubbin, E. A. Thompson, A. I. Thompson, & J. E. Fromer (Eds.), *Resiliency in ethnic minority families: Native and immigrant American families* (pp. 225-242). Madison: University of Wisconsin, Board of Regents and Center for Excellence in Family Studies.

Kim, M. S. (1993). Culture-based interactive constraints in explaining intercultural strategic competence. In R. L. Wiseman & J. Koester (Eds.), *Intercultural communication competence* (pp. 132-150). Newbury Park, CA: Sage.

Kitano, H., Yeung, W. T., Chai, L., & Hatanaka, H. (1984). Asian American interracial marriage. *Journal of Marriage and the Family, 46*, 179-190.

Kitayama, S., & Markus, H. R. (1994a). The cultural shaping of emotion: A conceptual framework. In S. Kitayama & H. R. Markus (Eds.), *Emotion and culture: Empirical studies of mutual influence* (pp. 339-351). Washington, DC: American Psychological Association.

Kitayama, S., & Markus, H. R. (Eds.). (1994b). *Emotion and culture: Empirical studies of mutual influence.* Washington, DC: American Psychological Association.

Klessig, J. (1992). The effect of values and culture on life-support decisions. *Western Journal of Medicine, 157*, 316-322.

Krantzler, N. (1982). *Treatment for cancer: Nurses and the sociocultural context of medical care.* Berkeley: University of California Press.

Kuo, E. (1974). The family and bilingual socialization: A sociolinguistic study of a sample of Chinese children in the United States. *Journal of Social Psychology, 92*, 181-191.

LEAP Asian Pacific American Public Policy Institute and UCLA Asian American Studies Center. (1993). *The state of Asian Pacific America: A public policy report.* Los Angeles: Leadership Education for Asian Pacifics and UCLA Asian American Studies Center.

Lebra, T. S. (1984). *Japanese women: Constraint and fulfillment.* Honolulu: University of Hawaii Press.

Lebra, T. S. (1992). Self in Japanese culture. In N. R. Rosenberger (Ed.), *Japanese sense of self* (pp. 105-120). Cambridge, UK: Cambridge University Press.

Lebra, T. S. (1994). Mother and child in Japanese socialization: A Japan-U.S. comparison. In P. M. Greenfield & R. R. Cocking (Eds.), *Cross-cultural roots of minority child development* (pp. 259-274). Hillsdale, NJ: Lawrence Erlbaum.

Lee, S. M., & Yamanaka, K. (1990). Patterns of Asian American intermarriage and marital assimilation. *Journal of Comparative Family Studies, 21,* 287-305.

Lee, Y. (1987). *Academic success of East Asian Americans: An ethnographic comparative study of East Asian American and Anglo American Academic achievement.* Seoul, South Korea: American Studies Institute, National University Press.

Leong, F. T. L. (1991). Career development attributes and occupational values of Asian American and White American college students. *Career Development Quarterly, 39,* 221-230.

Leong, F. T. L., & Chow, E. (1994, August). *Occupational barriers for Asian Americans: Glass ceiling and model minority effects and consequences.* Paper presented at the convention of the Asian American Psychological Association, Los Angeles.

Leong, F. T. L., & Hayes, T. J. (1990). Occupational stereotyping of Asian Americans. *Career Development Quarterly, 39,* 143-154.

Lew, A. S. (1994). *Achievement motivation orientation and fear of success in Asian American college students.* Unpublished doctoral dissertation, Long Island University.

Lin, C. Y. C., & Fu, V. R. (1990). A comparison of child-rearing practices among Chinese, immigrant Chinese, and Caucasian-American parents. *Child Development, 61,* 429-433.

Lin, K. M., Masuda, M., & Tazuma, L. (1982). Adaptational problems of Vietnamese refugees. Part III: Case studies in clinic and field: Adaptive and maladaptive. *Psychiatric Journal of the University of Ottawa, 7*(3), 173-183.

Lind, A. W. (1964). Interracial marriage as affecting divorce in Hawaii. *Sociology and Social Research, 49,* 17-26.

Liu, W. T., & Yu, E. (1985). Asian/Pacific American elderly: Mortality differentials, health status and use of health services. *Journal of Applied Gerontology, 4,* 35-64.

Lu, C. R. (1982). Ethnic and economic correlates of marital satisfaction and attitude towards divorce of Chinese American women. *Dissertation Abstracts International, 43,* 1293-A. (University Microfilm No. DA8219695)

Lutz, C. A. (1988). *Unnatural emotions: Everyday sentiments on a Micronesian atoll and their challenge to Western theory.* Chicago: University of Chicago Press.

Lynch, A., Detzner, D. F., & Eicher, J. B. (1995). Hmong American New Year rituals: Generational bonds through dress. *Clothing and Textiles Research Journal, 13,* 111-120.

Marsella, A. J., & Dash-Scheuer, A. (1988). Coping, culture, and healthy human development: A research and conceptual overview. In P. R. Dasen, J. W. Berry, & N. Sartorius (Eds.), *Health and cross-cultural psychology: Toward applications* (pp. 162-178). Newbury Park, CA: Sage.

Marsella, A. J., Oliveira, J. M., Plummer, C. M., & Crabbe, K. M. (1995). Native Hawaiian (*Kanaka Maoli*) culture, mind, and well-being. In H. I. McCubbin, E. A. Thompson, A. I. Thompson, & J. E. Fromer (Eds.), *Resiliency in ethnic minority families: Native and immigrant American families* (pp. 93-113). Madison: University of Wisconsin, Board of Regents and Center for Excellence in Family Studies.

McClure, E. (1981). Formal and functional aspects of the code-switched discourse of bilingual children. In R. Duran (Ed.), *Latino language and communicative behavior* (pp. 69-94). Norwood, NJ: Ablex.

McCubbin, H. I., Thompson, A., & McCubbin, M. A. (1996). *Family assessment: Resiliency, coping and adaptation—Inventories for research and practice.* Madison: University of Wisconsin Press.

McDermott, J. F., Jr., Char, W. F., Robillard, A. B., Hsu, J., Tseng, W. S., & Ashton, G. C. (1983). Cultural variations in family attitudes and their implications for therapy. *Journal of the American Academy of Child Psychiatry, 22,* 454-458.

McIntosh, J. L., & Santos, J. F. (1981). Suicide among minority elderly: A preliminary investigation. *Suicide Life Threat Behavior, 11,* 151-166.

Min, P. G. (1993). Korean immigrants' marital patterns and marital adjustments. In H. P. McAdoo (Ed.), *Family ethnicity: Strength in diversity* (pp. 287-299). Newbury Park, CA: Sage.

Mirande, A. (1991). Ethnicity and fatherhood. In F. W. Bozett & S. M. H. Hanson (Eds.), *Fatherhood and families in cultural context* (pp. 53-82). New York: Springer.

Miyamoto, S. F. (1986-1987). Problems of interpersonal style among the Nisei. *Amerasia, 13,* 29-45.

Mok, T. A. (1995). Looking for love: Factors influencing Asian Americans' choice of dating partners. In J. Y. Fong (Ed.), *Proceedings of the Asian American Psychological Association 1994 convention* (pp. 83-87). Atascadero, CA: Asian American Psychological Association.

Moon, A., & Williams, O. (1993). Perceptions of elder abuse and help-seeking patterns among African-American, Caucasian American, and Korean-American elderly women. *The Gerontologist, 33,* 386-395.

Mordkowitz, D., & Ginsburg, H. (1987). Early academic socialization of Asian-American college students. *Quarterly Newsletter of the Laboratory of Comparative Human Cognition, 9,* 85-91.

Morton, D. J., Stanford, E. P., Happersett, C. J., & Molgaard, C. A. (1992). Acculturation and functional impairment among older Chinese and Vietnamese in San Diego County, California. *Journal of Cross-Cultural Gerontology, 7,* 151-176.

Muller, J. H., & Desmond, B. (1992). Ethical dilemmas in a cross-cultural context: A Chinese example. *Western Journal of Medicine, 157,* 323-327.

Munet-Vilaro, F., & Egan, M. (1990). Reliability issues of the family environment scale for cross-cultural research. *Nursing Research, 39,* 244-247.

Nagata, D. K. (1989). Japanese American children and adolescents. In J. T. Gibbs & L. N. Huang (Eds.), *Children of color: Psychological interventions with minority youth* (pp. 67-113). San Francisco: Jossey-Bass.

Nagata, D. K. (1993). *Legacy of injustice: Exploring the cross-generational impact of the Japanese-American internment.* New York: Plenum.

Naidoo, J. C., & Davis, J. C. (1988). Canadian South Asian women in transition: A dualistic view of life. *Journal of Comparative Family Studies, 19,* 311-327.

National Asian Women's Health Organization. (1996). *A health needs assessment of South Asian women in 3 California counties: Alameda, Santa Clara, Sutter.* San Francisco: Author.

Nguyen, N. A., & Williams, H. L. (1989). Transition from East to West: Vietnamese adolescents and their parents. *Journal of the American Academy of Child and Adolescent Psychiatry, 28,* 505-515.

Nishi, S. (1995). Japanese Americans. In P. G. Min (Ed.), *Asian Americans: Contemporary trends and issues* (pp. 95-133). Thousand Oaks, CA: Sage.

Nishimura, M., & Yeo, G. (1992, October). *Ethnicity, medical decisions, and the care of Japanese American elders.* Poster presented at the annual meeting of the American Geriatric Society, Washington, DC.

Noda, F., Noda, M., & Clark, C. (1990). Family factors affecting adjustment in Japanese immigrant housewives. *Canadian Journal of Psychiatry, 35,* 689-692.

Nydegger, C. N. (1983). Family ties of the aged in cross-cultural perspective. *The Gerontologist, 23,* 26-32.

Ogawa, B. K. (in press). *E Hana Pono:* Issues of responsibility, justice, and culture in the design and practice of prevention programs. In B. W. K. Yee, N. Mokuau, & S. Kim (Eds.), *Cultural competence in Asian American and Pacific Islander communities: Opportunities in primary health and substance abuse prevention* (Cultural Competence Series 5). Rockville, MD: Center for Substance Abuse Prevention and Bureau of Primary Health Care.

Ogbu, J. (1981). Origins of human competence: A cultural-ecological perspective. *Child Development, 52,* 413-429.

Okano, Y., & Spilka, B. (1971). Ethnic identity, alienation and achievement orientation in Japanese-American families. *Journal of Cross-Cultural Psychology, 2,* 273-282.

O'Reilly, J., Tokuno, K., & Ebata, A. (1986). Cultural differences between Americans of Japanese and European ancestry in parental valuing of social competence. *Journal of Comparative Family Studies, 17,* 87-97.

Orona, C. J., Koenig, B. A., & Davis, A. J. (1994). Cultural aspects of nondisclosure. *Cambridge Quarterly of Health Care Ethics, 3,* 338-346.

Osako, M. M., & Liu, W. T. (1986). Intergenerational relations and the aged among Japanese Americans. *Research on Aging, 8,* 155-188.

Phinney, J. S. (1992). The multigroup ethnic identity measure: A new scale for use with diverse groups. *Journal of Adolescent Research, 7*(2), 156-176.

Phinney, J. S., & Alipuria, L. L. (1990). Ethnic identity in college students from four ethnic groups. *Journal of Adolescence, 13,* 171-183.

Phinney, J. S., & Chavira, V. (1992). Ethnic identity and self-esteem: An exploratory longitudinal study. *Journal of Adolescence, 15,* 271-281.

Phinney, J. S., Lochner, B. T., & Murphy, R. (1990). Ethnic identity development and psychological adjustment in adolescence. In A. R. Stiffman & L. E. Davis (Eds.), *Ethnic issues in adolescent mental health* (pp. 53-72). Newbury Park, CA: Sage.

Phinney, J., & Rotheram, M. (1987). *Children's ethnic socialization: Pluralism and development.* Newbury Park, CA: Sage.

Preto, N. G. (1988). Transformation of the family system in adolescence. In B. Carter & M. McGoldrick (Eds.), *The changing family life cycle: Framework for family therapy* (pp. 255-283). Boston: Allyn & Bacon.

Pukui, M. K., & Elbert. S. J. (1971). *Hawaiian dictionary.* Honolulu: University of Hawaii Press.

Ramola, J. (1992). *Perceived changes of immigrants in the United States: A study of* Kerala *(Asian Indian) immigrant couples in greater Chicago.* Unpublished doctoral dissertation, Loyola University.

Rosenbaum, M. (Ed.). (1990). *Learned resourcefulness: On coping skills, self-control, and adaptive behavior.* New York: Springer.

Rosenberg, M. (1979). *Convicting the self.* New York: Basic Books.

Rosenthal, D. A., & Feldman, S. S. (1992). The relationship between parenting behavior and ethnic identity in Chinese-American and Chinese-Australian adolescents. *International Journal of Psychology, 27*(1), 19-31.

Ross-Sheriff, F. (1992). Adaptation and integration into American society: Major issues affecting Asian Americans. In S. M. Furuto, R. Biswas, D. K. Chung, K. Murase, & F. Ross-Sheriff (Eds.), *Social work practice with Asian Americans* (pp. 45-63). Newbury Park, CA: Sage.

Rutter, M. (1994). Family discord and conduct disorder: Cause, consequence, or correlate? *Journal of Family Psychology, 8,* 170-186.

Sampson, E. (1988). The debate on individualism: Indigenous psychologies of the individual and their role in personal and societal functioning. *American Psychologist, 43,* 15-22.

Sanborn, K. O. (1977). Intercultural marriage in Hawaii. In W. Tseng, J. F. McDermott, & Maretzki (Eds.), *Adjustment in intercultural marriage* (pp. 41-50). Honolulu: University of Hawaii Press.

Sasao, T., & Chun, C. (1994). After the *Sa-I-gu* (April 29) Los Angeles riots: Correlates of subjective well-being in the Korean-American community. *Journal of Community Psychology, 22,* 136-152.

Sata, L. S. (1983). Mental health issues of Japanese-American children. In G. J. Powell (Ed.), *The psychosocial development of minority group children* (pp. 362-372). New York: Brunner/Mazel.

Schellenberger, S., & Hoffman, S. S. (1995). The changing family-work system. In R. H. Mikesell, D. Lusterman, & S. H. McDaniel (Eds.), *Integrating family therapy: Handbook of family psychology and systems theory* (pp. 461-479). Washington, DC: American Psychological Association.

Schneider, B., Hieshima, J., Lee, S., & Plank, S. (1994). East Asian academic success in the United States: Family, school, and community explanations. In P. Greenfield & R. Cocking (Eds.), *Cross cultural roots of minority child development* (pp. 323-350). Hillsdale, NJ: Lawrence Erbaum.

Serafica, F. C. (1990). Counseling Asian-American parents: A cultural-developmental approach. In F. C. Serafica, A. I. Schwebel, R. K. Russell, P. D. Isaac, & L. B. Myers (Eds.), *Mental health of ethnic minorities* (pp. 222-244). New York: Praeger.

Seymour, S. (1993). Sociocultural contexts: Examining sibling roles in South Asia. In C. W. Nuckolls (Ed.), *Siblings in South Asia: Brothers and sisters in cultural context* (pp. 45-69). New York: Guilford.

Shawtaylor, Y., & Benokratis, N. (1995). The presentation of minorities in marriage and family. *Teaching Sociology, 23*(2), 122-135.

Sheth, M. (1995). Asian Indian Americans. In P. G. Min (Ed.), *Asian Americans* (pp. 169-198). Thousand Oaks, CA: Sage.

Shinagawa, L. H. (1996). The impact of immigration on the demography of Asian Pacific Americans. In B. O. Hing & R. Lee (Eds.), *Reframing the immigration debate* (pp. 59-126). Los Angeles: Leadership Education for Asian Pacifics and UCLA Asian American Studies Center.

Shook, E. V. (1985). Ho'oponono: *Contemporary uses of a Hawaiian problem-solving process*. Honolulu: University of Hawaii Press.

Shu, R. (1985-1986). Kinship system and migrant adaptation: Samoans of the United States. *Amerasia, 12*(1), 23-47.

Slaughter-Defoe, D. T., Nakagawa, K., Takanishi, R., & Johnson, D. J. (1990). Toward cultural/ecological perspectives on schooling and achievement in African- and Asian-American children. *Child Development, 61*, 363-383.

Sollenberger, R. T. (1968). Chinese American child-rearing practices and juvenile delinquency. *Journal of Social Psychology, 74*, 13-23.

Spencer, M. (1987). Black children's ethnic identity formation: Risk and resilience of castelike minorities. In J. Phinney & M. Rotheram (Eds.), *Children's ethnic socialization: Pluralism and development* (pp. 103-116). Newbury Park, CA: Sage.

Stevenson, H. W., & Stigler, J. W. (1992). *The learning gap: Why our schools are failing and what we can learn from Japanese and Chinese education*. New York: Simon & Schuster.

Stiffman, A., & Davis, L. (1990). *Ethnic issues in adolescent mental health*. Newbury Park, CA: Sage.

Sue, D. W. (1973). Ethnic identity: The impact of two cultures on the psychological development of Asians in America. In S. Sue & N. Wagner (Eds.), *Asian Americans: Psychological perspectives* (pp. 140-149). Palo Alto, CA: Science and Behavior Books.

Sue, S., & Kirk, B. (1973). Differential characteristics of Japanese-American and Chinese-American college students. *Journal of Counseling Psychology, 20*, 142-148.

Sue, S., & Okazaki, S. (1990). Asian-American educational achievements: A phenomenon in search of an explanation. *American Psychologist, 45*, 913-920.

Sue, S., & Zane, N. (1987). The role of culture and cultural techniques in psychotherapy: A critique and reformulation. *American Psychologist, 42*, 37-45.

Sung, B. L. (1990). Chinese American intermarriage. *Journal of Comparative Family Studies, 21*, 337-352.

Szapocznik, H., & Kurtines, W. (1993). Family psychology and cultural diversity. *American Psychologist, 48*, 400-407.

Takamura, J. C., Nitz, K., & Haruki, G. (1991, March). *Ethnicity and caregiving: Developing research-based support programs for multigenerational caregivers from diverse ethnocultural groups*. Paper presented at the annual meeting of the American Society on Aging, New Orleans, LA.

Tam, V. C., & Detzner, D. F. (1995). Grandparents as a family resource in Chinese-American families: Perceptions of the middle generation. In H. I. McCubbin, E. A. Thompson, A. I. Thompson, & J. E. Fromer (Eds.), *Resiliency in ethnic minority families: Native and immigrant American families* (pp. 243-263). Madison: University of Wisconsin, Board of Regents and Center for Excellence in Family Studies.

Tamura, E. H. (1994). *Americanization, acculturation, and ethnic identity: The Nisei generation in Hawaii*. Urbana: University of Illinois Press.

Thompson, E. A., McCubbin, H. I., Thompson, A. K., & Elver, K. M. (1995). Vulnerability and resiliency in Native Hawaiian families under stress. In H. I. McCubbin, E. A. Thompson, A. I. Thompson, & J. E. Fromer (Eds.), *Resiliency in ethnic minority families: Native and immigrant American families* (pp. 115-131). Madison: University of Wisconsin Press.

Tinker, J. N. (1982). Intermarriage and assimilation in a plural society: Japanese-Americans in the United States. *Marriage and Family Review, 5,* 61-74.

Triandis, H. (1989). The self and social behavior in differing cultural contexts. *Psychological Review, 96,* 506-520.

True, R. H. (1981). The profile of Asian American women. In S. Cox (Ed.), *Female psychology: The emerging self* (pp. 124-135). New York: St. Martin's.

Truitner, K., & Truitner, N. (1993). Death and dying in Buddhism. In D. P. Irish, K. F. Lundquist, & V. J. Nelson (Eds.), *Ethnic variations in dying, death, and grief: Diversity in universality* (pp. 125-136). Washington, DC: Taylor & Francis.

Tseng, W. S. (1973). The development of psychiatric concepts in traditional Chinese medicine. *Archives of General Psychiatry, 29,* 569-575.

Tung, T. M. (1990). Death, dying and hospice: An Asian-American view. *American Journal Hospital Palliative Care, 7,* 23-25.

Uba, L. (1994). *Asian Americans: Personality patterns, identity, and mental health.* New York: Guilford.

Wellenkamp, J. (1995). Cultural similarities and differences regarding emotional disclosure: Some examples from Indonesia and the Pacific. In J. W. Pennebaker (Ed.), *Emotion, disclosure, and health* (pp. 293-311). Washington, DC: American Psychological Association.

Werner, E. E., & Smith, R. S. (1982). *Vulnerable but invincible.* New York: McGraw-Hill.

White, G. M., & Watson-Gegeo, K. A. (1990). Disentangling discourse. In K. A. Watson-Gegeo & G. M. White (Eds.), *Disentangling: Conflict discourse in Pacific societies* (pp. 3-49). Stanford, CA: Stanford University Press.

White, L. (1990). Determinants of divorce: A review of research in the eighties. *Journal of Marriage and the Family, 52,* 904-912.

Wong, M. (1980). Model students? Teachers' perceptions and expectations of their Asian and White students. *Sociology of Education, 53,* 236-246.

Yanagisako, S. J. (1985). *Transforming the past: Tradition and kinship among Japanese Americans.* Stanford, CA: Stanford University Press.

Yao, E. (1985a). Adjustment needs of Asian immigrant children. *Elementary School Guidance and Counseling, 19,* 222-227.

Yao, E. L. (1985b). A comparison of family characteristics of Asian-American and Anglo-American high achievers. *International Journal of Comparative Sociology, 26,* 198-208.

Yee, B. W. K. (1992). Markers of successful aging among Vietnamese refugee women. *Women and Therapy, 13,* 221-238.

Yee, B. W. K. (1997). The social and cultural context of adaptive aging among Southeast Asian elders. In J. Sokolovsky (Ed.), *The cultural context of aging* (2nd ed., pp. 293-303). Westport, CT: Greenwood.

Yee, B. W. K. (in press). Impact of gender and age upon evaluation of alcohol and drug abuse prevention with Asian and Pacific Islander communities. In B. W. K. Yee, N. Mokuau, & S. Kim (Eds.), *Cultural competence in Asian American and Pacific Islander communities: Opportunities in primary health and substance abuse prevention* (Cultural Competence Series 5). Rockville, MD: Center for Substance Abuse Prevention and Bureau of Primary Health Care.

Yee, B. W. K., Chiriboga, D. A., & Catron, L. (1991). Minority issues in the study of divorce. In D. A. Chiriboga & L. Catron (Eds.), *Divorce: Crisis, challenge or relief?* (pp. 248-279). New York: New York University Press.

Yee, B. W. K., & Hennessey, S. T. (1982). Pacific/Asian families and mental health. In F. U. Munoz & R. Endo (Eds.), *Perspectives on minority group mental health* (pp. 53-70). Washington, DC: University Press of America.

Yee, B. W. K., Mokuau, N., & Kim, S. (Eds.). (in press). *Cultural competence in Asian American and Pacific Islander communities: Opportunities in primary health and substance abuse prevention* (Cultural Competence Series 5). Rockville, MD: Center for Substance Abuse Prevention and Bureau of Primary Health Care.

Yeh, C., & Huang, K. (1994). *The collectivistic nature of ethnic identity development among Asian-American college students.* Unpublished manuscript, University of California, Los Angeles.

Yu, E. S. (1991). The health risks of Asian Americans. *American Journal of Public Health, 81,* 1391-1393.

Yu, E. S., Kim, K., Liu, W. T., & Wong, S. C. (1993). Functional abilities of Chinese and Korean elders in congregate housing. In D. Barressi & D. Stull (Eds.), *Ethnic elderly and long term care* (pp. 87-100). New York: Springer.

Yu, K. H., & Kim, L. I. C. (1983). The growth and development of Korean-American children. In G. J. Powell (Ed.), *The psychosocial development of minority group children* (pp. 147-158). New York: Brunner/Mazel.

Yu, L. C. (1983). Patterns of filial belief and behavior within the contemporary Chinese American family. *International Journal of Sociology of the Family, 13,* 17-36.

Yu, L. C., & Wu, S. (1985). Unemployment and family dynamics in meeting the needs of Chinese elderly in the United States. *The Gerontologist, 25,* 472-476.

Zane, N., Park, S., & Aoki, B. (in press). The development of culturally valid measures for assessing prevention impact in Asian communities. In B. W. K. Yee, N. Mokuau, & S. Kim (Eds.), *Cultural competence in Asian American and Pacific Islander communities: Opportunities in primary health and substance abuse prevention* (Cultural Competence Series 5). Rockville, MD: Center for Substance Abuse Prevention and Bureau of Primary Health Care.

4

PSYCHOSOCIAL STATUS OF CHILDREN AND YOUTHS

Lee C. Lee
Ginny Zhan

According to the 1990 census, 36% of the 7.44 million Asian Americans in the United States are age 19 years or under (U.S. Bureau of the Census, 1991a, 1991b). Of these 2.7 million children, 22% are preschool children (age 4 years or under), 40% are elementary or middle school children (ages 5-13 years), 17% are of high school age (ages 14-17 years), and 20% are of college age (18-22 years). Approximately 35% of these children are foreign born. Although there are slightly more females than males in the general Asian American population (51% vs. 49%), the reverse is true for the children and youth population; males outnumber females in every age group by approximately 3%.

This chapter appraises the status of these children and youths through a review of the relevant research literature, government reports, and various print media. First, there is a review of what is known about the experiences of Asian American children and youths during their formative years. Second, findings regarding the psychological status of Asian American children and youths are summarized. The third section of this chapter examines how these children and youths are perceived by others within U.S. society and the impact these perceptions may have on their adjustment. The chapter concludes with a discussion of the necessary directions in research if we are to better understand the status of Asian American children and youths.

EXPERIENCES OF ASIAN AMERICAN
CHILDREN AND YOUTHS

This section deals with the lives of Asian American children and youths in the context of their home, school, and social milieus. Thus, their experiences are discussed under the following topics: parent-child relationships, parental attitudes toward schooling, peer group influences, and the social and economic milieus. Within each of these topics, the unique experiences of Asian American ethnic groups are presented as necessary. To the extent possible, however, the commonalties of these groups are emphasized.

Parent-Child Relationships

In all families, regardless of background, the parent-child relationship and sibling relationships have a great impact on children's development. Under the most facilitative of circumstances, families serve as a secure base to which children can turn for support and help. It is commonly the case that as children grow up, especially during adolescence, parent-child conflicts increase because parents impose their expectations on children's activities contrary to children's striving for greater autonomy. In Asian American families, especially those in which the parents are immigrants, the conflicts often are greater because many parents adhere to traditional values of their homeland, whereas their children, who are eager to become Americanized, are influenced strongly by the American value system (Chan & Leong, 1994; Chen, 1989; Dinh, Sarason, & Sarason, 1994; Lee & Eng, 1989; Szapocznik & Kurtines, 1993; Yu, 1984). Conflicts can arise as children sense the differences between the views of the mainstream U.S. society and those of their parents. These children have to deal with the incongruity between their parents' values and the values held by their American peers and society in general. Children see that their parents are different and sometimes reject those differences. Although this is not an uncommon occurrence in immigrant families in general, there are some unique aspects worthy of examination specific to the various Asian American ethnic groups.

To understand the dynamics of parent-child relationships in Asian American families, it is necessary to examine parental values and expectations as well as their child-rearing attitudes and behaviors. Research findings suggest that, in general, Asian American parents hold on to certain attitudes and child-rearing practices unique to their Asian cultures. Chiu (1987) found that Chinese American mothers are similar to Chinese mothers in expecting that children should deify the parents, that parents are to approve (or disapprove) their children's activities, and that it is not only acceptable but desirable for parents to actively intrude in their children's lives. Similarly, it also was found that immigrant Chinese parents reported that they put more emphasis on parental control and children's achievement than was reported by White parents (Lin & Fu, 1990) and that immigrant Chinese parents scored higher than Caucasian parents on physical punishment and yelling at children (Kelley & Tseng, 1992).

Japanese American parents also have expectations in line with their traditional Japanese culture. They expect their children to have self-control, to be humble, and to avoid being "different" (Gehrie, 1976). Gray and Cosgrove (1985) found that Japanese American parents do not show overt emotion and affection and provide relatively little praise to their children. Japanese American parents were further found by O'Reilly, Tokuno, and Ebata (1986) to rank "behaves well" as the most important attribute in evaluating children's social competence. White parents, by contrast, ranked "self-directed" as the most important.

Some aspects of traditional Asian cultures can be particularly problematic for young people who wish to appear as "American" as possible. In an ongoing project on Asian American college students' personal histories, Lee found that many students described feelings of shame and denial of their heritage during their childhood.

> Although I'm not really sure when I began really hating everything that was Korean . . . I wouldn't let my mom bring out Korean food when my friends were in the house. If they saw something in the refrigerator and asked what it was, I would say, "gross stuff, I don't know," and slam it shut. I would yell at my mother if she spoke Korean to me in front of my friends. "We're in America now, speak American!" (Lee, ongoing project, Case 92-2-14)

> I refused to go to Filipino parties, eat Filipino food, and use the Filipino language. When my parents would talk to me in Tagalog, I would admonish them and tell them, "We're in America, speak English." And when they did talk in English, I would make fun of their accents. . . . I thought Asian girls were ugly and unexciting. (Lee, ongoing project, Case 92-3-14)

Many Asian American families are very protective of their children (Gray & Cosgrove, 1985). As one Vietnamese American student reported in the personal history project,

> I was instructed by my mother not to mention my Vietnamese heritage, so I lied and always said my father was Thai. Although we left Vietnam long before the Vietnam war, she worried that my classmates would shun me because memories of America's involvement were still fresh. When my father speaks about Vietnam, it is like a bad secret. (Lee, ongoing project, Case 93-1-3)

Gray and Cosgrove (1985) also reported that Vietnamese parents use physical punishment, call children nicknames (some based on physical characteristics such as "fat" or "big head"), and use folk remedies to cure sickness. These practices might be common among less educated parents in Vietnam, and many refugee parents seem to carry them over to the United States. Such practices often engender negative feelings in children and youths as they strive to be "Americans."

Some traditional Asian expectations for youth and early adulthood contrast markedly with those of the American culture. Many Asian Indian parents maintain the tradition of arranged marriages for their children; therefore, they do not approve of dating and strongly forbid premarital sex (Saran, 1985; Segal, 1991;

Yao, 1989). They expect young people to be obedient and to listen to their parents' advice (Segal, 1991). In general, Asian American parents expect that decisions regarding adolescent children are to be made jointly by parents and children, not just by children themselves (Dornbusch, Ritter, Mont-Reynaud, & Chen, 1990). Parental control is emphasized by immigrant Chinese parents more than by White parents (Lin & Fu, 1990). Japanese American parents strongly believe that important family decisions should involve all family members and that family members should share their deepest thoughts with one another (McDermott et al., 1983). Korean immigrant parents express a strong sense of responsibility to the family when reporting on their own accomplishment needs (DeVos, 1983).

To some extent, acculturation effects would be expected to modify the views and practices of Asian American parents. There is some evidence to this effect (Uba, 1992; Yao, 1985a, 1985b). Although Chinese American mothers scored higher than White American mothers on authoritarian-control dimensions, they did score lower than Chinese mothers from Taiwan (Chiu, 1987). Similarly, Korean American parents reported that they encourage children to think independently and allow children to have different opinions (Strom, Daniels, & Park, 1986), indicating that parental expectations for their children no longer are very traditional. Compared to self-reports by second-generation Chinese American adolescents, first-generation adolescents reported their families as being more controlling. On the other hand, Vietnamese parents are reported to overwhelmingly endorse traditional family values regardless of their length of stay in the United States (Nguyen & Williams, 1989), although they do favor some independence and autonomy in adolescent children. Likewise, Hmong parents are perceived by their adolescent children as having maintained strong traditional family values (Rick & Forward, 1992). Acculturation effects evidently proceed at different rates within the various ethnic Asian American groups (Cooper, Baker, Polichar, & Welsh, 1993).

The experience of growing up in an Asian American household where parents still hold some traditional Asian cultural values is likely to have an impact on children's value formation. Research findings suggest that traditional Asian values are transmitted from parents to children in these families, although many children are discriminating in what they accept or reject.

Feldman and Rosenthal (1990) examined age expectations for behavioral autonomy (e.g., staying out late, choosing friends, making decisions) in adolescents. They found that both first- and second-generation Chinese adolescents reported later age expectations than did White Americans on behavioral autonomy scales. It appears that acculturation in age expectations for behavioral autonomy occurs slowly among Chinese American youths, even among second-generation youths. This finding is consistent with the earlier findings by Chiu (1987) that Chinese American parents score higher on the authoritarian-control dimensions than do their White American counterparts. Furthermore, Chinese American adolescents' self-image in sexual attitudes and behavior is more conservative than that of White American adolescents (Chen & Yang, 1986). These characteristics are consistent with Asian traditional values. Connor's (1974, 1976) research suggests that Japanese American youths, even though very Americanized, still retain some Japanese traditional characteristics of being more deferent, less abusive, less dominant, more affiliative, less aggressive, more sensitive to others' opinions, and so forth. Japanese American college students in Hawaii were found to have different attribution styles from those of White students. They tended to attribute academic successes to external causes rather than to their own efforts (Powers, Choroszy, & Douglas, 1987; Tamura, 1994).

Cultural transmission within the family also occurs in other aspects of attitudes and values. For example, Asian American children's and youths' attitudes toward mental health seem to be influenced by Asian cultures. Sue, Wagner, Ja, Margullis, and Lew (1976) found that many Asian American college students believe that (a) avoidance of morbid thoughts enhances mental health, (b) too much sex can cause health-related problems, (c) mentally healthy persons do not become overly angry at minor insults, and (d) mental illness is a disease of organic origin that is more physiological than psychological in nature. Other researchers have found that Asian American college students tend to downplay interpersonal/emotional problems because there is a stigma attached to having these problems (Tracey, Leong, & Glidden, 1986) and that they are more willing to discuss academic or career-related problems than problems related to relationships (Gim, Atkinson, & Whiteley, 1990). Also, Suan and Tyler (1990) found that Japanese American college students perceive negative personal traits (e.g., untrustworthiness) as indicators of poor mental health and view good interpersonal relations as relevant to good mental health.

Asian cultural beliefs and values passed on by parents also seem to influence Asian American children's help-seeking behavior. Sue and Sue (1985) reported that Asian American parents tend to promote emotional self-reliance and restraint and to view the seeking of outside help as being weak and dependent. Many Asian American college students report that they turn to family members (e.g., parents, siblings) for help (Atkinson, Whitely, & Gim, 1990) or turn to "self-reliance" (Suan & Tyler, 1990) rather than to professional psychologists, indicating that they might feel uncomfortable seeking help from persons outside their families.

Parental Attitudes About Schooling

Apart from home, school has perhaps the greatest impact on children's lives. Parental and teacher attitudes about schooling greatly affect the nature of the school experience. There is a great deal of information regarding the perceptions of Asian American parents about their children's education. Asian American parents have high academic expectations for their children, and children are well aware of these expectations (Campbell & Mandel, 1990; Chen & Stevenson, 1995; Hieshima & Schneider, 1994; Mordkowitz & Ginsburg, 1987; Reglin & Adams, 1990; Schneider & Lee, 1990; Whang & Hancock, 1994; Yao, 1985b). Asian American parents express a commitment to education and to showing respect for teachers (Mordkowitz & Ginsburg, 1987). Furthermore, Asian American parents structure learning activities and the home environment (Schneider

& Lee, 1990) and monitor children's homework (Caplan, Choy, & Whitmore, 1992). Sue and Okazaki (1990) proposed that Asian Americans value educational success as functional for upward mobility. They maintained that education has been viewed by Asian American parents as providing the opportunity for their children to move upward in U.S. society as opposed to the general belief that Asian cultures value the educational process per se. These findings were supported by Alva (1993).

Despite strong concerns for academic achievement and school success across Asian American ethnic groups, there are some variations in parental and cultural beliefs. The traditional Khmer culture, for example, holds that ability in children is intrinsic and, therefore, that parents are less inclined to push their children to succeed (Smith-Hefner, 1990).

Peer Relationships

Peer relationships have been found to have a great impact on adolescent and young adult adjustment (Parker & Asher, 1987). There is evidence to suggest that children who are accepted by peers tend to grow up to be socially well-adjusted adults, whereas children who are rejected by peers tend to demonstrate adjustment problems later in life (e.g., dropping out of school, juvenile and adult criminality, adult psychopathology). For Asian American children, peer relationships may be more complex. Many U.S.-born Asian American students tend to socialize with White students and seldom feel isolated. They tend to have close friends of other races (Wang, Sedlacek, & Westbrook, 1992). However, language differences might prevent immigrant and refugee students from facilitating interactions with nonethnic peers. Many of these children also lack the time that is needed to form friendships because they often are relied on to care for their younger siblings (Cicirelli, 1994; Lee & Eng, 1989). Furthermore, being non-White, Asian American students might encounter some negative responses from peers that are related to their physical appearance. There is some evidence that this is the case. Asian Indian and Filipino students, for example, were reported to be teased for their darker skin (Dasgupta, 1989; Santos, 1983; Yao, 1989). Of course, how other students react to Asian American students can be influenced by many factors such as the racial composition of the school and neighborhood in which they live and how teachers portray and treat Asian American students.

As a consequence of this social context, a pecking order often is established in young people's minds. When they find someone who embodies those stereotypes even more visibly, they disassociate themselves from that person, which can happen through teasing, harassment, or avoidance. One Asian American student recounted,

> I distinctly remember in junior high school there was a Chinese immigrant student who did very well in math and sciences but very poorly in English and French. His hair was never combed, he wore coke bottle glasses, and his English was terrible. . . . My French teacher was very antagonistic toward him. . . . I

wonder now if it was because she expected more from him because he was Asian. She never seemed to take into account that it might be more difficult for recent immigrants to do well in certain subjects. He needed extra help, and no one offered it. . . . I empathized with his difficulties, although I never did anything about it for fear that people would think I was his friend or that I was anything like him. (Lee, ongoing project, Case 92-3-11)

Rejection by peers might be less acute in ethnic enclaves such as New York City's Chinatown, where Chinese immigrant children have a large group of ethnic peers to interact with and from whom they can receive social support (Huang, Leong, & Wagner, 1994; Lee & Eng, 1989; Sung, 1985). In fact, immigrant Chinese children reported that they interact mainly with children who speak their native dialect (Lee & Eng, 1989). In these situations, of course, there is the concern about the lack of preparation of children for participation in the broader, multiethnic society within which Chinatown is embedded.

Social and Economic Milieus

The social and economic experiences of Asian American children and youths are tremendously varied. Some Asian American children come from highly educated and economically advantaged homes and have parents who might be many generations distant from an immigrant experience. As described earlier, some seldom interact with non-Asians or with other Asian groups. Others, such as residents of Hawaii, are accustomed to great ethnic diversity. Some immigrants have moved from a privileged life in their homeland to a privileged life as an Asian American. By contrast, some Southeast Asian children and youths and their parents might have experienced the stressful life associated with war in their home countries. Some might have a strong cultural identity. Others, such as Amerasian adolescents, might lack a strong sense of identity. The Amerasian youths comprise a unique group due to their particular circumstances and experiences. They grew up in Vietnam as a stigmatized group and had very little formal education. In recent years, many Amerasian youths came to the United States under the Amerasian Homecoming Act, which took effect in March 1989 (Mydans, 1991a). Many of these youths are experiencing serious problems that are related to their adjustment to life in U.S. society.

In summary, the experiences of many Asian American children have been characterized as potentially traumatic due to discrepancies between the traditional cultural values of their parents' homeland and those held by mainstream America. One area of difficulty is the difference in the extent to which parents might expect to dominate and direct their children's behavior and actions. Furthermore, Asian American families expect superior performance from their children in school and might have a greater commitment to showing respect for teachers than do many other American parents. The problems of language differences and physical appearance differences also plague some young Asian Americans in their interactions with peers. Other specific factors of social and economic diversity also were discussed as influential in forming the experiences of Asian American children and youths. The discussion in this chapter now turns to what is known about the psychological status of this group. Although the causal connections between the described experiences and psychological status are, in general, not established, there is room for fruitful speculation on these relationships.

PSYCHOLOGICAL STATUS OF ASIAN AMERICAN CHILDREN AND YOUTHS

What is the status of psychological and emotional well-being of Asian American children and youths in general? This broad question encompasses several different dimensions such as emotion, mental health, and adjustment. Clearly, how Asian American children and youths fare psychologically is related to their family background (e.g., native-born/immigrant/refugee status, socioeconomic status [SES], parents' education, parental value system, neighborhood in which they live), their relationship with their social milieu and/or society at large (e.g., interaction with peers, treatment at school by teacher and schoolmates), and their own individual temperament and personality. For example, socialization practices within the families will vary according to the degree of the parents' acculturation, which in turn affects the children's ability to accept or respond to parental demands. In addition, psychological adjustment for an immigrant adolescent is very different from that for a native-born Asian American. Furthermore, even within the immigrant population, the age of migration will engender different experiences. All these experiential factors contribute to variations in Asian American children's and youths' psychological and emotional state. This section discusses the following topics: the impact of parents' attitudes on children's well-being, self-concept/self-esteem, and psychological adjustment.

Impact of Parents' Attitudes on Children's Well-Being

Asian American children and youths are aware of value differences between their parents and themselves and sometimes evidence distress related to these disparities. Korean American students and Americanized Hmong youths feel a great deal of disparity in cultural values between parents and themselves (Aldwin & Greenberger, 1987; Rick & Forward, 1992). This is also the case for Asian Indian children (Gonzalez, 1991; Saran, 1985; Segal, 1991; Yao, 1989). These conflicts pose serious psychological challenges for children as they strive to deal with the two worlds in which they live: the American world outside the home and the world of their non-Americanized families. Aldwin and Greenberger (1987) found that for Korean American students, the extent to which they perceive parents as having traditional values is related to the severity of these students' depression.

Parental commitment to cultural and ethnic traditions has a significant impact on children's adjustment (Phinney & Chavira, 1992; Phinney, Lochner, & Murphy, 1990). Some Asian American parents create difficult circumstances for their children's adjustment because they themselves have ambivalent attitudes. They seem at once to have some Americanized ideas and beliefs while still holding on to certain traditional values. The mixed feelings and attitudes are reflected in their expectations for their children. Dasgupta (1989) reported that Asian Indian immigrant parents, for example, have two standards in socializing their children. On the one hand, parents encourage their children to be independent and assertive in dealing with U.S. society; on the other hand, children are expected to be obedient, dependent, and deferent to their parents at home. Vietnamese parents express a similar ambivalence toward their adolescent children. They strongly endorse Asian traditional values, but they also approve autonomy and independence in their adolescents (Nguyen & Peterson, 1993; Nguyen & Williams, 1989). This type of ambivalent attitude makes it very difficult for their children to behave in "appropriate" ways so as to be accepted by their parents. For children, parental acceptance is important. For example, Hahn (1981) found that for Korean American children, perceived parental acceptance is positively related to children's self-esteem and school achievement.

Self-Concept/Self-Esteem

Several studies have examined self-concepts among certain groups of Asian American children and youths. Generation differences are reported by Rosenthal and Feldman (1992) in that first-generation Chinese American adolescents identify with being Chinese (58%) more than do second-generation Chinese American adolescents (18%). Second-generation Chinese identified themselves as American (42%) more often than did first-generation Chinese (16%).

Chen and Yang's (1986) research compared first-generation Chinese adolescents' self-image to that of White American adolescents. It was found that Chinese American adolescents responded in a similar way as the White sample and very differently from Chinese adolescents in China. Lee and Eng (1989) not only found generation differences among Chinese American children and adolescents who lived in and around New York's Chinatown but also found that length of stay in the United States and age of migration were related to mean scores on the Harter Self-Perception Scale. Those who were native born and who migrated at an early age and had been in the United States for more than 3 years had self-concept scores similar to those of Harter's normative sample. By contrast, recent immigrants had lower self-concept scores and different patterns of response on the various subscales from those of the normative sample. Similarly, Japanese American children, most of whom are third- and fourth-generation Americans, reported very similar self-concept scores as White American children (Pang, Mizokawa, Morishima, & Olstad, 1985). There might be greater within-group differences on self-concept scores than differences between different ethnic groups. For example,

Korean American children from middle-class backgrounds reported higher self-esteem than did those from working-class families (Hahn, 1981).

In one area in particular, Asian American children and youths have different self-esteem ratings from those of other Americans of comparable ages. Asian American young people are more likely to have lower scores on physical self-esteem measures. Using the modified Piers-Harris Children Self-Concept Scale, Pang et al. (1985) found that Japanese American children scored lower on the physical self-concept subscale, and Chang (1975) found that Korean American children scored lower than Black children on the same subscale. Lee and Eng (1989) also found that native-born Chinese American children scored lower on the physical self-concept subscale on the Harter Self-Perception Scale. Similarly, Japanese American female college students reported more dissatisfaction with their physical appearance than did White Americans or Japanese male students (Arkoff & Weaver, 1966). Asamen and Berry (1987), in their study of alienation and self-concept, found that physical self-concepts were negatively related to perceived prejudice among Japanese American college students.

It appears that some Asian American children and youths are not very happy about their physical appearance. This is not surprising given U.S. society's Eurocentric view of physical attractiveness. Skin color is clearly a salient characteristic that Asian American students use to judge attractiveness, and they show greater sensitivity to it than do either White or Asian/White mixed students (Grove, 1991).

For minority children, ethnic identity development is intertwined with general identity development. Therefore, their attitudes toward their physical appearance might have significant effects on their identity development. Phinney's (1989) research found that more Asian American adolescents than either Black or Hispanic American adolescents reported that they would prefer belonging to a White group if they had a choice, indicating a somewhat negative attitude toward their ethnic identity. This negative attitude can be influenced by certain Asian cultural values that affect ethnic identity such as the socialization of shame. Yeh and Huang (1996) found that Asian American college students' sense of ethnic identity was influenced by an avoidance of shame.

Similarly, in the College Student Personal History Project, Lee found that many Asian American college students report that they grew up feeling that they were uglier or less socially accepted than other students because they did not measure up to the White standards held by their peers, teachers, and popular media. As one student recounted,

> I went through junior high school wishing that I was not Chinese but rather a blue-eyed blond . . . petite American girl that all the boys liked. I didn't like my mushroom-shaped head of thick hair and my slanted eyes for which I was mistaken for a boy more than once. (Lee, ongoing project, Case 95-1-5)

It is possible that Asian American children's lower scores on physical self-concept measures reflect a response tendency toward modesty and undervaluation. Schwartz (1971) found a negative relationship between self-esteem and school achievement among Japanese American children, suggesting that children who do well in school might be teased by peers, which decreases their self-esteem, or that there is some modesty factor. However, this modesty factor does not seem to affect Asian American children's scores on other self-concept subscales that are comparable with those of other non-Asian American children. Perhaps the more likely explanation is that racism in society, although subtle in many cases, affects Asian American children's views on their appearance. Their self-evaluations of their physical appearance might be influenced by the Eurocentric notion of physical attractiveness in U.S. society. Interview data from Zhan's (1991) research, for example, support this explanation. She found that female Vietnamese refugee adolescents mentioned models in magazines as the criteria for physical attraction and expressed dissatisfaction with their Asian appearance. In addition, given the Asian traditional characteristic that people are sensitive to others' opinions (Connor & Joge, 1976), negative/racist portrayals and views in U.S. society toward Asian Americans might affect Asian American children's and youths' self-concept and self-esteem.

Because there has been relatively little empirical research on direct examination of Asian American children's and youths' self-concept/self-esteem, it is worthwhile to include studies that have examined correlates to Asian American children and youths' self-concept/self-esteem or identity. The relationship between children's self-concept and other areas might shed some light on our understanding. Asamen and Berry (1987) found that for both Chinese and Japanese American college students, low self-concept is negatively related to high alienation. Hahn (1981) found that there is a positive relationship among perceived parental acceptance, children's self-esteem, and school achievement. Children's reported self-esteem also was found to be related to family SES in that higher family SES is related to children's higher self-esteem. Kim (1983) found that for Korean immigrant children in New York City, there is a positive relationship among levels of self-concept, English proficiency, and school adaptation and achievements. Ting-Toomey (1981) found that for Chinese American youths, ethnic identity was not predictive of a close friendship network, indicating that these students do not choose their close friends based on ethnicity. Similarly, Rosenthal and Feldman (1992) suggested that length of stay in the United States (first generation vs. second generation) is not associated with Chinese American adolescents' friendship networks. Lee (ongoing project) reported that Asian American college students indicate a differential ethnic link between close and "regular" friends. They generally characterize their friendship patterns as not ethnically based in that they do seek out friends of similar ethnicity to "hang out" with, but close friendships do not appear to be tied to ethnicity. Wang et al.'s (1992) findings concur in that native-born college students were more likely to have close friends that were of other races. However, there is some evidence that friendship patterns among Asian Americans might be the product of racism. As one college student recounted,

> With the exception of one close Chinese American friend, I avoided making friends with the other Asian Americans in school. I felt that by associating with

them, this would confirm other people's suspicions that I was a grade-monger-ing, socially inept Asian. (Lee, ongoing project, Case 92-4-2)

In sum, self-concept/self-esteem among Asian American children and youths has been found to be negatively related to alienation and positively related to parental acceptance, SES background, English proficiency (for immigrant chil-dren), school adjustment and achievement, and perceived social acceptance for Vietnamese children. Although no causal links can be established between self-concept/self-esteem and various factors in the social milieu, the research findings suggest that much can be done in these other areas to enhance Asian American children's self-concept/self-esteem.

Psychological Adjustment

One approach to assessing Asian American children's and youths' state of psychological adjustment is to examine how these children and youths fare in their daily lives. Indicators of adjustment/maladjustment can be seen through self-reports of perceived levels of stress, the individual's perceived ability to deal with these everyday stresses, and self-reports or clinical observations of depression.

Kinzie, Ryals, Cottington, and McDermott (1973) examined depressive symp-toms among different ethnic groups of college students in Hawaii. They found that Chinese and Japanese American students in the sample reported higher levels of depression than did White students. Similarly, Aldwin and Greenberger (1987) found that Korean American college students reported more symptoms of de-pression and felt more pressured than did White American students. In addition, there appears to be a gender difference in that Asian American females were more likely to be in the more severely depressed category. Factors that appear to be related to depression in these studies were an unhappy family life, being away from home, and perceived conflict with parents' traditional values. Fraier and Schauben (1994) also found that Asian American female college students reported a greater number of psychological symptoms and higher levels of stress compared to European American students. The most frequent stressors were test pressures, financial problems, and relationship breakups. Chang (1996), Greenberger and Chen (1996), and Okazaki (1997) also found higher rates of depression in Asian American college students than in White American students.

Research findings show that children and youths in Hawaii might face specific challenges that are different from those faced in the U.S. mainland. Hawaii, being a multiracial, multiethnic, and multicultural context with unique characteristics, might have psychological impacts on Asian American children and youths that are not apparent. Stephan and Stephan (1989) found that Asian American college students in Hawaii reported more anxiety when interacting with Whites and had more negative attitudes toward Whites than did Hispanic Americans on the main-land. It appeared that contacts with Whites were associated with anxiety and stress. This might be a residual effect of Hawaii's "colonial" history. In addition, Waldron and Whittington (1985) found that many unique problems facing children in Hawaii are due to cultural diversity within the family because of interracial marriages, difficulties that are associated with constant mobility in military families, the incursion of tourism, and the high cost of living. All these factors pose serious potential challenges to children's and youths' psychological adjustment.

There is evidence that immigrant children and youths suffer higher levels of stress than do native-born children and youths. Abe and Zane's (1990) research suggests that foreign-born Asian American college students reported greater psychological maladjustment than did White and U.S.-born Asian American students. This finding held true after controlling for many confounding variables, indicating that foreign-born Asian American youths are at greater risk for psychological maladjustment. Padilla, Wagatsuma, and Lindholm (1985) also found that Japanese American immigrant college students reported greater stress levels than did native-born students. Asian Indian immigrant college students also were found to suffer from a number of depressive symptoms such as moodiness, anxiety, loneliness, and paranoid feelings (Pais, 1990). These symptoms appear to be related to their social interactions with White students; many reported having misunderstandings in relationships with White friends and peers. It appears that acculturation played an important role; less acculturation was related to higher stress levels, whereas high acculturation was related to lower stress levels.

Asian American children and youths emigrating from Southeast Asia experience not only stress related to present life events but also stress related to the traumas associated with war in their home countries. In general, the early group of Vietnamese children who came right after the fall of Vietnam (approximately 1974-1975) have fared quite well in the United States. These children and youths appear to be adjusting well. Their parents (including foster parents) have reported very few social, psychological, and/or school problems (Sokoloff, Carlin, & Pham, 1984). However, these children generally came to the United States at an early age and were from well-to-do (educationally and economically) families. On the other hand, children who came to the United States during the second wave (1979 to the early and mid-1980s) as refugees have not fared as well. Most of the second-wave Vietnamese were from lower SES backgrounds and had parents who were less educated or illiterate. Charron and Ness (1981) studied these second-wave refugee children and youths using a self-report questionnaire. They found a high degree of distress among these adolescents. Female Vietnamese adolescents had a higher rate of distress and also reported more intense distress than did male adolescents. High emotional distress was found to be related to having few American friends, conflicts with parents, low English proficiency, and fewer years in U.S. schools.

It appears that refugee status has a negative impact on children's and youths' psychological adjustment. Kinzie, Sack, Angell, Manson, and Rath (1986) found that many Cambodian adolescents were diagnosed as having "depressive disorder" and were rated by teachers as withdrawn (Sack, Angell, Kinzie, & Rath, 1986). Many of these Cambodian youths who were traumatized in their earlier lives showed posttraumatic stress disorder over a long period of time, indicating the enduring nature of these traumatic experiences (Abe, Zane, & Chun, 1994;

Kinzie, Sack, Angell, Clarke, & Rath, 1989). For Indochinese adolescents, not living with their own families was related to a higher incidence of depression (Porte & Torney-Purta, 1987). In addition, parents of Cambodian youths were found to show higher than normal symptoms of stress (Sack et al., 1986), suggesting that these children and youths probably are living in a stressful environment. Tobin and Friedman (1984) proposed that these refugee adolescents might experience difficulties in establishing a cultural identity because of distress during their formative years and that they need to have ethnic adults in the family who can understand their behaviors and provide appropriate support to establish an identity.

Within this group of Southeast Asian refugee children and adolescents, the Amerasian youths mentioned earlier comprise a unique group because of their particular circumstances and experiences. How are these children and adolescents adjusting in U.S. society? Most came thinking that they had finally, after many years of longing, come to their fathers' land where they would belong and where life would be different. However, many have been disappointed. Mydans (1991a) reported that many of these children and adolescents have language problems and feel rejected by the Vietnamese community in the United States. Many have the sense that they do not really belong anywhere. Mothers of these Amerasian children and adolescents rated their children very high on somatization, depression, withdrawal, and symptoms of psychosis as compared to White mothers' ratings of their children (Nicassio, LaBarbera, Coburn, & Finley, 1986). Male children and adolescents in particular were rated high on these dimensions. Carlin (cited in Mydans, 1991a) also reported high levels of depression among Amerasian children. These findings suggest that there might be significant psychological distress among Amerasian children and youths. However, the problems of Amerasian children and youths need to be compared with those of other Vietnamese children and youths to identify the problems that are unique to Amerasians.

In sum, Asian American college students reported more symptoms of depression than did White American students. The general interpretation is that Asian Americans suffer from more stress related to their minority status. Several sources of psychological stress have been identified. Sue and Chin (1983) pointed out that different cultural values in socialization, racism in the United States, and changes in life (which are more relevant to immigrants and refugees) tend to negatively affect the mental health of Chinese American children and youths. Demands for excellence from families and social isolation also were found to have a negative impact on Asian American children's and youths' psychological health (Bourne, 1975). Other common sources of stress that were identified in previous studies are degrees of acculturation, socialization/cultural factors, and parental value orientations. In general, less acculturated Asian American college students reported more stress than did those who were more acculturated. Perceiving parents as having traditional views is related to increased depression, whereas perceiving parents as having modern views is related to decreased depression. Socialization practices that are influenced by Asian cultures also might have a bearing on Asian American children's and youths' psychological health.

Studies on Southeast Asian refugee children and youths suggest that refugee children and youths appear to have higher stress levels and show more depressive symptoms than do normative samples. In general, the earlier arrivals adjusted well, both in natural homes and in adoptive or foster homes. The younger the age on migration to the United States, the better the adjustment. However, the later arrivals and Amerasian adolescents have had problems of adjustment. Vietnamese high school students' emotional stress is related to their interpersonal relationships with White peers at school, their relationships with parents, and their English proficiency. The clinical diagnosis of depression in Southeast Asian youths is related to their living situations. Those who live at home or live in ethnic foster homes are less likely to be diagnosed as depressive than are those who live in Caucasian foster homes. As discussed earlier, parents of Cambodian youths showed higher symptoms of stress than did a normal sample, which might suggest that these children live in a stressful immediate environment. These daily stresses combined with their early traumatic experiences, which appear to be expressed in the form of posttraumatic symptoms, leave Cambodian youths at high risk for maladjustment.

SOCIETY'S VIEW OF ASIAN AMERICAN CHILDREN AND YOUTHS

The ways in which Asian American children and youths are viewed within the mainstream society of the United States may both enhance and limit the possibilities for personal fulfillment and societal contributions of this population. Therefore, it is important to examine not only what is really the case but also what is believed to be the case. Such views include perceptions of Asian Americans as the "model minority" that possesses superior academic abilities, especially in mathematics and science, and as the economically self-sufficient and culturally superior minority group that is not in need of special support to become independent and successful in U.S. society. In contrast to this model minority image are increasing concerns over the recent growth of Asian youth gangs in the United States. This section discusses these issues under the following topics: the concept of Asian Americans as a model minority—its origin, development, and impact on Asian Americans—and Asian gang and criminal activities.

Model Minority

It is important to understand the image of the model minority within a historical context. Contrary to today's image, Asians who came to the United States in the mid-1800s to early 1900s were considered a backward people who were so culturally and morally deviant that they were unassimilable to American ways of life. Although different nationalities of Asians came to and stayed in the United States for different reasons, they encountered racism that tended to homogenize their identities. Throughout this period of history, Asians who migrated to the

United States were met with hostility born from xenophobia, perceptions of economic threat, and racism. A vast difference exists between the negative depiction of the past and the model minority characterizations of the present.

The most prominent of the model minority stereotypes applied to Asian Americans by the U.S. media is that of the "bootstraps" family that has managed to scrimp and save to build a better life for the next generation. Politically, this idealized picture of Asian families has been used to criticize everything from the woes of other minorities and their dependence on big government to the consequences of our country's departure from traditional family roles.

The model minority image often depicts Asian parents as placing a high value on education, self-improvement, family honor, and (most important) hard work. Asian children respond by being obedient, filial, uncomplaining hard workers and overachievers. When Asian families face a crisis or when there are difficulties within Asian families, they tend to deal with those issues at home rather than air their "dirty laundry" or seek the aid of public agencies. Even those immigrants "fresh off the boat," who came from war-torn countries, are said to have been able to overcome their enormous psychological trauma and prosper economically on their own.

The model Asian and Asian American student is integral to the image of the model Asian family (Kim, 1973; Kitano & Sue, 1973; Lee & Rong, 1988; Minatoya & Sedlacek, 1981). Lee and Rong (1988), in reviewing the educational and economic achievements of Asian Americans, state,

> The superior performance of Asian American students from kindergarten through graduate school is so well known that it hardly needs recounting. Asian children, only a few years off the boat, have won national spelling bees. They have taken a major share of Westinghouse Science Awards, are disproportionately represented in the student bodies of prestigious colleges and universities, and sometimes outnumber all the other students in mathematics and science classes. In 30 years, four Asian Americans have won the Nobel prize in physics, and another has won the prize in chemistry. (p. 546)

This popular conception of the academically successful Asian American is supported by much research. Asian American students, in general, have demonstrated outstanding academic achievement (Sue & Okazaki, 1990). Even immigrant and refugee (especially Vietnamese) students in public schools are doing very well in academic work (Caplan et al., 1992; Caplan, Whitmore, & Choy, 1989; Hirayama, 1985; Rumbaut & Ima, 1988; Sung, 1987). Researchers also have reported that Asian American students spend more time studying than do non-Asian American students (Reglin & Adams, 1990; Tsang, 1984), indicating that extrinsic efforts rather than genetic factors might account for their school achievement. There are, however, variations within Asian American groups in regard to academic success. For example, Khmer and Laotian students lag behind. As cited earlier, within the traditional Khmer culture, academic effort is not stressed because there is the belief that success, or lack thereof, is due to intrinsic abilities rather than effort (Smith-Hefner, 1990).

Most researchers explain Asian American students' outstanding academic achievement from a cultural perspective that concentrates on family socialization factors such as parental expectations. However, the relationship is not so simple. Dornbusch, Ritter, Leiderman, Roberts, and Fraleigh (1987) investigated the relationships between parenting styles and adolescents' school performance with a diverse high school population in the San Francisco Bay area. Using Baumrind's topology (authoritarian, permissive, and authoritative) to assess parenting style, Dornbusch et al. found that, in general, students' grades were negatively related to authoritarian parenting styles and positively related to authoritative parenting styles regardless of ethnicity. Interestingly enough, even though the Asian American sample reported a higher mean on authoritarian parenting style and a lower mean on authoritative style as compared to those of White families, on the whole, the group demonstrated higher grades, indicating that the success of Asian American students cannot be adequately explained by parenting styles alone. Steinberg, Dornbusch, and Brown (1992) further reported that peer support for academic achievement offsets the negative consequences of the authoritarian parenting style among Asian American high school students.

There is the widespread belief that Asian Americans are model students who are respectful to teachers and diligent but not necessarily vocally assertive and who consistently excel in mathematics and science but are less able in other areas (Allis, 1991; Bagasao, 1989). For example, teachers view Asian American students as not competent at expressing feelings, persuasiveness, assertiveness, and leadership skills (Bannai & Cohen, 1985) and as more passive, quieter, and less capable at social tasks than White students (Kim, Y. J., 1983; Sung, 1987). These beliefs often influence the ways in which teachers and counselors relate to Asian American students. Schneider and Lee (1990) compared the social and academic skills of Asian American 6th and 7th graders to those of White students of similar socioeconomic background and found that teachers' actions were related to their perceptions of Asian American students as quiet students. Teachers tended to call on Asian Americans less often than on Anglo students. As one teacher described an Asian student in her class: "She is quiet, she tends to do her tasks, and . . . she is also self-disciplined. But she is a little more outgoing than other Oriental children. She asks questions." This attitude is supported by Feng and Cartledge's (1996) findings that teachers tended to attribute Asian American students' behaviors to internal characteristics.

What impact do these images have on Asian American children and youths? Some college students reported that they felt pigeonholed.

> This stereotype controlled my life. I came home from school and studied. Weekends I studied. And why? Because White society created an image of me that I needed to keep up or else suffer the consequences of being rejected from society. I would be talked about if I did not score an A on exams. I was unhappy because I could not live my life at a time when I should have had no worries. My high school years were spent in a room surrounded by four walls, a bed, a desk, and a bookshelf. If this is what being a model minority entails, I would rather pass. (Lee, ongoing project, Case 97-4-30)

Some students described situations in which they turned to teachers or counselors for help but found them insensitive or ignorant.

[My adviser] just kept recommending that I take more advanced physics and math classes. Academically, I was stereotyped as the typical Asian "geek," even though my grades in history and social studies were always above average. I think the teachers assumed that I would like math and science more because I was Chinese and did so well in these classes. (Lee, ongoing project, Case 92-1-8)

When my friend, who was second generation, moved to Dallas, when she was registering in school—the counselor there was ready to make her take an English exam and was considering placing her in a remedial course because she assumed that she knew little English. (Case 96-3-15)

As can be seen, the confluence of parental expectations and societal expectations for academic prowess might, in some instances, inappropriately channel the life course of some Asian American youngsters and might inhibit the development of other types of abilities. Tan (1994) reported that many Asian American college students believed that the model minority stereotype was more of a hindrance than encouragement to their productivity. Apprehensiveness about evaluation (Sue, Ino, & Sue, 1983) might prove dysfunctional in some Asian American students. Two college students reported the following:

My mother's friend's daughter committed suicide by jumping out of the county library window because she felt that she couldn't graduate from Columbia with honors. (Lee, ongoing project, Case 92-2-5)

My brother at this time was rebelling against everything. It hurt me to see how bad he was treating my parents. He was a victim of all the whiz kid media portrayal of Asian kids because he was not one of them. He excelled in the arts and resented the fact that teachers thought he should go into math and science. (Lee, ongoing project, Case 95-3-7)

Similarly, Kubany, Gallimore, and Buell (1970) reported that Filipino American children were found to show more competitiveness in public than in private situations, indicating an extrinsically based motivation to be seen as capable.

Clearly, the societal expectation for academic success, and especially as narrowly focused on in the areas of mathematics and science, might be less than a good fit for some Asian American children and youths (Hsia, 1987). Such stereotypes ignore individual differences. When Asian American children do not fit this model, they might experience the intense pressure to fit in with these expectations as a source of stress (Lee, 1994, 1996).

One other consequence of the model minority image is the notion that resources of social service agencies and governmental bodies are less necessary for Asian American groups than for other minorities within the U.S. society (Federal Civil Rights Commission, 1992). There is, however, some evidence that these groups might not be as self-sufficient as is believed. Apart from the misconception that Asian Americans can survive in this society without help is the indication that even when these agencies provide resources, Asian Americans generally underutilized available mental health and psychological services. The underutilization of professional help can be partially explained by Asian cultures. As discussed earlier, Asian Americans tend to rely on family members or themselves in dealing with emotional or other personal problems. However, the tendency of Asian Americans to underutilize professional mental health services also might bring to question the effectiveness of psychological services offered to Asian Americans. Research findings suggest that Asian American students view a counselor's cultural sensitivity as a strong indicator of the counselor's credibility and competence (Gim, Atkinson, & Kim, 1991) and that the ethnicity of the counselor per se plays only a small role in Asian American students' preference for a specific counselor (Atkinson, Poston, Carlos, Michael, & Mercado, 1989; Gim et al., 1991). The issue of counselor competence or effectiveness in dealing with Asian American clients has been discussed by a number of researchers (Cohon, 1983; Ford, 1987; Hartman & Askounis, 1989; Hong, 1988; Steiner & Bansil, 1989; Sue & Sue, 1985; West, 1983; Yao, 1985a). These authors agree that to serve Asian American clients more effectively, it is essential for professional counselors, regardless of their own ethnicity, to acquire some knowledge of Asian American culture in general and to have an understanding of Asian American communities' current circumstances. However, it also is important to view Asian American clients as unique individuals because there is some evidence that counselors sometimes stereotype them. For example, one college student reported that she

> only went to see the counselor once because . . . right off the bat, he attributed all my problems to my relationship with my family. He said they put too much pressure on me to succeed, even though in reality they hardly put any pressure on me at all. (Lee, ongoing project, Case 92-3-8)

Criminal and Gang Activities

The generally favorable picture of Asian American children and youths in the United States has been countered by arrest statistics published by the U.S. Department of Justice (1988, 1992, 1996). The number of Asian American and Pacific Islander youths (under 18 years of age) arrested increased steadily from 1987 to 1995, whereas arrests of those age 18 years or older were stable in the population at large. The types of offenses that contributed to this increase were crimes against families and children, curfew violations, embezzlement, gambling, robbery, runaways, and sex offenses. The runaway problem among Chinese immigrant youths in San Francisco also has been reported to be related in some way to an increase in gang membership (Louie, Joe, Lu, & Tong, 1991). These runaways usually end up in some gang group house and are at risk of getting involved in criminal activities.

Within the past few years, national attention has focused on the reported increase of Asian youth gang activities (Dao, 1992). Membership of these youth gangs appears to be clustered by ethnicity. Chinese youth gang activities in and around Chinatown in New York City (Lubasch, 1991; Sung, 1987) have been reported to be on the rise. Vietnamese gang activities were reported to be increasing and reported to be more dangerous because the members grew up in chaotic Vietnam and witnessed many atrocities. These members were described by the New York police as wild and uncontrollable (Hays, 1990; Lorch, 1990). Vietnamese gang activities also were reported to cause gang terror in some areas of California (Gross, 1991; Mydans, 1991b). These "problem youths" were described as being disappointed with life in the United States, experiencing difficulties in school in both academic and social areas (Peters, 1988), experiencing conflicts in the home (Furuto & Murase, 1992), and believing that they will be protected by joining gang groups (Hays, 1990; Lorch, 1990).

In a recent ethnographic study of Vietnamese youth gangs in Orange County, California, Vigil, Yun, and Long (1992) reported that poverty and an intense desire to obtain money played a major role in convincing adolescents to join gangs. As one youth revealed to the researchers,

> I didn't want my parents' money. I wanted my own money. . . . I feel like maybe they need the money. I always tried to get my own money . . . so I got the job [as a hotel bellboy] to save money. But the money was too slow. I didn't have enough money. I wanted more money. So I quit. . . . With my homeboys [gang members], I could make $10,000 a day. (p. 45)

According to Vigil et al. (1992), gang activities usually involve property crimes, car thefts, and "home invasion robberies." The most lucrative of these activities are the home invasion robberies, in which an evening's take ranges from $20,000 to $100,000. These robberies are well organized and planned. Gangs receive information about families who keep their savings in their homes, invade the homes, and force the victims to reveal their hiding places. Much of the information comes from family members or relatives who are gang members. These home invasions might be related to the increase in crimes against families by Asian American and Pacific Islander youths under 18 years of age cited earlier.

It appears, however, that problems with alcohol and drug use might not be as prevalent with Asian American children and youths as with other groups. Gillmore et al. (1990) observed that Asian American adolescents' use of alcohol and drugs is much lower than that of White youths. U.S. Department of Justice (1988, 1992, 1996) statistics also showed a decrease in arrests related to drug abuse violations by Asian American and Pacific Islander youths under 18 years of age. It is likely that much of this relatively low drug use is related to parental disapproval and control.

There is a need to better understand the factors that have led to the increases in gang and criminal activities among Asian American youths. It may well be that a broader spectrum of options for the engagement of immigrant youths within the American mainstream culture will be necessary before these trends can be reversed.

CONCLUSION

This review of the state of Asian American children and youths in U.S. society is incomplete because of the dearth of systematic research on Asian American children and youths. Even when there are studies, they are focused mainly on Chinese Americans, Japanese Americans, Korean Americans, and Vietnamese Americans. Very little has been reported about other groups such as Asian Indian Americans, Filipino Americans, and other Southeast Asian American groups. Many of the published reports are of the nature of "impressionistic discussions" rather than empirical studies. Although these reports are useful in highlighting the various qualitative aspects of the lives of Asian American children and youths, they cannot take the place of empirical research during which data are generated.

There are few baseline data that describe the diversity of family life and activities of the various ethnic groups that comprise Asian America. Given the importance of family in traditional Asian cultures, understanding family dynamics (parent-child relations, sibling relations, and the role of extended family members such as aunts, uncles, and grandparents) is central to assessing the psychological state of Asian American children and youths. In addition, it is important to understand the state of children and youths through their own perceptions of their world; we need to know how they view their own existence in this society, whether they experience stress, and what their perceptions are of the social supports within their social milieu.

At least 10% of the growing Asian American children and youth population are immigrants and refugees who arrived in the United States in the past 3 years. Except for a small segment of Vietnamese refugees, little research has been undertaken to assess the health and well-being of these children. There is a great need for in-depth studies of the lives of children and youths of the various ethnic groups within the Asian American community. The production of a set of descriptive data related to the various spheres of their lives would be useful. Also, an increasing number of White families have adopted children from Asian countries in recent years, yet there is little knowledge or understanding of how these children are functioning within a social milieu that is ethnically and racially different from themselves.

The ultimate goal is to allow Asian American children to have access to the variety of options available to other Americans (e.g., choose majors at school and later careers) without feeling obligated or pressured to fit a certain image of Asian Americans. We need to broaden the scope of opportunities for Asian Americans to participate and to attempt development in areas not seen as special strengths and thus to modify their own views of limitations and the views of others in mainstream society.

REFERENCES

Abe, J. S., & Zane, N. W. (1990). Psychological maladjustment among Asian and White American college students: Controlling for confounds. *Journal of Counseling Psychology, 37,* 437-444.

Abe, J. S., Zane, N. W., & Chun, K. (1994). Differential responses to trauma: Migration-related discriminants of post-traumatic stress among Southeast Asian refugees. *Journal of Community Psychology, 22*(2), 121-135.

Aldwin, C., & Greenberger, E. (1987). Cultural differences in the predictors of depression. *American Journal of Community Psychology, 15,* 789-813.

Allis, S. (1991, March 25). Kicking the nerd syndrome. *Time,* pp. 64-66.

Alva, S. A. (1993). Differential patterns of achievement among Asian-American adolescents. *Journal of Youth & Adolescence, 22,* 407-423.

Arkoff, A., & Weaver, H. B. (1966). Body image and body dissatisfaction in Japanese-Americans. *Journal of Social Psychology, 68,* 323-330.

Asamen, J. K., & Berry, G. L. (1987). Self-concept, alienation, and perceived prejudice: Implications for counseling Asian Americans. *Journal of Multicultural Counseling and Development, 15*(4), 146-160.

Atkinson, D. R., Poston, W., Carlos, F., Michael, J., & Mercado, P. (1989). Ethnic group preferences for counselor characteristics. *Journal of Counseling Psychology, 36*(1), 68-72.

Atkinson, D. R., Whiteley, S., & Gim, R. H. (1990). Asian American acculturation and preferences for help providers. *Journal of College Student Development, 31*(2), 155-161.

Bagasao, P. Y. (1989, November-December). Student voices: Breaking the silence. *Change,* pp. 28-37.

Bannai, H., & Cohen, D. A. (1985). The passive-methodical image of Asian American students in the school system. *Sociology and Social Research, 70*(1), 79-81.

Bourne, P. G. (1975, August). The Chinese student: Acculturation and mental illness. *Psychiatry, 38,* 269-277.

Campbell, J. R., & Mandel, F. (1990). Connecting math achievement to parental influences. *Contemporary Educational Psychology, 15,* 64-74.

Caplan, N., Choy, M. H., & Whitmore, J. K. (1992, February). Indochinese refugee families and academic achievement. *Scientific American,* pp. 36-42.

Caplan, N., Whitmore, J. K., & Choy, M. H. (1989). *The boat people and achievement in America.* Ann Arbor: University of Michigan Press.

Chan, S., & Leong, C. W. (1994). Chinese families in transition: Cultural conflicts and adjustment problems. *Journal of Social Distress and the Homeless, 3,* 263-281.

Chang, E. C. (1996). Cultural differences in optimism, pessimism, and coping: Predictors of subsequent adjustment in Asian American and Caucasian American college students. *Journal of Counseling Psychology, 43,* 113-123.

Chang, T. S. (1975, October). The self-concept of children in ethnic groups: Black American and Korean American. *Elementary School Journal, 75,* 54-58.

Charron, D. W., & Ness, R. C. (1981). Emotional distress among Vietnamese adolescents: A statewide survey. *Journal of Refugee Resettlement, 1*(3), 7-15.

Chen, C., & Stevenson, H. W. (1995). Motivation and mathematics achievement: A comparative study of Asian-American, Caucasian-American and East Asian high school students. *Child Development, 66,* 1215-1234.

Chen, C. L., & Yang, D. C. Y. (1986). The self-image of Chinese-American adolescents: A cross-cultural comparison. *International Journal of Social Psychiatry, 32*(4), 19-26.

Chen, V. W. (1989). Communication and conflict between American born Chinese and their immigrant parents. *Dissertation Abstracts International, 49*(12), 3883A.

Chiu, L. H. (1987). Child-rearing attitudes of Chinese, Chinese-American, and Anglo-American mothers. *International Journal of Psychology, 22,* 409-419.

Cicirelli, V. G. (1994). Sibling relationships in cross-cultural perspective. *Journal of Marriage and the Family, 56,* 7-20.

Cohon, J. D., Jr. (1983). Southeast Asian refugees and school health personnel. *Journal of School Health, 53,* 151-158.

Connor, J. W. (1974). Acculturation and family continuities in three generations of Japanese Americans. *Journal of Marriage and the Family, 36,* 159-165.

Connor, J. W. (1976). Persistence and change in Japanese-American value orientation. *Ethos, 4*(1), 1-44.

Connor, J. W., & Joge, K. (1976). A key concept for an understanding of Japanese-American achievement. *Psychiatry, 39,* 266-279.

Cooper, C. R., Baker, H., Polichar, D., & Welsh, M. (1993). Values and communication of Chinese, Filipino, European, Mexican and Vietnamese American adolescents with their families and friends. *New Directions for Child Development, 62,* 73-89.

Dao, J. (1992, April 1). Asian street gangs emerging as new underworld. *The New York Times,* p. B2.

Dasgupta, S. S. (1989). *On the trail of an uncertain dream.* New York: AMS Press.

DeVos, G. A. (1983). Achievement motivation and intra-family attitudes in immigrant Koreans. *Journal of Psychoanalytic Anthropology, 6*(1), 25-71.

Dinh, K. T., Sarason, B. R., & Sarason, I. G. (1994). Parent-child relationships in Vietnamese immigrant families. *Journal of Family Psychology, 8,* 471-488.

Dornbusch, S. M., Ritter, P. L., Leiderman, P. H., Roberts, D. F., & Fraleigh, M. J. (1987). The relation of parenting style to adolescent school performance. *Child Development, 58,* 1244-1257.

Dornbusch, S. M., Ritter, P. L., Mont-Reynaud, R., & Chen, Z. Y. (1990). Family decision making and academic performance in a diverse high school population. *Journal of Adolescent Research, 5,* 143-160.

Federal Civil Rights Commission. (1992). *Civil rights issues facing Asian Americans in the 1990s: A report of the United States Commission on Civil Rights.* Washington, DC: Government Printing Office.

Feldman, S. S., & Rosenthal, D. A. (1990). The acculturation of autonomy expectations in Chinese high schoolers residing in two Western nations. *International Journal of Psychology, 25,* 259-281.

Feng, H., & Cartledge, G. (1996). Social skill assessment of inner city Asian, African, and European American students. *School Psychology Review, 25*(2), 228-239.

Ford, R. C. (1987). Cultural awareness and cross-cultural counseling. *International Journal for the Advancement of Counseling, 10,* 71-78.

Fraier, P. A., & Schauben, L. J. (1994). Stressful life events and psychological adjustment among female college students. *Measurement & Evaluation in Counseling and Development, 27*(1), 280-292.

Furuto, S. M., & Murase, K. (1992). Asian Americans in the future. In S. M. Furuto, R. Biswas, D. K. Chung, K. Murase, & F. Ross-Sheriff (Eds.), *Social work practice with Asian Americans* (pp. 240-253). Newbury Park, CA: Sage.

Gehrie, M. J. (1976). Childhood and community: On the experience of young Japanese Americans in Chicago. *Ethos, 4*(3), 353-383.

Gillmore, M. R., Catalano, R. F., Morrison, D. M., Wells, E. A., Iritani, B., & Hawkins, J. D. (1990). Racial differences in acceptability and availability of drugs and early initiation of substance use. *American Journal of Drug and Alcohol Abuse, 16*(3/4), 185-206.

Gim, R. H., Atkinson, D. R., & Kim, S. J. (1991). Asian-American acculturation, counselor ethnicity and cultural sensitivity, and ratings of counselors. *Journal of Counseling Psychology, 38,* 57-62.

Gim, R. H., Atkinson, D. R., & Whiteley, S. (1990). Asian-American acculturation, severity of concerns, and willingness to see a counselor. *Journal of Counseling Psychology, 37,* 281-285.

Gonzalez, D. (1991, June 11). Indians balance change and tradition. *The New York Times,* p. B3.

Gray, E., & Cosgrove, J. (1985). Ethnocentric perception of childrearing practices in protective services. *Child Abuse and Neglect, 9,* 389-396.

Greenberger, E., & Chen, C. (1996). Perceived family relationships and depressed mood in early and late adolescence: A comparison of European and Asian Americans. *Developmental Psychology, 32,* 707-716.

Gross, J. (1991, April 6). Six are killed as 8-hour siege by gang ends in California. *The New York Times,* p. A6.

Grove, K. J. (1991). Identity development in interracial, Asian/White late adolescents: Must it be so problematic? *Journal of Youth and Adolescence, 20,* 617-628.

Hahn, B. C. (1981). Relationship among perceived parental acceptance-rejection, self-evaluation and academic performance of Korean-American children. *Dissertation Abstracts International, 41*(8), 3488A-3489A.

Hartman, J. S., & Askounis, A. C. (1989). Asian American students: Are they really a "model minority"? *School Counselor, 37*(2), 109-112.

Hays, C. L. (1990, July 31). Amid gang violence, Chinatown casts off quiet image. *The New York Times,* p. B1.

Hieshima, J. A., & Schneider, B. (1994). Intergenerational effects on the cultural and cognitive socialization of third- and fourth-generation Japanese Americans. *Journal of Applied Developmental Psychology, 15,* 319-327.

Hirayama, K. K. (1985). Asian children's adaptation to public schools. *Social Work in Education, 7*(4), 213-230.

Hong, G. K. (1988). A general family practitioner approach for Asian American mental health services. *Professional Psychology Research and Practice, 19,* 600-605.

Hsia, J. (1987). Asian Americans fight the myth of the super student. *Educational Record, 68*(4), 95-97.

Huang, K., Leong, F., & Wagner, N. S. (1994). Coping with peer stressors and associated dysphoria: Acculturation differences among Chinese-American children. *Counseling Psychology Quarterly, 7*(1), 53-68.

Kelley, M. L., & Tseng, H. (1992). Cultural differences in child rearing: A comparison of immigrant Chinese and Caucasian American mothers. *Journal of Cross-Cultural Psychology, 23,* 444-455.

Kim, B. L. C. (1973). Asian Americans: No model minority. *Social Work, 18,* 44-53.

Kim, S. P. (1983). Self-concept, English language acquisition, and school adaptation in recently immigrated Asian children. *Journal of Children in Contemporary Society, 15*(3), 71-79.

Kim, Y. J. (1983). Problems in the delivery of the school based psycho-educational services to the Asian immigrant children. *Journal of Children in Contemporary Society, 15*(3), 81-89.

Kinzie, J. D., Ryals, J., Cottington, F., & McDermott, J. F. (1973). Cross-cultural study of depressive symptoms in Hawaii. *International Journal of Social Psychiatry, 19*(1), 19-24.

Kinzie, J. D., Sack, W. H., Angell, R. H., Clarke, G., & Rath, B. (1989). A three-year follow-up of Cambodian young people traumatized as children. *Journal of American Academy of Child and Adolescent Psychiatry, 28,* 501-504.

Kinzie, J. D., Sack, W. H., Angell, R. H., Manson, S., & Rath, B. (1986). The psychiatric effects of massive trauma on Cambodian children: The children. *Journal of the American Academy of Child Psychiatry, 25,* 370-376.

Kitano, H. H. L., & Sue, S. (1973). The model minorities. *Journal of Social Issues, 29,* 1-10.

Kubany, E. S., Gallimore, R., & Buell, J. (1970). The effects of extrinsic factors on achievement-oriented behavior: A non-Western case. *Journal of Cross-Cultural Psychology, 1,* 77-84.

Lee, E. S., & Rong, X. L. (1988). The educational and economic achievement of Asian Americans. *Elementary School Journal, 88,* 545-560.

Lee, L. C. (ongoing project, 1991-). *College Student Personal History Project.* Ongoing project, Cornell University.

Lee, L. C., & Eng, R. (1989, June). The world of Chinese immigrant children of New York City. In *Proceedings of the International Conference on Chinese Mental Health.* Taipei, Taiwan.

Lee, S. J. (1994). Behind the model-minority stereotype: Voices of high- and low-achieving Asian American students. *Anthropology and Education Quarterly, 25,* 423-429.

Lee, S. J. (1996). *Unraveling the "model minority" stereotype: Listening to Asian American youth.* New York: Teachers College Press.

Lin, C. Y. C., & Fu, V. R. (1990). A comparison of child-rearing practices among Chinese, immigrant Chinese, and Caucasian-American parents. *Child Development, 61,* 429-433.

Lorch, D. (1990, July 30). Mourners returned fire, police say. *The New York Times,* p. B1.

Louie, L., Joe, K., Lu, M., & Tong, B. (1991, August). *Chinese American adolescent runaways.* Paper presented at the convention of the Asian American Psychological Association, San Francisco.

Lubasch, A. H. (1991, May 18). Thirteen are charged in violence tied to Queens gang. *The New York Times*, p. A27.

McDermott, J. F., Jr., Char, W. F., Robillard, A. B., Hsu, J., Tsent, W. S., & Aston, G. C. (1983). Cultural variations in family attitudes and their implications for therapy. *Journal of the American Academy of Child Psychiatry, 22*, 454-458.

Minatoya, L. Y., & Sedlacek, W. E. (1981). Another look at the melting pot: Perceptions of Asian American undergraduates. *Journal of College Student Personnel, 22*, 328-336.

Mordkowitz, E. R., & Ginsburg, H. P. (1987). Early academic socialization of successful Asian-American college students. *Quarterly Newsletter of the Laboratory of Comparative Human Cognition, 9*(2), 85-91.

Mydans, S. (1991a, May 28). Children rejected in Vietnam find a sad sanctuary in U.S. *The New York Times*, p. A1.

Mydans, S. (1991b, April 8). For Vietnamese, a wave of gang terror. *The New York Times*, p. A11.

Nguyen, L., & Peterson, C. (1993). Depressive symptoms among Vietnamese-American college students. *Journal of Social Psychology, 133*, 65-71.

Nguyen, N. A., & Williams, H. L. (1989). Transition from East to West: Vietnamese adolescents and their parents. *American Academy of Child and Adolescent Psychiatry, 28*, 505-515.

Nicassio, P. M., LaBarbera, J. D., Coburn, P., & Finley, R. (1986). The psychosocial adjustment of the Amerasian refugees: Findings from the personality inventory for children. *Journal of Nervous and Mental Disease, 174*, 541-544.

Okazaki, S. (1997). Sources of ethnic differences between Asian American and White American college students on measures of depression and social anxiety. *Journal of Abnormal Psychology, 106*(1), 52-60.

O'Reilly, J. P., Tokuno, K. A., & Ebata, A. T. (1986). Cultural differences between Americans of Japanese and European ancestry in parental valuing of social competence. *Journal of Comparative Family Studies, 17*(1), 87-97.

Padilla, A. M., Wagatsuma, Y., & Lindholm, K. J. (1985). Acculturation and personality as predictors of stress in Japanese and Japanese-Americans. *Journal of Social Psychology, 125*, 295-305.

Pais, A. (1990, May 11). Immigrant students' campus blues. *India Abroad*, p. 14.

Pang, V. O., Mizokawa, D., Morishima, J. K., & Olstad, R. G. (1985). Self-concepts of Japanese-American children. *Journal of Cross-Cultural Psychology, 16*, 99-109.

Parker, J. G., & Asher, S. R. (1987). Peer relations and later personal adjustment: Are low-accepted children at risk? *Psychological Bulletin, 102*, 357-389.

Peters, H. A. (1988). *A study of Southeast Asian youth in Philadelphia*. Philadelphia: Institute for the Study of Human Issues.

Phinney, J. S. (1989). Stages of ethnic identity development in minority group adolescents. *Journal of Early Adolescence, 9*(1/2), 34-49.

Phinney, J. S., & Chavira, V. (1992). Ethnic identity and self-esteem: An exploratory longitudinal study. *Journal of Adolescence, 15*, 271-281.

Phinney, J. S., Lochner, B. T., & Murphy, R. (1990). Ethnic identity development and psychological adjustment in adolescence. In A. R. Stiffman & L. E. Davis (Eds.), *Ethnic issues in adolescent mental health*. Newbury Park, CA: Sage.

Porte, Z., & Torney-Purta, J. (1987). Depression and academic achievement among Indochinese refugee unaccompanied minors in ethnic and nonethnic placements. *American Journal of Orthopsychiatry, 47*, 536-547.

Powers, S., Choroszy, M., & Douglas, P. (1987). Attributions for success and failure of Japanese-American and Anglo-American university students. *Quarterly Journal of Human Behavior, 24*(3), 17-23.

Reglin, G. L., & Adams, D. R. (1990). Why Asian American high school students have higher grade point averages and SAT scores than other high school students. *High School Journal, 73*(3), 143-149.

Rick, K., & Forward, J. (1992). Acculturation and perceived intergenerational differences among Hmong youth. *Journal of Cross-Cultural Psychology, 23*, 85-94.

Rosenthal, D. A., & Feldman, S. S. (1992). The nature and stability of ethnic identity in Chinese youth. *Journal of Cross-Cultural Psychology, 23*, 214-227.

Rumbaut, R. G., & Ima, K. (1988). *The adaptation of Southeast Asian refugee youth: A comparative study*. San Diego: San Diego State University Press.

Sack, W., Angell, R. H., Kinzie, J. D., & Rath, B. (1986). The psychiatric effects of massive trauma on Cambodian children: The family, the home, and the school. *Journal of the American Academy of Child Psychiatry, 25*, 377-383.

Santos, A. R. (1983). The social and emotional development of Filipino-American children. In G. J. Powell, J. Yamamoto, A. Romero, & A. Morales (Eds.), *The psychosocial development of minority group children* (pp. 131-178). New York: Brunner/Mazel.

Saran, P. (1985). *The Asian Indian experience in the United States*. New Delhi, India: Vikas.

Schneider, B., & Lee, Y. (1990). A model for academic success: The school and home environment of East Asian students. *Anthropology and Education Quarterly, 21*, 358-377.

Schwartz, A. J. (1971). The culturally advantaged: A study of Japanese-American pupils. *Sociology and Social Research, 55*, 341-353.

Segal, U. (1991). Cultural variables in Asian Indian families. *Families in Society, 72*, 233-241.

Smith-Hefner, N. J. (1990). Language and identity in the education of Boston-area Khmer. *Anthropology and Education Quarterly, 21*, 250-268.

Sokoloff, B., Carlin, J., & Pham, H. (1984). Five-year follow-up of Vietnamese refugee children in the United States. *Clinical Pediatrics, 10*, 565-570.

Steinberg, L., Dornbusch, S. M., & Brown, B. B. (1992). Ethnic differences in adolescent achievement: An ecological perspective. *American Psychologist, 47*, 723-729.

Steiner, G., & Bansil, R. (1989). Cultural patterns and the family system in Asian Indians: Implications for psychotherapy. *Journal of Comparative Family Studies, 20*, 371-375.

Stephan, W. G., & Stephan, C. W. (1989). Antecedents of intergroup anxiety in Asian-Americans and Hispanic-Americans. *International Journal of Intercultural Relations, 13*, 203-219.

Strom, R., Daniels, S., & Park, S. (1986). The adjustment of Korean immigrant families. *Educational and Psychological Research, 6*, 213-227.

Suan, L. V., & Tyler, J. D. (1990). Mental health values and preference for mental health resources of Japanese-American and Caucasian-American students. *Professional Psychology: Research and Practice, 21*, 291-296.

Sue, D., Ino, S., & Sue, D. M. (1983). Nonassertiveness of Asian Americans: An inaccurate assumption? *Journal of Counseling Psychology, 30*, 581-588.

Sue, D. M., & Sue, D. (1985). Asian-Americans. In N. Vace, J. Wittmer, & S. DeVaney (Eds.), *Experiencing and counseling multicultural and diverse populations* (pp. 239-262). Muncie, IN: Accelerated Development.

Sue, S., & Chin, R. (1983). The mental health of Chinese-American children: Stressors and resources. In G. J. Powell, J. Yamamoto, A. Romero, & A. Morales (Eds.), *The psychosocial development of minority group children* (pp. 385-397). New York: Brunner/Mazel.

Sue, S., & Okazaki, S. (1990). Asian American educational achievements: A phenomenon in search of an explanation. *American Psychologist, 45*, 913-920.

Sue, S., Wagner, N., Ja, D., Margullis, C., & Lew, L. (1976). Conceptions of mental illness among Asian and Caucasian-American students. *Psychological Reports, 38*, 703-708.

Sung, B. L. (1985). Bicultural conflicts in Chinese immigrant children. *Journal of Comparative Family Studies, 16*, 255-269.

Sung, B. L. (1987). *The adjustment experience of Chinese immigrant children in New York City*. New York: Center for Migration Studies.

Szapocznik, H., & Kurtines, W. (1993). Family psychology and cultural diversity. *American Psychologist, 48*, 400-407.

Tamura, E. H. (1994). *Americanization, acculturation, and ethnic identity: The Nisei generation in Hawaii*. Chicago: University of Illinois Press.

Tan, D. L. (1994). Uniqueness of the Asian-American experience in higher education. *College Student Journal, 28*, 412-421.

Ting-Toomey, S. (1981). Ethnic identity and close friendship in Chinese-American college students. *International Journal of Intercultural Relations, 5*, 383-406.

Tobin, J. J., & Friedman, J. (1984). Intercultural and developmental stresses confronting Southeast Asian refugee adolescents. *Journal of Operational Psychiatry, 15*, 39-45.

Tracey, T. J., Leong, F. T. L., & Glidden, C. (1986). Help seeking and problem perception among Asian Americans. *Journal of Counseling Psychology, 33*, 331-336.

Tsang, S. (1984). The mathematics education of Asian Americans. *Journal for Research in Mathematics Education, 15*(2), 114-122.

Uba, L. (1992). Cultural barriers to American health care among Southeast Asian refugees. *Public Health Reports, 107,* 544-548.

U.S. Bureau of the Census. (1991a). *Census of population and housing, 1990: Summary Tape File 2B* (machine-readable data files). Washington, DC: Author.

U.S. Bureau of the Census. (1991b). *1990 Census: Summary Tape File 1* (machine-readable data files). Washington, DC: Author.

U.S. Department of Justice. (1990). *Sourcebook of criminal justice statistics—1989.* Washington, DC: Hindelang Criminal Justice Research Center.

U.S. Department of Justice. (1992). *Sourcebook of criminal justice statistics—1991.* Washington, DC: Hindelang Criminal Justice Research Center.

U.S. Department of Justice. (1996). *Sourcebook of criminal justice statistics—1995.* Washington, DC: Hindelang Criminal Justice Research Center.

Vigil, J. D., Yun, S., & Long, J. M. (1992, June). *Youth gangs, crime, and the Vietnamese in Orange County.* Paper presented at the convention of the Association of Asian American Studies, San Jose, CA.

Waldron, J. A., & Whittington, R. R. (1985). Aloha and ambiguity: Social work with children in Hawaii. *Child and Adolescent Social Work Journal, 2,* 258-264.

Wang, Y., Sedlacek, W. E., & Westbrook, F. D. (1992). Asian Americans and student organizations: Attitudes and participation. *Journal of College Student Development, 33,* 214-221.

West, B. E. (1983). The new arrivals from Southeast Asia. *Childhood Education, 60*(2), 84-89.

Whang, P. A., & Hancock, G. R. (1994). Motivation and mathematics achievement: Comparisons between Asian-American and non-Asian students. *Contemporary Educational Psychology, 19,* 302-322.

Yao, E. L. (1985a). Adjustment needs of Asian immigrant children. *Elementary School Guidance and Counseling, 19,* 222-275.

Yao, E. L. (1985b). A comparison of family characteristics of Asian-American and Anglo-American high achievers. *International Journal of Comparative Sociology, 26*(3/4), 198-208.

Yao, E. L. (1989). Understanding Indian immigrant learners. *Elementary School Guidance and Counseling, 23,* 298-305.

Yeh, C., & Huang, K. (1996). The collectivistic nature of ethnic identity development among Asian-American college students. *Adolescence, 31,* 645-661.

Yu, L. C. (1984). Acculturation and stress within Chinese American families. *Journal of Comparative Family Studies, 15,* 77-94.

Zhan, G. Q. (1991). *Vietnamese refugee children's global self-worth and their perceived competence.* Master's thesis, Cornell University.

5

THE ELDERLY

Their Stress, Coping, and Mental Health

PAUL T. P. WONG
K. VICTOR UJIMOTO

How do elderly Asians adapt to contemporary North American society? This question cannot be answered adequately without addressing broader issues of ethnicity, mental health, stress, and coping. This chapter begins with a discussion of the role of ethnicity in aging and then describes the demographic profile of Asian and Pacific Islander (API) American elderly. The third section presents the Resource-Congruence (R-C) Model of coping as a theoretical framework to investigate major issues of acculturation and adaptation. The main portion of the chapter examines factors affecting the adaptation and mental health of Asian American elderly. These include their cultural heritage, immigration experience/history, and stress and coping. Finally, the chapter discusses methodological issues in cross-cultural and multinational research.

THE ASIAN AND PACIFIC ISLANDER AMERICAN
ELDERLY AND THEIR HEALTH NEEDS

API Americans are a highly diverse group. Kii (1984) identified 16 Asian and 6 Pacific Islander ethnic groups. Morioka-Douglas and Yeo (1990) included more than 20 different ethnic groups in the API category. However, because most of the research on Asian American elderly has been on the Chinese and Japanese, these two ethnic groups are the focal point of our analysis. Given the similarities in culture and patterns of Asian immigration in America and Canada, we have drawn on materials from both countries. In the absence of reference to specific

Asian groups, the term "Asian Americans" is used to encompass all API groups in North America.

Kalish and Moriwaki (1973) were among the pioneers in studying elderly Asian Americans. They reported many cultural differences between elderly Asian Americans and their White counterparts. They recommended that culturally appropriate services be made available to elderly Asian Americans. In spite of the continued emphasis on the mental health needs of Asian minority elderly (Cheung, 1989; Sue & Morishima, 1982), very little research has been done on the adjustment patterns and mental health of this group.

Similarly, there has been little progress in terms of mental health services for Asian American elderly. Escovar (1983) observed the paradoxical state of affairs that "the more aware social scientists become of the problems posed by service delivery to clients from different cultural backgrounds, the less they appear to have to say about how to remedy those problems" (p. 789). A similar situation exists in Canada. There has been a lot of lip service regarding the importance of ethnicity in aging. For example, the National Workshop on Ethnicity and Aging (1988) made a wide range of recommendations including that "the concerns and needs of ethnic seniors be given priority in mental health studies for which government funding is provided [and that] funding for culturally appropriate services in the area of mental health for seniors be declared a priority" (p. 26). There is little evidence that these recommendations have been implemented. In fact, given today's social and economic climate, the mental health needs of ethnic seniors are given an even lower priority by government funding agencies as compared to 10 years ago. It is hoped that this chapter will provide the impetus for research support on ethnic aging and will stimulate adequate funding for culturally appropriate mental health services to elderly Asian Americans.

There are several reasons why the Asian American elderly warrant special attention from policymakers, health professionals, and granting agencies. First, the number of ethnic minority elderly will grow much faster than the number of White elderly in the next 50 years (Angel & Hogan, 1991), and Asian groups are growing faster than is any other ethnic minority group (Browne, Fong, & Mokuau, 1994). Second, there is a sharp contrast between traditional Asian cultures and the dominant American culture. When two cultures are drastically different in basic values and beliefs, the potential for conflict and misunderstanding is enormous. Little is known about how cultural transitions of such magnitude affect the mental and physical health of aging immigrants. Research on how the Asian elderly adjust to American society will shed light on their adaptation to the dual challenge of aging and acculturation. Third, the Asian elderly are a group at risk. As a whole, Asian Americans appear to be doing quite well economically. According to the 1990 census, the 1989 average per capita income of Asian Americans was comparable to that of Caucasian Americans ($14,000 vs. $14,900). However, this should not obscure the fact that large segments of the Asian American population remain disadvantaged and poor. For example, the final report of the Pacific/Asian Elderly Research Project (Special Services for Groups, 1978) indicated that Asian American elderly tend to have lower-status jobs and lower incomes as compared to those of the total aging population. Peralta and Horikawa (1978) reported that many of the Asian American elderly in the greater Philadelphia area had inadequate incomes, had poor health, and lacked information and access to public facilities and other sources of assistance. Yoh and Bell (1987) studied the living arrangements and service needs of Korean elderly in the United States. They identified six major difficulties: inadequate command of the English language, health conditions, loneliness, and problems related to transportation, income, and housing. According to a conference on elder abuse prevention (Nerenberg & Yap, 1986), elder abuse might be worse in the Asian community than in the general population because Asian elders in the United States often lack community support systems and do not want to report abuses to outsiders. In terms of suicide rates, the Asian elderly also are at risk. Baker (1994) reported that API American elders age 65 years or over had the highest rate of completed suicides per 100,000 seniors (11.5), followed by Hispanics (10.3), American Indian/Alaskan Natives (6.7), and African Americans (6.6).

It is important to keep in mind that the Asian American elderly are a heterogeneous group. Lee (1992) studied five groups of Asian elderly living in Chicago: Chinese, Japanese, Filipino, Korean, and Vietnamese. Lee reported that the Asian American elderly as a group are in a better socioeconomic position than other ethnic minority groups; however, there were differences among Asian Americans. For example, Chinese and Vietnamese elderly were more likely to live in poverty than were those of other ancestries. Lee also reported that Asian American elderly were underserved, if not neglected, by non-Asian social agencies. Lee urged social agencies to dispel the myth that Asian Americans represent a "homogeneous model minority." Sue and Morishima (1982) argued,

> Racial conditions also act as stressors for Asian Americans, and research and theory on the mental health of these people have often been based on faulty assumptions. By understanding the problems and needs of Asian Americans, we may be able to gain insight into broader mental health issues. (p. 3)

They considered the elderly, immigrants, refugees, and Chinatown youths as disadvantaged, vulnerable Asian American groups. Unfortunately, the mental health needs of these at-risk groups have long been overlooked by mainstream professionals and policymakers; this neglect can be attributed to the stereotyping of Chinese Americans and/or to a more subtle, unintentional form of racism. This woeful situation will likely only deteriorate in the current climate of fiscal restraints and government cutbacks on health and social services.

ETHNICITY AND AGING

Lifestyles, attitudes, life experiences, social status and affiliations, and values associated with a person's ethnicity can substantially influence aging processes among minority individuals. To fully explore the issues affecting Asian Americans, we need to have a clear understanding of the meaning and parameters of ethnicity. Ethnicity shapes both subjective perceptions and objective environments. The construct of ethnicity generally encompasses race, culture, and history. To be Chinese means more than just belonging to a race; it also means the combination of a unique set of historical events and cultural characteristics. Ethnicity often is equated with minority status on the basis of race, nationality, religion, or language (Jackson, 1980). Broadly speaking, it is based on "shared history, collective identity, sense of people-hood, unique heritage, tradition, common expectations, values, attitudes, and meaningful symbols" (Holzberg, 1982, p. 254). According to Rosenthal (1986), ethnicity may be viewed in three ways: as social inequality, as traditionalism, and as culture.

The structural perspective considers ethnic influences to be the result of the social stratification processes. Bengtson (1979) argued that "any examination of ethnicity as a factor in social behavior must begin from the premise of social stratification" (p. 15). According to the stratification model (George, 1980; McCallum, 1987), older people with a low social position tend to experience greater distress. McKenzie and Campbell (1987) found that race and socioeconomic status (SES) of older Americans affected their self-assessments of health and the number of problems experienced—which, in turn, influenced subjective well-being. In spite of considerable empirical support, the structural perspective cannot be readily applied to Chinese Americans, who come from all levels of social strata. Many Chinese began their life in America working in restaurants and "sweat shops," but their children often grew up to enter prestigious professions. Recent "investor" immigrants from Hong Kong are wealthy businessmen.

The modernization hypothesis no longer adequately differentiates between mainstream society and Asian minorities. Various parts of Asia, such as Hong Kong, Taiwan, Japan, and Korea, have made great strides at modernization, even though they still maintain their traditional cultures. Furthermore, Asian communities in America have been able to maintain some form of their traditional values over succeeding generations, and there also is some evidence of a resurgence in their cultural heritage and ethnic pride.

Some social scientists have proposed that ethnicity is basically cultural in its origin, characterized by a common heritage (e.g., Haller, 1973). Culture has been shown to be the most prominent factor in ethnic aging (Holzberg, 1982; Kalish, 1971). Discriminant analysis of an Australian sample (Shadbolt & McCallum, 1988) showed that mainstream Australians, British migrants, and non-British migrants, who were mostly from Hong Kong and Southeast Asia, differ on a range of variables. The non-British migrants with poor English skills differ the most from mainstream Australians. This result suggests a simple way of defining ethnic strata in terms of cultural and language differences from the mainstream culture.

Recent years have witnessed a growing interest in the role of ethnicity in aging (Gibson, 1988; Jackson, 1989; Palmore, 1983). Evidence is accumulating that being an ethnic minority does make a difference in the experience of aging in American society (Gelfand & Kutzik, 1979; Holzberg, 1982; Jackson, 1980;

TABLE 5.1. Size and Percentages of Asian and Pacific Islander Elderly (age 65 years or older) by Ethnic Group

Country	Total Population	Age 65 Years or Older	Percentage of Group Age 65 Years or Older	Percentage of All Asians and Pacific Islanders Age 65 Years or Older
United States	248,709,873	31,241,831	12.5	n.a.
Chinese	1,645,472	133,977	8.1	29.5
Japanese	847,562	105,932	12.5	23.3
Filipino	1,406,770	104,206	7.4	22.9
Korean	798,849	35,247	4.4	7.8
Asian Indian	815,447	23,004	2.8	5.1
Vietnamese	614,547	18,084	2.8	4.0
Cambodian	147,411	3,724	2.5	0.8
Laotian	149,014	3,697	2.5	0.8
Hmong	90,082	2,535	2.8	0.5
Thai	91,275	1,416	1.6	0.3
Other Asian	302,209	7,901	2.6	1.7
Hawaiian	211,014	10,233	4.8	2.3
Samoan	62,964	2,047	3.3	0.5
Guamanian	49,345	1,523	3.1	0.3
Other Pacific Islander	41,701	932	2.2	0.2
All Asians and Pacific Islanders	7,273,662	454,458	6.2	100.0

SOURCE: U.S. Bureau of the Census (1995).

Markides & Mindel, 1987). Holzberg (1982) emphasized the importance of learning about cultural expectations of different ethnic groups and how "these expectations and structural pressures actually mold the way in which a person perceives, defines, and seeks solutions to problems associated with aging" (p. 255). It is from this cultural perspective that we examine the adaptation of older Asian Americans.

A DEMOGRAPHIC PROFILE OF ASIAN AMERICAN ELDERLY

The most recent (1990) U.S. census revealed that since the 1980 census, API American populations had more than doubled to nearly 7.3 million or 2.9% of the total population. The percentages of increase during the same period for four of the largest Asian American groups—namely, the Chinese, Filipino, Japanese, and Korean groups—were 104.09%, 81.55%, 20.97%, and 125.07%, respectively (U.S. Bureau of the Census, 1992b). Table 5.1 shows the size and percentage of API elderly by ethnic group. The Chinese, Japanese, Filipino, and Korean elderly remain the largest groups in terms of size or percentage of all API elderly (U.S. Bureau of the Census, 1992a).

These new census figures show that Asians remain the fastest-growing ethnic group in America. This impressive growth has largely been fueled by immigration. According to the U.S. census, more than 60% of the Chinese living in America are recent immigrants. U.S. Immigration and Naturalization Service figures further indicate that the percentages of elderly immigrants from Asian countries are much higher than those from other countries. For example, 13.6% of the immigrants from mainland China are age 65 years or over, whereas only 2.8% of immigrants from non-Asian countries are seniors.

Many Asian elderly have come to America because it is the only way in which to be close to their children and maintain family ties. Based on the statistics provided by the U.S. Department of Justice from 1980 to 1984, Cheung (1989) reported that during this period, total immigrants age 60 years or over numbered 161,679. Of these, 22,317 were Chinese immigrants from China, Hong Kong, Macau, Singapore, and Taiwan. An increase in the elderly Asian population also has occurred in Canada. According to Statistics Canada (1994), an increasing number of immigrants are older. Before 1961, only 2% of the immigrants were age 45 years or over; between 1981 and 1991, 15% of the immigrants were in this age bracket. In 1991, one out of every four persons age 65 years or over in Canada was an immigrant. The data also showed that the source countries for immigrants to Canada have shifted from Europe to Asia and South America. These demographics indicate that Asian elderly in North America are a diverse and growing group and need to be treated as such in both research and interventions. The following sections discuss their stress and coping and mental health needs from the R-C Model of adaptation (Wong, 1993).

RESOURCE-CONGRUENCE MODEL OF ADAPTATION

Issues of adaptation are particularly important in aging because of multiple losses and the decline of resources that occur in old age. Immigration and cultural differences in ethnic aging complicate these issues. Interest in the role of ethnicity in adaptation and aging is a rather recent development (McCallum & Shadbolt, 1989; Rosenthal, 1986; Wong & Reker, 1985). There is a paucity of data and very little theoretical development in this area. This section presents a conceptual framework in which to examine the variables and issues of ethnic aging and adaptation. Currently, the most popular theory is the double or multiple jeopardy hypothesis (Dowd & Bengtson, 1978; Havens & Chappell, 1983; Jackson, 1985), which contends that belonging to an ethnic minority group is an additional source of stress because of the group's disadvantaged condition. For example, many Chinese, Japanese, and Filipino American elders are reluctant and fearful to use public social and health services because of language barriers, lack of information, and past discrimination (Fujii, 1976). Although ethnic minorities, especially immigrants, may indeed experience more adjustment difficulties, the double jeopardy hypothesis proves to be inadequate because ethnicity also can be regarded as a resource rather than a disadvantage (Black, 1985; Driedger & Chappell, 1987; Holzberg, 1982). For example, ethnic communities have their own systems of support and caring (Kobata, Lockery, & Moriwaki, 1980). Ethnicity can facilitate adjustment to aging because it helps maintain a sense of continuity, identity, and meaning in a foreign land.

Yee (1977) proposed a life-span developmental approach in studying elderly minorities. She suggested that learned helplessness in elderly Asian Americans could be understood in terms of their personal history, their ethnic group history, their cultural values regarding old age, and the very different set of conditions in American society. Gibson (1988) emphasized similar points. She criticized the double jeopardy hypothesis, which "deals inadequately with the personal meaning of aging, the social context of aging, and life domains such as psychological well-being and social support, as Jacqueline Jackson and Kyriakos Markides have frequently pointed out" (p. 559). She then proposed a life course perspective that takes into account personal history, social history, changing social structures, life cycles, and personal coping resources.

The R-C Model of adaptation developed by Wong (1993) promises to be heuristically useful because it takes into account cultural factors and examines both the advantages and disadvantages of ethnic aging. From this new perspective, resources and deficits can coexist (Wong, 1993) and a person can be high in both internal and external locus of control beliefs (Wong & Sproule, 1984). This dualistic emphasis differs from dichotomous thinking so prevalent in American psychological theorizing but is consistent with the Chinese tendency "to try to synthesize the constituent parts into a whole so that all parts blend into a harmonious relationship at this higher level of perceptual organization" (Yang, 1986, p. 148). One of the major issues in current stress research is determining why similar misfortunes lead one person toward distress and another toward satisfaction and resilience. The differential outcomes among individuals with similar experiences suggest the important role of mediating variables. Sue and Morishima (1982) proposed that some individuals have better personal and social resources to cope with stress, whereas others have physiological abnormalities and inadequate coping resources. They suggested the need for a diathesis-stressor-resource model of psychopathology that takes into account constitutional, racial, and cultural factors. They also emphasized the importance of person-environment fit. The present R-C Model follows the same line of thinking.

The R-C Model is an extension of the cognitive-relational model developed by Lazarus and Folkman (1984). Their main thesis was that stress is experienced only when the demands of the environment are appraised by the person as exceeding his or her resources. Wong (1993) contended that the problem does not always stem from person-environment interactions given that an individual's inner conflicts also can be a source of stress. Thus, what is actually appraised by the person is the interaction between available resources and potential stressors, which include environmental demands and intrapsychic conflicts. The importance of culture is recognized for every component of the stress process. A schematic presentation of this expanded cognitive-relational theory of stress is shown in Figure 5.1. According to this view, stress is an interactive, dynamic process that takes place in a cultural context. Notice that interactions between resources and stressors occur in appraisal, coping, and outcome. The R-C Model, which is based on the cognitive-relational view, posits that sufficient personal resources and appropriate use of these resources are the necessary and sufficient conditions for successful adaptation. A schematic presentation of the R-C Model of effective coping is shown in Figure 5.2. It begins with the development of various types of personal resources in anticipation of potential problems. When a stressful encounter does occur, ideally an individual will rationally assess his or her resources and the nature of the stressor and then use the appropriate coping strategies. The person is able to relax and conserve his or her resources once some level of success is achieved. This cycle may be repeated many times in the case of a serious or chronic adjustment problem.

Personal Resources

The key to successful adaptation, whether it is adjusting to aging or to a new culture, is to develop and maintain a sufficient stock of resources as described in Figure 5.2. Therefore, in studying the adaptation of Asian American elderly, the first question is whether they possess the necessary resources in adapting to life in North America. A related question is whether factors associated with ethnicity enhance or constrain their coping resources. The importance of personal resources in coping has gained increasing attention (Holahan & Moos, 1991; Kobasa, 1979; Moos & Billings, 1982). Most of the research has focused on psychological and social resources.

■ Psychological Resources

Images and stories about the Olympics have made it clear that the battle is won or lost in the minds and hearts of athletes. In elite competition, many contestants are at about the same physical and technical level, but the winning edge belongs to those who possess greater inner strength. The triumphant are those who can maintain confidence and concentration, can endure pain and fatigue, and have the determination and willpower to win in spite of overwhelming obstacles and odds. The same type of psychological resources are needed to cope with life stress. Kobasa (1979) emphasized three personality characteristics that help people cope with stress: the belief that they can control or influence their life events, the ability to feel deeply involved and committed in life activities that minimize feelings of alienation, and the optimistic anticipation of change as a challenge. Pearlin and Schooler (1978) found that personality characteristics such as mastery and self-esteem are important psychological resources in stress resistance. There is extensive literature on control beliefs and related constructs such as mastery and efficacy (see Wong, 1992, for a review). The health benefits of control in the elderly have received a great deal of attention (Rodin, Timko, & Harris, 1985; Schulz, 1976; Slivinske & Fitch, 1987). The role of optimism in

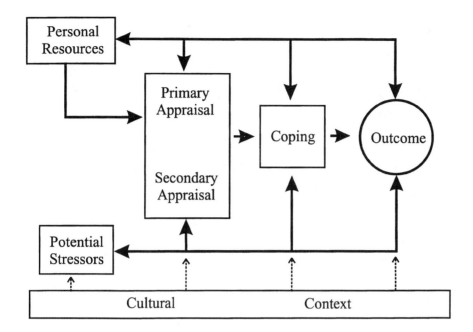

Figure 5.1. Schematic Presentation of Stress and Coping

health promotion also has been recognized (Reker & Wong, 1984; Scheier & Carver, 1985, 1987; Snyder, 1989). The contribution of personal meaning to stress resistance and successful aging is the latest addition to the study of psychological resources (Antonovsky, 1987; Reker, Peacock, & Wong, 1987; Reker & Wong, 1988; Wong, 1989; Wong & Fry, in press).

▨ Social Resources

The role of social support in buffering stress has already been well established (Cobb, 1976; Cohen & Wills, 1985; Gottlieb, 1988). The importance of social support in dealing with life stress in the elderly also has been well documented (Barrera, 1986; Krause, 1987a; Wan, 1982; Wong, 1991). Hobfoll's conservation of resources theory of social support (Hobfoll, 1988; Hobfoll, Freedy, Lane, & Geller, 1990) views social support as a major means of extending personal resources. Social resources include relationships, practical and moral social support, and social validation from significant others; these resources can be cultivated and conserved to supply individual needs. Caspi and Elder (1986), in a longitudinal study of life satisfaction in old age, emphasized that successful aging requires skills and resources. Problem-solving skills include the ability to search for information, to identify difficulties, and to generate appropriate acts to manage life crises. This personal resource was indexed by general intelligence scores and facility of language. Emotional health or resiliency is a source of resistance to the

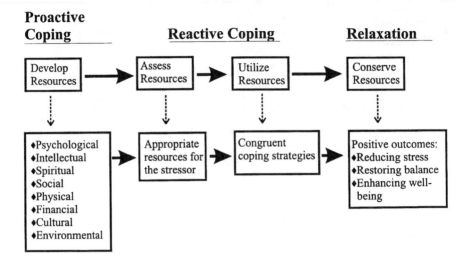

Figure 5.2. Schematic Presentation of the Resource-Congruence Model of Effective Coping

negative effects of successful life problems. Emotional health was measured by interviewers' ratings on cheerful, self-assured, and unworried scales. Social involvement was a composite index of the number of formal groups (including church) in which the individuals participate. Results suggested that the antecedents of successful aging partly involve adaptive personal resources and historical factors interacting with social conditions. Analysis of pathways showed that, for working-class women, intellectual ability predicted life satisfaction indirectly through social involvement, whereas for middle-class women, emotional health directly predicted life satisfaction. Caspi and Elder concluded,

> Adaptive resources consist of any property of the individual (e.g., intellectual ability, emotional health) or the environment (e.g., social network supports) that has the potential capacity to meet demands and lead to adequate psychological functioning. The ideal transaction between individual and environment is represented by a match between demands and resources. (p. 23)

In sum, host resistance depends on the availability of resources. One becomes vulnerable to stress to the extent that coping resources become deficient. However, it is important to realize that resources and deficits are not necessarily opposite poles on the same continuum. For example, positive and negative psychological factors are assumed to coexist in a state of dynamic tension as depicted by the Chinese symbolism of Ying-Yang. Self-confidence and self-doubt might be waging a constant tug-of-war, whereas hope and fear are vying for ascendancy. The net resources available to the person depend not on the actual amount of resources possessed but rather on the balance between resources and deficits. To enhance host resistance, one must aim at enhancing resources and reducing deficits at the same time.

The question of whether ethnic factors constitute resources or impediments to adjustment for the elderly can be more fully addressed using the R-C Model. For example, family, friends, and ethnic ties are assets in terms of social resources, whereas intergenerational conflict in an extended family and separation from ethnocultural communities are liabilities. Thus, whether ethnicity is a resource depends on factors such as the extent to which traditional values are practiced in one's family and whether one is connected with an ethnic community in the host country. In terms of psychological resources, ethnic associations or experiences can be assets and/or liabilities. For example, self-esteem is important for maintaining psychological well-being (Kaplan, 1975; Krause, 1987a; Thoits, 1983). Pride in one's heritage culture and traditional family values can contribute to a sense of self-worth and facilitate adjustment. However, self-esteem depends on self-validation and social validation (Ishiyama, 1989; Ishiyama & Westwood, 1992). Immigration threatens both types of validation because moving to a new country often means a loss of social status and supportive networks. Deficiencies in cultural competence further diminish one's self-worth, making the individual vulnerable to stress. Therefore, we need to know a great deal about the resources and deficits of Asian American elderly to determine whether ethnicity facilitates or hinders adjustment.

Potential Stressors

Accurate diagnosis of life stress is a prerequisite to its resolution. To cope effectively, one needs to know what the problems are and where they originate. Prior stress research has focused on major life events (Holmes & Rahe, 1967). This stems from the environmental bias of mainstream psychology. Unfortunately, the widely used list of major life events devised by Holmes and Rahe (1967) hardly contains any items relevant to acculturation stress. The inadequacy of the traditional measures of major life events has been critically evaluated (Wong, 1990). A comprehensive assessment of life stress was proposed by Wong (1993). The major domains of stress for such an assessment are shown in Figure 5.3. Most of the potential stressors of Asian American elderly are either intrapersonal or interpersonal. For example, unresolved conflicts between traditional beliefs and the values of contemporary society, existential crises regarding one's identity and social role, and memories about past racial abuse and concerns about discrimination are just some of the common inner tumults that might be experienced by Asian American elderly. The interpersonal domain includes common experiences such as having difficulty relating to mainstream society because of language/cultural barriers, perceived and actual prejudice, and discrimination. Stress researchers in the West have focused almost exclusively on individuals and overlooked the systemic and structural aspects of stress.

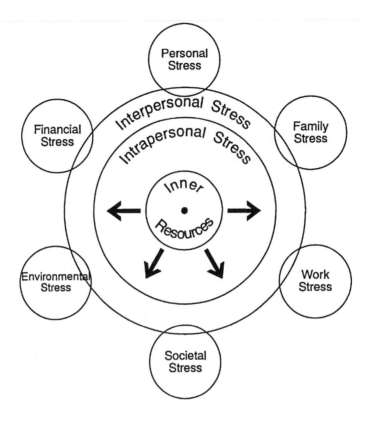

Figure 5.3. Domains of Stress in Everyday Life

Stress Appraisal

A central assumption of cognitive-relational theory is that appraisal plays a key role in the stress process. Primary appraisal is concerned with questions such as "Is there a problem?" and "What is going to happen to me?" Secondary appraisal is concerned with the assessment of the nature of the stressor as well as one's resources and coping options; one would ask questions such as "Can I handle it?" "What type of help do I need?" and "Is the situation beyond my control?" Accurate assessment is important. For example, Fitch and Slivinske (1988) proposed that the misappraisal of a lack of congruence between personal resources and environmental demands can lead to the experience of stress. Misappraisal can be due to an exaggerated assessment of the situation or one's coping capabilities. Insufficient cultural knowledge can lead to an inaccurate assessment of situational demands and the availability of external resources. Lack of confidence in one's cultural competence can generalize to other areas, resulting in lowered self-esteem. Ethnicity can be a handicap to stress appraisal unless immigrants have achieved a certain level of cultural competence in the host country.

Coping Strategies

There is an evolution of coping in terms of the history of conceptual development. Cannon's discovery of instinctual coping mechanisms, such as the fight-or-flight reaction, and Freud's concept of defense mechanisms have become a part of our cultural knowledge. Contemporary psychology has focused on behavioral and cognitive strategies (Folkman & Lazarus, 1980; Lazarus & Folkman, 1984). These conceptions of coping reflect the mechanistic bias of mainstream American psychology and do not adequately represent the coping strategies of Asian elderly. Recently, Wong and his associates (Peacock, 1992; Peacock & Wong, 1996; Peacock, Wong, & Reker, 1993; Wong & Reker, 1985; Wong, Reker, & Peacock, 1987) developed a schema-based coping inventory that includes coping strategies such as proactive, collective, existential, and spiritual strategies. The development of this coping measure was influenced by Wong's prior research on the coping behaviors of both Chinese and Caucasian elderly (Wong & Reker, 1985).

Cultural Context

The preceding discussion has shown that the cultural background of Asian Americans plays a major role in effective coping for several reasons. First, cultural expectations determine what is stressful. Second, culture predisposes an individual to react to stress in a certain fashion. Third, culture delimits resources and dictates their use. Fourth, cultural knowledge of what is appropriate coping behavior in a given situation increases the likelihood of congruent coping. Finally, it should be noted that culture also influences the expression of coping outcomes. Sue and Sue (1987) reviewed the relevant literature on how the Chinese culture influences the expression of distress. For example, Kleinman's (1979) model emphasized the pervasiveness of the cultural influence on psychopathology and illness behavior. Chinese patients' low level of complaints about psychological problems was attributed to their tendency to deny or to express affective disorders in somatic terms. In short, culture touches every aspect of the stress process.

Congruence and Successful Adaptation

The notion that person-environment fit contributes to successful aging has been discussed by a number of researchers (French, Rodgers, & Cobb, 1974; Fry, 1990; Kahana, 1975, 1982; Kahana, Liang, & Felton, 1980; Kahana, Kahana, & Riley, 1988). The basic concept is that adjustment is likely to be successful to the extent that an individual's needs and abilities are congruent with environmental demands. Kahana's (1975, 1982) model emphasized the importance of choosing environments that are congruent with an individual's needs and preferences. When such choices are not possible (for whatever reason), the person is likely to experience stress. Carp (1978-1979) proposed that one should consider both the environmental demands and the resources in meeting the needs of the elderly. Fry (1990) pointed out that the person-environment fit model "proposes a putative relation between individual and environmental resources and the mental health of the aging individual. As individual resources become limited and scarce with aging, environmental resources are presumed to become more plentiful" (p. 95). The implication of this dynamic, transactional view of person-environment fit is that the counselor should not always emphasize mastery or expect the individual to always control the situation. Once recognizing the limits of the individual's personal resources and functioning skills, therapeutic efforts must be made to mobilize external resources and social supports to compensate for any inadequacies of the older person. For the present R-C Model, we are concerned with both the congruence between demands and personal resources and the congruence between demands and coping strategies. When Asian American elderly lack adequate resources and culturally appropriate coping knowledge, they suffer a double handicap in adaptation.

CULTURAL HERITAGE OF ASIAN AMERICANS AND ADAPTATION

Because culture plays a crucial role in the adjustment of ethnic minorities, we need to examine the main features of traditional Asian cultures. Most API groups have a distinct heritage culture. Space permits only a detailed examination of the Chinese and Japanese.

The dominant influence of the Chinese culture is Confucius, who was born in 551 B.C. Confucianism was embraced by most Chinese rulers throughout the history of China (Fairbank, 1966; Fairbank & Reischauer, 1973). One of the fundamental dogmas of Confucianism is that humans are relational beings and that their behaviors should be defined by their relationships with others (Bond & Hwang, 1986; King & Bond, 1985). The so-called Five Cardinal Relations specify the relationships between sovereign and subject, father and son, elder brother and younger brother, husband and wife, and friend and friend. Socially correct behaviors are prescribed according to hierarchical arrangements in which the senior member in each relationship is accorded authority and privilege over the junior member. The father is viewed as the highest authority in the family (Ho, 1981). Conforming to parental demands and expectations is expected. This emphasis on hierarchy ensures social order, group harmony, and family stability. Chinese traits such as collective orientation, social conformity, respect for elders, and submission to authority stem directly from Confucianism.

Social Interactions

Bond and Hwang (1986) described Hwang's conceptual model, which characterized the social interactions and resource distributions in Chinese society.

Hwang employed four Chinese concepts: *quanxi, renqing, mianzi,* and *bao. Quanxi* means connections, ties, or relationships. Hwang differentiated between expressive ties and instrumental ties. The former governs the social exchange in a Chinese family in which members are expected to satisfy each other's needs. Thus, children are expected to support parents when they no longer can look after themselves. Instrumental ties are similar to networking for the purpose of achieving personal goals. Gift giving and reciprocation are important. The equity rule is necessary to maintain such ties. It is a common practice to present gifts before requesting favors, especially in dealing with those in higher positions. Such practices are considered blatant bribery in Western society.

Renqing literally means human kindness and is concerned with doing a favor or showing kindness to others. Renqing is based on affective (*ganqing*) and practical considerations. *Ganqing* refers to how one feels toward another person and how much one values his or her relationship with that person. Practical considerations involve the likelihood of reciprocation. In Western society, Chinese Americans are likely to be disappointed that ganqing seldom matters in social interactions and that kind deeds and warm feelings often are not reciprocated in business transactions. *Mianzi* literally means face. It is concerned with protecting one's dignity and self-esteem. In social interactions, *li*, which entails politeness, good manners, and courteous rituals, serves as an important safeguard for each other's face. Developing and maintaining quanxi, such as exchange of gifts and showing proper respect, have something to do with face. All kinds of defensive mechanisms are used to save each other's face. Pretending nothing has happened, playing down the event, making self-effacing remarks, and expressing dissatisfaction in subtle and indirect ways are some of the coping strategies to protect mianzi. Direct rejection and criticism, which is commonplace in North America, can be devastating to a Chinese because of his or her concerns about mianzi. The abrasive, aggressive, and confrontational style of social interaction so prevalent in American business and professional circles can be very stressful to first-generation Asian Americans. *Bao* or *baoying* has to do with reciprocating a favor. It is a deeply ingrained concept. Bao often is extended beyond individuals. For example, if A has done B a great favor, then B would treat A's family with special kindness, even if A had passed away. Most of these concepts, which make social interactions smooth and predictable in the Chinese culture, are foreign to the American culture. That is one of the reasons why elderly Chinese Americans find it difficult to socialize and interact with mainstream American society.

Filial Piety and Respect for the Elderly

Filial piety has long been a cardinal cultural norm in Asian societies influenced by Confucius (Hsu, 1971). It has been institutionalized in China, Japan, and Korea for a long time and involves many obligations. This norm involves the expectation that children have successful careers to honor their parents and ancestors. It also is expected that a married son and his wife support and serve the needs and wishes of the husband's parents (Lang, 1946; Lin, 1985; Osako & Liu, 1986; Sung, 1990). Old age to the Chinese is a source of status (J. Chen, 1980; Cheng, 1978; Cheung, Cho, Luan, Tang, & Yan, 1980; Ikels, 1983; Lum, Cheung, Cho, Tang, & Yau, 1980; Nagasawa, 1980). The image of the Chinese aged is one of honor, authority, and custodians of the cultural heritage. As such, aging parents expect to be respected by their children. Generally, Asians are more likely to practice filial piety than are their Caucasian counterparts. For example, in a study comparing Korean American and White American caregivers, Sung (1994) found that obligation, affection, and reciprocity were the three most frequently mentioned motivational responses by both Korean and American caregivers. However, respect for parents, family harmony, and filial sacrifice emerged as important motivational responses for the Korean sample only.

Traditional Japanese Culture

Similar to the Chinese, traditional Japanese culture emphasizes discipline and perseverance. The Japanese term *gaman* was most frequently cited by the Japanese elderly in the Ujimoto, Nishio, Wong, and Lam (1992) study as the most important factor that contributed to their successful aging. According to Kobata (1979), gaman is literally translated as "self-control." The outward manifestation of this is the tendency to suppress emotions, whether positive or negative. In traditional Japanese society, gaman was seen as virtuous, and Kobata argued that "the tendency to suffer in silence with a great deal of forbearance provides some insights into the nature of the family as the source for dealing with problems rather than the outside service provider" (p. 100). However, this practice can have a negative effect on the elderly. For example, Tomita (1994) pointed out that Japanese culture encourages the sick or weak to gaman. This quiet suffering makes it more difficult for social service practitioners to identify Japanese victims of elder abuse.

Associated with the concept of gaman, or self-control, is *enryo*. According to Kobata (1979), "the norm of *enryo* includes, but is not limited to, reticence, self-effacement, deference, humility, hesitation, and denigration of one's self and possessions" (p. 100). Because of the plethora of terms that can be associated with enryo, it is extremely difficult to assess the supportive aspects of social support activities of the Japanese elderly. For example, it often becomes difficult to differentiate between ritualistic behavior and genuinely supportive behavior in the Japanese social interaction context. As Kobata noted, "The concept had its origins in the cultural norms of knowing one's position in relation to another when interacting with others perceived as 'inferior' or 'superior' to oneself" (p. 100). Thus, in interactions with authority figures such as doctors, the Japanese elderly very often do not volunteer their true feelings of how they feel.

The extent to which various cultural values are retained by the Chinese, Japanese, and Korean elderly is related to the socialization processes experienced earlier, whether in the country of emigration or in the host society. Sugiman and

Nishio (1983) argued that the retention of cultural norms also is a function of the immigrant's attitudes toward acculturation. Consequently, the Issei (i.e., first-generation Japanese immigrants) made only modest demands on their children to fulfill filial obligations. This view appears to be supported even in contemporary Japan. The *Japan Times* reported that the elderly in Japan look less to their children to look after them and prefer their spouses to take care of them ("Elderly Look Less to Children," 1987). Another aspect to consider is support, or the lack thereof, for one's cultural heritage in the host country. For example, the lack of institutional support for the transmission of Japanese culture and language during the time of Japanese internment cannot be compared to today's multicultural environment that encourages the retention of the traditional cultural heritage.

IMMIGRATION EXPERIENCES AND HISTORY

The adjustment and well-being of any ethnic minority cannot be fully understood apart from its social history. This point is illustrated by a brief review of the Chinese and Japanese immigration experiences in Canada. According to Li (1988), the experiences of Chinese Canadians can be grouped into three distinct periods: the pre-exclusion era (1858-1923), the exclusion era in which no Chinese were allowed into Canada (1923-1947), and the post-1947 era in which the Chinese gained their civil rights. Each of these periods left a lasting effect on the well-being of the first-generation elderly Chinese. An interesting observation made by Li (1988) was that the Chinese who came to North America in the early 19th century were viewed "as aliens who could be utilized in lower-paying jobs but were not to be trusted as social equals" (p. 20). The Chinese were perceived to be mere "sojourners" and not permanent immigrants. They were subject to racial abuse and discrimination. White workers were concerned about Chinese laborers' undercutting wages and working long hours. Anti-Asian racism resulted in the Chinese Immigration Act of 1885, which imposed a head tax of $50 on every Chinese immigrant entering Canada. In 1900, the head tax was increased to $500. Other restrictive legislation followed that denied the Chinese their basic citizenship rights. Evidence of systemic discrimination of the Chinese in Canada was documented by Li (1988). The Chinese were allowed to participate in labor-intensive industries but were effectively excluded from professional occupations. These restrictions resulted in a labor market that was highly segmented into a low-wage, highly exploited sector made up mostly of Asians and a higher-paying job sector monopolized by White workers.

The early immigrant experiences of the first-generation Japanese were similar to those of these Chinese pioneers. Japanese Canadian history also can be classified according to the legal status of Japanese Canadians. Shimpo (1973) suggested the following four periods: free immigration (1877-1907), controlled immigration (1908-1940), deprived civil rights (1941-1948), and restored civil rights (1949-present). The first period can be characterized as one in which racial conflict based on economic competition gradually developed to such an extent that it resulted in the race riot of 1907 in Vancouver. General hostility against Chinese and Japanese immigrants in British Columbia was already on the increase when immigration restriction was legislated in 1885. The provincial government took steps to disenfranchise the Japanese in 1896. The Chinese had already been disenfranchised at the provincial level in 1885. Preventing the Chinese and Japanese from participating in the electoral process was a form of social control that clearly illustrates the racist ideology of the time. Such "institutional racism" (Wilson, 1973) was in force until after World War II.

South Asian immigrants began to arrive in Canada just as the anti-Asian hostilities were on the rise. Buchignani (1980) observed that South Asians were identified as part of the "Asian menace." They faced formidable discriminatory barriers that prevented them from productive participation in Canadian society. Although there was a ban on South Asian immigration between 1909 and 1947, Buchignani (1980) noted that wives and dependent children of legal South Asian residents were permitted to immigrate after 1920. The Chinese in Canada before World War II, however, were denied the conjugal family as a result of the anti-Chinese policy of the time. In the case of the Japanese, the Gentlemen's Agreement of 1908 restricted immigration to only four specified classes of people (Woodsworth, 1941).

Since the end of World War II, there has been a fundamental shift in the treatment of Asians in Canada. For the South Asians, the formal barriers to citizenship and the franchise were removed in 1947 and 1948. Similarly, the Chinese and Japanese gained access to citizenship and to the rights and privileges accorded Canadian citizens. Although the formal barriers to equality have been removed, subtle forms of racism and discrimination still are manifested in Canadian society.

It can be seen from the preceding account that there was a great difference in the political and social climates before and after World War II. Because of these differences, it is impossible to generalize regarding the well-being of Asian Canadian elderly of those who recently immigrated to those who came before World War II. It is even difficult for us to comprehend the psychological impact of years of systemic racial discrimination, economic exploitation, and deprivation of basic human rights on Canadian Asian elderly. The history of immigrants provides the necessary backdrop for understanding the social and political climate of North America. Some of the anti-immigrant, anti-Asian forces still are here, but they operate under the guise of nationalism or patriotism. Historical events also are important in understanding the immigration experiences of seniors. Yeo and Hikoyeda (1992) conducted a cohort analysis of the historical profiles of Chinese, Filipino, Mexican, and African American elders. These profiles indicate that many of the elders from all four samples have experienced racism, discrimination, segregation, and violence. These massive discontinuities in their lifetimes might have significantly influenced their self-esteem, health beliefs, and attitudes toward service providers.

POTENTIAL STRESSORS FACING
ASIAN AMERICAN ELDERLY

We have briefly described the R-C Model and shown how ethnicity can have both a positive and a negative impact on adaptation. We now examine the available empirical evidence from the conceptual framework of the R-C Model.

The primary stressors experienced by Asian Americans discussed by Sue and Morishima (1982) are culture conflict, minority status, and social change. In an extensive study of the needs of Chinese, Japanese, Korean, and Filipino Americans, Kim (1978) found that language/cultural barriers, low income, and employment problems were common. Lack of proficiency in English was of particular concern to Chinese Americans. Racism and discrimination also were problems. As reported by Okuley (1992), the U.S. Commission on Civil Rights recently issued a report titled "Civil Rights Issues Facing Asian Americans in the 1990s." It clearly states that Asian Americans, regardless of their levels of education, still face widespread prejudice and discrimination. Economic competition with Asian countries, the resentment of perceived success of Asian Americans, and scapegoating during economic recession are some of the causes of bigotry and violence against Asian Americans.

For elderly Asian Americans, these stressors are compounded by problems related to aging. In her review of the literature on the Chinese elderly living in the United States, Cheung (1989) identified several common problems experienced by elderly Chinese Americans. These included isolation, alienation, poverty, loss of power, lack of language proficiency and education, lack of access to services, immobility and transportation problems, lack of respect and caring, fear of racial discrimination and assimilation into a foreign culture, and health problems. Although some of these problems are common to all aged people, most of the stressors are unique to immigrant elderly.

A number of studies have identified poverty, cheap labor, unemployment, and low income as problems for the Asian elderly (Carp & Kataoka, 1976; Chen, 1979; Cheng, 1978; Fujii, 1976; Wong, 1984; Yu & Wu, 1985). For example, Chen (1979) interviewed older Chinese Americans living in hotel rooms in Los Angeles's Chinatown. The study provided clear evidence of poverty in terms of poor living conditions, malnutrition, and dependence on social security as their major source of income. These seniors lived in isolation and loneliness with little or no support from their children. Chen's study brings to mind a vivid picture of frail Chinese elderly living alone in dingy, dirty, cluttered rooms filled with the putrid smell of garbage, rotten food, and urine. They have lived a hard life full of discrimination, alienation, and backbreaking, low-paying jobs. With no family members to care for them and with very little government assistance, they struggle on their own to get through each day. In their old age, they live in isolation and often die alone. They can be found in almost any city in North America. They are a forgotten people because they do not have any political clout or any interest group to speak on their behalf. Income level, as well as health, has been consistently related to psychological distress in the elderly (George, 1980; Palmore, Burchett, Fillenbaum, George, & Hallman, 1985). Low SES not only means more strains and distress but also means fewer resources to help cope with life stress (Kessler, 1979; Krause, 1987b). The financial difficulties faced by many Asian American elderly is a serious problem that needs to be addressed.

Immigration, Acculturation, and Stress

In addition to the preceding social and economic hardships experienced by Asian American elderly, immigrants and refugees face additional stressors. The clashing of different cultures generates stress and tension. The greater the disparity between the immigrant culture and the host culture, the greater the acculturative stress (Berry & Annis, 1974; Kunz, 1981). Numerous studies have already shown that immigration, particularly from a non-Western culture, can be stressful and might have long-term, adverse psychological effects (Brislin, 1981; Handlin, 1951; Murphy, 1977; Nann, 1982). Some of the problems associated with immigration include role conflicts (Naditch & Morrissey, 1976), status loss (Abramson, 1966), loss of self-esteem (Padilla, Wagatsuma, & Lindholm, 1985), intergenerational conflicts (Cheung, 1989; Ikels, 1983; Yamamoto, 1968), and the loss of meaning (Marris, 1980; Westwood & Lawrence, 1990).

Nicassio, Solomon, Guest, and McCullough (1986) differentiated between immigration stress and acculturative stress of refugees. The former includes life events such as the loss of property and relatives in their homeland and confinement in a refugee camp prior to emigration. The latter refers to adjustment difficulties such as learning to speak English, finding a job, conflict over Indochinese and American ways of behavior, and not having enough money for basic necessities. Nicassio et al. reported that immigration stress and a lack of English proficiency were associated with depressive symptoms and that English proficiency reduced the impact of acculturative stress on depression. The National Workshop on Ethnicity and Aging (1988) also recognized the stressful experiences of immigrant seniors who came to Canada as sponsored dependents under the family reunification program. They are sponsored by their adult children, who often are recent immigrants still struggling to get established in the host country. The workshop described the special needs of sponsored dependents:

> Some immigrant seniors encounter financial hardship. During an up to ten-year period, sponsors are financially responsible for their dependents. Sponsorship sometimes becomes a great burden for families. If family circumstances change or the sponsorship threatens to break down, immigrant seniors can find themselves in extremely problematic situations.
>
> Also, the majority have only small pensions from their homelands or none at all. In any case, no immigrant senior can collect a Canadian government old age pension for ten years after becoming a landed immigrant. As a result, they might be unhappy in Canada, unable to return home, ineligible for financial

assistance, unable to speak English or French, and ashamed to ask friends or ethnocultural associations for help. (p. 25)

There is considerable evidence of acculturation stress in Chinese Americans (Yu, 1984; Yu & Harburg, 1980), Korean Americans (Hurh & Kim, 1984; Kim, Kim, & Hurh, 1991; Moon & Pearl, 1991), and Southeast Asian refugees (Nicassio et al., 1986; Strand & Jones, 1985). In one of the early studies on elderly Chinese immigrants in Los Angeles, Wu (1975) found that they experienced a wide range of practical and psychological problems in adjusting to life in America. Language barriers and lack of transportation and leisure time activities were cited as the most serious problems. They also experienced the difficulties of role reversal in the family and the loss of social status. Morton, Stanford, Happersett, and Molgaard (1992) studied the relationship between acculturation and functional impairment among Chinese and Vietnamese elderly; they reported that the level of acculturation and structural assimilation emerged as major contributors to functional impairment in both groups.

Similarly in Canada, a recent survey of the Chinese community in metro Toronto ("Racial Discrimination," 1992) showed that 63% felt there was some prejudice toward them by the majority culture and 24% said a great deal or quite a bit of prejudice was directed toward them. Many of them experienced discrimination on the job, in stores, and in public places. Among the respondents, 52% felt that prejudice toward the Chinese in Toronto had remained about the same, whereas 33% felt that it was increasing. Many felt that they will never be accepted in Canadian society because they are a visible minority. Chinese are among the best and the worst educated in Toronto. In Chinatown, there still are many immigrant pieceworkers who work long hours for very low wages because they do not know enough English to find better jobs. About 70% of the homeworkers are Chinese. In Canada, many Asian immigrants are unable to receive old age security because they need to establish residency for 10 years before they qualify. Recession and financial hardships exacerbate intergenerational conflict and increase the likelihood of elder abuse. Some aging parents have been forced out of their family homes by their adult sons or daughters because of irreconcilable conflicts.

Elderly Korean immigrants face similar adjustment problems (Kiefer et al., 1985; Kim, 1978; Moon & Pearl, 1991). In addition to culture shock, their problems often include financial difficulties and the lack of control over their living conditions. Successful adjustment was found to be positively related to level of education, length of residence in the United States, and a multigenerational household structure (Kiefer et al., 1985). Kim et al. (1991) summarized their difficulties as follows:

When elderly immigrants come to the United States, their immigrant status generally signifies the following three types of disadvantaged experience in the United States: (1) the substantial loss of preimmigration socio-economic resources or ties, (2) the continuous attachment to significant parts of their preimmigration lifestyle and belief system, and (3) the limited experience of Americanization. (p. 234)

These disadvantages translate to decreased coping resources and increased stress. Kim et al. (1991) reported that Korean immigrants tend to retain their social and cultural ties and only become barely Americanized regardless of the length of residence in the United States. They generally do not speak English and remain unfamiliar with the American way of life. This handicap makes it more difficult for Korean elderly to adjust to the aging process and makes them more dependent on adult children. Moon and Pearl (1991) reported that elderly Korean immigrants in Los Angeles exhibited less alienation than did their counterparts in Oklahoma because Los Angeles has a larger Korean community. This finding suggests that adjustment problems might be negatively related to the size and cohesiveness of the ethnic community. The study also showed that older Korean immigrants felt more alienated than did younger Korean immigrants. One plausible explanation is that older immigrants have stronger roots in traditional beliefs and experience more difficulty adjusting to a new culture.

A different set of stressors face Indochinese refugees. Some of them suffer from both acculturation stress and posttraumatic stress (Kinzie et al., 1990; Kroll et al., 1989). Many also have experienced economic problems during the early stages of resettlement (Strand & Jones, 1985). Tran (1992) studied relationships between SES, age, gender, ethnicity, and adjustment patterns among three groups of Indochinese refugees: Chinese Vietnamese, lowland Laotians, and Vietnamese. The results showed that education, occupation, gender, age, and length of residence in the United States were significantly related to adjustment. Men had a lower level of adjustment than did women. Older refugees have greater difficulties adjusting to the host society. They have more disadvantages than do their younger counterparts because they have lost their properties, positions, and careers and it is too late and too difficult to reestablish themselves in a new culture. From the perspective of exchange theory, older refugees also lack the social and economic resources to maintain their well-being (Dowd, 1983; Tran, 1991). It is not surprising that older Indochinese refugees tend to have a higher level of physical and mental dysfunctioning as compared to their younger counterparts (Lin, Tazuma, & Masuda, 1979; Rumbaut, 1985).

Cultural Transition and the Changing Role of the Asian American Elderly

Cultural transition remains the greatest challenge facing older Asian immigrants. In traditional Chinese culture, elders are valued and respected. They exercise considerable authority over the younger generations, even when their adult children are married and maintain separate households. Traditional values, including respect for the elderly, are replaced by a different set of values in North

America. Individualism and the nuclear family are accepted as the norm; youth and productivity are valued over age and experience. Research has shown that veneration of the elderly is inversely related to modernization (Maxwell & Silverman, 1980). The image of the elderly in North America is largely a negative one (Bengtson, Reedy, & Gordon, 1985). It is difficult for Asian elderly to feel at home in a society where the elderly are devalued and marginalized. It is even more difficult for them to accept the loss of respect from their children and grandchildren.

Young people in North America can generally support themselves and are less dependent on their parents. In many immigrant families, the elderly have to depend on their adult children financially. Moving to an adult child's home can make life very difficult for aging parents because it further undermines their self-respect and authority. Asian elders' lack of knowledge of English makes them dependent on their children, who have received a Western-style education. Those who fail to adjust to role reversal are likely to experience a high level of intergenerational conflict and life stress. Yee (1992) examined the effect of cultural transition on elders in Southeast Asian refugee families. She pointed out that migration to a new culture often changes the definition of life stages. For example, many Asian immigrants discover that they are too young to be considered as elderly by the American societal definition of seniors because they are not yet 50 years of age. Furthermore, they no longer are able to perform the traditional roles of elders in the host culture. Their credibility in advising younger family members also is diminished by their deficiency in English and cultural competence. For immigrant women, their situation is even more discouraging. Typically, these women stay at home to provide household and child care services so that younger members of the family can go to work. As a result, they are isolated at home, with no opportunity to learn the English language and acquire cultural knowledge. When the younger members of the family become more acculturated, these older women find themselves not only strangers in a new country but also strangers in their own homes.

Intergenerational Conflict

Contrary to the common assumption that Chinese elderly are well respected and well cared for by their adult children, there is mounting evidence of intergenerational conflict in the Chinese family. Many Chinese seniors still hang on to the unrealistic expectations of filial duties from their adult children in North America, where belief in filial piety has been undermined by a more individualistic orientation. Many older Chinese American elderly believe that traditional values about family, aging, and filial piety should continue, even when the traditional Chinese social structure no longer exists in America (Cheng, 1978; Markides & Mindel, 1987). Because of different cultural expectations, Chinese elderly often are frustrated and confused by the way in which they are treated (Cheung, 1989). Different rates of acculturation create more distance between the elderly, who cling to their traditional culture, and their children, who are more likely to embrace American cultural norms (Yu, 1983).

Kim et al. (1991) reported that Korean immigrants encounter a great deal of conflict and difficulty in practicing filial piety in the United States. Goode (1963) pointed out that as a society becomes industrialized, the family kinship system changes toward the conjugal family (i.e., the nuclear family). For Koreans who have immigrated to a highly industrialized American society, their traditional family system has undergone a similar change. However, despite this change, most Korean immigrants still are committed to filial obligation and maintain strong kinship ties. Married children are expected to take in and care for their aging parents whenever necessary. This adaptation of the traditional family system is characterized as the extended conjugal family. It is difficult for the Korean family to fulfill the traditional expectation of filial piety. The expectation that married children and their spouses should sacrifice their marital lives by caring for their parents creates pressure for the married children and severely strains intergenerational relationships. Kim et al. (1991) proposed that for aging parents to reduce adjustment problems, they need to adjust their cultural beliefs and accept a more limited range of filial obligation to physical care and social-psychological comfort. This realistic adjustment will facilitate coping and improve their relationships with their married children and spouses.

Another major source of conflict involves child-rearing practices. Asian seniors often are shocked and saddened by the attitude and behavior of their American-born grandchildren. The youngsters' lack of respect for both parents and grandparents, their rejection of traditional Chinese culture and language, and their total identification with American youth culture are matters of grave concern to Asian grandparents. Chinese American elderly are quite aware of the social problems such as sexual promiscuity, teenage pregnancy, drug abuse, AIDS, and drunken driving. These seniors are concerned not only about the decline of traditional Chinese values but also about what they perceive as the destructive influence of Western culture on their grandchildren. Many Chinese elderly believe that the Chinese culture is superior because it has survived more than 5,000 years. They are convinced that traditional Chinese virtues, such as being family minded, socially harmonious, self-restrained, and conscientious (Yang, 1986), are far more beneficial to young people than are the undisciplined, self-absorbed, pleasure-seeking tendencies of the average American youth. They are proud of their cultural heritage, which they believe provides enduring moral principles necessary for survival in a rapidly changing world. Accordingly, Asian elderly are eager to pass on traditional values to their grandchildren. Caring for family members, self-discipline, hard work, and striving to make something of one's life can have a positive influence on the younger generation. In fact, grandparents can be a useful source of wisdom and inspiration as they share the family history and their own life experiences with the young (Wong, 1995; Wong & Watt, 1991). However, conflict can occur when they try to assert their authority over young people whose sense of filial piety often has lessened with acculturation.

COPING RESOURCES AND STRATEGIES

Aging may be viewed as a process of adaptation to change. "The process of aging is lifelong, requiring the individual to adapt constantly to the fact of his or her changing capabilities" (Ikels, 1983, p. 241). In later years, adaptation becomes more demanding because of multiple losses and continued decline in various capabilities. How do Asian Americans manage to adapt to the dual task of aging and acculturation? How does their cultural heritage affect the adaptation outcomes?

According to Markus and Kitayama (1991), cultural differences in construals of the self, others, and their interdependence can influence the nature of individual experiences. Many Asian cultures emphasize the relatedness and interdependence of individuals, whereas the American culture construes the self as independent. This difference between East and West has profound implications for coping. From the Eastern perspective, coping is a collective effort, and maintaining harmony is more desirable than is problem solving. From the Western perspective, coping is largely a solo effort aimed at changing each problematic situation. Given these cultural differences, coping strategies downgraded by the Western culture often are valued by Chinese seniors. For example, passive acceptance is generally considered a weakness to the Western mind, whereas it is a virtue to the traditional Chinese elderly. Taoist philosophy has encouraged passive acceptance of change and endurance in the midst of adversity. Wu (1975) found that the Chinese traditional values of endurance, frugality, and religious faith helped elderly Chinese immigrants to adjust to the difficulties of life in the new world.

Whereas Westerners favor internal locus of control, the Chinese are more likely to make external attributions for both positive and negative outcomes. Hsien, Shybut, and Lotsof (1969) found that Hong Kong Chinese had a stronger external orientation on the Rotter's Scale than did Anglo-Americans. Lao (1977) found that Chinese students had a stronger belief in "powerful others" than did their American counterparts. Lee (1985) found that interpersonal difficulties were attributed to *yuan,* which roughly means relationship as preordained by fate or providence; this is a defense mechanism that minimizes blame. The Chinese also have a tendency to give credit to others and make self-effacing attributions after success. However, endorsement of external beliefs does not necessarily mean a lack of internal control or self-reliance. This external orientation simply reflects the socialization process of the Chinese that promotes respect of authority and acceptance of yuan (Bond, 1983, 1986). There are very few studies that have explicitly examined ethnic/cultural factors in coping. Cheung (1986) provided a useful review of the coping patterns of the Chinese, and the major studies reviewed by her are summarized in the following.

Hwang (1977, 1978, 1979) studied the coping behaviors of married men in Taiwan. He discovered four major coping strategies. First, *self-reliance* includes facing the problem, striving and persevering, and maintaining self-confidence. Perseverance (*ren-nai*) emphasizes the virtue of endurance, tolerance, patience, and persistence. Second, *social support* includes drawing on one's own social resources, especially relatives and friends. Third is *prayer and appealing to supernatural power.* Fourth, *acceptance* is based on the Taoist philosophy of accepting reality and letting nature take its course. Hwang also found that his participants often employed several strategies in dealing with their problems. Cheung (1986) commented that most of the coping strategies employed by Taiwanese men were related to cognitive processes. Active problem-solving strategies were more often employed by younger participants from a higher SES. Cheung, Lee, and Chan (1983) studied the coping strategies of university students in Hong Kong. They identified the following types of coping: *psychological endurance,* which includes strategies such as telling oneself to calm down and accepting or trying to forget the problem, and *active coping,* which includes analyzing the problem and resetting goals. These self-reliant, cognitive solutions were used to deal with mild problems such as feeling anxious or empty. However, when problems were severe, individuals tended to seek consultation and professional help. Cheung, Lau, and Wong (1984) found that most of the psychiatric patients in Hong Kong initially used self-directed methods such as controlling oneself, ignoring or avoiding the problem, and passive endurance. Cheung (1986) concluded that the tendency to resort to self-directed cognitive coping strategies may be understood in terms of the Confucian tradition of self-discipline, which emphasizes the virtue of controlling one's own mind and maintaining an even temperament so that one is not easily disturbed. She also suggested that self-control and frustration tolerance, which are emphasized in the Chinese culture, can be a source of resistance to stress.

In contrast to the Western emphasis on instrumental action and problem solving, Asian elderly favor existential coping. From the hardships of life and from the painful lessons of history, they have learned that being philosophical about unavoidable suffering can make it more bearable. Another interesting finding is that Chinese elderly tend to use a variety of coping strategies. This is consistent with the Chinese tendency to be holistic, eclectic, practical, and cautious (Yang, 1986); they would do everything possible to make life easier. Wong and Reker (1985) compared a sample of first-generation elderly Chinese immigrants to their Caucasian counterparts in subjective well-being and coping strategies. The authors reported that the Chinese sample rated growing old in Canada a more stressful experience, reported lower psychological well-being, and employed more palliative strategies (i.e., trying to ignore or forget the problem) and more external strategies (i.e., trying to get help from family and friends) than did Caucasians. They also found that Chinese elderly employed a greater number of strategies from various categories but perceived their coping as being less efficacious. In a subsequent study, Wong and Ujimoto (1988) performed a more detailed comparison using a larger sample of elderly Chinese Canadians and Caucasians. Assessing life satisfaction and coping strategies, Wong and Ujimoto found that in most specific domains, such as family and government services, the Chinese elderly reported lower satisfaction. However, with respect to general satisfaction with life as a whole, the Chinese scored higher. The results also showed that the Chinese elderly employed more coping strategies in every coping category (i.e., internal, external, palliative, existential, preventive) except the religious coping category, in which the Caucasians scored higher. The Chinese depended equally on internal and external coping strategies, whereas the Caucasians employed significantly more internal strategies than external ones. Generally, the Chinese elderly tended to try harder and use a greater variety of coping strategies.

Kim (1978) reported that different Asian American groups differed in coping strategies. When asked the hypothetical question as to where they would seek help for mental illness, Chinese Americans were most likely to use public and professional resources such as hospitals and doctors, whereas Japanese Americans were most dependent on private resources such as family and friends. Koreans and Filipino Americans responded somewhere in between. Desbarats (1986) investigated differences in adaptation between Sino-Vietnamese and ethnic Vietnamese refugees. However, the dependent variables actually measured patterns of acculturation rather than coping. She found that ethnic Vietnamese refugees were superior in the use of English and in taking vocational training, whereas Sino-Vietnamese were more likely to find their first jobs through the ethnic community. Desbarats concluded that Chinese ethnicity had an adverse effect on adaptation. However, this conclusion is based on the faulty assumption that the greater the assimilation, the better the adaptation. The author failed to recognize the adaptive values of different types of acculturation and different stages of racial/cultural identity (Sue & Sue, 1990).

Ethnic Community and Social Support

The importance of support from one's own ethnic community needs to be recognized as a major protective factor in acculturation stress. Minority elderly are particularly inclined to be associated with people with the same ethnic background (Hoyt & Babchuk, 1981; Lin, Simeone, Ensel, & Kuo, 1979). Older Chinese immigrants always have tried to maintain their traditional values and customs through association with their peer group (Cheung, 1989). They often take an active part in Chinese ethnocultural associations or Chinese churches. Many Chinese elderly prefer to live in Chinatown so that they can speak Chinese, socialize with other Chinese, and consult traditional Chinese doctors and herbalists. Their tendency to seek help from the ethnic community partially explains their underutilization of mainstream health and social services. In a study of Chinese Americans in Washington, D.C., Kuo and Tsai (1986) found a positive relationship between stress and psychiatric symptoms but also found that non-kin social supports, such as friends and involvement in Chinese associations, had a stronger negative correlation with symptoms. These results showed that active cultivation of social networks protects immigrants from distress and psychological impairment.

Family Support

Close kinship ties in traditional Chinese families satisfy individuals' needs for intimacy and provide social support against the adverse effects of stress (Hsu, 1973). Family support, in terms of love and encouragement, advice, and tangible help, plays a major role in caring for the old and the young (Li, 1985) and in maintaining mental health (Cheung, 1986). Chinese mental patients typically rely on family members before seeking professional help (Cheung et al., 1984; Lin, Tardiff, Doretz, & Goresky, 1978). Research in Canada has documented the salience of ethnicity in family support. For example, Tseng and Wu (1985); England (1986); Chappell, Strain, and Blandford (1986); Driedger and Chappell (1987); Disman (1987); and Ujimoto (1987a, 1987b, 1988, 1991) have found that family support plays an important role in caring for the old in Asian groups.

Many Chinese Americans believe in filial responsibilities, but they do not always practice what they believe (Yu, 1983). Many overseas Chinese continue to provide various forms of support to their aging parents, although not to the extent expected by their parents. Elderly Chinese immigrants tend to depend on their adult children for psychological, financial, and other types of support (Yu & Harburg, 1980; Yu & Wu, 1985). However, meeting the financial and housing needs of elderly relatives depends on the employment status, marital status, and gender of the adult children. Yu and Wu (1985) found that married, employed females were more likely to give money to their parents and in-laws than were single, unemployed females. Employed respondents reported less discomfort in meeting the needs of elderly relatives.

With respect to other Asian groups, Blust and Scheidt (1988) conducted a study on the perceptions of filial responsibility by elderly Filipino widows and their primary caregivers and found that the widows' reports of actual support received exceeded their expectations. Interestingly, daughters, the primary caregivers, held higher filial expectations than did their mothers. This indicates that daughters accept and practice various filial responsibilities such as providing financial aid and personal care and showing respect, warmth, and affection. The result suggests that the widows might have lowered their expectations to avoid disappointments. Tran (1991) studied the importance of family living arrangements on social adjustment in elderly Indochinese refugees in the United States. Tran found that those who lived within the nuclear or extended family were more satisfied than those living outside the family context. This result suggests that living with the family is a major source of life satisfaction.

Asian American seniors prefer to live in their home countries. They often reluctantly move to North America to be close to their children. Many of them still believe that depending on their children in older age is the proper thing to do. They expect their adult children to take care of them to the same degree that the children were cared for when they were young. Institutionalization is not an acceptable alternative because it means rejection and abandonment by their children. However, because of the potential conflicts and difficulties of living with their children, they are prepared to live in separate residences until they no longer can manage on their own. Ikels (1983) reported that Hong Kong elderly were apprehensive of moving to America because they were afraid of separation, financial problems, and having to spend old age in nursing homes. They found life in Hong Kong to be more enjoyable. They would consider moving to America to be with their children only when they no longer could manage on their own. Coresidence was the preferred alternative to institutionalization for these frail Chinese elderly. The data on living arrangements tend to reflect these attitudes. Using data from the 1980 U.S. census, Kamo and Zhou (1994) showed that elderly Japanese and Chinese were more likely to live in extended family households than were White Hispanic elderly. The results also showed that, for the Asian American elderly, the lower their level of acculturation, the greater the likelihood of living in an extended family household.

Although filial piety continues to be accepted in various Asian American communities, its practice has been on the decline. Hendricks and Leedham (1989) made the astute observation that filial piety is "nearly always undergirded by an ironclad control over whatever younger people aspire to. Principles of veneration are likely to result from the leverage older people have to ply" (p. 7). It is less likely that the elderly will exercise resource control in North America, where the younger generation is less dependent on the elderly for expertise, goods, and services. Nevertheless, family support and filial piety still are valued greatly by the many Asian elderly. A recent study of aging Chinese, Japanese, and Koreans in Canada by Ujimoto et al. (1992) indicated that Chinese elderly had the highest frequency in seeing their relatives. However, Korean elderly spent considerably more time with their relatives in numerous familial activities. In response to the question, "What aspects of your cultural heritage do you feel have enabled you to grow old successfully?" 26% of the Korean elderly indicated filial piety as the key cultural variable for successful aging. This contrasted with the Chinese and Japanese elderly respondents, of whom 12% and 7%, respectively, indicated filial piety. The Korean respondents in the survey also indicated that pride in their cultural heritage was important. Being the most recent immigrants to Canada, Koreans still maintain a strong attachment to traditional Korean values. The Chinese responses tended to fall between the Korean and Japanese responses. Supportive activities in the Asian Canadian family can take many forms. For Asian Canadian families, the time spent together over meals serves as a very cohesive factor and an opportunity to discuss daily happenings in addition to discussing important family matters. Another important supportive activity is the time spent with relatives in shopping activities. Assistance with shopping for groceries and for other necessities is quite strong. The Chinese respondents in the research just cited indicated a high level of daily contact with their elderly relatives.

Considering all the available evidence, ethnicity is indeed a valuable resource in more than one way. Cultural heritage and traditional values provide an anchor in a sea of change. Strong family ties and connections with the ethnic community provide both moral and practical social support. The human spirit of hard work, endurance, and self-reliance enables immigrants to overcome obstacles and succeed in the host country. In short, ethnicity strengthens both the social and psychological coping resources and more than compensates for the deficiency in cultural competence. This overall positive assessment of ethnicity should not obscure the fact that there are hidden pockets of Asian American elderly at risk because of ethnicity. They tend to be poor and speak little or no English. Many of these seniors do not have the financial means to support themselves and often are unwelcome dependents living with their adult children. Some are victims of elder abuse, but they would not report this abuse to outsiders because their culture dictates that families should not "hang their dirty laundry in public." They often do not receive proper medical and social services because of language barriers and a lack of translation services. In almost every city, there are Asian American elderly living and dying alone in poverty or living out their old age in nursing homes where no one speaks their language and no one brings them the food they used to eat. They do not have the coping resources to fend for themselves. To our knowledge, there is little or no research on these "hidden" and forgotten victims, but they can be found almost anywhere.

LIFE SATISFACTION AND MENTAL HEALTH OF ASIAN AMERICANS

Given the additional stresses associated with immigration and acculturation, and considering that ethnicity can be either an asset or a liability, how do Asian American elderly fare in terms of mental health? The mental health problems of Asian Americans have been dealt with thoroughly elsewhere (e.g., Sue & Morishima, 1982; Sue & Sue, 1987). One of the messages from this body of research is that the mental health needs of Asian Americans have been underestimated because of their underutilization of mainstream mental health services (Sue & Sue, 1987). With respect to life satisfaction, there has been no large nationwide survey on Asian Americans. Nandi's (1980) exploratory study on the life quality of Asian Americans had a small sample of 45 individuals. P. Chen (1980) interviewed a sample of 150 Mexican, Black, and Chinese American elderly who were participants in nutrition programs in Los Angeles. The focus was on diet patterns and health rather than on life satisfaction.

Recently, Ying (1992) studied life satisfaction in a random sample of 142 San Francisco Chinese Americans. The participants, with a mean age of 36.7 years (ranging from 19 to 85), participated in face-to-face interviews. Overall life satisfaction was assessed on a Likert scale by the question, "When you think about the things you want from life, would you say that you are very satisfied, satisfied, neither satisfied nor dissatisfied, dissatisfied, or very dissatisfied with your current life?" (with a score of 5 indicating very satisfied). Subjective satisfaction with specific life domains such as work, health, marriage, and biculturality (e.g., life as a Chinese person living in America) also was rated. Mean overall life satisfaction was 3.62, which reflects a moderate level of satisfaction. Chinese Americans also were moderately satisfied in specific life domains, with the highest level of satisfaction (mean = 4.11) in the domain of friendship. American-born Chinese had significantly greater bicultural satisfaction than did immigrants. Ying suggested that the American-born Chinese have more access to various resources and are less likely to experience the cultural and language barriers. The study showed that overall life satisfaction did not vary by sex, age, marital status, or years of residence in the United States. The only significant difference was that higher SES status was associated with higher overall life satisfaction. Subjective satisfaction with life domains accounted for 37% of the variance in overall life satisfaction. Subgroup analyses showed that bicultural satisfaction was the most powerful predictor of overall life satisfaction in immigrants, whereas friendship satisfaction was the best predictor of quality of life in American-born Chinese. Immigrants had a significantly lower SES than did American-born Chinese but did not report lower overall life satisfaction. Ying proposed that immigrants have likely reduced their expectations.

Kim (1987) reported that Korean immigrants to Canada appear to have adapted well. However, his intensive interviews with medical and social support staff revealed that Koreans tend to internalize their problems, making it difficult to assess their real problems. Kim also observed that Koreans do not want to admit that they are sick or show any signs of weakness and that they tend to somatize their psychological problems because of the stigma attached to mental illness. Self-reported health satisfaction was studied by Ujimoto et al. (1992) in a large sample of elderly Japanese, Chinese, and Korean women. The study revealed that the Chinese and Korean elderly reported lower satisfaction than did elderly Japanese women. Their dissatisfaction might stem from the fact that both Chinese and Korean women immigrated to Canada as "captive immigrants," a term used by Kim (1987) to describe Korean parents or grandparents who came to Canada because of their sense of responsibility toward their families. In a Korean household that operates a small business or has dual income earners, the babysitting role most often is provided by grandparents.

Studies comparing Asian Americans to mainstream Americans are particularly rare, and the results are inconclusive. Loo (1991), in her comprehensive study of Chinese adults in San Francisco's Chinatown, found that they reported lower life satisfaction than did Americans overall in many areas such as education, job, health, housing, and family life. They described their lives as less enjoyable, less hopeful, and offering fewer opportunities. Raskin and Chien (1992) compared Chinese elderly to Caucasian American elderly on measures of psychic distress, somatic complaints, and social competence. They found less psychic distress and emotionality in Chinese seniors than in their Caucasian counterparts. Chinese Americans also performed better on empirical tests of memory but registered more attention and memory complaints. There was no evidence of more somatic distress or somatic symptoms in Chinese Americans. In terms of social competence, Chinese American women saw themselves as less able than their Caucasian counterparts. In another study, Morioka-Douglas and Yeo (1990) found that Asian American elders visited a doctor's office only about half as often as did White Americans; however, the underutilization of Western medical services by elderly Asians does not necessarily mean that they enjoy better physical health.

Morioka-Douglas and Yeo (1990) also reported that death rates for foreign-born Chinese are almost six times higher than those reported for American-born Chinese, implicating the negative effects of migration on physical health. Berkanovic and Hurwicz (1992) examined 16 indicators of physical, mental, and social health status of older Chinese in Los Angeles, Beijing, and Guangzhou. They reported that the older Chinese in Los Angeles rated their health status as better and had fewer chronic conditions than did their counterparts in Beijing and Guangzhou. They also reported fewer mobility limitations; however, Los Angeles respondents spent more days in bed due to illness than did respondents in Beijing and Guangzhou. The results of the Barkanovic and Hurwicz (1992) study are inconclusive with respect to the effects of living in America on the Chinese elderly.

McCallum and Shadbolt (1989) demonstrated that ethnicity was a significant predictor of psychological distress in the context of other relevant variables. Here, ethnicity was defined in terms of the four different ethnic strata, namely mainstream Australians, British migrants, and non-British migrants with either good or poor English. Network variables were related to psychological distress only for non-British migrants. The number of nonhousehold relatives was important for those with poor English, whereas the number of nonrelatives and neighbors predicted distress for those with good English. By contrast, for mainstream Australians, living arrangements, health, and gender, rather than network variables, were the significant predictors of distress. The authors concluded, "Ethnicity, then, makes a difference to the individual's need to organize social networks to avoid feelings of psychological distress" (p. 95). Note that the majority of non-British migrants came from various parts of Asia. The main limitation of this study is that psychological distress was measured by four items on subjective feelings of loneliness, boredom, and depression (e.g., "Would you say that you find yourself feeling lonely quite often, sometimes, or almost never?"). This is a restricted measure with little evidence of validity. The emphasis seems to be on underload rather than on overload. Still, the study is important in demonstrating that comparative studies of distress and mental health need to consider other factors such as social and personal resources.

Stanford (1990) investigated the prevalence and level of functional impairment among API Americans and American Indians age 45 years or over. The Older American Resources and Services (OARS) instrument was used to measure five different levels of impairment. Additional data on acculturation, depression, nutritional risk, and alcohol use also were collected. The Vietnamese tended to be least acculturated, and the older Vietnamese experienced higher levels of activities of daily living impairment than did other minority samples. Females age 65 years or over had the highest prevalence rate and level of impairment regardless of ethnicity. Lack of cultural competence (e.g., poor English language skills) contributed to all five levels of functional impairment for the Chinese and Vietnamese samples. Lew (1991) described the Older Southeast Asian Health Project, which was designed to improve access to health care among older Cambodians in Long Beach, California. About 10% of the Cambodian immigrants were age 55 years or over. These elders suffered from many physical and mental health problems but were prevented from using available health services because of numerous social, cultural, and economic barriers.

Browne et al. (1994) provided a review of the research literature on the mental health service utilization of API American elders. They pointed out that previous research focused on the underutilization of mental health services by API Americans, whereas more recent studies focused on the risk factors of the underutilization of such services. These authors highlighted the prevalence of mental health problems of Chinese, Japanese, and Hawaiian elderly, taking particular note of the special needs of recent elderly immigrants such as Koreans and Indochinese. In a recent review of the social and health needs of API elderly, Tanjasiri, Wallace, and Shibata (1995) pointed out that these elderly might be in equal or better health as compared to Whites. However, the authors cited several studies showing that there were numerous pockets of Asian American seniors who were both in poverty and in poor health. They pointed out that aggregate data clouds the bimodal distribution in SES and health status. There have been pockets of needy and helpless API seniors who have fallen through the cracks of health and social services unnoticed. The authors suggest, "These results raise the possibility of health status inequality and demonstrate the need for more research with larger samples of API elderly" (p. 758).

Mental Health Implications

Successful adaptation for API Americans depends on a number of factors such as the presence of an ethnic community, adequate financial resources, and cultural competence in the host country. The greatest disadvantage and stress of being an elderly API American is racial discrimination, especially the type of systemic discrimination described earlier. One of the emphases in Sue and Sue's (1990) book was that the broader sociopolitical climate of racism and oppression can have a devastating effect on ethnic minorities. Being visible minorities and unable to communicate in English often can mean that they do not receive the same type of medical attention as does the majority. Furthermore, a lack of access to culturally relevant health and social services means that they have fewer external resources to resort to in times of need.

Kalish and Moriwaki (1973) pointed out that the early socialization and expectations regarding old age can be maladaptive to life in America. However, complete assimilation is not the answer because this would mean loss of cultural heritage as a coping resource. Stress that stems from basic conflicts of different values can be best reduced by modifying ethnic cultural expectations and selectively integrating the best from both cultures. For example, one should have more realistic expectations in terms of filial piety and respect for the elderly. At the same time, one can accept the values of autonomy and self-expression without embracing the unbridled individualism of American culture. This type of selective acculturation calls for education and dialogue, not indoctrination.

Given the effects of culture on coping and help seeking, there is some consensus that mental health services and interventions should be more culturally appropriate to Asian Americans. There also is the need for more ethnic resources to care for the elderly (Cheung, 1989; Holzberg, 1983-1984; Kobata et al., 1980; Snow & Gordon, 1980; Sue & Morishima, 1982). Cheung (1989) recommended that "services should focus on the person's need for a cohesive family structure by providing services in a simulated family setting" (p. 459). She further emphasized the importance of accepting Chinese clients' values and using peer support groups, as exemplified in a drug addiction treatment program in New York (Deely, Kaufman, Yen, Jue, & Brown, 1979).

The R-C Model emphasizes the importance of developing resources and using appropriate strategies to deal with various types of stressors. This would require more than the efforts of individuals. For example, the societal stress of racism and discrimination requires structural change. Language barriers can be overcome by publicly funded lessons in English. To increase the likelihood of congruence in adaptation, we need to provide training in cultural competence for new immigrants. Government and private agencies can play a key role to improve the coping resources of Asian American elderly. More attention needs to be given to the "hidden" Asian elderly; they probably are the most vulnerable group of seniors because they fall through the cracks unnoticed.

The R-C Model also emphasizes inner resources as a buffer against stress. In their study of Asian immigrants, Kuo and Tsai (1986) found that hardiness, in terms of internal locus of control and mastery, can reduce migration stress. More recently, Dion, Dion, and Pak (1992) also reported that hardiness served as a buffer against discrimination-related stress in members of Toronto's Chinese community. Wong (1993) proposed that by cultivating psychological resources, we can enhance stress resistance and improve mental health. To increase inner resources, "we need to foster a sense of mastery while recognizing external constraints and internal limitations; we need to explore sources of personal meaning; we can also cultivate our capacity for dreaming and hoping" (p. 59). Implementation of these suggestions can go a long way in improving the mental health of Asian elderly in a foreign land.

METHODOLOGICAL LIMITATIONS
AND FUTURE RESEARCH DIRECTIONS

The study of Asian American elderly must be viewed within a broader cross-cultural perspective. Cross-cultural research is interested in both the universal principles (etic) and culture-specific aspect (emic) of aging and adaptation. We need to identify the common experiences from different cultural groups as well as the culture-specific issues. The major methodologies in cross-culture research, such as linear research and parallel research, have been critically evaluated (Sue

& Sue, 1987; Zane & Sue, 1986). The assumption of universality in the constructs and assessment instruments in mainstream American culture has been questioned. Triandis (1972) called this approach "pseudo-etic" rather than etic because it imposes the categories of Western culture (which is emic rather than etic) on other cultures. Sinha (1983) criticized ethnocentrism in cross-cultural research, especially the practice of using a model of Western personality as the standard to measure psychological development in other cultures. He also questioned the validity of trying to interpret data collected from a different culture without any firsthand experience and real understanding of that culture. Similar criticisms were voiced by Sue and Sue (1987).

Recently, Gibson et al. (1993) published a 17-nation study of perceived problems and coping strategies in youth. An international research team met regularly during the design, data collection, and coding stages of the project. Members of the team also consulted one another frequently in interpreting the results. It was truly a multicultural, collaborative effort. However, Western influence is evident in the design of the questionnaire, which inevitably biases the results and interpretation. For example, to obtain information on coping strategies, respondents were asked, "When you have this problem, what do you do about it? That is, what are the things you do in order to deal with this concern, pressure, or difficulty?" (p. 205). This question clearly reflects the dominant influence of Western psychology, which favors individualistic, action-oriented coping. No wonder the results showed that close to 50% of the coping strategies reported belonged to the "individual problem-solving" category. On the other hand, the coping question could have been broadened to include, "How do you handle the problem mentally and emotionally? How does your family respond to the problem?" The results might have been very different if a more inclusive type of coping question were employed.

According to Sinha, true cross-cultural research should begin with many emic studies within each culture. "When emic understanding of behavior which reflects one's own societal base is supplemented by a comparative analysis of these variations, emergence of pan-culture regularities and the establishment of whatever universal features are found become possible" (p. 8). In other words, he proposed a derived etic approach, which is based on common features of a wide range of emic studies by psychologists from different cultures. His notion is similar to our suggestion of a "synemic" approach, which might be viewed as a form of integrated, parallel research. From the outset, the development of conceptualization and research instruments using this approach does not take part separately in several cultural groups; rather, it takes part cooperatively, involving different cultures. It also means that data collection and interpretations of the results are based on the synthesis of ideas from several cultures. This approach calls for equal partnership between participating countries. Truly etic principles will emerge when synemic research incorporates more and more cultures. The R-C Model and the coping assessment employed in our research may be considered an example of the synemic approach because they were based on constructs from both mainstream American culture and Oriental culture. Ideally, cross-cultural research should involve members from different cultures who formulate research ideas and develop theories and instruments from scratch, as was done in the development of the coping schema (Peacock et al., 1993; Wong, 1993; Wong & Reker, 1985). This approach would avoid domination by Western constructs and instruments in cross-cultural research.

In terms of future directions in research, Gibson (1988) emphasized continued research on measurements of physical and psychological well-being as well as the development of valid instruments for minority elderly. She also emphasized the need to disentangle multiple intercorrelated variables. More important, she proposed that instead of simply looking for ethnic differences on a number of variables, one should be concerned with when these variables operate and how they relate to each other differently for majority and minority groups. For example, one should study "whether stress is differentially buffered by personal resources of minority and majority group members [rather] than simply to know that minorities have higher levels of stress" (p. 560). Kuo and Tsai (1986) emphasized the importance of studying the hardy personality associated with immigrants. From the perspective of the R-C Model, hardy individuals may be viewed as possessing a great deal of psychological resources such as mastery, optimism, and personal meaning. A great deal can be learned about hardiness and resilience by studying how Asian American elderly have survived tough times both in their own land and in the host country.

The study of Asian American elderly is further complicated by the fact that within each ethnic group, there are subgroups. For example, the overseas Chinese are a very heterogeneous group. Prewar Asians in Canada have experienced formidable barriers, whereas postwar immigrants have been relatively well protected at the social and political levels. It is necessary to place the life experiences of each group in the context of the social and political environments at the time of their immigration. Consistent with this emphasis, Holzberg (1982) called for a more rigorous investigation of the qualitative dimensions of ethnicity (e.g., values, traditions, family, support systems) that are of significance to the aging experience. We need to know how these dimensions affect adjustment to various problems associated with aging such as health and housing needs. These questions certainly are relevant to research on the Asian American elderly population.

REFERENCES

Abramson, J. H. (1966). Emotional disorder, status inconsistency and migration. *Milbank Memorial Fund Quarterly, 44,* 23-48.

Angel, J. L., & Hogan, D. P. (1991). The demography of minority aging populations. In *Minority elders: Longevity, economics and health building a public policy base.* Washington, DC: Gerontological Society of America.

Antonovsky, A. (1987). *Unraveling the mystery of health.* San Francisco: Jossey-Bass.

Baker, F. M. (1994). Suicide among ethnic minority elderly: A statistical and psychosocial perspective. *Journal of Geriatric Psychiatry, 27,* 241-264.

Barrera, M. (1986). Distinction between social support concepts, measures, and models. *American Journal of Community Psychology, 14,* 413-445.

Bengtson, V. L. (1979). Ethnicity and aging: Problems and issues in current social science inquiry. In D. E. Gelfand & A. J. Kutzik (Eds.), *Ethnicity and aging: Theory, research, and policy* (pp. 9-31). New York: Springer.

Bengtson, V. L., Reedy, M. N., & Gordon, C. (1985). Aging and self-conceptions, personality processes and social contexts. In J. E. Birren & K. W. Schaie (Eds.), *Handbook of psychology and aging* (pp. 544-593). New York: Van Nostrand Reinhold.

Berkanovic, E., & Hurwicz, M. (1992). Illness episodes, physician visits, and depressive symptoms. *Journal of Aging and Health, 4,* 331-348.

Berry, J. W., & Annis, R. C. (1974). Acculturative stress. *Journal of Cross-Cultural Psychology, 5,* 382-405.

Black, M. (1985). Health and social support of older adults in the community. *Canadian Journal on Aging, 4,* 213-226.

Blust, E. P. N., & Scheidt, R. J. (1988). Perceptions of filial responsibility by elderly Filipino widows and their primary caregivers. *International Journal of Aging and Human Development, 26*(2), 91-106.

Bond, M. H. (1983). A proposal for cross-cultural studies of attribution. In M. Hewstone (Ed.), *Attribution theory: Social and functional extensions* (pp. 144-157). Oxford, UK: Basil Blackwell.

Bond, M. H. (Ed.). (1986). *The psychology of the Chinese people.* Hong Kong: Oxford University Press.

Bond, M. H., & Hwang, K. K. (1986). The social psychology of Chinese people. In M. H. Bond (Ed.), *The psychology of the Chinese people* (pp. 213-266). Hong Kong: Oxford University Press.

Brislin, R. (1981). *Cross-cultural encounters.* New York: Pergamon.

Browne, C., Fong, R., & Mokuau, N. (1994). The mental health of Asian and Pacific Island elders: Implications for research and mental health administration. *Journal of Mental Health Administration, 21,* 52-59.

Buchignani, N. L. (1980). Accommodation, adaptation, and policy: Dimensions of the South Asian experience in Canada. In K. V. Ujimoto & G. Hirabayashi (Eds.), *Visible minorities and multiculturalism: Asians in Canada* (pp. 121-150). Toronto: Butterworths.

Carp, F. M. (1978-1979). Effects of the living environment on activity and use of time. *International Journal of Aging and Human Development, 9,* 75-91.

Carp, F. M., & Kataoka, E. (1976). Health care problems of the elderly of San Francisco's Chinatown. *The Gerontologist, 16*(1), 30-38.

Caspi, A., & Elder, G. H., Jr. (1986). Life satisfaction in old age: Linking social psychology and history. *Journal of Psychology and Aging, 1,* 18-26.

Chappell, N. L., Strain, L. A., & Blandford, A. A. (1986). *Aging and health care: A social perspective.* New York: Holt, Rinehart & Winston.

Chen, J. (1980). *The Chinese of America.* New York: Harper & Row.

Chen, P. N. (1979). A study of Chinese-American elderly residing in hotel rooms. *Social Casework, 60*(2), 89-95.

Chen, P. N. (1980). Continuing satisfying life patterns among aging minorities. *Journal of Gerontological Social Work, 2,* 199-211.

Cheng, E. (1978). *The elder Chinese.* San Diego: San Diego State University, Center on Aging.

Cheung, F. M. C. (1986). Psychopathology among Chinese people. In M. H. Bond (Ed.), *The psychology of the Chinese people* (pp. 171-211). Hong Kong: Oxford University Press.

Cheung, F. M., Lau, B. W. K., & Wong, S. W. (1984). Paths to psychiatric care in Hong Kong. *Culture, Medicine and Psychiatry, 8,* 207-208.

Cheung, F. M., Lee, S. Y., & Chan, Y. Y. (1983). Variations in problem conceptualizations and intended solutions among Hong Kong students. *Culture, Medicine and Psychiatry, 7,* 263-278.

Cheung, L. Y. S., Cho, E. R., Luan, D., Tang, T. Y., & Yan, H. B. (1980). The Chinese elderly and family structure: Implications for health care. *Public Health Reports, 95,* 491-495.

Cheung, M. (1989). Elderly Chinese living in the United States: Assimilation or adjustment? *Social Work, 34,* 457-461.

Cobb, S. (1976). Social support as a moderator of life stress. *Psychosomatic Medicine, 3,* 300-314.

Cohen, S., & Wills, T. A. (1985). Stress, social support, and the buffering hypothesis. *Psychological Bulletin, 98,* 310-357.

Deely, P. J., Kaufman, E., Yen, M. S., Jue, A., & Brown, E. (1979). The special problems and treatment of a group of elderly Chinese opiate addicts in New York City. *British Journal of Addiction, 74,* 403-409.

Desbarats, J. (1986). Ethnic differences in adaptation: Sino-Vietnamese refugees in the United States. *International Migration Review, 20,* 405-427.

Dion, K. L., Dion, K. K., & Pak, A. W. P. (1992). Personality-based hardiness as a buffer for discrimination-related stress in members of Toronto's Chinese community. *Canadian Journal of Behavioral Science, 24,* 517-536.

Disman, M. (1987). Explorations in ethnic identity, oldness and continuity. In D. E. Gelfand & C. M. Barresi (Eds.), *Ethnic dimensions of aging* (pp. 64-74). New York: Springer.

Dowd, J. (1983). Social exchange, class, and old people. In J. Sokolovsky (Ed.), *Growing old in different societies* (pp. 29-42). Belmont, CA: Wadsworth.

Dowd, J., & Bengtson, V. (1978). Aging in minority populations: An examination of the double jeopardy hypothesis. *Journal of Gerontology, 33,* 427-436.

Driedger, L., & Chappell, N. (1987). *Aging and ethnicity: Towards an interface.* Toronto: Butterworths.

Elderly look less to children for care. (1987, October 3). *Japan Times.*

England, J. (1986). Cross-cultural health care. *Canada's Mental Health, 34,* 13-15.

Escovar, L. A. (1983). Not of service for cultural minorities. *Contemporary Psychology, 28,* 789-792.

Fairbank, J. K. (1966). How to deal with the Chinese Revolution. *New York Review of Books, 6,* 12.

Fairbank, J. K., & Reischauer, E. O. (1973). *China: Tradition and transformation.* Boston: Houghton Mifflin.

Fitch, V. L., & Slivinske, L. R. (1988). Situational perceptions of control in the aged. In P. S. Fry (Ed.), *Psychological perspectives of helplessness and control in the elderly* (pp. 155-186). Amsterdam: North Holland.

Folkman, S., & Lazarus, R. S. (1980). An analysis of coping in a middle-aged community sample. *Journal of Health and Social Behavior, 22,* 457-459.

French, J. P. R., Rodgers, W., & Cobb, S. (1974). Adjustment as person-environment fit. In C. V. Coelho, D. A. Hamburg, & J. E. Adams (Eds.), *Coping and adaptation* (pp. 316-333). New York: Basic Books.

Fry, P. S. (1990). The person-environment congruence model: Implications and applications for adjustment counselling with older adults. *International Journal for the Advancement of Counselling, 13,* 87-106.

Fujii, S. M. (1976, Fall). Older Asian Americans: Victims of multiple jeopardy. *Civil Rights Digest,* pp. 22-29.

Gelfand, D. E., & Kutzik, A. J. (Eds.). (1979). *Ethnicity and aging: Theory, research and policy.* New York: Springer.

George, L. K. (1980). *Role transitions in later life.* Pacific Grove, CA: Brooks/Cole.

Gibson, J. T., Westwood, M. J., Ishiyama, F. I., Borgen, W. A., Showalter, S. M., Al-Sarraf, Q., Atakan, S. A., Guimares, I. R. F., Guisti-Ortiz, A. L., Robertson, M., Benjamin, S., De Weerdt, P., Velazco, G. A., Baker, C. E., Dikaiou, M., Gabay, T., Kashyup, L., Lee, I., Di Paula, M. E. F., Ngunangwa, H., & Talzina, N. F. (1993). Youth and culture: A seventeen nation study of perceived problems and coping strategies. *International Journal for the Advancement of Counselling, 24,* 203-216.

Gibson, R. C. (1988). Minority aging research: Opportunity and challenge. *The Gerontologist, 28,* 559-560.

Goode, W. J. (1963). *World revolution and family patterns.* Glencoe, IL: Free Press.

Gottlieb, B. H. (1988). *Marshaling social support: Formats, processes, and effects.* Newbury Park, CA: Sage.

Haller, M. (1973). Recurring themes. In A. Davis & M. Haller (Eds.), *The peoples of Philadelphia.* Philadelphia: Temple University Press.

Handlin, O. (1951). *The uprooted.* Boston: Little, Brown.

Havens, B., & Chappell, N. (1983). Triple jeopardy: Age, sex and ethnicity. *Canadian Ethnic Studies, 15*(3), 119-132.

Hendricks, J., & Leedham, C. A. (1989). Making sense: Interpreting historical and cross-cultural literature on aging. In P. V. D. Bagnell & P. S. Soper (Eds.), *Perceptions of aging in literature: A cross-cultural study* (pp. 1-16). Westport, CT: Greenwood.

Ho, D. Y. F. (1981). Traditional patterns of socialization in Chinese society. *Acta Psychologica Taiwanica, 23,* 81-95.

Hobfoll, S. E. (1988). *The ecology of stress.* New York: Hemisphere.

Hobfoll, S. E., Freedy, J., Lane, C., & Geller, P. (1990). Conservation of social resources: Social support resource theory. *Journal of Social and Personal Relationships, 7,* 465-478.

Holahan, C. J., & Moos, R. H. (1991). Life stressors, personal and social resources, and depression: A 4-year structural model. *Journal of Abnormal Psychology, 100,* 31-38.

Holmes, T. H., & Rahe, R. H. (1967). The Social Readjustment Scale. *Journal of Psychosomatic Research, 11,* 203-218.

Holzberg, C. S. (1982). Ethnicity and aging: Anthropological perspectives on more than just the minority elderly. *The Gerontologist, 22,* 249-257.

Holzberg, C. (1983-1984). Anthropology, life histories and the aged: The Toronto Baycrest Centre. *International Journal of Aging and Human Development, 18,* 255-275.

Hoyt, D., & Babchuk, N. (1981). Ethnicity and the voluntary associations of the aged. *Ethnicity, 8,* 67-81.

Hsien, T., Shybut, J., & Lotsof, E. (1969). Internal versus external control and ethnic group membership: A cross-cultural comparison. *Journal of Consulting and Clinical Psychology, 33,* 122-124.

Hsu, F. L. K. (1971). Filial piety in Japan and China: Borrowing, variation and significance. *Journal of Comparative Family Studies, 2,* 67-74.

Hsu, F. L. K. (1973). Kinship is the key. *Center Magazine, 6,* 4-14.

Hurh, W. M., & Kim K. C. (1984). *Korean immigrants in America: Structural analysis of ethnic confinement and adhesive adaptation.* Rutherford, NJ: Fairleigh Dickinson University.

Hwang, K. K. (1977). The patterns of coping strategies in a Chinese society. *Acta Psychologica Taiwanica, 19,* 61-73.

Hwang, K. K. (1978). The dynamic processes of coping with interpersonal conflicts in a Chinese society. *Proceedings of the National Science Council, 2,* 198-208.

Hwang, K. K. (1979). Coping with residential crowding in a Chinese urban society: The interplay of high-density dwelling and interpersonal values. *Acta Psychologica Taiwanica, 21,* 117-133.

Ikels, C. (1983). *Aging and adaptation: Chinese in Hong Kong and the United States.* Hamden, CT: Archon Books.

Ishiyama, F. I. (1989). Understanding foreign adolescents' difficulties in cross-cultural adjustment: A self-validation model. *Canadian Journal of School Psychology, 5,* 41-56.

Ishiyama, F. I., & Westwood, M. J. (1992). Enhancing client-validating communication: Helping discouraged clients in cross-cultural adjustment. *Journal of Multicultural Counseling and Development, 20,* 50-63.

Jackson, J. J. (1980). *Minorities and aging.* Belmont, CA: Wadsworth.

Jackson, J. J. (1985). Race, national origin, ethnicity and aging. In R. H. Binstock & E. Shana (Eds.), *Handbook of aging and the social sciences* (2nd ed.). New York: Van Nostrand Reinhold.

Jackson, J. S. (1989). Race, ethnicity, and psychological theory and research. *Journal of Gerontology: Psychological Sciences, 44*(1), 1-2.

Kahana, E. (1975). A congruence model of person-environment interaction. In P. C. Windley, T. Byerts, & E. C. Ernst (Eds.), *Theoretical developments in environments for aging* (pp. 181-214). Washington, DC: Gerontological Society of America.

Kahana, E. (1982). A congruence model of person-environment interaction. In M. P. Lawton, B. C. Windley, & T. O. Byerts (Eds.), *Aging and the environment: Theoretical approaches* (pp. 97-120). New York: Garland.

Kahana, E., Kahana, B., & Riley, K. (1988). Person-environment transactions relevant to control and helplessness in institutional settings. In P. S. Fry (Ed.), *Psychological perspectives of helplessness and control in the elderly* (pp. 121-154). Amsterdam: North Holland.

Kahana, E., Liang, J., & Felton, B. (1980). Alternative models of person-environment fit: Prediction of morale in three homes for the aged. *Journal of Gerontology, 35,* 584-595.

Kalish, R. A. (1971). A gerontological look at ethnicity, human capacities, and individual adjustment. *The Gerontologist, 11,* 78-87.

Kalish, R. A., & Moriwaki, S. (1973). The world of the elderly Asian American. *Journal of Social Issues, 29,* 187-209.

Kamo, Y., & Zhou, M. (1994). Living arrangements of elderly Chinese and Japanese in the United States. *Journal of Marriage and the Family,* pp. 544-558.

Kaplan, H. B. (1975). *Self-attitudes and deviant behavior.* Pacific Palisades, CA: Goodyear.

Kessler, R. (1979). Stress, social status, and psychological distress. *Journal of Health and Social Behavior, 20,* 259-272.

Kiefer, C. W., Kim, S., Choi, K., Kim, L., Kim, B. L., Shon, S., & Kim, T. (1985). Adjustment problems of Korean American elderly. *The Gerontologist, 25,* 477-482.

Kii, T. (1984). Asians. In E. B. Palmore (Ed.), *Handbook on the aged in the United States* (pp. 201-217). Westport, CT: Greenwood.

Kim, B. L. C. (1978). *The Asian Americans: Changing patterns, changing needs.* Montclair, NJ: Association of Korean Christian Scholars in North America.

Kim, K. C., Kim, S., & Hurh, W. M. (1991). Filial piety and intergenerational relationship in Korean immigrant families. *International Journal of Aging and Human Development, 33,* 233-245.

Kim, U. (1987). Illness behavior patterns of Korean immigrants in Toronto: What are the hidden costs? In K. V. Ujimoto & J. Naidoo (Eds.), *Asian Canadians: Contemporary perspectives* (pp. 194-219). Guelph, Ontario: University of Guelph.

King, A. Y. C., & Bond, M. H. (1985). The Confucian paradigm of man: A sociological view. In W. S. Tsang & D. Y. H. Wu (Eds.), *Chinese culture and mental health* (pp. 29-46). New York: Academic Press.

Kinzie, J. D., Boehnlein, J. K., Leung, P. K., Moore, L. J., Riley, C., & Smith, D. (1990, July). The prevalence of posttraumatic stress disorder and its clinical significance among Southeast Asian refugees. *American Journal of Psychiatry, 147,* 913-917.

Kleinman, A. M. (1979). *Patients and healers in the context of culture.* Berkeley: University of California Press.

Kobasa, S. C. (1979). Stressful life events, personality and health: An inquiry into hardiness. *Journal of Personality and Social Psychology, 37,* 1-11.

Kobata, F. (1979). The influence of culture on family relations: The Asian American experience. In P. Ragan (Ed.), *Aging parents* (pp 94-106). Los Angeles: University of Southern California Press.

Kobata, F., Lockery, S., & Moriwaki, S. (1980). Minority issues in mental health and aging. In J. Birren & R. Sloane (Eds.), *Handbook of mental health and aging* (pp. 448-467). Englewood Cliffs, NJ: Prentice Hall.

Krause, N. (1987a). Life stress, social support, and self-esteem in an elderly population. *Psychology and Aging, 2*(4), 1-8.

Krause, N. (1987b). Stress in racial differences in self-reported health among the elderly. *The Gerontologist, 27,* 72-76.

Kroll, J., Habenicht, M., Mackenzie, T., Yang, M., Chan, S., Vang, T., Nguyen, T., Ly, M., Phommasouvanh, B., Nguyen, H., Vang, Y., Souvannasoth, L., & Cabugao, R. (1989, December). Depression and posttraumatic stress disorder in Southeast Asian refugees. *American Journal of Psychiatry, 146,* 1592-1597.

Kunz, E. F. (1981). Exile and resettlement: Refugee theory. *International Migration Review, 15,* 42-45.

Kuo, W. H., & Tsai, Y. M. (1986). Social networking hardiness and immigrants' mental health. *Journal of Health and Social Behavior, 27,* 133-149.

Lang, O. (1946). *Chinese family and society.* New Haven, CT: Yale University Press.

Lao, R. C. (1977). Levinson's IPC (internal-external control) scale: A comparison of Chinese and American students. *Journal of Cross-Cultural Psychology, 9,* 113-124.

Lazarus, R. S., & Folkman, S. (1984). *Stress, appraisal and coping.* New York: Springer.

Lee, J. J. (1992). *Development, delivery, and utilization of services under the Older Americans Act: A perspective of Asian American elderly.* New York: Garland.

Lee, R. P. L. (1985). Social stress and coping behavior in Hong Kong. In W. S. Tseng & D. Wu (Eds.), *Chinese culture and mental health* (pp. 193-214). New York: Academic Press.

Lew, L. S. (1991). Elderly Cambodians in Long Beach: Creating cultural access to health care. *Journal of Cross-Cultural Gerontology, 6,* 199-203.

Li, P. (1988). *The Chinese in Canada.* Toronto: Oxford University Press.

Li, X. T. (1985). The effect of family on the mental health of the Chinese people. In W. S. Tseng & D. Wu (Eds.), *Chinese culture and mental health* (pp. 83-94). New York: Academic Press.

Lin, C. (1985). *Intergenerational relationships among Chinese immigrant families: A study of filial piety.* Unpublished doctoral dissertation, University of Illinois, Chicago.

Lin, K. M., Tazuma, L., & Masuda, M. (1979). Adaptational problems of the Vietnamese refugees. Part 1: Health and mental health status. *Archives of General Psychiatry, 36,* 955-961.

Lin, N., Simeone, R. S., Ensel, W. M., & Kuo, W. (1979). Social support, stressful life events, and illness: A model and an empirical test. *Journal of Health and Social Behavior, 20,* 108-119.

Lin, T. Y., Tardiff, K., Donetz, G., & Goresky, W. (1978). Ethnicity and patterns of help-seeking. *Culture, Medicine and Psychiatry, 2,* 3-13.

Loo, C. M. (1991). *Chinatown: Most time, hard time.* Westport, CT: Greenwood.

Lum, D., Cheung, L. Y. S., Cho, E. R., Tang, T. Y., & Yau, H. B. (1980). The psychosocial needs of the Chinese elderly. *Social Casework, 61*(2), 100-106.

Markides, K. S., & Mindel, C. H. (1987). *Aging and ethnicity.* Newbury Park, CA: Sage.

Markus, H. R., & Kitayama, S. (1991). Culture and the self: Implications for cognition, emotion, and motivation. *Psychological Review, 98,* 224-253.

Marris, P. (1980). The uprooting of meaning. In G. Coelho & P. Ahmed (Eds.), *Uprooting and development.* New York: Plenum.

Maxwell, R., & Silverman, P. (1980). Information and esteem. In J. Hendricks (Ed.), *In the country of the old.* Farmingsdale, NY: Baywood.

McCallum, J. (1987). Aging and adjustment: A resource theory approach. *Advances in Behavioral Medicine, 4,* 259-273.

McCallum, J., & Shadbolt, B. (1989). Ethnicity and stress among older Australians. *Journal of Gerontology: Social Sciences, 44*(3), 89-96.

McKenzie, B., & Campbell, J. (1987). Race, socioeconomic status, and the subjective well-being of older Americans. *International Journal of Aging and Human Development, 25,* 43-61.

Moon, J. H., & Pearl, J. H. (1991). Alienation of elderly Korean American immigrants as related to place of residence, gender, age, years of education, time in the U.S., living with or without children, and living with or without a spouse. *International Journal of Aging and Human Development, 32*(2), 115-124.

Moos, R. H., & Billings, A. G. (1982). Conceptualizing and measuring coping resources and processes. In L. Goldberger & S. Breznitz (Eds.), *Handbook of stress: Theoretical and clinical aspects* (pp. 212-230). New York: Free Press.

Morioka-Douglas, N., & Yeo, G. (1990). *Aging and health: Asian/Pacific Island American elders* (Working Paper Series No. 3). Stanford, CA: Stanford Geriatric Education Center.

Morton, D. J., Stanford, E. E., Happersett, C. J., & Molgaard, C. A. (1992). Acculturation and functional impairment among older Chinese and Vietnamese in San Diego County, California. *Journal of Cross-Cultural Gerontology, 7*(2), 151-176.

Murphy, H. (1977). Migration, culture, and mental health. *Psychological Medicine, 7,* 677-684.

Naditch, M. P., & Morrissey, R. F. (1976). Role stress, personality, and psychopathology in a group of immigrant adolescents. *Journal of Abnormal Psychology, 85,* 113-118.

Nagasawa, R. (1980). *The elderly Chinese: A forgotten minority.* Chicago: Pacific/Asian American Mental Health Research Center.

Nandi, P. (1980). *The quality of life of Asian Americans: An exploratory study in a middle-size community.* Chicago: Pacific/Asian American Mental Health Research Center.

Nann, R. (1982). Uprooting and surviving: An overview. In R. Nann (Ed.), *Uprooting and surviving* (pp. 1-10). Boston: D. Reidel.

National Workshop on Ethnicity and Aging. (1988, February). *Report: Ethnicity and aging.* Ottawa, Ontario: Canadian Public Health Association.

Nerenberg, L., & Yap, P. (Eds.). (1986). *Elder abuse in the Asian community: A conference sponsored by Self-Help for the Elderly and the San Francisco Consortium for Elder Abuse Prevention.* San Francisco: U.S. Administration on Aging.

Nicassio, P. M., Solomon, G. S., Guest, S. S., & McCullough, J. E. (1986). Emigration stress and language proficiency as correlates of depression in a sample of Southeast Asian refugees. *International Journal of Social Psychiatry, 32,* 22-28.

Okuley, B. (1992, July). The Asian equation. *Asia Magazine,* pp. 17-20.

Osako, M. M., & Liu, W. T. (1986). Intergenerational relations and the aged among Japanese Americans. *Research on Aging, 8,* 128-155.

Padilla, A. M., Wagatsuma, Y., & Lindholm, K. J. (1985). Acculturation and personality as predictors of stress in Japanese and Japanese-Americans. *Journal of Social Psychology, 125,* 295-305.

Palmore, E. B. (1983). Cross-cultural research. *Research on Aging, 5,* 45-57.

Palmore, E. G., Burchett, B. M., Fillenbaum, G. G., George, L. K., & Hallman, L. M. (1985). *Retirement causes and consequences.* New York: Springer.

Peacock, E. J. (1992). Coping with anticipatory stress: A study of appraisal, personality, and situational variables. Unpublished doctoral dissertation, University of Toronto.

Peacock, E. J., & Wong, P. T. P. (1996). Anticipatory stress: The relation of locus of control, optimism, and control appraisals to coping. *Journal of Research in Personality, 30,* 204-222.

Peacock, E. J., Wong, P. T. P., & Reker, G. T. (1993). Relations between appraisals and coping schemas: Support for the congruence model. *Canadian Journal of Behavioral Science, 25,* 64-80.

Pearlin, L. I., & Schooler, C. (1978). The structure of coping. *Journal of Health and Social Behavior, 19,* 2-21.

Peralta, V., & Horikawa, H. (1978). *Needs and potentialities assessment of Asian American elderly in greater Philadelphia* (Report No. 3). Chicago: Pacific/Asian American Mental Health Research Center.

Racial discrimination in Toronto. (1992, July 12). *Toronto Star,* pp. A6-A7.

Raskin, A., & Chien, C. (1992). Elderly Chinese- and Caucasian-Americans compared on measures of psychic distress, somatic complaints and social competence. *International Journal of Geriatric Psychiatry, 7*(3), 191-198.

Reker, G. T., Peacock, E. J., & Wong, P. T. P. (1987). Meaning and purpose in life and well-being: A life-span perspective. *Journal of Gerontology, 42,* 44-49.

Reker, G. T., & Wong, P. T. P. (1984). Personal optimism, physical and mental health: The triumph of successful aging. In J. E. Birren & J. Livingston (Eds.), *Cognition, stress and aging* (pp. 134-173). Englewood Cliffs, NJ: Prentice Hall.

Reker, G. T., & Wong, P. T. P. (1988). Towards a theory of personal meaning. In J. E. Birren & V. L. Bengtson (Eds.), *Emergent theories of aging* (pp. 214-246). New York: Springer.

Rodin, J., Timko, C., & Harris, S. (1985). The construct of control: Biological and psychological correlates. In M. P. Lawton & G. L. Maddox (Eds.), *Annual review of gerontology and geriatrics* (Vol. 5, pp. 3-55). New York: Springer.

Rosenthal, C. J. (1986). Family supports in late life: Does ethnicity make a difference? *The Gerontologist, 26,* 19-24.

Rumbaut, R. G. (1985). Mental health and the refugee experience: A comparative study of Southeast Asian refugees. In T. C. Owan et al. (Eds.), *Southeast Asian mental health: Treatment, prevention, services, training, and research.* Rockville, MD: National Institute of Mental Health.

Scheier, M. F., & Carver, C. S. (1985). Optimism, coping, and health: Assessment and implications of generalized outcome expectancies. *Health Psychology, 4,* 219-247.

Scheier, M. F., & Carver, C. S. (1987). Dispositional optimism and physical well-being: The influence of generalized outcome expectancies on health. *Journal of Personality, 55,* 169-210.

Schulz, R. (1976). Effects of control and predictability on the physical and psychological well-being of the institutionalized aged. *Journal of Personality and Social Psychology, 33,* 563-573.

Shadbolt, B., & McCallum, J. (1988). Ethnicity and psychological distress. *Migration Monitor, 3,* 9-14.

Shimpo, M. (1973). Social history of the Japanese in Canada. *RIKKA, 1,* 2-3.

Sinha, D. (1983). Cross-cultural psychology: A view from the Third World. In J. B. Deregowski, S. Dzivrawiec, & R. D. Annis (Eds.), *Expectations in cross-cultural psychology* (pp. 3-17). Lisse, Netherlands: Swets & Zeitlinger.

Slivinske, L. R., & Fitch, V. L. (1987). The effect of control enhancing interventions on the well-being of elderly individuals living in retirement communities. *The Gerontologist, 27*, 176-181.

Snow, D., & Gordon, J. (1980). Social network analysis and intervention with the elderly. *The Gerontologist, 20*, 463-467.

Snyder, C. R. (1989). Reality negotiation: From excuses to hope and beyond. *Journal of Social and Clinical Psychology, 8*, 130-157.

Special Services for Groups. (1978). *Pacific/Asian Elderly Research Project: Final report* (mimeo). Los Angeles: Author.

Stanford, E. P. (1990). *Health status and lifestyles of Asian and Pacific Islanders and American Indians*. San Diego: San Diego State University, College of Health and Human Services, Center on Aging.

Statistics Canada. (1994). *Canada's changing immigrant population* (Catalogue No. 96-311 E). Ottawa: Author.

Strand, P. J., & Jones, W., Jr. (1985). *Indochinese refugees in America: Problems of adaptation and assimilation*. Durham, NC: Duke University Press.

Sue, D., & Sue, S. (1987). Cultural factors in the clinical assessment of Asian Americans. *Journal of Consulting and Clinical Psychology, 55*, 479-487.

Sue, D. W., & Sue, D. (1990). *Counseling the culturally different: Theory and practice* (2nd ed.). New York: John Wiley.

Sue, S., & Morishima, J. K. (1982). *The mental health of Asian Americans*. San Francisco: Jossey-Bass.

Sugiman, P., & Nishio, H. K. (1983). Socialization and cultural duality among aging Japanese Canadians. *Canadian Ethnic Studies, 15*(3), 17-35.

Sung, T. K. (1990). A new look at filial piety: Ideas and practices of family-centered parent care in Korea. *The Gerontologist, 30*, 610-617.

Sung, T. K. (1994). Cross-cultural comparison of motivations for parent care: The case of Americans and Koreans. *Journal of Aging Studies, 8*, 195-209.

Tanjasiri, S. P., Wallace, S. P., & Shibata, K. (1995). Picture imperfect: Hidden problems among Asian Pacific Islander elderly. *The Gerontologist, 35*, 753-760.

Thoits, P. A. (1983). Dimensions of life stress that influence psychological distress: An evaluation and synthesis of the literature. In H. B. Kaplan (Ed.), *Psychosocial stress: Trends in theory and research* (pp. 33-103). New York: Academic Press.

Tomita, S. K. (1994). Consideration of cultural factors in the research of elder mistreatment with an in-depth look at the Japanese. *Journal of Cross-Cultural Gerontology, 9*(1), 39-52.

Tran, T. V. (1991). Family living arrangement and social adjustment among three ethnic groups of elderly Indochinese refugees. *International Journal of Aging and Human Development, 32*(2), 91-102.

Tran, T. V. (1992). Adjustment among different age and ethnic groups of Indochinese in the U.S. *The Gerontologist, 32*, 508-518.

Triandis, H. C. (1972). *The analysis of subjective culture*. New York: John Wiley.

Tseng, W., & Wu, D. Y. U. (1985). *Chinese culture and mental health*. New York: Academic Press.

Ujimoto, K. V. (1987a). The ethnic dimensions of aging in Canada. In V. Marshall (Ed.), *Aging in Canada: Social perspectives* (pp. 111-137). Toronto: Fitzhenry & Whiteside.

Ujimoto, K. V. (1987b). Organizational activities, cultural factors and well-being of aged Japanese Canadians. In D. E. Gelfand & C. M. Barresi (Eds.), *Ethnic dimensions of aging* (pp. 145-160). New York: Springer.

Ujimoto, K. V. (1988). Variations in the allocation of time among aged Japanese Canadians. In K. Altergott (Ed.), *Daily life in later life: A comparative perspective* (pp. 186-204). Newbury Park, CA: Sage.

Ujimoto, K. V. (1991). Multiculturalism, ethnic identity and inequality. In B. S. Bolaria (Ed.), *Canadian society: Issues and contradictions* (p. 133). Orlando, FL: Harcourt Brace Jovanovich.

Ujimoto, K. V., Nishio, H. K., Wong, P. T. P., & Lam, L. (1992). Cultural factors affecting the self-assessment of health satisfaction. In R. Masi, L. Mensah, & K. McLeod (Eds.), *Health and cultures: Explaining the relationships* (pp. 229-240). Toronto: Canadian Council on Multicultural Health.

U.S. Bureau of the Census. (1992a). *Census of the population, 1990 (U.S.): General population characteristics* (CP-1-1). Washington, DC: U.S. Department of Commerce, Bureau of the Census.

U.S. Bureau of the Census. (1992b). *Statistical abstract of the United States: The national data book* (112th ed.). Washington, DC: U.S. Department of Commerce, Bureau of the Census.

U.S. Bureau of the Census. (1995). *Statistical abstract of the United States: The national data book* (115th ed.). Washington, DC: U.S. Department of Commerce, Bureau of the Census.

Wan, T. T. H. (1982). *Stressful life events, social-support networks, and gerontological health: A prospective study.* Lexington, MA: Lexington Books.

Westwood, M. J., & Lawrence, S. (1990). Uprooted: Towards a counsellor understanding of the refugee experience. *International Journal for the Advancement of Counselling, 13,* 145-153.

Wilson, W. J. (1973). *Power, racism, and privilege.* London: Collier-Macmillan.

Wong, M. G. (1984). Economic survival: The case of Asian American elderly. *Economic Perspectives, 27,* 197-217.

Wong, P. T. P. (1989). Personal meaning and successful aging. *Canadian Psychology, 30,* 516-525.

Wong, P. T. P. (Ed.). (1990). Advances in measuring life stress [special issue]. *Stress Medicine, 6*(2/3).

Wong, P. T. P. (1991). Social support functions of group reminiscence. *Canadian Journal of Community Mental Health, 10*(2), 151-161.

Wong, P. T. P. (Ed.). (1992). The psychology of control [special issue]. *Canadian Journal of Behavioral Science, 24*(2).

Wong, P. T. P. (1993). Effective management of life stress: The Resource-Congruence Model. *Stress Medicine, 9,* 51-60.

Wong, P. T. P. (1995). The adaptive processes of reminiscence. In B. Haight & J. D. Webster (Eds.), *Reminiscence: Theory, research methods, and applications* (pp. 23-35). Washington, DC: Taylor & Francis.

Wong, P. T. P., & Fry, P. (Eds.). (in press). *The human quest for meaning: A handbook of psychological research and clinical applications.* Mahwah, NJ: Lawrence Erlbaum.

Wong, P. T. P., & Reker, G. T. (1985). Stress, coping, and well-being in Anglo and Chinese elderly. *Canadian Journal on Aging, 4*(1), 29-37.

Wong, P. T. P., Reker, G. T., & Peacock, E. J. (1987). *The Revised Coping Inventory.* Unpublished manuscript, Trent University.

Wong, P. T. P., & Sproule, C. F. (1984). Attributional analysis of locus of control and the Trent Attribution Profile (TAP). In H. M. Lefcourt (Ed.), *Research with the locus of control construct,* Vol. 3: *Limitations and extension* (pp. 309-360). New York: Academic Press.

Wong, P. T. P., & Ujimoto, K. V. (1988, June). *Stress as coping in the Chinese elderly.* Paper presented at a Symposium on Cross-Cultural Research, University of Windsor.

Wong, P. T. P., & Watt, L. M. (1991). What types of reminiscence are associated with successful aging? *Psychology and Aging, 6,* 272-279.

Woodsworth, D. J. (1941). *Canada and the Orient: A study in international relations.* Toronto: Macmillan Canada.

Wu, F. Y. T. (1975). Mandarin-speaking aged Chinese in the Los Angeles area. *The Gerontologist, 15,* 271-275.

Yamamoto, J. (1968). Japanese American identity crisis. In E. B. Brody (Ed.), *Minority group adolescents in the United States.* Baltimore, MD: Wilkins & Wilkins.

Yang, K. S. (1986). Chinese personality and its change. In M. H. Bond (Ed.), *The psychology of the Chinese people* (pp. 106-170). Hong Kong: Oxford University Press.

Yee, B. W. K. (1977, August). *Asian American elderly: A life-span developmental approach to minorities and learned helplessness.* Paper presented at the annual meeting of the American Psychological Association, San Francisco.

Yee, B. W. K. (1992). Elders in Southeast Asian refugee families. *Generations, 17*(3), 24-27.

Yeo, G., & Hikoyeda, N. (1992). *Cohort analysis as a clinical and educational tool in ethnogeriatrics: Historical profiles of Chinese, Filipino, Mexican, and African American elders* (Working Paper Series No. 3). Stanford, CA: Stanford Geriatric Education Center.

Ying, Y. W. (1992). Life satisfaction among San Francisco Chinese-Americans. *Social Indicators Research, 26,* 1-22.

Yoh, J. Y., & Bell, W. G. (1987). Korean elders in the United States: Intergenerational relations and living arrangements. *The Gerontologist, 27,* 66-71.

Yu, L. C. (1983). Patterns of filial belief and behavior within the contemporary Chinese American family. *International Journal of Sociology of the Family, 13*(1), 17-36.

Yu, L. C. (1984). Acculturation and stress within Chinese American families. *Journal of Comparative Family Studies, 15,* 77-94.

Yu, L. C., & Harburg, E. (1980). Acculturation and stress among Chinese Americans in a university town. *International Journal of Group Tensions, 10,* 99-119.

Yu, L. C., & Wu, S. C. (1985). Unemployment and family dynamics in meeting the needs of Chinese elderly in the United States. *The Gerontologist, 25,* 472-476.

Zane, N., & Sue, S. (1986). Ethnic minority issues: Divergent reasoning and diverse solution. In E. Seidman & J. Rappaport (Eds.), *Redefining social issues* (pp. 289-304). New York: Praeger.

6

WOMEN

Maria P. P. Root

Despite vilification, exotification, subjugation, and infantilization, Asian American women have demonstrated resilience. Resilience reflects a process of adaptation and transformation. In a country and in many cultures where gender carries a secondary status, women's resilience is remarkable. This chapter provides an overview of the growing body of psychological research on Asian American women. An overview of social factors and stereotypes provides hypotheses as to why research on Asian American women emerges slowly. Subsequently, the rest of this chapter summarizes the research in five general areas of existing research: family, identity, sexuality, violence, and general mental health.

Social Factors

Demographic and cultural factors might offer partial explanations for the paucity of research on Asian American women. The most relevant demographic hypothesis suggests that the small size of this population relative to the rest of the country would produce few Asian American women researchers. Researchers in the social sciences often inquire into personally relevant content areas. Few Asian American women psychologists have been positioned in research institutions. Concomitantly, until we entered the current "postmodern" era that values the personal experience and connection of participants and researchers to the content and substance of the research questions, minority researchers were discouraged from developing research agendas outside of mainstream psychology. Consequently, few Asian American female psychologists exist as role models for subsequent generations of women (Nagata, 1995) or therapists in the mental health fields (Homma-True, 1990). Since the Immigration and Naturalization Act of 1965, the size of the Asian American population has increased significantly. Just in the past decade, the recorded population has doubled to 7.3 million (Homma-True, 1991). Subsequently, we could expect more Asian American women positioned to research issues relevant and specific to Asian American women.

The second demographic hypothesis suggests that the generation of the individual has a bearing on educational attainment. With the tremendous growth in the Asian American population over several decades, the typical profile of the Asian American woman has been transformed. Fujitomi and Wong (1973), authors of the first psychology chapter on Asian American women, observed that the average Asian American woman was modally represented by a Sansei (third-generation Japanese American) or a first- or second-generation Chinese American. However, the modal Asian American woman now extends significantly beyond these two groups. The term has even expanded to include Pacific Islanders. She may be Filipino, Korean, Vietnamese, Laotian, Cambodian, East Asian, Chamorro, Thai, Taiwanese, Hawaiian, or Samoan. She still may be first or second generation, but she also may be at least fourth or fifth generation, as we see in the Japanese American population. She may be multiethnic or multiracial as a result of the high rates of intermarriage for many Asian and Pacific Island communities (see Chapter 7, this volume). Extended generations in this country increase the opportunity for education, which increases the chance of the educational system producing researchers who will pursue issues relevant to Asian American women.

These demographic factors may interact with cultural and generational factors. Psychology seeks to expose the private world of the psyche whether the unit of study is the individual, the married couple, or the family unit. Cultural proscriptions across various Asian groups have demarcated private and public lives. Private lives are not for outsiders to view. A second cultural factor that might dissuade Asian Americans from going into psychology is the conflict between worldviews. For those persons who are more closely aligned with traditional Asian cultures that tend to be collectively oriented, psychology is oriented within an individualistic framework. Parents might not be willing to finance their children's educations for a field of study that does not make sense or seems frivolous. Leong and Serafica (1995) observed the generational conflicts and parental influence that Asian American parents exert on their children's choice of college majors. Parents might be concerned with increasing the family's future economic stability. A psychology major might even feel like a threat or loss to the financial security of the future family as compared to an engineering or a business major. With increased financial stability over generations and with acculturation, it seems that parents are allowing their children to choose their majors. Although Asian American women have contributed to dual-income families, their work has had to place family and child rearing first. Thus, until recently, an advanced degree in psychology was not practical. With increased acculturation, young women have been able to assert more control over the directions of their lives.

Stereotypes

Although research on Asian American women need not be carried out only by Asian American women, "inside" researchers might be able to critically evaluate prevailing hypotheses, theories, and stereotypes in a way that might even formulate different questions or interpret results in a different way. Inside information about culture and gender may challenge stereotypes that might otherwise turn into self-fulfilling prophecies and guide realities (Chow, 1989). Stereotypes limit both the behavior to which the observer will attend and the possible meaning assigned to behavior, cognitions, and emotions.

Never has there existed as much specific legislation toward a broad cultural group as there has been toward Asian Americans (Chan, 1991). Very specific legislation has been directed to prevent women from immigrating or assisting in the development of permanent Asian American communities. The stereotypes that exist for Asian American women might be analyzed as reflective of sentiments of anxiety and hostility that ebb and flow with economic depressions, wartime, and societal transformation. These sentiments are embodied in enduring stereotypes of Asian American women.

The diabolical, cunning, manipulative stereotype exemplified by the daughter of Fu Manchu in American films depicts this woman as being immoral and hypersexual with a penchant for White men—a "dragon lady." She began to emerge shortly after and concomitantly with economic hardship in which Asian laborers were accused of taking up jobs that were entitled to American White men and with legislation barring Chinese women from immigration as current-day mail-order brides. This stereotype is attributed to assertive Asian American women who do not cater to men, particularly White men.

A contrasting, nonthreatening stereotype emerged during World War II through the Vietnam war in which U.S. military personnel were distributed throughout the Pacific region. World War II brought home the stereotype of the subservient woman and exotic geisha girl who catered to men's sexual fantasies. A second nonthreatening stereotype is particularly paternalistic. Asian or Asian American women are characterized as childlike, fragile, and innocent as in "China dolls," "Polynesian babies," and "Asian Thumbelinas" (the latter appearing in some of the reptilian monster movies). These two stereotypes, among others, combine to produce the "Suzie Wong" stereotype of the "hooker with a heart of gold" who is portrayed as having a penchant for White men. The main White character of the same-titled movie, again, is cast in a paternalistic role as a justification for his attraction and use of this Asian woman.

A different stereotype characterizes the Asian American woman as a laborer, asexual, and smart and/or industrious. Glenn's (1986) now classic work on three generations of Japanese American women in domestic service highlights the invisibility these women experienced in their role as domestics. Some women reported that when they tired of a job, they could have friends replace them without their employers necessarily noticing these substitutions or trades. Contemporarily, Asian American women employed in the garment industry are stereotyped in this role.

A final stereotype that runs through all the stereotypes except that of the dragon lady is that of the Asian American woman as passive, subservient, and deriving her pleasure from domestic spheres. Fujino's (1992) dissertation examined images of Asian American women by Asian American men and White American men. Some of this stereotype comes through in the differences between Asian American and White American men's images of Asian American women compared to those of White American women. The issue is not whether Asian American women are more domestic but rather the meaning placed on it.

Thinking about the research available on Asian American women, one must contend with the tensions between gender roles and their transformation between and across generations. Many Asian American women must find their way in a world where they might simultaneously struggle with gratitude to their mothers for their hardships and feel critical of their mothers' lives. Chan (1987a) reflected, "When Asian American women speak of their conflicts, they frequently focus first upon their familial relationships, then [upon] their work relationships, and only later upon their relationship with the rest of American society" (p. 13). Thus, separation or challenging of patriarchal structures without rejection of the family or betrayal of the community can be a tenuous accomplishment.

FAMILY

Few studies have examined Asian American marital relationships; fewer studies have researched parent-child relationships. However, with time and generational transformation, the Asian American family in its various ethnic cultural contexts (e.g., Chinese, Korean, Vietnamese) has changed. When most Asian Americans lived in ethnic enclaves with multiple wage earners to pay rents, multigenerational households were common. Although they still exist, many households are comprised of partners and their children (if they have children). Concurrent with this transformation of who comprises the household, marriage also has been transformed. No longer primarily a utilitarian arrangement to ensure settlement in America and the progeny of the future, love now is a critical and necessary requirement for entering into most marriages (Takagi, 1988). However, the continued infusion of immigrants continues to reinforce traditional values while younger people are quickly acculturating to American values. This juxtaposition of value systems can be the source of conflict between generations. It often is a source of discussion in therapy. Homma-True (1990) suggested that therapist self-disclosure may provide role modeling when working with Asian American women if the therapist is Asian American.

Gender role expectations of women can vary widely based on class of origin, current class, ethnic group of origin, and generation in the United States. Furthermore, many Asian American women will report performing different gender roles at home, in private, at work, and in public. Conflicts for women subsequently may arise from differences in roles and expectations at work and at home. Homma-True (1987) suggested that these differences might cause conflict if an Asian American woman is partnered with an Asian American man who expects her to fulfill a gender role modeled by his mother if she followed more traditional gender expectations. One might extend this observation to any partnership regardless of race or ethnicity.

Marriage

Communication, designated a key to successful relationships, may have different definitions and requirements by ethnic group. For example, Card (1978) found that communication style between Filipino American spouses was situationally dynamic. Couples tended not to confront problems between themselves but instead would discuss problems regarding their children. This pattern is absolutely consistent with Filipino values around subjugating the needs of the self to the greater good of the relationship. However, being responsible for teaching children values, parents would need to talk about their children. Agbayani-Siewert (1991) suggested that as couples become more assimilated and have fewer sources of support with the diminished proximity to extended families, such styles of communication as Card (1978) observed might be less effective. Homma-True (1990) suggested that family therapy might be an effective intervention for adjusting to changes in gender expectations and general social stress.

Although few in number, empirical marital studies support the hypothesis that conflicts in gender role expectations and transformations in roles can be a major source of marital conflict and dissatisfaction. For immigrant groups, class status changes, struggles with language barriers, and trying to make ends meet become everyday sources of stress that might interact with shifts in gender role performance (Loo, 1991). Among a sample of Filipinos in Los Angeles County, Agbayani-Siewert (1991) found that shifts in sex-role behavior that conflicted with a spouse's expectations of the performance of gender roles were correlated with increased marital conflict and dissatisfaction. In a study of Chinese American couples, Ying (1991) found that 42% of the variance in marital satisfaction for women, compared to 30% for men, was accounted for by subjective ratings of life aims, friendships, and communication. The best predictor for marital satisfaction was sharing goals with partners. In some families, gender expectations might not include sharing or even communicating goals between partners. In Southeast Asian communities, women working alongside men and earning similar or more income changes their relationships with their male partners. Luu (1989) observed that these changing roles were correlated with divorce, particularly among Vietnamese. Tien (1994) noted that many of these women, although they might have worked in their countries of origin, must work in roles that cause work to be perceived as a "necessary evil."

Interracial Dating and Intermarriage

Asian American women as a group have the highest rate of interracial marriage. Several factors account for this: skin color, socioeconomic status (SES), degree of acculturation, higher education, generation, occupation, income, proximity to different groups, and small numbers of one group (Adams, 1937; Miller, 1992; Shinagawa & Pang, 1996; Sung, 1990). Rates of intermarriage also differ by gender, generation, and geographic region of the country. For example, the rates of intermarriage are extremely high in Hawaii (Kitano, Yeung, Chai, & Hatanaka, 1984). Geographic differences were summarized by Sung (1990), who observed that Chinese American intermarriage is highest in Hawaii (more than 75% combining men and women), high in Los Angeles, and relatively low in New York. However, in contrast to other studies showing that women had higher rates of intermarriage than did men, the rates for New York Chinese American men and women are similar. Based on Los Angeles County, Kitano, Fujino, and Sato (Chapter 8, this volume) reported that generation in this country, acculturation, time in this country, and proximity to other groups play significant roles in determining rates of interracial marriage, with women always having higher rates than men. Each successive generation generates higher rates of intermarriage.

Although Ho (1984) and Sung (1990) suggested that interracial marriages would be difficult, this does not necessarily mean that these marriages end in divorce. Ho and Johnson (1990) examined the longevity of interracial marriages among residents in Hawaii, the majority of which consisted of an Asian or Hawaiian partner. The divorce rate was proportionately lower for between-group marriages (which included some interethnic marriages among Asians and Hawaiians) than for within-group marriages. Sung's (1990) study of 50 interracially married New York Chinese showed that the divorce rate was relatively low, 12% to 18%, compared to a 40% divorce rate for the general population in 1982.

Current theories no longer explore individual pathology as the motivation for interracial dating or marriage. In fact, Ahern, Cole, Johnson, and Wong (1981) found no evidence of psychopathology in their study of interracial and interethnic marriage in Hawaii. However, the women, more so than the men, were less traditional.

Fujino (1992) suggested that interracial dating is partly a response to trading status by gender and race. Although Asian American women were viewed as less attractive than their White female peers, they were seen as more obedient, more willing to do chores, and more willing to take care of men than were their White female peers (Fujino, 1993), which may be viewed as attractive in a relationship but not necessarily reality based.

The intermarriage of Asian American women also has long been associated with war, from the Spanish-American War in the Philippines, to the war brides of World War II and the Korean war (Kim, 1977), to the Vietnam war. Currently, the largest source of international brides of Asian origin stems from correspondence marriages. Controversy abounds around the reasons for these marriages and concerns about the isolation of the women coming to the United States. Isolation from extended family systems also puts these women at risk for harm from abusive spouses with few people to intervene. Serita (1984) noted that the mail-order bride business is a transformation of colonization and imperialism of Asian women through sexual, racial, and economic oppression of women from poor countries such as the Philippines, Malaysia, and Singapore. Villapando (1989) observed that the men seeking wives through this means are buying into racial stereotypes of Asian women as obedient, subservient, and agreeable. Despite the concerns around exploitation that have been documented (Ordoñez, 1997), two extensive studies show that the women generally report being happy (Lin, 1991; Yung, 1991). By contrast, Villapando (1989) reported preliminary findings of a University of Texas study showing that many of the women subsequently endured bitter divorces. Various anecdotal reports and qualitative interviews suggested that many of the women left their countries of origin for both individual and family reasons (Ordoñez, 1997). They felt that there were limited options to make good incomes in their countries of origin. At the same time, having an opportunity to work for a better wage or income in the United States allows the possibility of sending money home to countries such as the Philippines to improve the lot of the extended family.

Changes in Family Constellations

Patriarchally structured societies seem to place more responsibility on women for upholding the success and smooth running of the domestic sphere, which includes relationships. Although divorce is becoming more prevalent in many Asian American families, the stigma of divorce tends to be greater for Asian American women than for Asian American men. This stigma originates not only in the failure to make a successful marriage but possibly also in the failure to fulfill obligations to one's family and in-laws. Chu (1988) suggested that this pressure on women might contribute to lower divorce rates, which is what she found in her analysis of 1980 Los Angeles County census data comparing Asian American women to other women. Other factors also might contribute to lower divorce rates. A substantial increase in the Asian American population stems from immigration since 1965. Thus, it is possible that orientation toward the collective versus the individual and staying together for the children's sake might contribute to lower divorce rates. Chu's (1988) Los Angeles County study produced many interesting results. With lower divorce rates, proportionally fewer Asian women are single heads of households compared to other groups of women. However, differences exist between and among Asian groups. In general, divorce was correlated with generational distance from immigration. For example, Japanese had higher divorce rates than did Vietnamese. However, Korean women had relatively high divorce rates. Chu suggested that the familiarity of divorce in the country of origin also might influence the woman's ability to use this strategy as a solution to marital dissatisfaction.

Most recently, a new family constellation has evolved, and distress has arisen over recent immigrating Hong Kong families in which the wives and children reside in the United States and the husband frequently travels between countries. These men, called "astronauts" because of the frequency and distance of travel, maintain business and work ties in Hong Kong. Subsequently, gender-role expectations are strained as the women, resilient to adapting to the demands for change, head their households, make unilateral decisions, discipline their children, and acculturate to American ways of conducting daily life. When their husbands return, some are able to shift back into the previous method of interaction, which might include the women deferring decision making or including their husbands in decision making. However, many women have changed, and conflicts ensue over their transformation in the performance of gender roles.

Generation Gaps

Within families, value differences create cultural generation gaps between Asian parents and Asian American children (Nguyen, 1992; Shon & Ja, 1982). These conflicts are particularly intense between immigrant generations and their children raised in America (Nguyen, 1992). Homma-True (1991) found that mothers bear the brunt of much of this conflict because, throughout their children's lifetimes, mothers adjust to their children's wishes to move toward the American middle-class value of autonomy and independence and try to instill the closeness and interdependency that have value in Asian families (Bradshaw, 1990). Despite distance from immigration, some vestiges of cultural patterns appear to be evident in child-rearing practices of Asian American women compared to those of White women (Lui, 1990). Thus, despite acculturation, many culturally derived values persist, although perhaps in evolved, adaptive forms.

Cultural generation gaps become evident in the conflicts between elderly parents and their children. Whereas in traditional families it has been assumed that elderly parents will be cared for by their children, particularly eldest sons (Shon & Ja, 1982), value conflicts are increasingly apparent regarding this responsibility. Like women in many cultures, Asian American women have been socialized to put family first; in operating more from a collective philosophy than from an individualistic one, not only is caretaking of elderly parents (and in-laws) assumed but not to follow through with these obligations violates implicit or explicit role expectations. Yu and Wu (1985) documented gender effects in support of parents, with daughters (94%) providing support for aging relatives' needs more often than sons (86%). Although caretaking of elderly parents has been primarily a son's designated responsibility in many Asian cultures, it often was and is delegated to the son's wife. Caretaking of elderly parents has become an issue because most Asian American women work. Furthermore, with a movement away from multigenerational households and with geographic mobility and acculturation, although many Asian American women care about their parents, living and caring for them at home becomes a difficult proposition.

IDENTITY

The positive valuation and empowerment of the self as an Asian American woman is a balancing act in which gender, race, culture, class, and psychosocial aspects of dynamic senses of self must be integrated in daily life (Robinson, 1993). This integration might include the different roles one enacts in a day as worker, student, mother, daughter, wife, lover, and friend. The self as a relational entity also must achieve a balance between individual needs and significant others' needs (e.g., family, partners, children). The totality of valuation of self and identities comprises the self-concept, which might not be supported by the people and within all the social contexts in which one operates.

In this balancing act, one must develop reference standards by which to judge himself or herself and others. The valuation of women, more so than that of men, places undue emphasis on physical attractiveness. This is a dilemma in a nation that prizes European standards of beauty. Thus, the desire for approval from the mainstream culture leads many young people to attempt to divest themselves of cultural values and an Asian American identity.

A combination of racism and sexism contributes to negative feelings that many Asian American women have about their racial features (Chan, 1985; Hall, 1996) such as small breasts, eye and nose shapes, skin color, straight hair, and short stature. Although women of color have suffered from being compared to the European-based standard of attractiveness, perhaps no other group of women has attempted to change its racial features as much and by as drastic measures as have Asian American women. They have subjected themselves to eye surgery, nose construction, and breast implants (Kaw, 1993).

Lack of identity, powerlessness, struggles with self-acceptance, feelings of diminished worth and diminished attractiveness, and difficulties with assuming adult roles all are part of the development of chronic eating disorders (Root, 1990). Yoshimura (1992) observed that a history of greater body image dissatisfaction among Japanese American children and adolescents poses a risk factor for developing eating disorders. However, neither Yi (1989) nor Yoshimura (1992) found acculturation to be associated with eating disorder symptomatology among Asian American women. Ironically, although the petiteness of many Asian American women is seen as physically attractive, when combined with short stature, this equates with diminished power and childlikeness. Asian American women's eating disorders are more likely to include dissatisfaction with or loathing of specific racial features that are not related to body weight and fatness but that are projected onto a general feeling of body dissatisfaction, reflecting the struggles with identity, empowerment, and self-esteem.

Some of the social origins of alcohol and drug abuse are similar to those of eating disorders. Sue, Zane, and Ito (1979) found that patterns of Asian American drinking are associated with assimilation. However, Sun (1991) found that the importance of family identity, restrictiveness of the female role, importance of moderation, and lack of emphasis on drinking contribute to Asian American women drinking less than other women and less than Asian American men. This result is empirically documented for Koreans in Los Angeles (Lubben, Chi, & Kitano, 1989) and Chinese and Japanese Americans (Sue et al., 1979).

Bradshaw (1994) noted that conventional ethnic identity models are not sufficient to explain how Asian American women accomplish a positive ethnic identity that asserts equal social value with Asian American men. These models suggest that at some point, individuals seek refuge in their ethnic or racial communities to shield themselves from the denigrating messages they receive. However, gender is another status around which women receive denigrating messages even within their own communities. Thus, Bradshaw noted that Asian American women must attain a positive sense of self by maintaining simultaneous contact with a majority culture that supports their personal achievements and increased freedom as well as their ethnic group that affirms their ethnic self.

Identity development is further complicated for multiracial Asian American women. Kich (1992) observed, "The assertion of the self as biracial requires both the personal organizing structure of a biracial self label and the interpersonal and social recognition of the individual as biracial. The assertion creates and fosters a coherent, whole sense of self" (p. 317). However, given the subscriptions to notions of racial purity and hypodescent rules within some Asian cultures, biracial women might be marginalized and put through authenticity tests for acceptance as Asian. Identity is further complicated by the objectification of mixed-race women (Root, 1994). Valverde (1992) observed the operation of objectification and oppression by race rules on Vietnamese Amerasian women who are viewed as prostitutes whether or not they really are prostitutes. Some multiracial women lost in the identity process might play on their exoticness to gain acceptance from men or search for acceptance through their sexuality with men.

Many immigrant Asian American women struggle with a loss of satisfaction and esteem when their specialized training in their countries of origin does not allow them reciprocal credentials. Subsequently, many women with graduate educations are working in jobs that require little or no schooling. Some of these women suffer psychologically for having a lower status, often with a loss of self-esteem. Yet, other women seem to demonstrate the capacity for resilience and adaptation to the multitude of changes presented in immigration.

Kanuha (1990) observed the triple jeopardy—sexism, racism, and homophobia—faced by Asian American lesbians. Until recently, there were few places for lesbians to retreat for recognition of all three significant aspects of their lives (Ordona, 1994). H. (1989) suggested, "An Asian American lesbian must first strive to develop a basic sense of self-identity before taking the next step of developing a sexual identity" (p. 285). Chan (1987b) stated that declaring a lesbian identity is a revolutionary act in that one does not derive her identity from partnership with a man. "Coming out" might be accompanied by difficulty in achieving full adult status in her family's eyes. Adult status often is conferred through marriage and the birth of children. Thus, the coming-out process is fraught with anticipation of the loss of benefits associated with an expected role in the family.

SEXUALITY

Although there is a history of erotica in Asian countries, only recently have narratives and anthologies offered information about Asian American sexualities (Kudaka, 1995; Lim-Hing, 1994). Tsui (1985) observed that certain notions of propriety and, again, the distinction between private and public selves (Chan, 1994) might preclude certain types of written information on this topic. Chan (1994) suggested that sexuality subsequently might be a conflicted subject for young Asian Americans who are influenced by both familial rules and peer behavior. Hirayama and Hirayama (1986) further suggested that sexuality can be hard to study because it is both a private behavior and associated with emotion that often is controlled.

The literature that does exist suggests that Asian Americans tend to be sexually conservative in outward expressions of sexuality, which can serve to maintain social order within the family and community (Chan, 1994). This conservatism is correlated with lower rates of sexually active young adults, as Cochran, Mays, and Leung (1991) found in comparing Asian American college students with other ethnic and racial groups. Sexual conservatism makes it difficult to discuss many topics and may provide a more subtle form of culture generation gap between youths and their parents. The relative absence of written information on sexuality until now has far-reaching implications for Asian American women about the meaning of and right to sex, safe sex, sexual identity, birth control, pregnancy, and abortion.

Discussion of, much less declaration of, a gay, lesbian, or bisexual identity can be more difficult in the various Asian American communities (Chan, 1994). A lesbian identity can run in direct conflict with important cultural values on children and men. Support networks now exist specifically for Asian and Pacific Islander American lesbians and bisexuals to negotiate this life experience and to facilitate a positive sense of personal empowerment and negotiation of gender roles, ethnicity, and sexual orientation (Ordona, 1994). A woman has many obstacles to face in trying to negotiate a new role in the family if the family will allow its members to listen and obtain information to correct their misinformation about the meaning and origin of same-sex orientations and lesbian identity.

Sexually conservative attitudes also might contribute to some abused women staying in abusive partnerships for sexual companionship (Rimonte, 1989). Asking for help regarding sexual information and sexual functioning also could be very difficult. In addition, lack of information on sexuality and the importance of preserving the family name might make it difficult to disclose extrafamilial sexual abuse and rape.

Homma-True (1991) pointed out other implications of the lack of openness with which many families shy away from sexuality. Although Cochran et al. (1991) found that unsafe sex practices occurred at similar frequencies in their Asian and non-Asian American samples, Homma-True (1991) summarized the research indicating a dramatic increase in AIDS and HIV infection in the Asian American community. Given the role of women in sexuality, this can be an extremely difficult topic to address openly with partners, particularly with immigrant women from class and cultural backgrounds that do not regard their sexual safety or satisfaction as important. Homma-True suggested that aggressive outreach might be necessary to prevent the spread of AIDS and HIV infection in the Asian American community, particularly because the next risk group worldwide might be women.

VIOLENCE

A misdirected use of cultural sensitivity would be to interpret the dearth of information on sexual and physical violence against Asian American girls and women as a positive reflection on cultural values (Rimonte, 1991). More likely than not, a multitude of factors conspire to keep this evidence from public record. Traditional Japanese, Chinese, Korean, Filipino, South Asian, and Southeast Asian cultures reinforce power differentials based on gender (Ho, 1990; Kim, 1977; Rimonte, 1989, 1991; Song, 1994).

The insular nature of the family and cultural imperatives to protect the name of the family make it particularly difficult to report sexual abuse and domestic violence (Rimonte, 1991; Tsui, 1985). Such a disclosure might separate the girl or woman from familial support, amplifying the shame and humiliation that survivors often feel. From philosophical or religious origins, some Asian cultures have ascribed a positive trait to the ability to endure suffering (Ho, 1990) and even consider suffering as one's fate (Rimonte, 1989). Thus, a woman might be abused by male relatives, and the abuse might be accepted, either tacitly or overtly. Rimonte (1989) further observed that immigration disrupts the role and possible protective factor that the extended family might otherwise offer to women abused by spouses. Even if elderly parents are part of the family system, acculturation and disruption of traditional authority patterns might render elderly parents unable to effectively intervene on behalf of a daughter.

Abuse is an important area of study for determining what specific aspects of a culture, and what specific parts of patriarchal privilege, are correlated with abuse. In one of the few studies of child maltreatment, which includes a large number of Asian Americans, Ima and Hohm (1991) studied Southeast Asians, Filipinos, Koreans, and Pacific Islanders who were part of the database for a San Diego agency serving immigrants and refugees. They found that the differences among ethnic groups in which children had been mistreated were most likely attributable to cultural differences in life experiences, family structure, and child-rearing patterns. Samoans and Vietnamese reported high rates of child sexual abuse, whereas it was not frequently reported in the Filipino sample. In the latter group, the abuser often was a non-Filipino, military-enlisted stepfather. Nevertheless, in comparing the authors' sample to general statistics for the U.S. population, rates of physical abuse were similar and sexual abuse was either lower or underreported in their sample.

Domestic violence is a significant unexposed problem in Asian American communities. Rimonte (1989) reported on the presence of a shelter agency to help Pacific Asian women and their children subjected to violence in Los Angeles County. She emphasized diversity by group, income, and education. Of 3,000 women served by this Los Angeles center between 1978 and 1985, one third were Korean, one third were Southeast Asian, and the rest were other Asians and Pacific Islanders. Between 1982 and 1985, the majority of these women were immigrant women, 90% of whom had been battered, and the remainder were seeking services for rape. Rimonte observed several key factors that prevented women from leaving their abusers: economic hardship, the need for sexual companionship, and the fear of being deported. Since her initial report, immigration laws have been changed so that a woman who has been abused in a marriage will not be deported if she separates or divorces from her spouse.

In specifically working with Southeast Asian American refugee women, researchers and therapists must have an informed, broad contextual framework for understanding domestic problems that includes a consideration of the traumas incurred before resettlement in the United States, expectations of marriage, and relationship disequilibrators such as women being employed (Tien, 1994) before offering formulaic approaches to domestic problems. Pre- and postmigration exposure to violence must be considered. The life experiences of Southeast Asian refugee women subjected to horrific war atrocities were correlated with rape and sexual abuse, and the prevalence approached 100% (Mollica, Wyshak, & Lavelle, 1987). Subsequently, many of these refugee women have a particular fear of calling authorities; in their countries of origin, the authorities committed many of the war atrocities (e.g., murder, pillage, rape) (Rozee & van Boemel, 1989; Tien, 1994). As for postmigration, Luu (1989) observed that the economic hardships in the United States require many Vietnamese American women to move away from traditional roles through employment. Significant financial provision for the family threatens the foundation on which order has been maintained. She noted that men have had tremendous difficulty with this as they struggle in a country where it is difficult for them to find employment. Luu suggested that spousal abuse will be present under extreme duress and dislocation and when gender-role changes threaten authority and the distribution of power that determines the hierarchy; some men will attempt to assert their authority through spousal abuse.

Song (1994) offered similar explanations for the high rate of spousal violence she observed in her sample of 150 Korean immigrant women, 60% of whom reported abuse by their spouses. The battering often started once they were in the United States or intensified from its previous level. Kim (1977) and Song-Kim (1992) spoke to the cultural factors, immigration stresses, and isolation many Korean women experience after the immigration process that makes it difficult to leave these relationships.

In a study of immigrant Filipinos, Agbayani-Siewert (1991) found a similar pattern of marital role strain related to increased rates of domestic violence. She suggested that the role strain originated in conflicts in gender-role expectations between spouses. These two studies, as well as the Luu (1989) study, also suggested that the decreased presence of extended family kinship systems might serve to isolate women. Isolation is a key factor in spousal abuse.

It is important that researchers recognize and explore the diversity present among Asian and Pacific Americans (Ho, 1990; Ima & Hohm, 1991). Ho (1990) started this process with a focus group methodology in her study of attitudes toward physical violence in four Southeast Asian American communities in Seattle, Washington: Khmer, Laotian, Vietnamese, and Southeast Asian Chinese. She found that although similarities existed on the basis of patriarchal Confucianism,[1] asserting that men are superior to women and have the authority to dominate, there also are differences in the groups' attitudes toward violence.

Generational differences also must be considered in drawing conclusions from all the data presented heretofore. Ho (1990) observed that breaking the silence that keeps women and children prisoners of domestic violence is particularly difficult for first-generation individuals because of language facility, lack of familiarity with the system and resources, and family obligations. Leaving the family home for safety, although a viable strategy in communities that provide assistance and shelters, confronts the value of honor and name associated with the family hearth (Luu, 1989), is considered an "extraordinary gesture of self-assertion" (Rimonte, 1989, p. 332), and is perceived as selfish and at odds with the "best interest of the collective."

Empirical data are lacking on rape statistics for Asian American women. Again, we know that rape occurs in that it is the aftermath that can cause a woman to seek counseling. However, rape too is an underreported crime. In an increasing atmosphere of Asian bashing, my colleagues and I have hypothesized that rates of physical assault against women might have increased in the form of rape.

GENERAL MENTAL HEALTH

Perhaps two wide assertions about the mental health of Asian Americans are that emotional distress tends to be somatized and that Asian Americans underutilize the mental health system. These assertions are linked through the European invention that splits mind and body. Rozee and van Boemel (1989) stated, "Somatization is probably a universal phenomenon with varying degrees of acceptability in different cultures, and . . . an understanding of the client's cultural background may help us to understand the significance and meaning of the symptom" (p. 36). If someone experiences distress through physical symptoms, it is unlikely that the individual will seek the help of a psychotherapist. In essence, psychotherapy does not make sense as a first-line intervention for many Asian Americans (Chao, 1992; Loo & Ong, 1982). Many immigrants and refugees have their own beliefs about who and what can help them that are consistent with their personal theories about the origins of their distress. Ying (1990) found that, even when a problem might be conceptualized psychologically, Chinese Americans turned toward relational strategies (e.g., family, friends, themselves) to address problems of a psychological nature. She noted, "Harmony in one's relationships as well as within oneself (e.g., balance of mind and body) are paramount in the [mental] health of the Chinese person" (p. 394). Thus, it makes sense that the solution be relational in nature.

Use of mental health services also might be effected by client-therapist match. Fujino, Okazaki, and Young (1994) analyzed Los Angeles County mental health data from the mid-1980s. They found that ethnic and gender matches were correlated with longer use of therapy and less severe diagnoses. This match was found to be more important for Asian American women than for Asian American men or White men or women.

Several studies have documented that certain psychosocial stressors particularly present for immigrants and refugees increased their risk for continued psychological distress and need for mental health services after they left or fled their countries (Chao, 1992; Felsman, Leong, Johnson, & Felsman, 1990; Gong-Guy, 1987; Leong & Johnson, 1992; Tien, 1994). These samples are composed largely of Chinese and Southeast Asians. Depression among women appears to be particularly salient in some reports, whether on the West Coast (Fujino & Chung, 1991; Homma-True, 1989; Ying, 1988) or the East Coast (Yu, Liu, & Wong, 1987). However, if SES or birthplace and length of residence in the United States was controlled for, then the differences between genders disappeared in a San Francisco immigrant Chinese sample (Ying, 1988). In this same study, if SES was controlled and education and occupation were allowed to vary, age was correlated with depression, with younger respondents reporting more depressive symptomatology.

Homma-True (1990) noted that when some of the obstacles to psychotherapy were removed (e.g., language barriers, scheduling conflicts, distrust) (Root, 1985), she found that approximately half of the clients using San Francisco Bay area public mental health services were Asian American women. Like American women in general, these women seemed to struggle with depression more frequently than did Asian American men. She attributed these differences largely to role strain, the stress of living biculturally and unappreciated in both cultures, and often denying one's needs. Risk factors for depression, such as low self-esteem, devalued social status, and poverty, are simultaneously relevant variables describing much, but not all, of Asian America, particularly Asian American women closer to immigrant status and old women. On the other hand, women had lower rates of schizophrenia than did Asian American men based on service utilization. Homma-True (1991) suggested that the spectrum of disorders that includes psychotic symptoms might impinge more on men's ability to work in gender-role proscriptions than on women's, which might bring them to the attention of mental health service systems even though the range of symptoms is approximately evenly distributed by gender (American Psychiatric Association, 1994).

Fujino and Chung (1991) obtained results similar to those of Homma-True (1989) using Los Angeles County data. There were no gender differences for Asian Americans for depression. This finding departs from the typical finding of depression that is diagnosed more frequently in women (American Psychiatric Association, 1994). However, Asian American men had higher rates of depression than did men in other ethnic groups. Asians and African Americans had higher rates of schizophrenia across gender, and men had higher rates across groups than did women. Asian American women had significantly more adjustment disorders than did Asian American men, but they were not significantly different from other groups of women.

Immigration poses many stresses to immigrant women, who might have less support and help from extended family who are not present and might feel alienated by customs of interaction, language, and/or knowledge of resources (Homma-True, 1991). Gender-role strain that may follow adaptation to the need to work to support the family might contribute to immigrants' stress levels. Furthermore, immigrant women and men might end up taking lower-status and lower-paying jobs because certification or credentialing procedures in the United States differ from those in their countries of origin. This lends itself to depression, low self-esteem, and alienation even from oneself.

Refugee Mental Health

Mental health concerns are particularly salient for Southeast Asian refugees, Vietnamese, Laotian, and Khmer who have migrated involuntarily, have not necessarily preferred to reside in the United States, and have most frequently endured a significant number of war atrocities (Kinzie, Fredrickson, Ben, Fleck, & Karls, 1984). For women, these atrocities include witness to murder of family and friends as well as rape or the torture of their spouses, children, and other family members. Rozee and van Boemel's (1989) study of functionally blind female Cambodian refugees documented that 90% of the participants had lost 1 to 10 relatives; the women had witnessed many of the deaths. Many of these women were widowed because of the war. Tien (1994) observed that therapists should attend to dates of departure. Vietnamese women who left before 1975 or in the first wave tended to have money and resources; they did not go through the camp experiences. Many of the relational resources to which young adult refugees might turn are not available; many mothers of these now young adults are distressed and unable to provide the psychological caregiving their children might need because of their traumas (Leong & Johnson, 1992).

Chung (1991) used data from one of the first statewide needs assessment studies that used a nonclinical, representative sample to study the well-being of Southeast Asian refugees in California. The differences between groups and by gender were explained by pre- and postmigration variables. Premigration trauma experiences were a consistent predictor of distress, as measured by depression and anxiety. In general, men's distress, more so than women's, could be predicted in part by postmigration issues that involved employment and income and sources of traditional identity. Of three groups studied—Cambodians, Laotians, and Vietnamese—Cambodians were the most distressed group, followed by Laotians and Vietnamese. The women in all groups were more distressed than the men.

Chung explained these results. Cambodians reported more and multiple traumas; the women, more so than the men, had lost partners and other family members. Cambodians resided in camps much longer than did the other groups and Vietnamese the least. Cambodian and Laotian women, compared to Vietnamese women, had less facility with English and more frequently were not involved in the decision to flee. These same groups of women, compared to Vietnamese women, tended to be unemployed and had low family incomes. Cambodian men and women still were preoccupied with premigration issues, having been in the United States for a shorter time than the other two groups.

FUTURE DIRECTIONS

The consideration of specific political and cultural legacies must become the domain of psychology if psychologists are to move away from stereotypes to understand the psychology of Asian American women in context and in a framework that includes notions of adaptation and positive transformation indicative of resiliency. Contemporarily, being an Asian American woman has many complexities. We do not currently understand all of the complexities of being located at the intersection of gender, ethnicity, social class, generation, geographic region, and educational achievement. Now more than ever, the Asian American woman has many representatives. Generation, age, religion, ethnicity, geographical region, values, and orientations to family and society guarantee diversity among Asian American women (Bradshaw, 1994). Compared to 20 years ago, the Asian American woman is less defined by the man with whom she is in a relationship.

We have more Asian Americans in graduate school in psychology than ever before. Many of these students are women. This fact increases the likelihood that more research will be conducted on Asian American women in the future. What are some of the directions to which past research points us? What research needs to be done? The increased size and variability of Asian America underscores the importance of studying the differential impact that specific cultural and political legacies exert on behavior, identity, values, and ultimately mental health. Researchers must resist amalgamating Asian American groups across ethnicities without a rationale beyond convenience. We need to carefully consider gender differences in the issues studied. Research studies must anticipate the complex braid of variables (e.g., gender, class, ethnicity, generation) that may help us to decipher the meanings of results. We need studies to be ethnic-group specific for rape, abuse, divorce, identity development, mental health, sexuality, and intermarriage. Additional areas of study not reviewed in this chapter include the elderly (particularly because women tend to outlive men); health practices that decrease risks; contemporary child rearing; educational aspirations and attainment as they combine with decisions about family, pregnancy, and childbearing; management of stereotypes of Asian American women in the workplace; transgenerational trauma, particularly for children of refugees; the reporting of rape, sexual abuse, physical abuse, and domestic violence; the impact of welfare reform and managed care on mental health and on responsibilities adult women take for elderly parents; and changes in alcohol and drug use for Asian American women.

NOTE

1. Confucionism, however, neither condones nor advocates violence.

REFERENCES

Adams, R. (1937). Chinese familialism and interracial marriage. In R. Adams (Ed.), *Interracial marriage in Hawaii*. New York: Macmillan.

Agbayani-Siewert, P. (1991). *Filipino American social role strain, self-esteem, locus of control, social networks, coping, stress and mental health outcome*. Unpublished doctoral dissertation, University of California, Los Angeles.

Ahern, F. M., Cole, R. E., Johnson, R. C., & Wong, B. (1981). Personality attributes of males and females marrying within vs. across racial/ethnic groups. *Behavior Genetics, 11*, 181-194.

American Psychiatric Association. (1994). *Diagnostic and statistical manual of mental disorders* (4th ed.). Washington, DC: Author.

Bradshaw, C. (1990). A Japanese view of dependency: What can Amae psychology contribute to feminist theory and therapy? In L. S. Brown & M. P. P. Root (Eds.), *Diversity and complexity in feminist therapy* (pp. 67-86). New York: Haworth.

Bradshaw, C. (1994). Asian American women. In L. Comas Diaz & B. Greene (Eds.), *Women of color: Integrating ethnic and gender identities in psychotherapy* (pp. 72-113). New York: Guilford.

Card, J. (1978). Correspondence of data gathered from husband and wife: Implications for family planning studies. *Social Biology, 25*, 196-204.

Chan, C. S. (1985). Self-esteem and body-image of Asian American adolescent girls. *Journal of the Asian American Psychological Association, 4*, 24-25.

Chan, C. S. (1987a). Asian-American women: Psychological responses to sexual exploitation and cultural stereotypes. *Journal of the Asian American Psychological Association, 6*, 11-15.

Chan, C. S. (1987b). Asian lesbians: Psychological issues in the "coming out" process. *Journal of the Asian American Psychological Association, 6*, 16-18.

Chan, C. S. (1994). Asian American adolescents: Issues of sexuality. In J. Irvine (Ed.), *Sexual cultures: Adolescence, communities, and the constructions of identities* (pp. 88-99). Philadelphia: Temple University Press.

Chan, S. (1991). *Asian Americans: An interpretive history*. Boston: Twayne.

Chao, C. M. (1992). The inner heart: Therapy with Southeast Asian families. In L. A. Vargas & J. D. Koss-Chioino (Eds.), *Working with culture: Psychotherapeutic interventions with ethnic minority children and adolescents* (pp. 157-181). San Francisco: Jossey-Bass.

Chow, E. N.-L. (1989). The feminist movement: Where are all the Asian American women? In Asian Women United of California (Ed.), *Making waves: An anthology of writings by and about Asian American women* (pp. 362-377). Boston: Beacon.

Chu, J. (1988). Social and economic profile of Asian Pacific American women: Los Angeles County. In G. Y. Okihiro, S. Hune, A. A. Hansen, & J. M. Liu (Eds.), *Reflections on shattered windows: Promises and prospects for Asian American studies* (pp. 193-205). Pullman: Washington State University Press.

Chung, R. C. (1991, August). *Predictors of distress among Southeast Asian refugees: Group and gender differences*. Paper presented at the annual convention of the Asian American Psychological Association, San Francisco.

Cochran, S., Mays, V. Y., & Leung, L. (1991). Sexual practices of heterosexual Asian-American young adults: Implications for risk of HIV infection. *Archives of Sexual Behavior, 20*, 381-391.

Felsman, J. K., Leong, F. T. L., Johnson, M. C., & Felsman, I. C. (1990). Estimates of psychological distress among Vietnamese refugees: Adolescents, unaccompanied minors and young adults. *Social Science Medicine, 31,* 1251-1256.

Fujino, D. (1992). *Extending exchange theory: Effects of ethnicity and gender on Asian American heterosexual relationships.* Doctoral dissertation, University of California, Los Angeles.

Fujino, D. (1993, August). *Cultural standards of beauty, power, and interracial relationships.* Paper presented at the annual convention of the Asian American Psychological Association, Toronto.

Fujino, D. C., & Chung, R. C.-Y. (1991, August). *Asian American mental health: An examination of gender issues.* Paper presented at the annual convention of the Asian American Psychological Association, San Francisco.

Fujino, D. C., Okazaki, S., & Young, K. (1994). Asian-American women in the mental health system: An examination of ethnic and gender match between therapist and client. *Journal of Community Psychology, 22,* 164-176.

Fujitomi, I., & Wong, D. (1973). The new Asian-American woman. In S. Sue & N. N. Wagner (Eds.), *Asian Americans: Psychological perspectives* (pp. 252-263). Ben Lomond, CA: Science and Behavior Books.

Glenn, E. N. (1986). *Issei, Nisei, warbride: Three generations of Japanese American women in domestic service.* Philadelphia: Temple University Press.

Gong-Guy, E. (1987). *The California Southeast Asian Mental Health Needs Assessment.* Oakland, CA: Asian Community Mental Health Services.

H., P. (1989). Asian American lesbians: An emerging voice in the Asian American community. In Asian Women United of California (Ed.), *Making waves: An anthology of writings by and about Asian American women* (pp. 282-290). Boston: Beacon.

Hall, C. I. (1996). Asian eyes: Body image and eating disorders of Asian American women. *Eating Disorders: Journal of Prevention and Treatment, 4*(1), 1-12.

Hirayama, H., & Hirayama, K. (1986). The sexuality of Japanese Americans. *Journal of Social Work and Human Sexuality, 4,* 81-98.

Ho, C. K. (1990). An analysis of domestic violence in Asian American communities: A multicultural approach to counseling. In L. Brown & M. P. P. Root (Eds.), *Diversity and complexity in feminist therapy* (pp. 129-150). New York: Haworth.

Ho, F. C., & Johnson, R. C. (1990). Intraethnic and interethnic marriage and divorce in Hawaii. *Social Biology, 37,* 44-51.

Ho, M. K. (1984). *Building a successful intermarriage.* St. Meinrad, IN: St. Meinrad Archabbey.

Homma-True, R. (1987, August). *Psychotherapeutic issues with Asian American women.* Paper presented at the annual convention of the Asian American Psychological Association, New York.

Homma-True, R. (1989, August). *Mental health service utilization by Asian American women in San Francisco.* Paper presented at the annual convention of the Asian American Psychological Association, New York.

Homma-True, R. (1990). Psychotherapeutic issues with Asian American women. *Sex Roles, 22,* 477-486.

Homma-True, R. (1991, August). *Psychological impact of immigration on Asian women.* Paper presented at the annual convention of the Asian American Psychological Association, San Francisco.

Ima, K., & Hohm, C. F. (1991). Child maltreatment among Asian and Pacific Islander refugees and immigrants: The San Diego case. *Journal of Interpersonal Violence, 6,* 267-285.

Kanuha, V. (1990). Compounding the triple jeopardy: Battering in lesbian of color relationships. In L. S. Brown & M. P. P. Root (Eds.), *Diversity and complexity in feminist therapy* (pp. 169-184). New York: Haworth.

Kaw, E. (1993). Medicalization of racial features: Asian American women and cosmetic surgery. *Medical Anthropology Quarterly, 7,* 74-89.

Kich, G. K. (1992). The developmental process of asserting a biracial, bicultural identity. In M. P. P. Root (Ed.), *Racially mixed people in America* (pp. 304-320). Newbury Park, CA: Sage.

Kim, B.-L. C. (1977). Asian wives of U.S. servicemen: Women in shadows. *Amerasia, 4,* 91-115.

Kinzie, J. D., Fredrickson, R. H., Ben, R., Fleck, J., & Karls, W. (1984). Posttraumatic stress disorder among survivors of Cambodian concentration camps. *American Journal of Psychiatry, 141,* 645-650.

Kitano, H. L. L., Yeung, W.-T., Chai, L., & Hatanaka, H. (1984). Asian American interracial marriage. *Journal of Marriage and the Family, 46,* 179-190.

Kudaka, G. (Ed.). (1995). *On a bed of rice: An Asian American erotic feast.* New York: Anchor Books.

Leong, F. T. L., & Johnson, M. C. (1992). *Vietnamese Amerasian mothers: Psychological distress and high-risk factors.* Washington, DC: Department of Health and Human Services, Office of Refugee Resettlement.

Leong, F. T. L., & Serafica, F. C. (1995). Career development of Asian Americans: A research area in need of a good theory. In F. T. L. Leong (Ed.), *Career development and vocational behavior of racial and ethnic minorities* (pp. 67-101). Mahwah, NJ: Lawrence Erlbaum.

Lim-Hing, S. (Ed.). (1994). *The very inside: An anthology of writing by Asian and Pacific Islander lesbian and bisexual women.* Toronto: Sister Vision Press.

Lin, J. (1991). *Marital satisfaction and conflict in intercultural correspondence marriage.* Doctoral dissertation, University of Washington, Seattle.

Loo, C. (1991). *Most time, hard time Chinatown.* New York: Praeger.

Loo, C., & Ong, P. (1982). Slaying demons with a sewing needle: Feminist issues for Chinatown women. *Berkeley Journal of Sociology, 27,* 77-88.

Lubben, J. E., Chi, I., & Kitano, H. (1989). The relative influence of selected social factors on Korean drinking behavior in Los Angeles. *Advances in Alcohol and Substance Abuse, 8,* 1-17.

Lui, B. (1990). *Asian American childrearing practices and acculturation: A cross-cultural examination.* Doctoral dissertation, University of Washington, Seattle.

Luu, V. (1989). The hardships of escape for Vietnamese women. In Asian Women United of California (Eds.), *Making waves: An anthology of writings by and about Asian American women* (pp. 60-72). Boston: Beacon.

Miller, R. L. (1992). The human ecology of multiracial identity. In M. P. P. Root (Ed.), *Racially mixed people in America* (pp. 24-36). Newbury Park, CA: Sage.

Mollica, R., Wyshak, G., & Lavelle, J. (1987). The psychological impact of war trauma and torture on Southeast Asian refugees. *American Journal of Psychiatry, 144,* 1567-1571.

Nagata, D. K. (1995). Understanding the training experiences of Asian-American women. In J. Adleman & G. Enguidanos-Clark (Eds.), *Racism in the lives of women: Testimony, theory, and guides to antiracist practice.* New York: Haworth.

Nguyen, N. A. (1992). Living between two cultures: Treating first-generation Asian Americans. In L. A. Vargas & J. D. Koss-Chioino (Eds.), *Working with culture: Psychotherapeutic interventions with ethnic minority children and adolescents* (pp. 204-224). San Francisco: Jossey-Bass.

Ordona, T. A. (1994). The challenges facing Asian and Pacific Islander lesbian and bisexual women in the U.S.: Coming out, coming together, moving forward. In S. Lim-Hing (Ed.), *The very inside: An anthology of writing by Asian and Pacific Islander lesbian and bisexual women.* Toronto: Sister Vision Press.

Ordoñez, R. Z. (1997). Mail order brides: The emerging community. In M. P. P. Root (Ed.), *Filipino Americans: Transformation and identity* (pp. 121-142). Thousand Oaks, CA: Sage.

Rimonte, N. (1989). Domestic violence among Pacific Asians. In Asian Women United of California (Eds.), *Making waves: An anthology of writings by and about Asian American women* (pp. 327-337). Boston: Beacon.

Rimonte, N. (1991). A question of culture: Cultural approval of violence against women in the Pacific-Asian community and the cultural defense. *Harvard Law Review, 43,* 1311-1326.

Robinson, T. (1993). The intersections of gender, class, race, and culture: On seeing clients whole. *Journal of Multicultural Counseling and Development, 21*(1), 50-58.

Root, M. P. P. (1985). Guidelines for facilitating therapy with Asian American clients. *Psychotherapy: Theory, Research, and Practice, 22,* 349-356.

Root, M. P. P. (1990). Disordered eating in women of color. *Sex Roles, 22,* 525-536.

Root, M. P. P. (1994). Mixed race women. In L. Comas Diaz & B. Greene (Eds.), *Women of color: Integrating ethnic and gender identities in psychotherapy* (pp. 455-478). New York: Guilford.

Rozee, P. D., & van Boemel, G. (1989). The psychological effects of war trauma and abuse on older Cambodian refugee women. *Women and Therapy, 8,* 23-50.

Serita, T. (1984). Mail order sexploitation. *Bridge, 9,* 39-41.

Shinagawa, L. H., & Pang, G. Y. (1996). Asian American panethnicity and intermarriage. *Amerasia Journal, 22*(2), 127-152.

Shon, S. P., & Ja, D. (1982). Asian families. In M. McGoldrick, J. K. Pearce, & J. Giordano (Eds.), *Ethnicity and family therapy* (pp. 208-228). New York: Guilford.

Song, Y. (1994). *Battered women in Korean immigrant families.* New York: Garland.

Song-Kim, Y. I. (1992). Battered Korean women in urban United States. In S. M. Furuto, R. Biswas, D. K. Chung, K. Murasse, & F. Ross-Sheriff (Eds.), *Social work practice with Asian Americans* (pp. 213-226). Newbury Park, CA: Sage.

Sue, S., Zane, N., & Ito, J. (1979). Alcohol drinking patterns among Asian and Caucasian Americans. *Journal of Cross-Cultural Psychology, 10,* 41-56.

Sun, A.-P. (1991). Issues for Asian American women. In P. Roth (Ed.), *Alcohol and drugs are women's issues* (Vol. 1, pp. 125-129). Metuchen, NJ: Women's Action Alliance/Scarecrow Press.

Sung, B. L. (1990). *Chinese American intermarriage.* New York: Center for Migration Studies.

Takagi, D. Y. (1988). Personality and history: Hostile Nisei women. In G. Y. Okihiro, S. Hune, A. A. Hansen, & J. M. Liu (Eds.), *Reflections on shattered windows: Promises and prospects for Asian American studies* (pp. 184-192). Pullman: Washington State University Press.

Tien, L. (1994). Southeast Asian women. In L. Comas Diaz & B. Greene (Eds.), *Women of color: Integrating ethnic and gender identities in psychotherapy* (pp. 479-503). New York: Guilford.

Tsui, A. M. (1985). Psychotherapeutic considerations in sexual counseling for Asian immigrants. *Psychotherapy: Theory, Research, and Practice, 22,* 357-362.

Valverde, K. C. (1992). From dust to gold: The Vietnamese Amerasian experience. In M. P. P. Root (Ed.), *Racially mixed people in America* (pp. 144-161). Newbury Park, CA: Sage.

Villapando, V. (1989). The business of selling mail-order brides. In Asian Women United of California (Eds.), *Making waves: An anthology of writings by and about Asian American women* (pp. 318-326). Boston: Beacon.

Yi, K. Y. (1989). *Symptoms of eating disorders among Asian-American college female students as a function of acculturation.* Doctoral dissertation, California School of Professional Psychology, Los Angeles.

Ying, Y. W. (1988). Depressive symptomatology among Chinese-Americans as measured by the CES-D. *Journal of Clinical Psychology, 44,* 739-746.

Ying, Y. W. (1990). Explanatory models of major depression and implications for help-seeking among immigrant Chinese-American women. *Culture, Medicine, and Psychiatry, 14,* 393-408.

Ying, Y. W. (1991). Marital satisfaction among San Francisco Chinese-Americans. *International Journal of Social Psychiatry, 37,* 201-213.

Yoshimura, K. K. (1992). *Acculturative and sociocultural influences on the development of eating disorders in Asian-American females.* Doctoral dissertation, California School of Professional Psychology, Los Angeles.

Yu, L. C., & Wu, S. (1985). Unemployment and family dynamics in meeting the needs of Chinese elderly in the United States. *The Gerontologist, 25,* 472-476.

Yu, W. S. H., Liu, W. T., & Wong, S. C. (1987). Measurement of depression in a Chinatown health clinic. In W. T. Liu (Ed.), *A decade review of mental health research, training, and services.* Chicago: Pacific/Asian American Mental Health Research Center.

Yung, J. (1991). The social awakening of Chinese American women as reported in *Chung Sai Yat Po,* 1900-1911. In C. DuBois & V. L. Ruiz (Eds.), *Unequal sisters: A multicultural reader in U.S. women's history* (pp. 195-207). New York: Routledge.

INTERRACIAL MARRIAGES

Where Are the Asian Americans and Where Are They Going?

HARRY H. L. KITANO
DIANE C. FUJINO
JANE TAKAHASHI SATO

It was not that long ago that the rhetorical question "But do you want your daughter to marry one?" was sufficient to discourage all but the most committed to cancel marital plans across racial lines. But the attitudinal barrier did not stand alone; there were antimiscegenation laws, fines, and even jail sentences. It was clear that society looked on interracial marriages as something negative and to be avoided in spite of the American image of the "melting pot."

By contrast, the answer to the rhetorical question today might be "Yes, but under certain conditions." Does the suitor have an acceptable professional and occupational background? Is there role compatibility? And, of course, are they in love? This change is interesting given that the ideology of the melting pot—that we all should melt and become one—has been replaced by a pluralistic ideology that encourages ethnic retention.

The purpose of this chapter is to present a short history of Asian Americans, review past major findings, present current data, and provide a model to understand and to make future predictions. The following groups are covered: Chinese, Filipinos, Japanese, Koreans, and Vietnamese.

Definitions

There are a variety of terms that are used concerning marital relationships between and among the Asian American groups. *In-marriage* or *intragroup marriage* is used whenever an Asian American marries within his or her own ethnic group such as a Chinese American male marrying a Chinese American female. *Out-marriage* or *intergroup marriage* is used whenever an individual of a specific Asian American group marries out of his or her ethnic group; for example, a Chinese American marrying a person who is not of Chinese ancestry is an out-marriage. An *interracial marriage* occurs when the individual not only marries out of his or her own ethnic group but also marries a person who is not of Asian ancestry.

Ethnicity is used to identify specific Asian American groups by their ancestry. Therefore, in the present study, there are Americans of the following ancestries: Chinese, Filipino, Japanese, Korean, and Vietnamese.

Sources of Data

There are two major sources of data concerning intermarriage. One source is the U.S. census, which provides data on existing marriages (prevalence). The other is marriage license records maintained by local sources, which provide data on new marriages on a year-by-year basis (incidence). There are limitations of both of these sources including the following:

1. They are self-reports, and categories for people of mixed ancestry are arbitrary.
2. Ethnic and racial categories have not been consistently recorded. In 1959, civil rights legislation prohibited racial identification on marriage license applications. Another problem has been the lumping together of the various Asian American groups into an "Asian" or "other" category. The 1970 to 1990 census reports have been the most thorough in providing detailed information on Chinese, Japanese, and Filipinos.
3. Hawaii has been an exception; there are data for each of the Asian American groups.
4. Although local marriage license records provide more detailed information (e.g., place of birth, birthplace of parents, number of previous marriages, occupation), the gathering of the data is costly and tedious. For example, in Los Angeles, researchers have to go through more than 35,000 marriage licenses for any given year and identify the various Asian American applicants by surname and birthplace while competing with other groups for access to the microfilm records.

Units of Analysis

The most common ways of computing intermarriage rates are by counting individuals or counting marriages (Cretser & Leon, 1982; Shinagawa & Pang, 1988). Counting individuals will give higher rates of out-marriage than when marriages are used as the unit of analysis.

Sociologists and others studying macrolevel phenomena may use another level of analysis such as the community or the society. Lichter, LeClere, and McLaughlin (1991) used a labor market area as their unit of analysis. They explored mate selection on variables such as labor force participation and relative supply of men within each labor market area to explain variances in marriage.

Historical Factors

By the importance of history, we refer to time, motivation, conditions of immigration, and sociodemographic factors such as age and sex composition of the immigrating Asian groups. In addition, the interaction with the host society is important because racial prejudice, discrimination, and segregation have limited equality and access to the American mainstream. Each Asian group entered the United States with a variety of backgrounds and in different historical time periods so that instead of homogeneity in terms of marital preferences, it is expected that there will be differences.

THE CHINESE

The Chinese were the first Asian group to arrive in the United States. Their initial immigration took place between 1850 and 1882 and was composed primarily of young male sojourners. Some were already married; only a few brought their wives and children to America, so it was basically a single male community living in "Chinatowns" (Kitano & Daniels, 1995).

The Chinese Exclusion Act of 1882 closed the door to further Chinese immigration so that from 1882 to 1943, no Chinese could come to America legally. As a consequence, there was an abnormally high male-to-female ratio, which, along with antimiscegenation laws, resulted in a lack of family life and very small numbers of American-born Chinese children.

In 1943, the Chinese Exclusion Act was repealed. In addition, the Immigration and Naturalization Act of 1965 abolished national origin quotas. Consequently, there has been a rise in the numbers of Chinese entering the United States. In 1980, the U.S. census reported 812,178 Chinese; in 1990, their numbers had grown to 1,643,621. The great majority of the Chinese population is foreign born (Kitano & Daniels, 1988).

Panunzio (1942) conducted one of the earliest studies on intermarriage in Los Angeles County. Marriage license data were analyzed from 1924, when immigration from Asia was totally stopped, to 1933, when antimiscegenation laws included Filipinos. Although Panunzio indicated that "Yellow" and "Brown" people were lumped together so that interethnic and interracial rates were impossible to obtain, she also reported on the out-marriage rates for Chinese, Filipino, Japanese, and Mexican Americans (Table 7.1).

The Chinese, who comprised 0.2% of the Los Angeles County population with a sex ratio of 377 men to 100 women, had an out-marriage rate of 23.7%

TABLE 7.1. Out-Marriage Rates, Sex Ratios, and Population Percentages for Various Ethnic Groups in Los Angeles County, 1924-1933

Ethnicity	Out-Marriage Rate (percentage)[a]	Percentage of Total Married to Whites[a]	Sex Ratio[b,c]	Percentage of County Population[b]
African American	1.1[d]	0.1	84	2.1
Chinese American	23.7	1.0	377	0.2
Filipino American	70.1	35.0[e]	2,416	0.2
Japanese American	2.3	0.6	125	1.6
Mexican American	17.0	15.6	114	7.6

SOURCE: Panunzio (1942).
a. Based on marriage license data, 1924 to 1933.
b. Based on 1930 U.S. census data.
c. Refers to number of men per 100 women.
d. Technically refers to interracial marriage rate for African Americans.
e. This figure represents an estimation of the Filipino marriage rate to Whites, which was approximately half the Filipino out-marriage rate.

(Panunzio, 1942). Of the 23 intermarriages, 14 were to Japanese, 5 to African Americans, 1 to a Filipino, and 2 to other "Yellow-Browns." There also was 1 recorded Chinese-White marriage, although antimiscegenation laws existed in California at that time.

African Americans had an out-marriage rate of 1.1%, with 0.1% married to Whites. Their sex ratio balance was 84 men to 100 women.

Mexican out-marriage was estimated to be 17.0%. The Mexican groups were different from the Asian American groups in that they were more numerous and were not subject to antimiscegenation legislation. The majority of Mexican Americans married Whites.

Studies of Chinese out-marriage rates in California covering the years 1955 to 1959 were analyzed by Barnett (1963). He found rates of 14% in 1955, 16.9% in 1957, 15.8% in 1958, and 17.0% in 1959. Chinese out-marriage rates in Los Angeles County between 1948 and 1959 were 5.83% for males and 4.94% for females (Burma, 1963).

These early studies indicate that the rates of Chinese out-marriage in Los Angeles and in California were consistently below 20%.

Urban and rural comparisons of out-marriage were analyzed based on data from the 1970 census (Table 7.2). The 1970 census published a separate volume titled *Japanese, Chinese, and Filipinos in the United States* so that comparisons could be made among the interracial marriage rates of the three groups by using the category of "marriage with spouse of the same race." Urban areas were defined as (a) persons living in places of 2,500 inhabitants or more incorporated as cities, villages, or boroughs but excluding those persons living in the rural portions; (b) unincorporated places of 2,500 inhabitants or more; or (c) other territories, incorporated or unincoporated, included in urbanized areas. The population not classified as urban constitutes the rural population. The great majority of Chinese lived in urban areas. The interracial marriage rate for urban Chinese males was

TABLE 7.2. National Interracial Marriage Rates for Urban, Rural Nonfarm, and Rural Farm Residence, by Ethnicity and Gender, 1970

Gender and Residence	Chinese		Filipino		Japanese	
	Number	Percentage	Number	Percentage	Number	Percentage
Women						
Urban	82,500	12	50,876	28	137,619	33
Rural nonfarm	2,763	38	7,580	28	14,831	42
Rural farm	151	12	306	32	3,313	12
Men						
Urban	84,525	13	55,146	33	105,154	12
Rural nonfarm	2,634	33	8,493	35	10,049	14
Rural farm	165	14	416	51	3,138	7

SOURCE: U.S. Bureau of the Census (1973).

13%. The rural farm population was defined as (a) persons living on places of 10 acres or more in which sales of farm products amounted to $50 or more in the preceding year or (b) persons living on places less than 10 acres from which sales of farm products amounted to $250 or more in the preceding year. Their interracial marriage rate was 14%. The highest rates of out-marriage were among the rural nonfarm sample, defined as all residents not living in rural farm areas, where 33% were married to spouses not of the same race. The picture of the Chinese female in terms of interracial marriage was similar to that of the Chinese male. Most were urban dwellers, where the out-marriage rate was 12% and where the rural nonfarm sample had the highest out-marriage rate (38%).

Kitano and Yeung (1982), using U.S. census reports for 1970, found the following out-marriage rates by sex and by state for the Chinese. Hawaii had the highest rates of out-marriage (29.7% for females, 30.6% for males), followed by Illinois (11.2% females, 11.0% males), Massachusetts (8.0% females, 10.2% males), California (8.9% females, 9.2% males), and New York (3.7% females, 7.3% males). The sex breakdown was about equal in all of the states, with the exception of New York, where male out-marriages were higher than female out-marriages.

Intermarriage rates during the 1980s were reported in a number of studies. Lee and Yamanaka (1990) presented national data on Chinese, Filipino, Japanese, Korean, and Vietnamese as well as on African American, Latino, and White American intermarriages using the Public Use Microdata Samples for 1980 (Table 7.3). Using individuals as the unit of analysis, the out-marriage rates were 16.8% for Chinese females, with 12.2% married to Whites, and 14.4% for Chinese males, with 8.3% married to Whites. It is interesting to note that only 1.5% of African Americans were married to Whites, whereas 99% of Whites married other Whites.

Shinagawa and Pang (1988), using the 1980 U.S. Census, reported on intermarriage rates for California (Table 7.4). They covered the same Asian American groups as did Lee and Yamanaka (1990) but did not present gender differences. The Chinese out-marriage rate, this time using marriages as the unit of analysis, was 22.2%, with 13.7% married to Whites.

TABLE 7.3. Out-Marriage Rates in the United States for Various Ethnic Groups by Gender, 1980 (percentages)

Ethnicity and Gender	Out-Marriage Rate	Intraethnic Rate	Interethnic Rate	Interracial Rate	Percentage Married to Whites
Chinese female[a]	16.8	83.2	3.4	13.4	12.2
Chinese male[a]	14.4	85.6	5.1	9.3	8.3
Filipino female[a]	35.5	64.5	3.2	32.3	27.5
Filipino male[a]	22.2	77.8	4.0	18.2	15.1
Japanese female[a]	41.6	58.4	4.7	36.9	33.9
Japanese male[a]	21.3	78.7	6.1	15.1	13.7
Korean female[a]	4.5	55.5	3.3	41.2	36.1
Korean male[a]	7.5	92.5	2.9	4.6	4.4
Vietnamese female[a]	28.9	71.1	2.0	26.9	24.9
Vietnamese male[a]	5.5	94.5	1.0	4.5	4.2
Asian American[b]	25.4	74.6	3.6	21.4	19.5
African American[b]	–	–	–	2.2	1.5
Latina/Latino[b]	–	–	–	12.7	10.5
White American[b]	–	–	–	1.0	99.0

SOURCE: Lee and Yamanaka (1990).
NOTE: Based on 1980 U.S. Census data using individuals as the unit of analysis.
a. Refers to Asians in America.
b. No information is provided by gender.

Sung (1990) used data from the 1980 census, marriage license applications, and personal interviews to study intermarriage rates in New York City. She indicated that because immigration to that city is more recent and is overwhelmingly foreign born, the rates of out-marriage were about 25%.

Out-marriage data for Chinese, Filipinos, Japanese, Koreans, and Vietnamese in Los Angeles County, based on marriage license data for 1975, 1977, 1979, 1984, and 1989, were gathered by Kitano and Yeung (1982) and Kitano (1988, 1997). As shown in Table 7.5, the out-marriage rates for the Chinese were 44.0% in 1975, 49.7% in 1977, 41.2% in 1979, 30.0% in 1984, and 33.9% in 1989. The percentage figures are somewhat deceptive because they show a drop from a high of 49.7% in 1977, to 30.0% in 1984, and back up slightly to 33.9% in

TABLE 7.4. Out-Marriage Rates in California for Various Ethnic Groups, 1980 (percentages)

Ethnicity and Gender	Out-Marriage Rate	Intraethnic Rate	Interethnic Rate	Interracial Rate	Percentage Married to Whites
Chinese American	22.2	77.8	5.7	15.3	13.7
Filipino American	38.4	61.6	2.8	31.5	23.9
Japanese American	43.4	56.6	5.8	35.4	31.6
Korean American	30.6	69.4	6.8	22.0	18.8
Vietnamese	21.2	78.8	3.5	16.8	14.6

SOURCE: Shinagawa and Pang (1988).
NOTE: Based on 1980 U.S. Census data using marriages as the unit of analysis.

TABLE 7.5. Out-Marriage Rates of Chinese, Filipinos, Japanese, Koreans, and Vietnamese, Total and by Gender for 1975, 1977, 1979, 1984, and 1989, Los Angeles County

Ethnicity	Year	Marriages	Out-Marriages		Percentage of Out-Marriages by Gender	
			Number	Percentage	Women	Men
Chinese	1989	1,836	622	33.9	63.0	37.0
	1984	1,881	564	30.0	56.6	43.4
	1979	716	295	41.2	56.3	43.7
	1977	650	323	49.7	56.3	43.7
	1975	596	250	44.0	62.2	37.8
Filipino[a]	1989	1,384	565	40.8	74.2	25.8
Japanese	1989	1,134	588	51.9	58.3	41.7
	1984	1,404	719	51.2	60.2	39.8
	1979	764	463	60.6	52.7	47.3
	1977	756	477	63.1	60.6	39.4
	1975	664	364	54.8	53.6	46.4
Korean	1989	1,372	151	11.0	74.8	25.2
	1984	543	47	8.7	78.6	21.4
	1979	334	92	27.6	79.6	20.4
	1977	232	79	34.1	73.4	26.6
	1975	250	65	26.0	63.1	36.9
Vietnamese[b]	1989	555	147	26.5	54.4	45.6
	1984	560	34	6.0	74.7	25.3

SOURCE: Los Angeles County Marriage License Bureau.
a. Data for Filipinos is limited to 1989.
b. Data for Vietnamese is limited to 1984 and 1989.

1989, yet the actual numbers of out-marriages have continued to rise. For example, there were 323 out-marriages in 1977 (with more than 49%), whereas there were 564 in 1984 and 622 in 1989. The percentages obviously are affected by the increasing number of total Chinese marriages for any given year. The percentage of females who out-married remained consistently higher than that of males who did so, ranging from 56% to 63% of total out-marriages. It also is interesting to note that in 1979, 21.8% of the out-marriages of the Chinese were to Japanese, 4.4% to Koreans, and 73.7% to others, presumably to Whites (Kitano & Yeung, 1982).

THE JAPANESE

The Japanese followed the Chinese immigration, and in common with them, the first immigrants were primarily single males with a sojourner's orientation. The major immigration occurred between 1890 and 1924; the Immigration Act of 1924 closed the door to further immigration until the McCarran Walter Act of 1952, which allowed naturalization privileges and a token quota (Ichioka, 1988; Kitano & Daniels, 1995).

One major difference between the Chinese and the Japanese was the start of family life. Although most Issei (the first-generation Japanese to live in America, born in Japan) came with a sojourner's mentality, many of them remained in America and sent for brides (including the picture brides) so that they had an opportunity to marry within their ethnic group. As one consequence, there was an American-born second generation (the Nisei) and succeeding generations (the Sansei [third] and the Yonsei [fourth]). As we shall see, this has had an effect on marital patterns.

Another incident, unique in the annals of Asian American history, was the wartime evacuation of the Japanese Americans during World War II. All Japanese residing along the Pacific Coast were "relocated" to America's version of the concentration camps from 1942 to 1945. We have no statistics concerning marriage, but it would be safe to say that the probability of marrying out of the group while in the camps would have been extremely low.

Some of the early studies on out-marriages for the Japanese were already reported in the section on the Chinese (Tables 7.1, 7.3, 7.4, and 7.5). Panunzio (1942) reported that the Japanese American out-marriage rate between 1924 and 1933 was 2.3%, with 0.6% married to Whites. Of the 27 Japanese Americans who out-married, 17 were men.

Tinker (1982), using U.S. census data, reported that in the period 1940 to 1949, 14.9% of Japanese American marriages throughout the nation were out-marriages.

Barnett (1963), using individuals as the unit of analysis, indicated that 12.3% of Japanese American women and 6.8% of Japanese men in California out-married in 1955. In terms of interracial unions, in 1955, 8.7% of the women and 5.4% of the men were married to Whites. By 1959, the out-marriage rates were 19.8% for women and 10.7% for men. In terms of interracial unions, 13.6% of women and 8.2% of men were married to Whites.

Burma (1963), examining data from Los Angeles County, indicated that 11.8% of Japanese American women and 5.5% of the men married Whites between 1949 and 1959. Tinker (1982), using marriages as the unit of analysis, reported that in 1960 and 1961, there was a 67.9% out-marriage rate for Japanese Americans in Los Angeles County. Kikumura and Kitano (1973) summarized Japanese American out-marriages in Los Angeles County from 1924 to 1972 and found the following trend: From a low of 2% in 1924, Japanese American out-marriages rose from 10% to 20% in 1955, to the 20% to 25% range up to 1959, before rising sharply to 47% and 49% in 1971 and 1972. Female rates of out-marriage have consistently been higher than male rates for the same period, with the exception of the very early years. The highest female-to-male ratio was in 1954, when the out-marriage rate was 74% female to 26% male. In 1972, the rate was 56% female to 44% male.

Urban and rural differences for the Japanese, based on the 1970 census, are shown in Table 7.2. The great majority of the population, both male and female, resided in urban areas. Male rates of interracial marriage in the urban area were 12%; for females, the rate was 33%. The rural nonfarm sample of male interracial marriages was 14%, whereas their female counterparts had an interracial marriage rate of 42%. Finally, 12% of women and 7% of men in rural farm areas married interracially. It is clear that female rates of out-marriage were consistently higher than male rates.

Tinker (1973) reported out-marriage rates for Japanese Americans in Fresno County in California from 1958 to 1971. From 1958 to 1963, the out-marriage rates were below 20%; from 1964 to 1968, they had risen above the 30% level and reached the 40% and 50% levels between 1969 and 1971. He also reported that about 50% of marriages in San Francisco also were out-marriages.

Lee and Yamanaka (1990) (see Table 7.3), using national census figures for 1980, indicated that the out-marriage rates were 41.6% for Japanese females, with 33.9% married to Whites, and 21.3% for Japanese males, with 13.7% married to Whites. Shinagawa and Pang (1988), using 1980 U.S. census data for California, reported that the Japanese out-marriage rate was 43.4%, with 31.6% married to Whites (Table 7.3).

Based on marriage license data, Kitano (1988) provided out-marriage data in Los Angeles County for the Chinese, Japanese, Koreans, and Vietnamese for 1975, 1977, 1979, and 1984; the 1989 data are new (Table 7.5). The out-marriage rates for the Japanese were 54.8% in 1975, 63.1% in 1977, 60.6% in 1979, 51.2% in 1984, and 51.9% in 1989. The percentage figures for out-marriages can be somewhat deceiving, just as with the Chinese data, because they show a low of 51.2% in 1984 even though the actual number of out-marriages reached an all-time high of 719 in the same year. However, the total number of out-marriages dropped to 588 in 1989, with a corresponding drop in the total number of marriages. More females out-married than did males, with a low of 52.7% in 1979 and a high of 60.6% in 1977. It also should be noted that the Japanese, as well as all Asians who out-married in California prior to 1948, were violating the antimiscegenation law, but there is no evidence that anything was done to them.

THE KOREANS

Although there was an early, small migration of Koreans to the United States (mainly to Hawaii), the bulk of their immigration has taken place over the past decade. The growth of the Korean population has been dramatic. In 1970, there were approximately 70,000 Koreans in the United States; in 1980, the U.S. census reported 354,529, and by 1990 the number had grown to 799,993. The rise has been due to the Immigration and Naturalization Act of 1965, which abolished national origin quotas. Much of their migration has been as families and extended families, so that there is a high degree of social interaction within the community (Kitano & Daniels, 1988). It also should be noted that they are primarily a first-generation immigrant population, although there is a reference to a "knee-high" group, which refers to immigrants who arrived in the United States while still very young.

One distinctive group of Korean immigrants who came to the United States between 1952 and 1960 included "war brides" and children of American servicemen (Kim, 1980). Possible conflicts in these marriages were analyzed by Ratliff, Moon, and Bonacci (1978). They mentioned that most marriages in the old country were arranged and sanctioned by parents, whereas many of these wartime marriages apparently did not go through the usual parental sanctioning procedures. In interviewing a sample of the war brides, they reported that 72.9% of the women responded that they had married because of financial reasons, and 68% answered that they would not marry American servicemen again (Ratliff et al., 1978).

Kim (1977) summarized some of the social characteristics of the Koreans who arrived in the United States since the Immigration and Naturalization Act of 1965. They plan to remain permanently, although the relative ease of travel makes trips to Korea popular. They are unfamiliar with the United States; a major barrier is the English language, which forces a high dependence on the ethnic community. They are highly educated, but their education and training are difficult to translate into equivalent jobs in the United States. A large number go into private business, but the move may be attributed more to limited opportunities than to profitable free enterprise, although many have become successful.

There are very little data on Korean marital practices in the United States prior to the 1970s; however, it is our impression that many of those who came as students prior to 1965 married non-Koreans because there were so few Koreans. Furthermore, there were no established Korean settlements, and most were scattered throughout the country. For example, a Korean male, who currently is a college professor and who married a Caucasian, indicated that when he was here in the early 1960s, there simply were no Korean females, especially on the East Coast. Or, a Korean female indicated that when she came to America in 1968, she was already 20 years old and could not find an appropriate Korean partner. She had to learn English and about America by herself, and the Korean males who arrived after her were too far behind in speaking English and knowing about the United States (Kitano & Chai, 1982).

The previously mentioned study by Lee and Yamanaka (1990) indicated that in 1980, the out-marriage rates were 44.5% for Korean females, with 36.1% married to Whites, and 7.5% for Korean males, with 4.4% married to Whites (Table 7.3). Shinagawa and Pang (1988), focusing on California, reported that the Korean out-marriage rate for 1980 was 30.6%, with 18.8% married to Whites (Table 7.4).

Table 7.5 shows the Korean out-marriage rates for 1975, 1977, 1979, 1984, and 1989 in Los Angeles County. The Korean rates of out-marriage differ from those of the Chinese and Japanese in that their initial rates were low (26.0% in 1975) and were even lower, both in actual number (47) and in percentage (8.7%), in 1984. The ratio of female-to-male out-marriages showed a very high percentage of female out-marriages, from a low of 63.1% in 1975 to well over 70.0% in the succeeding years.

THE FILIPINOS

Filipino history is unique in that of all the Asian groups, Filipinos were a direct and unforeseen result of American imperialism. For a short period of time following the United States' acquisition of their country after the Spanish-American War of 1898, Filipinos were not considered aliens but rather were considered American nationals, so they were not excluded by the Immigration Act of 1924. Therefore, Filipino laborers were prominent in the 1920s and 1930s as replacements for Asian groups who could not legally immigrate. However, the Tydings-McDuffie Act of 1934 coupled independence for the Philippines in 1945 with an annual quota of 50 Filipinos (Kitano & Daniels, 1995).

Antimiscegenation laws in California, which forbade only marriage of Negroes (the commonly used term in that era), mulattoes, and Mongolians to Whites, did not apply to Filipinos, so this group of primarily single men had an opportunity to marry interracially. However, in 1933, California amended its statute to include members of the "Malay race," so that the Filipinos also became targets of antimiscegenation laws.

The growth of the Filipino population has been high due to the passage of the Immigration and Naturalization Act of 1965. In 1970, there were approximately 336,000 Filipinos in the United States; the number had grown to more than 774,000 in 1980 and to more than 1,403,000 by 1990. The new immigrants are different from the laborers who came in the 1920s and 1930s. They are apt to be highly educated professionals and fluent in English. Therefore, in comparison to the recent Korean immigrants, the English-speaking Filipinos, especially those with degrees in medicine or nursing, can find employment relatively easily outside of the ethnic community (Kitano & Daniels, 1995). As one consequence, they are less apt to have their own separate ethnic communities, and this has an effect on social interaction as well as on dating and marital patterns.

The early study by Panunzio (1942) (see Table 7.1) indicated that the Filipinos, who were not subject to antimiscegenation legislation until 1933, had an out-marriage rate of 70.1%. They also had an extremely skewed male-to-female ratio.

Data from the 1970 census (Table 7.2) indicated that the great majority of the Filipinos, both males and females, were living in urban areas. The interracial marriage rate of Filipinos residing in urban areas was 28% for females and 33% for males. In the rural nonfarm areas, female rates were 28% and male rates were 35%. The highest proportion of interracial marriages was found in the rural farm sample, where 32% of females and 51% of males married interracially. It is clear from Table 7.2 that each of the three Asian groups—Chinese, Filipino, and Japanese—has a different pattern of interracial marriage by gender and by urban-rural residence.

The previously reported study by Lee and Yamanaka (1990) (see Table 7.3), based on the 1980 census and using national figures, indicated that the out-marriage rates were 35.5% for Filipino females, with 27.5% married to Whites, and 22.2% for Filipino males, with 15.1% married to Whites. The study by Shinagawa and Pang (1988) (see Table 7.4), using U.S. census data for California, showed that the Filipino out-marriage rate was 38.4%, with 23.9% married to Whites. As shown in Table 7.5, 40.8% of Filipinos who applied for marriage licenses in Los Angeles County in 1989 were marrying non-Filipinos. Women comprised 74.2% of these out-marriages.

THE VIETNAMESE

The Vietnamese are among the newest of the Asian groups. Their presence in the United States is a direct result of the American intervention in Vietnam, which began as early as the Truman and Eisenhower administrations with aid to the French and closed in 1975 with the signing of a peace treaty.

The fall of Saigon in 1975 set off a wave of Southeast Asia refugees fleeing from the victorious North Vietnamese. There were several waves of refugees who arrived in America; many of those who fled in the 1980s and were named the "boat people" suffered terrible hardships. The Vietnamese are but one of the groups that have come from Southeast Asia; there also are the Laotians, the Hmong, and the Cambodians.

There were 245,500 Vietnamese in the United States in 1980; the number had grown to more than 610,000 in 1990. Although initially scattered throughout the country as part of government policy, many have clustered together in communities, especially in California, and have developed "Little Saigons" (Kitano & Daniels, 1988).

The study by Lee and Yamanaka (1990), using the 1980 census, found that the out-marriage rates were 28.9% for Vietnamese females, with 24.9% married to Whites, and 5.5% for Vietnamese males, with 4.2% married to Whites (Table 7.3). Shinagawa and Pang (1988) (see Table 7.4), using California rates for 1980, indicated that the Vietnamese out-marriage rate was 21.2%, with 14.6% married to Whites.

Vietnamese out-marriages in Los Angeles County are shown in Table 7.5. Of the total 560 marriages in 1984, 34 (or 6.0%) were to non-Vietnamese; in 1989, the out-marriage rate had grown to 26.5%. Females out-married more than did males, with 74.7% selecting non-Vietnamese spouses in 1984 and 54.4% in 1989.

The important features of the historical background and a review of the studies indicate the following:

1. Motives for immigration have varied. Asians came to America as sojourners, contract laborers, voluntary immigrants, and refugees. Some have wanted to enter the mainstream, whereas others have preferred a pluralistic existence.

2. Demographic characteristics such as sex ratio, family composition, education, social class background, and age of arrival also were different.

3. They developed and maintained a variety of ethnic communities. Some Asian groups lived in cohesive communities with large numbers and with ample opportunities for social, within-group interaction, whereas others were much more scattered and prone to interact primarily outside of their ethnic groups.

Most eventually settled in urban areas, and their marital preferences were different from those residing in rural areas.

4. Time of entrance into the United States varied. Some have been here for more than a century, whereas others are relative newcomers. There are within-group and between-group generational differences.

5. Reception by the host society has varied. Those who came prior to the 1950s faced antimiscegenation laws as well as other barriers to participation in the host society, whereas newcomers have benefited from equal opportunity and affirmative action legislation. However, economic recessions and Asian "bashing" also have been a part of the current scene.

6. There has been a consistent rise in the number of out-marriages by the Chinese and Japanese. The Japanese rates are the highest, with figures above 50%, followed by the Chinese at the 30% to 40% level. The Korean and Vietnamese rates of out-marriage show no consistent pattern.

7. Asian females out-marry at a higher rate than Asian males.

8. There were and continue to be differences in marital patterns by ethnic group, by sex, by geographic area, and by urban-rural residence.

INTERMARRIAGE IN HAWAII

We present a study that will further explore these differences after a presentation of Asian American out-marriage patterns in Hawaii. Marital patterns of the Asians in Hawaii are different from those in other areas of the United States for a number of reasons. Historic and demographic factors, as well as the racial ambiance of the island, created a different climate so that there were the following differences:

1. Numbers and proportion: The 1990 U.S. census showed that although California has the largest number of Asians, the proportion of Asians in Hawaii is the highest. Asian and Pacific Islanders (APIs) make up 61.8% of the Hawaiian population; of the total state population of 1,108,229 in 1990, 685,236 were APIs, whereas 396,616 were White. Hawaii is the only state in which Whites do not constitute the majority.

2. There were early intermarriages between racial groups in Hawaii. For example, there were numerous marriages between high-ranking Hawaiian women of royal blood and commoners of Anglo descent.

3. As on the mainland, there were disproportionate sex ratios; however, because of the relative tolerance of interracial unions (there were no antimiscegenation laws, and interracial marriage has been legally sanctioned since 1840), rather than remaining as bachelors, many Asian American men out-married. Adams (1934) labeled the continuing intermixture of races as Hawaii's "unorthodox race doctrine."

Although there was discrimination, prejudice, and inequality (Fuchs, 1961), the barriers toward economic, educational, and social mobility were not as rigid as in California and the West Coast states. Most Asians were recruited to work on the plantations; they were segregated, exploited, and oppressed (Takaki, 1989), yet this background did not hinder them from eventually achieving a degree of equality that has not yet been achieved by their peers on the mainland. The state has been represented by Asian Americans in the Senate and the House of Representatives, in the governorship, and in many of the influential boards and business groups.

Glick (1970) indicated that the development of Hawaii's interracial population has been a consequence of successive waves of immigration. Based on the entrance of different ethnic groups into the islands, the following phases emerged. Phase 1 was characterized by extensive intermingling between foreign men and local women, resulting in casual relations and marriages of convenience (Horman, 1948). Phase 2 saw a decline of interracial relationships as each immigrant group attempted to establish its own ethnic society by discouraging out-marriages. Finally in Phase 3 (the current phase), there is an increase in out-marriages based on romantic love by the more Americanized members of the descendants of Asian immigrants.

There are several factors that contribute to out-marriage rates. First, Cheng and Yamamura (1957) indicated that groups with more balanced sex ratios show an inverse tendency toward out-marriage among the females than among the males. Therefore, when ethnic differences decline as barriers to marriage, the greater availability of unmarried males in other groups is reflected in more out-marriages of females from the groups with more balanced sex ratios. Second, Hawaii out-marriage data supported the thesis proposed by Blau (1977), namely, that a group's relative size is inversely related to its out-marriage rate; the smaller the group, the higher the out-marriage rate (Blau, Blum, & Schwartz, 1982). Koreans and Puerto Ricans, both small ethnic groups, tended to show higher out-marriage rates for females than did larger groups such as the Japanese (Glick, 1970). Third, time of arrival and generation also were contributing factors. The Chinese and Portuguese tended to have higher out-marriage rates than did those with shorter histories in the islands such as the Japanese and Filipinos (Glick, 1970).

Yamamoto (1973) wrote about the marital choices of those who did out-marry in Hawaii. For example,

> In 1965, the 793 Caucasian men who intermarried selected the following brides: 12 Hawaiian, 312 part-Hawaiian, 59 Chinese, 155 Filipino, 152 Japanese, 35 Puerto Rican, 20 Korean, 4 Negro, and 44 others. In the same year, the 380 Japanese women who intermarried selected the following grooms: 152 Caucasian, 1 Hawaiian, 91 part-Hawaiian, 53 Chinese, 54 Filipino, 6 Puerto Rican, 17 Korean, and 6 others. (p. 318)

Questions have been raised about the stability of interracial relationships and the personality development of the offsprings of such unions. Schwertfeger (1982) examined the relationship among ethnicity, interethnic marriages, and divorce. Of the 3,405 first marriages of Hawaii residents recorded in 1968, 544 (or 16%) ended in divorce by 1976. Interethnic marriages, which comprised 41% of the original sample, were more likely to end in divorce (19.2%) than were homogamous marriages (13.8%). Whereas slightly lower divorce rates were found for Japanese and Chinese men and women, it is interesting to note that there were no divorces among the in-married Chinese.

In regard to personality development of biracial individuals, Johnson and Nagoshi (1986) used the Adjective Check List to study the children of couples in Hawaii. In general, the children of interracially married couples were similar to the children of intraracially married couples. However, the multiracial children were found to be more extroverted, scored higher on socially desirable traits, and scored lower on a factor measuring intraception. The ethnic identities of multiracial college students in Hawaii and in New Mexico were examined by Stephan and Stephan (1989). Of the part-Japanese Americans in Hawaii, 67% reported having multiple ethnic identities, as did 44% of the part-Hispanics in New Mexico. The finding suggested that ethnic boundaries among Americans might be eroding through intermarriage.

Finally, the notion that interracial births were more often illegitimate in comparison to same-race births was studied in samples from Hawaii and California. However, no conclusions could be reached regarding this relationship because 67% of illegitimate births lacked information regarding the ethnicity of the father (Monahan, 1977).

Parkman and Sawyer (1967), in looking at Hawaii's high intermarriage rate, assessed the relative distance separating eight major ethnic groups. Based on an analysis of 50,000 marriages, they found that in Hawaii, as in most other places, there were similarities of the past and similarities of the present, so that there was some ethnic clustering, and the basic generalization was that "like marries like."

Labov and Jacobs (1986), in studying intermarriage in Hawaii from 1950 to 1983, noted that both cultural and structural change are important in explaining Hawaii's marital patterns. The growth of the Caucasian population has tended to depress intermarriage rates, whereas cultural predispositions to intermarry increased during the period under study. They expected that as group size and heterogeneity are studied in a variety of places in longitudinal research, the more we will understand the processes that lead to populations remaining separate or becoming mixed.

Data From Hawaii

To bring together the marriage data from Hawaii, official data from the Department of Health, Office of Health Status Monitoring, for the state of Hawaii were obtained. The data contained information on Chinese, Filipinos, Japanese, Koreans, and Vietnamese from 1912 to 1989.

Hawaii collects ethnic identification information on its marital records so that it provides information on interethnic and interracial marriages. However, given the high incidence of interracial marriages in Hawaii, the recording of ethnicity among those of mixed racial ancestry is problematic. Data were gathered from marriage certificates after marriage ceremonies were completed. Based on

TABLE 7.6. Out-Marriage Rates of Chinese, Filipinos, Japanese, Koreans, and Vietnamese in Hawaii, by Decade

Ethnicity	Years	Total Marriages	Percentage of Out-Marriages	Percentage of Out-Marriages, by Gender	
				Women	Men
Chinese	1912-1916	777	27.9	5.7	41.7
	1920-1929	3,059	20.5	15.7	24.8
	1930-1939	3,925	28.6	28.5	28.8
	1940-1949	6,041	34.8	38.0	31.2
	1950-1959	5,358	44.4	45.2	43.6
	1960-1969	5,023	59.9	61.5	58.2
	1980-1989	7,683	65.4	66.9	63.7
Filipino	1912-1916	1,234	13.3	2.82	1.8
	1920-1930	5,877	15.0	1.0	25.6
	1930-1940	5,932	24.3	4.03	7.5
	1940-1949	8,830	33.1	21.0	42.0
	1950-1959	11,390	40.5	35.8	44.5
	1960-1969	13,026	49.3	47.9	50.6
	1980-1989	24,643	49.9	54.3	44.6
Japanese	1912-1916	12,771	3.5	2.0	5.0
	1920-1930	16,562	2.9	3.1	2.7
	1930-1940	20,445	5.3	6.3	4.3
	1940-1949	31,589	11.0	16.9	4.3
	1950-1959	33,007	14.2	19.1	8.7
	1960-1969	28,278	24.1	28.1	19.6
	1980-1989	30,097	44.8	47.6	41.6
Korean	1912-1916	472	15.5	0.0	26.4
	1920-1930	827	32.2	49.0	17.6
	1930-1940	937	32.0	39.0	23.5
	1940-1949	1,742	59.8	66.7	49.0
	1950-1959	1,368	72.5	74.5	70.3
	1960-1969	1,404	79.3	82.3	75.1
	1980-1989	4,187	67.4	76.4	47.3
Vietnamese	1980-1989	653	51.6	62.8	30.7

SOURCE: Hawaii Department of Health.
NOTE: Data were not available from 1970 to 1979.

self-reports, only one ethnicity was recorded per person. When two or more ethnic groups were reported, the following procedure was used. When Hawaiian was listed among the multiple ethnicities, the person was coded as Hawaiian. Therefore, an individual who listed Korean, Chinese, and Hawaiian was classified as Hawaiian. If a person listed Caucasian (White) as part of his or her mixed ethnic heritage, then the ethnic category that was mentioned first was used. When more than one non-White ethnicity was reported, the first non-White ethnicity was recorded (V. Kong, state statistician, Department of Health Office, Honolulu, personal interview, December 1991).

The Chinese in Hawaii. The overall Chinese rate of out-marriage prior to 1940 was consistently in the 20% range (Table 7.6). There was a rise to 34.8% in the

1940s and then a jump to 65.4% by the 1980s. The rate of out-marriage from 1912 to 1916 for males was very high (41.7%) compared to the 5.7% rate for females, which reflected the male-to-female ratio of that era. The unbalanced sex ratio began to change during the 1930s, and from 1940 on there was a higher proportion of females who out-married.

The Filipinos in Hawaii. The overall rate of out-marriages for Filipinos has shown a steady rise, from 13.3% in the 1912 to 1916 era to 49.9% in the 1980s (Table 7.6). There was a predominance of male out-marriages from 1912 to 1969, but in the past decade, 1980 to 1989, there was a higher percentage of female out-marriages (54.3%) than male out-marriages (44.6%).

The Japanese in Hawaii. The Japanese pattern of out-marriage shows a very low rate of below 10% between 1912 and 1940, a slightly higher rate of 11% to 14% from 1940 to 1959, an increase to 24.0% in the 1960s, and then a sharp jump to 44.8% in the 1980s (Table 7.6). There was a slightly higher male out-marriage rate up through 1916; from that time on, more females than males were out-marrying.

The Koreans in Hawaii. The overall out-marriage rates for the Koreans show a steady rise, from a low of 15.5% in the 1912 to 1916 era to 67.4% in the most recent decade (Table 7.6). Korean males out-married at a higher rate than did females in the 1912 to 1916 era; since that time, female rates of out-marriage have been higher. The most startling statistic is the drop in Korean male out-marriages, from 75.1% in the 1960s to only 47.3% in the 1980s. The Korean female out-marriage rate of 76.4% is the highest among all Asian groups.

The Vietnamese in Hawaii. The Vietnamese have been relative newcomers to both the mainland and Hawaii. The earliest available data are from the 1980s; they show that the Vietnamese out-marriage rate was 51.6%, with females out-marrying at a higher rate (62.8%) than males (30.7%) (Table 7.6). The out-marriage rate appears rather high for a first-generation immigrant group.

In summary, the marital patterns of Asian Americans in Hawaii show the following. First, there has been a general rise in out-marriage rates since 1912 for all groups. Second, the early periods show higher rates of male out-marriage for all groups, which was a reflection of the male-to-female ratio. Third, later periods show a higher proportion of females who out-married, with the exception of Filipinos. Fourth, all Asian American groups in the 1980 to 1990 period had out-marriage rates of more than 60%, which indicates that there is a considerable amount of interethnic and interracial contact in Hawaii. Fifth, as on the continent, each of the Asian groups shows differences. We cannot determine the extent to which the coding of ethnicity in Hawaiian records affects the data.

THEORIES

There are a variety of models and theories concerning out-group marriage. From our review of the Asian Americans, the following appear to be the most appropriate.

Relative Group Size, Heterogeneity, and Sex Ratio

One common explanation for out-group marriage looks at variables such as group size, the heterogeneity of the population, and an unbalanced sex ratio (Blau, 1977; Blau et al., 1982; Guttentag & Secord, 1983). The smaller the group, the higher the rates of out-marriage (Blau, 1977). The more unbalanced the sex ratio, the higher the rates for the oversupplied gender (Guttentag & Secord, 1983). In addition, the more diverse the group (e.g., generation, living in different locales, the number of different Asian American groups), the higher the rates.

All of these variables provide partial explanations for the out-marriage rates of different Asian American groups. We would add that there are factors that lead to *lower* rates of out-marriage: ethnic community cohesion with ample opportunities to meet fellow ethnics, strong parental control over children, and a high preference for ethnic peers and ethnic interaction. Therefore, one model that helps to explain in- and out-marriage includes group size, heterogeneity, and an unbalanced sex ratio.

Acculturation and Assimilation

Another explanation for out-marriage is related to acculturation, assimilation, and length of time in the United States. Marcson (1950) found that higher rates of out-marriage were related to high education, middle-class status, professional occupations, generation, and nonfarm residence.

Tinker (1982), in studying the Japanese Nisei, found that those who approve of intermarriage are generally those who by their religion, education, occupation, place of residence, and friendship patterns are culturally and structurally assimilated.

Related to acculturation is *propinquity*. Physical closeness, such as being with other non-Asian groups in terms of work, school, housing, and play, leads to increased out-group contact. There is a higher likelihood of meeting and liking those from other groups (Festinger, Schachter, & Back, 1950; Saegert, Swap, & Zajonc, 1973). The assumption is that with length of time in the country, there will be acculturation (with the exception of the elderly and some who arrived as adults) and mobility in housing, education, and occupation. Mobility in housing and the breakup of ethnic ghettos have been especially influential in changing patterns of interaction.

Acculturation also would affect the "traditional" Asian family structure, where strict controls over the marital preferences of children would be modified toward the less traditional model of choosing one's own mate.

Acculturation also is related to *generation;* the American-born generations will generally be less apt to follow parental preferences in terms of dating and marriage. We present data in the final section of the article analyzing the role of generation in Asian American out-marriage.

Legal Barriers and Changing Norms

One of the most important barriers in intermarriage facing Asian Americans, as well as other racial minorities (although not in Hawaii), has been the laws concerning marriage into the host society. The first antimiscegenation law was enacted in Maryland in 1661 and prohibited the marriage of a Caucasian woman to a Negro slave. The penalty for violating the statute was that the woman would be sent into slavery.

California first introduced antimiscegenation legislation in 1850 with the Marriage Regulation Act, which prohibited marriages between Whites and Negroes. The code was extended in 1901 to include Mongolians (i.e., Chinese, Japanese, Koreans) and in 1933 to include Malays (i.e., Filipinos). However, these antimiscegenation laws were overturned by the California court in *Perez v. Lippold* in 1948 and by the U.S. Supreme Court in *Loving v. Virginia* in 1967 (Kikumura & Kitano, 1973).

If laws can be taken as symptoms of the changing attitudes of the country, then it is apparent that there have been changes—from strict sentiments against interracial marriages to tolerance of such unions. We are not sure whether norms against interracial unions have changed significantly in the general public, but a few experiences with undergraduate and graduate students at the University of California, Los Angeles, indicate that Asians dating and marrying Caucasians no longer is considered unusual. Greek fraternities and sororities, once considered as bastions of "Whites only," now have a scattering of Asian Americans. There undoubtedly have been changes in the norms of both the Asian and non-Asian communities; there seems to be a higher tolerance of intergroup and interracial relationships.

Hypergamy

The concept of hypergamy explains interethnic unions on the basis of differential status. Females of lower status marry males of higher status. Cretser and Leon (1982), referring to a study by Davis (1941), presented an example in which the male of a higher status exchanged his social position for the beauty and other desirable characteristics of the lower-status female.

Shinagawa (1990) found that hierarchy in marital preference was consistent among Asian Americans and Whites. From samples drawn from California universities, he found that Asian Americans gave priority to skin color and socioeconomic status, whereas Whites felt that the degree of acculturation and social integration into the mainstream were more important.

Based on marriage license data for Los Angeles County, Fujino (1991) found that interracially married Chinese and Japanese Americans tended to exchange their higher educational attainment for the higher racial status of their White spouses.

Psychological Theories

Other explanations draw from psychological and psychoanalytic perspectives. The basic assumption is that an individual marries away from his or her ethnic group as an acting out of a psychological problem or what we would label as "marginal meets marginal." Freeman (1955) charted this process as follows. Individuals feel rejected by their own group and become hostile and rebellious. They are exposed to another rejected group. They identify with this new group, internalize its norms, and idealize its way of life. Dating and mate selection may follow, but mainly rebels and the "marginals" from each of the groups will be attracted to each other. The pairs will possess similar psychological backgrounds and patterns of social adjustment, and intermarriage becomes a possibility.

Other psychological models of intermarriage include low self-esteem and guilt feelings. Biegel (1966) and Brayboy (1966) indicated that individuals with low self-esteem and feelings of inferiority might marry members of a lower-status group because they feel that they deserve nothing better. Conversely, members of a lower-status group intermarry through overcompensation.

Guilt, associated with the need to punish oneself for the exploitation of a group, also can be a motive for intermarriage. Grier and Cobbs (1968) alluded to intermarriage, especially between Blacks and Whites, as a means of managing oedipal fantasies. The inadequate repression of attraction to the opposite-sex parent may lead to a relationship with an individual who is different from the parents—in this case, of a different race.

Porterfield (1978, 1982) indicated that studies of Black-White intermarriages, using psychological models, have limited explanatory value. They are difficult to measure, lack unity, and are primarily dependent on individual case histories. The motives for Black-White marriages do not appear to be any different from the motives for those who marry in the more conventional within-group style.

Other theoretical explanations include variables such as physical attractiveness (Critelli & Waid, 1980), skin color (Feinman & Gill, 1978), rewards and costs (Thibaut & Kelley, 1959), similarity and complementarity (Byrne, 1969), and the attraction of opposites (Winch, 1958).

From our review of research and analysis of our data, it is clear that no one variable or one model can fully explain the phenomenon of two individuals joining together in matrimony. We have talked with many couples, both in-married and out-married, some who approached an ideal and others who had almost nothing in common, and their universal answer was that they were in love. We also have talked with many parents, and although they might have had reservations about the choices made by their children, many also accepted the marriages as long as "they love each other."

The purpose of the present study is twofold. The first is a follow-up of the studies conducted in Los Angeles County in 1975, 1977, 1979, and 1984 to indicate historical patterns of out-marriage by ethnic group and gender. The question for analysis deals with trends: Are the rates of out-marriage for the Chinese, Japanese, Koreans, and Vietnamese rising or falling from the earlier periods? The second purpose is to present a model for predicting out-marriage.

METHOD

Data were gathered through an examination of marital records available from the Los Angeles County Marriage License Bureau. The method for the selection of each Asian group for 1975, 1977, 1979, 1984, and 1989 was generally the same. The data from the studies prior to 1989 have already been published in a number of articles (Kikumura & Kitano, 1973; Kitano & Chai, 1982; Kitano & Daniels, 1995; Kitano & Yeung, 1982; Kitano, Yeung, Chai, & Hatanaka, 1984), whereas the data for 1989 are new.

Every application with an identifiable Asian surname was drawn. Ethnicity could not be reported since 1959, so the surname provided the primary means of identification. The identification was supported by information on the application that included applicant's and parents' birthplaces, mother's maiden name, and father's surname. Other variables included highest completed grade, number of marriages, age, and occupation. Asians who had changed their surnames or whose surnames were not readily identifiable were missed.

Any marriage to a person who was not a member of the same ethnic group was considered an out-marriage (e.g., Japanese surname to a Chinese surname, Japanese surname to a non-Asian surname). An interracial marriage was defined as one in which one partner did not have an Asian surname. We estimate that we have correctly identified more than 95% of the Asian Americans who were married in Los Angeles County.

RESULTS

The overall findings were already discussed and presented in Table 7.5. In summary, although each of the Asian American groups showed a different pattern (with the exception of the Koreans), there was a general trend over the years toward increasing out-marriages. The Japanese had the highest rates of out-marriage, and the Koreans had the lowest. The one consistent finding was that Asian females out-married at a higher rate than did males.

The remaining analyses concentrated on the Chinese, Filipinos, Japanese, Koreans, and Vietnamese in Los Angeles County in 1989.

TABLE 7.7 Mean Ages, Educations, Generations, and Numbers of Marriages Between In- and Out-Married Asian Americans, by Gender in Los Angeles County, 1989

	Female		Male	
	In-Marriage	Out-Marriage	In-Marriage	Out-Marriage
Chinese				
First generation	555 (68.2)	259 (31.8)*	541 (78.0)	153 (22.1)*
Second generation	41 (35.3)	75 (64.7)*	46 (52.9)	41 (47.1)
Third generation	9 (13.4)	58 (86.6)*	20 (35.7)	36 (64.3)
Age (mean years)	29.6	30.1	32.9	30.9*
Education[a]	14.9	15.4	15.8	15.8
Number of marriages[b]	1.15	1.17	1.16	1.12
Filipino				
First generation	377 (53.1)	333 (46.9)	371 (77.5)	108 (22.6)*
Second generation	26 (34.2)	50 (65.8)*	22 (51.2)	21 (48.8)
Third generation	6 (14.3)	36 (85.7)*	17 (51.5)	16 (48.5)
Age (mean years)	28.9	29.3	30.7	30.0
Education[a]	15.1	14.9	15.0	14.6
Number of marriages[b]	1.12	1.23*	1.20	1.21
Japanese				
First generation	108 (59.0)	75 (41.0)*	99 (71.7)	39 (28.3)*
Second generation	17 (50.0)	17 (50.0)	15 (51.7)	14 (48.3)
Third generation	147 (37.1)	249 (62.9)*	160 (45.5)	192 (54.6)
Age (mean years)	30.8	30.4	33.2	32.3
Education[a]	15.0	15.3	15.3	15.8
Number of marriages[b]	1.19	1.19	1.15	1.21
Korean				
First generation	608 (86.7)	93 (13.3)*	599 (96.3)	23 (3.7)*
Second generation	3 (37.5)	5 (62.5)	4 (66.7)	2 (33.3)
Third generation	0 (00.0)	15 (100.0)*	6 (31.6)	13 (68.4)
Age (mean years)	28.8	30.0	31.5	28.6
Education[a]	14.6	14.6	15.3	15.6
Number of marriages[b]	1.22	1.34	1.24	1.21
Vietnamese				
First generation	202 (74.5)	69 (25.5)*	202 (75.7)	65 (24.3)*
Second generation	2 (66.7)	1 (33.3)	1 (100.0)	0 (00.0)
Third generation	0 (00.0)	10 (100.0)*	1 (33.3)	2 (66.7)
Age (mean years)	27.3	27.3	31.4	28.5*
Education[a]	13.9	14.4	14.7	14.9
Number of marriages[b]	1.04	1.06	1.05	1.06

NOTE: Figures are numbers and percentages (in parentheses) unless otherwise noted.
*To control for simultaneous alpha rate, $p < .001$ is used as the significance criterion. For variables testing proportions as denoted by percentages, test for significance of difference between two proportions was used. For variables testing means, t test was used.
a. Refers to the number of years of education completed.
b. Refers to the total number of marriages including the marriage presently being applied for.

The Chinese

Table 7.7 shows generation, age, education, and number of marriages for the Chinese by sex and marital preference in Los Angeles County for 1989. First-generation Chinese, both female and male, tend to marry within the group, but there is a definite move toward out-marriage with each succeeding generation. For example, for the females, out-marriage rates rose from 31.8% in the first generation, to 64.7% in the second, to 86.6% in the third. Similarly, male rates of out-marriage rose from 22.1% in the first generation, to 47.1% in the second, to 64.3% in the third. The differences between in- and out-marriages by generation for both sexes were statistically significant.

The Filipinos

As shown in Table 7.7, the trend for the Filipinos, both male and female, appears to be similar to that of the Chinese. Female rates of out-marriage rose from 46.9% in the first generation, to 65.8% in the second, to 85.7% in the third. The second- and third-generation differences between in- and out-marriages for women were statistically significant. Male out-marriage rates also rose by generation: 22.6% in the first generation, 48.8% in the second, and 48.5% in the third. The only statistically significant difference between in- and out-marriages was for the first-generation males. It also should be noted that the Filipinos (and Chinese) who were married in Los Angeles in 1989 were primarily of the immigrant generation, so the numbers of second- and third-generation Filipinos were very small.

The Japanese

As with the Chinese and Filipinos, there was a rising rate of Japanese out-marriages by generation (Table 7.7). For example, the out-marriage rates of the first-generation females were 41.0%, followed by 50.0% for the second generation and 62.9% for the third. Japanese male rates also increased by generation, as 28.3% of the first generation, 48.3% of the second, and 54.6% of the third out-married. The differences between the in- and out-marriage rates for the first-generation females and males, and for the third-generation females, were statistically significant. In contrast to the Chinese and Filipinos, the Japanese who were married in 1989 were primarily a third-generation group. It also was surprising that the number of first-generation immigrants who were married in 1989 far exceeded the number of second-generation marriages.

The Koreans

As shown in Table 7.7, there was a similar trend toward increasing out-marriages by generation among the Koreans, although the actual numbers of Koreans in the second and third generations were extremely small. Female out-marriage rates were 13.3% in the first generation, 62.5% in the second, and 100% in the third (although there were only 15 total marriages). Male out-marriage rates also were related to generation: 3.7% in the first generation, 33.3% in the second, and 68.4% in the third. Differences between in- and out-marriages for females and males in the first generation, and those for females in the third generation, were

TABLE 7.8 Odds Ratios for Variables Predicting Out-Marriage by Gender

Variable	Female	Male
Chinese[a]	1.34*	0.98
Filipino[a]	2.25**	0.89
Korean[a]	0.45**	0.18**
Vietnamese[a]	1.03	1.08
Second generation[b]	3.11**	3.35**
Third generation[b]	5.63**	4.57**
Age	1.00	0.97**
Education	1.01	1.00
Number of marriages (two or more)[c]	1.62**	1.69**

*$p < .05$, **$p < .001$.
a. Compared to Japanese American.
b. Compared to first generation.
c. Compared to one marriage.

statistically significant. The Koreans also were similar to the Chinese and Filipinos in that the bulk of those who were married in 1989 were of the immigrant generation.

The Vietnamese

Because the great majority of the Vietnamese were of the first generation, figures for the other generations are extremely limited. Nevertheless, even with very small numbers for the second and third generations, the trend toward increasing out-marriages by generation follows that of the other Asian groups (Table 7.7). For example, the out-marriage rate for females was 25.5% for the first generation, 33.3% for the second, and 100% for the third. The male first-generation out-marriage rate was 24.3%; there were no second-generation males who out-married (but there was only one who in-married), and 66.7% (two out of three marriages) out-married in the third. Female and male rates of in- and out-marriages in the first generation, and female rates in the third generation, were statistically significant.

Analyses of Variables

The data indicated that (a) generation was related to out-marriage for all of the Asian groups and that (b) with the exception of the Japanese, the Chinese, Filipinos, Koreans, and Vietnamese who were married in 1989 came primarily from the first (or immigrant) generation.

Logistic regression analyses were performed to determine the variables that would best predict out-marriage. For the analyses, the contribution of each predictor variable was controlled in relation to the others by simultaneously entering all predictor variables into the model. The dependent variable was *out-marriage* and the predictor variables were *ethnicity, generation, age, education,* and *number of marriages.* Analyses were performed separately for women and for men.

Table 7.8 shows the odds ratio of each predictor variable after controlling for the other variables. The results indicate that generational status was the strongest predictor of out-marriage for both women and men. Compared to first-generation Asians, second-generation Asians were more than three times as likely to out-marry, and third-generation Asians were approximately five times as likely to out-marry.

Ethnicity also played an important role in predicting who would out-marry. For both genders, Koreans were less likely than Japanese to out-marry. Among women, Chinese and Filipinos were more likely than Japanese to out-marry when controlling for the effects of generation. In addition, women and men who had been married previously were more likely to out-marry. Younger men, in comparison to older men, were slightly more likely to out-marry.

DISCUSSION

It is not too surprising that generation was the most important predictor of out-marriage given that the concept takes into account length of time in the United States, acquisition of language skills, and exposure to American norms, especially in relation to dating and marriage. It also includes loss of family control over marriage; growing independence of children; issues of an American and/or ethnic identity; acquisition of language and social skills; value changes; mobility in housing; and educational, occupational, and social integration. The study was limited by the data source to using the gross measure of generation; in subsequent studies, it would be important to study the previously mentioned variables as independent predictors of out-marriage.

Gender also was important; females consistently out-married at a higher rate than did males. Asian American women might be more "accepted" by the dominant culture; they might acculturate more rapidly and have stereotypes and images (e.g., sexy, dedicated to serving men) that increase their value as mates in comparison to Asian men, whose stereotypes include being sneaky, fanatic, feminine, and nerdy. In addition, one study found that racial discrimination had differential effects on the dating behaviors of Asian women and men (Fujino, 1992). Although no gender differences were found in the extent of discriminatory experiences, racial discrimination was found to be a significant and negative predictor of interracial dating for Asian men but not for Asian women. Fujino (1992) inferred that because it is men who initiate the majority of dates, Asian men who perceive White racism might not initiate dates with White women. By contrast, as the recipients of dating bids, Asian American women can more easily distinguish between more racist White men and less racist White men. Finally, in our discussions with Asian women who out-married, there also was mention of the dislike of the traditional male-female roles in which the male ruled with absolute authority, as was seen in the parents' relationship.

It is clear that both area and numbers also affect marital practices. Los Angeles and Hawaii represent the largest concentrations of Asian Americans. Studies from other locales are likely to show higher rates, as predicted by the relative group size thesis (Blau, 1977).

The ability of an ethnic group to provide resources, such as social activities and organizational support, is another factor related to marital practices. For example, the Korean community in Los Angeles has a large number of churches and other resources that enable young adults to interact with each other. The ethnic community facilities are especially helpful to the newly arrived immigrant. It will be interesting to see whether the Korean experiences will be similar to those of the Japanese in terms of out-marriage as Koreans enter into the second, third, and subsequent generations.

There were a number of important variables that could not be evaluated from the data. One was the practice of seeking and marrying persons from the ancestral homeland (e.g., Korea, Hong Kong, the Philippines). There was no information on the extent of this practice by ethnic group or on the profiles of those who have taken this route. Data also were lacking on Asians who opted to marry in Nevada. Given the fairly strong parental preferences against interracial marriages found in Asian families (Fujino, 1992), it is possible that some who have married interracially have done so in Las Vegas. It is unclear how they would differ, if at all, from those who marry in Los Angeles or San Francisco. Finally, the study was limited in the measure of social class; educational level represented socioeconomic status.

The presence of interracial relationships has permeated society, as seen in the popular media. In January 1992, the popular television program *L.A. Law* showed an African American lawyer kissing and living with a White woman. Previously, sexually laden interracial scenes were forbidden in the media. Then it became acceptable for White men to kiss and make love to African and Asian American women. Perhaps the next step will be an Asian American man in an intimate relationship with a White woman.

But not all Americans take a relaxed stance concerning interracial relationships. Ezekiel (1995), in discussing the racist mind, indicated that White hate groups feel that their special blood is being tainted by inferior blood and that the White race is near destruction unless they take steps to preserve their "superiority."

In summary, we have presented data covering five Asian American groups. Although all of them are different, it appears that length of time, exposure to American society, and acculturation—all related to generation—begin a process leading to higher rates of out-marriage. The Japanese Americans, primarily a third-generation group, had the highest rates of out-marriage. The Koreans, primarily a first-generation immigrant population, had the lowest rates. Females, especially of the American-born generations, also were more likely to marry non-Asians than were those who were born in the old country.

In a private conversation with Larry Shinagawa in 1995, it was noted that, although out-marriages are quite common, there has been a strong tendency for Asian Americans to marry other Asian Americans rather than to choose interracial partners. It will be interesting to follow this trend.

Future studies might look at the relative "success" of both in- and out-married couples and their children as well as analyze the motives for out-marriages. The profile of the non-Asian who marries an Asian also will be important. It will be valuable to gather data from other parts of the country and from rural and urban settings. The marital practices of Asian Americans in terms of "melting," or of ethnic retention and pluralism, will have important implications for future trends in U. S. society.

REFERENCES

Adams, R. (1934). *Interracial marriage in Hawaii.* New York: Macmillan.

Barnett, L. D. (1963). Interracial marriage in California. *Marriage and Family Living, 25,* 424-427.

Biegel, H. G. (1966). Problems and motives in interracial relationships. *Journal of Sex Research, 2,* 185-205.

Blau, P. M. (1977). *Inequality and heterogeneity.* New York: Free Press.

Blau, P. M., Blum, T. C., & Schwartz, J. E. (1982). Heterogeneity and intermarriage. *American Sociological Review, 47,* 45-62.

Brayboy, T. L. (1966). Interracial sexuality as an expression of neurotic conflict. *Journal of Sex Research,* 2(3), 179-184.

Burma, J. H. (1963). Interethnic marriage in Los Angeles, 1948-1959. *Social Forces, 42,* 156-165.

Byrne, D. (1969). Attitudes and attraction. *Advances in Experimental Social Psychology, 4,* 35-89.

Cheng, C. K., & Yamamura, D. S. (1957). Interracial marriage and divorce in Hawaii. *Social Forces, 36,* 77-84.

Cretser, G., & Leon, J. (1982). Intermarriage in the U.S.: An overview of theory and research. In G. Crester & J. Leon (Eds.), *Intermarriage in the United States* (pp. 3-15). New York: Haworth.

Critelli, J. W., & Waid, L. R. (1980). Physical attractiveness, romantic love, and equity restoration in dating relationships. *Journal of Personality Assessment, 44,* 624-629.

Davis, K. (1941). Intermarriage and caste societies. *American Anthropologist, 43,* 376-395.

Ezekiel, R. (1995). *The racist mind.* New York: Viking.

Feinman, S., & Gill, G. W. (1978). Sex differences in physical attractiveness preferences. *Journal of Social Psychology, 105,* 43-52.

Festinger, L., Schachter, S., & Back, K. (1950). *Social pressures in informal groups: A study of a housing community.* New York: Harper & Row.

Freeman, L. (1955). Homogamy in interethnic mate selection. *Sociology and Social Research, 39,* 369-377.

Fuchs, L. (1961). *Hawaii pono: A social history of Hawaii.* New York: Harcourt, Brace & World.

Fujino, D. C. (1991, August). *Asian American interracial relationships: Moving from description information to a theoretical framework.* Paper presented at the convention of the American Psychological Association, San Francisco.

Fujino, D. C. (1992). *Extending exchange theory: Effects of ethnicity and gender on Asian American heterosexual relationships.* Unpublished doctoral dissertation, University of California, Los Angeles.

Glick, C. (1970). Interracial marriage and admixture in Hawaii. *Social Biology, 17,* 278-291.

Grier, W. H., & Cobbs, P. M. (1968). *Black rage.* New York: Basic Books.

Guttentag, M., & Secord, P. F. (1983). *Too many women? The sex ratio question.* Beverly Hills, CA: Sage.

Horman, B. L. (1948). Racial complexion of Hawaii's future population. *Social Forces, 27,* 68-72.

Ichioka, Y. (1988). *The Issei: The world of the first generation Japanese immigrants, 1885-1924.* New York: Free Press.

Johnson, R. C., & Nagoshi, C. (1986). Marriages: A comparison of personality scores. *Journal of Marriage and the Family, 48,* 279-284.

Kikumura, A., & Kitano, H. (1973). Interracial marriage: A picture of the Japanese Americans. *Journal of Social Issues,* 29(2), 67-81.

Kim, B. (1980). An appraisal of Korean immigrant service needs. *Social Casework, 57,* 139-148.

Kim, H. (1977). Korean communities in America: Their characteristics and problems. In H. Kim (Ed.), *The Korean diaspora* (pp. 65-83). Santa Barbara, CA: Clio Press.

Kitano, H. H. L. (1988). *Race relations.* Englewood Cliffs, NJ: Prentice Hall.

Kitano, H. (1997). *Race relations* (5th ed.). Englewood Cliffs, NJ: Prentice Hall.

Kitano, H., & Chai, L. (1982). Korean interracial marriage. *Journal of Marriage and the Family, 5,* 75-78.

Kitano, H., & Daniels, R. (1988). *Asian Americans.* Englewood Cliffs, NJ: Prentice Hall.

Kitano, H., & Daniels, R. (1995). *Asian Americans* (2nd ed.). Englewood Cliffs, NJ: Prentice Hall.

Kitano, H., & Yeung, W. T. (1982). Chinese interracial marriage. *Journal of Marriage and the Family, 5,* 35-48.

Kitano, H., Yeung, W. T., Chai, L., & Hatanaka, H. (1984). Asian American interracial marriage. *Journal of Marriage and the Family, 46,* 179-190.

Labov, T., & Jacobs, J. (1986). Intermarriage in Hawaii, 1950-1983. *Journal of Marriage and the Family, 48,* 79-88.

Lee, S. M., & Yamanaka, K. (1990). Patterns of Asian American intermarriage and marital assimilation. *Journal of Comparative Family Studies, 21,* 287-305.

Lichter, D. T., LeClere, F. B., & McLaughlin, D. K. (1991). Local marriage markets and the marital behavior of Black and White women. *American Journal of Sociology, 4,* 843-867.

Marcson, S. (1950). A theory of intermarriage and assimilation. *Social Forces, 29,* 75-78.

Monahan, T. P. (1977). Illegitimacy by race and mixture of race. *International Journal of Sociology of the Family, 7,* 45-54.

Panunzio, C. (1942). Intermarriage in Los Angeles, 1924-1933. *American Journal of Sociology, 47,* 690-701.

Parkman, M., & Sawyer, J. (1967). Dimensions of ethnic intermarriage in Hawaii. *American Sociological Review, 32,* 593-607.

Porterfield, E. (1978). *Black and White mixed marriages.* Chicago: Nelson-Hall.

Porterfield, E. (1982). Black-American intermarriage in the United States. *Marriage and Family Review, 5,* 17-34.

Ratliff, B., Moon, H., & Bonacci, G. (1978). Intercultural marriage: The Korean-American experience. *Social Casework, 59,* 221-226.

Saegert, S. C., Swap, W., & Zajonc, R. B. (1973). Exposure, context, and interpersonal attraction. *Journal of Personality and Social Psychology, 25,* 234-242.

Schwertfeger, M. M. (1982). Interethnic marriage and divorce in Hawaii: A panel study of 1968 first marriages. *Marriage and Family Review, 5,* 49-59.

Shinagawa, L. (1990). *Marriage patterns of Asian Americans in California, 1980.* Unpublished manuscript, California State University, Sonoma.

Shinagawa, L. H., & Pang, G. Y. (1988). Intraethnic, interethnic, and interracial marriages among Asian Americans in California, 1980. *Berkeley Journal of Sociology, 33,* 95-114.

Stephan, C., & Stephan, W. (1989). After intermarriage: Ethnic identity among mixed heritage Japanese Americans and Hispanics. *Journal of Marriage and the Family, 51,* 507-519.

Sung, B. L. (1990). Chinese American intermarriage. *Journal of Comparative Family Studies, 21,* 337-352.

Takaki, R. (1989). *Strangers from a different shore: A history of Asian Americans.* Boston: Little, Brown.

Thibaut, J. W., & Kelley, H. H. (1959). *The social psychology of groups.* New York: John Wiley.

Tinker, J. (1973). Intermarriage and ethnic boundaries: The Japanese American case. *Journal of Social Issues. 2,* 49-66.

Tinker, J. N. (1982). Intermarriage and assimilation in a plural society: Japanese Americans in the U.S. In G. A. Cretser & J. J. Leon (Eds.), *Intermarriage in the United States* (pp. 61-74). New York: Haworth.

U.S. Bureau of the Census. (1973, July). *Japanese, Chinese, and Filipinos in the United States (based on 20 per cent sample)* (PC [2], 1G). Washington, DC: Government Printing Office.

Winch, R. F. (1958). *Mate selection.* New York: Harper.

Yamamoto, G. (1973). Interracial marriage in Hawaii. In I. R. Stuart & L. E. Abt (Eds.), *Interracial marriage: Expectations and realities* (pp. 309-321). New York: Grossman.

8

MULTIRACIAL AMERICANS

Changing the Face of Asian America

Maria P. P. Root

Hapa, mestizo, Amerasian, Eurasian, Afro-Asian, Black Japanese. These are polite terms, but nevertheless, they are terms that have come into existence because multiracial Asian Americans often are perceived as "outsiders" or "foreigners" to the Asian American experience by many other Asian Americans. The American mixed-race Asian must sort through America's "original sin" of racism (Chao, 1995), a "sin" also present in many Asian countries and cultures (Mrazek, 1987; Valverde, 1992; Wagatsuma, 1976; Weisman, 1996; Williams, 1992a, 1992b). Multiracial Asian Americans are the human "inkblots" on which fears based on xenophobia and racism are projected.

Not only are they hyphenated Americans, but this segment of the Asian American population is a "minority among minorities" (Motoyoshi, 1990). This attitude reflects the degree to which ethnicity and culture have been reduced to race (Omi & Winant, 1986) and to which race and ethnicity are implicitly assumed to be synonymous. The multiracial Asian requires us to reconsider this assumption (Mass, 1992). Multiracial Asians and Asian Americans are conscripted "stimulus objects" for glimpsing the racism and ethnocentrism that exists within Asian and Asian American communities.

There is no single, universal term with which to refer to Asian Americans of multiple racial heritages. However, the term *Amerasian*, originally coined by Buck

AUTHOR'S NOTE: Several colleagues were generous with the amount of time they took to provide extensive, insightful, scholarly feedback on an earlier draft of this chapter and/or to provide original manuscripts: Gordon Nagayama Hall, George Kitahara Kich, Stephen Murphy-Shigematsu, Michael Thornton, and Teresa Kay Williams.

(1930) in her novel *East Wind, West Wind* (referring to children of Asian and White American ancestry living in Asia), has undergone many transformations of usage. More recently, it was a term used to connote mixed-heritage Vietnamese children fathered by American servicemen living in Asia or, even more recently, Vietnamese Amerasian refugees. In contemporary times, many persons use it as an inclusive term, at times cutting across nationalities, across racial mixtures, and across social contexts within which parents have met as well as among generations of mixture (parents vs. grandparents).

In the United States, the presence of multiracial Asians is now normative and growing. We must consider how we define ethnicity and how we confront the racism especially levied toward this growing segment of the Asian American population. This chapter focuses on multiracial Asian Americans living in the United States. Thus, the literature on mixed-heritage Asians living in Asia will not be reviewed here. At times, I refer to this population most inclusively as Amerasians, multiracial Asians, or mixed-heritage Asian Americans. I also refer to subsets of this population specifically as Vietnamese Amerasians, Eurasians (to connote White European ancestry), or Afro-Asians (to connote African heritage).

With a significant number of Amerasians now in a position to research and conceptualize the social, psychological, and political phenomenology and implications of this experience, there has been a proliferation of research and theory on racial and ethnic identity guided by an "insider" perspective (e.g., Grove, 1991; Hall, 1980, 1992; Kich, 1982, 1992; King & DaCosta, 1996; Mass, 1992; Motoyoshi, 1990; Murphy-Shigematsu, 1987, 1988; Nakashima, 1988; Root, 1990, in press; Standen, 1996; Thornton, 1983; Williams, 1992a, 1992b). This insider perspective is important for formulating questions that make sense, interpreting the data in context, and challenging existing frameworks of race and ethnicity that cannot accommodate dual identities or affiliations. The literature to date focuses primarily on nonclinical samples, uses ethnographic research methods more essential to anthropology and sociology than to psychology, and essentially ceases investigation of this phenomenological experience after early adulthood or the college years. Furthermore, the contemporary investigations take place since the civil rights movement, in which much of culture and ethnicity was reduced to race; thus, there is a greater focus on racial identity than on understanding components of ethnicity (Omi & Winant, 1986). As in almost all literature on gender, sexual orientation, or race, the intersection of presumably simultaneous and important aspects of identity are not considered.

This chapter was written at the time a special issue of *Amerasia Journal* (edited by Velina Hasu Houston and Teresa Kay Williams) was planned and a special 1995 holiday issue of *Pacific Citizen* (the newspaper of the Japanese American Citizen's League) was published, both on mixed-heritage Asian Americans. My hope is that this chapter will alert the reader to a significant demographic and phenomenological trend that is transforming the "face" of Asian America. As with any other demographic change in Asian America over the past century, this one surely will have lasting social and political implications for families, communities, and our nation. We must reconsider Murphy-Shigematsu's (1988) question, "Who is an Asian American?" (p. 113), and the implicit question probed by many of the researchers of multiracial identity, "What does it mean to be Asian American?" A third question also emerges out of the ethnographic studies: "Will Asian Americans be able to accept multiracial Asian Americans as equals?" After all, how can one enact being one half Chinese American or one half African American and one half Japanese? This fragmentation serves only to deploy the oppressive mechanics of race that have always disenfranchised those who are the object of it (Root, 1996a, 1996b).

The data on multiracial Asian Americans require that we challenge "racial purity" as a necessary condition for Asian American identity. Mass (1992) and Murphy-Shigematsu (1988) noted that without this change, the Asian community might indeed realize its fears that intermarriage is a portent of the end of Asian America.

UNDERSTANDING THE EMERGENCE
OF MIXED-HERITAGE ASIAN AMERICANS

The increased numbers of Amerasians stem primarily from two sources: intermarriage and America's significant male military presence in the Pacific Rim for more than 50 years. The latter source accounts for the initial surge in the presence of Amerasians in the World War II and Korean war eras. During the Korean war in particular, a significant number of Japanese, Filipino, and Korean-heritage children were born of American fathers, many in their mothers' homelands. The era of the Vietnam war witnessed the increase of multiracial Asians fathered by American military personnel in the Philippines and Vietnam.

Approximately 40,000 to 50,000 Vietnamese Amerasians were born because of U.S. military presence in Vietnam. Many of them have sought refuge in America as a result of the Amerasian Homecoming Act of 1987. This piece of legislation was the result of more than a decade of distress, difficulties, and obstacles for Amerasians attempting to leave Vietnam for the United States because of maltreatment and persecution for being racially mixed and fatherless, although fathered by Americans, in their homeland (Mrazek, 1987; Valverde, 1992). This act initially allotted a 2-year period (to end March 21, 1990) in which Amerasians born between January 1, 1962, and December 31, 1976, would be given immigrant status and refugee benefits in the United States along with their immediate families. (Reaching and processing the large numbers of Vietnamese Amerasians [an estimated 30,000] that qualified under this legislation required further legislation removing the 2-year deadline.)

Many Amerasians and their family members have been subject to cruel social conditions in various Asian countries for their mixed heritage and/or for their fatherlessness, a major stigma in a patriarchal society (Valverde, 1992; Weisman, 1996). Furthermore, these children have been the scapegoats for anti-American sentiments (Valverde, 1992) when Americans were not well regarded in Vietnam, Japan, Thailand, the Philippines, and Korea. Reference in Vietnam to these Amerasians as *bui doi* (dust of life) reflects the politically and socially marginalized position they experience by the failure of two governments to responsibly and quickly attend to the needs of these children (Felsman, Johnson, Leong, & Felsman, 1989; Valverde, 1992), most now adults, which has tremendous implications for psychosocial adjustment. Valverde (1992) observed that with the change in U.S. legislation giving Amerasians priority immigration and ability to have family members accompany them, the "dust of life" has become a ticket for immigration or "gold" in Vietnam.

Since the Vietnam war, however, a biracial baby boom has occurred in the United States rooted in intermarriage of American citizens (Chapter 8, this volume; Root, 1992). The U.S. Supreme Court's repeal of antimiscegenation laws in the remaining 14 states in 1967 and changes in anti-Asian immigration legislation, particularly the Immigration and Naturalization Act of 1965, no doubt have contributed to the increased rates of intermarriage (Thornton, 1992) evidenced in the early 1970s. Chew, Eggebeen, and Uhlenberg (1989) noted that of all racially mixed households in the United States, Asian Americans represent the largest number (this includes transracial adoption). Although these households have largely been Asian American women with men of other ethnic groups, statistics in New York City (Sung, 1990) and Los Angeles County (Chapter 8, this volume) suggest that rates of intermarriage are becoming more similar for Asian American men and women.

Nevertheless, one would have expected significant numbers of biracial Amerasian children to have emerged sooner in the history of Asian America than they did given that several factors associated with intermarriage were present over an extended period of time, for example, imbalanced sex ratios of early Asian immigrants (Degler, 1971; Chan, 1991) due to Asian exclusionary laws (Thornton, 1992), small immigrant groups relative to the indigenous population (Adams, 1937), and a largely unacknowledged history of interracial unions in this country since Columbus. However, the anti-Asian sentiment and the prevailing antimiscegenation attitudes were significant obstacles to intermarriage. Ironically, intermarriage is now a fact in Asian American communities, the rates of which have increased with each successive generation in this country (Chapter 8, this volume) and will likely produce an increased ratio of multiracial Asians to monoracial Asians over time.

Currently, the Population Reference Bureau (1992) estimated that there are almost 40% more Japanese-White births than monoracial Japanese-heritage births, a figure larger than that for Chinese-White births. When all Asians and Pacific Islanders were collapsed into one group in 1989, births to interracial couples with one parent of Euro-American ancestry and one parent of Asian/Pacific Island ancestry was two thirds the number of births to both parents being of Asian/Pacific Island ancestry.

The various social and political contexts within which the Amerasian has emerged have very different implications for identity, adjustment, and cultural transmission. In contrast to 25 years ago, a binational experience is less common today for young Amerasians because they are largely the product of intermarriage between American parents. Multiracial Asians whose parents met in Asia largely because of military assignments during wartime had mothers who were Asian nationals; they often were born in their mothers' countries of origin, might have immigrated themselves, might have spoken another language or be bilingual, might have been cultural liaisons for their mothers in America, and might have been raised more frequently on U.S. military bases (Hall, 1980; Thornton, 1983; Williams, 1992a, 1992b). Although many of these unions included intermarriage, America's anti-intermarriage sentiment and need to maintain rigid racial boundaries perpetuated reference to these Amerasians as "war babies"; similar sentiment in Japan against interracial marriage made reference to these children as *konketsuji* (Strong, 1978). This reference has been extremely damaging because it relegates all Asian and American unions of this time to illicit sex in the context of "one-night stands" and only about sex, thus diminishing the personal worth attributed to earlier cohorts of multiracial Asians in this country. Despite data to the contrary, this mythology has been extended to the Vietnamese Amerasians. A recent report by the U.S. Catholic Conference (Felsman et al., 1989) found that mothers and fathers of Vietnamese Amerasians had been in committed relationships, often cohabitating for an average of 2 years.

The process of social adjustment, determination of belonging, and ethnic identity for Amerasians has been complicated by the assertion that a socially constructed notion of race, with boundaries that change to serve those in power, has been reified through scientific research (Spickard, 1992). The construct of race in this country is particularly harmful because it denies and discourages the possibility of dual racial affiliations. Hypodescent rules create this obstacle. Thus, racial categories are viewed as mutually exclusive (replicated every 10 years in the U.S. census counts) and hierarchically arranged with White seen as superior and Black as inferior.

The result of combining these rules can only be irrational and oppressive. White society labels the Eurasian as non-White, although in the process it might misidentify the non-European contribution to physical appearance. It has been assumed that the multiracial individual will be "better off" or accepted by non-White communities. However, many Asian groups can be equally oppressive in their belief in racial purity and their avoidance of racial "contamination" represented by mixed-heritage Asian Americans (Murphy-Shigematsu, 1987; Thornton, 1983; Wagatsuma, 1976). Similarly, racist attitudes are projected onto the Eurasian for his or her inferiority due to racial hybridity and contamination of superior racial strains. This fallout of oppressive practices is only magnified in situations of persons who are of African and Asian heritage because of even a more negative valence attributed to "Blackness" due to Asians having adopted the oppressive racial hierarchy viewing African American ancestry as inferior not only to Asian ancestry but to European ancestry as well. Many Asian Americans have not only internalized an attitude of superiority but also internalized the American attitude that has relegated the African American to a class status that appears to be unchangeable in its essence even by economics or marriage.

Ironically, the discrimination can be a two-way street, creating a squeeze of oppression (Root, 1990) that results from racial authenticity tests. Thornton's (1983) Black Japanese Asian Americans reflected that African Americans tended to be less accepting of them than were many other people. Lack of acceptance by many African Americans rests in the oppressive interpretation of race mixing centuries earlier between Blacks and Whites (Daniel, 1992; Thornton, 1983). Thus, the Amerasian is not guaranteed full acceptance by any group. The Amerasian's racial and ethnic legitimacy may be challenged because of the observer's internalized oppression around the rules of race and the legacy of colorism in many ethnic communities. Furthermore, the definitions of ethnic solidarity seem to be increasingly narrowly defined and almost simultaneous with race.

Acceptance or rejection by one group appears to play a critical part in identity (Hall, 1980; Kinloch, 1983; Thornton, 1983). Thus, the internalization of rigid racial boundaries based on pseudoscience (Spickard, 1992) (i.e., racism) results in a "squeeze of oppression" commonly experienced by Amerasians (Root, 1990) and fractionation of the self that obstructs, but does not prevent, the motivation to integrate divergent experiences.

America's racial politics makes the multiracial experience an issue. In addition to experiences of a person of color, many Amerasians, particularly adults, have had to deal with a marginalized status that is a consequence of how embedded the tool of race is in our culture (Root, 1996a). Bradshaw (1992) notes, "The biracial individual must disentangle internalized prohibitions against gaining privileges not accorded to the 'other' (lower status) racial heritage (internalized racism) from legitimate claims to privileges existing in both heritages" (p. 80). This is why marginal status is not inherent to being multiracial but, rather, is created by the society (Root, 1990). Currently, the case of the Vietnamese Amerasian both in Vietnam and in America illustrates this so well (Felsman et al., 1989; Valverde, 1992). Root (1997) recently explored how Filipinos who make no claims to racial purity are accommodating a racial definition of Filipino as part of acculturation to life in the United States. This certainly will change the experience of offspring of cross-cultural and interracial Filipino relationships.

LIMITATIONS OF RESEARCH ON MULTIRACIAL ASIAN AMERICANS

A line of demarcation between old and new research occurred in the 1970s, corresponding to the repeal of the last antimiscegenation laws, the first large cohort of Amerasians coming of adult age, the articulation of ethnic and racial pride from the civil rights movement, the removal of barriers to Asian immigration to the United States, and the beginning of the biracial baby boom. Although the research on multiracial Asians is between its adolescence and adulthood, there are many strengths. The contemporary research and conceptualization has been largely by Asians of mixed heritage and by others critical of the political and social biases that guided earlier research on racially mixed persons. The research has been approached with more optimism and awareness of how the construction of race and ethnicity has limited our explanations of findings and processes. Questions that are relevant to the adjustment and identity of Amerasians are being asked in context through combined methods of quantitative measures and qualitative methods informed by insider experience. Nonclinical samples have been exclusively used to answer questions about identity and adjustment. Thus, we have data on normative processes for working through racial and ethnic identity for Amerasians.

There also are weaknesses in the research that pose limitations to some of our conclusions. First, almost all the research uses nonrandomized samples, often using college-age students and a snowballing method in which groups to which multiracial Asians belong are approached for research participants; participants are then asked about other potential participants. This is hard to avoid because Amerasians are not randomly distributed in this country or within counties or cities. Chew et al. (1989) noted that more than 50% of children in multiracial households live in six states: California, Hawaii, Washington, New York, Texas, and Illinois. The majority of these children are Eurasian. Randomization also is difficult because the U.S. Bureau of the Census accounts for persons according to monoracial categories. Lastly, because of the American custom for women to adopt their husbands' surnames in marriage, many Amerasians cannot be identified by surname.

Second, many studies have not used control groups. This is a problem only when comparative statements are made. Most of the research that does not include control groups has attempted to describe the experiences of multiracial Asians including their identity resolution processes. Control groups have not been necessary. When control groups are necessary to the research inquiry, researchers have been cautious and have questioned what constitutes appropriate controls. For example, Cauce et al. (1992) used monoracial Asian adolescents as the control group for their multiracial Asians as they shared the experience of being treated as people of color in U.S. society.

Another limitation has been that the majority of studies have focused on Japanese-heritage individuals. We do not know which results we can generalize across Asian groups. For example, it would make sense conceptually to hypothesize that Filipinos, who are multiracial by heritage and were wards of the United States, base group ethnic membership on different or fewer criteria; racial purity is not as significant a criterion as it might be for other Asian groups, although the interpretation of physical appearance and colorism might be significant in the context of 350 years of colonization by Spain and then 50 more by the United States (Root, 1997). Vietnamese Amerasians' experiences include larger binational conflicts, immigration and/or refugee experiences, and extreme overt stigmatization by the Vietnamese community (Felsman et al., 1989; Valverde, 1992). Korean-heritage Amerasians recently have been studied by Standen (1996). Their experience, although often originating in the U.S. military presence in Korea, also is intertwined with the oppression experienced by Japan. This tension still is present in some aspects of Korean identity.

Related to this previous limitation is that research has used participants who have identified as Asian and/or biracial. We do not know much about those persons who have not done so or who have chosen to identify monoracially and monoethnically or even to avoid the issue. Given America's politics of race, one would predict that the adjustment of these individuals might be more difficult because race is a critical social address.

I consider one of the most eminent weaknesses at this point in time to be the limited age window from which conclusions about the Amerasian experience and the process of integrating social experiences around race and ethnicity into identity are drawn. Thornton (1996) noted that many other aspects of identity are not considered in the process of understanding identity. This research is subject to the same limitations of other identity research. Simultaneous aspects of identity such as gender, job or career, sexual orientation, and other aspects of being have not been explored for their co-influences. Lerner (1986) suggested that race and gender are co-constructed and that understanding one without the other creates a circumscribed understanding. Recently, several people have begun to tackle the co-influence and confoundedness of other oppressed status (Allman, 1996; Kich, 1996). Given that contemporary theory and research on multiracial identity asserts the importance of situationality, it is time for researchers to explore the influence of other aspects of identity on racial identity (Root, in press). The life span will need to be broadened to understand identity processes more fully.

Root (1990) suggested that many multiracial people struggle with different aspects of identity over their lifetimes. For Amerasians, the centrality of race and ethnicity and the resolution of duality or multiplicity seem to span into the 20s and even 30s. Thornton (1983) suggested that it often took as long as 20 years with his Black Japanese participants. I suggest that the process of identity is characterized by a spiral in which issues are revisited at different times in one's life driven by internal conflicts that are externally produced. During this process, it is very likely that although the essence of who one is remains the same, what is critical in determining identity might change. Furthermore, the co-influence of other social critical aspects of identity inform this process. Thus, I suggest that gender or sexual orientation, for example, will influence this process because of the conflict over secondary status that threatens one's sense of value in the community or society at large. Other ecological contexts affect identity such as generation, geographical history of race relations, class, family influences, and interpersonal interactions in different significant communities (Root, in press). Furthermore, developmental milestones such as choice of partner, having children, dealing with a parent's death, or dealing with one's own mortality may have a significant impact on which issues are foreground versus background to identity.

The research needs to consider the influence of generation-specific influences. Until recently, multiracial Asians generally had Asian or Asian American mothers and white American fathers. For example, for those Amerasians born in Asian countries but living in the United States, how has this experience and the attendant variables (e.g., serving as liaisons for their mothers in the United States, bilingualism, being separated from their fathers for periods of time, living on military bases) affected their experience of being multiracial Asian Americans compared to Amerasians born of American-born parents? For example, Nakashima's (1988) young adult sample of Japanese Eurasians does not describe the pain that Kich's (1982) older sample of Asian Americans of mixed heritage described in their first stage of identity resolution. As more Asian American men are marrying women who are not Asian American, how will this influence child rearing given that research has shown that mothers have been explicitly and implicitly charged with the task of imparting culture? How will persons born of Asian American fathers and first-generation immigrants from other countries be influenced in their identification process?

We also need to understand the interaction of various mixes. To date, only three studies of Black Japanese exist (Hall, 1980; Thornton, 1983; Williams, 1992a, 1992b). How are the experiences of Afro-Asians different from those of Eurasians?

With this awareness of the salient strengths and limitations in the contemporary research, the rest of this chapter summarizes the research in four areas: self-esteem and adjustment, identity, sexuality, and adaptation.

SELF-ESTEEM AND ADJUSTMENT

The question "What of the children?" posed to biracial couples assumes that this experience is inherently negative and problematic. Thornton (1983) noted, "It is simply because interracial marriage and mixtures are deemed *socially* significant events that they are of any consequence" (p. 48, emphasis in original). By contrast, those who approach this issue "color-blind" suggest that the individual has free choice in identity. Other naive assumptions are that the Amerasian inherits the best of both worlds and is even a superior being.

Prior to the emergence of the contemporary research, the predicted maladjustment of the multiracial person was hypothesized to be the manifestation of parental pathology (who is likely to intermarry), marital instability (as the result of differences), and marginal belonging of children due to their ambiguous status. Thornton (1983) summarized it well: "Most of these arguments for motives of out-marriage are inherently weak, for they are impressionistic, speculative, and often fragmentary. So while true of individual cases and particular marriages, they hardly provide a valid picture for all mixed marriages" (p. 68). It is difficult to assess these hypotheses because the early empirical studies, in their uncontrolled reflection of the time's bias against intermarriage, did not separate out which difficulties in marriage that affected children were the psychological effects of war, language boundaries in the marriage, the mother's loss of support systems that followed immigration to America, the mother's grief over leaving her homeland, and the social ostracism of many interracial couples. Ignored in this literature was the significant role that the larger society played in its rejection of the multiracial child, often manifested in the extended family's rejection of the child or ostracism of the family (Hall, 1980; Murphy-Shigematsu, 1987; Root, 1990; Stephan & Stephan, 1989; Thornton, 1983).

Despite the adverse experiences some multiheritage Asian children have, contemporary studies in different areas of the country have found multiracial Asians raised in the United States to evidence good adjustment and self-esteem. Thus, although there can be additional stresses to the multiracial experience, as a group, the people studied do not evidence ill effects. The results of significant studies are reviewed in the area of adjustment.

Several studies have been conducted in Hawaii, where almost 50% of resident marriages are interracial, and thus a significant proportion of the population is racially mixed. The first significant published study of any Amerasian sample was conducted in Hawaii by Dien and Vinacke (1964) on 15 freshmen from the University of Hawaii with White fathers and Nisei mothers. This was a complicated exploration of discrepancy between self-concept and ideal self-concept of multiracial Japanese, monoracial Japanese, and Whites. Generally, there were no differences among groups. However, multiracial males' pattern of scores showed less discrepancy between self and ideal scores than did that of monoracial counterparts. The authors advanced several explanations for the meaning of the male results. For example, the multiracial male results might reflect higher self-esteem or lower aspirations for the ideal self. They felt that the difference between male and female patterns of results might be best explained by the important "identificand" being the same-sex parent for young women but could not test this hypothesis because of the imbalanced design of parentage.

Subsequent studies conducted in Hawaii primarily with Japanese-White samples, similar to Dien and Vinacke (1964) with mothers being Asian American and fathers being White, found that self-esteem and psychological adjustment appear to be on the "good" adjusted end of the spectrum. When there were differences, the multiracial Asians tended to score between the groups of their heritage, with the differences having no real-world implications (Johnson & Nagoshi, 1986). Duffy (1978) compared the self-concepts of 41 Japanese-White participants to those of monoracial Japanese and White participants and found them to be similar to both control groups on measures of self-concept, patterns of parental interactions, and parental concepts. Johnson and Nagoshi (1986) compared 180 late adolescents of interethnic/interracial Asian-White marriages to 1,024 offspring of intraethnic marriages on personality variables indicative of adjustment. They found no significant differences on 11 of 14 scales that included ego strength, self-regard, and neuroticism. Stephan and Stephan (1989) explored the impact of intermarriage on personality; they compared 57 predominantly Japanese-White heritage college students to 100 monoracial Asian Americans and 34 Whites. Mixed-heritage Asian Americans scored between Whites and monoracial Asians on self-esteem, a difference that did not appear to have real-world significance. There were no differences among groups on psychological symptomatology.

Mainland samples have yielded similar results. In Seattle, Washington, Cauce et al. (1992) reported on one of the youngest samples of biracial Asians yet in a study exploring psychosocial adjustment. The authors found no differences between the five preadolescents of Asian-White ancestry and their monoracial Asian American cohort, so they were combined into one group. No differences were found on self-esteem, peer acceptance, stressful life events, or psychological adjustment. Other researchers have deliberately picked at least college-age students to attempt to rule out the confound of normal identity crises that might be typical of adolescence and for multiracial Amerasians (Hall, 1980). Hall (1980) found that a second significant period in which Amerasians may experience challenges to adjustment past early childhood became apparent around 15 years of age, which corresponded to dating, where again issues of acceptance and nonacceptance by peers and the larger community became apparent. Self-esteem was independent of ethnic identity choice in Hall's study of Afro-Asians of college age in Los Angeles. Mass (1992), a decade later, found no differences between monoracial and biracial Japanese Americans of White parentage in her Los Angeles area sample on self-esteem and psychological adjustment.

In contrast to the studies on multiracial Japanese Americans, studies on Vietnamese Amerasians have yielded significant adjustment problems and low self-esteem related to many of the harsh adversities correlated with the persecution related to their racial status in Vietnam and their fatherless status. Subsequently, the refugee status granted under the Amerasian Homecoming Act meant more adjustments and being placed in a foreign culture and land that did not guarantee them acceptance. Valverde (1992) noted that it was normative to settle into areas that had immigrant Vietnamese populations. However, the harsh and discriminatory attitudes that were held in Vietnam toward mixed-heritage children were prevalent in these communities. Felsman et al. (1989) provided an excellent review of the research on Vietnamese Amerasians; the Vietnamese Amerasians studied ranged in age from their early teens to late 20s.

Several studies have developed risk profiles for adjustment problems including psychological distress indicating the centrality of the primary caregiver and the color of the father. One study indicated that 83% of the sample had problems within a couple years of resettlement (Felsman et al., 1989) that were significantly associated with male gender, the father being Black, living outside the Vietnamese community, and an unstable home environment. The first attempt at a large study was conducted by the U.S. Catholic Conference (Felsman et al., 1989) of 350 Amerasians resettled during 1983 and 1984. The majority (71%) were "free cases," meaning that they were not sponsored by relatives. Adjustment problems were correlated with being an unaccompanied minor and not being accompanied by the primary caregiver, both variables of which occurred much more frequently among Afro-Amerasians. Felsman et al. (1989) provided the largest randomly selected sample of Vietnamese Amerasian adolescents ($N = 259$, with an even distribution of males and females) who were selected prior to their arrival in the United States. The majority (81%) were raised with their biological mothers, and the vast majority (88%) knew little or nothing of their fathers, although 67% knew their fathers were White, 17% knew their fathers were Black, and 54% hoped for reunions. The powerful role of discrimination in their countries of origin was evident in that 22% indicated leaving school early because of discrimination. The authors were impressed by the resiliency of these Amerasians in the face of experiencing enormous adversities in youth and in the resettlement process. In contrast to Felsman et al.'s (1989) study, female gender was correlated with more general psychological distress and specific depression. Thus, gender was included in a risk profile for psychological distress and school failure that also included being Afro-Amerasian, having completed less than 9 years of schooling in Vietnam, having low reading scores, being raised apart from the biological mother, not being accompanied by the mother, not being accompanied by siblings, having a history of serious illness, and having a history of missing school.

Felsman et al.'s (1989) data suggest that many of the earlier arriving Amerasians were likely to have been separated from their birth families, living in orphanages and monasteries and immigrating with fewer family members than is the case with Amerasians immigrating now. They also suggest that there appears to be a change in where Amerasians are coming from; the earlier arrivals were from urban areas, and the most recent arrivals in Ho Chi Minh's Amerasian Departure Center appear to have rural origins. The delay in rural Amerasians arriving in the city might have been due to local and sometimes corrupt bureaucracy and the cost of such a trip (Valverde, 1992). This difference in origin and experiences can lead to different expectations by Vietnamese Amerasians in the United States (Felsman et al., 1989) and can have implications for adjustment. Tien and Hunthausen (1990) described a sample of 33 Vietnamese Amerasian free cases (non-relative sponsored) between 15 and 24 years of age who resettled in Tacoma, Washington, from September 1989 to March 1990. These authors, as well as Felsman et al. (1989), observed that Amerasians have not necessarily been equipped with the English and job skills they need to move freely in the United States; thus, they might feel alienated. The resettlement experience is all the more difficult when family relations are strained from all the stresses of adjustment and life is harder than anticipated. In this sample, the authors noted that the multiracial Vietnamese, in contrast to their monoracial cohorts, are quicker to attempt American ways of doing things, which they suggested might be aided by their physical appearance. It also is possible that there is some intrinsic sense of belonging to America by parentage, even though there is a conflict inherent in the sorting through of identity and belonging in America (Valverde, 1992). Lastly, it is distinctly possible that lack of acceptance by the Vietnamese American community, as is the case in other Asian American communities, contributes to the racially mixed Asians looking to be accepted or to blend into society at large.

In summary, we lack data on the psychological profiles and adjustment of multiracial Filipino- and Chinese-heritage Asian Americans. That contemporary adjustment of multiracial Asian Americans raised in the United States is similar to peers but significantly different from Vietnamese Amerasians allows us to conclude more emphatically the significance of racism, war trauma, and stigmatized fatherlessness as systemic influences on psychological adjustment. Drawing on ecological models of identity development, the significance of the social interactions for determining the meaning and assignation of identity becomes apparent. This view is tied to economic theories and symbolic interactionism. More systematic studies are needed at younger ages; it has been hypothesized from interviews with Amerasians that the developmental hurts and challenges are particularly acute in early childhood, when the "squeeze of oppression" first surfaces (Root, 1990).

Mass (1992) suggested that rather than ask "What will happen to the children?" we might ask "What is the best way to facilitate a positive growing up experience for interracial children?" The Eurasian and Afro-Asian participants in Williams' (1992a, 1992b) study pointed to the importance of parents, grandparents, and other kin in accepting Amerasian children and welcoming them to the world. In addition, the children need permission and examples for how to cope with intrusive questions and comments and possible irrational rejections. Motoyoshi (1990) underscored familial influence and responsibility in orienting biracial children to the harsh realities and irrationalities of racism. King and DaCosta (1996) noted that understanding the ways in which race is performed and the ways in which this understanding is facilitated by family, community, and peers influences the experience and interpretation of being multiracial.

IDENTITY

In a society where there is significant variance in race and ethnicity, these become significant variables in the establishment of identity and determination of belonging (Phinney, 1990). America's racial legacy poses a problem to many multiracial Asians who are challenged to prove their ethnic legitimacy within the African and Asian American communities in particular (Chao, 1995; Murphy-Shigematsu, 1987, 1988; Thornton, 1983). Murphy-Shigematsu (1988) observed,

> The biracial Asian American also is subjected to these types of ambivalent and confusing messages in the Asian American media: "Although Amerasian, she is interested in and proud of her Chinese heritage"; "The half Black, half Japanese looks just like Ben Vereen"; and "Though she is Eurasian, . . . " (p. 114)

Sentiments that racial mixing will dilute the cultural integrity of the group and that racially mixed persons will disavow or identify less with their Asian heritage than with other heritages originate in the assumption that race and ethnicity are synonymous. It further perpetuates the assumption that mixed people, particularly of European heritage, aspire to be White (Root, 1995). Furthermore, such a statement devalues the contribution of the Amerasian to the Asian community, particularly in the potential growth of the various Asian American communities across America. In contrast to this sentiment, several studies find no differences in the strength of ethnic identity between groups such as multiracial and monoracial Chinese (Grove, 1991) or monoracial and biracial Japanese (Nakashima, 1988); other studies find tremendous variability (Mass, 1992; Stephan, 1991).

With Amerasians, race and ethnicity are not interchangeable constructs. How ethnicity is measured becomes extremely important. Nakashima (1988) observed that her same sample of American-born Japanese Eurasians scored differently on Asian ethnicity depending on the point of reference for determining ethnicity. In fact, she observed that for many Amerasians, their search for rootedness leaves them knowing much more about their Asian heritage than do their monoracial peers.

Race influences identity to some degree because physical appearance mediates acceptance and rejection of the individual by groups of his or her heritage *and* reflects a construction of reality that serves those who have desired resources and privileges (Murphy-Shigematsu, 1987, 1988; Root, 1990). As researchers had found with other Amerasian samples, Grove (1991) found in her study of the ethnic identity of predominantly multiracial and monoracial Chinese that biracial Chinese Amerasians perceived race to be less important to identity formation than did monoracial Chinese Asians. Stephan (1991) found that race was neither a necessary nor a sufficient condition for determining ethnicity in her Hawaiian sample of predominantly Japanese Americans.

Ethnicity has long been assumed to be an objective social status or identity. However, this is not the case for Amerasians and other racially mixed persons where congruence in identity is extremely variable between the self and the other. Furthermore, multiracial Asians claim simultaneous identities (Duffy, 1978; Hall, 1980; Thornton, 1983), situationally specific identities (Duffy, 1978; Stephan, 1992), and different identities over a lifetime (Root, 1990). A fairly salient finding across studies is that Amerasians are able to establish integrated identities that are different from either group of their heritage (Hall, 1980, 1992; Kich, 1982, 1992; Murphy-Shigematsu, 1987; Nakashima, 1988; Thornton, 1983). This finding suggests that the dichotomous way in which identity traditionally is approached (i.e., Asian/not Asian) is a flawed approach to identity research with this population. Thus, the research on multiracial Asian Americans directs us to the phenomenology of what it means to be Asian American.

The dynamic identity and multiple affiliation evidenced among many Amerasians have been misunderstood as instability or attempts to negate certain aspects of heritage. Thus, terms such as "passing" have been applied negatively to Eurasians who appear to function in the White world and identify as White. What is not considered is that the very concept of passing reflects internalized racism and the desire for distinct boundaries and racial segregation. Instead, much as Daniel (1992) observed of multiracial African Americans and Bradshaw (1992) and Chao (1995) observed of Amerasians, passing also can be viewed as an adaptive strategy that does not necessarily inform the observer of the core self-identity of the Amerasian. I observed this as a possibility with my sample of multiracial Filipinos in Honolulu, Hawaii. I observed that it was to the multiethnic Filipino's social advantage in Hawaii to claim a primary ethnic identity different from Filipino in many situations, particularly when asked to give a singular identity, because of the ethnic hierarchy in which Filipino occupies a low rung on the ladder. This does not mean that they deny their ethnic heritage; rather, they are subverting a hierarchy in which they occupy a low status and lay legitimate claim to their other heritages.

The ecological environment (Miller, 1992) is critical to understanding how the observer assigns identity to the multiracial individual, how the Amerasian identifies in given situations, and how self-other incongruence affects identity formation and retention. Miller (1992) observed that for the minority individual, and particularly for the multiracial individual, the content of his or her experience is critical to establishing a sense of belonging to a group or a foundation for positive esteem and identity. She further observed that Eriksonian models, which have been used to explore multiracial identity to give salience to the content of one's experience in a social group and proscriptions of social group behaviors, assume that social ascription and personal identity are convergent; one claims status with a group along a dimension considered static, such as race. However, this is not necessarily an accurate reflection of the Amerasian's experience (Stephan, 1992).

Several variables are part of an ecological matrix including community and family members' acceptance or rejection (Hall, 1980; Kinloch, 1983; Mass, 1992; Stephan, 1991), fatherlessness (Valverde, 1992), physical appearance (Kinloch, 1983; Stephan, 1991), the possession (Root, in press; Stephan, 1992) or reclamation of Asian names (Murphy-Shigematsu, 1987), the gender by ethnicity interaction of parents, the exposure and socializing with specific ethnic groups (Hall, 1980; Mass, 1992; Stephan, 1991), the social status of heritage groups in relation to one another (Kinloch, 1983; Vallangca, 1987), age (Hall, 1980), parental identification (Dien & Vinacke, 1964), generation, and life experiences.

Using an ecological approach to her data analysis, Hall (1980, 1992) found that four variables accounted for 56% of the variance in identity choice in her sample of 30 Afro-Asians. Younger respondents, who had primarily Black friends, had knowledge of Black culture, and had experienced rejection by Japanese Americans, tended to identify as Black. Participants who identified as other than Black (Japanese or other) had the opposite characteristics. Hall suggested that it was possible that the age of respondents might have been related to their ethnic identity choice, with younger respondents treating race as a more unidimensional construct with distinct boundaries.

Research on ethnic populations suggests that generation contributes to ethnic identity. Surprisingly, Hall (1980, 1992) found a lack of correlation between these two variables in her sample of multiracial Black Japanese given that 24 of the 30 Japanese mothers were first generation. She suggested that the multiracial nature of her respondents' experiences might have contributed to a uniqueness in their experience more powerful than generational effects. It also is distinctly possible that the era in which this research took place, the age of participants, and the role of African Americans in society influenced her participants' identification beyond what she could measure.

This ecological matrix for Asian Americans also is embedded in history, which is variable to the degree that the following issues are relevant to the specific Asian group: nationalism, colonialism, the legacy of war, military occupation, language differences, religion differences, and economic standing in the world community. These components of a matrix coexist through recurring cycles of anti-Asian sentiment in this country that is imposed on Asian Americans. The variability in self-identification also may be influenced by the Asian group's history of racial mixing. Thus, Filipinos, being of multiracial origin for centuries, do not manifest the same degree of concern with purity of race as do other Asian groups. However, for a younger generation born and raised in the United States, ethnicity takes on a symbolic representation (Root, 1997). Being of Filipino heritage adds to their sense of uniqueness but might not be represented in their lives in any overt or significant ways of which they have awareness. Felsman et al. (1989) observed the traumatic sequelae of war in the identity struggles of the Vietnamese Amerasians who have been colored by the "psychological meaning embodied in being 'half-American' " (p. 8). Valverde (1992) emphasized that a correlate of war for Vietnamese Amerasians was fatherlessness, which Felsman et al. (1989) noted to be the predominant experience of Vietnamese Amerasians and a detriment to identity development: "In a society in which identity and self-definition are derived through patriarchal lineage, the trauma of an unknown father follows an individual through life" (p. 147). In a different context, Williams' (1992a, 1992b) study of 43 binational Japanese-heritage Amerasians of White (29) and Black (14) American heritage, ages 16 to 35 years, who spent a significant part of their adolescence on military bases of Yokohama and Yokosuka in Japan, often claimed the saliency of their identity as military dependents and then children of international marriages over their biracial status. This finding was observed earlier by Cottrell (1978) and Thornton (1983). Thornton further observed that "identity crises" arose outside the military environment. Being raised on bases with other biracial persons protected children from Japanese racism that was experienced on "outings" and allowed them to forge a "biracial community and culture" (Williams, 1992a, 1992b). For Afro-Asians, coming to the United States began their first significant contacts with American racism and a chance to embrace their African American heritage. Many respondents talked about switching identities to be most congruent with the demands of the situation. Sometimes this included language switching and behavior switching (Williams, 1992a, 1992b).

The multiracial experience poses some unique challenges to conventional theories of ethnic identity formation (Root, 1990) that suggest that achievement of positive ethnic identity requires rejection of the mainstream for a period of time to explore and subsequently immerse oneself in the ethnic community. Root (1990) suggested that this is a dilemma that poses problems in multiracial families, particularly color-color mixes, and indeed does not tend to happen because for the "biracial individual to reject either part of their racial heritage continues an internalized oppression. . . . To reject the dominant culture is to reject one parent and, subsequently, an integral part of themselves that is unchangeable, particularly if it is the same-sex parent" (p. 193). Hall (1980) found that Blackness and Japaneseness could coexist and, thus, pointed out the absurdity of the "please choose one" dilemma (Hall, 1992). In fact, 10 of the 30 participants in her study of Afro-Asians (Japanese) designated themselves as "other" when forced to choose between Black and Japanese. Duffy (1978) concluded in her study of multiracial Japanese Eurasians in Honolulu that they, too, did not choose one culture over the other. She asserted that the Eurasians in her sample evidenced a "situationally dynamic ethnic identity" that Stephan (1991) found in Honolulu more than 10 years later. That identity can be situationally determined is not evidence of instability but might be evidence of situation saliency for certain roles, behaviors, and expressions of attitudes and beliefs.

To a greater extent than among monoracials, there is an active identity process among many Amerasians (Grove, 1991; Hall, 1980; Thornton, 1983) that may extend well into the adult years, lasting as long as 20 years (Thornton, 1983), worked through a bit more with significant developmental markers (e.g., choice of life partners, having and naming children, death of parents). Hall (1980) found that 60% of her participants said they had faced ethnic identity choices that occurred around 14 or 15 years of age. Of these participants, 10 ended up identifying as Black at the time of her study and 8 identified as "other." Similarly, Grove (1991) found that the majority of her largely Chinese Eurasian sample had questioned their racial identity and achieved resolution around it. Based on simultaneous interview data from these respondents, Grove suggested that the "social and cultural status of being half White facilitated and allowed questioning Asian identity from a 'safe place,' a place where their race was not a salient issue" (p. 623). Thornton (1983) found that 91% of his Black Japanese sample had actively addressed their identity resolution.

The goal of identity is to develop a whole identity that reflects the successful integration of diverse aspects of self rather than a fractionation of self. As such, a healthy identity requires that racial boundaries are not experienced as fixed and rigid as one is taught they are. Kich (1982) developed an identity development stage model to explain the experience of Amerasians from his sample. He described three stages. The first stage, most prominent between 3 and 8 years of age, is characterized by feeling different and separate from peers and the community. This difference is promoted by the awareness of the incongruence between self and other perceptions based on the rigidity of racial boundaries. Thus, Root (1990) observed that the child is likely to compartmentalize and separate racial components (e.g., asking a parent, "What part of me is your color? What part of me is Daddy's color?"). On a more subtle level, Bradshaw (1992) observed, "Reconciling the conflict between internal experience of differentness and external attribution of the meaning of this difference is likely a lifelong developmental process affected by the vicissitudes of both social and personal change" (p. 78). This differentness is more salient when race has not been talked about in the family and when children have not been provided a means of understanding their experiences. In the second stage, an active process of labeling self occurs, and attempts to connect and value different aspects of heritage are sought. In contrast to the third stage, the individual in the second stage (usually from preadolescence to young adulthood) searches for affirmation and acceptance from others. In the third stage, the individual has labels for his or her experience and ethnic identity and often asserts a multiracial label. The ability to do this is accomplished when the individual is able to break free from the system of racial classification and can assert an identity that is congruent with his or her experience.

In summary, the Amerasian self-identity cannot confidently be determined based on physical appearance. A host of ecological factors through time, within a community, and within a family exert influence on identity (Figure 8.1) (Root, in press). Furthermore, life-span developmental milestones undoubtedly must affect the process of racial identity resolution and the salience of race to identity. Models of ethnic identity must challenge linear notions of race and ethnicity, which assume that only one aspect of self can be affirmed at a time and promote fractionation rather than integration. Creative solutions for achieving integration must be explored and outlined. Marginalization is not necessarily an experience that has a negative result. It is a negative experience when one does have alternatives (Thornton, 1983) and wishes not be marginal. Thus, for many multiracial persons, I suggest that we consider the experience of feeling marginal a normative experience, as Kich (1982) observed and developmental psychologists have observed as normative experience for adolescence (Erikson, 1968). Feeling that one is different in a way that raises internal tension seems to be part of a human process for clarifying values (Root, 1990). As Park (1937) originally noted, marginalization may lead to flexibility. Indeed, several researchers have noted such cognitive flexibility (e.g., Hall, 1980, 1992) just in the ability to think about race (Root, 1996b) and in racial attitudes of acceptance (Thornton, 1983). It does not necessarily have to be painful, but it can be a time of reflection. Situational ethnicity and "reflective marginalization" by choice may be common adaptive strategies to situational demands and sensitivity to changes in the meaning of ethnicity and acceptance (Root, 1996b).

The presence of multiracial Asian Americans forces us to reconsider several issues. The face of Asian America is changing dramatically. It forces us to recognize that the meaning of being Asian American has been, and will continue to be, dynamically influenced by history. Multiracial Asians are only a physical embodiment of one aspect of what is driving the issues to reconsider the meaning of being Asian American identified in the United States.

PHYSICAL APPEARANCE

Multiracial Asians often have a "flexible look" (Root, 1994) that frequently results in misidentification racially and/or ethnically: Black, White, Latino, Hawaiian, American Indian, Eskimo, Aleut, Indonesian, and Polynesian (Hall, 1980, 1992; Williams, 1996). Amerasians can have brown, black, blonde, or even reddish hair that is straight, wavy, curly, or kinky. Likewise, eye color, although usually brown or dark brown, can be blue or hazel. Many of Mass's (1992) participants volunteered that they felt comfortable in Hawaii, where people were used to the vari-

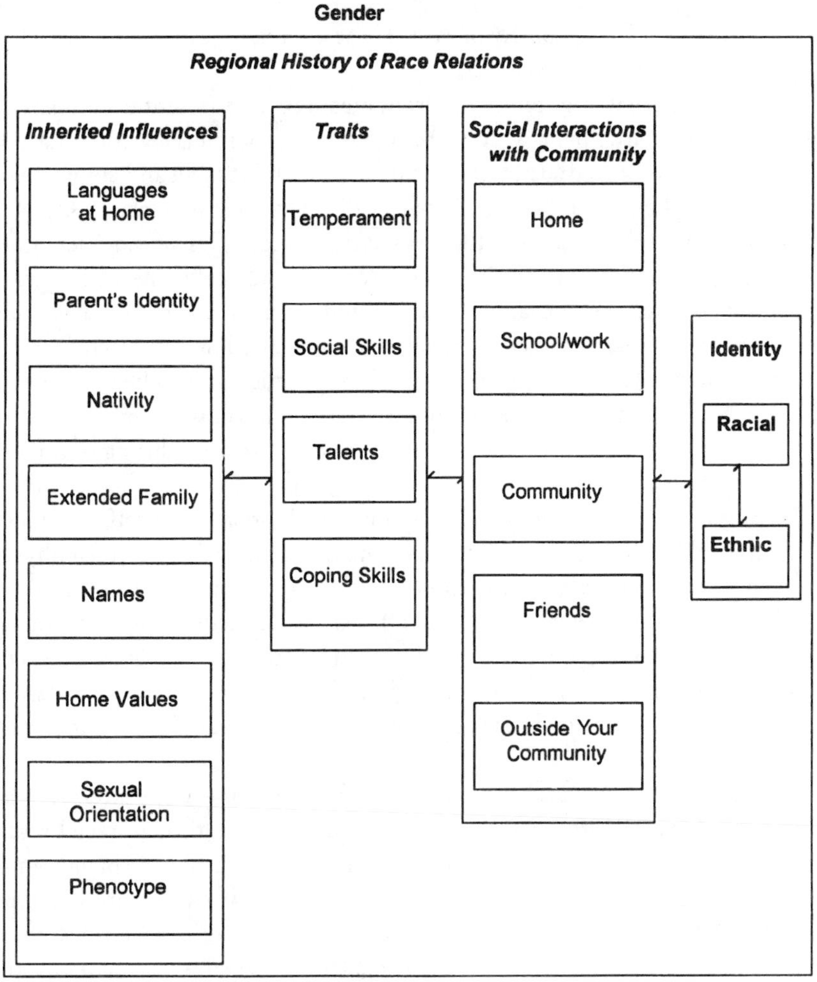

Gender

Figure 8.1. Ecological Identity Model

ability produced by racial mixing. Clearly, the multiracial Asian does not broadcast a well-understood "social address."

Clearly, physical appearance is an issue that must be contended with, particularly when one's private experience does not necessarily coincide with the observer's categorization. Racial features such as hair color and texture, skin color, and the presence or arrangement of racial features confuse the observer as to the boundaries of race. As Bradshaw (1992) observed, "A person's awareness of his or her racial ambiguity contributes to a sense of vulnerability and a feeling of being an outsider in some situations" (p. 77). Because of America's legacy of racism, unconscious exclusionary categorization goes on. Murphy-Shigematsu (1988) and Chao (1995) observed that intrusive comments and questions of the Amerasian reflect an underlying process aimed at excluding the individual from full membership to the group of the observer, preserving racial boundaries, and protecting the belief in the purity of race. These experiences are painful and have served to silence the Amerasian voice.

Looking different might have different meanings at different developmental stages. Research participants who were retrospectively interviewed about their childhoods have reported sustaining significant hurtful teasing and comments by both groups of their heritage (e.g., Grove, 1991; Hall, 1980; Kich, 1982; Mass, 1992). Valverde (1992) observed the most extreme examples among Vietnamese Amerasians in Vietnam in the daily name calling and nickname of *lai* (which means "mixed") attached to names or substituted for given names that continually reminded them of being mixed in a way that objectified and rejected them. By contrast, Williams (1992a, 1992b) reported that participants in her studies who spent much of their adolescence on military bases in Japan were insulated somewhat from this discrimination and found more of a curiosity during outings off the military bases.

During a time when belonging is hypothetically related to self-esteem and identity formation, the negations that Amerasians experience regarding their physical appearance, such as in reference to monoracial Asian Americans (e.g., "You can't be," "You don't look like it," "I can't tell"), may be particularly hurtful and isolating until they develop coping strategies for these comments. Chao (1995) observed that Amerasians stand "disqualified by each group, orphaned by each group, grappling with the questions such as 'What makes one "really" Asian or "really" white?' " (p. 10).

Stephan's (1992) research indirectly corroborates some of the interview data provided by Mass's (1992) respondents. She found that although racial resemblance was significantly associated with ethnic identity in her Hispanic sample in New Mexico it was not with her mixed-heritage Hawaiian Japanese sample. She suggested that, although in New Mexico Hispanic heritage did distinguish participants from other groups, Asian heritage did not separate participants from the majority of the population, in which mixed marriages are the norm. However, in semistructured interviews of other multiheritage individuals in Hawaii that did not include Japanese, respondents' physical appearance did contribute to their identification.

Mass (1992) shared coping strategies used by her Japanese Eurasian participants gleaned from interviews. Some participants described how they let people know how they identified in a conversation because they had accepted that their ambiguous racial features did not neatly identify them with being Japanese American. Indeed, Kich (1982, 1992) noted that this conflict between internal psychological experience is disturbing. It does not provide a "mirror" such as that which Cooley (1902) suggested facilitates identity and esteem. Several anecdotes from research suggest that one of the markers employed by multiracial Asian Americans is the use of Asian middle names or the adoption of Asian surnames from their Asian heritage when they do not have given surnames that provide a marker of "Asianness" to facilitate the observer's identification of them. However, Hall (1980) and Grove (1991) found that adult participants talked about the advantages of being ambiguous. Hall's (1980) participants largely liked the way they looked. Valverde (1992) found that some Vietnamese Amerasians in a society otherwise prejudiced against the idea of their existence were able to merge into the Vietnamese community because their physical appearance was not that distinguishable from the rest of the population.

Several researchers have postulated that physical appearance mediates ethnic identity for racially mixed Asians (Kinloch, 1983; Stephan, 1991), although findings from empirical studies have been inconsistent. For example, Posadas (1989) suggested that the particularly close relationships between mestiza Filipina daughters and their Filipino fathers might be explained by the fact that they appeared to look more like their fathers than their mothers to the majority culture. By contrast, Hall (1980, 1992) did not find this result in her study of Afro-Asians. Self-perceived racial appearance neither contributed to the explanation of variance in ethnic identity nor correlated with it. However, with her Black Japanese sample, almost all participants thought that they looked Black; thus, she thought that a lack of correlation might simply have represented a lack of variance in the sample. Again, internalization of rules of race create for accommodation to more variation in what is considered African American and relatively very little variance to physical features associated with other racial groups. It is very possible that issues of skin color have a very salient impact on how physical appearance mediates identity.

"Colorism," or skin color discrimination, pervades Asian American communities, particularly immigrant generations. Thus, the experiences related to phenotype are more pronounced and more difficult for multiheritage persons of either extreme light or darker skin, with more pronounced negative prejudice against persons of darker skin and/or possessing African heritage. Light-skinned Amerasians might have a more difficult time in African American communities where colorism has oppressive tones. This has been observed in Japanese American (Williams, 1992a, 1992b), Vietnamese (Felsman et al., 1989; Valverde, 1992), and Filipino (Posadas, 1989; Vallangca, 1987) communities.

SEXUALITY

Historically, racially mixed people have been stereotyped as exotic because of an ambiguous physical appearance. Exoticness carries with it an objectification and sexualization of the individual, particularly the multiracial Asian American woman (Root, 1994). In contrast to the racially mixed man, the exotic descriptor as applied to the Amerasian woman is associated with uniqueness or hypersexuality, as illustrated by the significant use of Amerasians in the pornography industry (Nakashima, 1992) and the stereotyping of Vietnamese Amerasians in the United States as prostitutes (Valverde, 1992). This stereotype depersonalizes the Amerasian woman, turning her into a sexual object to be possessed. Subsequently, many multiracial women have internalized this stereotype or alternately been very reserved in their expressions of sexuality (Root, 1994). Multiracial women are particularly vulnerable to internalizing the oppressive expectations of the exotic woman because of society's socialization to the importance of physical appearance, mixed messages of women's sexuality, and the oppressive beliefs about multiracial women's sexuality. Accepting the role of exotic might provide the permission to be sexual. Conversely, some mixed-race women might curtail the expression of their sexuality so as not to be stereotyped.

Some researchers have suggested that when one generalizes the experience of making racial boundaries more permeable and fluid, this might change one's willingness to consider the fluidity of other seemingly mutually exclusive boundaries (Allman, 1996; Kich, 1996). Although anecdotal evidence is available, it has not yet been corroborated by more systematic study of the co-influence of fluidity in racial identification and fluidity in sexual orientation.

ADAPTATION OF ASIAN AMERICA

One prevalent conjecture is that the increasing presence of Amerasians will contribute to an erosion, and ultimately the disappearance, of the Asian American community. Mass (1992) investigated this question in her research with 53 multiracial and 52 monoracial Japanese Americans culled primarily from the student body at the University of California, Los Angeles. Although she found a trend for multiracial Japanese Americans to be less strongly ethnically identified with Japanese and more acculturated by her measures, she also noted that one must look at the individual cases; some multiple-heritage participants were more strongly identified as Japanese than their monoracial counterparts. Grove (1991) found no differences in ethnic identification between her multi- and monoracial Asian samples of young adults. Nakashima (1988) found that Asianness measured in her sample in two different ways yielded different results, with Japanese Eurasians appearing very ethnically identified on one measure and less so when adherence to ethnic values was assessed versus comfort in socializing with Whites.

It has been suggested that the increased rates of intermarriage for Asian Americans stem from the increased fluidity of the borders between social groups. Some Asian Americans fear that this is the portent of the end of the Asian American community. Futhermore, they fear that multiracial Asians will tend to "marry out" (Tinker, 1973). This assumption that Amerasians will marry out, and that this is a reflection of a less legitimate ethnic identity, is oppressive and lacks a sound conceptual basis. Virtually all dating and marriage for multiracial Asians can be considered interracial, whereas it might not be considered interethnic. In Sung's (1990) New York study of Chinese American intermarriage, she found that approximately one third of Chinese Amerasians married Chinese, another one third married other people of color, and the other one third married Whites.

Many observations must be considered. First, with successive generations, rates of intermarriage increase (Chapter 8, this volume); the tendency for Amerasians to marry other than Asian (Sung, 1990; Tinker, 1973) might only reflect this trend. Williams (1992a, 1992b) observed that much of her Amerasian sample preferred to date or envision themselves partnered with other multiracial persons. Indeed, at the time of her interviews with Amerasians raised during their adolescence on military bases in Japan, 26 of the 43 respondents were dating other Amerasians. Second, many Amerasians have experienced quite painful experiences and rejections by other Asian Americans (Hall, 1980; Kich, 1982; Kinloch, 1983; Mass, 1992; Williams, 1992a, 1992b). It is possible that marrying out represents moving out of a "marginal status" or anomic position to one of belonging that will facilitate psychological well-being, particularly for those who are less distinguishably Asian in physical appearance. Third, exchange theory as applied to interracial marriage suggests that different statuses are exchanged. These hypotheses are likely interconnected and mediated by other variables such as geographic region, family, neighborhood, community, and school experiences. What is largely forgotten is that the racial experience of the multiracial person may render any relationship virtually interracial. Thus, assumptions in this area must be studied carefully. Furthermore, given that race must become less central to the definition of who is Asian American, ethnic identification might be the significant variable to study in assessing intermarriage.

The totality of these hypotheses suggests that increased assimilation of Amerasians by the mainstream or other ethnic communities might not be the doing of the Amerasian wanting to deny being Asian American; rather, it might reflect an interactive process in which the Amerasian seeks a more comfortable place in which he or she is not tested for ethnic legitimacy—and may in fact experience less rejection. Because the mainstream does not reflect a clearly defined ethnic heritage, Amerasians can attempt to be "just American," although in reality they will have a lesser status because they will not be perceived as White. It also is possible that Eurasians will have less opposition to marrying into less valued communities such that an increasing African American heritage will start to emerge in the Asian American population.

Mass (1992) suggested that the Asian American community and researchers must question more seriously than ever how ethnic identity is determined. If it is by subjective experience, as previous research on ethnicity contends, then many Amerasians will reflect a continuity in Asian American identity. If it is by appearance, then Asian American identity will change. It is largely a choice for which the Asian American community must hold itself responsible (Murphy-Shigematsu, 1988). If it evolves, as have American Indian and Latino groups, then persons sharing this heritage might be embraced and it is likely that the Asian American community will remain viable.

CONCLUSIONS

Whereas the 1970s might have been the context for openly affirming a positive Asian identity for monoracial Asians, the 1990s might be the beginning of expanding the meaning of Asian American identity. Much of the contemporary research on mixed-heritage Asian Americans challenges the necessity of race in declaring ethnicity and exposes the internalized racism of many Asian Americans. Mixed-heritage Asian Americans are a growing subset of the Asian American population and undoubtedly will have an influence on the continued transformation of various dialogues about race, ethnicity, and belonging within the various Asian American communities in the United States. Race must necessarily be considered more separate from ethnicity for these dialogues to make progress and make sense.

Research reflects that with the exception of Vietnamese Amerasians, multiracial Asian Americans in contemporary times show good adjustment. Asian American heritage does influence identity. When it is disavowed, there usually is a significant story about painful rejection and exclusion by Asians.

Resolution of identity may span over a longer period of time because of life events and developmental markers that revive race as a significant issue for others. Furthermore, it reflects the attempt to integrate racial features with ethnic group membership within a particular community and to find acceptance. The enactment of ethnicity may be separate from the individual's core sense of self and reflect a response to the specific meaning of ethnicity in a given situation (Stephan, 1991). The presence of intermarriage and the Amerasian is not a threat to the viability of the Asian American community unless exclusionary attitudes based on the myth of racial purity persist within Asian America.

Studying from an insider perspective, many researchers have reinterpreted the pattern of results and offered conceptualizations that reflect a broader acknowledgment of the environmental ecology to explain the variability in identity within same-age, same-heritage cohorts and to explain the differences in mixed-heritage Asian Americans within an ecological matrix. As such, the experiences of Vietnamese Amerasians epitomize the effects of adversity created by war, fatherlessness in a patriarchal society, and racial intolerance. The explanations point to how these individuals cannot be understood without understanding history, racial politics, and oppression. Given this context, one of the ways in which to further expand our understanding of how Amerasians are making a place in Asian America or being turned away from it would be to study Amerasians who do and do not identify as Asian or Amerasian, particularly in longitudinal studies, and to study multiracial Asians throughout the life span.

One role that Amerasians have contributed to Asian American psychology is the social deconstruction of race by attempting to free themselves from an oppressive reality while skillfully negotiating a very real reality for many persons outside this experience. Murphy-Shigematsu (1988) offered some sage observations:

> Addressing the concerns of biracial Asian Americans also teaches all of us about ourselves as human beings. It teaches us tolerance for difference and diversity, where individuals can exist without apology and denial of an important part of themselves that is their ethnic heritage. The minority voice, the voice of the person who is seen as marginal, in some way, is often a valuable one to hear, for its relevance extends beyond the particular experience of the minority to that of the larger group. (p. 114)

REFERENCES

Adams, R. C. (1937). *Interracial marriage in Hawaii: A study of the mutually conditioned processes of acculturation and amalgamation.* New York: Macmillan.

Allman, K. M. (1996). (Un)Natural boundaries: Mixed race, gender, and sexuality. In M. P. P. Root (Ed.), *The multiracial experience: Racial borders as the new frontier* (pp. 277-290). Thousand Oaks, CA: Sage.

Bradshaw, C. K. (1992). Beauty and the beast: On racial ambiguity. In M. P. P. Root (Ed.), *Racially mixed people in America* (pp. 77-88). Newbury Park, CA: Sage.

Buck, P. S. (1930). *East wind, west wind.* New York: John Day.

Cauce, A. M., Hiraga, Y., Mason, C., Aguilar, T., Ordonez, N., & Gonzales, N. (1992). Between a rock and a hard place: Social adjustment of biracial youth. In M. P. P. Root (Ed.), *Racially mixed people in America* (pp. 207-222). Newbury Park, CA: Sage.

Chan, S. (1991). *Asian Americans: An interpretive history.* Boston: Twayne.

Chao, C. M. (1995). A bridge over troubled waters: Being Eurasian in the U.S. of A. In J. Adleman & G. Equinados (Eds.), *The significance of racism in the psychology of women: Building consciously anti-racist models of feminist therapy* (pp. 33-44). New York: Haworth.

Chew, K., Eggebeen, D., & Uhlenberg, P. (1989). American children in multiracial households. *Sociological Perspectives, 32,* 65-85.

Cooley, C. H. (1902). *Human nature and social order.* New York: Scribner.

Cottrell, A. (1978). Cross-cultural marriage as an extension of an international lifestyle: A study of Indian-Western couples. *Journal of Marriage and the Family, 35,* 739-741.

Daniel, G. R. (1992). Passers and pluralist: Subverting the racial divide. In M. P. P. Root (Ed.), *Racially mixed people in America* (pp. 91-107). Newbury Park, CA: Sage.

Degler, C. N. (1971). *Neither Black nor White: Slavery and race relations in Brazil and the United States.* New York: Macmillan.

Dien, D. S., & Vinacke, W. E. (1964). Self-concept and parental identification of young adults with mixed Caucasian-Japanese parentage. *Journal of Abnormal Psychology, 69,* 463-466.

Duffy, L. K. (1978). *The interracial individuals: Self-concept, parental interaction and ethnic identity.* Master's thesis, University of Hawaii, Honolulu.

Erikson, E. H. (1968). *Identity, youth and crisis.* New York: Norton.

Felsman, J. K., Johnson, M. C., Leong, F. T. L., & Felsman, I. C. (1989). *Vietnamese Amerasians: Practical implications of current research.* Washington, DC: Department of Health and Human Services, Family Support Administration, Office of Refugee Resettlement.

Grove, K. J. (1991). Identity development in interracial, Asian/White late adolescents: Must it be so problematic? *Journal of Youth and Adolescence, 20,* 617-628.

Hall, C. C. I. (1980). *The ethnic identity of racially mixed people: A study of Black-Japanese.* Doctoral dissertation, University of California, Los Angeles.

Hall, C. C. I. (1992). Please choose one: Ethnic identity choices for biracial individuals. In M. P. P. Root (Ed.), *Racially mixed people in America* (pp. 250-264). Newbury Park, CA: Sage.

Johnson, R. C., & Nagoshi, C. T. (1986). The adjustment of offspring of within-group and inter-racial/intercultural marriages: A comparison of personality factor scores. *Journal of Marriage and the Family, 48,* 279-284.

Kich, G. K. (1982). *Eurasians: Ethnic/racial identity development of biracial Japanese/White adults.* Doctoral dissertation, Wright Institute Graduate School of Psychology, Berkeley, CA.

Kich, G. K. (1992). The developmental process of asserting a biracial, bicultural identity. In M. P. P. Root (Ed.), *Racially mixed people in America* (pp. 304-319). Newbury Park, CA: Sage.

Kich, G. K. (1996). In the margins of sex and race: Difference, marginality, and flexibility. In M. P. P. Root (Ed.), *The multiracial experience: Racial borders as the new frontier* (pp. 263-276). Thousand Oaks, CA: Sage.

King, R. C., & DaCosta, K. M. (1996). Changing face, changing race: The remaking of race in the Japanese American and African American communities. In M. P. P. Root (Ed.), *The multiracial experience: Racial borders as the new frontier* (pp. 227-244). Thousand Oaks, CA: Sage.

Kinloch, G. C. (1983). Racial identity among mixed adolescents in Hawaii: A research note. *Explorations in Ethnic Studies, 6,* 38-41.

Lerner, G. (1986). *The creation of patriarchy.* New York: Oxford University Press.

Mass, A. I. (1992). Interracial Japanese Americans: The best of both worlds or the end of the Japanese American community? In M. P. P. Root (Ed.), *Racially mixed people in America* (pp. 265-279). Newbury Park, CA: Sage.

Miller, R. L. (1992). The human ecology of multiracial identity. In M. P. P. Root (Ed.), *Racially mixed people in America* (pp. 24-36). Newbury Park, CA: Sage.

Motoyoshi, M. (1990). The experience of mixed-race people: Some thoughts and theories. *Journal of Ethnic Studies, 18,* 77-94.

Mrazek, J. (1987). *Analysis of the Vietnamese Amerasian situation and the need for congressional action.* Washington, DC: Government Printing Office.

Murphy-Shigematsu, S. (1987). *The voices of Amerasians: Ethnicity, identity, and empowerment in interracial Japanese Americans.* Doctoral dissertation, Harvard University.

Murphy-Shigematsu, S. (1988). Addressing issues of biracial Asian Americans. In G. Y. Okihiro, S. Hune, A. A. Hansen, & J. M. Liu (Eds.), *Reflections on shattered windows: Promises and prospects for Asian American studies* (pp. 111-116). Pullman: Washington State University Press.

Nakishima, C. L. (1988). Research notes on Nikkei Happa identity. In G. Y. Okohiro, S. Hune, A. A. Hansen, & J. M. Liu (Eds.), *Reflections on shattered windows: Promises and prospects for Asian American studies* (pp. 206-213). Pullman: Washington State University Press.

Nakashima, C. L. (1992). An invisible monster: The creation and denial of mixed-race people in America. In M. P. P. Root (Ed.), *Racially mixed people in America* (pp. 162-178). Newbury Park, CA: Sage.

Omi, M., & Winant, H. (1986). *Racial formation in the United States: From the 1960s to the 1980s.* New York: Routledge.

Park, R. E. (1937). Introduction. In E. V. Stonequist (Ed.), *The marginal man: A study in personality and culture conflict* (p. xvii). New York: Russell & Russell.

Phinney, J. S. (1990). Ethnic identity in adolescents and adults: Review of research. *Psychological Bulletin, 108,* 499-514.

Population Reference Bureau. (1992). *Minority markets alert: Critical trends among non-European Americans.* Washington, DC: Author.

Posadas, B. M. (1989). Mestiza girlhood: Interracial families in Chicago's Filipino American community since 1925. In Asian Women United of California (Ed.), *Making waves: An anthology of writings by and about Asian American women* (pp. 273-282). Boston: Beacon.

Root, M. P. P. (1990). Resolving "other" status. In L. S. Brown & M. P. P. Root (Eds.), *Diversity and complexity in feminist therapy* (pp. 185-205). New York: Haworth.

Root, M. P. P. (Ed.). (1992). *Racially mixed people in America.* Newbury Park, CA: Sage.

Root, M. P. P. (1994). Mixed-race women. In L. Comas-Diaz & B. Greene (Eds.), *Women of color: Integrating ethnic and gender identities in psychotherapy* (pp. 455-478). New York: Guilford.

Root, M. P. P. (1995). The psychological browning of America. In N. Zack (Ed.), *American mixed race: The culture of microdiversity* (pp. 231-236). Lanham, MD: Rowman & Littlefield.

Root, M. P. P. (1996a). A Bill of Rights for racially mixed people. In M. P. P. Root (Ed.), *The multiracial experience: Racial borders as the new frontier* (pp. 3-14). Thousand Oaks, CA: Sage.

Root, M. P. P. (1996b). The multiracial experience: Racial borders as a significant frontier in race relations. In M. P. P. Root (Ed.), *The multiracial experience: Racial borders as the new frontier* (pp. xiii-xxviii). Thousand Oaks, CA: Sage.

Root, M. P. P. (1997). Contemporary mixed heritage Filipino Americans: Fighting colonized identities. In M. P. P. Root (Ed.), *Filipino Americans: Transformation and identity* (pp. 80-94). Thousand Oaks, CA: Sage.

Root, M. P. P. (in press). The biracial baby boom: Understanding ecological construction of racial identity in the twenty-first century. In R. H. Sheets & E. Hollins (Eds.), *Racial, ethnic, cultural identity and human development: Implications for education.* Mahwah, NJ: Lawrence Erlbaum.

Spickard, P. R. (1992). The illogic of American racial categories. In M. P. P. Root (Ed.), *Racially mixed people in America* (pp. 12-23). Newbury Park, CA: Sage.

Standen, B. C. S. (1996). Without a template: The biracial Korean/White experience. In M. P. P. Root (Ed.), *The multiracial experience: Racial borders as the new frontier* (pp. 245-262). Thousand Oaks, CA: Sage.

Stephan, C. W. (1991). Ethnic identity among mixed-heritage people in Hawaii. *Symbolic Interactionism, 14,* 261-277.

Stephan, C. W. (1992). Mixed-heritage individuals: Ethnic identity and trait characteristics. In M. P. P. Root (Ed.), *Racially mixed people in America* (pp. 50-63). Newbury Park, CA: Sage.

Stephan, C. W., & Stephan, W. G. (1989). After intermarriage: Ethnic identity among mixed heritage Japanese-Americans and Hispanics. *Journal of Marriage and the Family, 51,* 507-519.

Strong, N. (1978). *Patterns of social interaction and psychological accommodation among Japan's Konketsuji populations.* Ph.D. dissertation, University of California, Berkeley.

Sung, B. L. (1990). *Chinese American intermarriage.* New York: Center for Migration Studies.

Thornton, M. C. (1983). *A social history of multiethnic identity: The case of Black Japanese Americans.* Doctoral dissertation, University of Michigan.

Thornton, M. C. (1992). The quiet immigration: Foreign spouses of U.S. citizens, 1945-1985. In M. P. P. Root (Ed.), *Racially mixed people in America* (pp. 64-76). Newbury Park, CA: Sage.

Thornton, M. C. (1996). Hidden agendas, identity theories, and multiracial people. In M. P. P. Root (Ed.), *The multiracial experience: Racial borders as the new frontier* (pp. 101-120). Thousand Oaks, CA: Sage.

Tien, L., & Hunthausen, G. (1990). The Vietnamese Amerasian resettlement experience: From initial application to the first six months in the United States. *Vietnam Generation, 3*(2), 23-35.

Tinker, J. N. (1973). Intermarriage and ethnic boundaries: The Japanese American case. *Journal of Social Issues, 29,* 49-66.

Vallangca, C. C. (1987). *The second wave: Pinay and Pinoy (1945-1960).* San Francisco: Strawberry Hill Press.

Valverde, K. L. C. (1992). From dust to gold: The Vietnamese American experience. In M. P. P. Root (Ed.), *Racially mixed people in America* (pp. 144-161). Newbury Park, CA: Sage.

Wagatsuma, J. (1976). Mixed-blood children in Japan: An exploratory study. *Journal of Asian Affairs, 2,* 9-16.

Weisman, J. R. (1996). An "other" way of life: The empowerment of alterity in the interracial individual. In M. P. P. Root (Ed.), *The multiracial experience: Racial borders as the new frontier* (pp. 152-166). Thousand Oaks, CA: Sage.

Williams, T. K. (1992a). *Bilingualism, transnationality, and the multiethnic identity of Japanese-descent Amerasians.* Unpublished manuscript, University of California, Los Angeles.

Williams, T. K. (1992b). Prism lives: Identity in binational Amerasians. In M. P. P. Root (Ed.), *Racially mixed people in America* (pp. 280-303). Newbury Park, CA: Sage.

Williams, T. K. (1996). Race as process: Reassessing the "what are you?" encounters of biracial individuals. In M. P. P. Root (Ed.), *The multiracial experience: Racial borders as the new frontier* (pp. 191-210). Thousand Oaks, CA: Sage.

9

ETHNIC IDENTITY

DAVID SUE
WINNIE S. MAK
DERALD W. SUE

According to population statistics,

the 1990 population of American Indians/Eskimos/Aleuts (2 million), Asians (7.3 million), [African Americans]/Blacks (30 million), and Latinos (22.4 million) represented growth rates of, respectively, 38%, 108%, 13%, and 53% from the figures in 1980. Early in the twenty-first century, one-third of the United States population will be members of an ethnic minority group. (Sue, 1991, p. 52)

Given the increasing diversity within American pluralistic cultures, researchers are highly interested in the study of the interactions within and between various ethnic groups and the dominant group, namely European Americans. Among the topics covered within the area of interethnic and intraethnic relations, ethnic identity garnered much momentum with the changing demographics and its significance in affecting psychological functioning. Not only did researchers propose various general ethnic identity models (Atkinson, Morten, & Sue, 1989; Helms & Carter, 1991; Parham, 1989; Phinney, 1989; Smith, 1989; Sue & Sue, 1990), they also pursued delineating models for specific ethnic groups. Models for African Americans (Cross, 1971; Helms, 1989; Jackson, 1975), Hispanic Americans (Cuellar, Harris, & Jasso, 1980; Lopez, Lopez, & Fong, 1991; Sanchez & Atkinson, 1983), American Indians (Bennett & BigFoot-Sipes, 1991; Zitzow & Estes, 1981), and Asian Americans (Kitano, 1989; Sodowsky, Kwan, & Pannu, 1995; Sue & Sue, 1971) have been developed. This interest in ethnic identity arose primarily because of three lines of inquiry.

First, the oppressive nature of our society has been responsible for ethnic identity confusion and for influencing the transformation of ethnic minority among African Americans (Carter, 1995; Cross, 1971; Helms, 1990; Jackson, 1975; Parham, 1989; Parham & Helms, 1981; Thomas, 1970, 1971; Vontress, 1971), Hispanic Americans (Ruiz, 1990; Szapocznik, Santisteban, Kurtines, Hervis, & Spencer, 1982), American Indians (Choney, Berryhill-Paapke, & Robbins, 1995; Swinomish Tribal Mental Health Project, 1991), and Asian Americans (Maykovich, 1973; Sue & Sue, 1972). Political underrepresentation, economic disadvantages, social discrimination, physical attacks, and biased portrayals of ethnic groups in the media all differentially affect the attitudes of ethnic groups toward themselves as well as toward each other (Harwood, 1994; Phinney, 1990). Other groups, such as women and homosexuals, also have implicated the sociopolitical nature of our society in identity development. Hence, many researchers believe that it is important to trace the identity process involved from a developmental and sociopolitical perspective.

Second, ethnic minority researchers became concerned that information on minorities was being accepted on a stereotypical basis and that within-group differences were not being explored. For example, many educators and mental health practitioners often responded to ethnic minority populations as if they were "the same." Little thought was given to the stage of identity development of the culturally different individuals that would affect their attitudes, beliefs, and behaviors. Furthermore, research studies have made it increasingly clear that ethnic identification is a fluid and dynamic process in which individuals can possess multiple ethnic identities through the interactions of various contextual factors (e.g., age, educational level, gender, sexual orientation, socioeconomic status, language usage, generational status, length of residence, cultural distance, type of neighborhood, community, religion) and the demands of different social situations (Cortes, 1994; Harwood, 1994; Ibrahim, Ohnishi, & Sandhu, 1997; Phinney, 1990). Thus, a failure to acknowledge the heterogeneity within each ethnic group and the intricate interactions with the social context would lead to continued stereotyping.

Third, the implications of ethnic identity for minority individuals' presentation of problems, acceptance of counseling, and preference for counseling style or ethnicity of the counselor became areas of increasing research (Atkinson & Gim, 1989; Gim, Atkinson, & Whiteley, 1990; Sue & Sue, 1990). Some research seemed to suggest that minority clients prefer members of their own ethnic group as counselors/therapists, whereas others found no such preference (Atkinson & Matsushita, 1991; Atkinson & Schein, 1986; Parham & Helms, 1981; Ponterotto & Wise, 1987). Whether an ethnically similar counselor is preferred might actually be a function of ethnic identity of the individual rather than of ethnicity per se. The interaction of both the client's and the counselor's ethnic identities also will influence the salience of ethnicity and the effectiveness of client-counselor match or mismatch. Thus, by careful examination of the individual's ethnic identity within a particular context, the psychologist can better develop suitable and effective counseling strategies for his or her particular client.

The goals of this chapter are fivefold. First, the constructs of ethnic identity and acculturation are differentiated and clarified because many studies have used the terms synonymously and have disregarded their variances and distinctions. Second, after clarifying the terminology, we provide an overview of major ethnic identity and acculturation models from the Asian American perspective. Third, we attempt to relate the process of ethnic identity development and acculturation to mental health; the attitudes of individuals' ethnicity and self-concept and their relations with the dominant culture affect their psychological adjustment and functioning. Fourth, given the malleability and the multifaceted nature of ethnic identity for Asian Americans, we pose some questions and discussion of the models' shortcomings with respect to Asian Americans. Lastly, we present current research on the impact of cultural variables on ethnic identity and suggest alternative ways in which to study ethnic identity in the attempt to fulfill the missing portions of the picture. Through our examination, it will become clear that research and conceptual development in this area are in need of further advancement with respect to Asian Americans.

DEFINITIONS: ETHNIC IDENTITY AND ACCULTURATION

Despite researchers' interest in ethnic identity and acculturation research, the two constructs were not clearly defined and differentiated. They often were used interchangeably in the literature, which fostered confusion and ambiguity in their description of and explanation about different ethnic groups. A number of studies have defined ethnic identity as being a part of one's social identity (Hutnik, 1991). According to this conception, ethnic identity refers to "that part of an individual's self-concept which derives from his [or her] knowledge of his [or her] membership of a social group (or groups) together with the value and emotional significance attached to that membership" (Tajfel, 1981, p. 255, as cited in Phinney, 1990). Acculturation is generally described as the changes in cultural attitudes, values, and behaviors due to contact between two cultures (Berry, Trimble, & Olmedo, 1986). Although acculturation originally was conceptualized at the group level, researchers also assessed acculturation at the individual level. This is what Berry (1989) referred to as psychological acculturation and is defined as changes within an individual in cultural attitudes, values, and behaviors as a result of continuous firsthand contact between the cultural group to which he or she belongs and another cultural group (Berry, 1989; Phinney, 1990).

According to the preceding definitions, the level of focus between ethnic identity and acculturation is different. Ethnic identity focuses mainly on the relationships between individuals and their own ethnic group within the dominant society, whereas acculturation emphasizes the relationships between ethnic individuals and the dominant society (Phinney, 1990). Ethnic identity generally reflects the degree of identification individuals have toward their ethnic group, and acculturation emphasizes the extent of knowledge individuals have toward a cultural group. In addition to the difference in orientation of interests, ethnic identity and acculturation also have relevance to different target populations. Ethnic identity models were derived mainly from the experiences of American-born adolescents and adults. On the other hand, acculturation models are more applicable to the immigrant populations because the American-born populations are already enculturated into the dominant culture. For some immigrants, their ethnic identity development begins in their culture of origin and is affected by forces of socialization that might be different from those in the host culture, where they are considered minorities. Therefore, immigrants may experience stages of ethnic identity development differently or may even undergo different forms of ethnic identity development, depending on various pre- and postmigration factors.

ASIAN AMERICAN ETHNIC IDENTITY MODELS

Ethnic identity models attempt to account for the interactions between personal variables and characteristics, traditional ethnic group values, dominant group values, and racism. The following example shows some of the confusion that a child might go through in developing an ethnic identity:

> Some years ago, my five-year-old son came home from school, shortly after entering kindergarten in a predominantly White neighborhood, and asked me, "What am I? Am I a Korean or an American?" Trying to be a good mother, I told him he was a Korean American—he was born in the United States of Korean parents, and thus he had a rich heritage from two cultures. This did not comfort my son, nor did he feel enlightened by the knowledge of his bicultural background. Instead he protested, "If I am a Korean, why can't I speak Korean like you do? And if I'm an American, how come I don't look like the American kids in my class?" He paused for a moment and then delivered the final blow: "Besides, they call me Chinese!" (Kim, 1980, p. 1)

Many Asian Americans have gone through the process of questioning who they are. Identity is first formed through the family, but as exposure to different ethnocultural values and standards increases through socialization in the schools and other mainstream social institutions, confusion might develop. The Korean child, for example, became a pawn between the social psychological forces of the dominant society that is advocating assimilation and acculturation and the parents' attempt to have their son be proud of his cultural heritage. In this case, an attempt by the parents to have the son become bicultural was subverted by societal forces such as stereotypes (e.g., "they call me Chinese!").

Components of Ethnic Identity

An understanding of how Asian Americans develop their personal and social sense of identity is important in many ways. Researchers discussed several major components of ethnic identity in the process of identity development and formation. The components basically can be divided into three main areas: affect, cognition, and behavior. The affective component involves ethnic self-identification, or the ethnic label, that individuals use for themselves (Phinney, 1990, 1991, 1992). Self-identification is one of the first signs that ethnic membership is a salient aspect of individuals' identity. However, it must be differentiated from one's ethnicity because one's self-identification might not be congruent with one's ethnicity. Furthermore, self-labeling might differ from the identity imposed by dominant society that may be used as an easily accessible way in which to categorize physically distinct ethnic groups (e.g., African Americans, Asian Americans).

The affective component also includes individuals' sense of belonging and commitment with members of their own ethnic group (Ibrahim et al., 1997; Phinney, 1990, 1991, 1992; Phinney & Kohatsu, 1997). The sense of belonging and commitment entails having positive attitudes and a certain level of acceptance toward the ethnic group with which individuals identify. "Positive attitudes include pride in and pleasure, satisfaction, and contentment with one's own group" (Phinney, 1990, p. 504). On the other hand, the lack of positive affect or the presence of negative attitudes implies a sense of rejection and displeasure of individuals' ethnicity. It is important to note that individuals might have mixed feelings toward different aspects of their ethnicity and culture, and these differences must be carefully assessed and weighed in their significance to individuals' ethnic identity.

The cognitive component of ethnic identity encompasses interest in and knowledge about one's ethnic group including its history, traditions, values, norms, and mores. It is broadly referred to as cultural awareness or ethnic consciousness (Padilla, 1994; Uba, 1994). It can be subdivided into either passive or active learning. Passive learning includes inculcation of cultural information to the individuals by socializing agents such as parents, teachers, and the media. Active learning, on the other hand, involves self-searching of one's cultural heritage by reading and interacting with other cultural means. The ethnic knowledge that individuals acquire subsequently will influence the way in which they register and process various information, events, and situations within their particular ethnic group, other ethnic cultures, and the dominant society (Uba, 1994). Individuals develop schemata that are derived from their ethnic identity and can influence the way in which they approach and interpret the world. Their utility of such ethnic schemata depends on the salience of their ethnic identity within a particular social context, which is affected by factors such as investment in their ethnic group, perceived benefits of their ethnic identity, generational status, place of residence, and racism (refer to Uba, 1994, for details). Thus, to varying degrees, individuals' psychological reality is shaped by their knowledge and conceptualization of their ethnic identity.

The behavioral component refers to the amount of ethnic involvement with which individuals participate in various cultural practices and activities. For many Asian Americans, it includes language usage (Phinney, 1992). In addition to the actual practice of cultural behaviors, this component includes the level of competence that individuals have in carrying out each behavior. Furthermore, the timing and setting of a particular situation must be taken into account to determine the feasibility for individuals to actually initiate and complete the behaviors.

Although the three components of ethnic identity interact and influence each other in determining the level and form of ethnic identity individuals have at a particular context, they also can operate independently from each other. For instance, having ample knowledge about a particular cultural custom does not necessarily lead to pride or actual practice of that particular tradition. On the other hand, individuals' sense of efficacy in carrying out a cultural act is influenced by their knowledge about the practice as well as by their attitudes and feelings toward their ethnic group. Therefore, individuals can have variable combinations of these components, which interact with their personality characteristics and the sociocultural context in determining the resultant adoption and manifestation of ethnic identity (Uba, 1994). Individuals select and integrate certain cultural patterns and beliefs into their repertoire and invoke these ethnic schemata as found to be appropriate in specific social situations.

In a study on first- and second-generation Chinese American and Chinese Australian adolescents, Rosenthal and Feldman (1992a) examined various aspects of ethnic identity by measuring the adolescents' ethnic identification, level of ethnic knowledge and cultural practice, importance of culturally related behaviors, and judged value of their ethnic heritage. Findings indicated that, over time, participants were weaker in their ethnic identification, engaged in fewer culturally relevant behaviors, and acquired less knowledge about their culture. Nevertheless, generational status did not have an eroding effect on the importance or the evaluative components of identity. Furthermore, the ethnic identity measures were only moderately correlated (r's ranged from −.62 to .78), indicating that although the aspects of ethnic identity might overlap, they were not identical. These findings confirm the importance of separately analyzing various dimensions of ethnic identity because certain aspects of culture might be less vulnerable to erosion than others.

Strong identification with a particular culture was found to be related to an increase in culture-linked behaviors or activities. Research found that Chinese youths in the Netherlands and Chinese Australians, who identified themselves as Chinese, participated in the most ethnic practices and preferred in-group friendships and relationships (Rosenthal & Feldman, 1992a; Verkuyten & Kwa, 1996). In a study with Chinese-English bilinguals, Yang and Bond (1980) found that Chinese identification was higher when participants responded to the English version of the attitude questionnaire. This finding was attributed to the association among the level of ethnic affirmation, the level of identification with the Chinese culture, and the availability of behaviors that would affirm or deny that culture. Thus, the English questionnaire heightened participants' ethnic salience, which led to stronger endorsement of their Chinese identification.

One major force that influences the components of ethnic identity is the relationship among the self, other ethnic groups, and the dominant society. The experiences of racism and discrimination and the subjective interpretation of these experiences critically affect the way in which individuals define themselves ethnically. Some researchers have argued that the experience of discrimination inhibits individuals from adopting and displaying their ethnic identity for fear of becoming its victims (Uba, 1994). However, others have asserted that such experience and awareness of racism actually provoke individuals to espouse their ethnic identity and connect with other ethnic groups in battling against discrimination (Phinney & Kohatsu, 1997). Thus, minority status of ethnic individuals and their relationships with other ethnic groups in a particular setting and in the general society are important factors in the development of their ethnic identity. Given the background information about ethnic identity, let us briefly explore some of the early and contemporary models of Asian American ethnic identity, their implications to mental health and psychotherapy, and their limitations in the conceptualization of ethnic identity.

Typologies of Ethnic Identity

The following typologies of Sue and Sue (1971) and Kitano (1989) represent early attempts to conceptualize ethnic identity. Specific categories are established, and individuals within each are presumed to share similar characteristics. The typologies do not focus on the process or components of ethnic identity; rather, they merely focus on the final product. As such, they are more useful in a conceptual rather than an explanatory framework.

▦ Sue and Sue Typologies

Sue and Sue (1971) developed an ethnic identity model for Chinese Americans but believed that it was appropriate for other Asian Americans as well. Instead of focusing merely on acculturation, Sue and Sue believed that ethnic identity was formulated from the forces of acculturation, ethnic values and family upbringing, and oppressive aspects of American society. Out of this interaction, three possible types—traditional, marginal, and Asian American—were identified.

Traditional Asian Americans identify strongly with their ethnic group's values. Primary allegiance is to the parents, and self-esteem is defined as the ability to increase the status of the family through educational and occupational achievements. There is much less emphasis on the self than on the family of origin. When successful, they feel a sense of pride and respect because they have brought honor to the family name. By contrast, *marginal* Asian Americans reject their own ethnic group and attempt to identify with the dominant culture's (e.g., European American) values and expectations. They may view their own ethnic group unfavorably. Hostility and conflict over physical and psychological aspects of the self might be manifested as "racial self-hatred" because the dominant culture's physical and behavioral standards are accepted as the norm. Identity exists not within the family but rather in the self. Marginal persons have a tendency to deny the impact or existence of racism. The *Asian American* type, on the other hand, is in a stage of self-definition. Pride is developed in the formation of a new identity that incorporates certain ethnic and mainstream values and sociopolitical elements. This may result in a bicultural orientation. Certain values such as unquestioning obedience to parents might be challenged or transformed, whereas there is pride for other aspects of Asian culture. There is less a rejection of Asian values than an identification of those that need to be maintained. A pan-Asian identification might develop. There is a recognition of problems such as racism, and emphasis is placed on organizing and raising group esteem. Political action might be undertaken to protect Asian American group interests.

Based on these typologies, predictions were made for the possible reactions of the different types to counseling/therapy. Traditional Asian Americans might show little understanding of the counseling process, are unlikely to reveal information of a personal nature, and are more likely to expect a directive and problem-solving approach. Conflicts over personal feelings and parental expectations might develop. Because they do not have a strong individual identity, guilt feelings emerge when an identity outside of the family begins to develop. Asian Americans with a traditional identification also might become stressed when interacting with the dominant society. Expectations, roles, and values often differ between the two. The patterns of deference and respect to others might be interpreted by the dominant society as passivity and a lack of self-confidence or assertiveness. Marginal individuals probably are receptive to counseling and will tend to see traditional cultural values as contributing to their problems. Blame and denial often are exhibited by individuals in this category. They might be resentful that personal goals are being blocked by the values of their ethnic group. At this stage, there might be feelings of rejection and anger toward ethnically similar counselors. The Asian American type might be suspicious of the goals of counseling because counselors are thought to represent the dominant societal perspective. Personal problems might be externalized, and blame is placed on society and racism.

Sue and Sue (1971) presented several limitations of their typologies. They acknowledged the fact that typologies limit the number of variables that can be considered. Moreover, the categories were taken to their "logical extremes" so that the dynamics of each type could be considered. The authors noted that individual differences and variations among the types do occur. Some marginal individuals do not exhibit self-hatred, and some traditionalists are aware of the social and political forces surrounding them. Sue and Sue also cautioned that the descriptions were for heuristic purposes and were not to be considered as representing actual individuals.

▓ Kitano Typologies

Kitano (1989) formulated similar typologies but stressed the importance of two variables: assimilation and ethnic identity. He defined *assimilation* as the process of acculturation and *ethnic identity* as the retention of attitudes and beliefs of the culture of origin. These two dimensions are different from one another, and the combinations form four different types. Type A (*high assimilation, low ethnic identity*) is associated with individuals who are Westernized to a great extent. Little impact of the ethnic background is noted. Kitano believed that individuals in this category are basically Westerners with an "Asian face." Type B (*high assimilation, high ethnic identity*) individuals are considered to be bicultural. They are comfortable and relaxed in both cultures. Kitano believed that few people fall into this category, although it might increase in the future. Type C (*low assimilation, high ethnic identity*) individuals maintain a traditional ethnic orientation. They include recent immigrants and individuals who live in ethnic communities. There is little desire to assimilate due to the interactions of personal preferences and societal restrictions. Type D (*low assimilation, low ethnic identity*) individuals are considered to be "dropouts" of society who have no sense of belonging to either culture.

Kitano (1989) also postulated possible implications of these typologies to mental health and counseling. For Type A individuals, traditional counseling approaches often are effective because they are receptive to mainstream values and Western conceptualization of their problems. On the other hand, counselors may experience difficulty in working with bicultural individuals (Type B) whose values and knowledge might incorporate more than one culture. Therefore, counselors must be sensitive to their clients' ethnic identification, as well as a wealth of other personal factors, and attune to their needs accordingly. Type C individuals, who adhere to their ethnic culture, are more likely to present somatic complaints, reveal little emotionality, and have a difficult time discussing material of a personal nature in counseling because they usually are unfamiliar with the Western concept of mental health and the Western-oriented psychotherapy framework. Finally, individuals in the Type D category might suffer from severe mental disorders and conflicts if their lack of support from both the dominant culture and their ethnic culture is coupled with multiple stressors and insufficient personal resources.

Kitano's (1989) typologies were useful in that he separated assimilation from ethnic identity. The struggle for Asian Americans is "how American can or should they become, and how much of their ethnic culture can or should they retain?" (p. 143). He believed that the "straight line model" fits the Asian American experience in that with each successive generation ethnic identity becomes weaker. Ethnic identity is seen as correlated with assimilation.

Orthogonal Model of Cultural Identification

Extending Kitano's (1989) four typologies that considered individuals' espousal of both ethnic culture and the dominant culture, Oetting and Beauvais (1990-1991) proposed the orthogonal cultural identification theory, which allows a more flexible depiction of individuals' identification with the two cultures. They argued that identification with one culture is independent of identification with another culture. Therefore, by independently assessing individuals' cultural identification with their ethnic culture and the dominant culture, any combination and movement of cultural identification is possible without any systematic association between the two cultures. Their conception allows identification with two cultures to be examined independently of and concurrently with each other without diminishing the significance of either culture in the assessment. Thus, individuals can have variable levels of cultural identification under this model. Sodowsky et al. (1995) believed that this model follows a bidirectional system. Individuals can move back and forth over the four orientations in their attitudes, feelings, and behaviors toward the ethnic and dominant cultures over time and across situations. Oetting and Beauvais (1990-1991) further asserted that individuals' source of strength and psychological well-being rests in having a positive identification with any culture. So long as individuals can identify with one culture, they are able to derive meaning and benefits from such culture, which sustains their psychological health. Therefore, it is weak (not mixed) cultural identification that creates adjustment problems for the individuals (LaFromboise, Coleman, & Gerton, 1993).

This model of orthogonal identification could be validated by obtaining separate measures of individuals' feelings, attitudes and values, beliefs, or observable behaviors toward both cultures within various contexts (e.g., familial, social, cultural, linguistic, professional). Depending on the types and purposes of research, various indexes could be used to indicate ethnic identification. The scores for each index could then be plotted along each orthogonal dimension. Thus, individuals' feelings, attitudes, beliefs, and behaviors can differentially reflect their level of ethnic identification within different social contexts (Sayegh & Lasry, 1993). Furthermore, individuals' level of ethnic identification can be used to predict their level of psychological adjustment based on various indicators (e.g., self-esteem, family support, academic adjustment) (Oetting & Beauvais, 1990-1991).

Stage Models of Ethnic Identity Development

Several stage models of ethnic identity were proposed in the attempt to more clearly delineate the processes that ethnic individuals go through in the formation of their ethnic identity. Generally, these models acknowledge the struggle that ethnic individuals undergo as they negotiate the conflicts among their cultural values and orientation, the influences of the dominant culture, and the prejudice and discrimination that they encounter. Although there has not been a specific stage model developed for Asian Americans, models have been applied in depicting their development of ethnic identity (e.g., Sue & Sue's, 1990, racial/cultural identity development model; Atkinson et al.'s, 1989, minority identity development model; Marcia, Waterman, Matteson, Archer, & Orlofsky's, 1994, ego identity model; Cross's, 1991, and Helms's, 1990, racial identity theory; Phinney's, 1989, 1993, three-stage model of identity formation). Table 9.1 depicts the relationships between different identity development models and the specific terminology used for each model.

Given the similarities of these models, we present the Racial/Cultural Identity Development (R/CID) Model in detail (Sue & Sue, 1990), which is an expanded and refined version of the Minority Identity Development Model (Atkinson et al.,

TABLE 9.1. Terminology of Other Identity Models Corresponding to the Racial/Cultural Identity Development Model

Racial/cultural identity (Sue & Sue, 1990)	Conformity	Dissonance	Resistance and immersion	Introspection	Integrative awareness
Minority identity (Atkinson et al., 1989)	Conformity	Dissonance	Resistance and immersion	Introspection	Synergetic articulation and awareness
Ego identity (Marcia et al., 1994)	Diffusion/ foreclosure	←	Moratorium	↑	Identity achievement
Racial identity (Cross, 1991; Helms, 1990)	Preencounter	Encounter	Immersion/emmersion	Internalization	Commitment
Ethnic identity (Phinney, 1989, 1993)	Unexamined	←	Exploration	↑	Achievement

TABLE 9.2. Stages of the Racial/Cultural Identity Development Model and Their Corresponding Attitudes

Stage	Attitude Toward Self	Attitude Toward Others of the Same Minority	Attitude Toward Others of Different Minority	Attitude Toward Dominant Group
Stage 1: Conformity	Self-depreciating	Group-depreciating	Discriminatory	Group-appreciating
Stage 2: Dissonance	Conflict between self-depreciating and self-appreciating	Conflict between group-depreciating and group-appreciating	Conflict between dominant-held views of minority hierarchy and feelings of shared experience	Conflict between group-appreciating and group-depreciating
Stage 3: Resistance and immersion	Self-appreciating	Group-appreciating	Conflict between feelings of empathy for other minority experiences and feelings of culturocentrism	Group-depreciating
Stage 4: Introspection	Concern with basis of self-appreciation	Concern with nature of unequivocal appreciation	Concern with ethnocentric basis for judging others	Concern with basis of group depreciation
Stage 5: Integrative awareness	Self-appreciating	Group-appreciating	Group-appreciating	Selective appreciation

1989). The five-stage (conformity, dissonance, resistance and immersion, introspection, and integrative awareness) R/CID Model is presumed to apply to the Asian American population. Table 9.2 outlines the R/CID Model and the interactions between the stages and the corresponding attitudes.

During the *conformity stage* (Stage 1) (this is similar to the marginal type described earlier), individuals accept the superiority of the dominant group's values and norms. They believe in the superiority of the dominant culture in terms of lifestyles and traditions, and they evaluate their own culture negatively. This is due, in large part, to the constant barrage of mass media that portrays Asian Americans in an unflattering light (e.g., passive, sneaky, sly, inhibited). Because of this, some individuals at this stage will tend to feel negatively toward themselves and their ethnic group and will attempt to identify with the dominant group (e.g., European Americans). Some might believe that their physical appearance is less desirable than that of European American individuals and will avoid interactions with other ethnic minorities. Arkoff and Weaver (1966) found that Japanese American males were dissatisfied with their height and upper body development, whereas Japanese American females wanted to have larger breasts and slimmer thighs. Korean American children also displayed more dissatisfaction with their physiques than did a comparison group (Chang, 1975). On the Piers-Harris Self-Concept Scale, Japanese American children (third and fourth generations) were less satisfied with their physical characteristics than were their European American counterparts (Pang, Mizokawa, Morishima, & Olstad, 1985). Using the 40-item Narcissistic Personality Inventory, Asian American women were found to rate themselves significantly lower than European American women on their physical attractiveness (Smith, 1990). Weiss (1970) indicated that among young Asian Americans, European American dating standards and behaviors were accepted as the ideal. Although individuals at this stage might denigrate their ethnic group with negative stereotypes and deny their ethnic group membership, family and community support of the individuals might alleviate the internalization of negative attitudes (Phinney & Kohatsu, 1997). Cross (1995) believed that many individuals at this stage do not show self-hatred and consider race to be of little relevance in the pursuit of happiness.

The *dissonance stage* (Stage 2) is entered when individuals begin to question the wholesale rejection of their own ethnic identity and their total acceptance of the dominant culture. Often this process may develop as a reaction to incidents that shake individuals' cultural assumptions. For example, Asian Americans might be subjected to racism in a manner that cannot be denied, or they might come into contact with another Asian American who has positive qualities and is proud of his or her cultural heritage. Admiration might develop for Asian American leaders who have demonstrated qualities unrelated to the stereotypes that individuals received in the dominant society. During this process, individuals become more aware of their minority status, that racism does exist, and that positive qualities are prevalent among Asian Americans. Individuals are in conflict over the attempt to reconcile group-depreciating and group-appreciating attitudes.

They may experience feelings of "confusion, alarm, anomie, or even depression" (Cross, 1991, p. 201).

During the *resistance and immersion stage* (Stage 3), individuals begin to identify totally with the Asian American culture and actively reject the values of the dominant society. The dominant society is perceived as the source of all problems, and examples of racism are actively sought out. Individuals might feel guilty and shameful at having reacted negatively to their group and focus attention on appreciating the history and values of their ethnic group. A strong sense of commitment is formed with other members of the ethnic group, and a new identity is formed. There is a sense of distrust and dislike for the oppressors of the group. Norms and values of the dominant culture are not seen as valid, and attempts to obtain knowledge about the cultural group are evident. Instead of shame, feelings of pride now develop in the individuals over their cultural heritage. Empathy and a sense of camaraderie develop with persons of other ethnic groups. However, commitment remains the strongest for individuals' own ethnic group. Social support from parents and other positive role models and participation in ethnic organizations are likely to foster exploration of their own and other groups' cultures and to enhance their affirmation of their ethnic membership (Phinney & Kohatsu, 1997). For example, in a study with first- and second-generation Chinese American and Chinese Australian high school students, Rosenthal and Feldman (1992b) found that ethnic pride was associated with home environments that are characterized as being warm, controlling, and autonomy promoting. This finding indicated that parenting practices, which are inclusive of family care, do contribute to the formation of ethnic pride and positive evaluation of one's ethnic culture.

The move to the *introspection stage* (Stage 4) occurs when individuals realize that too much energy has been channeled to their anger toward the dominant society. Little energy remains for self-identity. Individuals might raise questions on the utility and correctness of submerging their individual autonomy into the ethnic group. They might experience conflicts over the degree of adherence to the goals of their ethnic group and their personal independence and autonomy. Individuals might increasingly resent their ethnic group's pressures to make commitments that might be inconsistent with their self-identity or personal values. Individuals become less ethnocentric and begin to reach out to other ethnic minorities to identify similar experiences with oppression. However, they still might have doubts in their relationship with the dominant culture. Does the acceptance of some elements of the dominant culture represent a sellout to their own ethnic group? How can they be incorporated into their ethnic culture?

The final stage, *integrative awareness* (Stage 5), is represented in individuals who have worked out earlier conflicts and are now secure in their own ethnic identity. They are more likely to view elements of different ethnic groups as well as those of the dominant society objectively and appreciatively. Individuals understand that all cultures have positive and negative features. They accept healthy aspects of the dominant culture and reject those that are negative (e.g., racism, sexism). A desire to eliminate all forms of oppression becomes a motivating force.

They have a strong positive ethnic identity and cultural pride but also a high sense of autonomy. Ethnic values do not have to be accepted unequivocally. They might strongly identify with and reach out to other ethnic minorities. They also might perceive that some European American individuals can be victims of racism in the society.

Stages of the R/CID Model have implicated to influence the counseling process. Individuals at the conformity stage often prefer European American counselors and may reject counselors of the same ethnicity. Attempts to explore cultural identity or issues will likely be met with resistance or rejection because individuals are attempting to repress feelings of racial self-hatred. Having to admit problems in these areas would be threatening and bring to awareness their Asian qualities. However, individual differences exist in individuals' endorsement of the various aspects of the dominant culture and their ethnic culture. Therefore, therapists must assess the extent of negative affect and their corresponding beliefs and behaviors rather than assume that individuals will manifest their "conformed" identity uniformly. Contrary to the conformed individuals, individuals at the dissonance stage might be preoccupied with self-identity and receptive to self-exploration during counseling. There is a growing sense of mistrust with the dominant group; therefore, counselors perceived to be from the dominant group must be sensitive to their clients' concerns and process these issues appropriately. As individuals enter the resistance and immersion stage, they are likely to view problems as stemming from oppression and racism. They might perceive counselors from the dominant group as members of the "establishment." The counselors' goals might be viewed with suspicion. Individuals might be willing to discuss only issues involving racism. Counselors working with individuals at this stage must realize that they will be viewed suspiciously; therefore, they should act in a nondefensive manner. Furthermore, it is important for the counselors to be open to address both the issue of racism and personal problems with Stage 3 individuals. Individuals at the introspection stage still might prefer counselors of the same ethnic group but might be receptive to counselors who understand or share the same worldview. Individuals may desire to explore group versus individual issues and their new sense of identity in counseling. Finally, for individuals who have achieved the integrative awareness, attitudinal and worldview similarity becomes much more important than membership group similarity in counselor selection.

In addition to the relevance of different stages of ethnic identity to counseling, higher stages also correspond to better psychological adjustment. Tenth-grade Asian Americans of Chinese, Filipino, Japanese, Korean, and Vietnamese ancestry who had achieved ethnic identity were found to have higher scores in self-evaluation, sense of mastery, social and peer interactions, and family relations. Scores of ego identity and adjustment also increased along with progression in the ethnic identity developmental stages (Phinney, 1989). Ethnic identity search and commitment also were positively related to self-esteem among a sample of Asian American adolescents and adults over time (Phinney & Alipuria, 1990; Phinney & Chavira, 1992). Nonetheless, although the majority of the sample progressed through the stages of ethnic identity development, stability and regression also were evident among the participants (Phinney & Chavira, 1992). Thus, individual variation exists in the process of ethnic identity development.

▓ Cautions/Limitations of the R/CID Model

Although Sue and Sue (1990) proposed five distinct stages, they warned that what is represented are only possible processes that individuals might undergo. First, not everyone going through the stages will do so in the same way. Factors such as coping responses, contextual cues, situational variables, and cultural orientations have not been considered (Berry et al., 1986). In addition, features of certain stages may overlap with one another. Second, it is not clear whether or not ethnic identity development is a linear process. For example, Parham (1989) believed that three distinct possibilities exist in the development of racial identity among African Americans: (a) stagnation, which represents individuals who stay within one stage throughout their lives; this state is considered to be an unhealthy one because individuals are not considered to be open to new ideas, feelings, and experiences; (b) linear progression, which is represented by the stage models; and (c) recycling. Individuals at this latter process can repeat earlier stages as a function of new experiences. Myers et al. (1991) believed that identity development proceeds as an expanding spiral whose beginning is similar to the end of the process. Parham (1989) also believed that ethnic identity models may form complex loops through the various stages. The proliferation of different stage models raises questions about their applicability and validity in describing ethnic identity development.

Third, do you have to start from Stage 1 that involves interaction with a racist society? Does this model apply to recent Asian immigrants who already have a strong ethnic identity and then encounter cultural biases in the United States? How might they differ from second-, third-, and fourth-generation Asian Americans in identity formation? Using the present ethnic identity measures, researchers often failed to obtain responses indicative of the early stages of ethnic identity (Pomales, Claiborn, & LaFromboise, 1986). For example, in a Dutch study of 119 Chinese youths, the majority of whom were born in the Netherlands (92%), the sample was predominant in identifying themselves as either Chinese or bicultural, with only a few identifying themselves as Dutch or neither (Verkuyten & Kwa, 1996).

Fourth, can you move backward from a "higher" to a "lower" stage? Most stage models indicate a forward progression. However, Parham (1989) believed that individuals can recycle through the stages as they gain new experiences. Under what types of conditions would this occur? Would individuals who moved back to a lower stage be similar to those in the same stage but who never had shown characteristics of a higher stage?

Fifth, many of the typologies and stage models were developed during the civil rights movement and might represent the characteristics or set of experiences of a particular time rather than a universal process (Myers et al., 1991). Are they still applicable to recent immigrants or later-generation Asian Americans? Also, although ethnic minorities have a shared set of experiences with oppression, differences also might exist. The R/CID Model was based on earlier models developed for African American experiences (Cross, 1971; Jackson, 1975). We are not certain whether or not these stages also develop in Asian Americans in the same manner. In one study (Liu, Sue, & Dinnel, 1992), the short form of the Racial Identity Attitude Scale developed by Helms (1990) for African Americans was modified (the term "Asian" was substituted for "Black") to make it appropriate for Asian Americans. A multidimensional scaling was performed on the responses of 81 Asian American students on the questionnaire. The items related to the specific stages did not cluster together according to the stages proposed by Parham (1989) and Helms (1989). Therefore, instruments reflective of the proposed stages must be developed and empirically validated among individuals of various ethnicities and other demographic distinctions.

Sixth, identity has been described in global terms. Values associated with particular stages might not move in a uniform manner. Chen and Yang (1986) reported that Chinese American adolescents were similar to European American adolescents in dating and sexual standards; however, they found that these same adolescents retained values such as loyalty, conformity, and respect for elders. The question about which values remain or change has to be addressed.

Seventh, it is clear that researchers have associated certain stages of ethnic identity development with a healthier adjustment than at other stages. Whether or not this is the case needs to be determined empirically.

The Multigroup Ethnic Identity Measure

Ethnic identity constitutes an important part of self-definition that affects the way in which individuals feel about themselves, process information, and present themselves in the social environment. Concurrently, individuals modify and redefine themselves ethnically as they interact and negotiate with different people in various settings who provide feedback to their identity. Given the increasingly multiethnic nature of the American society, individuals (whether ethnic minorities or European Americans) will experience increased salience in their ethnic identity. Given the belief that ethnic identity is a general phenomenon that is relevant to all ethnic groups, Phinney (1992) developed the Multigroup Ethnic Identity Measure (MEIM) to measure the extent of ethnic identity among diverse ethnic groups. Based on the assumption that all individuals, regardless of their unique cultural traditions and values, develop a sense of identification with their own group, Phinney extracted elements that are believed to be common among all individuals in their ethnic identity development. The dimensions in the MEIM include self-identification (e.g., ethnic label used for oneself), ethnic behaviors and practices (e.g., social activities with one's group, participation in cultural traditions), affirmation and belonging to an ethnic group (e.g., ethnic pride, sense of attachment), and the stages of ethnic identity achievement (e.g., exploring and resolving ethnic identity issues). The scale consists of 14 items, which can be divided into two subscales: the 5-item Affirmation/Belonging subscale and the

7-item Ethnic Identity Achievement subscale (subscale on ethnic behaviors cannot be reliably developed with 2 items).

Two samples were used in the validation of the MEIM. The first sample was composed of 417 high school students, ages 14 to 19 years. Among them, there were 134 Asian Americans, 131 African Americans, 89 Hispanic Americans, 41 of mixed backgrounds, 12 European Americans, and 10 of other ethnicities. The second sample was composed of college students in which there were 35 Asian Americans, 11 African Americans, 58 Hispanic Americans, 8 of mixed backgrounds, 23 European Americans, and 1 American Indian. The MEIM full scale achieved overall reliability coefficients of .81 for the high school sample and .90 for the college sample. The reliabilities for the Affirmation/Belonging subscale were .75 and .86 for the high school and college samples, respectively. The Ethnic Identity Achievement subscale had reliabilities of .69 and .80 for the respective groups (Phinney, 1992).

The college students were found to have higher ethnic identity achievement scores than the high school students, $t = 2.18$, $p < .05$. This finding, together with the greater reliability coefficients for the college sample, indicated that ethnic identity may be more established with age. No significant gender differences were found among two groups, with the exception of high school girls having higher scores in ethnic behaviors and practices than their male counterparts, $t = 2.45$, $p < .05$. Also, socioeconomic status was not related to ethnic identity but was marginally significant for high school students whose parents were unskilled workers, $F(2, 378) = 2.94$, $p = .054$. Higher ethnic identity scores were found to be related to better high school grades, $t = 2.7$, $p < .01$, and higher self-esteem among both groups ($r = .31$, $p < .001$ for the high school sample and $r = .25$, $p < .01$ for the college sample). However, no relationship between ethnic identity and self-esteem was found among the European American samples ($r = .05$). These findings suggested that ethnic identity affects the psychological adjustment and self-concept of ethnic individuals. However, because ethnic identity is not salient among European Americans, who are the majority, their self-identity and evaluation are not influenced by it. But the relationship may change as the situation changes, when European Americans become the minority and the salience of their ethnicity increases (Phinney, 1992). Therefore, the effects of social context on ethnic identity and mental health must be assessed in later studies.

ACCULTURATION MODELS

Besides the within-group relationship that contributes to the development of individuals' ethnic identity, their relationship with the dominant culture also influences the way in which they conceptualize themselves in relation to their own ethnic group and the larger society. Changes in identity are bound to occur as the individuals continue contacts with various ethnic groups in a multiethnic culture such as the United States. The way in which individuals alter their ethnic identification might be a function of their level of cultural adaptation or acculturation.

A variety of models describing acculturation styles have been suggested, ranging from linear models to independent ones. The models that have been developed to measure acculturation levels can be divided into two broad categories: (a) scales measuring acculturation on a cultural continuum, defined by a single line or dimension, with each pole representing one of the two cultures that are in contact, and (b) scales measuring acculturation in a cultural space, defined by multiple dimensions that signify the variability of the cultures in contact (Olmedo, 1979).

The Linear Model

A linear model of acculturation uses the cultural continuum as the measure of cultural change. It assumes that change in cultural knowledge progresses in a unidirectional manner, from the ethnic minority culture to the dominant culture. It suggests that any cultural change is in terms of adaptation to the mainstream; thus, it is biased toward acculturation to the dominant culture. Individuals not achieving full assimilation into the dominant culture are presumed to be distressed and are psychologically affected negatively. Furthermore, due to its bipolar nature, strengthening reception of the dominant culture will lead to automatic weakening of ethnic endorsement, and the process is assumed to be linear with each succeeding generation (Oetting & Beauvais, 1990-1991).

Researchers have developed instruments based on the linear model. Examples of this type of acculturation scale are the Ethnic Identity Questionnaire (EIQ) (Masuda, Matsumoto, & Meredith, 1970) and the Suinn-Lew Asian Self-Identity Acculturation Scale (SL-ASIA) (Suinn, Rickard-Figueroa, Lew, & Vigil, 1987). The EIQ consists of 50 items that respondents rate on a 5-point scale, with 1 indicating *strongly disagree* and 5 indicating *strongly agree*. It was developed specifically for Japanese Americans and contains items that indicate preference for Japanese things (e.g., food, movies, schools), personality characteristics (e.g., obedience, emotionality, displays of affection), child-rearing practices, family orientation, Japanese cultural heritage, community social relationships, sex roles, dating practices, and prejudice. The total ethnic identity score is the sum of the 50 items. This instrument was used in several studies. The findings indicated that among Japanese Americans living in Hawaii the first generation (Issei) scored higher on ethnic identity than did the second (Nisei) and third (Sansei) generations. In addition, Japanese Americans living in Seattle, Washington, scored higher on ethnic identity than did those living in Hawaii. Females also tended to be less ethnically identified than males. In addition, a search for, sense of, and commitment to ethnic identity were found to be positively related to self-esteem (Matsumoto, Meredith, & Masuda, 1973).

The SL-ASIA (Suinn et al., 1987) is based on the Acculturation Rating Scale for Mexican Americans (Cuellar et al., 1980). It is composed of 21 items covering behaviors, identity, friendship choices, language, generation, geographic history, and attitudes that reflect the five dimensions of Padilla's (1980) multidimensional model of acculturation (i.e., language familiarity and usage, cultural heritage, ethnic pride, ethnicity, and interethnic distance). The respondents could rate the items on a 5-point scale, with 1 representing *low acculturation* and 5 representing *high acculturation*. Scoring the scale involved summing the 21 scores and then dividing the total by 21. Suinn et al. (1987) believed that the scale could identify three dimensions: *Asian identified, bicultural,* and *Western identified*. The questionnaire was developed using college students from Colorado State University ($n = 35$) and the University of California, Los Angeles ($n = 47$). Consistent and high reliability coefficients of .88, .89, and .91 for the 21 items were reported in three studies (Suinn et al., 1987; Atkinson & Gim, 1989; and Suinn, Ahuna, & Khoo, 1992, respectively). The scores on the SL-ASIA were found to be correlated with generational status, length of residence, and years of schooling in the United States (Suinn et al., 1987, 1992). A highly significant relationship, $F = 14.26, p = .00001$, between the mean scores and Item 20 of the questionnaire (evaluated as if it were a separate scale), "How would you rate yourself?", also was found. The choices and means were as follows: *very Asian* ($M = 2.49$), *mostly Asian* ($M = 2.91$), *bicultural* ($M = 3.36$), *mostly Anglicized* ($M = 3.81$), and *very Anglicized* ($M = 4.14$).

Suinn and colleagues (1987, 1992) raised several issues to consider in the use and development of the scale. First, it is a generic instrument. Asian American groups are not identified or separated. Whether specific scales have to be developed for the different Asian American groups is not known. Second, the study was based on student samples. It is not clear whether the instrument can be used with older or younger samples or with immigrants. Third, it is not clear whether the important dimensions associated with acculturation have been assessed with the instrument. Lastly, this linear measure is limiting because it does not acknowledge the possibility of high or low cultural endorsement with both cultures.

Related to the last point, in a study comparing value orientations of Japanese Americans from 1952 to those of Japanese and European Americans from 1974, Connor (1974) found that Japanese Americans acculturated differentially depending on the particular target values. Two samples of Japanese Americans were similar with a higher need for abasement, affiliation, nurturance, and order and a lower need for change, heterosexuality (masculinity), and intraception than those of European Americans. However, the 1974 group valued autonomy and aggression more strongly than did the 1952 group. Contrary to the linear model of acculturation, the samples seemed to retain salient aspects of their ethnic culture while selectively integrating various aspects of the dominant culture that might be deemed useful in their adaptation to the larger society.

Other problems with these two paper-and-pencil measures existed when used in research on Asian Americans. Both the EIQ and the SL-ASIA scales tap different behavioral, attitudinal, and affective dimensions. The items are added up, and the score indicates the degree of identity. This process gives all the items equal weight. It is quite possible that certain items might be more important in terms of how identity is defined. This possibility needs to be examined empirically.

Three studies (Atkinson & Matsushita, 1991; Gim et al., 1990; Leong & Tata, 1990) used the SL-ASIA. All three reported finding few or no participants scoring in the low acculturation range. In the Leong and Tata (1990) study, which involved Chinese American 5th and 6th graders, the authors reported results that were consistent with the "straight line" acculturation model. The first generation was less acculturated than each successive generation. The Atkinson and Matsushita (1991) and Gim et al. (1990) studies attempted to determine the relationship between acculturation levels and counseling receptivity. The differences found were minimal, and Atkinson and Matsushita (1991) speculated that acculturation might not have a direct linear relationship with attitudes toward counseling services. In the Gim et al. (1990) study, the Asian American university sample included Chinese Americans, Filipino Americans, Japanese Americans, Korean Americans, and Southeast Asian Americans. The latter group had the most individuals in the low to medium acculturation level. Japanese Americans, on the other hand, were the most highly acculturated among various Asian American groups sampled. Low (actually midrange scores on the SL-ASIA) acculturated participants exposed to Asian American and European American counselors, who were described as either "culturally blind" or "culturally sensitive" to clients, least preferred the culturally blind European American counselor. Hence, ethnic similarity and credibility may be highly important for individuals who are not highly acculturated. In general, level of acculturation as measured by the SL-ASIA does seem to be related to certain counseling variables. Nevertheless, replication studies are necessary to confirm these relationships.

The Independent Model

In contrast to the linear model, the independent model of acculturation views cultural change within a cultural space. This particular type of acculturation model was proposed as a result of the criticism arising from the linear model's basic assumption that adaptation to the dominant culture involves low cultural endorsement with the ethnic culture (Sayegh & Lasry, 1993). Similar to the orthogonal model of cultural identification, proponents of the independent model argued that acculturation to one culture is independent of knowledge about another culture (Oetting & Beauvais, 1990-1991). Therefore, in the assessment of cultural adaptation, rather than placing cultures at either end of a bipolar continuum, the dimensions assessing cultural adaptation are placed at right angles to each other in a cultural space (Oetting & Beauvais, 1990-1991). According to this model, individuals can have varying degrees of cultural values, knowledge, affiliation, and lifestyles from either their culture of origin or the host culture. Moreover, a full range of possibilities for each relevant dimension can be measured by assessing it along the two cultures separately.

Based on this independent model of acculturation, researchers have outlined four possible acculturation styles (Berry, 1989; Sayegh & Lasry, 1993). The four styles are derived from two separate acculturation scores (one for the ethnic culture and the other for the dominant culture). Before these styles are described, it must be kept in mind that they were used mainly for heuristic purposes. Any combination of ethnic and dominant cultural adaptation is possible under the independent model. According to the categorization of acculturation styles, strong relationships with both the ethnic and dominant cultures result in *integration*. Ethnic individuals incorporate new attitudes and behaviors from the dominant culture without conflicting with the established attitudes and behaviors of their ethnic culture. They can develop a sense of belonging and commitment to both cultures without feeling estranged or conflictual. A balance is maintained in which individuals retain the integrity of their ethnic knowledge and adjust their particular cultural repertoire accordingly to effectively regulate their interactions with different ethnic groups. This acculturation style corresponds to LaFromboise et al.'s (1993) alternation model. It is an additive model that assumes the ability of individuals to fluidly adjust their "problem-solving, coping, human relational, communication, and incentive motivational styles, depending on the demands of the social context" (LaFromboise et al., 1993 p. 399).

When individuals have weak relationships with both cultures, *marginalization* results. Individuals in this case do not culturally identify with either of the two groups. Researchers have related this category with psychological stress and confusion wherein individuals lacked meaningful affiliation and contact with their ethnic culture and were being excluded or alienated in the dominant culture (Berry, 1989). Individuals experience *assimilation* when they have strong relationships with the dominant culture but weak relationships with their ethnic culture. Individuals strive for acceptance into the dominant culture by rejecting and denigrating their ethnic culture. Finally, strong relationships with their ethnic culture together with weak relationships with the dominant culture is labeled as either *separation* or *segregation*. Individuals in this case tend to resist aspects of the dominant culture while they maintain their traditional ways of life. Whereas separation is initiated by ethnic individuals who choose to lead separate and independent ways of life from the dominant culture, segregation results from the force of the dominant group to keep these individuals in place (Berry, 1989).

RESEARCH PROBLEMS WITH
CURRENT ETHNIC IDENTITY DEVELOPMENT
AND ACCULTURATION MODELS

Myers et al. (1991) indicated that "few development models have been systematically developed, and even fewer have been empirically validated. . . . Little research has been done to test the validity of these conceptualizations" (p. 55). Research has been hampered because of the variety of ways in which ethnic identity has been defined and the inconsistency in relating it with acculturation. As

Leong and Chou (1994) noted, the various models have not clearly identified the distinctions between ethnic identification and acculturation, although the two concepts are interrelated. Each theoretical model is individually specific, which makes it difficult to draw general conclusions about the processes of cultural adaptation and the formation of ethnic identity. Before the models can be refined and consolidated, the constructs of ethnic identity and acculturation must be defined specifically in reference to a particular group.

Kitano (1989) referred to ethnic identity mostly in behavioral terms by describing it as the degree of "retention of the customs, attitudes, and beliefs of the culture of origin" (p. 142). He distinguished this from assimilation, which was defined as the "processes of acculturation and becoming 'Americanized.' " However, ethnic identity also encompasses an affective component—the feeling of "Asianness" or the acceptance of group identification. In writings and research of African Americans, Helms and Carter (1991) described racial identity as the "quality of a person's commitment to her or his socially ascribed racial group" (p. 446). The "process of becoming Black" in terms of African American identity has been used by Cross (1971, 1978) and Parham (1989). Given the proposed components of ethnic identity, researchers have to decide empirically whether ethnic identity is a psychological state of feeling "Asian" or "Black," commitment to the ascribed ethnic group, retention of cultural values and beliefs, or variable combinations of these plus other unexplored dimensions. In the more recent research, different components of ethnic identity such as context—internal and external aspects— were examined. Isajiw (1990) separated ethnic identity into external aspects (e.g., language, group friendships, ethnic behavior patterns) and internal features (e.g., self-images of the cultural group, feelings of group obligation, attachment). Under these circumstances, an individual may show few observable signs of ethnic identity but have a strong sense of emotional identification.

Most identity models deal with identity with the culture of origin, whereas acculturation models center around relationships with the dominant culture. Although different in focus, ethnic identity may be related to acculturation in complex ways. Many of the current identity models presume that the people who have the strongest ethnic identity are those who maintain the traditional cultural orientation. However, many individuals who are highly acculturated still maintain a strong personal identity with their ethnic culture. In the study of Asian Americans by Gim, Atkinson, and Kim (1991), few low-acculturated individuals were found using the SL-ASIA (Suinn et al., 1987). Most of them scored in the middle or high acculturation range. Matsumoto, Meredith, and Masuda (1973) also reported that acculturation was occurring in their Japanese American samples. Does acculturation or a weakening of adherence to the traditional customs, beliefs, and attitudes necessarily lead to a weak ethnic identity? We do not believe so. Unfortunately, most of our identity models do not assess this possibility. Because of the complexity of the constructs, acculturation and ethnic identity, it is prudent to separate out these variables and be able to relate their effects to each other.

As the independent model of ethnic identification suggested, individuals are enculturated and acculturated in various aspects of both their ethnic and the dominant cultures at variable levels. "Ethnic identity is not a unidimensional quality of persons; it is a characteristic of persons in relation to social situations" (Harwood, 1994, p. 10). Given the interpersonal and dynamic nature of individuals, their definitions, adoptions, and manifestations of ethnic identity are bound to be changed by cultural influence, situational forces, and their subjective interpretations of them. For example, the numerical and social minority status of ethnic individuals will affect their interactions with each other as well as with the dominant group (Harwood, 1994; Padilla, 1994). Their relative positions in society are coupled with cultural and personality attributes (i.e., allocentrism and face concern, which are discussed in a later section) in influencing their interpretation of a particular situation and their definition, adoption, and manifestation of their ethnic identity. Therefore, we need to look at and separate acculturation and ethnic identity at multiple levels (personal, social, political, economic, and cultural), in multiple areas (feelings, attitudes, values, knowledge, and practice), and in multiple settings (being alone, being with members of own ethnic group, other ethnocultural groups, the dominant group, or a mix).

Another major problem in confronting Asian American identity development and acculturation models is the lack of attention to the diversity of the Asian American population in the United States. The U.S. Commission on Civil Rights (1992) identified 29 to 32 separate Asian groups in the United States, each with its own cultural values, language or dialect, history, and traditions. Along with the heterogeneity across Asian American groups, wide variability can be found within each Asian ethnic group. Fully 62% of Asians who now reside in the United States are foreign born (U.S. Commission on Civil Rights, 1992). They also differ in their length of residence, degree of permanence (sojourner vs. resident), gender, age, sexual orientation, years of education, occupation, amount of social support, acceptance of own ethnic group in the dominant society, English proficiency, cultural competence, and many other factors (Cortes, 1994). Most of the early acculturation instruments and conceptualizations of Asian American identity were formulated prior to the massive Asian immigration of the 1980s. The Asian American population is the fastest growing minority group in the United States, increasing by 108% over a 10-year period, which is 2 times faster than the Hispanic American population, 8 times faster than the African American population, and 15 times faster than the European American population (Ong & Hee, 1993).

The implications drawn from these demographic shifts are enormous and important. First, the Asian American community is becoming even more heterogeneous. There are Asians who have resided in the United States for many generations and those who immigrated here recently and cannot speak English. The socioeconomic statuses of Asians are quite diverse, from those considered affluent to those far below the poverty line. Coupling these factors with the varying ethnicities (e.g., Asian Indian, Cambodian, Chinese, Filipino, Hmong, Japanese, Korean, Laotian, Samoan, Thai, Tongan, Vietnamese) it does not take much to conclude that any single theory of Asian American identity development would be an oversimplification and inadequate.

Second, it is becoming clear that Asian American ethnic identity models might be extremely limited in application to recent immigrants. Our own clinical experience and subjective interactions with immigrants lead us to conclude that they already possess an intact ethnic identity. How would we classify them on any of the typologies or stages postulated by researchers? We believe that these models possess serious shortcomings when applied to these populations. However, an interesting question to ask is whether the American-born sons and daughters of the immigrants will experience the postulated dynamics in the stage theories. Certainly, our historical study of the early Chinese, Japanese, and Filipino immigration and their offspring seems to imply an affirmative answer. Nevertheless, even if they do arrive at the proposed stages, how can we more clearly understand the course of their identity development and compare theirs to those of recent immigrants, later-generation ethnic individuals, and even other ethnic groups (Padilla, 1994)? Given the heterogeneity of the Asian American population, it is important that researchers study different Asian ethnic groups (rather than aggregate Asian Americans as a group to garner an adequate sample size) and gather sufficient demographic and cultural information from their samples to either covary out or study their effects directly.

Another important issue that must be considered when examining the ethnic identity and acculturation process of ethnic individuals is the social context and the cultural milieu in which individuals are situated. The presence of a particular group of individuals and the dominance of certain values in a particular setting would affect how the individuals define themselves ethnically in that particular situation. Similarly, the salience of cultural differences in a particular setting with a particular group of individuals would affect the attitudes, cognitions, and behaviors of the individuals and their acculturation process (Uba, 1994; Yeh & Huang, 1996). The importance of contextual factors may be accentuated, especially among individuals who have a collectivistic tendency.

INDIVIDUALISM-COLLECTIVISM ON IDENTITY

Recent studies have identified various cultural dimensions to better understand and explain the psychological and behavioral patterns of individuals from different cultures (Hofstede, 1980). Among these efforts, Triandis and his colleagues' work on individualism-collectivism generated the most attention within and across different Asian groups (Triandis et al., 1986, 1993; Triandis, Bontempo, Villareal, Asai, & Lucca, 1988; Triandis, McCusker, & Hui, 1990). Originally developed as a cultural-level construct, the implications of individualism and collectivism have been investigated by researchers at the individual level and been referred to with terminology such as idiocentrism/independent self-construals and allocentrism/interdependent self-construals, respectively (Markus & Kitayama, 1991; Triandis, Leung, Villareal, & Clack, 1985; Yamaguchi, Kuhlman, & Sugimori, 1995).

Individuals with strong independent self-construals tend to give priority to personal goals over in-group goals, to feel distinct from their in-groups, to accept confrontation with in-groups, and to define themselves independently from the in-groups to which they belong. By contrast, individuals with strong interdependent self-construals are more likely to give priority to the collective goals over their own, to feel interdependent with their in-groups, to avoid confrontation so as to maintain harmony with their in-groups, and to define themselves in terms of their in-groups (Markus & Kitayama, 1991; Rhee, Uleman, & Lee, 1996; Yamaguchi et al., 1995).

In addition to the differences in idiocentric and allocentric individuals, individuals who are in either a numerical or a social minority are more likely to rate their in-groups more positively and to perceive less variability in their in-groups compared to their out-groups (Triandis et al., 1990; Verkuyten & Kwa, 1996). These differences in interpersonal orientation would influence the way in which ethnic individuals conceptualize and define themselves. However, the definition of in-group/out-group is complicated given the variability in age, gender, sexual orientation, socioeconomic status, language, and other sociocultural factors within a multiethnic context such as the United States. Based on the aforementioned discussion, ethnic individuals, who have strong interdependent self-construals and are relegated to a disadvantaged social status, tend to espouse collective self-schemata and are more likely to rely on external sources in defining themselves than are those who have independent self-construals and internal orientation. In other words, allocentric individuals are more likely to describe themselves in social and collective terms specific to a particular context than are idiocentric individuals, who tend to describe themselves abstractly and independent from others (Bochner, 1994; Rhee, Uleman, Lee, & Roman, 1995; Triandis, 1989).

Studies have repeatedly found that Asian Americans tend to have stronger interdependent self-construals (Cross, 1995; Gaines et al., 1997; Singelis & Sharkey, 1995; Yamaguchi et al., 1995) and weaker independent self-construals than do European Americans (Gudykunst, Gao, & Franklyn-Stokes, 1996; Singelis & Sharkey, 1995; for exceptions, see Cross, 1995, and Gaines et al., 1997, which found no significant differences in independent self-construals). They have a greater affiliative tendency, have a higher sensitivity to rejection and embarrassment, and are stronger self-monitors compared to European Americans (Gudykunst et al., 1996; Triandis, 1989; Yamaguchi et al., 1995). Moreover, Asian Americans are found to have high face concern and to use shame as a mechanism for social control. According to Yeh and Huang (1996), "Face includes the positive image, interpretations, or social attributes that one claims for oneself or perceives others to have accorded one. If one does not fulfill expectations of the self, then one loses face" (p. 651). The shame and pain of losing one's face are felt strongly by the collective to which the individual belongs. Therefore, the prospect of losing face triggers loss of support and threat of ostracism from one's in-groups. For this reason, individuals with high face concern are more likely to conform to interpersonal expectations and to threaten others and themselves with shame to control other people's and their own behaviors (Shon & Ja, 1982).

Given their allocentric emphasis, Asian Americans are more likely to be influenced by the situational context and their in-group members in defining their identities. Using the Ethnic Identity Development Exercise, a qualitative assessment tool, Yeh and Huang (1996) found that Asian Americans' ethnic identification was significantly influenced by interpersonal relationships and external forces such as geographic location and the attitudes of the larger culture. Moreover, 40% of the sample described shame as the motivating force in shaping their ethnic identity, whereas only 6% of the sample cited anger as an important factor, which was implicated as an important mechanism in many stage models of ethnic identity. In a study of Chinese youths in the Netherlands (Verkuyten & Kwa, 1996), the majority of whom were born in the Netherlands (92%), allocentric individuals (as measured by 4 items from the short form of Hui's, 1988, INDCOL scale) were significantly more likely to describe themselves in ethnic terms. They also practiced significantly more ethnic activities and preferred in-group formation and relationships but did not differ in their interactions with the dominant group (Dutch) and other ethnic groups as compared to those who were less allocentric (Verkuyten & Kwa, 1996).

Using quantitative instruments (i.e., Individualism-Collectivism Questionnaire, Ethnic Behavior and Knowledge Scale, Importance of Ethnic Behaviors and Knowledge Scale, and Evaluation of Ethnic Origins Scale), Rosenthal and Feldman (1992a) found that individualism-collectivism was not directly related to the strength of ethnic identity among a sample of Chinese Americans and Chinese Australians. Nevertheless, both collectivism and the affective components of ethnic identity (the importance and evaluation of one's ethnic identity) were found to remain stable relative to ethnic knowledge and behaviors in the first two generations (Rosenthal & Feldman, 1992a). In another study of Chinese immigrants, internal ethnic identity (e.g., sense of belonging and attitudes toward one's ethnic group) was found to be predictive of fear of loss of face, $R^2 = .20$, $p < .00001$. Salience of ethnicity, external ethnic identity (e.g., ethnic and cultural activities and practices), loss of face, and income significantly predicted cultural stress, $R^2 = .32$, $p < .002$ (Kwan & Sodowsky, 1997). Thus, although the relationships among interpersonal orientation and ethnic identity cannot be discussed in a simplistic fashion, for many Asian Americans who espouse the interpersonal orientation and have high face concern, ethnic identity is likely to be shaped by forces in addition to those suggested by traditional ethnic identity models (e.g., anger toward and conflict with the dominant group).

Concurrent with the interaction between allocentrism and ethnic identity formation, ethnic identity development also would interact with the acculturation process as Asian Americans continue to function within various cultural contexts and to deal with different cultural values and situations (e.g., Rhee et al., 1995). Combining with one's personality attributes, both forces within one's ethnic group and factors in the larger culture and the surrounding environment will variably affect one's ethnic identity development. Under this paradigm, many Asian Americans, especially those with strong interdependent self-construals, are likely to possess and manifest different ethnic identities according to the conditions and demands of a particular context (Harwood, 1994). Furthermore, their ethnic identification will be highly malleable, diverse, and evolving over time and situations (Yeh & Huang, 1996). Given the interpersonal and dynamic nature of ethnic identity for many Asian Americans, the existing models of ethnic identity and acculturation, which are described as individuocentric and linear (Betancourt & Lopez, 1993; Lee, 1994), might not adequately account for the diversity among Asian Americans.

RECOMMENDATIONS FOR FUTURE RESEARCH

Recognizing and appreciating the heterogeneity within the Asian American population, researchers increasingly have advocated the adoption of emic approaches to examine specific target groups and to interpret their findings in light of particular ecological and cultural features. Measures indigenous to the targeted ethnic groups and specific hypotheses framed within a particular cultural context are necessary to augment the existing standardized etic measures and theories. Not only does the emic approach avoid the problems of linguistic and conceptual equivalence, it also allows researchers to incorporate culture-specific concepts into their instruments. By relying on the imposed etic approach, which basically borrows measures developed in one culture (usually the dominant European American culture) for use in another, researchers run into the danger of omitting important ethnocultural characteristics that are unique to a particular ethnic group. Although it still is important to acknowledge and extract the commonalities across groups with respect to ethnic identity and acculturation and the worth of using standardized measures for comparisons and contrasts, ethnic-specific characteristics also must be assessed to complement the limitations of etic measures (Phinney, 1992). Etic instruments "will measure only those characteristics that are common to [all ethnic groups], while characteristics that are salient only in one culture will be neglected" (Lee, 1991, p. 301).

Some approaches that have been recommended by researchers include the use of ethnographic and qualitative methods. In such open-ended measures, individuals or focus groups are allowed to express their own perspectives about the characteristics of their own culture, the important values and behaviors emphasized by their particular ethnic group, and the meaning of being "American," "Asian," or their particular ethnic group (Cortes, 1994; Harwood, 1994). Their criteria of acculturation also are important in designing appropriate measures. Their desires and purposes to acculturate or to maintain their ethnic heritage can be evaluated in personal and group interviews. For individuals who are limited in their language capability due to developmental level, cultural etiquette, and personality attributes, alternative means such as writing, drawing, and behavioral demonstrations can be useful to access important information.

These alternative methods can supplement the limitations of traditional self-reported paper-and-pencil questionnaires. Different ethnocultural groups may have various response sets such as the tendency to acquiesce and to moderate extreme responding. Moreover, given the sensitivity of the issues surrounding one's identity, participants' responses are likely to be influenced by social desirability or face concern. Therefore, self-reported questionnaires might not accurately reflect the feelings, attitudes, and behaviors that individuals endorse and actually engage in. This points directly to the idea that Asian Americans might be more self-effacing and allocentric, so that they might not report honestly to avoid shame and preserve face in front of the experimenter, who may be perceived to be from the same or different ethnic group and be regarded as an out-group member. Furthermore, because allocentric individuals are more likely to adjust their attitudes and behaviors according to whom they are interacting with and where they are situated, their identity must be assessed across different settings. Researchers can include in their research process methods such as observations of the participants in multiple settings and interviews with individuals who interact with the participants in different capacities (e.g., family members, peers, coworkers) to get a more comprehensive picture of the participants.

To further enrich the experience, researchers from the same ethnic group and those different from the target group can collaborate to impart unique knowledge and objectivity on their investigations. The combination of diverse backgrounds would enhance the comprehensiveness and understanding of the target groups in the topic of interest (Phinney & Kohatsu, 1997). In addition to the use of qualitative approaches, longitudinal studies should be done to understand the interactions of various contextual factors in the process of acculturation and ethnic identity formation over time. Longitudinal research also would allow researchers to better study and understand the changes of these processes and their implications to individuals' psychological adjustment and mental health.

SUMMARY

Asian American ethnic identity and acculturation models were developed through personal observations in working with clients who reported conflicts in adjusting to the dominant culture. The earliest models were typologies that indicated the different responses that individuals might make in traversing values from their ethnic group and those of the larger society. Typologies were used for illustrative rather than explanatory purposes and in no means suggested that individuals are fixed in any certain composition. The EIQ and SL-ASIA were the first instruments used to quantify the degree of acculturation for Asian Americans. The MEIM was a measure for ethnic identity that was developed to be applicable to various ethnic groups based on an extraction of common factors in ethnic identity formation. In general, the instruments had adequate reliability and validity. Independent models of acculturation and cultural identification were proposed to assess cultural adaptation of the ethnic culture and the dominant culture separately to examine the possible combinations of various cultural components. Stage models such as the R/CID Model described the movement of individuals as they react to racism in the dominant society and struggle in their ethnic identity formation. Although all models of ethnic identity fit with clinical observations, adequate research support for these perspectives still does not exist. No empirical method yet is developed reflecting the dynamics of various ethnic identity models.

Efforts should be made to clearly conceptualize the constructs of ethnic identity and acculturation given that the present literature reflects ambiguity and confusion in their specification and usage. The interrelationships of ethnic identity and acculturation together with various contextual factors should be examined and organized to allow a more complete picture of ethnic individuals' psychological reality. The effects of various cultural value orientations (e.g., individualism-collectivism) on individuals' self-definition should be examined systematically to understand their relations to ethnic identity. Cultural value dimensions are proximal variables that can influence the salience of ethnic identity and affect the way in which individuals define themselves in a particular context. However, the mechanisms in which they shape individuals' schemata and influence the salience of a particular identity have not yet been examined. What situations make ethnic identity salient to individuals and how cultural value dimensions affect their interpretations are important questions that should be explored and answered.

Emic methods can be more widely employed along with standardized measures to better understand both the similarities and uniqueness among different ethnic groups. Longitudinal research can be done to examine the process of acculturation and identity formation and their impact on individuals' mental health. By considering the intricate relationships among a wide range of variables both unique to and shared by different ethnic groups and individuals, researchers can refine their conceptualizations and develop dynamic models that can more adequately capture the evolving identity development of ethnic individuals in relation to their own ethnic group, other ethnocultural groups, and the dominant society.

REFERENCES

Arkoff, A., & Weaver, H. B. (1966). Body image and body dissatisfaction in Japanese-Americans. *Journal of Social Psychology, 68*, 323-330.

Atkinson, D. R., & Gim, R. (1989). Asian-American cultural identity and attitudes toward mental health services. *Journal of Counseling Psychology, 36*, 209-212.

Atkinson, D. R., & Matsushita, Y. J. (1991). Japanese-American acculturation, counseling style, counselor ethnicity, and perceived counselor credibility. *Journal of Counseling Psychology, 38*, 446-457.

Atkinson, D. R., Morten, G., & Sue, D. W. (1989). A minority identity development model. In D. R. Atkinson, G. Morten, & D. W. Sue (Eds.), *Counseling American minorities* (3rd ed., pp. 35-47). Dubuque, IA: William C. Brown.

Atkinson, D. R., & Schein, S. (1986). Similarity in counseling. *The Counseling Psychologist, 14*, 319-354.

Bennett, S. K., & BigFoot-Sipes, D. S. (1991). American Indian and White college student preferences for counselor characteristics. *Journal of Counseling Psychology, 38*, 440-445.

Berry, J. W. (1989). Acculturation and psychological adaptation. In J. P. Forgas & J. M. Innes (Eds.), *Recent advances in social psychology: An international perspective* (pp. 511-520). Amsterdam: Elsevier Science.

Berry, J. W., Trimble, J. E., & Olmedo, E. L. (1986). Assessment of acculturation. In W. J. Lonner & J. W. Berry (Eds.), *Field methods in cross-cultural research* (pp. 291-324). Beverly Hills, CA: Sage.

Betancourt, H., & Lopez, S. R. (1993). The study of culture, ethnicity, and race in American psychology. *American Psychologist, 48,* 629-637.

Bochner, S. (1994). Cross-cultural differences in the self concept: A test of Hofstede's individualism/collectivism distinction. *Journal of Cross-Cultural Psychology, 25,* 273-283.

Carter, R. T. (1995). *The influence of race and racial identity in psychotherapy.* New York: John Wiley.

Chang, T. (1975). The self-concept of children in ethnic groups: Black American and Korean American. *Elementary School Journal, 76,* 52-58.

Chen, C., & Yang, D. (1986). The self-image of Chinese-American adolescents. *Pacific Asian American Mental Health Research Center Review, 3/4,* 27-29.

Choney, S. K., Berryhill-Paapke, E., & Robbins, R. R. (1995). The acculturation of American Indians: Developing frameworks for research and practice. In J. G. Ponterotto, J. M. Casas, L. A. Suzuki, & C. M. Alexander (Eds.), *Handbook of multicultural counseling* (pp. 73-92). Thousand Oaks, CA: Sage.

Connor, J. W. (1974). Acculturation and changing need patterns in Japanese-American and Caucasian-American college students. *Journal of Social Psychology, 93,* 293-294.

Cortes, D. E. (1994). Acculturation and its relevance to mental health. In R. G. Malgady & O. Rodriguez (Eds.), *Theoretical and conceptual issues in Hispanic mental health* (pp. 54-68). Malabar, FL: Krieger.

Cross, S. E. (1995). Self-construals, coping, and stress in cross-cultural adaptation. *Journal of Cross-Cultural Psychology, 26,* 673-697.

Cross, W. E., Jr. (1971). The Negro-to-Black conversion experience: Towards a psychology of Black liberation. *Black World, 20,* 13-27.

Cross, W. E. (1978). The Thomas and Cross models of psychological nigrescence: A review. *Journal of Black Psychology, 5*(1), 13-31.

Cross, W. E., Jr. (1991). *Shades of Black: Diversity in African-American identity.* Philadelphia: Temple University Press.

Cross, W. E., Jr. (1995). The psychology of nigrescence: Revising the Cross model. In J. G. Ponterotto, J. M. Casas, L. A. Suzuki, & C. M. Alexander (Eds.), *Handbook of multicultural counseling* (pp. 93-122). Thousand Oaks, CA: Sage.

Cuellar, I., Harris, L. C., & Jasso, R. (1980). An acculturation scale for Mexican American normal and clinical populations. *Hispanic Journal of Behavioral Sciences, 2,* 199-217.

Gaines, S. O., Jr., Marelich, W. D., Bledsoe, K. L., Steers, W. N., Henderson, M. C., Granrose, C. S., Barajas, L., Hicks, D., Lyde, M., Takahashi, Y., Yum, N., Rios, D. I., Garcia, B. F., Farris, K. R., & Page, M. S. (1997). Links between race/ethnicity and cultural values as mediated by racial/ethnic identity and moderated by gender. *Journal of Personality and Social Psychology, 72,* 1460-1476.

Gim, R. H., Atkinson, D. R., & Kim, S. J. (1991). Asian American acculturation, counselor ethnicity and cultural sensitivity, and ratings of counselors. *Journal of Counseling Psychology, 38,* 57-62.

Gim, R. H., Atkinson, D. R., & Whiteley, S. (1990). Asian-American acculturation, severity of concerns, and willingness to see a counselor. *Journal of Counseling Psychology, 37,* 281-285.

Gudykunst, W. B., Gao, G., & Franklyn-Stokes, A. (1996). Self-monitoring and concern for social appropriateness in China and England. In J. Pandey, D. Sinha, & D. P. S. Bhawuk (Eds.), *Asian contributions to cross-cultural psychology* (pp. 255-267). New Delhi, India: Sage.

Harwood, A. (1994). Acculturation in the postmodern world: Implications for mental health research. In R. G. Malgady & O. Rodriguez (Eds.), *Theoretical and conceptual issues in Hispanic mental health* (pp. 4-17). Malabar, FL: Krieger.

Helms, J. E. (1989). Considering some methodological issues in racial identity counseling research. *The Counseling Psychologist, 17,* 227-252.

Helms, J. E. (1990). *Black and White racial identity: Theory, research and practice.* Westport, CT: Greenwood.

Helms, J. E., & Carter, R. T. (1991). Relationships of White and Black racial identity attitudes and demographic similarity to counselor preferences. *Journal of Counseling Psychology, 38,* 446-457.

Hofstede, G. (1980). *Culture's consequences.* Beverly Hills, CA: Sage.

Hui, C. H. (1988). Measurement of individualism-collectivism. *Journal of Research on Personality, 22,* 17-36.

Hutnik, N. (1991). *Ethnic minority identity: A social psychological perspective.* Oxford, UK: Oxford University Press.

Ibrahim, F., Ohnishi, H., & Sandhu, D. S. (1997). Asian American identity development: A culture specific model for South Asian Americans. *Journal of Multicultural Counseling and Development, 25,* 34-50.

Isajiw, W. W. (1990). Ethnic identity retention. In R. Breton, W. W. Isajiw, W. E. Kalbach, & I. G. Reitz (Eds.), *Ethnic identity and equality* (pp. 34-91). Toronto: University of Toronto Press.

Jackson, B. (1975). Black identity development. *Journal of Education Diversity, 2,* 19-25.

Kim, B. L. C. (1980). *Korean American child at school and at home.* Technical report to the Administration for Child, Youth, and Families, Washington, DC.

Kitano, H. H. L. (1989). A model for counseling Asian Americans. In P. B. Pedersen, J. G. Draguns, W. J. Lonner, & J. E. Trimble (Eds.), *Counseling across cultures* (3rd ed., pp. 139-151). Honolulu: University of Hawaii Press.

Kwan, K. L. K., & Sodowsky, G. R. (1997). Internal and external ethnic identity and their correlates: A study of Chinese American immigrants. *Journal of Multicultural Counseling and Development, 25,* 51-67.

LaFromboise, T., Coleman, H. L. K., & Gerton, J. (1993). Psychological impact of biculturalism: Evidence and theory. *Psychological Bulletin, 114,* 395-412.

Lee, K. C. (1991). The problem of appropriateness of the Rokeach value survey in Korea. *International Journal of Psychology, 26,* 299-310.

Lee, Y. T. (1994). Why does American psychology have cultural limitations? *American Psychologist, 49,* 524.

Leong, F. T. L., & Chou, E. L. (1994). The role of ethnic identity and acculturation in the vocational behavior of Asian Americans: An integrative review. *Journal of Vocational Behavior, 44*(2), 155-172.

Leong, F. T. L., & Tata, S. P. (1990). Sex and acculturation differences in occupational values among Chinese-American children. *Journal of Counseling Psychology, 37,* 208-212.

Liu, C., Sue, D., & Dinnel, D. (1992). *Use of the Racial Identity Attitude Scale (RIAS) on Asian Americans.* Unpublished master's thesis, Western Washington University.

Lopez, S. R., Lopez, A. A., & Fong, K. T. (1991). Mexican Americans' initial preferences for counselors: The role of ethnic factors. *Journal of Counseling Psychology, 38,* 487-496.

Marcia, J., Waterman, A., Matteson, D., Archer, S., & Orlofsky, J. (1994). *Ego identity: A handbook of psychosocial research.* New York: Springer-Verlag.

Markus, H. R., & Kitayama, S. (1991). Culture and the self: Implications for cognition, emotion, and motivation. *Psychological Review, 98,* 224-253.

Masuda, M., Matsumoto, G. M., & Meredith, G. M. (1970). Ethnic identity in three generations of Japanese-Americans. *Journal of Social Psychology, 81,* 199-207.

Matsumoto, G. M., Meredith, G. M., & Masuda, M. (1973). Ethnic identity: Honolulu and Seattle Japanese-Americans. In S. Sue & N. N. Wagner (Eds.), *Asian-Americans: Psychological perspectives* (pp. 65-74). Ben Lomond, CA: Science and Behavior Books.

Maykovich, M. H. (1973). Political activation of Japanese American youth. *Journal of Social Issues, 29,* 167-185.

Myers, L. J., Speight, S. L., Highlen, P. S., Cox, C. I., Reynolds, A. L., Adams, E. M., & Hanley, C. P. (1991). Identity development and worldview toward an optimal conceptualization. *Journal of Counseling and Development, 70,* 54-63.

Oetting, E. R., & Beauvais, F. (1990-1991). Orthogonal cultural identification theory: The cultural identification of minority adolescents. *International Journal of the Addictions, 25,* 655-685.

Olmedo, E. L. (1979). Acculturation: A psychometric perspective. *American Psychologist, 34,* 1061-1070.

Ong, P., & Hee, S. J. (1993). Twenty million in 2020. In *The state of Asian Pacific America* (pp. 11-24). Los Angeles: Leadership Education for Asian Pacifics and UCLA Asian American Studies Center.

Padilla, A. (1980). The role of cultural awareness and ethnic loyalty in acculturation. In A. Padilla (Ed.), *Acculturation: Theory, models, and some new findings* (pp. 47-84). Boulder, CO: Westview.

Padilla, A. M. (1994). Bicultural development: A theoretical and empirical examination. In R. G. Malgady & O. Rodriguez (Eds.), *Theoretical and conceptual issues in Hispanic mental health* (pp. 20-51). Malabar, FL: Krieger.

Pang, V. O., Mizokawa, D. T., Morishima, J. K., & Olstad, R. G. (1985). Self-concepts of Japanese American children. *Journal of Cross-Cultural Psychology, 16,* 99-109.

Parham, T. A. (1989). Cycles of psychological nigrescence. *The Counseling Psychologist, 17,* 187-226.

Parham, T. A., & Helms, J. E. (1981). Influence of a Black student's racial identity attitudes on preference for counselor race. *Journal of Counseling Psychology, 28,* 250-257.

Phinney, J. S. (1989). Stages of ethnic identity development in minority group adolescents. *Journal of Early Adolescence, 9*(1-2), 34-49.

Phinney, J. S. (1990). Ethnic identity in adolescents and adults: Review of literature. *Psychological Bulletin, 108,* 499-514.

Phinney, J. S. (1991). Ethnic identity and self-esteem: A review and integration. *Hispanic Journal of Behavioral Sciences, 13,* 193-208.

Phinney, J. S. (1992). The multigroup ethnic identity measure: A new scale for use with diverse groups. *Journal of Adolescent Research, 7*(2), 156-176.

Phinney, J. S. (1993). A three-stage model of ethnic identity development in adolescence. In M. E. Bernal & G. P. Knight (Eds.), *Ethnic identity: Formation and transmission among Hispanics and other minorities* (pp. 61-79). Albany: State University of New York Press.

Phinney, J. S., & Alipuria, L. (1990). Ethnic identity in college students from four ethnic groups. *Journal of Adolescent Research, 13,* 171-183.

Phinney, J. S., & Chavira, V. (1992). Ethnic identity and self-esteem: An exploratory longitudinal study. *Journal of Adolescence, 15,* 271-281.

Phinney, J. S., & Kohatsu, E. L. (1997). Ethnic and racial identity development and mental health. In J. Schulenberg, J. L. Maggs, & K. Herrelmann (Eds.), *Health risks and developmental transitions during adolescence* (pp. 420-443). New York: Cambridge University Press.

Pomales, J., Claiborn, C. D., & LaFromboise, T. D. (1986). Effects of Black students' racial identity on perceptions of White counselors varying in cultural sensitivity. *Journal of Counseling Psychology, 33,* 57-61.

Ponterotto, J. G., & Wise, S. L. (1987). Construct validity study of the Racial Identity Attitude Scale. *Journal of Counseling Psychology, 34,* 123-131.

Rhee, E., Uleman, J. S., & Lee, H. K. (1996). Variations in collectivism and individualism by ingroup and culture: Confirmatory factor analyses. *Journal of Personality and Social Psychology, 71,* 1037-1054.

Rhee, E., Uleman, J. S., Lee, H. K., & Roman, R. J. (1995). Spontaneous self-descriptions and ethnic identities in individualistic and collectivistic cultures. *Journal of Personality and Social Psychology, 69,* 142-152.

Rosenthal, D. A., & Feldman, S. S. (1992a). The nature and stability of ethnic identity in Chinese youth: Effects of length of residence in two cultural contexts. *Journal of Cross-Cultural Psychology, 23,* 214-227.

Rosenthal, D. A., & Feldman, S. S. (1992b). The relationship between parenting behaviour and ethnic identity in Chinese-American and Chinese-Australian adolescents. *International Journal of Psychology, 27,* 19-31.

Ruiz, A. S. (1990). Ethnic identity: Crisis and resolution. *Journal of Multicultural Counseling and Development, 18,* 29-40.

Sanchez, A. R., & Atkinson, D. R. (1983). Mexican-American cultural commitment, preference for counselor ethnicity, and willingness to use counseling. *Journal of Counseling Psychology, 30,* 215-220.

Sayegh, L., & Lasry, J. (1993). Immigrants' adaptation in Canada: Assimilation, acculturation, and orthogonal cultural identification. *Canadian Psychology, 34,* 98-109.

Shon, S. P., & Ja, D. Y. (1982). Asian families. In M. McGoldrick, J. K. Pearce, & J. Giordano (Eds.), *Ethnicity and family therapy* (pp. 208-228). New York: Guilford.

Singelis, T. M., & Sharkey, W. F. (1995). Culture, self-construal, and embarrassability. *Journal of Cross-Cultural Psychology, 26,* 622-644.

Smith, B. M. (1990). The measurement of narcissism in Asian, Caucasian, and Hispanic American women. *Psychological Reports, 67,* 779-785.

Smith, E. M. J. (1989). Black racial identity development: Issues and concerns. *The Counseling Psychologist, 17,* 277-288.

Sodowsky, G. R., Kwan, K.-L. K., & Pannu, R. (1995). Ethnic identity of Asians in the United States. In J. G. Ponterotto, J. M. Casas, L. A. Suzuki, & C. M. Alexander (Eds.), *Handbook of multicultural counseling* (pp. 123-154). Thousand Oaks, CA: Sage.

Sue, D. W., & Sue, D. (1990). *Counseling the culturally different.* New York: John Wiley.

Sue, D. W., & Sue, S. (1972). Counseling Chinese-Americans. *Personnel and Guidance Journal, 50,* 637-644.

Sue, S. (1991). Ethnicity and culture in psychological research and practice. In J. D. Goodchilds (Ed.), *Psychological perspectives on human diversity in America* (pp. 47-85). Washington, DC: American Psychological Association.

Sue, S., & Sue, D. W. (1971). Chinese-American personality and mental health. *Amerasia Journal, 1,* 36-49.

Suinn, R. M., Ahuna, C., & Khoo, G. (1992). The Suinn-Lew Asian Self-Identity Acculturation Scale: Concurrent and factorial validation. *Educational and Psychological Measurement, 52,* 1041-1046.

Suinn, R. M., Rickard-Figueroa, K., Lew, S., & Vigil, P. (1987). The Suinn-Lew Asian Self-Identity Acculturation Scale: An initial report. *Educational and Psychological Measurement, 47,* 401-407.

Swinomish Tribal Mental Health Project. (1991). *A gathering of wisdoms.* Mount Vernon, WA: Veda Vangarde.

Szapocznik, J., Santisteban, D., Kurtines, W. M., Hervis, O. E., & Spencer, F. (1982). Life enhancements counseling: A psychosocial model of services for Cuban elders. In E. E. Jones & S. J. Korchin (Eds.), *Minority mental health* (pp. 296-329). New York: Praeger.

Tajfel, H. (1981). *Human groups and social categories.* Cambridge, UK: Cambridge University Press.

Thomas, C. W. (1970, September). Different strokes for different folks. *Psychology Today,* pp. 49-53.

Thomas, C. W. (1971). *Boys no more.* Beverly Hills, CA: Glencoe.

Triandis, H. C. (1989). The self and social behavior in differing cultural contexts. *Psychological Review, 96,* 506-520.

Triandis, H. C., Bontempo, R., Betacourt, H., Bond, M., Leung, K., Brenes, A., Georgas, J., Hui, C. H., Marin, G., Setiadi, B., Sinha, J. B. P., Verma, J., Spangenberg, J., Touzard, H., & de Montmollin, G. (1986). The measurement of the etic aspects of individualism and collectivism across cultures. *Australian Journal of Psychology, 38,* 257-267.

Triandis, H. C., Bontempo, R., Villareal, M. J., Asai, M., & Lucca, N. (1988). Individualism and collectivism: Cross-cultural perspectives on self-ingroup relationships. *Journal of Personality and Social Psychology, 54,* 323-338.

Triandis, H. C., Leung, K., Villareal, M., & Clack, F. L. (1985). Allocentric vs. idiocentric tendencies: Convergent and discriminant validation. *Journal of Research in Personality, 19,* 395-415.

Triandis, H. C., McCusker, C., Betacourt, H., Iwao, S., Leung, K., Salazar, J. M., Setiadi, B., Sinha, J. B. P., Touzard, H., & Zaleski, Z. (1993). An etic-emic analysis of individualism and collectivism. *Journal of Cross-Cultural Psychology, 24,* 366-383.

Triandis, H. C., McCusker, C., & Hui, C. H. (1990). Multimethod probes of individualism and collectivism. *Journal of Personality and Social Psychology, 59,* 1006-1020.

Uba, L. (1994). *Asian Americans: Personality patterns, identity, and mental health.* New York: Guilford.

U.S. Commission on Civil Rights. (1992). *Civil rights issues facing Asian Americans in the 1990s.* Washington, DC: Author.

Verkuyten, M., & Kwa, G. A. (1996). Ethnic self-identification, ethnic involvement, and group differentiation among Chinese youth in the Netherlands. *Journal of Social Psychology, 136,* 35-48.

Vontress, C. (1971). Racial differences: Impediments to rapport. *Journal of Counseling Psychology, 18,* 9-13.

Weiss, M. S. (1970). Selective acculturation and the dating process: The patterning of Chinese-Caucasian interracial dating. *Journal of Marriage and the Family, 32,* 273-282.

Yamaguchi, S., Kuhlman, D. M., & Sugimori, S. (1995). Personality correlates of allocentric tendencies in individualist and collectivist cultures. *Journal of Cross-Cultural Psychology, 26,* 658-672.

Yang, K., & Bond, M. H. (1980). Ethnic affirmation by Chinese bilinguals. *Journal of Cross-Cultural Psychology, 11,* 411-425.

Yeh, C. J., & Huang, K. (1996). The collectivistic nature of ethnic identity development among Asian-Americans college students. *Adolescence, 31,* 645-661.

Zitzow, D., & Estes, G. (1981). The heritage consistency continuum in counseling Native American children. In *American Indian issues in higher education* (pp. 133-139). Aberdeen, SD: ERIC Document Reproduction Service.

10

ACADEMIC ACHIEVEMENT
AND PERFORMANCE

JAYJIA HSIA
SAMUEL S. PENG

Starting in the 1980s, the American public has been exposed to a spate of media reports about high levels of achievement on the part of Asian Americans in a number of fields. The focus most often has been on academic achievement of young Asian Americans. Each spring, pictures of National Merit Scholars, Presidential Scholars, and Westinghouse Science Talent Search finalists with Asian faces have smiled from their hometown newspapers. Success stories about the growing presence of Asian American students on this nation's most selective college campuses have been featured in print and broadcast media. Often there have been companion op-ed pieces that speculated on the etiology of Asian American academic success.

Polemicists have used such publicity to serve their own interests—to commend particular individuals or Asian groups, to chide or goad the majority or other minority groups, and sometimes to sow dissension among the increasingly diverse peoples in North America. Media and political attention, coupled with public concern about the deteriorating status of U.S. public education in an era of growing economic competition from other Pacific Rim nations, has contributed to widely held notions of Asian American students as super achievers and Asian Americans in general as a homogeneous "model minority" group. Media attention is one factor leading to a growing backlash, reflected in symptoms such as expressions of distrust or hatred, evidence of institutional discrimination, acts of violence against Asian Americans, and anti-immigrant legislation.

How much of the information we hear on radio, see on television, or read in the press about Asian American academic achievement is valid, and what ought to be relegated to the realm of folk myth? This chapter reviews recent literature and examines available databases to describe the current status of Asian American academic achievement. The first myth to be examined is the notion that Asian Americans constitute a uniformly high performance group.

DEMOGRAPHICS OF DIVERSITY

Far from being a homogeneous model minority group, "Asian American" is an umbrella term that covers all peoples whose origins could be traced to Asia or the Pacific Islands. Asians and Pacific Islanders (APIs) were grouped together for bureaucratic convenience in census counts and other databases. Over time, Asian Americans have learned to form alliances to advance common interests.

There have been remarkable changes in both size and composition of the Asian American population since the enactment of two laws: the Immigration and Naturalization Act of 1965 and the Civil Rights Act of 1964. The former allowed Asian immigrants entry to the United States after having been shut out for decades through a series of Asian exclusion laws. The latter opened up educational and economic opportunities that had been long denied members of minority groups including Asian Americans. The legislation freed those already in this country from more than a century of legally sanctioned discrimination that ensured prolonged and severe curtailment of APIs' access to citizenship, housing, education, and jobs.

New immigrants arrived from Asia in substantial numbers from 1968 onward, when liberalized Eastern Hemisphere quotas set by the Immigration and Naturalization Act took effect. Since 1975, the end of the war in Vietnam, waves of Southeast Asian refugees have landed via a series of parole authorizations granted by the U.S. attorney general. The number of Asian Americans has grown more than fivefold in 25 years, from 1.4 million in 1970 to 7.5 million by 1995, when Asian Americans constituted just over 3% of the total U.S. population (U.S. Bureau of the Census, 1993).

Asian Americans were much more heterogeneous than they had been in the past. The 1990 census counted 17 specified Asian groups as well as 8 Pacific Islander groups. Table 10.1 shows counts and proportions for the 11 largest groups in 1990 in comparison to their corresponding numbers a decade earlier. The relative proportions of ethnic groups under the API rubric also have changed. The Japanese American population had been augmented by only a handful of immigrants in the interval between census counts, so their relative proportion in the total API population has fallen. Chinese, Asian Indian, and Filipino Americans, on the other hand, had substantially increased their numbers and have become proportionally larger segments of the API population. Immigration has doubled the 1980 Korean American population, whereas Vietnamese have tripled their population during the interval. Percentage changes over time are difficult to estimate because earlier census counts did not include the same groups.

One implication of changing patterns of population growth is that to understand puzzling phenomena such as the disparity between verbal and quantitative

TABLE 10.1 Asian American Population Counts and Percentage Distributions, 1980 and 1990

| | 1990 | | 1980 | |
	Number	Percentage	Number	Percentage
Total	7,273,652	100.0	3,726,440	100.0
Chinese	1,645,472	22.6	812,178	21.8
Filipino	1,406,770	19.3	781,894	21.0
Japanese	847,562	11.7	716,331	19.2
Asian Indian	815,447	11.2	387,223	10.4
Korean	798,849	11.0	357,393	9.6
Vietnamese	614,547	8.4	245,025	6.6
Laotian	149,014	2.0	52,887	1.4
Cambodian	147,411	2.0	16,044	0.4
Samoan/				
Guamanian/Tongan	129,915	1.8	76,441	2.1
Thai	91,275	1.3	45,279	1.2
Parkistani	81,371	1.1	15,792	0.4
Other	546,021	7.5	219,953	5.9

SOURCES: U.S. Bureau of the Census (1991) and O'Hare and Felt (1991).

achievement, one must take into account substantial differences within some ethnic groups that included high proportions of newcomers. Students of the same ethnic groups presented different profiles of typical performance, with those of limited English proficiency (LEP) typically holding their own in quantitative tasks while having difficulties with verbal tasks. In addition to recency of migration, achievement differences between individuals, as well as within and among groups, should be considered in terms of disparities in educational experiences and socioeconomic background before and after their arrival in the United States. Educated, English-proficient immigrants, given preferential status for their professional or technical expertise, are more likely to adapt quickly to new living conditions and educational or occupational changes. Individuals and families from preliterate societies, who might have spent years in refugee camps, would need more time and greater effort before they could find their niche in American society. Diversity in national origin, ethnic identity, socioeconomic background, and experiences after arrival in the United States differentiated immigrants and refugees from each other and from native-born Asian Americans. Another myth holds that all API youths are model minority students. Let us examine the validity of this myth by looking at empirical data.

ACHIEVEMENT IN ELEMENTARY AND SECONDARY SCHOOLS

Information about the achievement of specific Asian American groups remains scarce. Small sample sizes and/or biased sampling procedures of some published studies diminish validity of findings. Therefore, results from such studies should be interpreted with caution. Validity coefficients of assessment instruments for measuring true developed abilities and achievement were not always available. Despite these limitations, there have been trends across a variety of assessment methods that have shown consistently strong performance in mathematics achievement and lower than average scores in language achievement tasks among Asian American students at elementary and secondary school levels.

The National Education Longitudinal Study of 8th Graders in 1988 (NELS:88) is the most recent national longitudinal study undertaken by the National Center for Education Statistics of the U.S. Department of Education. The base year survey in 1988 included achievement measures in four areas—reading and vocabulary, mathematics, science, and social studies—for a national representative sample of 8th graders. There also was a second-stage selection to obtain supplemental samples of Hispanic and Asian American students. Students judged by their schools to have had LEP were systematically eliminated from base year data collection, but subsequent follow-up surveys have included some LEP students. The base year sample of 1,500 Asian American 8th graders was large enough to permit some reporting of achievement scores by subgroups. Table 10.2 shows sample sizes and mean Achievement Test scores for nine Asian American groups and for their White, Black, and Hispanic peers. There were significant variations in mean Achievement Test scores by subgroups. Seven Asian subgroups' mean standard scores in reading were above the national average, and eight Asian subgroup means in mathematics were above the national average standard score. Pacific Islander pupils reported the lowest reading score among all racial/ethnic groups. This subgroup recorded low mathematics scores as well. Because LEP pupils were eliminated from the base year sample, the reported reading scores of those Asian subgroups with substantial proportions of newcomers who have acquired some knowledge of English would have been spuriously high if a truly representative sample had been included. Lumping Asian Americans together as a group, as most published reports have done, certainly masked problems and educational needs among some subgroups, particularly Southeast Asians and Pacific Islanders (Peng & Lee, 1991).

Continuing differences in achievement, particularly in reading, were observed among six Asian American groups during the second follow-up survey of NELS:88, conducted in 1992, when the students were in the 12th grade. The differences were associated with nativity and socioeconomic factors among 961 high school seniors identified as ethnically Chinese, Filipino, Korean, Southeast Asian, South Asian, or Japanese (Kim, 1997). Three out of four Southeast Asian and Chinese seniors were foreign born, compared to 71% of Filipino students who were native born. Native-born seniors recorded higher reading scores than did their foreign-born peers. The native-born students also reported more extracurricular activities and believed in efficacy of hard work. Their parents had more education and held higher status jobs than did parents of the foreign-born students. The parents of the native-born students had higher educational aspirations for, and discussed college plans more often with, their offsprings. Approximately 66% of foreign-born seniors recorded standardized mathematics scores above the 50th percentile

TABLE 10.2 Achievement Test Score of 1988 8th Graders, by Race/Ethnicity

Race/Ethnicity	Reading	Mathematics	Sample Size
Hispanic	46.01	45.70	3,170
Black	44.62	43.82	3,007
White	51.72	51.81	16,316
American Indian	44.33	44.67	299
Asian American	51.35	53.79	1,501
Chinese	52.19	56.72	309
Filipino	51.66	52.03	288
Japanese	52.75	56.33	92
Korean	55.06	58.24	187
Southeast Asian	49.42	52.56	240
Pacific Islander	42.86	44.91	99
South Asian	55.13	56.73	126
West Asian	53.15	56.38	33
Middle Eastern	51.36	54.06	42
Other	50.19	51.13	88

SOURCE: U.S. Department of Education (1988).
NOTE: The scores are standardized with a national mean of 50 and a standard deviation of 10. Southeast Asians included Vietnamese, Laotians, Cambodians, Thais, and so forth. Pacific Islanders included Samoans, Guamanians, and so forth. South Asians included Asian Indians, Pakistanis, Bangladeshis, Sri Lankans, and so forth. West Asians included Iranians, Afghans, Turks, and so forth. Middle Eastern included Iraqis, Israelis, Lebanese, and so forth.

of all NELS:88 students, compared to 65% of native-born Asian American seniors who did so. The foreign-born students spent more time on homework, reported better school attendance records, and believed that good luck was more important than hard work.

South Asian students, ethnically Indian and Pakistani, were most likely to be socioeconomically advantaged, with more educated parents and higher family incomes and occupational status. South Asian parents held higher educational aspirations for their offsprings and discussed grades and college plans with them more often. South Asian students recorded the highest reading scores, followed by Korean, Filipino, Chinese, Japanese, and Southeast Asian students. South Asian seniors also had the highest mathematics achievement scores, followed by Chinese, Korean, Japanese, Filipino, and Southeast Asian students. Southeast Asian students reported the lowest family socioeconomic indicators among all Asian groups. In 1990, the median family income among all Asian Americans was $41,251. Among Cambodian, Laotian, and Hmong families, median incomes were reported by the census as $18,126, $23,101, and $14,327, respectively.

NELS:88 follow-up data show that group differences in achievement observed in middle school continued through high school. These differences were associated with ethnicity and with generational and socioeconomic status.

National Assessment of Educational Progress (NAEP) is an ongoing survey of educational progress mandated by Congress. In the 1983-1984 and 1985-1986 periods, NAEP surveys that included language minority students were conducted by Educational Testing Service (Baratz-Snowden & Duran, 1987; Baratz-Snowden, Rock, Pollack, & Wilder, 1988). The 1983-1984 Reading Assessment used a stratified, three-stage sampling procedure to select nationally representative samples of schoolchildren in the 4th, 8th, and 11th grades. Less than 2% of the pupils tested at each grade were Asians. Testing was done with a balanced incomplete block design, and score analyses used item response theory to estimate reading proficiency levels. A common scale was developed across grades with a range of 0 to 500, a mean of 250, and a standard deviation of 50.

Data from the Reading Assessment were undermined by the same problem as was NELS:88. Pupils whose English language proficiency was judged inadequate were excluded from participating in the Reading Assessment test, resulting in elevated mean score reports for Asian Americans, whose proportion of LEP pupils was higher than those of all other groups. The proportions of LEP pupils excluded from the survey ranged from 11% to 13% of Asians sampled in each grade. Among Asian Americans who did participate in the NAEP assessment, proportions of language minority status ranged from 41% in the 4th grade to 48% in the 11th grade. Asian pupils who mostly spoke a non-English language at home, weighted to yield population estimates, were 56%, 51%, and 74% of all language minority Asian pupils in the 4th, 8th, and 11th grades, respectively. Policymakers who base their decisions on aggregated data of Asian American pupils might not have been informed about Asian subgroup differences or the fact that LEP pupils were excluded from baseline data altogether.

Mean reading scores by grade of White and Asian students, classified by language status, are shown in Table 10.3. Reading performance also was reported as percentage of students at or above anchor points designated in five categories: rudimentary, basic, intermediate, adept, and advanced. In the 4th grade, 30% of English-proficient API students and 25% of English-proficient White students read at or above the intermediate anchor point of 250. Among language minority students, 25% of Asians who spoke mostly English at home and 10% of their White peers performed at the intermediate level or above. Among those who did not speak English at home, 18% of Asian and 6% of White pupils read at the intermediate level or above. Reported percentages were possibly overestimated for Asian and White language minority students because students with limited English were excluded.

In the 8th grade, 24% of Asian and 16% of White English-speaking pupils read at or above the adept level. In addition, 14% of Asian and 9% of White language minority pupils read at the adept level. Among students who spoke another language besides English at home, 7% of White and 6% of Asian pupils read at the adept level. In the 11th grade, 56% of English-speaking Asian students and 47% of White students were classified as adept readers, whereas 13% of Asian and 7% of White students were classified as advanced readers. Among language minority students, about one out of four White students, as well as Asian students, who spoke mostly English at home had attained adept or advanced reading levels. Among those who spoke another language at home, 22% of White and 17% of Asian pupils were adept or advanced readers. After controlling for background and process variables, Asian language minority students in the 4th and 8th grades were reported to read significantly better than language minority pupils from other groups (Baratz-Snowden & Duran, 1987).

TABLE 10.3 Mean Reading Scale Scores and Percentages of Pupils at Specified Reading Proficiency Levels of White and Asian Pupils by Grade and Language Status

	EP		LM		LM:SHL		LM:SE	
	n	Mean	*n*	Mean	*n*	Mean	*n*	Mean
4th grade								
White	11,214	226 (1.0)	442	204 (3.7)	218	198 (3.8)	217	210 (4.6)
Asian	175	227 (2.3)	217	226 (4.1)	122	221 (6.5)	92	233 (4.4)
8th grade								
White	12,494	267 (0.7)	316	251 (2.6)	150	249 (3.7)	163	254 (3.5)
Asian	171	270 (2.8)	181	268 (4.8)	98	256 (6.4)	83	281 (4.3)
11th grade								
White	13,511	296 (0.9)	277	274 (2.9)	144	271 (4.5)	125	280 (4.7)
Asian	233	305 (2.3)	213	269 (5.1)	152	262 (5.5)	56	291 (6.3)

		% Reading Proficiency				
		Rudimentary	Basic	Intermediate	Adept	Advanced
4th grade						
EP	White	98.5	76.2	25.1	1.6	—
	Asian	96.5	74.4	29.9	3.4	—
LM	White	93.2	53.8	10.4	0.2	—
	Asian	98.6	75.3	24.7	2.7	—
LM:SHL	White	91.1	46.4	6.2	—	—
	Asian	97.4	70.5	18.4	2.2	—
8th grade						
EP	White	100.0	97.4	70.1	15.5	0.3
	Asian	100.0	97.8	72.2	20.4	1.4
LM	White	99.6	90.5	53.9	8.6	—
	Asian	100.0	96.6	71.7	14.3	0.8
LM:SHL	White	100.0	90.2	51.1	6.6	—
	Asian	100.0	94.4	56.1	6.3	—
11th grade						
EP	White	100.0	99.4	89.3	47.0	6.5
	Asian	100.0	99.1	93.5	55.6	13.2
LM	White	100.0	96.3	75.5	21.9	2.9
	Asian	100.0	96.4	66.4	21.6	2.6
LM:SHL	White	100.0	96.2	73.5	20.5	1.9
	Asian	100.0	95.96	1.41	6.5	0.5

SOURCE: Baratz-Snowden and Duran (1987).
NOTE: Reading scale scores range from 0 to 500, with a mean of 250 and a standard deviation of 50. Standard errors are in parentheses. Proficiency levels are as follows: rudimentary, 150; basic, 200; intermediate, 250; adept, 300; and advanced, 350. EP = English proficient (pupils from homes where only English is spoken or where English is dominant); LM = language minority (pupils from homes where most people speak languages other than English); LM:SHL = speaks home language (language minority pupils who speak mostly in languages other than English at home); LM:SE = speaks English (language minority pupils who speak mostly English at home).

In the period 1985-1986, NAEP conducted a special survey of reading and mathematics performance of language minority Asian and Hispanic pupils in the 3rd, 7th, and 11th grades. On the whole, Asian students reported higher grades than did their Hispanic peers after controlling for background, language use, school attitudes, and school characteristics. Asian American pupils received higher grades even when they performed at lower levels than some of their Hispanic classmates on assessment exercises, as they did in reading in the 3rd and 11th grades. Variables that explained the largest proportion of the differential in favor of Asian pupils included the following: having positive attitudes toward school, doing more homework, and taking more demanding courses (Baratz-Snowden et al., 1988).

A districtwide study of Southeast Asian pupils in San Diego schools also found higher grade point averages (GPAs) but lower Achievement Test scores among Asian pupils than among their White classmates. Vietnamese and ethnic Chinese pupils reported the highest GPAs, Hmong GPAs were slightly higher than those of White students, and Laotian and Cambodian pupils typically recorded grades at or below those of their White peers. In the 11th and 12th grades, reading test scores of Southeast Asian students were lower than all other group means except those of Samoans. Southeast Asian mathematics scores also were lower than those of their White classmates despite the fact that LEP pupils were not included in citywide testing programs. Higher grades coupled with lower Achievement Test scores support the hypothesis that teachers might have given greater weight to criteria other than grasp of subject matter.

Average proficiency in algebra and functions was reported for 8th-grade pupils from the 1990 NAEP assessment program (Mullis, Dossey, Owen, & Phillips, 1991). Relatively higher proportions of API pupils enrolled in 8th-grade mathematics, pre-algebra, or algebra than did their White, Black, or Hispanic classmates. Their average proficiency was consistently higher than that of their peers. In the 12th grade, proportions of all students who took algebra II, algebra III, or calculus were 1.3%, 0.7%, and 0.4%, respectively. Among Asians, the corresponding percentages were 4.7%, 3.6%, and 3.2%. Reports of higher mathematics achievement among API students in comparison to their White peers held true even when the former came from socioeconomically disadvantaged refugee families (Caplan, Whitmore, Bui, & Trautman, 1985).

In summary, findings from a current national representative longitudinal study (NELS:88) from cross-sectional studies such as the periodic NAEP reports, and from school district or special population studies, such as those of pupils in San Diego schools and of children from Southeast Asian refugee families, were consistent in their reports that most API students recorded higher mathematics performance at all grade levels than did their peers. Higher API achievement was related to completing more course work and taking more demanding courses in mathematics.

In language arts, API pupils presented more complex patterns of performance. LEP pupils were excluded from most assessment programs, and API students were more likely to have been classified as LEP than were students from other groups. Therefore, average Asian reading test scores were likely to have been higher than they would have been if all enrolled API pupils had been included. In elementary and middle schools, English-proficient API pupils did better than their peers, language minority Asian pupils who spoke mostly English at home performed as well as or better than their classmates, but language minority Asian pupils who did not speak English at home did less well. Nevertheless, teachers assigned higher grades in language arts to their Asian pupils, even when those pupils' test scores were lower than those of their peers. API pupils reported that they did more homework and held more positive attitudes toward school than did their classmates, and these behavioral factors might have influenced their teachers' grading despite some Asian groups' lower performances when assessed by objective measures.

Staying in school is another criterion of pupil performance. Differential high school dropout rates have not always been taken into account in examining achievement among groups. The loss of data from student who dropped out because of inadequate prior schooling, LEP, or other social and economic handicaps could have spuriously elevated average achievement scores. Several school districts with high proportions of Southeast Asian refugees have reported rising dropout rates among API students. Boston Public Schools reported that dropout rates among Cambodian and Laotian students had more than doubled during the 1980s. Dropout rates of these two groups were rising faster than any other groups of students in Boston (Boston Public Schools, Office of Research and Development, 1986). Similar retention data have been reported among Hmong pupils in the Midwest (Podeschi, 1987). The 1980 census reported that 22% of Hmong and 31% of Laotians had graduated from high school compared to 67% of all U.S. citizens. Family values and parents' educational levels could have been factors in making high school persistence decisions.

The studies cited heretofore suggest that achievement differences reported among Asian subgroups might have been associated with differences in recency of migration as well as pre- and postmigration learning experiences. Furthermore, contrary to academic achievement measured by objective tests, Asian American pupils from all groups, including LEP pupils, typically received higher grades from their teachers than did classmates of all other racial, ethnic, and linguistic groups in language-related subjects as well as in mathematics. Reasons for teachers' favorable assessment of Asian Americans' ability to communicate in English, unsupported by objective measures of the latter's grasp of rules for standard written English or their writing samples, have not yet been investigated. Although effort might count in teacher evaluation of language arts performance, a "halo effect" from arithmetic performance—unwarranted, positive academic stereotyping of Asian pupils—cannot be ruled out as a reason for inflated grades from teachers.

HIGH SCHOOL GRADUATION AND COLLEGE ADMISSIONS TEST SCORES

The second follow-up survey of the NELS:88 cohort reported that about 9% of students who began 8th grade in 1988 had dropped out of school. Asian Americans constituted 2% of all dropouts and 4% of the cohort who had graduated from high school in 1992 (Policy Information Center, 1995). Greater numbers of Asian Americans have been graduating from high school each year, in keeping with Asian population growth. In the 1985-1986 period, there were 62,000 Asian American public high school graduates, and 36,700 of those were from western states. By 1995, total Asian public high school graduates approached 98,000, with 55,400 from the West.

Proportionally more Asian American high school graduates continued on to college. Two thirds of Asian American high school seniors took the Scholastic Aptitude Test (SAT) each year. More APIs also were sitting for the American College Test (ACT) in addition to or instead of the SAT. Academic qualifications and admissions test trends of Asian American applicants to colleges and universities have been reviewed elsewhere (Hsia, 1988). During the 1980s, public and private institutions, state departments that serve substantial Asian populations, and the U.S. Department of Education undertook a variety of studies on API qualifications for college and access to institutions of higher learning. A number of institutional and system studies were initiated by API students and communities. Other studies were undertaken by selective institutions in the spirit of self-examination. Some institutional studies began in response to charges by Asian students and their communities that there were growing restrictions that denied qualified applicants access to certain highly selective schools (Nakanishi, 1989).

It is reasonable to conjecture that recent rapid demographic changes could have been accompanied by changes in qualifications of typical college-bound Asian Americans, so let us examine score trends among college-bound Asian Americans in the 1990s. Tables 10.4 through 10.7 summarize Asian American and White performance on tests widely used to assist admissions officials in making admissions decisions.

Table 10.4 shows that White and Asian American males obtained higher mean scores than did females in Preliminary Scholastic Aptitude Tests/National Merit Scholarship Qualifying Tests (PSAT/NMSQT). Such gender-related phenomena, studied and reported extensively during the 1970s and 1980s, were found to be related to choice of high school courses. In addition, a higher proportion of young women chose to go straight on to college from high school, so that female test takers were a less select group than were males. Asian Americans typically scored slightly lower, about one fifth of a standard deviation, than did Whites in the verbal section. Asian American means were about one third of a standard deviation higher than White means in the mathematics section of the assessment program. The reported statistics were based on the entire population of test takers, not a random sample of the total, where statistical significance must be taken into account. Consistency of group performance patterns over time support the notion that differences were real.

Table 10.5 shows typical SAT performance of college-bound high school seniors by gender and ethnicity in 1990. Self-reported English-language status of White and API seniors showed that 94% of White students' first language was

TABLE 10.4 Average Preliminary Scholastic Aptitude Test/National Merit Scholarship Qualifying Test Verbal and Mathematical Scores of Asian American and White College-Bound High School Juniors, 1990-1991

| | Asian American | | | White | | |
	Male	Female	Total	Male	Female	Total
n	31,846	33,734	65,599	375,283	453,087	828,726
Verbal						
Mean	40.1	39.1	39.6	42.4	41.3	41.8
SD	12.2	12.0	12.1	10.0	9.7	9.8
Mathematical						
Mean	51.7	47.6	49.6	48.3	44.1	46.0
SD	12.8	12.0	12.6	11.4	10.2	11.0

SOURCE: College Board (1991).

English compared to 30% of Asian Americans. Their test results were similar to PSAT/NMSQT scores already described, with White students showing a modest advantage in verbal tasks and Asian American students doing somewhat better in mathematical tasks.

College Board's Admissions Testing Program (ATP) instruments have been modified during the 1990s. Wording of the Student Descriptive Questionnaire (SDQ) items addressing language proficiency was changed in 1990. Students were asked whether English was their *first* language instead of their *best* language. As a result, subsequent student response trends could not be validly compared to

TABLE 10.5 Average SAT Scores and First Languages of Asian American and White College-Bound Seniors, 1990

| | Asian American | | | White | | |
	Male	Female	Total	Male	Female	Total
n	38,686	37,814	76,500	346,226	383,019	729,245
First language (percentage)						
English			30			94
English and other			27			4
Other			43			2
SAT verbal score						
Mean	413	406	410	447	438	442
SD	132	130	131	106	102	104
SAT mathematical score						
Mean	549	506	528	515	469	491
SD	132	128	132	119	110	117
Test of standard written English score						
Mean	39.3	40.6	39.9	43.7	45.3	44.6
SD	12.0	12.0	12.0	10.2	9.7	10.0

SOURCE: College Board (1990-1991).
NOTE: SAT = Scholastic Aptitude Test.

TABLE 10.6 Average SAT I Scores of College-Bound Seniors, 1995

	n	Percentage of Total	Verbal Mean	Mathematical Mean
American Indian	8,936	1	403	447
Asian/Pacific American	81,514	8	418	538
African American	103,872	11	356	388
Hispanic				
Mexican American	36,323	4	376	426
Puerto Rican	13,056	1	372	411
Other Hispanic	30,713	3	389	438
White	674,343	69	448	498
Other	25,113	3	432	486
Nonrespondents	94,123			

SOURCE: College Board (1995).

data from before 1990. SAT tests also have been altered. Since 1995, SAT scores have been based on the revised SAT I. The result was that, nationwide, more than half of all high schools experienced 1-year changes of school means of at least 10 points. In 1996, a change in score scale was introduced. Differences among groups in patterns of performance remained, as shown in Table 10.6. In 1994, the API mean mathematics score of 535 was higher than the White mean score of 495. The Asian mean verbal score was 416, lower than the White mean score of 443.

Delivery systems also were evolving, as automated computer testing and scoring gradually were replacing paper-and-pencil tests. ATP instrument changes were based on substantial bodies of program research and test theory. Nevertheless, the consequences of these changes were that cross-year comparisons no longer can be made with confidence either for the college-bound population as a whole or specific subgroups such as Asian Americans. Relative rankings of group performance on SAT I, however, remained the same as those of SAT. The 1996 SAT I mean verbal and mathematical scores of 505 and 508, respectively, were recorded for all college-bound seniors. The corresponding Asian American mean scores of 496 and 558 continued to show a pattern of slightly lower than average verbal scores and higher mathematical scores.

The 1995 ACT results for juniors and seniors who participated in the American College Testing Program during the 1994-1995 academic year, detailed in Table 10.7, showed patterns similar to those of ATP participants. Students who enrolled in college-preparatory core programs typically scored at higher levels than did their peers who signed up for fewer academic courses. More than two thirds of API participants of ACT had enrolled in core programs in high school compared to 6 out of 10 of their Caucasian peers and lower proportions among other minority classmates. Asian Americans scored higher than all other groups in mathematics and scored lower than their White peers in English and reading. The composite scores of White and Asian American students were virtually the same. Asian composite scores in 1991 and 1995 both were 21.5, whereas the

TABLE 10.7 Average American College Test Assessment Scores of 1995 High School Graduates

	African American	American Indian	Asian American	Mexican American	Puerto Rican	White
n	89,155	11,361	27,784	24,431	24,054	650,664
English	16.4	17.7	20.2	17.6	17.8	21.0
Mathematics	16.8	18.1	22.8	18.6	18.7	20.7
Reading	17.1	19.1	21.3	18.8	18.9	22.1
Science and reasoning	17.4	19.1	21.5	19.0	19.1	21.6
Composite	17.1	18.6	21.6	18.6	18.7	21.5

SOURCE: American College Testing Program (1995).

White composite score in 1995 was 21.5 and in 1991 was 21.3. English, reading, and science and reasoning are assessment exercises with substantial verbal components, which were more challenging for students whose best language was not English (American College Testing Program, 1995).

Data from national assessment programs of the ATP and ACT already described consistently recorded relative strength of Asian American high school students in measures of their developed mathematical abilities, accompanied by lower than typical White performance in verbal tests. These observations can be explained in large part by choice of courses during high school. Asian American students devoted greater amounts of time to mathematics classes, shown by self-reports of curricular choices. Asian Americans were more likely to report LEP related to home language use. Asian Americans also were more likely than their White classmates to be assigned to English as a Second Language classes rather than regular or honors English.

When test results have so consistently shown Asian Americans to do better than average in quantitative tasks and below average in verbal tasks, it is reasonable that questions about the validity of standardized testing programs to measure Asian American academic achievement have been raised by members of various Asian communities. Were assessments of communicative skills somehow systematically biased against Asians, whereas mathematics tests measured their true developed abilities?

Test scores have, in fact, been shown in reliability and validity studies to have been biased in favor of, or against, Asian American test takers in unexpected directions, particularly among those with LEP (Bleistein & Wright, 1985; Kulick & Dorans, 1983; Petersen & Livingston, 1982). The lower than average scores recorded by Asian American test takers in multiple-choice, objective English tests had, in fact, overestimated their performance in actual writing tasks such as composing essays. Compared to Whites and other minority peers, Asian American writing samples were less competent than would have been predicted from their test scores. If teacher grades were entered into the regression equation, the results would have been even greater overprediction of essay quality.

Although multiple-choice, standardized group-administered and machine-scored tests of standard written English have consistency overpredicted API performance in essay writing, Asian American students themselves were realistic about their own linguistic capabilities. They were more likely than their classmates to have rated themselves as low in writing and speaking skills in the Student Descriptive Questionnaire.

As for the higher than average mathematical test scores reported among APIs, particularly those of newcomers from East and South Asian nations that have dominated the top tier of international mathematics assessment programs, the typically above average test scores were, in fact, understating their true developed mathematical reasoning abilities. Validity studies using diverse methods and criteria have demonstrated that API test takers had trouble with story problems where difficulties with reading English slowed them down. Purely mathematical reasoning problems, on the other hand, were not speeded tests for APIs. Overprediction of college-level writing tasks by objective English usage tests and high school grades and underprediction of developed mathematical abilities by quantitative problems stated in English hold significant policy implications. Stronger preparation in communicative skills is needed by Asian newcomers if they are to realize their full potential. Their strengths in mathematics, engineering, and physical sciences, on the other hand, are likely to remain underestimated and therefore underutilized.

Sue and Abe (1988) examined high school grades, SAT scores, and Achievement Test scores as predictors of success, as measured by freshman-year GPAs. Participants were 4,113 API and 1,000 randomly selected White freshmen enrolled at eight University of California campuses in the fall of 1984. One third of the APIs reported that English was not their best language. Their numbers permitted analyses by subgroups—Chinese, Filipino, Japanese, Korean, other Asian American, and East Indian/Pakistani. The mean freshman undergraduate grade point averages (UGPAs) of APIs and White students were 2.74 and 2.75, respectively. For all APIs, three predictor variables—*HSGPA* (high school GPA), *SAT-V* (SAT-verbal), and *SAT-M* (SAT-mathematics)—yielded a multiple R of .498 with UGPA, higher than the White multiple R of .451. For Asian Americans, *SAT-M* contributed 36% and *SAT-V* contributed 3% to the prediction of college grades. For White freshmen, *SAT-V* contributed 32% and *SAT-M* contributed 3%. The multiple R of .545 among East Indians/Pakistanis was highest, and those of Koreans and Filipinos were lowest at .408 and .391, respectively. Similar results were found when Achievement Test scores were used as predictors instead of SAT scores. The multiple R for English best language APIs was .505 and for English not best language students was .490. Although *SAT-M* was superior to *SAT-V* as a predictor among both groups, the difference was not large for English best language APIs. If White regression equations were applied to APIs, then there would have been serious underprediction of UGPA for Chinese, other Asian, and English not best language students. On the other hand, Japanese, Filipino, and

English best language API students' UGPAs would have been overpredicted with the White students' regression equation.

HIGH SCHOOL CURRICULAR AND EXTRACURRICULAR ACHIEVEMENTS

Proportionately more Asian American high school students than their classmates fulfilled core academic requirements for college admissions, according to self-reports from ATP and ACT of 1990 and 1991, respectively. These and other surveys, including the National Longitudinal Study of the High School Class of 1972 (NLS-72), High School and Beyond (HS&B), and NELS:88, have recorded that Asian American students completed more advanced courses in mathematics and other quantitative subjects and earned higher high school GPAs. They also reported longer hours of homework and lower rates of absenteeism. APIs learned more between their sophomore and senior years, according to objective measures, and stayed the course to graduation (Peng, Owings, & Fetters, 1984; Rock, Ekstrome, Goertz, & Pollack, 1985). Asian Americans were three times as likely as their classmates to enroll in advanced placement programs to earn college credits during high school (Rothman, 1986).

As for extracurricular activities, APIs were less likely than their classmates to hold part-time jobs after school. Sports, the most popular choice of their peers, were less often chosen by Asian American students. API extracurricular participation was more likely to center on special academic interest clubs (e.g., science, classical music) and social, ethnic, or community organizations (Peng et al., 1984, Ramist & Arbeiter, 1986).

Apart from grades and rank in class, relatively more Asian American high school students than their peers reported having received honors and awards in academics and performing arts. Students from immigrant families garnered honors, particularly in areas that did not demand superb communicative skills. The Westinghouse Science Talent Search and the Arts Recognition and Talent Search reward excellence in science or mathematics research and in performing arts, respectively. Higher than expected numbers of Asian American students have been recognized by these programs. Perfect command of English is not a prerequisite for success in either of these awards. There were, in fact, high proportions of first- and second-generation Asian Americans among honorees and winners. National Merit honors and awards, on the other hand, use scores of PSAT/NMSQT as criteria. The verbal score (V) is given more weight than the mathematical score (M) in the selection process by using the formula $2V + M$. Among Asian American PSAT/NMSQT participants, 1 out of 10 have been recognized as semifinalists, finalists, or winners, but the proportion would have been even higher if the verbal and mathematical scores had been given equal weight in award decisions (Hsia, 1988).

TABLE 10.8 Average GRE General Test Scores and Language Proficiency of Asian American, White, and Total U.S. Citizen Examinees, 1987-1988

	Asian American	White	Total
n	6,133	173,674	203,084
Percentage of total	3	86	100
GRE scores			
Verbal mean	480	520	508
SD	127	108	114
Quantitative mean	612	546	536
SD	131	128	134
Analytic mean	539	557	543
SD	134	118	125
English best language[a]	80	99	97

SOURCE: Wah and Robinson (1990).
NOTE: GRE = Graduate Record Examination.
a. These data are from 1986-1987.

GRADUATE AND PROFESSIONAL SCHOOLS ADMISSIONS

The pattern of relatively higher performance by Asian Americans in quantitative areas of study and lower performance than White peers in verbal areas among the college-bound also was observed in graduate and professional school admissions test takers. Tables 10.8 through 10.14 show recent Asian American mean test scores and reported standard deviations of Graduate Record Examination (GRE), Graduate Management Aptitude Test (GMAT), Law School Aptitude Test (LSAT), and Medical College Aptitude Test (MCAT) programs for graduate, graduate management, law, and medical schools, respectively. Admissions test scores and undergraduate records, in combination with essays and interviews, remain widely used criteria for admissions decisions.

Asian American mean GRE scores from 1976 through 1983 showed a continuous trend of increasing GRE-Q (quantitative) scores and decreasing GRE-V (verbal) scores, whereas White mean scores remained stable. These score trends were very likely associated with the changing Asian demographics during this period, with growing proportions of students from immigrant and refugee families (Hsia, 1988). Asian Americans constituted 3% of GRE candidates in the 1987-1988 period, as shown in Table 10.8. Results included GRE-V, GRE-Q, and GRE-A (analytical) scores. Asian American GRE-V, GRE-Q, and GRE-A mean scores were 480, 612, and 539, respectively, compared to corresponding White means of 520, 546, and 557. Asian Americans typically found quantitative items to be easier and verbally loaded items harder in the analytic section of GRE (Wah & Robinson, 1990).

A more meaningful way of looking at GRE scores is by graduate field of study choices among test takers. For the period 1991-1992, mean scores of Asian American, White, and total male and female GRE candidates by fields of planned study, as shown in Table 10.9, supported the notion that informed choices for

TABLE 10.9 Mean Graduate Record Examination Scores of Asian American, White, and Total Examinees Planning Graduate Work by Fields of Study, 1991-1992

Area of Study	Asian American Male	Asian American Female	White Male	White Female	Total Male	Total Female
Arts and humanities						
Number of examinees	233	396	11,199	13,643	12,618	15,608
Mean verbal	591	546	578	565	573	557
Mean quantitative	603	562	554	511	550	506
Mean analytic	586	561	578	575	571	566
Physical sciences, mathematics, and computer sciences						
Number of examinees	433	216	7,144	3,052	8,286	3,728
Mean verbal	476	468	561	543	549	524
Mean quantitative	684	656	688	654	680	640
Mean analytic	555	558	632	638	619	515
Social sciences						
Number of examinees	389	739	12,928	22,340	15,278	26,569
Mean verbal	530	521	540	519	532	510
Mean quantitative	609	563	567	517	557	508
Mean analytic	561	563	569	564	558	552

SOURCE: Grandy (1994).

graduate fields were made based not only on undergraduate majors but also on candidates' self-assessments of their developed academic strengths and weaknesses. Students who planned graduate studies in the physical sciences, mathematics, or computer science typically scored the highest GRE-Q scores. Arts and humanities students had higher GRE-V scores. Social science students reported GRE-V, GRE-Q, and GRE-A scores in the same ranges (Grandy, 1994). Gender differences of total, White, and Asian American students were in similar directions. Highest mean GRE-Q scores were recorded among Asian American males who planned graduate studies in physical sciences, mathematics, or computer science. Highest GRE-V scores were recorded among Asian American males who planned to concentrate on arts and humanities. White and Asian American scores in GRE-V, GRE-Q, and GRE-A were very similar among those who planned to study social sciences. These scores suggest that relatively greater proportions of Asian Americans who planned graduate studies in quantitative fields were from newcomer families, whereas those who planned to concentrate on arts and humanities or social sciences were English-fluent second- or later-generation Americans.

GMAT scores are required by most graduate schools of management for admissions decisions. In the 1990-1991 period, 4.6% of GMAT takers identified themselves as Asian Americans. Table 10.10 shows that the Asian American mean total score was 499 compared to the White mean total score of 512 (Graduate Management Admissions Council, 1992). By the 1992-1993 period, Asian Americans had risen to 7.6% of all test takers with a mean score of 507 compared to a White mean score of 517 (Barton & Lapointe, 1995).

TABLE 10.10 Average Graduate Management Aptitude Test Scores of Asian American, White, and Total Applicants to Graduate Schools of Management, 1990-1991

	Asian American	White	Total
n	6,934	125,888	240,869
Percentage of applicants	4.6	83.8	100.0
Mean score	499	512	494

SOURCE: Graduate Management Admissions Council (1992).

LSAT scores are used by law schools as one criterion for student selection. In 1989, LSAT scores were reported for 1,687 Asian American law school applicants. They constituted 4.2% of all applicants that year. As shown in Tables 10.11 and 10.12, the Asian American mean score of 32.16 was close to the White mean score of 33.33 (Wightman & Muller, 1990). In June 1991, the LSAT format was changed. The test included four section scores with logical reasoning items constituting one third to one half of the total and required a writing sample. By 1995, Asian American law school applicants had tripled their numbers to 5,402, or 6.4% of the total. The LSAT introduced a new score scale of 120 to 180 with mean of 150 and standard deviation of 10. The Asian American mean of 152 was the same as the total applicant mean and was very close to the White mean of 154. The LSAT mean of Asian Americans who were admitted to at least one American Bar Association-approved law school was 156, with 156 being the mean of all admissions and 157 the mean of White admissions. Asian Americans constituted 6.5% of all admissions and 6.2% of 1995 law school matriculants (personal communication, LSAC Research Department personnel, 1996). As in the case of graduate school applicants, self-selection was evident among Asian American applicants and their White and other minority peers. Few API college graduates of LEP would aspire to the law, which values eloquence.

MCAT scores are used by most medical schools as criteria for admissions. Table 10.13 shows that in 1990, more than 4,000 Asian Americans took the MCAT. They comprised 15% of all MCAT registrants. Asian Americans scored higher than White test takers, as well as all test takers, in four out of six areas: biology, chemistry, physics, and science problems. The mean reading and quantitative

TABLE 10.11 Comparison of LSAT Performance Among Selected Subgroups of Test Takers in September 1989

Subgroup	n	Percentage	LSAT mean	LSAT SD
Asian/Pacific Islander	1,687	4.2	32.1	68.74
Black/African American	2,183	5.5	24.11	8.44
Caucasian/White	31,539	78.8	33.33	7.54
Hispanic	866	2.2	28.68	8.68
Puerto Rican	241	0.6	25.68	9.73
Mexican American	445	1.1	27.89	8.56

SOURCE: Wightman and Muller (1990).
NOTE: LSAT = Law School Aptitude Test.

TABLE 10.12 Means and Standard Deviations of Law School Aptitude Test Section Scores of Asian American and White Test Takers, September 1989

	Analytic Reasoning	Reading Comprehension	Logical Reasoning
Asian/Pacific Islander (n = 1,687)			
Mean	18.83	19.78	20.98
SD	5.63	5.3	15.54
Caucasian/White (n = 31,539)			
Mean	18.45	20.66	22.34
SD	5.38	4.82	4.79
Percentage of Asian scores >			
Caucasian median score	54.03	45.64	42.70

SOURCE: Wightman and Muller (1990).

skills analysis scores of Asian Americans were lower than those of Whites and of all test takers (Association of American Medical Colleges [AAMC], 1992). This pattern was similar to Asian American performance on the MCAT a decade earlier, when their numbers were about one half of those in 1990. Medicine remains the top professional choice of Asian American college graduates. A much higher proportion of APIs had fulfilled requirements for admission to medical schools in comparison to their peers. In 1985, APIs constituted 8.2% of all medical college applicants. By 1995, they comprised less than 5% of new college graduates but 20.7% of medical school applicants (AAMC, 1996).

TABLE 10.13 Average Medical College Aptitude Test Area Scores of Asian American, White, and Total American Medical School Applicants, 1990

	Asian American	White	Total
n	4,345	19,871	29,243
Percentage	14.9	68.0	100.0
Area scores			
Biology			
Mean	8.38	8.18	7.94
SD	2.42	2.33	2.45
Chemistry			
Mean	8.51	7.70	7.60
SD	2.44	2.32	2.40
Physics			
Mean	8.51	7.81	7.64
SD	2.50	2.36	2.47
Science problems			
Mean	8.31	7.78	7.59
SD	2.44	2.30	2.39
Skills analysis			
Reading			
Mean	7.0	7.96	7.41
SD	2.59	2.19	2.51
Quantitative			
Mean	7.37	7.70	7.26
SD	2.46	2.28	2.46

SOURCE: Smith and van der Veen (1991).

Despite completion of more medial college admissions prerequisites, higher than average UGPAs, and competitive MCAT scores, 1994 API acceptance rates were lowest among all groups in 1994, as shown in the following table:

	Percentage Applicants	Percentage Matriculants
Asian Americans	18.4	16.4
Blacks	7.9	8.2
Other underrepresented minorities	3.1	4.3
Other Hispanics	3.0	3.0
Whites	62.9	63.7

Nevertheless, APIs comprised 14.4% of total U.S. medical school enrollment by 1991 (Smith & van der Veen, 1991) and 18.2% by 1995, after the MCAT format had been revised to emphasize communicative skills (AAMC, 1996). Beginning with the 1992 academic year, the MCAT format was changed to place more emphasis on verbal reasoning and writing skills. Two essays were required. The AAMC reporting format of the MCAT and medical school enrollment data also changed. Bar and pie charts replaced tables (AAMC, 1996). Although graphics are more intuitively readable than tables, they did not provide fine details. AAMC research and assessment staff have published few numbers. The graphs showed slightly wider variations among API applicants' performance in comparison to their White peers, but central tendencies of Whites and APIs were close. Mean 1995 verbal reasoning scores of Asian and White applicants were 9.55 and 9.85, respectively, with the median of both groups being 10.00. The mean UGPAs of Asians and Whites were 3.59 and 3.56, respectively (AAMC, personal communication from Danielle Masters, September 11, 1996). These patterns were similar to data of these groups before 1992.

Like law school applicants, medical school applicants are a self-selected, academically elite group. Profiles of all applicant groups are similar, and those of matriculants are more alike still. In 1994, mean science UGPAs of Asian applicants and matriculants were 3.28 and 3.56, respectively. Corresponding White means were 3.29 and 3.54. The matriculant mean science UGPAs of underrepresented groups ranged from 2.95 to 3.22. Overall UGPAs of API and White applicants were 3.35 and 3.36, respectively; for matriculants, the corresponding UGPAs were 3.59 and 3.56.

Verbal reasoning scores of API and White applicants were 8 and 9, respectively; among matriculants, both Asians and Whites scored 10. API applicants had to perform as well as or better than White peers to be accepted by at least one AAMC member college. By 1995, Asian and White students comprised 20.7% and 62.9%, respectively, of all medical school applicants. Asian and White matriculants comprised 18.2% and 64.9%, respectively, of the total.

The distribution of Asian American medical school matriculants has changed because verbal reasoning and writing skills are given greater weight in the MCAT. By 1994, Asian Indian/Pakistani was the largest subgroup among Asian American matriculants, whereas Southeast Asians was the smallest subgroup (AAMC, 1994). Demographically, Asian Indians and Pakistanis together constitute a substantially smaller group than do Chinese or Filipino Americans. NELS:88 baseline data had shown that South Asian families were the best educated and held the highest-status jobs among all Asian American groups. Not only had English been an official language during the British raj, but Indo-European languages, which include English and South Asian languages based on Sanskrit, share common linguistic roots. Asian Indian and Pakistani, even recent brain drain immigrants, were more likely to do better than other Asian groups in English assessment exercises. Southeast Asian applicants to medical schools, by contrast, were most likely to have been recent arrivals, mostly from refugee families, some from preliterate communities. As a group, they were least likely to do well in tests of English language skills. Changes in the MCAT that emphasized communicative skills have resulted not only in the plateauing of API matriculants after a decade of growth but also in skewing admissions decisions in favor of South Asians and against recent arrivals including Southeast Asian applicants.

HIGHER EDUCATION ENROLLMENT

In spite of growing numbers of Asian Americans, especially new immigrants, who manifested inadequate preparation in communicative skills, overall Asian American achievement in higher education has remained above average in terms of enrollment, persistence, and degree attainment. In the decade between 1984 and 1994, Asian American enrollment in all higher education institutions had almost doubled, from 390,000 to 774,000. Their numbers have more than doubled in 4-year institutions, from 223,000 to 462,000. By 1994, API enrollment in public and private institutions had reached 622,000 and 152,000, respectively. There were 674,000 API undergraduates, 73,000 graduate students, and 28,000 professional school students. Carter and Wilson (1996) predicted slowing down of the rapid rate of growth seen during the 1980s, but API enrollment has continued to increase in line with demographic trends. More Asian American women are continuing on to tertiary educations. Their numbers grew by 40% between 1990 and 1994, whereas the men's numbers grew by 30%.

The Longitudinal Studies Program of the National Center for Education Statistics of the Department of Education has undertaken three studies: NLS-72, HS&B, and NELS:88. The goal of each study was to collect long-term information about educational opportunity and its long-term effects on individual growth in terms of education and careers.

NLS-72 sampled small numbers of APIs, and higher education enrollment analyses for NELS:88 Asian American students are not yet available at this time.

Higher education enrollment data were available for the 420 Asian American high school seniors and their peers who took part in HS&B. Virtually all Asian American participants obtained high school diplomas. Overall, more than 36% of study participants did not continue beyond high school. Among Asian Americans, only 12% of participants failed to enroll in some type of postsecondary education during the following 4 years. A majority of HS&B Asian Americans chose to attend public institutions, 22% chose 2-year institutions, and 33% chose 4-year colleges and universities. About 12% began postsecondary schooling part-time (Owings, 1987).

Cross-sectional data confirmed findings from longitudinal studies. API enrollment in higher education institutions grew along with demographic growth. Between 1984 and 1994, Asian American enrollment at colleges and universities rose from 3.2% to 6.8% of all college students. Between 1993 and 1994, Asian American enrollment as undergraduates rose by 6.2%. API enrollment in graduate and professional institutions rose by 11.2% and 10.4%, respectively (Carter & Wilson, 1996).

Most Asian Americans live in metropolitan centers. More than half of Asian Americans graduated from high schools in the West. Of the 50 states, 9 reported more than 10,000 API students enrolled in higher education institutions by the fall of 1988. California headed the list, with more than 200,000 API students, followed by New York, Hawaii, Illinois, Texas, Massachusetts, Washington, New Jersey, and Pennsylvania (with 11,000).

The large pool of qualified Asian American aspirants to higher education has pressed the capacity of some institutions and departments to respond. Highly selective public and private institutions on both coasts, in particular, have been targeted by more applicants than expected. Among the growing number of new-comers with high aspirations, well-developed quantitative skills, but limited ca-pability to communicate effectively in English, fields of study would be limited to engineering, physical sciences, mathematics, and quantitative areas of business. Among the most popular institutions and departments, proportions of Asian Ameri-cans enrolled substantially exceeded figures predicted by demographics alone.

Asian Americans in Los Angeles County comprised nearly 11% of the total population (Ong & Azores, 1991). The freshman class of the University of Cali-fornia, Los Angeles (UCLA), was 39% APIs that year. University officials cited both high eligibility and high application rates among Asian Americans as causes for the disproportionately large number of API matriculants (Salazar, 1994). Once admitted, proportionately more API students registered as UCLA freshmen. Ad-missions rates of API groups varied from each other and from both the majority and other minority rates. The American Indian admissions rate was highest at 71%, followed by those of Chicanos (66%) and African Americans (61%). These three groups together constituted 18% of 3,984 freshmen. Among API applicants, admissions rates were as follows: Chinese (55%), East Indians/Pakistanis (50%), Thais/other Asians (49%), Koreans (46%), Japanese (46%), Filipinos (39%), and Pacific Islanders (38%). University officials acknowledged complexity of admis-sions criteria, with weights given to ethnicity, socioeconomic factors, and other variables.

Asian American students were more likely than their peers to enter higher education without financial aid, even though their financial resources were no better than those of other students (Peng, 1985, 1990). About half of API students used earnings and/or savings to pay for college. About a quarter received Pell grants. Asian Americans were less likely than other students to receive any type of financial aid in the form of grants or loans. Once enrolled in college, were there observable patterns among groups in course-taking behavior, grades earned, or persistence? Among 1980 HS&B seniors who were tracked, average months of persistence and percentage persisting normally for 8 or 9 months (in parentheses) at each type of higher education institution are shown in the following table:

Group	Public 2-Year Institution	Public 4-Year Institution	4-Year Private Institution
Asians	8.5 (85.4)	9.0 (99.6)	9.0 (99.4)
Blacks	7.5 (69.7)	8.4 (88.0)	8.5 (89.5)
Hispanics	8.1 (81.2)	8.3 (85.1)	8.6 (89.5)
Whites	7.9 (77.0)	8.5 (90.1)	8.7 (94.0)

Asian American students typically spent more time in all types of institutions and were more likely to persist throughout the normal academic year (Owings, 1987).

During the second year after high school graduation, Asian Americans who persisted during their freshman year were more likely than their peers to return to college. Only 1% of Asian Americans failed to reenter postsecondary education in the 1981-1982 academic year compared to 6%, 9%, and 12% among White, Black, and Hispanic peers, respectively. There were fewer dropout or "stopout" API college students during their initial 4 years of postsecondary schooling. About one third of Asian Americans persisted normally compared to one fifth of White peers. Among Black classmates, 13.5% showed a normal 4-year persistence pattern. Less than 1 out of 10 Hispanic peers persisted normally (Owings, 1987).

The sample size of HS&B Asian American seniors in 1980 did not allow analysis by Asian subgroups. Some persistence data among API subgroups, however, have been reported for students who enrolled as new-from-high-school freshmen at the University of California, Berkeley (Frank, 1988). These data were from a single selective, public 4-year institution and cannot be generalized to other regions or institutions. They are included here because the data were reported for all API students at Berkeley, were reliable and valid, and were in numbers sufficient for subgoup tabulations. In the 1980-1981 academic year, the 1-year retention rate for new-from-high-school freshmen was 87% overall. Group retention rates ranged from 65% among American Indians to 92% among Asian Americans (excluding Filipinos). Filipinos, counted as a historically underrepresented minority group at that time, recorded 83% retention.

By 1986, overall retention had risen to 90%. The Asian American 1-year retention rate was 91%, and Filipino retention had risen to 86%. There were differences in retention rates between regularly admitted students and specially admitted students under the Educational Opportunity Program in favor of regular admissions. Among 21,796 first-time regularly admitted freshmen in the fall of

TABLE 10.14 Combined 5-Year Graduation and Retention Rates of University of California, Berkeley, Asian/Pacific Islander and White Freshmen in Fall of 1980-1982 by Ethnic Group, Citizenship Status, and College

	Chinese	Asian Indian/ Pakistani	Filipino	Japanese	Korean	Other Asian	White	Total
Engineering and Chemistry								
Number of citizens	194	6	47	57	21	8	704	1,207
Graduated (percentage)	80	33	55	79	81	63	66	66
Retained (percentage)	85	33	60	83	86	63	74	73
Number of immigrants	73	8	8	4	23	17	19	178
Graduated (percentage)	70	88	75	75	52	59	68	64
Retained (percentage)	73	88	75	75	52	71	68	68
Letters and Science								
Number of citizens	729	23	209	295	85	37	4,364	6,847
Graduated (percentage)	69	74	44	70	59	43	67	62
Retained (percentage)	76	78	55	76	65	65	73	69
Number of immigrants	229	28	53	12	121	43	83	650
Graduated (percentage)	61	68	38	100	52	44	58	54
Retained (percentage)	66	75	47	100	61	47	71	62

SOURCE: Frank (1988).

1978, 6,376 (29%) had graduated and 4,152 (19%) were continuing as under-graduates at Berkeley 5 years later. The remainder had transferred, stopped out, or dropped out. Among 4,091 specially admitted students, 17% were continuing at Berkeley and 319 (7.8%) had graduated in 5 years. Among 1,396 regularly admitted Asian Americans, 32% had graduated and 26% had remained at Berkeley. There were 246 regularly admitted Filipinos, of whom 24% had graduated and 28% remained at Berkeley. Among 68 specially admitted Filipino students, 12% had graduated and 29% remained at Berkeley. There were 89 regularly admitted Pacific Islanders, of whom 25% had graduated and 19% remained at Berkeley. Among more than 12,000 non-Hispanic White students, 33% had graduated and 18% were continuing at Berkeley. The tracking rate, the sum of graduates and continuing students, was 48% for all regularly admitted students and 25% for specially admitted students. Among regularly admitted students, Asian (58%), Filipino (52%), and White (51%) students recorded higher than average tracking rates. Among specially admitted students, Filipino, Asian, Pacific Islander, and White students recorded higher than average tracking rates.

Because some ethnic groups attended Berkeley in limited numbers, Frank (1988) combined Asian Americans who entered Berkeley as freshmen in the fall during the period 1980-1982 for persistence analysis by ethnic groups, citizenship status, and college affiliation. Table 10.14 displays 5-year graduation and retention rates of White and Asian students by ethnic group. Chinese and Japanese American students recorded graduation/retention rates higher than those of their White peers, whereas other Asian groups recorded rates that were a little lower.

TABLE 10.15 Mean Numbers of Postsecondary Credits Earned by 1972 NLS and Percentages of 1980 HS&B Seniors Who Earned Bachelor's Degrees by 1984, Classified by Ethnicity and Curriculum Areas

	n	Science/ Mathematics	Humanities	Social Science	Education	Business	All
NLS-72 (Seniors: mean credits earned)							
Asian	92	39 (32)	27 (21)	27 (17)	5 (13)	12 (19)	124 (24)
Black	356	24 (22)	27 (16)	34 (19)	12 (19)	9 (17)	130 (21)
Hispanic	80	23 (26)	32 (22)	33 (20)	12 (21)	7 (14)	129 (24)
White	3,815	29 (28)	29 (23)	29 (19)	9 (17)	9 (17)	127 (23)
HS&B-80 (Seniors: percentage with bachelor's by 1984)							
Asian	38	60 (35)	17 (9)	21 (18)	2 (6)	5 (10)	123 (17)
Black	121	30 (27)	19 (10)	29 (17)	4 (11)	14 (18)	121 (24)
Hispanic	95	29 (26)	20 (9)	33 (19)	3 (12)	18 (22)	122 (17)
White	703	29 (28)	21 (14)	28 (17)	7 (16)	13 (18)	124 (18)

SOURCE: Owings (1987).
NOTE: Standard deviations are in parentheses. NLS = National Longitudinal Study; HS&B = High School and Beyond.

Immigrants' graduation and retention rates were 30% lower than those of U.S. citizens among Koreans. Chinese immigrants' rates were 10% below those of citizens. There were no significant differences among other ethnic groups, in part due to small numbers in these groups. Retention referred only to persistence at Berkeley and not to transfers among departments or colleges within Berkeley.

Asian Americans enrolled in higher education institutions at higher than average rates. They were more likely to enroll without financial aid of any type. Once enrolled, API students were more likely to persevere. It is the combined effects of higher proportions of API high school graduates going on to college, their persistence once enrolled, and their propensity for graduate and particularly professional degrees that resulted in the percentage of Asian Americans increasing at each higher level of university enrollment.

UNDERGRADUATE ACHIEVEMENT, DEGREES EARNED, AND MAJOR FIELDS

Academic performance and credits earned toward a degree are two achievement criteria. Owings (1987) reported that nearly a third of all credits earned by 1972 Asian American high school seniors who took part in NLS follow-up surveys, and who had earned their bachelor's degrees by 1984, were in the areas of science and mathematics. Among Asian American high school seniors who participated in HS&B in 1980, nearly one half of all credits earned by those who had attained bachelor's degrees by 1984 were in science and mathematics. Numbers of Asian American seniors in both studies were modest—260 in NLS-72 and 420 in HS&B-80. Attrition over 12 years in NLS and attainment of bachelor's degrees within

4 years of high school graduation by HS&B participants further reduced their numbers, as shown in Table 10.15.

Apart from credits or degrees earned over time, UGPAs are accepted indicators of academic success. There are differences among institutions, and among departments within an institution, in grading practices. Sue and Abe (1988) reported UGPAs of 4,113 Asian American freshmen and a random sample of 1,000 White classmates who were enrolled at eight University of California campuses in the fall of 1984. Mean UGPAs of White and Asian freshmen were 2.75 and 2.74, respectively. There were no significant gender differences among Asian Americans, but the White female mean UGPA of 2.78 was higher than the White male mean of 2.72. Asian Americans whose best language was not English achieved a mean UGPA of 2.79, higher than the mean (2.70) of peers whose best language was English. There were differences among Asian subgroups in mean UGPAs, as shown in the following table:

Group	Undergraduate Grade Point Average
Chinese	2.89
East Indians/Pakistanis	2.86
Other Asians	2.78
Japanese	2.78
Koreans	2.68
Filipinos	2.44

Although good grades are indicators of success in college, degree attainment is the sine qua non of achievement in higher education. Numbers of Asian Americans who have earned associate, bachelor's, master's, doctorates, and professional degrees have kept pace with rising demographic trends.

In the spring of 1987, HS&B participants responded to a follow-up survey that included items about degrees earned since their high school graduation in 1980. The percentages of Asian, White, and total participants who had earned higher education degrees by 1987 are shown in the following table:

Group	Associate	Bachelor's	Graduate/ Professional
Asians	8.7	27.3	1.7
Whites	6.6	20.2	0.9
Total	6.5	18.2	0.7

Among 1980 high school seniors, proportionately more Asian Americans had obtained postsecondary degrees by 1987.

Cross-sectional degree attainment data since 1980 supported longitudinal findings from HS&B. Table 10.16 shows the increase in numbers of degrees awarded to Asian Americans over time. The Asian American share of all degrees awarded

TABLE 10.16 Total Associate, Bachelor's, Master's, Doctorate, and First Professional Degrees Awarded as Well as Numbers and Percentages Awarded to Asian Americans, 1981, 1985, 1989, and 1992

	1981	1985	1989	1992
Associate degrees				
Total	410,174	429,815	432,144	494,387
Asian American	8,650 (2.1)	9,914 (2.3)	12,519 (2.9)	15,596 (3.2)
Bachelor's degrees				
Total	934,811	968,311	1,016,350	1,129,833
Asian American	18,794 (2.0)	25,395 (2.6)	37,674 (3.7)	46,720 (4.1)
Master's degrees				
Total	294,183	280,421	309,770	348,682
Asian American	6,282 (2.1)	7,782 (2.8)	10,335 (3.3)	12,658 (3.6)
First professional degrees				
Total	71,340	71,057	70,856	72,129
Asian American	1,456 (2.0)	1,816 (2.6)	2,976 (100)	4,455 (6.2)
Doctorates				
Total	32,839	32,309	35,659	40,090
Asian American	877 (2.7)	1,106 (3.4)	1,323 (3.7)	1,559 (3.9)

SOURCE: Snyder and Hoffman (1994).
NOTE: Percentages are in parentheses.

mirrored population growth. Bachelor's degrees awarded to Asian American candidates rose from 2% of the 1981 total to 3.8% of the total in 1989. By 1993, Asian Americans accounted for 4.4% of bachelor's degrees and 3.3% of associate degrees earned. Asian Americans represented 2.1% of master's degrees awarded in 1981 and 3.8% of those awarded in 1993. First professional degrees earned by Asian Americans rose from 2% of the total in 1981 to 6.9% of the total by 1993. Asian American doctorates who were U.S. citizens went from 1.9% in 1981 to 2.7% by 1989. Changes in degrees earned by Asian Americans over time varied by types of degree and by gender. Between 1992 and 1993, first professional degrees grew by 15.8%, whereas master's degrees rose by 9.5%. Asian women outpaced men in rate of change. First professional degrees to women rose 23.6%, whereas to men they rose 10.2% (Carter & Wilson, 1992, 1996; Snyder & Hoffman, 1994). The significant gender difference unrelated to demographic changes might have reflected changing attitudes toward higher education for women among Asian American communities. High proportions of advanced degrees awarded to Asians, particularly doctorates in physical sciences, engineering, and quantitative professions, went not just to Asian Americans but also to Asians who held permanent or temporary visas. Many Asian nationals with advanced degrees from U.S. institutions later opted to become naturalized U.S. citizens (Hsia, 1988).

The distribution of Asian American bachelor's degree holders by fields in 1989 showed that relatively more APIs chose to major in engineering, business, social, or biology/life sciences than in the humanities. Only 1,127 (1.1%) earned bachelor's degrees in education. The cohort was awarded 8,039 bachelor's degrees in business, 1,733 in health professions, and 3,992 in social sciences. Almost 3,000 bachelor's degrees in biology/life sciences and 7,000 in engineering meant that Asian American college graduates represented more than 8% of all degrees awarded in these two fields. Among women engineering graduates in 1989, 1 in 10 was Asian American. In 1993, in descending order, bachelor's degrees were awarded to Asian Americans in the following fields:

Field	Bachelor's
Business	11,780
Engineering	7,307
Social sciences	5,712
Biological/life sciences	5,205
Health professions	2,513
Education	1,100

By 1994, the graduation rate for Asian Americans at National Collegiate Athletic Association Division I institutions was 65%, highest among all groups. The Asian American women's graduation rate, 67%, was higher than the Asian American men's rate of 62% (Carter & Wilson, 1996).

In 1993, Asian Americans were awarded 13,866 master's degrees, an increase of 78% from their numbers in 1985. In descending order, they had concentrated in the following fields:

Field	Master's
Business	4,304
Engineering	2,441
Education	1,391
Health professions	864
Public affairs	466
Social sciences	422

First professional degrees awarded to APIs between 1985 and 1993 had increased by 184%, to 5,160, by 1993. Of all doctoral degrees awarded in 1994, 949 (3.5%) were to Asian American citizens. Almost half of all 1994 doctorates were awarded to non-U.S. citizens. A total of 9,359 doctorates were awarded to Asian nationals. They outnumbered Asian American doctorates by 9 to 1 (Carter & Wilson, 1996). Asian recipients of science and engineering doctorates doubled in the decade between 1983 and 1993. The growth was recorded for both Asian Americans and Asian immigrants with permanent resident visas. Asian American science and engineering doctorates rose from a total of 345 in 1983 to 710 in 1993. Asian permanent visa doctorates rose in the same interval from 433 to 892 (National Science Foundation, 1995).

The college/university graduation rate of Asian Americans has been the highest among all groups. Proportions of API college graduates who continued their higher education and obtained advanced degrees also have been high. These trends, augmented by Asian nationals (particularly those with permanent resident visas who obtained doctorates and continued on to become naturalized American citizens), have resulted in higher than expected numbers of Asian Americans holding advanced academic and professional degrees.

FACULTY AND ADMINISTRATION IN HIGHER EDUCATION

Did the unexpectedly high proportions of Asians and Asian Americans who earned advanced degrees throughout the 1980s and 1990s follow a traditional academic career path by staying on campus as faculty members, research staff, or administrators? Manpower data from annual reports of the National Science Foundation have suggested that, until recent population changes, the tiny fraction of faculty of Asian heritage were not Asian Americans but rather Asian nationals or naturalized U.S. citizens (Hsia, 1988).

Recent statistics on Asian American faculty members, particularly tenured faculty, and on administrators in higher education institutions have shown that numbers have grown as demographics changed but that their tenure rates have been low (Carter & Wilson, 1991). Between 1983 and 1991, Asian American full-time faculty rose from 16,899 (3.5%) to 26,545 (5.1%). Since 1991, their numbers have eroded. In 1993, their number was down to 25,269 (4.7%). The decrease in numbers was observed particularly among Asian males. Female Asian American faculty have continued to grow, doubling between 1983 and 1993, whereas male full-time faculty grew by 38% in the interval. By 1993, Asian Americans represented 4.5% of all full professors, 4.6% of associate professors, 6.1% of assistant professors, 3.4% of instructors and lecturers, and 4.6% of other faculty. In addition, 64% of Asian American faculty held tenure in comparison to 73% of White faculty (Carter & Wilson, 1996).

Between 1980 and 1990, 38% of Asian American recent doctorates with definite postdoctoral career plans were going into academic teaching or research. This figure was markedly lower than the 50%, 55%, 55%, and 57% reported for White, African American, American Indian, and Hispanic American peers, respectively. Science and engineering Asian American doctorates had the option to choose careers in industry. The lower than average Asian American career plans in academe might have been related, in part, to higher proportions of science and engineering doctorates among them. According to Carter and Wilson (1991), Asians on campuses were more likely to be those who obtained doctorates earlier, Asians who were recently naturalized U.S. citizens, or Asians who remained foreign nationals at the time of data collection. Departments in which Asian Americans were most likely to be found as faculty members were those that produced greater numbers of Asian doctorates as well—engineering, social sciences, physical sciences, mathematics and statistics, business, and biological sciences.

Asian Americans were thin in the ranks of administration and management positions in higher education. As to Asian American chief executive officers (CEOs) of colleges and universities, they were very rare. By 1996, there were altogether only 20 (0.6%) Asian American CEOs heading U.S. institutions, 13 at 4-year institutions. Out of 2,939 CEOs, 2,175 were White. African American, Hispanic, and American Indian CEOs numbered 192, 99, and 28, respectively. The renmaining CEOs' ethnicity could not be identified. Numerically and proportionately, Asian Americans were at the bottom of the list. The pool of Asian American administrators and managers, from which CEOs are likely to be drawn, remained small. in 1993, 1.6% of full-time administrators in higher education were Asian American. In 1983, they comprised 1.1% of all full-time administrators. Growth in the decade from 1983 to 1993 did not parallel higher education trends in enrollment, graduate degree attainment, or faculty positions (Carter & Wilson, 1996).

CONCLUSIONS AND POLICY IMPLICATIONS

This review of academic achievement among Asian Americans has shown above average performance in elementary and secondary schools. Statistical data from national longitudinal and cross-sectional studies, as well as regional or single school district research studies of Asian American pupils, supported the conclusion that Asian American pupils at all levels typically record higher than average performance in quantitative subjects. English-proficient APIs also performed well in language-related tasks. There were substantial differences in achievement within the API population. Differences were shown between the native born and immigrants or refugees, not always in favor of the native born. Performance varied among diverse ethnic and language groups, between students fluent in English and those of LEP, and among newcomers of different socioeconomic backgrounds and post-entry experiences. Asian American pupils typically received higher than average grades from their teachers, even when objective test scores show their verbal performance to have been below average.

Diversity notwithstanding, with some exceptions, Asian American academic achievement equaled or exceeded national averages by a variety of objective criteria, at every educational level, from elementary and secondary school through graduate and professional degrees. By the year 2000, Asian Americans are projected to reach 4% of the total U.S. population. Their impact on education could be greater than the numbers imply—first, because APIs enroll in, persist in, and graduate from every level of the educational pipeline; second, because the API population on both coasts and within metropolitan centers has resulted in greater pressure on educational resources in areas of concentration; and finally, because Asian newcomers with limited language ability but well-developed quantitative skills tend to restrict their fields of study to sciences or engineering.

Asian American success in education has, moreover, elicited growing signs of resistance from majority and other minority groups within academe. Institutional response was inevitable. Admissions of Asian Americans to highly selective undergraduate institutions, both private and public, are plateauing after two decades of growth, in line with demographic trends and the deep API talent pool. Admissions testing programs, particularly to medical schools, have been modified to demand greater communicative skills and less science and mathematics knowledge. Reporting of testing data by groups also has changed, with limited quantitative data and greater reliance on graphs. Preliminary data suggest that the distribution of medical students by Asian ethnic groups is changing as a result, with more South Asian matriculants who are strong in English and fewer newcomers, particularly Southeast Asians. The impacts of these institutional policy changes on aspiring Asian American youths have not been widely recognized by institutions or by most Asian communities.

The rapid growth of Asian American students at all levels and their academic achievements have not been accompanied by commensurate growth in Asian American faculty. The number of Asian higher education administrators, particularly CEOs, has remained minute. Despite a broad student base, high academic performance, and high proportions of advanced degree holders, Asian Americans have been unable to gain a foothold in the decision- and policy-making ranks of academic administration.

Policy implications of Asian American academic achievement should begin with recognition of differential validity of assessment instruments to assess Asian Americans' developed abilities and academic achievement. For students of LEP, strong language arts programs with an emphasis on writing remain a continuing need. Because existing measures of developed quantitative abilities underestimated true abilities due to verbally loaded content, interpretation of LEP Asian American mathematical performance ought to take bias into account to avoid underutilization of newcomers' quantitative skills. Scrutiny of selective higher education admissions policies and practices, as well as existing processes for faculty appointments, promotions, and tenure status, must continue so as to monitor academic progress of Asian Americans. There is a pressing need for Asian American communities and higher education decision makers to focus on development and recruitment of Asian American candidates for administrative and management positions in academe. Asian Americans have made progress in overcoming societal exclusion and racial discrimination. As we approach the 21st century, Asian Americans will be less and less likely to be candidates for affirmative action and more and more at risk for future academic limitations in the form of hidden quotas and invisible ceilings.

REFERENCES

American College Testing Program. (1995). *The high school profile report: High school graduating class, 1995.* Iowa City, IA: Author.

Association of American Medical Colleges. (1992). *Facts, applicants, matriculants and graduates: 1985 to 1991*. Washington, DC: Author.

Association of American Medical Colleges. (1994-1996). *Trends: U.S. medical school applicants, matriculants, graduates, 19_*. Washington, DC: Author.

Baratz-Snowden, J., & Duran, R. (1987). *The educational progress of language minority students: Findings from the 1983-84 NAEP Reading Survey*. Princeton, NJ: National Assessment of Educational Progress/Educational Testing Service.

Baratz-Snowden, J., Rock, D., Pollack, J., & Wilder, G. (1988). *The educational progress of language minority children: Findings from the NAEP 1985-86 special study*. Princeton, NJ: National Assessment of Educational Progress/Educational Testing Service.

Barton, P. E., & Lapointe, A. (1995). *Learning by degrees: Indicators of performance in higher education*. Princeton, NJ: Policy Information Center, Educational Testing Service.

Bleistein, C. A., & Wright, D. (1985). *Assessing unexpected differential item performance of Oriental candidates and of White candidates for whom English is not the best language on SAT Form 3FSA08 and TSWE Form E47* (Statistical Report No. SR85-123). Princeton, NJ: Educational Testing Service.

Boston Public Schools, Office of Research and Development. (1986). *A working document on the dropout problem in Boston public schools* (2 vols.). Boston: Author.

Caplan, N., Whitmore, J., Bui, Q., & Trautman, M. (1985). *Scholastic achievement among the children of Southeast Asian refugees*. Ann Arbor, MI: Institute for Social Research.

Carter, D. A., & Wilson, R. (1992). *Minorities in higher education, 1991: Tenth annual status report*. Washington, DC: American Council on Education.

Carter, D. A., & Wilson, R. (1996). *Minorities in higher education, 1995-96: Fourteenth annual status report*. Washington, DC: American Council on Education.

College Board. (1990-1991). *College-bound seniors profile reports*. New York: Author.

College Board. (1991). *Tabulations PSAT/NMSQT 1990-91*. New York: Author.

College Board. (1995). *1995 profile of SAT program test takers: College bound seniors national report*. Princeton, NJ: Educational Testing Service.

Frank, A. (1988, April). *UC Berkeley retention rates for entering freshmen*. Paper presented at the annual meeting of the American Educational Research Association, New Orleans, LA.

Graduate Management Admissions Council. (1992). *An admissions office profile of candidates taking the GMAT 1986-87 through 1990-91*. Princeton, NJ: Author.

Grandy, J. (1994). *GRE trends and profiles: Statistics about general test examinees by sex and ethnicity* (Report No. RR-94-1). Princeton, NJ: Educational Testing Service.

Hsia, J. (1988). *Asian Americans in higher education and at work*. Hillsdale, NJ: Lawrence Erlbaum.

Kim, H. (1997). *Diversity among Asian American high school students*. Princeton, NJ: Educational Testing Service.

Kulick, E., & Dorans, N. J. (1983). *Assessing unexpected differential item performance of Oriental candidates on SAT Form CSA6 and TSWE Form E33* (Statistical Report No. SR-83-106). Princeton, NJ: Educational Testing Service.

Mullis, I. V. S., Dossey, J. A., Owen, E. H., & Phillips, G. W. (1991). *The state of mathematics achievement executive summary: NAEP's 1990 assessment of the nation and the trial assessment of the states*. Washington, DC: National Center for Education Statistics.

Nakanishi, D. T. (1989, November-December). A quota on excellence? The Asian American admissions debate. *Change*, pp. 38-47.

National Science Foundation. (1995). *Science and engineering degrees, by race/ethnicity of recipients, 1985-93*. Washington, DC: Author.

O'Hare, W. P., & Felt, J. C. (1991). *Asian Americans: America's fastest growing minority group*. Washington, DC: Population Reference Bureau.

Ong, P., & Azores, T. (1991). Asian Pacific Americans in L.A.: A demographic profile. *Crosscurrents*, pp. 3-4, 8-9.

Owings, J. A. (1987, April). *Persistence and course taking behavior of Asian American students*. Paper presented at the annual meeting of the American Educational Research Association, Washington, DC.

Peng, S. S. (1985, April). *Enrollment patterns of Asian American students in postsecondary education*. Paper presented at the annual meeting of the American Educational Research Association, Chicago.

Peng, S. S. (1990). Attainment status of Asian Americans in higher education. In R. Endo, V. Chattergy, S. Chou, & N. Touchida (Eds.), *Contemporary perspectives in Asian and Pacific American education.* South El Monte, CA: Pacific Asia Press.

Peng, S. S., & Lee, R. M. (1991, February). *Diversity of Asian American students and its implications for education: A study of the 1988 eighth graders.* Paper presented at the annual conference of the National Association for Bilingual Education, Washington, DC.

Peng, S. S., Owings, J. A., & Fetters, W. B. (1984, April). *School experiences and performance of Asian American high school students.* Paper presented at the annual meeting of the American Educational Research Association, New Orleans, LA.

Petersen, N. S., & Livingston, S. A. (1982). *English composition test with essay* (Statistical Report No. SR-82-96). Princeton, NJ: Educational Testing Service.

Podeschi, R. L. (1987, April). *A case study of Hmong adolescents in community context.* Paper presented at the annual meeting of the American Educational Research Association, Washington, DC.

Policy Information Center. (1995). *Dreams deferred: High school dropouts in the U.S.* Princeton, NJ: Educational Testing Service.

Ramist, L., & Arbeiter, S. (1986). *Profile: College-bound seniors, 1985.* New York: College Entrance Examination Board.

Rock, D. A., Ekstrome, R. B., Goertz, M. E., & Pollack, J. M. (1985). *Determinants of achievement gain in high school* (Briefing paper prepared under Contract No. 300-83-0247 for the U.S. Department of Education, NCES). Princeton, NJ: Educational Testing Service.

Rothman, R. (1986, December). Record number of schools join advanced placement program. *Education Week.*

Salazar, M. (1994). Asian frosh admissions at 39%: What does it mean? *Crosscurrents,* pp. 3-4.

Smith, V. D., & van der Veen, P. (1991). *Trends in medical school applicants and matriculants 1981-90.* Washington, DC: Association of American Medical Colleges.

Snyder, T. D., & Hoffman, C. M. (1994). *Digest of education statistics.* Washington, DC: U.S. Department of Education.

Sue, S., & Abe, J. (1988). *Predictors of academic achievement among Asian American and White students,* (College Board Report No. 88-11). New York: College Entrance Examination Board.

U.S. Bureau of the Census. (1991, June 12). *Census Bureau releases 1990 census counts on specific census groups* (press release, Commerce Neal CB91-215). Washington, DC: U.S. Department of Commerce.

U.S. Department of Education. (1988). *National Education Longitudinal Study of the eighth graders in 1988.* Washington, DC: Author.

Wah, D. M., & Robinson, D. S. (1990). *Examinee and score trends for the GRE general test: 1977-78, 1982-83, 1985-87, and 1987-88.* Princeton, NJ: Educational Testing Service.

Wightman, L. F., & Muller, D. G. (1990). *Comparison of LSAT performance among select subgroups* (LSAC Statistical Report No. 90-01). Newtown, PA: Law School Admissions Council.

11

CAREER DEVELOPMENT AND VOCATIONAL BEHAVIORS

FREDERICK T. L. LEONG

As Leong (1985; see also Leong & Serafica, 1995) has observed repeatedly, very little research has been done on Asian Americans' career choices and development. This deficit exists in spite of the great need for career counseling services expressed by Asian Americans. For example, 34% of the Asian American students taking the Scholastic Aptitude Test (SAT) in 1980 expressed an intention to seek vocational-career counseling when enrolled in college compared to 27% of Whites, 24% of Blacks, and 30% of Mexican Americans (College Entrance Examination Board, 1980). In a more recent national survey conducted by the Gallup organization for the National Career Development Association (Brown, Minor, & Jepsen, 1991), it was found that large percentages of Asians and Pacific Islanders (APIs) (71%) and Hispanics (75%) reported being interested in getting more information about careers if they could start over. APIs (37%) also were significantly more likely to report using college career information centers than were Whites (21%), African Americans (19%), and Hispanics (15%). Whites (71%) were significantly more likely than APIs (61%) to report that the information they needed was available. When they found career information, 83% of APIs found the information useful compared to 88% of African Americans, 77% of Whites, and 83% of Hispanics.

In addition to their interest and need for career services, Asian Americans also constitute the fastest growing minority group in the United States. The combination of these factors highlights the immense disparity between what is needed and what is available by way of career theory and research on Asian Americans. Career counselors need information on how Asian American clients may be different from White American students so that they can provide culturally relevant and effective services. In addition to the present chapter, information on the career development of Asian Americans can be found in two recently published chapters (Leong & Gim-Chung, 1995; Leong & Serafica, 1995) that appeared in Leong's (1995) edited volume devoted to the career development and vocational behavior of racial and ethnic minorities. Leong and Leung (1994) also have addressed the issues involved in career assessment with Asian Americans.

This chapter is divided into three sections. The first section, consisting of an individual level of analysis, explores Asian Americans' career interests, career choices, occupational values, and vocational behaviors in the professions and in organizations. It also examines personality variables that affect Asian Americans' career development. The second section, using a group and societal level of analysis, examines the role of macrolevel processes such as occupational stereotypes, discrimination, occupational mobility, and occupational segregation and their potential impact on the career development of Asian Americans. The third section discusses the problems inherent in current research and ends with an outline of the directions for future research.

INDIVIDUAL LEVEL OF ANALYSIS

Career Interests

Over the past 20 years, there has been only a handful of studies of the career interest patterns of Asian Americans (Leong & Leung, 1994; Leong & Serafica, 1995). In a mid-1980s review of the literature on the career development of Asian Americans, Leong (1985) was able to identify only three published emperical articles and one dissertation related to the career interests of Asian Americans. In the first study, which focused on Chinese Americans and was done at the University of California, Berkeley, consisting of the School and College Ability Test (SCAT), the Strong Vocational Interest Blank (SVIB), and the Omnibus Personality Inventory (OPI), Sue and Kirk (1972) found that Chinese American students had higher quantitative and lower verbal scores than did the control group. Males in both groups did better than females in quantitative scores. Students at Berkeley generally do better than the national norm.

Chinese American males showed more of an interest in physical sciences, skilled technical trades, and business occupations than did all other males. They tended to be less interested in social service and welfare, sales and business contact, and verbal-linguistic occupations. The Chinese American males' vocational interests appeared more masculine than those of all other males. Also, Chinese American males seemed to aspire to a lower level of occupational status and responsibility.

Generally, Chinese American females tended to be more oriented toward the domestic occupations. Besides this, Chinese American females exhibited more interest in technical-applied fields, biological and physical sciences, and business and office-type activities and exhibited less interest in aesthetic-cultural fields, social sciences, and verbal-linguistic vocations.

Chinese American students were less oriented toward theoretical or abstract ideas and concepts and tended more to evaluate ideas on the basis of their immediate practical applications than did all other students. Chinese American males did not differ from all other males in interest in scientific activities employing logical, analytical, and critical thinking. Chinese American females, however, scored much lower in that area.

In the second study, which focused on both Chinese and Japanese Americans, Sue and Kirk (1973) found a similar pattern of vocational choices between the two groups of Asian men. The exception was that the Japanese American men did not express greater interest in physical sciences or lower interest in the social sciences than did White men. In addition, Japanese American women did not express greater interest in domestic fields than did White women. The authors explained these differences between the Chinese and Japanese participants in terms of differential rates of acculturation and assimilation into American society between these two groups.

In the third study, using a typological analysis of the same Chinese and Japanese American men who participated in the study already discussed, Sue and Frank (1973) found that these students clustered into groups with characteristics quite different from those of Whites. They confirmed the findings of the other two studies and concluded that those occupations that require "forceful self-expression, interaction with people, and communication in oral or written form" are the ones that Asian Americans feel most uncomfortable with and are most likely to avoid, given their preferences for "structured, logical, concrete, and impersonal" work activities (p. 141).

In an unpublished dissertation on career development of Asian Americans, Kwak (1980) examined the vocational interests of Asian American youths using Holland's (1977) Self-Directed Search. He found that the Asian American students revealed vocational types predominantly in the investigative (25.8%) and social (25.0%) categories.

In another unpublished study, Leong (1982) used the Vocational Preference Inventory to assess interest patterns within Holland's model and found that Asian American students at the University of Maryland had measured interest patterns that were predominantly in the investigative (30%) and social (21%) areas. These results are quite consistent with Kwak's (1980) earlier study. Interestingly, when Leong (1982) examined the Asian American students' expressed interests (i.e., what career fields they said they were interested in pursuing) as opposed to their measured interests (i.e., what the inventory said they were interested in pursuing), a different picture emerged. More than 50% of the Asian American students reported interests in investigative careers (vs. 30% who had measured interests), and only 7% expressed interests in social careers (vs. 21% who had measured interests). This discrepancy between measured and expressed interests among Asian American students seems to be a significant clinical phenomenon worthy of further investigation.

In a little-known study that was published as a technical report by the American College Testing service, Lamb (1976) analyzed the structural validity of Holland's model of career interests for the four ethnic minority groups including Asian Americans. He found that the hexagonal structure was consistent across all of the minority groups with the exception of the American Indian group. In other words, the internal structure of Holland's model was the same for Asian Americans as it was for White, Black, and Hispanic American high school students. Unfortunately, this study was based on a relatively small sample of Asian Americans ($N = 102$).

Another approach to understanding the career interests of Asian Americans would be to examine the courses they take and the academic majors they choose while in high school. Data from a recent National Science Foundation (1990) report indicate that

> fully twice the proportion of Asians as Whites had a calculus course while in high school: 36 percent versus 18 percent. Asians were also more apt to have been in honors math courses. . . . Whereas almost all students had taken biology, Asians reported taking a chemistry or physics course more often than Whites. (p. 41)

In terms of intended undergraduate major, Asian Amerians were twice as likely to choose an engineering discipline. Within the sciences, Asians tended more toward biology and computer science than did Whites. Asian Americans' greater interest in scientific majors also was paralleled by a high level of educational aspiration. More than two out of five Asian American freshmen planned their highest degree to be either a doctorate or a medical degree compared to one out of five White American freshmen who did so (National Science Foundation, 1990, p. 43).

According to the National Science Foundation (1990) report,

> coincident with their higher degree aspirations, over one-third of Asian freshmen plan to become either engineers or physicians; this fraction compares to only about a tenth of Whites. Among other careers, Asians choose elementary or secondary teaching as their probable profession to a much lesser extent than do Whites: 2 percent versus 9 percent. (p. 43)

Occupational Values

On the whole, there also has been a lack of empirical studies on the work values of Asian Americans. In an early dissertation, Tou (1974) compared the work value orientations of Chinese American and White American 7th- and 8th-grade students in Catholic schools and designed a career intervention. Using Super's (1970) Work Values Inventory, she found that cultural influences were associated with the Chinese American students' work value orientations. The intervention involved administering the Self-Directed Search in an attempt to increase the

Chinese Americans' awareness of work value alternatives. A small increase in awareness was produced, but it was not statistically significant.

More recently, Leong and Tata (1990) designed a study to determine what work values were important to Chinese American children. The relation between the Chinese American children's level of acculturation and work values also was examined. Sex differences in work values among Chinese American 5th and 6th graders were studied as well.

In the Leong and Tata (1990) study, 177 Chinese American 5th and 6th graders in a Los Angeles inner-city elementary school were given the Ohio Work Values Inventory (OWVI) and the Suinn-Lew Asian Self-Identity Acculturation scale (SL-ASIA). The OWVI yields scores on 11 scales. The two most important values for Chinese American children were money and task satisfaction. Object orientation and solitude appeared to be of considerably lower importance. Boys valued object orientation, self-realization, and ideas-data more than did girls. Girls valued altruism more than did boys. These sex differences may represent non-culture-specific sex differences in work values. The Chinese American children also were divided into three groups according to their SL-ASIA scores: the low-acculturation group, the medium-acculturation group, and the high-acculturation group. Significant acculturation differences were found only for self-realization. High-acculturation Chinese American children valued self-realization more than did low-acculturation Chinese American children. The major aspect of self-realization seems to be more a part of the White culture than of the Chinese American culture. There are several limitations of this study. The lack of a comparable White sample from a similar region, socioeconomic status, and time span was noted.

Knowledge of this pattern of occupational values among Chinese American children can serve as advance organizers for counselors who help this group of minority children with their career planning. The challenge lies in broadening the occupational options for Chinese American children while still respecting their cultural values, which might underlie their occupational values.

In another study that examined both career development variables and occupational values, Leong (1991) used Rosenberg's (1957) Occupational Values Scale to compare the work values of 83 White American (46% male and 54% female) and 63 Asian American (38% male and 62% female) college students. The results related to the career development variables are discussed subsequently. In terms of values, following the pattern used by Rosenberg, clusters of occupational values were formed for analyses in the study: the social cluster, the extrinsic cluster, the self-expression cluster, the power cluster, and the element of security.

The comparison of the two racial/ethnic groups revealed that Asian Americans showed significant differences in terms of placing greater emphasis on the extrinsic values than did White Americans. Asian Americans also significantly valued security more than did White Americans. Hence, Asian American college students, when compared to their White American peers, do show some significant differences on occupational values. These differences could be because of the Asian Americans' culture having a greater emphasis on pragmatism, a collectivistic orientation in decision making, and a mind-set influenced by the immigration experience.

The major implication of the Leong (1991) study for counseling is that Asian Americans do seem to have differential occupational values when compared to White Americans. Career counselors need to find ways of using a sufficiently structured approach that is mindful of the occupational values of Asian Americans (Leong & Gim-Chung, 1995; Leong & Leung, 1994). Asian American clients might not appreciate counselors who directly or indirectly promote the use of a more intrinsic set of work values with which to guide their career decision making.

Career Development

Research on career choice and development has been dominated by three major theoretial perspectives: the person-environment interaction model as exemplified by Holland's model, the developmental approaches as exemplified by Super's (1970) theory, and the social learning approaches as delineated by Krumboltz and Mitchell (see Brown & Brooks, 1990). Within the developmental perspective, the level and correlates of career maturity have been the most researched construct. Crites (1978) defined career maturity as comprising five attitudinal components: "(a) decisiveness in career decision making, (b) involvement in career decision making, (c) independence in career decision making, (d) orientation to career decision making, and (e) compromise in career decision making" (p. 3). As is evident from these culture-bound components, there are likely to be cultural variations in the construct of career maturity among Asian Americans (Leong & Serafica, 1995).

In a study examining the differential career development attributes of Asian American and White American college students, Leong (1991) used Crites's (1978) Career Maturity Inventory: Attitude Scale; Harren's (1978) Assessment of Career Decision-Making Style subscale; and Holland, Daiger, and Power's (1980) My Vocational Situation on a sample of 83 White American (46% male and 54% female) and 63 Asian American (38% male and 62% female) college students. The Asian Americans were primarily of Chinese and Korean descent.

The Asian Americans exhibited higher levels of dependent decision-making styles than did the White Americans. The Asian Americans also scored lower on career maturity. There were no significant cultural differences for vocational identity. Asian American college students, when compared to their White American peers, did show some significant differences on career development attributes and occupational values. These differences could be because of the Asian Americans' culture having a greater emphasis on a collectivistic orientation in decision making and could be influenced by the acculturation process (Leong, 1991).

The major implication of Leong's (1991) study for counseling is that Asian Americans do seem to have differential career development attributes when compared to White Americans. Career counselors need to be mindful that Asian Americans might have preferences for different decision-making processes and might on the surface appear less "career mature" than Whites. However, it also should be recognized that most of the career maturity models and measures have been developed from a White middle-class value orientation that might not be appropriate for Asian Americans (Leong & Brown, 1995; Leong & Serafica, 1995). Future research on the career development attributes of Asian Americans needs to examine this pattern of results and more directly test cultural differences in career decision-making styles and career maturity levels (Leong & Leung, 1994).

Career Choices

At first glance, it would seem that Asian Americans' career choices would be a direct reflection of their career interests. However, as Leong (1982) pointed out, due to a host of factors that have not yet been investigated empirically, Asian Americans' career choices might not be consistently related to their career interests. For example, many Asian American adolescents might be interested in artistic careers (reflected in measured interests) but eventually might choose careers in medicine or engineering (expressed interests or choices) because of parental guidance or pressure.

This is quite likely to occur because many Asian American parents are aware that discrimination in the work world is quite common and that their children would have an easier time if they were in respected and autonomous professions in which many Asian Americans already have succeeded. Hence, Asian American parents might be more likely than White American parents to exert direct influence on the career aspirations and choices of their children. In addition, the Asian American youths would be more likely than White American youths to defer to their parental guidance given the strong Asian value of respecting authority and submitting to the wisdom of the elderly. For example, in Chinese American culture, when parents give advice to their children they usually preface their remarks with an observation such as "In my lifetime, I have eaten more salt than you have eaten rice." Loosely translated, the saying implies that the elderly have much more experience and, by extension, much more wisdom than do the young on most matters. Therefore, to understand the career behavior of Asian Americans, it would be important to examine their career interests and career choices separately. It also would be important to examine when, why, and for whom the two processess do not converge.

On a more general level, Hsia (1988) analyzed the major occupational groupings that Asian Americans had chosen to enter using the 1980 U.S. census data. Of the nine groups examined, Asian Americans were more likely than White Americans to be in three of them. More than 18% of Asian Americans were in professional occupations compared to 12.8% of White Americans, 5.5% of Asian Americans were in technical occupations compared to 3.1% of White Americans, and 15.6% of Asian Americans were in service occupations compared to 11.6% of White Americans. Conversely, fewer Asian Americans were in sales (8.4%), production/craft (8.4%), and operator/laborer occupations (14.2%) compared to White Americans (10.7%, 13.4%, and 17.1%, respectively). Hsia also provided similar data on specific Asian American subgroups (e.g., Japanese, Chinese, Filipino, Korean).

The greater tendency for Asian Americans to work in the professional and technical occupations and the lower tendency to enter sales and laborer occupations are consistent with some of the earlier observations about the pattern of career interests made by Sue and Kirk (1972, 1973). Based on this set of data, one can see why it is so common for the concept of the "model minority" to be applied to Asian Americans. Using the criterion of occupational attainment alone, Asian Americans as a group have fared quite well relative to other minority groups. However, such an observation overlooks important intragroup differences. For example, although Asian Americans as a group constitute 18.3% of professional occupations relative to the 12.3% for White Americans, only 8.8% of Vietnamese Americans are in professional occupations. Furthermore, 29.3% of Vietnamese and 20.5% of Korean Americans are in operator/laborer occupations compared to 17.1% of White Americans and 14.2% of Asian Americans overall (Hsia, 1988). The model minority concept also ignores the problem of discrimination against Asian Americans. Being successful is no guarantee against prejudice and discrimination. This problem of occupational discrimination is discussed later in the chapter.

Asian Americans in the Professions

The representation of Asian Americans in their various professions was thoroughly discussed by Hsia (1988) in her book, *Asian Americans in Higher Education and at Work*. For our present purposes, we review some of the basic statistics to highlight some issues with regard to Asian Americans' career choices in the professions. Beginning with the legal profession, Hsia pointed out that data collected since 1971 have shown that Asian Americans represent less than 1% of the law student population. However, there has been a steady increase in Asian American enrollment in law schools since 1973. In fact, the total number of first-year Asian American students has doubled in the decade from 327 to 711. Hsia also pointed out that despite this increase in the number of Asian Americans in law schools, recent immigrants, because of their limited English-language ability, are at a certain disadvantage in terms of access to law school educations.

In terms of medical school, Asian Americans have been a very visible minority within this particular profession (Hsia, 1988). For example, in the 1979-1980 academic year, they constituted 3% of first-year and 2.8% of total medical student enrollment. As Hsia pointed out, by the 1984-1985 academic year, Asian Americans constituted 6.6% of first-year and 5.6% of total medical school enrollment. This compares to Asian Americans representing 1.2% of the general U.S. population in the 1970s and 3.0% in 1990. As the comparison has illustrated, Asian Americans are "overrepresented" in medical schools. However, Hsia also pointed out that, despite this overrepresentation relative to the proportion of Asians in the U.S. population, Asian Americans do experience a lower level of application-to-acceptance ratio than do other racial/ethnic groups. She further suggested that this might be due to some discriminatory admissions policies occurring. In essence, Asian Americans seem to gravitate toward medicine as a career choice. Unfortunately, for a variety of reasons that have not yet been explicated, they are not as likely to be accepted into medical school as are Whites and other minorities even when they fulfill all of the academic requirements.

Hsia (1988) did not examine Asian Americans' representation in business school; as such, no information was presented in her book. However, when we examined the 1980 census, we found that in terms of actual representation in the category of executive, administrative, and managerial occupations, the number or percentage of Asian Americans relative to their population was comparable for both groups. For example, White executive, administrative, and managerial occupations represented 13.5% of all White individuals who were age 16 years or over and employed. For Asian Americans, 13.2% of the Asian population were in executive, administrative, or managerial occupations. It would be interesting to determine whether the representation of Asians in business schools and the like also is comparable or whether the Asian executives and business managers enter those occupations without going through the traditional MBA and business school training—in other words, that there actually might be two paths to becoming an executive or a manager: White Americans might use business school as a way in which to enter the profession, whereas Asian Americans might be entering directly without the usual academic training.

Personality Variables and Asian Americans' Career Development

In a review of the literature on the career development of Asian Americans, Leong (1985) noted that there were three personality variables that were referred to repeatedly in various studies concerning the vocational behavior of Asian Americans. These three personality variables were locus of control, social anxiety, and intolerance of ambiguity. With regard to locus of control, different studies have pointed out that Asian Americans tend to be less autonomous, more dependent, and more obedient to authority (Meredith, 1966; Sue & Kirk, 1972, 1973). Meredith's (1966) study, which used the Personality Factor Questionnaire, found that Japanese American students were more "submissive, diffident, and regulated by external realities" than the White students. Relatedly, Sue and Kirk (1972) administered the Omnibus Personality Inventory to 236 Chinese American students and found that they were significantly more conforming and socially introverted than the White students. The authors went on to suggest that this high level of conformity might be due to the traditional Chinese cultural values of respect for authority and submergence of individuality. These findings seem to suggest that Asian Americans, or at least Chinese and Japanese Americans, are more externally oriented in terms of how they view issues of control and reinforcement. In fact, Hsieh, Shybut, and Lotrof (1969) already had discovered that Chinese Americans do score higher on Rotters' locus of control scale (i.e., more external) than do White Americans. As suggested by Leong (1985), if indeed Asian Americans perceived the locus of control for reinforcement as external, it could affect not only their career decision-making style but also the nature and scope of their career choices.

Social anxiety was the second personality characteristic that Leong (1985) identified as a converging theme within the literature. Besides clinical impressions that Asian Americans are more emotionally withdrawn, socially isolated, and verbally inhibited (Bourne, 1975; Sue & Sue, 1974), various empirical studies using objective and standardized personality instruments have found that Asian Americans do experience a greater degree of social anxiety. Sue and Sue (1974), in a Minnesota Multiphasic Personality Inventory comparison of Asian American and White American students, found that the former exhibit greater social introversion. In another study using the OPI, Sue and Kirk (1972) found that Chinese American students were significantly more inhibited, were more impersonal in their interpersonal relations, and appeared less socially concerned with other people. In a related study using the same database as did that study, Sue and Kirk (1973) found a similar pattern of social introversion and withdrawal among both Chinese and Japanese American samples. They concluded that the social discomfort experienced by these Asian American students might be due to conflict between the informal nature of social relationships within American culture and their own more formal and traditional cultural values and minority status.

Leong (1985) also found that Fenz and Arkoff (1962) provided additional confirming data on this social anxiety/discomfort phenomenon among Asian Americans. Administering the Edwards Personal Preference Schedule (EPPS) to their participants, Fenz and Arkoff found that both Chinese and Filipino Americans (and, to a lesser exent, Japanese Americans) scored higher on the deference and abasement scales than did Whites. The Asian ethnic groups also scored lower on the exhibition and aggression scales. Later on, but also using the EPPS with Japanese Americans and White Americans as participants, Connor (1975) found that the former exhibited greater need for deference, order, and abasement.

Sue (1975), in his chapter in Picou and Campbell's (1975) book, *Career Behavior of Special Groups,* already had pointed out the relevance of Asian Americans' social anxiety to their career aspirations and plans. Sue (1975) observed that Asian Americans tend to withdraw from social contacts and responsibility. Sue went on to point out that the tendency of Asian Americans to choose occupations in the physical sciences and technical trades might be due to this social anxiety, discomfort, and inhibition. In any event, Sue noted that Asian Americans are underrepresented in the social sciences and other vocations that require verbal/pursuasive skills and high levels of social interactions such as law and psychology.

Besides the personality dimensions identified by Leong (1985), Hsia (1980) also discussed the role of a field-independent cognitive style among Asian Americans in the occupational segregation and limited occupational mobility among Asian Americans. She noted that given their field-independent orientation, Asian Americans were much more likely to be limited to scientific and technical careers and were not likely to be successful in the people-oriented occupations such as managerial and administrative positions that require the more field-dependent cognitive style. The relationship between field dependence/independence and occupational choices already has been examined; the evidence supports Hsia's observation, and her hypothesis is definitely worthy of further exploration with various Asian American samples. Her observation about cognitive style and career choices also points to the need to examine the role of cognitive styles in the career choices and behaviors of Asian Americans.

Some of the data from personality inventories already provide some support for Hsia's (1980) and Leong's (1985) hypotheses about the influence of personality variables on the career behavior of Asian Americans. For example, Sue and Frank's (1973) study, which was done on 69% of entering freshman males at Berkeley in the fall of 1966, found that Asian males leaned toward occupations encompassing routine business-detail activities. They were overrepresented in engineering and underrepresented in the social sciences. Asian men tended to score low in autonomy; they tended to be more conforming, more obedient to authority, and more connected to familial control. They tended to dislike ambiguity. They also experienced strong feelings of isolation, loneliness, and rejection.

Similarly, Sue and Kirk (1972) found that Japanese American students were less oriented toward theoretical or abstract ideas and concepts than were White American students. Japanese American students also tended to dislike ambiguity in favor of structured situations. They tended to evaluate ideas based on immediate practical applications and were more socially conforming.

In a study examining the influence of the sex-role identity and occupational attainment of Asian American women's psychological well-being, Chow (1987) tested three hypotheses: (a) both masculine and androgynous Asian American women would have a higher level of occupational attainment than would those with feminine and undifferentiated sex-role identities; (b) androgynous Asian American women would have a higher level of self-esteem and greater work satisfaction than would those with other sex-role identities; and (c) the higher the level of occupational attainment secured by Asian American women, the higher their level of self-esteem and work satisfaction.

In Chow's (1987) survey, 161 Asian American women (Chinese, Japanese, Korean, and Filipino) were rated for occupational attainment, work satisfaction, and self-esteem. Most of the individuals were employed full-time, and information was obtained through the Bem Sex Role Inventory (BSRI), the Self-Esteem Scale, and interviews.

The results of the study supported all three of the hypotheses just stated. Chow (1987) also questioned Bem's assertion that androgyny benefits behavioral adaptivity and personal competence because it was masculinity and not androgyny that was linked to the greatest occupational attainment among Asian American women. However, this study points to androgyny as being a positive and healthy state for women given that androgynous Asian American women scored high levels of self-esteem.

Interestingly, feminine women scored higher in both self-esteem and work satisfaction than did masculine women. This is perhaps due to the stronger emphasis of femininity in women that is placed by Asian culture. The concluding results appeared to indicate that both masculine and feminine qualities are important for the career development and physiological well-being of Asian American women. Chow (1987) also suggested that enhancing both androgyny and occupational status would improve the self-esteem and work satisfaction of Asian American women.

Work Adjustment and Vocational Problems

Asian Americans experience both a unique set of work adjustment problems and vocational problems common to many minority groups. One work adjustment problem that many Asian Americans have to deal with concerns their academic abilities. As measured by tests such as the SAT, Asian Americans tend to have lower levels of verbal skills in English than do White Americans. In 1988, Asian SAT verbal scores averaged 408, which was 37 points lower than the average for Whites (445). On the other hand, the average mathematics score for Asians (552) was 62 points higher than that for Whites (490) (National Science Foundation, 1990). Although never investigated systematically, it is easy to envision that many Asian Americans experience career-related problems due to their limited ability with the English language. For example, Asian Americans might be perceived as less intelligent or less competent than their White counterparts on the job because they are not able to articulate what they know fully. This, in turn, could lead to consequences such as being passed over for promotion to managerial or supervisory positions or receiving lower ratings in performance appraisals.

Asian Americans' higher ability with mathematics also is a double-edged sword. Whereas the higher mathematics scores have helped balance out their lower verbal scores and increased their chances of admission into colleges and graduate programs, the combination of the two also creates a certain image. The popular stereotypical version of this image is of Asian Americans being engineering or computer science "geeks"—bespectacled, slide rules sticking out of their pockets, and spending all of their time buried in books. However one chooses to characterize this image, the impression is that Asian Americans are best at being "technicians," and not managers and supervisors, because they lack the social skills stemming from their lower verbal skills.

There is some evidence that Asian Americans do perceive themselves to be underemployed at work regardless of whether it is related to these stereotypes. In a recent national survey conducted by the Gallup organization, Brown et al. (1991) reported in their telephone survey of 1,350 adults (age 18 years or older) from three major minority groups—African Americans ($n = 737$), Hispanics ($n = 310$), and APIs ($n = 255$)—that APIs (47%) were less likely than Whites (54%), African Americans (60%), or Hispanics (63%) to report that their skills were being used very well. Large percentages of APIs (71%) and Hispanics (75%) also reported being interested in getting more information about careers if they could start over. More Asian Americans also reported experiencing stress on the job than did other minority groups; African Americans (59%) and Hispanics (61%) were significantly more likely than Whites (46%) or APIs (48%) to report little or no job stress.

In a study of Asian American students' help-seeking behavior and problem perception, Tracey, Leong, and Glidden (1986) found that Asian Americans were more likely to present vocational and career problems than personal-emotional problems to a counselor. They used archival data consisting of all clients seen at the student development center at the University of Hawaii at Manoa between the fall of 1980 and the spring of 1983. The final sample of 3,050 student clients consisted of the following ethnic groups: White, Chinese American, Filipino American, part Hawaiian, Korean American, Japanese American, Asian American-White mix, and Asian American mix.

Tracey et al. (1986) found that the problem endorsement rates differed significantly among the groups on each of the eight problem areas. Those problems reflecting interpersonal or intrapersonal concerns were disproportionately overendorsed by the Whites and fairly uniformly underendorsed by the Asian Americans. The Filipino American and Asian American-White mix students lay between the majority White students and the rest of the Asian American groups in endorsing these areas as concerns. All of the other areas (e.g., academic/career) seemed to be overendorsed by the Asian American students and underendorsed by the White students.

Asian American men were less likely to endorse more than one problem than were White men, whereas Asian American women were more likely to endorse more than one problem than were White women. Asian American clients were less likely to have had previous counseling. White clients were more likely to endorse a personal concern as paramount, especially if they had previous counseling. Asian American clients were more likely to endorse academic/vocational concerns as most important, but to a lesser degree if they had previous counseling (Tracey et al., 1986).

Yu and Wu's (1985) article addressed a unique work adjustment problem experienced by Chinese Americans, namely the stress from being unable to provide for extended family members. Because the ability to assist financially in the care of aged relatives often is dependent on one's employment and income, Yu and Wu examined the relationship among unemployment, marital status, and discomfort experienced by Chinese American adults when providing support to their parents and parents-in-law.

Combining the city directory with the university faculty and student directories, Yu and Wu (1985) found 1,005 people with Chinese surnames. They then cross-referenced the three directories and obtained a list of 872 unduplicated names with verifiable addresses. From this total sample, 510 respondents (59%) returned the self-administered questionnaires. Although the age of respondents ranged from 18 to 90 years, the sample population was relatively young (mean age 35 ± 15).

Yu and Wu (1985) found that 45% ($n = 88$) of the single respondents were employed and 55% ($n = 106$) were not employed; of the married respondents, 77% ($n = 228$) were employed and 23% ($n = 69$) were not employed (this was due mainly to respondents who were full-time students). Their data also showed that among the married couples, 64% reported that both spouses were employed,

28% reported that one spouse was working, and only 8% reported that both spouses were not employed.

The levels of stress reported in Yu and Wu's (1985) investigation were not the same for American-born (24% of their sample were American born) and naturalized Chinese Americans. The American-born respondents tended to be younger, to earn less money, and to be more acculturated to American traditions than did the naturalized Chinese Americans. The American-born respondents believed in giving financial support to aged parents, but few actually did so; many of them said that their parents did not need help because they still were young, that their parents' economic situations were better than their own, and/or that they did not believe in cohabitation with their parents.

Yu and Wu's (1985) sample did not exhibit the traditional Chinese pattern of family responsibility, as 46% of married females worked outside the home; some contributed economically to their in-laws through financial assistance and cohabitation, whereas others contributed economically to their own parents as well. The authors found that married women's parents lived with their families as often as did the husbands' parents. They also found that 44% of married women gave support to their in-laws, but when they explored the question of whether a difference existed between the husband's and the wife's discomfort toward their respective parents-in-law with regard to financial and housing issues, they found no difference in discomfort levels. In 58 (81%) out of 72 married couples, both husband and wife gave support to their own parents. In the sample, women were not only working outside the home but also contributing financially to their own parents' needs.

Employment status affected the discomfort level of males, with the unemployed reporting the highest discomfort among four groups in providing financial support to aged parents. Marital status interacted with employment status; married employed persons tended to give support to their parents (in 58 out of 72 couples, both spouses gave to their parents). The married respondents tended to be older; among the 72 married couples, the mean age of those for whom both spouses worked was 42 years. Among this group, 54% of married males and 46% of married females worked. Higher income, however, did not necessarily mean that these respondents had more money to spend. Some of them probably had college-aged children who also depended on them for support.

Yu and Wu (1985) also found an interaction between employment and marital status with the housing issue; married and employed respondents, regardless of gender, cohabitated with their parents or parents-in-law more often than did single respondents. Again, the married and employed respondents were older, had higher incomes, and probably resided in better housing. However, very few respondents reported that their parents-in-law were living with them or intended to live with them permanently as was the custom in traditional China. Moreover, a high correlation was found between the husband's and the wife's discomfort level with regard to giving money to parents and living with parents-in-law, indicating that the husband's discomfort in meeting financial and housing needs was related to his wife's discomfort and vice versa.

Yu and Wu (1985) concluded that employment decreased the discomfort levels of respondents if they met their aging relatives' needs but that employment status alone was not the deciding factor in meeting those needs. Marital status interacted with employment in the provision of both financial and housing assistance; employed married respondents gave money and lived with their aged relatives more often than did unemployed and/or single respondents. Furthermore, the discriminating factor in meeting aged relatives' needs was providing financial aid to parents-in-law; respondents who did not give support to their parents-in-law reported higher discomfort than did those who did give such support, regardless of whether they gave support to or lived with their own parents. Finally, one spouse's discomfort in meeting such needs affected the discomfort level of the other spouse.

Related to the preceding study, Sung (1987, as cited in Liu, Yu, Chang, & Fernandez, 1990) found that the lengthy absence of many Chinese American parents from home created a major stressor for the whole family. The absences were necessitated by both parents having to work long hours to support the family. Sung (1987) interpreted her data to support the idea that these long absences contributed significantly to Chinese teenagers becoming gang members to substitute for a sense of identity and belonging that was unavailable at home.

Redding and Ng (1982) also examined a culturally related work adjustment problem among the Chinese. They investigated the role of "face" in the organizational perceptions among Chinese managers. Although the study was conducted on Chinese and not Chinese Americans, it is included here because it investigated an important dimension that was worthy of exploration and might have parallels for Chinese Americans.

According to Redding and Ng (1982), face is particularly salient for the Chinese and is argued to be a key in explaining much of their behavior. Their article discussed the operation of face in the Chinese business context, indicating the power of face as a mediating force in social interactions, in business transactions, or in social situations inside formal organizations.

Redding and Ng (1982) described two dimensions to the Chinese concept of face and discussed it by using either of the two words *lien* or *mien-tzu*. Lien is good moral character and is more ascribed than achieved. Mien-tzu is the idea of the reputation based on one's own efforts and is more achieved than ascribed. Face is the individual's assessment of how others chose to see him or her. In business behavior, the great importance of trust in Chinese business relationships and the resulting informality as to contracts and agreements rest on the common adoption of lien as a moral foundation.

Research was conducted with 102 Chinese middle-level executives in commercial, trading, and engineering companies in Hong Kong. First, a bilingual questionnaire was administered covering different aspects of the perception of face and its operation. Second, in individual interviews, respondents were asked to describe specific face incidents from their experiences.

The salience of status and power was made clear. The reactions to losing face were shame (100% of respondents); worry (99%); feelings of uneasiness, anxiety, and tension (98%); difficulty in concentrating on work (72%); and symptoms such as blushing (64%). The main effect appears to be short term. Long-term effects such as loss of appetite and loss of sleep were reported as probable by only 33% and 21% of respondents, respectively.

When respondents were asked whether having face influenced success in daily business transactions and negotiations, the response was 100% strongly positive. Almost equally strongly negative (97%) was not having face. The process of being given face during a transaction also was seen as highly favorable (96%). To have one's face challenged or deliberately destroyed was seen as highly unfavorable (100%). In addition, 100% of the sample responded that if they were being given face, then they would give it back in return. If their face were being challenged or attacked, then 80% of the respondents indicated they would retaliate by destroying the other's face in return and 20% would retaliate by simply not giving face (Redding & Ng, 1982).

The objective of the content analysis of the incidents was to investigate themes. The first grouping of classification deals with *how* and *why* it operates, and the second deals with *where* and *when* it operates. There is commonly a fundamental clash between the behaviors needed when taking face into account and those needed to meet the rational needs of the organization. Typical problems referred to in the original accounts are having to restrain from criticizing a subordinate because of face obligation to a third party who has been a sponsor, extra costs involved in meeting customer requirements so as not to lose face with the customer, dilution of managerial authority due to loss of face, and the risks involved in transactions based on trust and on the maintenance of face. There is some acknowledgment of the advantage of using face in business transactions. The appropriateness of a Western bureaucracy form of organization to the Oriental context is a question of the clash of two Western values—rationality and individualism—with Oriental values of a different and not so simply classifiable nature. On these grounds, Redding and Ng (1982) argued that the introduction of Western managerial systems will either meet resistance or be subjected to extensive adaptation.

In one of only a few studies that examined gender issues in the work adjustment of Asian Americans, Fujii, Fukushima, and Chang (1989) examined the experiences and thoughts of Asian women psychiatrists who must deal with the impact of gender, race, and culture on the evolution of their careers. In the study, 10 Asian American women in the psychiatry field were given a 90-minute semistructured interview. This allowed for the collection of demographic data and for each respondent to relate her experiences in an open-ended fashion. Interviews were conducted with 2 Chinese, 2 Filipinos, 4 Japanese, 1 Vietnamese, and 1 Korean. Ages ranged from 26 to 44 years, with a mean age of 35.

There were significant differences between the foreign medical graduates (FMGs) and those who were trained in the United States. The FMGs were older, were married to men of the same ethnicity, had retained their religious ties, and were the eldest in their families. The non-FMGs were generally younger and were married to or involved with men who were ethnically dissimilar to themselves. Although some had been raised religiously, they did not have strong ties to their religions. Reasons for entering the field varied in a way not related to any variable (Fujii et al., 1989).

As a general rule, families of the women had disapproved of their career choices. There is not as much respect for psychiatrists in the United States and Asia as there is for surgeons. Racism and positive and negative stereotyping by residence faculty, colleagues, and patients appeared to be present, albeit sometimes subtly. Some of the women felt "pushed" into minority issues or felt pressure to behave in a certain way.

All of the women reported satisfaction with their professional lives. They were deeply committed to their profession. FMGs relied on family and religion to help them through difficult times. It appears that they assimilated but did not acculturate. Non-FMGs were more similar to their mainstream colleagues.

Both in the United States and in Asian countries, psychiatry is not considered a "typical" choice for Asians, who usually are expected to excel in mathematics, science, engineering, and computer science. The Asian women who chose medicine and eventually psychiatry differed from Asian women in the United States and in their native lands. Most were the eldest in their families and had experienced unusual life circumstances such as fleeing a native land that was under siege, facing the possibility of a fatal illness, having a life-changing mentor, or dealing with personal periods of emotional stress with self-recognized and acknowledged mood disturbance. The number of Asian women psychiatrists in the United States is small but growing. Fujii et al. (1989) pointed out that future inquiry into this subpopulation of Asian Americans might include issues related to stereotyping and its effects, training, transference, countertransference, and therapy for Asian women psychiatrists.

Another common problem experienced by many Asian American groups concerns the impact of migration on their work adjustment in the host country. Kincaid and Yum (1987) examined some of the socioeconomic consequences of the migration of Samoans, Koreans, and Filipinos in Hawaii in contrast to local Japanese and Caucasian residents. Special attention was given to income levels, occupational mobility, and difficulty of adjustment as indicated by the incidence of stressful life events.

Kincaid and Yum's (1987) results were obtained by means of a cross-sectional sample survey conducted in Honolulu and Hilo from 1978 to 1979 from independently drawn samples of first-generation immigrants from Korea, the Philippines, and Samoa as well as from resident Japanese Americans and Caucasian Americans who were born in Hawaii or migrated there from Japan or the U.S. mainland. All data were collected by face-to-face home interviews by native-language speakers from the same ethnic group. There were approximately similar-size samples of males and females from each ethnic group except for the Filipino sample, which was only 36% male.

Filipinos had the lowest average level of education with 8 years as compared to 11 years for Samoans, 12 years for Koreans, 13 years for Japanese, and 15 years for Caucasians. This order of educational experience corresponds exactly to the order of the average occupational status of these ethnic groups. The annual family income of Samoans is extremely low compared to that of any other ethnic group. They also have the lowest percentage of both spouses working and the highest percentage of both spouses not working. In addition, 76% earn less than $10,000 a year. One of the reasons why Samoans are low in household income is that Samoan women are not as active in the labor market as are women from the other ethnic groups.

According to Kincaid and Yum (1987), one of the main consequences of migration is the intensification of the differences in occupational prestige between the Caucasians and Japanese, on the one hand, and the three immigrant groups, on the other. The second most important consequence was the striking decrease in occupational status of Korean men relative to Caucasians from the U.S. mainland and the decrease in the mean occupational prestige of Samoan men relative to Filipino men. The third most important result of the analysis was the overall difference in occupational mobility across the four migrant groups after they arrived in Hawaii.

The Samoans had experienced greater amounts of stress as a group than had any of the other groups. Second were the Koreans, then the Caucasians, then the Japanese, and then the Filipinos. The Caucasians reported the highest incidence of outstanding personal achievement of 13% as compared to 3% for the Japanese, 2% for the Koreans, 1% for the Filipinos, and no occurrence at all for the Samoans. The greatest incidence of dissatisfaction was expressed by the Korean immigrants.

Samoans made greater use of the Social Security Administration (29%) than did the other two immigrant groups, with 25% of Filipinos and only 3% of Koreans reporting having used the Social Security Administration. More people were aware of social agencies than had ever used them. The most serious information gap or problem of awareness was among the Samoan immigrants.

Kincaid and Yum (1987) also observed that one of the main results of migration was a substantial drop in occupational prestige for the three immigrant groups and for the Caucasians. The Korean immigrants had experienced the greatest decrease of status among all ethnic groups in Hawaii. The authors concluded from this study that the needs of each immigrant group were different and that social policies should reflect these differences in their priorities.

Several studies also have examined the work adjustment problems experienced by Southeast Asian immigrants and refugees. In the first of these studies, Vertiz and Fortune (1984) reported on an intervention program for Blacks, Hispanics, Chicanos, American Indians, and Indochinese at J. E. B. Stuart High School in Fairfax County, Virginia. The program was designed to meet some of the employment and support service needs of the school's foreign-born students, with an emphasis on Indochinese. The program, which was geared to enrollees of English as a second language (ESL) classes (particularly to those who were not progressing rapidly in English), serves other foreign born as well. The authors also described some of the effects of cultural discrepancies on the employment of Indochinese youths.

Vertiz and Fortune (1984) observed that the majority of foreign-born students lacked necessary skills to obtain jobs because of language and cultural differences. For instance, to show respect, Indochinese children must keep their eyes lowered when speaking to adults. In the United States, during a job interview, eye contact is equated with honesty, sincerity, and straightforwardness. Hence, the Indochinese often were misread in their attempts to show respect.

These and other "cultural discrepancies" also caused obvious employer-employee misunderstandings in the American workplace, where subordinates were expected to ask questions to learn or to clarify instructions. The fact that most Indochinese are embarrassed about their limited knowledge of English also contributed to their hesitation to ask questions or to say what was on their minds.

Vertiz and Fortune's (1984) workshops employed the concept of self-directed placement and focused on developing the qualities necessary to communicate effectively in an interview. Based on trust building, activities were conducted in small groups and met the following broad objectives: (a) identification of personal values, interests, aptitudes, and abilities; (b) communication of personal qualities to others; (c) identification of at least two types of pre-entry-level jobs that would provide viable experience toward tentative career options; (d) location of possible employment sites; (e) establishment of personal contact with potential employers to inquire about part-time jobs; (f) completion of a job application; and (g) interviews in small groups with personnel specialists from business and industry as well as in a one-to-one situation with videotape. Vertiz and Fortune reported that the participants in the workshops showed considerable progress in learning job interviewing skills.

In another study examining the adjustment of Southeast Asian refugees in the United States, Nicassio and Pate (1984) sought to identify major obstacles to resettlement as perceived by the refugees, to evaluate interrelationships between problems of adjustment, and to study the influence of pertinent sociodemographic factors on various indexes of adjustment.

The first phase of the project consisted of a mail survey with a questionnaire. Information was obtained on the sociodemographic characteristics of the refugees, their awareness and use of social services, and their evaluation of the magnitude of their adjustment problems. A total of 968 completed instruments were received, representing a response rate of approximately 43%. The second and third phases of the project were a lengthier questionnaire administered to 349 Indochinese attending ESL classes and interviews with 460 heads of household who had not participated in the two previous phases. The combination of these three phases yielded a sample size of 1,638.

Data on two measures of adjustment were reported in Nicassio and Pate's (1984) article. The first measure was a problem index that consisted of the responses to 32 potential problems of adjustment. Also, refugees who were interviewed in their homes responded to a 10-item measure of alienation.

Respondents were predominantly male, young, and of Vietnamese extraction. There was considerable financial deprivation shown in the sample. The refugees reported an average of 4.45 residents per household and had been in the United States an average of 25.67 months at the time the research was conducted.

Problems of separation and emigration stress received major emphasis. Also regarded as very serious were problems such as learning to speak English, finances, job skills, and medical care, which reflected the most imminent survival needs of the refugees. The reporting of problems in specific areas was predictive of adjustment difficulty in all other areas.

From the pattern of correlations in the Nicassio and Pate (1984) study, it is evident that refugees who were more advanced in age, had less education and income, were unemployed, and had resided in the United States for shorter periods of time reported more adjustment difficulty. The social adjustment of refugees to the new cultural setting was very significantly related to their socioeconomic level. The socioeconomic, psychological, and cultural dimensions of adjustment among refugees and immigrants probably are interactive and mutually dependent.

Nicassio and Pate (1984) concluded that the results of their investigation had significant practical implications for services rendered to the Indochinese during their resettlement. First, interventions that consolidate or develop the support systems and networks of refugees would appear to be particularly valuable. Second, services that enhance the educational and job-related skills of refugees should receive major emphasis because improvement in the socioeconomic area might facilitate psychosocial adjustment. The results also indicated that work adjustment was a major problem.

In a similar study, Matsuoka and Ryujin (1989) collected panel data on 125 Vietnamese refugee families drawn from the San Diego area. Neighborhoods reflecting different income levels were selected to ensure a more representative sample. Letters were sent to potential respondents requesting interviews. Once a request was accepted, an interview was conducted with at least one member of that family. A team of six bilingual Vietnamese conducted the interviews. Generally speaking, the refugees were extremely suspicious of the interviewers.

The interviews were designed to collect information in several critical areas. These areas included (a) background information on each respondent (e.g., age, religious affiliation), (b) circumstances surrounding the respondent's evacuation from Vietnam, (c) sponsorship experiences, (d) patterns of mobility since arriving in the United States, (e) employment history, (f) the refugee community, (g) mental health, and (h) prospects for the future. Findings indicated that Vietnamese refugees were experiencing difficulties in adjustment associated with learning a new culture and leaving behind parts of an old one. Many of the respondents who stated that they had no problem adjusting to life in the United States were young people.

In Matsuoka and Ryujin's (1989) study, 75% of the respondents believed that their children would be more successful than they would, and 47% felt that they would not be able to attain what they had obtained in Vietnam. However, 40% felt that they would be able to climb back to where they had been or even surpass their accomplishments in Vietnam.

Fully 88% of parents wanted their children to retain traditional aspects of Vietnamese culture. Filial piety was an important issue for parents, as 39% thought that their children would retain this characteristic and 38% said that they could only hope for it. Only 11% of the respondents felt that its value would diminish among their children's generation.

Vietnamese enclaves in the resettlement and psychological adjustment of Vietnamese refugees were extremely important. These communities appear to be an important source of mutual support. The biggest adjustment problems for refugees deal with language, cultural differences, and employment. What refugees miss most about Vietnam are the emotional support of loved ones and the cultural way of life inherent to their country. Many refugees enjoy the freedom, opportunities, and comforts provided by the United States, but a quarter of the Vietnamese said that there was nothing they liked about the United States. Many restricted themselves materially to minimize their feelings of guilt.

Matsuoka and Ryujin (1989) argued that American social workers could provide services that help the refugees to survive in American society—language training, job training, access to employment, economic support, courses on the U.S. culture, and counseling on how to obtain all of these.

Haines (1987) also found employment to be a major source of stress for Southeast Asian refugees. His article addressed three distinct issues in the study of Southeast Asian refugee employment: the general patterns in Southeast Asian refugee employment in the United States, the major correlates of refugee employment, and statistical analysis of the relative effects of these different correlates. There were consistent patterns in refugee employment, consistently appearing correlates of employment success, but a somewhat less consistent set of statistical interpretations of these patterns and correlates.

As labor force participation rises in a consistent fashion, unemployment rates drop. Very severe employment problems are faced by refugees on their arrival in the United States, many of which are the result of refugee exodus. These problems are then reflected in the receipt of various forms of public assistance, whose figures decrease from very high initial levels to the approximate one third in assistance among refugees resident in the United States for more than 3 years. The consistent pattern of economic improvement has three elements: increasing labor force participation, declining unemployment, and declining receipt of public assistance.

There exists much documentation of these improvements. However, there is a difficult initial situation that permits such an impressive improvement, and figures have shown a potential downward shift over time in that starting point. Also, there is only limited improvement in wage and salary income, and economic self-sufficiency often is due to an increase in the number of jobs in the household rather than to any great increase in the income from individual jobs. Refugees may well end up in dead-end jobs and lack occupational mobility after arrival. Perhaps the most crucial issue is the jobs that refugees obtain. There is an initial downward step that might not be ameliorated over time.

Three correlates seem related to occupational attainment: ability to understand and communicate in English, occupational background in Southeast Asia, and education. All three can indicate occupational status in the United States, although they might overlap. To some extent, then, these correlations are not the separate effects of different variables but rather the effects of socioeconomic status (Haines, 1987).

In another study of Southeast Asians, Tang and O'Brien (1990) defined the vocational expectations of the Indochinese refugees by their willingness to stay on low-status jobs. The authors used existing vocational data from a social service organization. The data consisted mainly of demographic information related to the refugees and the positions into which they were placed.

Status inconsistency was operationally defined as the difference in occupational status between the refugees' previous positions in their homeland and their present positions. Vocational success was defined as the length of time the refugees spent on their present jobs.

Participants were 529 Indochinese refugees (337 males and 192 females) who used the employment placement services of the Center for Southeast Asian Refugee Resettlement between 1981 and 1984. The following variables were collected: (a) number of days worked before quitting or being fired from the most recent job placement, (b) job retention during the monitoring period (90 days), (c) starting wage in the most recent job placement, (d) welfare status, (e) English proficiency, (f) age, (g) number of languages spoken, (h) number of jobs held in the United States before placement, (i) education, (j) months in the United States before receiving job placement, and (k) prestige of the individual's current job placement, last job in Indochina, the position currently desired, and the ultimately desired career position. Intercorrelations among all variables were computed.

Participants who had been in America for fewer than 3 years worked an average of 53 days on their previous job placement, whereas those who had been in America for more than 3 years worked an average of 77 days. The longer the individual had stayed in America, the greater the likelihood of vocational success. Before 3 years of residence in America, individuals who had held low-prestige positions in Asia worked longer than did their high-prestige counterparts. After the 3-year period, the situation was reversed, with those individuals who previously held high-prestige positions working much longer than their previously low-prestige counterparts. Analyses of variance (ANOVAs) using gender, age, educational level, and public assistance as predictors of vocational success yielded nonsignificant results.

Tang and O'Brien's (1990) study provided evidence that status inconsistency affected the vocational success of the Indochinese refugees. Those refugees who had more than 3 years of residence exhibited fewer psychosocial problems than did those who had less than 3 years of residence. Once the immigrants had become culturally acclimated, achieving vocational goals that were consistent with their self-concept became more important. Former high-prestige refugees might attempt to reduce the dissonance produced by status incongruence by leaving low-status positions in a desire to seek positions more consistent with their expectations or self-image. Inability to find high-prestige positions could lead to a high turnover rate for this group.

The Tang and O'Brien (1990) findings have an important implication for refugee assistance efforts. Agency interventions with status-inconsistent individuals should be focused on maintaining and enhancing self-esteem. Also, the counselor might try to convince the refugees that there are other aspects to a job (e.g., learning new skills, helping to fulfill the goals of the larger organization, earning a wage or salary) that are as important as job prestige.

In the final study concerned with Southeast Asians, Anh and Healy (1985) examined the factors believed to affect the job satisfaction of Vietnamese refugees. Participants were 210 Vietnamese refugees drawn randomly from the public social service rosters of Los Angeles and Orange counties in California in 1979 and interviewed in 1980. Of these, 127 worked full-time, 23 worked part-time, and 60 were unemployed. There were 88 women and 122 men. The mean income was $5,423. The participants had been in the United States for an average of 3.4 years.

The questionnaire had 131 items related to aspects of work and resettlement in the United States. The authors used ANOVA and chi-square to ascertain whether being employed and feeling satisfied with one's job related to length of time in the United States, estimated English proficiency, and views about job-seeking resources.

On average, the immigrants were moderately satisfied with their jobs. Overall satisfaction related moderately and positively to wages and related negatively to number of obstacles to having the desired job. Among the participants, 39% believed they lacked job skills, 30% thought they needed more job information, 26% reported a scarcity of suitable jobs and inadequate transportation, 21% felt isolated, and 10% felt discouraged. On average, the refugees judged their English proficiency as moderate.

Ratings on the helpfulness of seven job-seeking resources were skewed negatively. Only Vietnamese friends were generally considered somewhat helpful; all other sources were considered somewhat less than helpful. The comparisons showed a significant positive relationship between time in the United States and employment status and satisfaction. The unemployed averaged 2.6 years in the United States, whereas part- and full-time workers averaged 3.6 years. Refugees in the United States for 3 or more years were more satisfied than were those present 1 or 2 years, and those in the United States 2 years were more satisfied than those present 1 year or less.

English proficiency was not found to be related to employment or employment status, but it was significantly related to job satisfaction. Of the variables considered in Anh and Healy's (1985) study, time was the most consistent in its relation to the refugees' resettlement. Refugees who were in the United States the longest were most likely to have jobs and to feel satisfied with their jobs. It is important, however, for future research to verify that increases in satisfaction over time do not merely indicate that refugees have settled for poor jobs.

Anh and Healy (1985) concluded that Vietnamese face many of the same obstacles that other refugees have encountered including nonrecognition of their degrees and skills, lack of information about the labor market, licensing restrictions, lack of an established ethnic support community, and regulations limiting training to citizens or established residents.

In another study related to job satisfaction, McNeely (1987) surveyed Asian American human service workers. A survey was mailed to 2,925 county human service workers located in geographically disparate areas of the United States and yielded 68 Asian American and 1,299 other respondents. A portion of the sample (210 respondents) was eliminated because they had moved, so the final response rate was 50.3%.

Participating respondents were given a questionnaire consisting of 115 Likert-type items. Several questions focused on demographic data—age, length of employment, education, income, and occupational status, among others. Three indexes were incorporated into the instrument. The Science Research Associates Attitude Survey determines precise correlates of job satisfaction; the 78 items pinpoint specific aspects of respondents' working conditions. The Index of Job Satisfaction (IJS) focuses on employees' subjective assessments regarding their jobs. It consists of 18 items, and its scores determine overall levels of job satisfaction. The third index, the Morse Index of Intrinsic Job Satisfaction, assesses intrinsic job satisfaction—those aspects of the job that satisfy what has been described as workers' fundamental need for creative and challenging work.

A statistically significant difference was observed for occupational status, with disproportionate underrepresentation of Asian Americans in both managerial and supervisory positions and overrepresentation in paraprofessional positions. The data did not reveal any significant differences between Asian American and non-Asian workers in length of employment. Even though the Asian American respondents had attained higher levels of education, they earned less. The Asian American families appeared to be more stable than those of other workers. No statistical differences were observed for age.

There were no significant differences between the Asian American and non-Asian respondents on either overall (Index of Job Satisfaction) or intrinsic (Morse Index) satisfaction. The job satisfaction of Asian American respondents was affected substantially by their perception of whether or not "most of the 'higher-ups' are friendly toward employees." This finding fits with the perhaps stereotypical belief that Asian Americans are more affected by their treatment at the hands of superiors than are other racial groups. The "most of the 'higher-ups' are friendly toward employees" variable was virtually unrelated to the non-Asian respondents' level of satisfaction (McNeely, 1987).

GROUP AND SOCIETAL LEVELS OF ANALYSIS

Psychology as a field of scientific inquiry has tended to employ an individual level of analysis with a few exceptions. These exceptions include social psychology, organizational psychology, and community psychology. However, much of psychological research and theorizing have focused on the individual. This emphasis also has been true within the field of vocational psychology. However, as Smith (1983) and many others have observed (Leong & Brown, 1995), the study of the experience of racial and ethnic minority members at the individual level of analysis misses many important factors (e.g., institutional racism, intergroup conflicts). Hence, although the analysis of the individual is the strength of psychology, a complete career psychology of the minority groups in general and of Asian Americans in particular will come about only with an extension to higher levels of analyses such as group or societal phenomena.

Family Influences on the Career Development of Asian Americans

Psychologists and other social scientists have long indicated that the family plays a central role in the lives of Asian Americans that is different from the role it plays in the lives of White Americans (e.g., Sue & Morishima, 1982). Yet very little research has been conducted on the influence of the family on the career choices and behaviors of Asian Americans. There have been, however, a few studies to date.

Evanoski and Tse (1989) described a career awareness program for Chinese and Korean American parents. They argued that education and career choices are of great importance to many Chinese and Korean families. The crucial role of Chinese and Korean parents in the career choice of their children makes it imperative that they not be omitted from the career counseling efforts of the educational institutions.

The main goal of the career awareness program for Chinese and Korean American parents was to establish a linkage whereby role models of similar cultures and backgrounds could use their prestige and knowledge to inform parents of career opportunities for their children. Another goal was to explain the concept of the community college and the academic and career programs available, thus offering a great variety of career choices to newly arrived immigrants and their children.

The role models were professionals identified by closely knit networks in the Chinese and Korean communities. They had to have several years of professional working experience, be good speakers, and be willing to serve the community by volunteering to make presentations. A series of 10 separate workshops for each school year were planned, with each workshop being a complete program. Each workshop was approximately 3 hours long. After the more formal presentations by the role models, there were question-and-answer exchanges with the parents.

The workshops served 1,140 Chinese and Korean parents and 551 students in the 1985-1986 school year as well as 1,413 Chinese and Korean parents and 1,987 students in the 1986-1987 school year. A survey was filled out by 550 persons during 1985-1986 and by 801 persons during 1986-1987. More than

90% of the respondents reported that they learned more about new jobs for themselves and their children, 86% reported that they were better informed about the employment outlook for particular occupations and the anticipated salary schedules, 85% reported that they were more knowledgeable about the educational requirements of the occupations discussed, and 94% reported that they were more informed about the types of financial aid available for college for themselves and for their children.

Evanoski and Tse (1989) pointed out that the most useful strategy in starting such programs seems to be the concept of a bilingual role model. It also was recommended that written materials be prepared in the native language of the target group. Linkage with community organizations of the special target population also was critical to the success of such programs.

In one of only a few empirical pieces, Johnson et al. (1983) designed a study to assess the relations of scores on standardized psychometric tests of personality and cognition with the educational and occupational levels attained by a group of middle-aged males and females. Along with sex differences, possible ethnic differences in the relative influence of background, ability, and personality were examined by comparing results obtained from Americans of European ancestry (AEA) to those obtained from Americans of Japanese ancestry (AJA).

More than 1,800 families consisting of two biological parents and one or more offspring over 13 years of age were tested on a battery of 15 cognitive tests. Respondents provided information regarding their own years of education and their occupations. Respondents also provided information regarding the years of education of their fathers and mothers and, during later years of testing, provided information regarding paternal occupations. Various subsets of respondents were administered personality measures as well. The majority of the subjects were AEAs, and the minority were AJAs.

The family background indexes were consistently positively correlated with respondents' educational attainment. Cognitive abilities were positively correlated with educational attainment, with verbal ability producing the highest correlations. An Adjective Check List (ACL) scale, Ego Organization, was positively correlated with educational attainment. Superego Strength declined in importance for college-aged respondents in predicting school achievement. Internal Discomfort (neuroticism) was negatively associated with educational attainment. Intraception, which measures rebelliousness, was positively related to final educational attainment. The obtained correlations of these variables with educational attainment were fairly consistent across both ethnicity and sex.

Educational attainment was a strong predictor of occupational attainment. The correlations of the family background items with occupational attainment were similar to those found for educational attainment and were consistent across ethnicities, in spite of the AJA respondents' parents coming from a lower socioeconomic stratum than those of the AEA respondents. The respondents' occupational status was positively correlated with cognitive ability for both the first principal component and some of the factor scores. Verbal ability showed the strongest relation to occupational attainment, as it did to educational attainment.

For verbal ability and the first principal component, the AJA correlation with occupational attainment was .15 to .20 higher than the same-sex AEA correlation. A respondent's father's occupational status did have an influence on the educational and occupational status of his adult children, although it was not as strong as is usually assumed. Associations did exist between family background and cognition and personality measures. Educational attainment remained a strong predictor of occupational attainment over and above the effect of family background and cognitive ability. In many cases, the correlations were actually higher for the AJA group than for the AEA group (Johnson et al., 1983).

In observing that most Chinese companies are started and run by families, Wong (1985) described a model of the family firm. According to Wong, prototypically, the father-entrepreneur is the founder of the business, which centralizes decision making and cuts down on the delegation of responsibility to subordinates. The father-entrepreneur is a busy man carrying the entire business on his shoulders. The father's children all will share the business evenly when the father leaves, weakening the business's power and centralization. There often is a tug-of-war between the father-entrepreneur and the sons-inheritors until fate intervenes by removing the former. The father often does not want to retire in fear of losing face or having the company fail.

It is clear that once the sons take over the business, the consensus among brothers cannot be taken for granted. The power of the new chief executive is greatly curtailed. He no longer enjoys his predecessor's flexibility in reinvestment and transferring funds laterally. Thus, the characteristic features of this phase are the outward expansion of the enterprise owing to segmentation and a reduction in the flexibility for reinvestment and risk taking.

Although relationships among Chinese brothers doubtlessly are brittle, the most fragile family bonds are to be found among first cousins if they remain in the same *jia* (Chinese family). The family business will either stay strong or be run into the ground by uncaring owners. The durability of the Chinese family firm is, of course, a relative matter. Compared to its Japanese equivalent, it would appear to be transitory. Because the Japanese practice primogeniture in the sense that only one male heir is chosen for succession, it is easier for the ownership and management of the family estate to remain intact. There are bound to be many external factors that would alter these cycles. However, the Chinese family firm, if left on its own, tends to evolve from the father-entrepreneur to his sons, with the sons eventually losing power. In describing the dynamics of the Chinese family firm, Wong (1985) pointed out the potential impact of family and cultural variables' interactions on the career behavior of some Chinese families.

Occupational Stereotyping

Although it has been known for a long time that Asian Americans often are the victims of occupational stereotyping, virtually no empirical study of this phenomenon had been undertaken until that of Leong and Hayes (1990). The purpose of their study was to determine empirically (a) whether occupational stereotyping of Asian Americans occurred among White college students and (b) what the *positive* and *negative* stereotypes of Asian Americans might be regarding occupations. The participants were 262 students enrolled in an introductory psychology class in a large eastern university. All were under 30 years old, and 97.5% of them were single. Only Whites were used (46% males and 54% females).

The questionnaire consisted of two parts. First, it gave a profile of a high school senior, alternating in description only between male and female and between White and Oriental. Because the questionnaires were identical in every way except race and gender of the profile, it was assumed that any differences in rating would be the result of stereotyping by race and sex. The second part of the questionnaire asked participants to rate, on a scale of 1 to 7, (a) how well qualified the student was to seek *training* in certain occupations, (b) the probability of *success* in 16 different occupations, and (c) how likely the individual was to be *accepted* by his or her coworkers in those occupations.

For the dimension of "qualified to seek training," only the main effect for gender was significant. Women were seen as less qualified to seek training as engineers, economists, and police officers but as more qualified to seek training as secretaries. For the dimension of "probability of success," both the race and gender main effects were significant, whereas the interaction was not. Significant gender stereotyping differences also were found for secretary and police officer. Also, women were rated as more likely to be successful as elementary school teachers and less likely to be successful as computer scientists. Asians were seen as being less likely to succeed in insurance sales but more likely to be successful as engineers, computer scientists, and mathematicians as compared to Whites. For the dimension of "likely to be accepted," neither the main effects nor the interaction was significant.

Asian American students were perceived as being less likely to be successful as insurance salespersons. They were rated more likely to be successful as engineers, computer scientists, and mathematicians. The lack of significant race by gender interactions seems to suggest that gender stereotyping by occupations might operate for both Whites and Asian Americans.

Occupational stereotyping by gender and race continues to exist despite the increasing sophistication among the public about the social undesirability of prejudicial attitudes. Further research is needed to determine how widespread these occupational stereotypes are before accepting the generalizability of the current findings. Future research also is needed to assess the psychological impact of these occupational stereotypes on Asian Americans and to study both internal and external barriers.

Occupational Discrimination

The myth that Asian Americans are a successful minority has been well documented and discussed within the social science literature (Endo, 1974; Kim, 1973; Lan, 1976; Leong, 1985; Okimoto, 1974; Owan, 1975; Schmid & Nobbe, 1965; Sue & Kitano, 1973; Suzuki, 1977). Many have questioned the myth, arguing that the stereotypes do not generalize to all Asian Americans (Sue & Kitano, 1973) and pointing out that labeling Asian Americans as a successful or model minority has resulted in their being neglected in terms of research or intervention programs (Chun, 1980; Hsia, 1980; Kim, 1973; Kitano & Sue, 1973; Leong, 1985; Minatoya & Sedlacek, 1981; Owan, 1975; Sue & Kitano, 1973; Sue, Sue, & Sue, 1975; Sue & Wagner, 1973).

The successful minority myth has arisen from the documentation of achievements Asian Americans have made in the United States. They have been portrayed as overcoming injustice and setbacks to become one of the most upwardly mobile minority groups in the country (Peterson, 1966, 1971). These findings would lead one to believe that Asian Americans had successfully assimilated into American culture and, therefore, would not experience discriminatory barriers to their success. Reference to their higher levels of educational attainment often is used as evidence of this successful assimilation. In addition, traditional Asian cultures often have emphasized the importance of educational performance in achieving success in society.

Leong and Raote (1992) used some national data sets to challenge both the successful minority myth and the economic uniformity myth regarding Chinese Americans. The successful minority myth maintains that Asian Americans have been able to use their own resources to achieve high levels of educational and occupational attainment relative to other minority groups. The economic uniformity myth consists of Asian Americans' assumption that economic returns from investment in education are uniformly consistent across all groups within the United States. Put differently, it is the assumption that there is a positive correlation between education and income and that the degree of this correlation is equal among different racial/ethnic groups. As Siegel (1965) pointed out, this assumption did not apply in regard to "Negroes" back in the early 1960s. Everything else being equal, Negroes paid a price for being Black. More specifically, Siegel found that it cost Negroes approximately $1,000 for being Black. A 1970 update of the Siegel study found that Black Americans still paid a price for being Black and that the cost had increased from $1,000 in 1965, or $1,380 in 1969 dollars, to $1,647 in 1970, an increase of $267 (Johnson & Sell, 1976). In Leong and Raote's (1992) study, a national data set was used to demonstrate the cost of being a Chinese American as well as that of being Black.

The specific results of Leong and Raote's (1992) study were obtained from two reports. Primary data for this study came from a single national data set called the Survey of Income and Education (SIE), which was collected in 1976 (U.S. Commission on Civil Rights, 1978). The second source of the data was a report based on the SIE data set conducted by Hirschman and Wong (1981), who compared the socioeconomic achievements among foreign-born Asian Americans.

The SIE, being a large national data set, not only was based on a representative sample but also had a sufficient number of Asian Americans to provide data for the study. Much of the federal statistical system does not collect such information, and if such information is collected, data on Asian Americans are not published. The few data sets that do publish data on Asian Americans will lump Asians (e.g.,

Chinese, Japanese, Koreans) together with Pacific Islanders (e.g., Samoans, other Polynesians). The SIE data set has the added advantage of not lumping Pacific Islanders with Asian Americans. In addition, it breaks down the Asian Americans into meaningful subgroups (e.g., Chinese, Japanese) for comparisons. Therefore, the quality and nature of SIE data on Asian Americans serves as a valuable resource for examining educational, economic, and occupational patterns among Asian Americans.

Leong and Raote (1992) pointed out that, when viewed in isolation, both the educational attainment data and the occupational status data in the SIE data set present a rather positive picture of the Chinese American. With a relatively high level of education and occupational prestige value of their occupations, one can readily understand how Chinese Americans can be viewed as a successful minority. However, a close examination of data would reveal that this is not really true. To reveal the occupational discrimination against Chinese Americans, Leong and Raote examined the adjusted mean earnings of the Chinese, Blacks, and White Americans with the level of education, occupation prestige, and number of hours/days worked statistically controlled for with multiple regressions. These analyses essentially told us what each group made while working in the United States if everything else was held constant. Everything else being equal, White males made $11,427, Black males made $9,741, and Chinese males made $8,817. In other words, it cost Chinese American males $2,610 for being Chinese. For Blacks, the cost was $1,686.

These figures provide an index of racial income inequity and also challenge the economic uniformity assumption concerning the education-income correlation. More specifically, they reveal that Chinese American men are not all that successful. In fact, with the same level of education, age, and occupational prestige and the same amount of time worked, Chinese American men lose much more than do Blacks. This surprisingly high level of inequity for Chinese American men should warrant not only a reversal of the successful minority myth for this particular Asian group but also a reevaluation by Chinese Americans of their underlying assumption of an automatic relationship between levels of educational attainment and economic success in the United States.

Many Asian American families have used education as a primary means of attaining upward mobility within American society. Although these families and their children, through their conscientiousness and persistence, have achieved a considerable amount of "success" in educational and occupational attainment, they have been unknowingly discriminated against by the American economic and occupational systems for a long time. A recognition and redress of this "hidden cost" for being Chinese American is long overdue. However, these families first need to be educated about the disparity within the economic system and informed that the "educational route" by itself is insufficient and that a parallel "political route" also is necessary if they are to succeed within American society. As Chun (1980) pointed out, the concept that Asian Americans are a successful or model minority often has covered up the occupational constraints and inequities experienced by Asian Americans.

Evidence that Asian Americans might have higher academic competencies and yet be paid less than White Americans comes from another national data set. The National Science Foundation (1990) found that "the self-reported grades of Asian freshmen were substantially higher than those of Whites in 1987. While almost half of Asians gave their grade point averages in the "A" range, the proportion for Whites was less than one-third" (p. 43). Furthermore, the same report revealed that Asian American psychologists earn only 66% of what White American psychologists earn, even though the entry-level degree for both groups is the doctorate (National Science Foundation, 1990).

There also is some evidence of occupational discrimination against Asian American scientists and engineers within our universities. A recent National Science Foundation (1990) report revealed that

> the tenure status and academic rank of Asian scientists and engineers also differ from those of Whites. Among doctoral scientists and engineers in 4-year colleges and universities, Asians are less likely than Whites to hold tenure: in 1987, roughly 43 percent of Asians, compared with 57 percent of Whites, held tenure. A higher proportion of Asians (12 percent) than Whites (9 percent) were in non-tenure-track positions. . . . Asians and Whites also show some differences in measures of academic rank. In 1987, 36 percent of Asians and 42 percent of Whites were full professors; at the associate level, the fraction was 22 percent for Asians and 24 percent for Whites. (p. 31)

It is important to note that these disparities exist despite the fact that Asian Americans enter colleges and universities with much higher academic credentials (course grades and SAT/Graduate Record Examination scores) than those of White Americans.

In the recent publication of *Projections of Education Statistics to 2002* of the U.S. Department of Education, it was estimated that Asian Americans would continue to invest in higher education; the expected increase in college education of Asian Americans was predicted to increase by 38% by the year 2002. Until and unless these families and policymakers recognize the economic uniformity myth that masks these "hidden costs," the system will continue to pay Asian Americans, particularly Chinese Americans, less money than it pays other Americans for the same work with the same training. It would be useful to determine to what extent these Chinese American families, the general public, policymakers, and social scientists are aware of this cost.

Despite the preceding information, in a recent empirical study similar to Leong and Hayes's (1990) stereotyping study, Carroll, Feren, and Olian (1987) found no evidence of prejudice against Asian Americans as managers. Respondents assumed the role of new members of an organization and assessed their attraction to a scripted manager in terms of general personal reactions (e.g., liking as a person or as a colleague) and as a potential mentor. The sample consisted of individuals who themselves were about to enter organizations in junior capacities and could relate to the issues of interest. Complete data were obtained from 267 participants who were randomly assigned to the experimental conditions.

The scripts described a newly hired manager interacting with a subordinate. The meeting included an attempt on the part of the manager to get acquainted with his subordinate, an engineer who had wanted the job ultimately obtained by the manager. Both the manager and subordinate were male. Each script contained 4.0 to 4.5 typed, double-spaced pages. The three scripts were created to reflect differences in the manager's interpersonal competence along the following dimensions: structuring and controlling the interaction, establishing rapport, reacting to stress, resolving conflict, developing the subordinate, and motivating the subordinate. The scripted manager was given the name Cesar Rodriguez (Hispanic), Ho Chen (Asian), or Dick Baxter (Anglo-Saxon) equally often across the three interpersonal competency levels. Otherwise, all of the information in the scripts was identical. In responding to the questionnaire, individuals were instructed to consider the individual portrayed in the script as their potential mentor and to assume the role of a young manager employed by the same company. This study provided no evidence of bias against Hispanic or Asian scripted managers. In fact, it was indicated that women preferred non-Anglo-Saxon managers as mentors. The study indicated that personal liking and acceptance of an Asian or a Hispanic manager as a work colleague, boss, and mentor is primarily related to the manager's interpersonal competence. The study also provided evidence showing that women were more sensitive in their reactions to the manager's interpersonal competence than were men because women typically responded more extremely to manifestations of the manager's high and low interpersonal competence. Further research would have to resolve the conflicting findings and examine the relationship between bias and actual discriminatory behaviors.

Occupational Segregation

As early as 1972, Sue and Kirk had observed that Asian Americans seem to be overrepresented in some occupations while being underrepresented in others. Over the years, more and more data have been accumulated to demonstrate that occupational segregation is a major problem for Asian Americans as it has been for women. The notion that occupational segregation is a problem comes from the assumption that a skewed distribution of any group in the occupational structure might represent restricted access to certain occupations. At the very least, a pattern of occupational segregation among a racial/ethnic group would call for investigations to determine whether there is differential access to various occupations.

In a review article, Chun (1980) noted that occupational segregation was a prevalent problem among Asian Americans. He cited various studies to show this pattern of occupational segregation and the tendency for Asian Americans to avoid the social sciences and humanities and to gravitate toward the biological and physical sciences. He stated that this segregation probably is a result of the societal and cultural barriers to Asian Americans' occupational aspirations. In fact, in a recent national survey (U.S. Commision on Civil Rights, 1978), it was discovered that the Chinese, Filipinos, and Japanese Americans exhibited the highest levels of occupational segregation among all minorities.

In another article, Sue and Frank (1973) explained this occupational segregation in terms of Asian Americans' ethnic identity and cultural background, which emphasizes reserve and formality in interpersonal relations, restraint and inhibition of strong feelings, and obedience to authority. Hence, this pattern of social anxiety and occupational segregation has important consequences for Asian Americans not only in terms of the lack of access to certain professionals (e.g., lawyers, psychologists, social workers) from their own culture but also in terms of the internal and external occupational stereotypes that might develop and result in additional occupational barriers.

The problem of occupational segregation has been investigated by social scientists for many decades. Much of this research has focused on occupational segregation, namely the pattern of women being overrepresented in some occupational fields (i.e., segregating into those occupations) and being underrepresented in other fields (i.e., segregating out of those fields). More recently, some attention has been shifted to the pattern of occupational segregation among minorities. For example, Arbona (1989) examined the occupational trends among Hispanics in the U.S. labor force by using the 1980 census data and the Holland Typology of Work. She was able to demonstrate that the Hispanic groups tend to segregate into certain Holland types and are overrepresented in some occupations and underrepresented in others.

A table in Hsia's (1988) book concerning the representation of Asian Americans in selected occupations using the 1980 census data provides a good illustration of the overall pattern of occupational segregation among Asian Americans. The table presents the representation index (or *RI*) of Asian Americans, which is derived by dividing the percentage of Asian Americans in a particular occupation by the percentage of Asian Americans in the total civilian labor force and multiplying that by 100. The representation index then provides a single numerical representation of the degree of segregation. For example, Asian Americans with an *RI* in a particular occupation of 100 means that they are representative according to their proportion in the general population. On the other hand, an *RI* of 200 means that twice the number of Asians are in that particular occupation relative to their proportion in the population.

Starting with the occupations in which Asian Americans tend to be most overrepresented or into which they tend to be heavily segregated, we find that this oversegregation pattern is represented by several fields. Consistent with Hsia's (1988) finding that Asian Americans are overrepresented in medical schools, the occupational group physicians has the highest *RI* (537). In other words, more than five times as many Asian Americans are physicians as one would expect given their representation in the general U.S. population. The other occupations into which Asians are highly segregated include medical scientists with an *RI* of 372, physicists and astronomers with an *RI* of 357, biological and life scientists with an *RI* of 316, engineers with an *RI* of 293, architects with an *RI* of 251, and accountants and auditors with an *RI* of 202.

The categories out of which Asian Americans are segregated or underrepresented include lawyers with an *RI* of 41, judges with an *RI* of 35, and chief executive officers and general administrators with an *RI* of 60. It is interesting to note that this pattern of occupational segregation among Asian Americans parallels the stereotyping literature, namely that Asians are stereotyped as being more qualified to enter the physical, biological, and medical sciences and are less qualified to enter or be successful in the verbal, persuasive, social careers such as being a lawyer, judge, or teacher. Hence, there seems to be some numerical basis for which Americans are stereotyping Asian Americans.

More recent data from the National Science Foundation (1990) continue to document this problem of occupational segregation among Asian Americans:

> Since 1978, employment of Asian scientists and engineers has increased faster than has employment of Whites: 146 percent (9 percent per year) versus 97 percent (7 percent per year). In 1988, the approximately 268,000 Asian scientists and engineers accounted for about 5 percent of the total S/E [science and engineering] workforce. In contrast, Asians represent only about 2 percent of the overall U.S. workforce. . . . Asians are somewhat more likely than Whites to be engineers rather than scientists. Among scientists, Asians are most likely to be computer specialists and least likely to be environmental scientists. The index of dissimilarity between Asians and Whites was 16 in 1988; that is, 16 percent of Asians would have to change fields to have a distribution similar to that for Whites. . . . Of the Ph.D. Asian scientists, more than three-fifths were either life or physical scientists. (p. 30)

One consequence of occupational segregation is that Asian Americans, like women, might be segregated into lower-paying occupations and denied access to higher-paying jobs. The same National Science Foundation (1990) report also noted that "Asians are less likely than Whites to be in management. About 28 percent of Whites—but only 22 percent of Asians—reported management as their major work activity" (p. 30). This pattern of segregation in career paths of Asian Americans in science and engineering is important because it is most commonly through rising into the administrative ranks that individuals are able to advance their careers in terms of both salary and prestige. Are Asian American bench scientists being passed over for promotion to science director positions for less qualified White bench scientists due to the former group's lack of social and managerial skills?

SUMMARY AND CONCLUSIONS

Current Status of Career and Vocational Research on Asian Americans

As indicated by this review of the literature on the career development and vocational behavior of Asian Americans, this research area is plagued by several problems (Leong & Brown, 1995; Leong & Serafica, 1995). First, there is a dearth of empirical studies, with the consequence that career counselors and psychologists charged with helping Asian Americans with their career concerns are left with a miniscule knowledge base with which to formulate interventions. Second, there is a very uneven pattern to our studies of the career behavior of Asian Americans. There are many more studies on the work adjustment problems of Asian Americans than on the role of family influences on their career choices. We know more about problems of Southeast Asian refugees than about the occupational segregation of all Asian American groups.

Third, the limited research that does exist seems to be more problem driven than theory driven. For example, there are many more studies about the work adjustment problems of Asian Americans than about their career development processes and outcomes from a theoretical point of view. There is no question that problem-driven research is needed and has its value. Take the example of studies related to the work adjustment of Southeast Asian refugees. These studies clearly were in response to the large influx of this group of Asians into the United States. Yet many of these studies were primarily descriptive in cataloging the problems experienced by this refugee group. What also is needed are studies that add to our theoretical knowledge base. For example, are there predictable cycles in the work adjustment of recent refugees and how the various Southeast Asian groups fit this modal path? If not, what cultural variables can account for their deviations? There are many established career theories (Brown & Brooks, 1990) that can be tested for their relevance to Asian Americans, yet they often are ignored (Leong & Serafica, 1995).

Finally, like much of the rest of the field of ethnic minority psychology, studies of the career development of Asian Americans still are stuck at the descriptive level. Most of the studies are based on the examination of ethnicity as a demographic variable and not a psychological one. The former approach is characterized by studies that tend to examine a specific ethnic group's experience (e.g., What is the level of job-interviewing skills of Vietnamese refugees?) or seek to compare two groups based solely on ethnic designation (e.g., Are Chinese American engineers more job satisfied than White American engineers?). What is needed are studies that examine psychological variables that might be related to these ethnic groups' behaviors. For example, how does Berry's acculuration model relate to the type of work adjustment problems experienced by the Vietnamese? Or, does Rokeach's system of values moderate whether Japanese Americans are congruent in their measured and expressed career choices? Can Bogardus's social distance model account for a significant portion of the variance for the occupational discrimination of Asian Americans?

Ethnicity per se is not a psychological variable and in the long run will yield very little information about the career behavior of Asian Americans. What is needed are studies that identify, evaluate, and test the role and impact of various culturally based psychological variables that are believed to influence the work behavior and career development of Asian Americans.

Directions for Future Research

The first observation concerning research on the career development and vocational behavior of Asian Americans is that despite the fact that work constitutes a major portion of the activity of Asian Americans as with all other populations, surprisingly little empirical research has been conducted on this particular topic with Asian Americans. Hence, there is a desperate need for more systematic empirical studies of the career and vocational experience and problems encountered by Asian Americans.

In terms of the existing studies, there are several methodological issues that will need to be addressed to improve our knowledge based on the career behavior of Asian Americans. The first of these is to attempt, wherever possible, to collect data on the career behavior of Asian Americans such that data are available from subgroups so that we can examine whether the same pattern of findings is true for Chinese Americans versus Korean Americans versus Filipino or Japanese Americans.

Currently, most of the research is focused on Asian Americans as a global group with very little attention paid to intra- or subgroup differences. Worse still, many of the data collected from the federal statistical system use the combined group of APIs that include the Eastern Asian groups such as Chinese, Japanese, Koreans, and Filipinos and then combine them with the Pacific Islanders, who are from a totally different culture including Samoans, Hawaiians, and so on. One possibility would be to mirror what has been done in the U.S. census since 1980, which is to encourage federal, state, and local statistical systems to collect data not only on the Asian subgroup but also on the specific groups such that, as in the 1980 census, a person indicates whether he or she is Asian or Pacific Islander and then also designates his or her subgroup. This provides a more refined level of analysis, and as we do that particular level of subgroup identification, much more of our research and statistical data will be meaningful.

A second area for future research is with regard to testing the models of career development that have been developed on White Americans to see whether they are culturally valid for Asian American subgroups and, if not, what modifications are needed for them to be culturally relevant and culturally appropriate in terms of career interventions for this particular minority group (Leong & Brown, 1995). As a part of translating or modifying and adapting these models for Asian Americans, one important advance that will need to take place is that of evaluating the validity of various career assessment instruments for Asian Americans. For example, very little validity research has been done to determine whether Holland's classification system, as represented in the Vocational Preference Inventory, the Self-Directed Search, or even the Strong-Interest Inventory, is appropriate for Asian Americans as a group. We need to know whether the interest patterns that we get from interest profiles as well as career decision scales, career maturity measures, and so on indicate whether these scales are appropriate to be used for Asian Americans. We certainly need more research on both the instruments and the process of career assessment with Asian Americans (Leong & Leung, 1994).

A third major dimension for future research in the career behavior of Asian Americans is to include two important moderating variables. The first of these is acculturation or ethnic identity (Leong & Chou, 1994). There is now substantive research to show that Asian Americans, either as an entire group or as subgroups, experience this temporal variable, which includes a process of acculturation that then differentiates these subgroups; namely, highly acculturated Chinese Americans might not be the same as low-acculturation Chinese Americans in terms of their occupational aspirations, interests, choices, and behaviors. Hence, future research on the career behavior of Asian Americans will have to take into account this moderating effect of acculturation or of ethnic identity so that traditional high ethnic identity Japanese Americans may be different from low ethnic identity assimilated Japanese Americans. The latter group might be more likely to go into law or politics, whereas the former group might choose a different set of occupations and socialize their children differently.

The second variable that is an important moderator for future research on Asian American career behavior also is important for all minority research, and that is social economic status. We are in desperate need of research that separates out the effects of social economic status from racial/ethnic minority group status. For Asian Americans, as with many of the racial/ethnic minority groups in the United States, the two often are highly confounded. We do not know to what extent the career patterns are due to the fact that Asian Americans might be from lower working classes or to the fact that they are from a distinct cultural group, namely Asians in the United States. To achieve this purpose of identifying the effects of these two moderating variables, we are in need of instruments that also will accurately and reliably measure their effects. For acculturation, there already are available instruments such as the SL-ASIA and the more recent work of Phinney (1992) in terms of the multigroup ethnic identity measure. Unfortunately, we do not have a short, reliable, practical social class measure that we can use in our research, and that certainly is one area in need of further exploration. It would be very valuable if we could develop a short, highly reliable, useful social class measure for various racial/ethnic minority groups that could be used across various studies and across various groups to provide comparable data on this very important moderated variable.

As the numbers of Asian Americans continue to increase in the United States, the need for solid empirical data to guide career assessment and interventions with this fastest-growing ethnic minority group also will increase. In one sense, this chapter is as much a call for more research on the career development of Asian Americans as it is a review of the state of the art.

REFERENCES

Anh, N. T., & Healy, C. C. (1985). Factors affecting employment and job satisfaction of Vietnamese refugees. *Journal of Employment Counseling, 22*(2), 78-85.

Arbona, C. (1989). Hispanic employment and the Holland Typology of Work. *Career Development Quarterly, 37,* 257-268.

Bourne, P. (1975). The Chinese student—acculturation and mental illness. *Psychiatry, 38,* 269-277.

Brown, D., & Brooks, L. (Eds.). (1990). *Career choice and development.* San Francisco: Jossey-Bass.

Brown, D., Minor, C. W., & Jepsen, D. A. (1991). The opinions of minorities about preparing for work: Report of the second NCDA National Survey. *Career Development Quarterly, 40,* 5-19.

Carroll, S. J., Feren, D. B., & Olian, J. D. (1987). Reactions to the new minorities by employees of the future: An experimental study. *Psychological Reports, 60,* 911-920.

Chow, E. N. (1987). The influence of sex-role identity and occupational attainment on the psychological well-being of Asian American women. *Psychology of Women Quarterly, 11*(1), 69-82.

Chun, K. T. (1980, Winter-Spring). The myth of Asian American success and its educational ramifications. *IRCD Bulletin,* pp. 2-13.

College Entrance Examination Board. (1980). *National college-bound seniors, 1980.* Princeton, NJ: Author.

Connor, J. W. (1975). Value changes in third generation Japanese Americans. *Journal of Personality Assessment, 39,* 597-600.

Crites. J. O. (1978). *Career Maturity Inventory: Administration and use manual.* New York: McGraw-Hill.

Endo, R. (1974). Japanese Americans: The "model minority" in perspective. In R. Gomez (Ed.), *The social reality of ethnic America.* Lexington, MA: D. C. Heath.

Evanoski, P. O., & Tse, F. W. (1989). Career awareness program for Chinese and Korean American parents. *Journal of Counseling and Development, 67,* 472-474.

Fenz, W. D., & Arkoff, A. (1962). Comparative need patterns of five ancestry groups in Hawaii. *Journal of Social Psychology, 58,* 67-89.

Fujii, J. S., Fukushima, S. N., & Chang, C. Y. (1989). Asian women psychiatrists. *Psychiatric Annals, 19,* 633-638.

Haines, D. W. (1987). Patterns in Southeast Asian refugee employment: A reappraisal of the existing research. *Ethnic Groups, 7,* 39-63.

Harren, V. A. (1978). *Assessment of career decision-making.* Carbondale: Southern Illinois University, Department of Psychology.

Hirschman, C., & Wong, M. G. (1981). Trends in socioeconomic achievement among immigrants and native born Asian Americans, 1960-1976. *Sociogical Quarterly, 22,* 495-514.

Holland, J. L. (1977). *Self-directed search: A guide to educational and vocational planning.* Palo Alto, CA: Consulting Psychological Press.

Holland, J. L., Daiger, D. C., & Power, P. G. (1980). *My Vocational Situation.* Palo Alto, CA: Consulting Psychologists Press.

Hsia, J. (1980, September). *Cognitive assessment of Asian Americans.* Paper presented at a symposium on bilingual research of the National Institute of Education, National Center of Bilingual Research, Los Alamitos, CA.

Hsia, J. (1988). *Asian Americans in higher education and at work.* Hillsdale, NJ: Lawrence Erlbaum.

Hsieh, T. T. Y., Shybut, J., & Lotrof, E. J. (1969). Internal versus external control and ethnic group membership: A cross-cultural comparison. *Journal of Consulting and Clinical Psychology, 33,* 122-124.

Johnson, M. P., & Sell, R. P. (1976). The cost of being Black: A 1970 update. *American Journal of Sociology, 82,* 183-190.

Johnson, R. C., Nagoshi, C. T., Ahern, F. M., Wilson, J. R., DeFries, J. C., McClearn, G. E., & Vandenberg, S. G. (1983). Family background, cognitive ability, and personality as predictors of educational and occupational attainment. *Social Biology, 30,* 86-100.

Kim, L. C. (1973). Asian Americans: No model minority. *Social Work, 18,* 44-53.

Kincaid, D. L., & Yum, J. O. (1987). A comparative study of Korean, Filipino and Samoan immigrants to Hawaii: Socioeconomic consequences. *Human Organization, 46*(1), 70-77.

Kitano, H. H., & Sue, S. (1973). The model minorities. *Journal of Social Issues, 29*(2), 1-9.

Kwak, J. C. (1980). Vocational development of Asian American youth. *Dissertation Abstracts International, 41,* 1956A.

Lamb, R. R. (1976). *Validity of the ACT Interest Inventory for minority group members* (ACT Research Report No. 72). Iowa City, IA: American College Testing Program.

Lan, D. (1976). *Prestige with limitations: Realities of the Chinese-American elite.* San Francisco: R&E Research Associates.

Leong, F. T. L. (1982). *Differential career development attributes of Asian American and White college students.* Unpublished master's thesis, University of Maryland.

Leong, F. T. (1985). Career development of Asian Americans. *Journal of College Student Personnel, 26,* 539-546.

Leong, F. T. L. (1991). Career development attributes and occupational values of Asian American and White American college students. *Career Development Quarterly, 39,* 221-230.

Leong, F. T. L. (Ed.). (1995). *Career development and vocational behavior of racial and ethnic minorities.* Hillsdale, NJ: Lawrence Erlbaum.

Leong, F. T. L., & Brown, M. (1995). Theoretical issues in cross-cultural career development: Cultural validity and cultural specificity. In W. B. Walsh & S. H. Osipow (Eds.), *Handbook of vocational psychology* (2nd ed., pp. 143-180). Hillsdale, NJ: Lawrence Erlbaum.

Leong, F. T. L., & Chou, E. L. (1994). The role of ethnic identity and acculturation in the vocational behavior of Asian Americans: An integrative review. *Journal of Vocational Behavior, 44,* 155-172.

Leong, F. T. L., & Gim-Chung, R. H. (1995). Career assessment and intervention with Asian Americans. In F. T. L. Leong (Ed.), *Career development and vocational behavior of racial and ethnic minorities* (pp. 193-226). Hillsdale, NJ: Lawrence Erlbaum.

Leong, F. T., & Hayes, T. J. (1990). Occupational stereotyping of Asian Americans. *Career Development Quarterly, 39,* 143-154.

Leong, F. T. L., & Leung, S. A. (1994). Career assessment with Asian Americans. *Journal of Career Assessment, 2,* 240-257.

Leong, F. T. L., & Raote, R. (1992). *On the hidden cost of being a Chinese American.* Unpublished manuscript, Ohio State University.

Leong, F. T. L., & Serafica, F. C. (1995). Career development of Asian Americans: A research area in search of a good theory. In F. T. L. Leong (Ed.), *Career development and vocational behavior of racial and ethnic minorities* (pp. 67-102). Hillsdale, NJ: Lawrence Erlbaum.

Leong, F. T., & Tata, S. P. (1990). Sex and acculturation differences in occupational values among Chinese-American children. *Journal of Counseling Psychology, 37,* 208-212.

Liu, W. T., Yu, E. S. H., Chang, C. F., & Fernandez, M. (1990). The mental health of Asian American teenagers: A research challenge. In A. P. Stiffman & L. E. Davis (Eds.), *Ethnic issues in adolescent mental health* (pp. 92-112). Newbury Park, CA: Sage.

Matsuoka, J. K., & Ryujin, D. H. (1989). Vietnamese refugees: An analysis of contemporary adjustment issues. *Journal of Applied Social Sciences, 14,* 23-45.

McNeely, R. L. (1987). Job satisfaction and other characteristics of Asian American human service workers. *Social Work Research and Abstracts, 23*(4), 7-9.

Meredith, G. M. (1966). Amae and acculteration among Japanese-American college students in Hawaii. *Journal of Social Psychology, 70,* 171-180.

Minatoya, L. A., & Sedlacek, W. E. (1981). Another look at the melting pot: Perceptions of Asian American undergraduates. *Journal of College Student Personnel, 22,* 328-336.

National Science Foundation. (1990). *Women and minorities in science and engineering.* Washington, DC: Author.

Nicassio, P. M., & Pate, J. K. (1984). An analysis of problems of resettlement of the Indochinese refugees in the United States. *Social Psychiatry, 19*(3), 135-141.

Okimoto, D. (1974). The intolerance of success. In R. Gomez (Ed.), *The social reality of ethnic America.* Lexington, MA: D. C. Heath.

Owan, T. (1975). *Asian Americans: A case study of benign neglect* (Occasional Paper No. 1). Chicago: Pacific/Asian American Mental Health Research Center.

Petersen, W. (1966, January 6). Success story, Japanese American style. *New York Times Magazine.*

Petersen, W. (1971). *Japanese Americans: Oppression and success.* New York: Random House.

Phinney, J. S. (1992). The Multigroup Ethnic Identity Measure: A new scale for use with diverse groups. *Journal of Adolescent Research, 7,* 156-176.

Picou, J. S., & Campbell, R. E. (Eds.). (1975). *Career behavior of special groups: Theory, research and practice.* Columbus, OH: Merrill.

Redding, S. G., & Ng, M. (1982). The role of "face" in the organizational perceptions of Chinese managers. *Organization Studies, 3*(3), 201-219.

Rosenberg, M. (1957). *Occupations and values.* Glencoe, IL: Free Press.

Schmid, C. F., & Nobbe, C. E. (1965). Socioeconomic differentials among non-White races. *American Sociological Review, 30,* 909-922.

Siegel, P. N. (1965). On the cost of being Negro. *Sociological Inquiry, 35,* 41-57.

Smith, E. J. (1983). Issues in racial minorities' career behavior. In W. B. Walsh & S. H. Osipow (Eds.), *Handbook of vocational psychology* (Vol. 1, pp. 161-222). Hillsdale, NJ: Lawrence Erlbaum.

Sue, D. W. (1975). Asian Americans: Social-psychological factors affecting their lifestyles. In J. S. Picou & R. E. Campbell (Eds.), *Career behavior of special groups: Theory, research and practice* (pp. 97-121). Columbus, OH: Merrill.

Sue, D. W., & Frank, A. C. (1973). A typological approach to the psychological study of Chinese and Japanese American college males. *Journal of Social Issues, 29,* 129-148.

Sue, D. W., & Kirk, B. A. (1972). Psychological characteristics of Chinese-American students. *Journal of Counseling Psychology, 19,* 471-478.

Sue, D. W., & Kirk, B. A. (1973). Differential characteristics of Japanese-American and Chinese-American college students. *Journal of Counseling Psychology, 20,* 142-148.

Sue, S., & Kitano, H. H. (1973). Stereotypes as a measure of success. *Journal of Social Issues, 29,* 83-98.

Sue, S., & Morishima, J. K. (1982). *The mental health of Asian Americans.* San Francisco: Jossey-Bass.

Sue, S., & Sue, D. W. (1974). MMPI comparisons between Asian American and non-Asian students utilizing a student health psychiatric clinic. *Journal of Counseling Psychology, 21,* 423-427.

Sue, S., Sue, D. W., & Sue, D. (1975). Asians as a minority group. *American Psychologist, 30,* 906-910.

Sue, S., & Wagner, N. (Eds.). (1973). *Asian Americans: Psychological perspectives.* Palo Alto, CA: Science and Behavioral Books.

Sung, B. L. (1987). *The adjustment experience of Chinese immigrant children in New York City.* Staten Island, NY: Center for Migration Studies.

Super, D. E. (1970). *Work Values Inventory.* Boston: Houghton Mifflin.

Suzuki, B. H. (1977). Education and the socialization of Asian Americans: A revisionist analysis of the "model minority" thesis. *Amerasia, 4*(2), 23-52.

Tang, J., & O'Brien, T. P. (1990). Correlates of vocational success in refugee work adaptation. *Journal of Applied Social Psychology, 20,* 1444-1452.

Tou, L. A. (1974). A study of work orientations of Chinese American and White American students of the 7th and 8th grades in Catholic elementary schools. *Dissertation Abstracts International, 35,* 831A. (Catholic University of America)

Tracey, T. J., Leong, F. T. L., & Glidden, C. (1986). Help seeking and problem perception among Asian Americans. *Journal of Counseling Psychology, 33,* 331-336.

U.S. Commission on Civil Rights. (1978). *Social indicators of equality for minorities and women.* Washington, DC: Author.

U.S. Department of Education. (1988). *Projection of education statistics to 2002.* Washington, DC: Author.

Vertiz, V. C., & Fortune, J. C. (1984). An ethnographic study of cultural barriers to employment among Indochinese immigrant youth. *College Student Journal, 18,* 229-235.

Wong, S. (1985). The Chinese family firm: A model. *British Journal of Sociology, 36*(1), 58-72.

Yu, L. C., & Wu, S. (1985). Unemployment and family dynamics in meeting the needs of Chinese elderly in the United States. *The Gerontologist, 25,* 472-476.

PART II

SOCIAL AND PERSONAL ADJUSTMENT

12

RACISM

KATHLEEN YOUNG
DAVID T. TAKEUCHI

One night in 1871, mobs in Los Angeles shot, hanged, or burned to death 21 Chinese in an anti-Chinese riot (Daniels, 1988). Numerous other acts of violence against Chinese followed throughout California and the Pacific Northwest and mountain states. In 1882, the U.S. Congress passed the Chinese Exclusion Act, which suspended the immigration of Chinese for 10 years and excluded Chinese from U.S. citizenship by naturalization. Still, the violence continued, as 22 to 50 Chinese were killed in an anti-Chinese riot in Rock Springs, Wyoming (Leadership Education for Asian Pacifics [LEAP], 1991).

After Japanese planes attacked Pearl Harbor on December 7, 1941, the Federal Bureau of Investigation (FBI) arrested and interrogated about 1,500 Issei (first-generation Japanese American immigrants). Two months later, on February 19, 1942, President Franklin D. Roosevelt issued Executive Order 9066, which resulted in the evacuation and relocation of more than 100,000 Japanese Americans into 10 concentration camps in the United States. Despite the fact that most of these Japanese Americans were U.S. citizens, this relocation and confinement was done without due process or allegation of wrongdoing by the incarcerated individuals (Commission on Wartime Relocation and Internment of Civilians, 1982a, 1982b; Daniels, 1988; LEAP, 1991).

On June 19, 1982, Vincent Chin, a Chinese American, was at a bar in Detroit with friends to celebrate his upcoming wedding when he was accosted by two White automobile factory workers. They apparently mistook Chin for a "Jap" and blamed him for the loss of jobs in the automobile industry. They chased him out of the bar, and when they caught him, one of the men held Chin while the other beat him with a baseball bat. Chin died 4 days later. Neither of his assailants went to prison for Chin's killing. Each was sentenced to 3 years' probation and fined $3,780. Although the U.S. Department of Justice brought federal civil rights charges against them, both eventually were acquitted (U.S. Commission on Civil Rights, 1992).

During a Marine Office Candidate School training that began in October 1989, Bruce Yamashita was a target of steady and often vicious racial/ethnic harassment (Schmitt, 1992). Throughout the 10-week training, Marine instructors taunted Yamashita, a Japanese American who was born and raised in Honolulu, Hawaii, with verbal assaults such as "go back to your country" and "kamikaze man." Prior to entering Office Candidate School, Yamashita counted among his accomplishments that he had served as his high school's student body president, had been an elected delegate to the 1978 Hawaii State Constitution Convention, and had earned a law degree from Georgetown University. A couple of days before the training ended, and despite passing all of his written examinations, Yamashita was discharged for "leadership failure."

These examples encompass qualitatively different attempts to exclude, isolate, or harm groups and individuals. A common element of these acts is that they were committed against Asian Americans simply because of their physical appearance or group membership. By definition, these acts are accounts of racism that are part of the historical record and continue into the present experiences of Asian Americans in the United States. Racism in the United States has been, and continues to be, a pervasive social problem despite the long-standing American ideals of the fundamental equality of human beings and human beings' inalienable rights to freedom, justice, and opportunity (Schlesinger, 1991). It is beyond the scope of this chapter to provide an extensive discussion of the use of the term *racism* (see Katz & Taylor, 1988, for a more comprehensive discussion of racism terminology). For the purposes of this chapter, racism is defined as the "prejudicial attitudes and discriminatory behavior toward people of a given race, or . . . institutional practices (even if not motivated by prejudice) that subordinate people of a given race" (Myers, 1990, p. 484).

According to the 1990 census, Asian Americans are the fastest growing ethnic minority group in the United States, having more than doubled in size to 7.1 million since 1980, which is 2.9% of the total population of the United States (Asian Week, 1991; U.S. Bureau of the Census, 1990). In this chapter, the term *Asian American* is used to refer to both Asians and Pacific Islanders who live in the United States. This includes people who are originally from, or whose ancestors originated in the countries of Asia, or the island groups of the Pacific Ocean. Asian ethnic groups include, but are not limited to, Bangladeshi, Burmese, Cambodian, Chinese, Filipino, Hmong, Asian Indian, Indonesian, Japanese, Korean, Laotian, Malayan, Okinawan, Pakistani, Sri Lankan, Thai, and Vietnamese. Pacific Islander ethnic groups tend to be grouped into Polynesian, Micronesian, and Melanesian categories by the U.S. census (Kitano & Daniels, 1988). These categories may include Fijian, Hawaiian, Guamanian, Samoan, Tahitian, and Tongan, among other Pacific Islander ethnic groups.

A 1991 *Wall Street Journal*/NBC News national poll found that most American voters believed that Asian Americans do not encounter discrimination in the United States (McQueen, 1991). However, these perceptions are divorced from the daily experiences of Asian Americans. The U.S. Commission on Civil Rights (1992) documented a wide array of prejudice and discrimination against Asian Americans including barriers to equal opportunity in education and employment, unequal access to social services, and victimization by racially motivated violence. One reason for the misperception of Asian Americans is the lack of discussion about issues related to discrimination, prejudice, and racism perpetuated against Asian Americans. There is a tendency to see racist acts as isolated incidents rather than as systematic attempts to subordinate Asian Americans. This chapter attempts to fill the gap by discussing different types of racist acts perpetuated against Asian Americans, providing an overview of psychological theories of racism and proposing future directions for psychological theory and research in the area of racism.

DIFFERENCES AMONG ASIAN AMERICANS

There have been varying degrees and qualities of racism experienced by Asian ethnic groups who migrated to the United States. Each specific Asian American ethnic group has experienced different receptions from American society depending on factors both *internal* to the ethnic group (e.g., historical circumstances for migration, demographic variables, cultural characteristics, originating-country power in the international arena) and *external* to the ethnic group (e.g., the political, economic, and sociocultural context of the United States at the time of the group's immigration) (Kitano & Daniels, 1988). What follows is a sketch of the differences in treatment some Asian American ethnic groups have received in the United States.

Chinese

Although there are scattered reports of Asians inhabiting parts of the United States as early as 498 A. D., the migration of significant numbers of Asians, specifically the Chinese, began with the California Gold Rush of 1849 (Daniels, 1988). Between 1849 and 1882, more than 275,000 Chinese entered the United States. Of these, more than 90% were male. Initially, the Chinese immigrants worked primarily in mines but labored on the western leg of the transcontinental Central Pacific Railroad, in agriculture, and in service trades. Some researchers have proposed that the Chinese, like other European ethnic groups who immigrated to the United States, were sojourners who intended only to work in the United States to make money and then return to their country of origin. However, unlike European immigrants, the Chinese became the first ethnic group to be legally barred from immigrating to the United States by the Chinese Exclusion Act of 1882. The Chinese Exclusion Act represented, at a federal level, the culmination of anti-Chinese sentiment that had been present throughout many western states and localities. Prior to the Chinese Exclusion Act, the Chinese had been the target of anti-Chinese legislation and racially motivated violence. Because of the Chinese Exclusion Act, the early Chinese population, consisting primarily of unmarried males, declined until the 1920s.

The advent of World War II marked a change in U.S. policy toward the Chinese. During World War II, China and the United States became allies, and there were movements within the American establishment to change U.S. exclusionary policies. The laws that had excluded Chinese immigration to the United States were repealed in 1943 by the Magnuson Act. The Magnuson Act also set a Chinese immigration quota of 105 per year and allowed those of Chinese descent to be eligible for naturalization. Despite the immigration quota, several other acts of Congress allowed the legal entry of a significant influx of Chinese wives and family members into the United States under family reunification provisions (Daniels, 1988).

Although there were concerns among the Chinese American community that the victory of Communist forces in China and the cold war between the United States and Communist countries would result in poor treatment of Chinese in the United States (Daniels, 1988; Kitano & Daniels, 1988), the ideological rather than racial focus during the cold war era actually resulted in some positive changes in immigration policies for Chinese who wanted to enter the United States. For example, for the first time, in 1953, the Refugee Relief Act allowed Chinese to enter the United States as refugees from the civil war in China. The negative repercussions of the cold war included ideologically motivated governmental prosecution of Chinese who were suspected of being Communist, but these well-known "red-hunting" organizations (e.g., the FBI under J. Edgar Hoover) targeted not only Chinese but also suspected Communists of many different ethnicities.

The McCarran-Walter Act of 1952 was a turning point in the United States' past policy of discrimination along racial lines in citizenship eligibility. The McCarran-Walter Act allowed the Chinese, and all Asians for that matter, to become naturalized citizens of the United States. Because of changes in immigration and refugee policies, between 1960 and 1985, the Chinese American population quadrupled (Kitano & Daniels, 1988).

Japanese

In the late 1800s, Japanese contract workers began arriving in Hawaii to work on the sugar plantations. These workers were brought to the Hawaiian Islands by the White American sugar plantation owners not only for their labor but also to provide an ethnic counterweight to the Chinese, who represented approximately one fifth to one fourth of Hawaii's population (Daniels, 1988). After the United States annexed Hawaii, many Japanese began moving to the West Coast of the U.S. mainland. By 1920, there were at least 110,000 Japanese

Americans living on the West Coast, predominantly in California (Kitano & Daniels, 1988).

Like the Chinese, the Japanese experienced significant racial discrimination. Due to anti-Japanese sentiment, President Roosevelt negotiated with Japan to limit the immigration of Japanese into the United States in the Gentlemen's Agreement of 1907. Despite the exclusionary character of the Gentlemen's Agreement, the immigration of Japanese women was allowed, which helped balance the sex ratio of Japanese men to women and resulted in a growing native-born Japanese American population.

Among the worst governmentally sanctioned acts imposed against Asian residents of the United States was the internment of Japanese Americans. As mentioned in the opening of this chapter, during World War II, more than 100,000 Japanese Americans were relocated and confined to concentration camps in the United States solely because of their ethnicity. As is discussed later in this chapter, this incarceration continues to have an impact on Japanese Americans today.

Filipinos

Initial Filipino immigration to the United States was markedly different from Chinese or Japanese immigration. Unlike earlier Asian immigrants who were considered "aliens," because of American imperialism in the Philippine Islands, Filipinos were considered to be American nationals (Kitano & Daniels, 1988). Between 1903 and 1910, the first wave of Filipino immigrants, the *pensionados,* was sponsored by a U.S. government program to attend American educational institutions. In what is considered to be a second wave of immigration, after World War I, significant numbers of Filipinos began arriving in the United States and Hawaii to work in agriculture, a labor niche previously occupied by the Chinese and Japanese immigrants.

Although the Tydings-McDuffie Act of 1934 provided the Philippines with commonwealth status and the promise of future independence, it also made Filipinos born in the Philippines, who were earlier granted the rights of American nationals, aliens ineligible for citizenship (U.S. Commission on Civil Rights, 1992). Anti-Filipino sentiment was further demonstrated by congressional resolutions in 1935 that provided free one-way passage to Filipinos who wanted to return to the Philippines, provided that they agreed not to return to the United States.

Asian Indians

There have been two major periods of migration of Asian Indians to the United States. The first wave started around 1900, when approximately 10,000 Asian Indians began migrating to the United States. The majority of these immigrants were Sikhs who came from the Punjab region of India. Many of them settled in California, initially working on the railroad or in lumbering and then in agriculture. Other smaller Asian Indian communities were formed in the eastern and midwestern United States; members of these communities tended to be Hindu and worked as merchants or in the professions (Kitano & Daniels, 1988).

The second major wave of Asian Indian immigration began after the U.S. Congress passed the Act of July 2, 1946, allowing "persons of races indigenous to India" (as cited in Kitano & Daniels, 1988, p. 96) to immigrate to the United States with the right of naturalization. This act is notable in that Asian Indians (in addition to Filipinos) became eligible for U.S. citizenship, unlike other Asian ethnic groups such as the Chinese and the Japanese who at the time still were considered aliens and were not allowed to become U.S. citizens. Nearly half a million Asian Indians entered the United States after 1946. These Asian Indians tended to be demographically different from the first wave of Asian Indian immigrants and from other Asian immigrants. Unlike the first group of Asian immigrants and other Asians, the second wave of Asian Indians settled throughout the United States. They tended to have a high level of education and significantly higher levels of occupational achievement than did Whites and other Asian Americans. In 1979, the median income of Asian Indian workers was higher than those of Whites and other Asian groups (Kitano & Daniels, 1988).

Koreans

There have been three waves of immigration of Koreans to the United States. The Tonghak Rebellion, the Sino-Japanese War, and the Russo-Japanese War in the late 1800s and early 1900s, as well as a cholera epidemic, a drought, a locust plague, and famine, created unstable conditions in Korea, prompting Koreans displaced by the wars to migrate to Hawaii to work on plantations (Kitano & Daniels, 1988). The first Korean immigrants tended to be primarily male, although some Korean "picture brides" immigrated to the United States before U.S. immigration policy barred Korean immigration in 1924 (Kitano, 1991). Between 1951 and 1964, the second wave of Korean immigration consisted of the wives of Americans who had gone to Korea during the Korean war, Korean children orphaned by the Korean war who were adopted by American families, and students (Kitano, 1991). The largest wave of Korean immigration, which continues today, followed the Immigration and Naturalization Act of 1965. The Koreans who are currently immigrating to the United States tend to come in family units, and the adults of these families tend to be highly educated.

Recent Korean immigrants tend to live in "Koreatowns," isolated from contact with other ethnic groups in the United States. A large proportion of Koreans own or work in small businesses. For example, in 1984, there were 7,000 Korean-owned businesses in Los Angeles County (Kitano & Daniels, 1988). A current major concern in the Korean community is the growing tensions between Korean Americans and other ethnic minority groups. In major cities such as Los Angeles and New York, conflict between immigrant Korean Americans and other ethnic minority groups, such as African Americans and Latinos, has escalated into violence.

Pacific Islanders

The history of relations between the United States and the people indigenous to the Pacific Islands is different from those between this country and many of the other Asian American ethnic groups whose relations have been affected primarily by immigration. In many cases, Pacific Islands were taken over by the United States—by threat of force in the case of the Hawaiian Islands and indirectly as a result of military victory such as in the case of Guam (which was acquired after the United States won the Spanish-American War of 1898). Although it is beyond the scope of this chapter to provide a history of U.S. relations with the various Pacific Islander ethnic groups, the most dominant U.S.-Pacific Islander relational pattern has been colonialism, resulting in the destruction of indigenous cultures.

The circumstances of Native Hawaiians provide an example of the consequences of colonialism. In contrast to most Asian American groups who migrated to the United States, Native Hawaiians are an indigenous people who settled in the Hawaiian Islands more than 2,000 years ago. At the time of Captain Cook's arrival in Hawaii in 1778, the population of Native Hawaiians might have been as large as 1 million people (Stannard, 1989). The impact of infectious diseases such as tuberculosis, syphilis, gonorrhea, measles, and influenza brought to the islands by Westerners decimated the Native Hawaiian population. From 1778 to 1883, the population was reduced to approximately 40,000 Native Hawaiians. Within this 50-year period, the number of foreigners outnumbered Native Hawaiians by more than 10,000 people (Blaisdell, 1989). In addition to the decimation of the population, over the past two centuries, Hawaiian cultural values, relationship to the land, and traditional methods for resolving problems have been devalued through Westernization and capitalism (Kame'eleihiwa, 1992). Some have argued that the effects of colonization account for much of the negative socioeconomic, health, and mental health problems the Native Hawaiians experience today (Trask, 1990).

Southeast Asians

Most of the Southeast Asian Americans, such as the Vietnamese, Laotians, and Cambodians, came to the United States after the Refugee Act of 1980; following the Refugee Act, the Southeast Asian population grew from 20,000 to a staggering 1.2 million in 1989 (O'Hare & Felt, 1991). Southeast Asian refugees left their home countries or, in some cases, were forcibly displaced due to wars, genocide, famine, and political repression. Many Southeast Asian immigrants were further traumatized by pirates, who attacked the boats that many refugees used to escape their homelands, and by the overcrowded and often unsanitary refugee camps in which they often waited for months before being resettled. Many Southeast Asian refugees died in their attempts to leave their countries (Chung & Okazaki, 1991).

The Southeast Asian refugees are distinct from many of the other Asian American groups because they were not voluntary immigrants to the United States. Many long to return to what they consider to be their home countries. Furthermore, as a group, Southeast Asian refugees have one of the lowest incomes of all ethnic groups in the United States, significantly less than the incomes of Chinese or Japanese Americans, whose earnings tend to be among the highest of the ethnic groups (O'Hare & Felt, 1991). Thus, the needs of the Southeast Asian refugees are significant. Yet, those needs have put Southeast Asians at odds with other ethnic groups, such as African Americans and Latinos, who resent the special assistance given to the refugees and perceive that the provision of services to refugees reduces the resources available to their own communities (Kitano & Daniels, 1988). Furthermore, racial tensions between Southeast Asian refugees and Whites have been documented throughout the country (U.S. Commission on Civil Rights, 1992).

DISCRIMINATORY PRACTICES
AGAINST ASIANS IN THE UNITED STATES

Anti-Asian Laws

In the past, fears and hostilities against Asian Americans often were commonplace and pervasive enough that discrimination against them had been codified into laws. Anti-Asian laws were enacted at all governmental levels, and anti-Asian sentiment could be found through all branches of the government (i.e., the executive, legislative, and judicial branches). At state and local levels, numerous laws and ordinances were passed specifically targeting Asian Americans. For example, in 1855, the California legislature passed an act that would have required that Asian immigrants not be allowed into California unless they could pay a tax of $50. Although this act was invalidated by the state supreme court, other legislation was passed in further attempts to limit Asian immigration (Daniels, 1988). The California Alien Land Acts of 1913 and 1920, which prohibited noncitizens from owning land and limited land lease terms to 3 years or less, targeted mainly Japanese farmers, who, by federal naturalization laws, were aliens ineligible for citizenship. City ordinances, such as the San Francisco Cubic Air Ordinance (which required each residence to have at least 500 cubic feet of air per inhabitant), were passed for the explicit purpose of driving the Chinese out of San Francisco to other regions and states (Daniels, 1988). In 1876, San Francisco passed an ordinance requiring that any Chinese who was arrested allow his pigtail to be cut off by the arresting officer (LEAP, 1991).

Throughout the history of the United States, antimiscegenation laws prohibiting the intermarriage of Whites and other racial groups were prevalent in many states. In 1880, California's antimiscegenation law prohibited the marriage of Whites to "Negroes," "mulattos," and "Mongolians" (U.S. Commission on Civil Rights, 1992). In 1933, when a Filipino won a court decision establishing his right to marry a White woman because Filipinos were Malaysian and not Mongolian, the California legislature extended antimiscegenation laws to prohibit intermarriage between Whites and Filipinos (Takaki, 1989). Anti-Asian legal discrimination was not limited to the laws and ordinances. In 1854, the chief justice of the California Supreme Court, extending a California statute that had been adopted from southern slave codes limiting Black or mulatto individuals' testimony in court, ruled that Chinese should be barred from testifying against a White person (Daniels, 1988; Takaki, 1990).

At the federal level, the history of the United States' immigration and naturalization laws regarding Asians displays a clear pattern of racial discrimination. (For a more comprehensive discussion of racial discrimination in immigration policies, see U.S. Commission on Civil Rights, 1980.) In the first 100 years of the United States, the eligibility to citizenship was limited to "free White persons" (U.S. Commission on Civil Rights, 1980). The naturalization rights of Asians, in particular the Chinese, was debated during congressional discussions prior to the ratification of the Fourteenth Amendment in 1870. Senator Charles Sumner of Massachusetts proposed that because persons of African descent were to be added to the category of those eligible for naturalization (a group that previously had been limited to "White persons"), naturalization statutes should be changed to be color-blind and apply equally to all persons regardless of race (Daniels, 1988). Given the social milieu of nativism and racial exclusion at the time, Sumner's bill ultimately was defeated, as were other attempts to allow Asians to be eligible for naturalization.

The Chinese Exclusion Act of 1882 and the Gentlemen's Agreement of 1907 reflect the pervasive anti-Asian sentiment in the United States and clearly illustrate federal attempts to limit the immigration of Asians to the United States. Other federal immigration laws targeting Asians in particular included the Immigration Act of 1917, which barred immigration from all Asian countries except the Philippines and Japan. The Immigration Act of 1924 limited immigration from Japan and barred immigration of those who were ineligible for citizenship; at the time, Asians were defined as being aliens ineligible for citizenship. As described earlier, the Tydings-McDuffie Act of 1934 and the Repatriation Act of 1935 limited Filipino immigration and provided funds to send Filipinos back to the Philippines if they promised not to return to the United States (U.S. Commission on Civil Rights, 1992).

It is clear that numerous anti-Asian laws were enacted throughout the history of Asians in the United States. Yet, probably the most shamefully racist federal-level anti-Asian policy was Executive Order 9066, which authorized the evacuation, relocation, and internment of at least 100,000 Japanese Americans, without due process, into concentration camps in the United States. The decision to incarcerate individuals was based solely on the persons' race and place of residence; Supreme Court Justice Frank Murphy called the relocation a "legalization of racism" and a violation of the U.S. Constitution (Commission on Wartime Relocation and Internment of Civilians, 1982a; Daniels, 1988; Kitano & Daniels, 1988; U.S. Commission on Civil Rights, 1992).

Anti-Asian Violence

Violence against a minority group represents one of the more primitive manifestations of racism and the most overtly threatening; many minority group individuals have lost their lives due to racist violence in the United States. The history of Asians in the United States is no exception. As mentioned in the opening of this chapter, in the 1870s, the early Chinese immigrants were targeted in violent anti-Chinese riots throughout the western United States. In some incidents, the Chinese were forced to leave the area. In others, the homes and stores of Chinese were burned or looted and Chinese were robbed. In the worst instances, Chinese were beaten, shot, mutilated, hanged, or burned to death (Daniels, 1988; Kitano & Daniels, 1988; U.S. Commission on Civil Rights, 1992). In most cases, the perpetrators never were brought to justice, and those who were caught were not convicted (Daniels, 1988; Kitano & Daniels, 1988). After the Chinese Exclusion Act of 1882, although violence toward Chinese continued, much of the anti-Asian sentiment focused on the Japanese and Filipinos. During the Depression, anti-Filipino riots and murders took place in areas along the West Coast (LEAP, 1991; U.S. Commission on Civil Rights, 1992).

Currently, racially motivated violence against Asian Americans is being targeted on a national level by the U.S. attorney general, who is required by the Hate Crimes Statistics Act to monitor and report hate crimes. Hate crimes are criminal acts that are motivated by hatred, bias, or extreme prejudice based on the perceived race, ethnicity, religion, or sexual orientation of the victims. Hate crimes against Asian Americans have been found to be a serious and growing national problem (U.S. Commission on Civil Rights, 1986, 1992; Wong, 1991). Yet, prior to the Hate Crimes Statistics Act of 1990, there was no federal mechanism to assess the extent of the problem on a national scale, and much of what is known about hate crimes has been collected by cities and states in the United States. For example, in Boston, Asians were found to represent a disproportionate number of hate crime victims; although they constitute only 3% of the population, they were victims of nearly a third of racially motivated attacks (Matsui, 1987). The Los Angeles County Human Relations Commission found that, compared to the first 6 months of 1989, hate crimes against Asians had more than doubled during the first half of 1990 (Siao, 1990). In a 1989 survey of hate crimes in Los Angeles County schools, Asians and Pacific Islanders were found to be disproportionately victimized by hate crimes and related incidents (e.g., racial slurs) than would be expected by their numbers in the population. Anti-Asian incidents accounted for 14.5% of the reported hate crimes, although Asians and Pacific Islanders represented only 8.6% of the population. Anti-immigrant sentiment was found to account for more than half of the anti-Asian incidents reported (Los Angeles County Commission in Human Relations, 1989).

Although there is diversity in the generational/immigration status of Asian Americans, perpetrators of hate crimes are unlikely to make such fine distinctions. If individuals who commit hate crimes are motivated by anti-immigrant Asian bias, then it is likely that, just as in the Vincent Chin case when a Chinese American was mistaken for Japanese, both immigrant and nonimmigrant Asians will be at risk simply due to their Asian appearance.

Colonialism

Racism usually is embodied in historical colonialism because in the institutionalized contact between racial or ethnic groups that have unequal power, race often is the major determinant that maintains the categorization of those with the power and those who are to be governed. Clearly, the policy of the United States to extend its power over other nations with disregard for the other nations' right to self-determination and the resultant destruction of indigenous cultures constitutes colonialism.

Some Asian American and Pacific Islander ethnic groups were subjugated by American colonialism. In the case of Filipinos and some Pacific Islander groups such as the Samoans and the Hawaiians, American colonialization was direct and invasive; Americans entered these societies, undermined their sociocultural systems, and ultimately wrested governance away from the indigenous islanders (Kitano, 1991). In the case of the Philippines and the Hawaiian Islands, political power was taken through the threat or use of the U.S. armed forces. However, colonialism might not always take a direct form; some researchers have argued that the contract labor immigration of Chinese and Japanese to the United States constitutes a semicolonial pattern (Kuo, 1981).

Anti-Asian Discrimination in Housing

Racial segregation was a social reality throughout much of the history of the United States. Past efforts to legislate the segregation of Asians ranged from 1879 California legislation that attempted to require all incorporated cities to remove the Chinese from their territories (Chan, 1991) to the actual relocation and confinement of more than 100,000 Japanese Americans in concentration camps during World War II. Although currently there are no active governmental attempts to segregate Asian Americans from the majority population, and indeed there are laws that prohibit segregation based on race or ethnicity, anti-Asian discrimination regarding housing still can be found in many communities across the United States.

The U.S. Commission on Civil Rights (1992) documented numerous incidents in which Asian Americans experienced racially motivated intimidation, harassment, or vandalism designed to prevent Asians from living in particular communities. For example, anti-Asian flyers, which encouraged the boycott of Asian businesses and of realtors who sold property to Asians, were distributed in the Bensonhurst and Gravesend neighborhoods of Brooklyn, New York, in 1987 and in Hayward, California, in 1992 (U.S. Commission on Civil Rights, 1992). In other incidents, egg or rock throwing, vandalism, and arson were accompanied by the clear message that Asians were not wanted in certain neighborhoods. Yinger (1988), in a review of fair housing audits conducted in cities across the United States between 1977 and 1983, found that, like African Americans and Hispanic Americans, Asian Americans face considerable discrimination in the provision of information about available housing by real estate agents. However, although Asian Americans continue to experience residential segregation, they have been found to be equally or slightly less segregated than Latino Americans and much less segregated than African Americans (Langberg & Farley, 1985; O'Hare & Felt, 1991).

Discrimination in School

Within the U.S. history of school segregation based on race, Asian Americans, like African Americans and American Indians, were barred from "White" public schools. For example, in 1859, the California superintendent of education decided that the schools should be racially segregated, and during the following year the California legislature authorized the superintendent to withhold funds from schools that did not exclude Black, American Indian, and Asian students (Takaki, 1990). However, the California Supreme Court ruled that barring such students from public schools was unconstitutional, and by 1885, "separate but equal" schools were set up for Asians by the state of California (U.S. Commission on Civil Rights, 1992). In 1906, San Francisco's school board decreed that Japanese and Korean children could not attend White schools and that all children of Asian ancestry should attend the segregated schools set up for the Chinese in Chinatown. An international incident followed, during which the Japanese government protested the school board's decision. As a result, President Roosevelt privately apologized to the Japanese ambassador and persuaded the San Francisco school board not to enforce its segregationist policy with Japanese children (Daniels, 1988; U.S. Commission on Civil Rights, 1992).

In Hawaii, although racially segregated schools were not formally instituted, in 1920 the school superintendent established what became known as "English standard schools," a two-tiered school system that trained, at the English standard level, "competent leaders," and, at the other level, "efficient workers." The ostensible justification for this system was the preservation of the English language from the "degradation" of pidgin English (which was generally spoken by Asians and other non-Whites in the islands). Although race supposedly was not to be used as a criterion for selecting students, the English standard schools had the effect of racial segregation. The majority of students in English standard schools were White, and the majority of those in the regular public schools were non-White (Okihiro, 1991).

Although public schools no longer are legally segregated in the United States, Asian Americans continue to face problems in access to educational opportunity. Because the majority of Asian Americans are foreign born and significant Asian immigration continues, the educational needs of foreign-born Asian Americans will likely increase in the future. In the primary and secondary schools, Asian immigrant children or American-born children of recently arrived Asian immigrant refugees encounter considerable obstacles. Numerous studies suggest that limited English language proficiency (LEP) Asian American students are underserved by the educational system (U.S. Commission on Civil Rights, 1992). Some Asian American children have LEP and enter schools whose teachers do not know their languages or cultures despite federal civil rights laws that require school districts to provide equal educational opportunity for children with LEP. In addition, the classmates of Asian American immigrant children might ridicule Asian-accented English or express anti-Asian or anti-immigrant sentiments through racial slurs or name-calling. Some Asian immigrant students have even been victims of racially motivated violence (Los Angeles County Commission on Human Relations, 1989; U.S. Commission on Civil Rights, 1992). This type of unfriendly or even hostile school environment is likely to hamper both the academic success and social adjustment of Asian American immigrant children.

In higher education, educational access for Asian Americans also is a concern. In addition to the types of problems faced by LEP students in the primary and secondary schools (e.g., inadequate supplemental language services), other issues include the underrepresentation of Asian Americans in faculty positions, discriminatory policies regarding financial aid to Asian American students, and discriminatory admissions policies toward Asian American students. The latter issue, admissions policies toward Asian Americans, has received significant nationwide publicity (Wang, 1988). Various investigations into the policies of different colleges and universities, such as Harvard, Brown, Princeton, Yale, and Stanford universities as well as the University of California, Berkeley, and the University of California, Los Angeles (UCLA), alleged that Asian Americans were admitted at a lower rate than were White applicants despite comparable academic qualifications. In 1988, the Office for Civil Rights of the U.S. Department of Education began civil rights compliance reviews and complaint investigations into the admissions policies of some colleges and universities. In 1990, the Office for Civil Rights concluded that the undergraduate admissions policy of Harvard did not discriminate against Asian Americans. However, in the review of graduate programs at UCLA, the Office for Civil Rights found that one graduate program had violated civil rights laws by discriminating against Asian American applicants (U.S. Commission on Civil Rights, 1992). Currently, several other colleges and universities are in the process of being reviewed by the Office for Civil Rights.

Discrimination in Employment Opportunities

Since the Civil Rights Act of 1866, and more recently Title VII of the Civil Rights Act of 1964, racial discrimination in employment is prohibited by law in the United States. However, Asian Americans continue to face employment discrimination. Some employment issues are specific to foreign-born Asian Americans. For example, Asian Americans who have learned English as a second language might have difficulty with some employment tests. Asian Americans who have been educated abroad usually encounter barriers in the certification procedures of professional boards and, as a result, often are unable to find employment commensurate with their education. Other issues of employment discrimination, such as the "glass ceiling," affect even fourth- or fifth-generation Asian Americans. Thus, employment discrimination affects all Asian Americans.

Much of the employment discrimination toward foreign-born Asian Americans centers around language proficiency rights and employment practices. Many foreign-born Asian Americans may have LEP or may speak English with a foreign accent. The validity of the common institutional practice of administering employment tests to potential workers has been called into question because these tests might have a discriminatory impact on Asian Americans. Some have claimed that certain employment tests require levels of English language skills that are beyond what is necessary for adequate job performance. Thus, such tests might unfairly discriminate against those who have LEP. Because of such concerns, the Equal Employment Opportunity Commission has published guidelines on the use of tests in employment selection. Currently, if employment tests are administered, then they must be shown to be job related and to measure success on the job rather than other factors (such as language proficiency) that might not be relevant to the job (U.S. Commission on Civil Rights, 1992).

Some Asian Americans are proficient in the English language but may speak with a foreign accent. In general, it is a violation of Title VII of the Civil Rights Act of 1964 to demote, fail to promote, or fail to hire an individual because of his or her foreign accent. However, in cases where communication is related to job performance and an individual's accent interferes with his or her ability to perform what is required, courts have ruled that Asian Americans can be denied employment due to their Asian-accented English (U.S. Commission on Civil Rights, 1992).

In addition to the obstacles encountered by foreign-born Asian Americans, many Asian Americans born in the United States believe that a glass ceiling bars Asian Americans from occupational attainment in the upper echelon of jobs in the United States. Research on various occupations, from managerial positions and administration to Fortune 500 business executives, suggests that Asian Americans are underrepresented in the higher positions and experience limits to occupational upward mobility. For example, a study by the U.S. Commission on Civil Rights (1988) found that Asian Americans were much less likely to occupy managerial positions than were Whites of comparable education and work experience. Other studies have found that Asian Americans are less likely to be promoted to administrative or managerial positions than are comparable Whites (U.S. Commission on Civil Rights, 1992). Although some Asian Americans think that racial prejudice is a primary factor affecting their upward mobility, others cite other factors such as their lack of access to networking support systems that would facilitate employment opportunities (Cabezas, Tam, Lowe, Wong, & Turner, 1989; U.S. Commission on Civil Rights, 1992).

Possibly the most compelling evidence supporting the notion of the glass ceiling, or institutional racism, is the finding that, when compared to non-Hispanic Whites of equivalent age and educational levels, Asian Americans earned significantly less; that is, Asian Americans receive less economic returns on their educational investments than did Whites (O'Hare & Felt, 1991). This finding often has been obscured by studies that simply compared the median family income of Asian Americans to that of non-Hispanic Whites and claimed that the incomes of some groups of Asian Americans were equivalent to that of Whites. Researchers who have attempted to analyze the component factors (e.g., education) that influence economic achievement have found that "the apparent equality between Asians and Whites is largely a function of educational overachievement by Asians" (Hirschman & Wong, 1984, p. 602). Thus, there remains a "cost" to being an Asian in the United States: Asian Americans must work harder to receive comparable economic gains (Wong, 1982).

Interminority Conflicts

More than many other countries, the ethnic composition of the United States is extremely diverse. Most studies have focused on the relationship between Whites and ethnic minority groups. However, the relations between the different ethnic minority groups in this country are important to recognize and address because conflict between minority ethnic groups is becoming an increasing concern as the United States becomes more diverse. There have been numerous interminority conflicts throughout the history of the United States. For example, during the anti-Chinese violence of the late 1800s, American Indians murdered five Chinese in Idaho (Daniels, 1988). During World War II, Chinese and Korean Americans expressed anti-Japanese sentiment both in response to the Japanese occupation of China and Japan and in order to distinguish themselves from the Japanese, who were perceived as enemies of the United States at the time.

Currently, interminority conflicts between Haitian and African Americans and recent immigrant Korean Americans have increased. For example, in New York in 1990, an incident between a Korean American grocer and a Haitian American escalated into a large boycott of the Korean-owned store, punctuated by racism and violence (U.S. Commission on Civil Rights, 1992). And in the worst civil unrest in U.S. history, the Los Angeles rebellion (during which approximately 4,000 businesses were destroyed, 43 people died, and more than 2,000 people were injured in the burning and looting), some have argued that the competition among Blacks, Latinos, and Koreans over scarce resources in the inner city provided the undercurrent of frustration and anger that overflowed after a "not guilty" verdict acquitted four White police officers who were accused of using unreasonable force in restraining the African American Rodney King (Johnson, Jones, Farrell, & Oliver, 1992; Johnson & Oliver, 1989). During the civil unrest following the verdict, Korean American-owned stores were targeted in some of the burning and looting, possibly because the tensions between the Black longtime residents of South Central Los Angeles and the more recent immigrant Koreans already were strained by a previous incident involving the probationary sentencing of a Korean shopkeeper who had shot and killed an African American high school girl, Latasha Harlins (Johnson et al., 1992).

Unfortunately, interminority conflicts are likely to continue without intervention. In a study after the Los Angeles rebellion, researchers found that Asians' attitudes toward Blacks had become significantly more negative; Blacks' attitudes toward Asians had not changed. In addition, Asians were the most likely to oppose residential contact with Blacks when compared to Whites and Hispanics (Bobo, Johnson, Oliver, Sidanius, & Zubrinsky, 1992).

INDIVIDUAL-LEVEL
THEORIES OF RACISM

Individual-level theories of racism focus on the individual as a unit of analysis rather than on, for example, the group or society. Theories that incorporate an individual perspective include research done on the attitudes and personality characteristics of prejudiced persons, the characteristics of minorities, the socialization processes in the development of racist attitudes, the social roles and status of prejudiced individuals, and cognitive sources of prejudice. The following comprise some of the major individual-level theories developed to explain racism.

The Authoritarian Personality

One approach to explaining prejudice and discrimination has been to locate the cause of prejudice in the particular dysfunctional personality characteristics of individuals. A prototypical model of this strategy is the "authoritarian personality" conceived by Adorno, Frenkel-Brunswick, Levinson, and Sanford (1950) to explain the anti-Semitism and Nazi war atrocities of World War II. In their study of more than 2,000 individuals (predominantly White and middle-class), Adorno et al. found that individuals who held hostile attitudes toward Jews tended to also have hostile attitudes toward all ethnic out-groups, an attitude that they termed "ethnocentric." Furthermore, Adorno et al. found that the ethnocentric individuals tended to manifest a particular pattern of characteristics that they termed an authoritarian personality. These characteristics included a punitive demeanor; a preoccupation with power and status; an intolerance for the weakness of others; and respect for, submission to, and obedience to in-group authority figures. They proposed that the cause of the authoritarian personality was the harsh and restrictive discipline received when these individuals were children. Such discipline resulted in psychodynamic processes such as the introjection of the parents, the repression of the criticism of the parents, and the repression of the hostility toward authority. As adults, the repressed criticism surfaces instead in a projection onto the out-group (prejudice), and repressed hostilities are then displaced onto the out-group (discrimination).

Adorno et al.'s (1950) research and theory of the authoritarian personality have been criticized on methodological, measurement, and theoretical/interpretive grounds (see Brown, 1965, for a review of these criticisms). Despite the various criticisms of the authoritarian personality theory, there continues to be some research investigating the relationship between an authoritarian personality (or attitudes), and prejudice and discrimination (Bierly, 1985; Ray, 1980; Ray & Lovejoy, 1983; Van Staden, 1987). Perhaps one of the most important criticisms of the authoritarian personality, and of other theories that would locate the cause of prejudice, discrimination, and racism in the relatively fixed personality characteristics of individuals, is that an individual-level explanation fails to fully account for certain group phenomena. If racism were simply the result of the dysfunctional personalities of individuals within groups, then the relationships between groups would be expected to also remain stable. However, the relationships between groups and collective shifts in intergroup attitudes have been known to change relatively quickly depending on the circumstances (Hogg & Abrams, 1988). For example, as mentioned earlier, prior to World War II, there continued to be negative attitudes toward Chinese Americans, and Chinese Americans were subjected to racism in many forms. However, when Japan attacked Pearl Harbor and the United States and China became allies, attitudes toward the Chinese underwent a large transformation and positive stereotypes of Chinese replaced what had been predominantly negative images of Chinese (Daniels, 1988; Kitano & Daniels, 1988).

Affective Causes of Prejudice

Dollard, Doob, Miller, Mowrer, and Sears (1939) proposed the frustration-aggression hypothesis to explain intergroup prejudice. In their model, any type of frustration eventually would lead to aggression. Operating within a psychodynamic framework, frustration that cannot be relieved is suppressed, and the ensuing aggression is redirected or displaced onto out-groups, typically minority group members. The problem with this model, as well as with the similar scapegoat theory, is that it cannot explain why certain minority groups are targeted instead of others, nor can it differentiate between other types of aggression perpetuated against minority group members (Hogg & Abrams, 1988).

Racist Attitudes

The underlying assumption in research on attitudes is that attitudes cause behavior. Therefore, racial prejudice is seen to be a necessary condition for racial discrimination. Given such a model, it would seem that if it were possible to change racial attitudes, then racism would decrease. There has been a tremendous amount of research documenting changing racial attitudes. It is generally accepted that racist attitudes are acquired through socialization processes. The major sources of socialization are the family, school, peers, and (more recently) the mass media (Ashmore & Del Boca, 1976; Katz, 1976). Intergroup contact, mentioned earlier, was seen as having the potential to affect racial attitudes. In a review of studies on the effects of school desegregation on the prejudicial attitudes of Blacks and Whites, Stephan (1986) concluded that, overall, desegregation was more likely to decrease prejudice in Blacks but more likely to increase prejudice in Whites.

Although the endorsement of blatantly racist attitudes, such as the support for racial segregation, is less likely to be elicited due to the current social norms and their accompanying social desirability factors, many researchers continue to find indications of racial prejudice, only in more subtle forms. For example, Bobo (1988) considered contemporary racial attitudes a "paradox"; on the one hand, White Americans are now less likely to endorse negative stereotypes of Blacks and are more likely to support the principle of racial equality than they were in the past, yet at the same time, Whites continue to oppose policies that would achieve racial equality. Thus, there is a gap between Whites' attitudes toward the *principle* of egalitarianism (i.e., racial equality) and the *implementation* of such principles (i.e., racial policy preferences).

There is very little research on Whites' attitudes toward Asian Americans, but in general, the current stereotype of Asian Americans differs from those of other ethnic minority groups in that Asian Americans tend to be stereotyped as a "model minority"; that is, from an outsider's perspective, Asian Americans appear to have made substantial educational and economic progress while accepting their less-than-equal status with passivity and few complaints. However, whatever achievement Asian Americans have attained does not necessarily mean that Asians do not face racial prejudice and discrimination, nor does it necessarily indicate that Asians have achieved equal opportunity on par with the majority group in the United States. The impact of the stereotype of the Asian American model minority should be investigated, especially given the past history of racism endured by Asian Americans (Sue & Sue, 1973; Toupin, 1980).

Symbolic Racism

The concept of symbolic racism initially was introduced to explain the effect of White American racial attitudes toward Blacks on their responses to racial issues in the political arena. It was conceptualized as a new type of racial attitude, a result of the combination of anti-Black affect and particular moral values such as those related to the Protestant work ethic (Sears, 1988). Symbolic racism is operationalized with items representing both anti-Black affect and traditional values (e.g., individualism, self-reliance) such as the antagonism toward the demands of Blacks, the resentment of special treatment of Blacks (e.g., racial quotas), and the denial that discrimination toward Blacks still exists (Sears, 1988). Theorists proposed that symbolic racism was a major determinant of White American voting behavior and racial policy preferences. Typically, the construct of symbolic racism has been tested by correlating, in a multiple regression analysis, items measuring symbolic racism with White American political behavior (e.g., attitudes toward particular racial policies, support of ethnic politicians). For example, in a study in Los Angeles, researchers found that symbolic racism could predict White voters' choices not to vote for the Black mayoral candidate, Tom Bradley (Kinder & Sears, 1981). Although findings have varied depending on the study and the number of items used to measure symbolic racism, in many cases symbolic racism has been a useful construct in predicting White political attitudes.

Self-Esteem

Researchers have suggested not only that groups compete for material resources such as jobs and educational opportunities but that intergroup discrimination is the result of intergroup competition for a positive social identity (Tajfel, 1982). In such a model of intergroup conflict, individuals within one group will try to achieve or maintain a distinctive and comparatively positive social identity relative to another group (Tajfel & Turner, 1979). This model combines both intergroup processes (such as the need for a positive social identity) and individual psychological processes (such as the need for positive self-esteem).

There have been numerous studies on self-esteem and prejudice. Although initial theories hypothesized a simple linear relationship between self-esteem and prejudice—a person with low self-esteem was considered to be more likely to be prejudiced against out-group members for the purposes of self-enhancement due to social comparison—subsequent findings were more complex. Low self-esteem individuals were found to be more prejudiced in that they rated *both* in-group and out-group members negatively rather than simply rating out-group members more negatively relative to in-group ratings (Crocker, Thomson, McGraw, & Ingerman, 1987).

Cognitive Sources of Prejudice

Recent research has begun to investigate cognitive sources of prejudice. This approach has tried to examine, at an information processing level (i.e., attention, encoding, and retrieval), how intergroup biases are created. At this level, biases are conceived as the result of normal, "automatic" cognitive functioning rather than of social or psychological processes.

Simply the categorization of individuals has been found to create intergroup bias effects (Gaertner, Mann, Murrell, & Dovidio, 1989; Messick & Mackie, 1989). Thus, a cognitive factor in intergroup conflict might be the result of in-group formation and identification rather than simply the denigration of out-group members. Furthermore, individuals within a group tend to be perceived as more similar to others in the group but are perceived as more different from the outside perceiver's perspective (Myers, 1990). Researchers also found that individuals perceived those within one's own group as more distinctive. For example, African Americans are more able to differentiate between African American faces than between White faces. Yet, even though one might automatically be better able to recognize the faces of one's own race, one investigator found that White students could improve the facial recognition of Japanese faces through training (Chance, 1985, as cited in Myers, 1990).

Another common cognitive error, known as the expectancy-confirmation bias, is the tendency to find evidence that will confirm prior expectations and not look for evidence that might disconfirm one's expectations (Stephan, 1987). This type of bias might explain stereotyping and the difficulty in changing existing racial attitudes.

In another type of cognitive process called the saliency bias, the more distinctive stimulus, such as a minority or an out-group member, is more likely to be the focus of one's attention. Furthermore, the cause of an event is more likely to be automatically attributed to that which is salient (Stephan, 1987). Thus, in the case of a negative event, the cause might automatically be attributed to what was perceived as distinctive, which might explain why individuals may tend to automatically blame minority group members rather than majority group members.

SOCIAL EXPLANATIONS OF RACISM

Social theories of racism focus on the environmental forces, such as institutional or societal systems, that contain and constrain race relations including, but not limited to, group conflict processes in the context of limited resources. Although individual and societal theories of racism differ in their unit of analysis, they obviously are not necessarily mutually exclusive. Whereas some have argued that individual-level issues, such as prejudicial attitudes, might reflect social forces (Bobo, 1988), others have argued just the opposite. However, it is beyond the scope of this chapter and the current knowledge in the field to determine which forces should be deemed conceptually or actually prior. Thus, at this time, both perspectives are conceived as having the potential to inform the other in providing a more comprehensive analysis of the problem of racism.

Cultural Deprivation

One of the earlier theories of racism assumed that the past history of discrimination and unequal treatment of minorities had resulted in a situation whereby the minority group did not perform as well as the majority group. This theory tended to focus on the comparative "inadequacy" of minority achievement relative to the achievement of the majority group and proposed that the differential achievement was due to differences in the groups' starting points and the absence of certain cultural necessities in the minority group, giving rise to the notion of cultural deprivation/disadvantage. For example, some sociogenic variables proposed to account for differential minority group educational performance included the characteristics of the minority family, community, and culture such as cultural differences in child-rearing practices, the lack of space in the home for studying, the lack of a stimulating home environment, the cultural tendency toward concrete reasoning rather than the abstract reasoning necessary in school, an inability to delay gratification, and the parental lack of value placed on education (Chesler, 1976; Gottfried & Gottfried, 1986; LeVine & White, 1986).

Theories of cultural deprivation or cultural disadvantage have been criticized because they hold the majority group achievement levels and cultural ideals as the standard by which to measure minority performance and do not value or even consider the possibility of cultural pluralism. Moreover, such theories contain the implicitly racist perspective that would assert the cultural superiority of one group over the other. To incorporate the concept of differing but equally legitimate cultural values, more recent theorists have preferred the notion of cultural *difference* rather than deprivation or disadvantage. This conception is especially relevant for Asian Americans, many of whom value and maintain the cultural and educational traditions of their countries of origin or ancestry over those of the dominant U.S. culture.

The cultural deprivation theory breaks down further when applied to Asian Americans. In contrast to some other minority groups, Asian Americans have been able to attain high levels of educational achievement despite cultural differences and societal discrimination (Hirschman & Wong, 1986). However, studies suggest that even though Asians surpass the White majority in educational attainment, they do not receive an economic return comparable to their level of education (O'Hare & Felt, 1991; Wong, 1982). Specifically, as mentioned earlier, Asian Americans received less income per year of education when compared to non-Hispanic Whites of the same age and educational levels.

Thus, Asian Americans provide a counterexample to the cultural deprivation/disadvantage theory. Asian Americans have been shown to achieve in the educational realm despite cultural differences, yet they still fail to achieve comparable economic rewards. Other critics of theories of cultural deprivation/disadvantage have suggested that cultural deprivation models of inequality have a tendency to posit the cause of continuing differential achievement in the qualities of the minority group. They have proposed that alternative sources of investigation, rather than a type of "blaming the victim," would be more productive in understanding continuing minority-majority inequality (Chesler, 1976).

Class-Based Explanations

Class theories argue that race and class are intertwined and should be seen as a single system of inequality rather than as separate dimensions. One class perspective argues that racism is a product of world capitalism. Capitalism creates a need for cheap labor, which has led to the colonization and exploitation of non-White cultures and the restricted immigration of minority groups. The result is the oppression of non-Whites, which benefits a select few in White-dominant societies (Nikolinakos, 1973). Modifications of this theme have explored the complexities of race and class in detail. For example, concepts of internal colonies and segmented labor economies seek to explore the racial and ethnic divisions as a function of powerful economic forces (Bonacich, 1976; Hechter, 1975).

The system of capitalism creates and maintains racism to prevent minority groups from recognizing that the inequities inherent in the economic system are common to all groups. One example of this thesis is especially applicable to Asian

Americans. As discussed previously, Asian Americans sometimes have been called the model minority. Even when that term is not specifically used, Asian Americans often are referred to as an ethnic group that has achieved economic success despite the barriers its members encountered when they first immigrated to the United States (Suzuki, 1977). The model minority label forces Asian Americans to become a buffer for the dominant class; that is, Asian Americans are used as an example to follow—which, in turn, creates resentment among other minorities. Accordingly, other minorities faced with inequities in the economic system channel their hostilities and frustrations toward Asian Americans.

Racial Segregation

An example of a theory that employs an alternative societal focus is the "contact hypothesis." The assumption of the contact hypothesis was that racism continued to be a problem because demographic or institutional segregation limited the contact between minority and majority group members, thus limiting the conditions for individual and societal change. Allport (1954) proposed that prejudice could be reduced if there were opportunities for majority and minority group members to have contact on an equal-status basis. To this end, Allport advocated the institutional support and enforcement of desegregation. Many of the researchers who followed attempted to clarify the relevant factors operating in the contact situation. According to Stephan (1987), early proponents of the contact model sought to improve intergroup relations by changing individual variables that researchers believed could be manipulated such as the negative attitudes toward another group, and later researchers added societal factors such as physical proximity, role relationships, and the norms of the in-group. In the 1980s, normal cognitive processes within the individual at an information processing level (e.g., categorization) that take place in the context of intergroup contact were incorporated into the contact model.

Some have suggested that the social science statement, titled "The Effect of Segregation and the Consequences of Desegregation: A Social Science Statement," signed by 36 prominent social scientists, and submitted to the U.S. Supreme Court as an appendix to the plaintiff's briefs in *Brown v. Board of Education,* influenced the court to rule that segregated education was discriminatory (Cook, 1988; Stephan, 1987). The subsequent school desegregation illustrates a governmental attempt to institute interracial contact. As discussed earlier, Asian Americans have been in the past, and to some extent continue to be, segregated and isolated from majority contact, and this segregation has included separate schooling (Chan, 1991; Daniels, 1988; Daniels & Kitano, 1970; Langberg & Farley, 1985; Takaki, 1989; U.S. Commission on Civil Rights, 1992; Wong, 1991).

In advocating desegregation, many social psychologists hoped that desegregation would reduce prejudice, improve the academic achievement of minority group students, and raise the self-esteem of minority group students (Aronson & Gonzalez, 1988; Stephan, 1986). The outcomes of governmentally imposed desegregation have been mixed. The actual desegregation of schools has proceeded very slowly, and there continues to be substantial opposition to school desegregation and busing (Stephan, 1986). In reviews of the research on racial attitudes, desegregation did not always reduce prejudice; in nearly half of the studies, desegregation was found to increase Whites' prejudice of Blacks and Blacks' prejudice of Whites (Stephan, 1978, 1986). In addition, even in desegregated schools, students may continue to stay within their own ethnic groups when choosing friends and acquaintances (Gerard & Miller, 1975), thus perpetuating segregation, albeit on a less formal basis. On the other hand, reviews of studies of the impact of desegregation on the academic achievement and educational achievement suggest a positive impact; desegregation was found to improve Blacks' scores on reading achievement tests and to increase the likelihood that Blacks would attend and adjust better to college (Stephan, 1986).

Thus, even though there has been a great deal of controversy over the effects of school desegregation on African Americans (e.g., Cook, 1988; Gerard, 1988), many researchers and reviewers have found benefits in the educational attainment of African Americans. Although there have been no comparable studies of the effects of desegregation on Asian American educational achievement (the existing research tends to look at factors other than the desegregation of schools such as cultural values or selective migration to explain the high levels of Asian American educational attainment), considering that historically Asian children in California were kept in segregated schools into the 1930s and were segregated in Mississippi until the 1950s, desegregation would be an interesting factor to explore.

Group Self-Interest

As noted earlier, many researchers have pointed out that interracial contact alone is insufficient to promote change in racial attitudes and to reduce racism. Segregation has been considered by some researchers to be a form of "boundary maintenance," and they have likened the defense of intergroup boundaries to the territorial defense of a perceived threat of loss of that which is considered to be one's own (Daniels & Kitano, 1970). In this model, majority economic and status self-interest underlies discrimination toward out-group members (Chesler, 1976). Group conflict arises when different groups have incompatible group interests; groups might be forced to compete with each other for limited resources. Many theorists focus on sociostructural group interests involving the distribution of power, money, and status. Like other societies, there are particular patterns of sociostructural inequality between groups in United States historically and currently. According to theories of group self-interest, the group that currently possesses power, wealth, and status will be unlikely to support policies that might redistribute resources if such redistribution results in an ultimate loss of resources for the group (Bobo, 1988). Not only is there no incentive for the group with the resources to share the resources, but it might be in the self-interest of the group to support policies that maintain the status quo.

Some theorists and researchers have proposed that the conditions of economic competition for scarce resources fueled anti-Asian sentiment in the past, such as the anti-Chinese riots in the late 1800s in the western states (Kitano, 1991) and the internment of Japanese Americans in World War II (Fugita & O'Brien, 1991). At that time, White workers perceived that the low-paid Chinese workers were reducing their wages, and in some instances, predominantly White labor unions encouraged anti-Chinese laws (Daniels, 1988).

Group Processes

Some researchers have tried to explain interracial conflict through the naturally occurring processes of group formation. An example of this type of research is Sherif's (1966) classic study of intra- and intergroup processes. Sherif proposed that simply the existence of two groups in a context where each competes for goals that only one can attain was a sufficient condition for the development of intergroup hostility. In a series of three experiments with 11- and 12-year-old boys, Sherif documented the formation of groups and experimentally varied the conditions under which groups were brought into contact. Initially, Sherif brought the groups of boys into contact under competitive situations such as a tournament of games in which the winner received prizes. These situations produced hostility between the groups, and each group developed negative attitudes toward members of the opposing group. Group members were more likely to overestimate the abilities of fellow group members while underestimating the abilities of out-group members. At the same time, within-group pride and cohesiveness increased under conditions of intergroup competition and conflict. Furthermore, intergroup conflict resulted in changes in status, role relationships, and previously established group practices within the group.

Sherif (1966) then tested a version of the contact hypothesis by bringing the groups together under pleasant conditions in which each group had equal status but interdependence between the groups was not required (e.g., going to the movies, eating together). These conditions did not reduce intergroup conflict; rather, they provided more opportunities for the groups to harass and attack each other. After eliminating the viability of simple contact in improving intergroup relations, Sherif devised situations in which cooperation between groups was necessary to achieve a common superordinate goal. Examples of superordinate goals used were a breakdown of the water supply and a pooling of resources to rent a movie that each group would not have been able to rent alone. The cumulative effect of the successful achievement of superordinate goals was that the hostility between groups was reduced and intergroup cooperation was facilitated.

The findings of Sherif's (1966) studies with young boys have been verified and replicated with other populations including adults (Blake & Mouton, 1979; Brewer & Miller, 1988; Sherif, 1966). These studies provide practical implications in reducing intergroup conflicts. For example, Gaertner et al. (1989) found that if members of two groups were regrouped into one group under the type of superordinate goal conditions outlined by Sherif, the creation of this new group tended to curtail the negative feelings of the former intergroup conflict.

Institutional Practices

Another type of societal force considered to cause and maintain racism is the normal functioning of institutions. Some theorists have proposed that current institutional practices embody the past historical patterns of injustice toward minorities and tend to maintain the status quo differential between groups. This concept of "institutional racism" suggests that racial discrimination does not necessarily require the conscious prejudice of an individual agent but merely requires the normal operations of current institutions (Chesler, 1976). For example, many public institutions, such as schools, attempt to provide equal treatment and rewards based on meritocratic achievement. However, this model assumes that all individuals in both the majority and minority begin at a relatively equal starting point. If individuals in the minority start out slightly behind because of past injustices or have more obstacles to overcome such as societal prejudice and the lowered expectations of others, then the institutional practices of apparent equal treatment of all becomes, in actuality, vehicles for the perpetuation of inequality.

There are significant social policy implications given the conceptualization of normal organizational practices as institutional racism. Advocates of affirmative action and other compensatory mechanisms tend to adopt this theoretical approach to justify the implementation of seemingly preferential practices (Chesler, 1976). It is beyond the scope of this chapter to detail the continuing debate over preferential practices or quota systems; however, for Asian Americans, the issue of discriminatory admissions policies to higher education provides a different perspective on how admissions quotas have been used against Asian American applicants. As detailed earlier, the U.S. Commission on Civil Rights found that in some prestigious private and public universities, Asian Americans were admitted at a lower rate than were Whites despite comparable academic qualifications. Furthermore, as mentioned earlier, Asian American educational attainment is higher than that of the majority White population, yet Asian Americans receive less of an income return on their educations per year of schooling when compared to that of Whites. It is apparent that Asian Americans do face institutional racism on many levels including the limitation of access to higher education and possibly the institutional forces that grant Asian Americans "less pay for equal education."

THE IMPACT OF RACISM: EFFECTS OF PREJUDICE AND DISCRIMINATION ON ASIAN AMERICANS

Although there have been some empirical investigations on the occupational and socioeconomic impact of racism on Asian American achievement in the United States, research on the psychological impact of racism for Asian Americans is lacking. The majority of past research efforts on the psychological impact of racism on the victim, like other areas discussed previously, have focused on African

Americans (although there has been some research on the effects of stereotyping, prejudice, and discrimination on groups characterized by qualities other than race such as obese individuals, the physically or mentally disabled, women, and homosexuals). When we review the major trends in the literature, it cannot be emphasized too strongly that more research is needed on Asian Americans, and it is questionable to what degree research on African Americans can be extended to Asian Americans.

A major area of investigation has been the impact of racism on the victimized individual's self-esteem and self-concept (Crocker & Major, 1989). Early investigations on the self-esteem of African Americans in the 1970s found no consistent differences between the self-esteem levels of African Americans and Whites, which some researchers explained by reconceptualizing the notion of self-esteem as developing through the evaluation of significant others and the social comparison of perceived similar individuals in one's social context rather than a social comparison to majority norms (Stephan, 1986). However, desegregation provided a context in which the self-esteem of minority individuals might change due to the exposure to majority norms. In an overview of past review articles on the impact of school desegregation on African American children's self-esteem, Cook (1988) reported that, due to methodological difficulties, alternative interpretations of the implications of past research, and divergent findings by a variety of reviewers, the research on self-esteem remains inconclusive.

Likewise, at this time, the available evidence does not provide a definitive answer to whether the self-esteem of Asians suffers because of racial discrimination. One study of Chinese Canadian male college students found that even if the students felt discriminated against, it did not appear to affect their self-esteem (Dion, Earn, & Yee, 1978, as cited in Asamen & Berry, 1987). By contrast, in a study of Japanese American and Chinese American college students, Asamen and Berry (1987) found that Japanese Americans who perceived more racial prejudice and inequality were more likely to have a lower self-concept (i.e., lower self-worth or self-satisfaction) than were those who perceived less racial prejudice. However, Asamen and Berry did not find a significant relationship between perceived prejudice and self-concept for Chinese Americans. They proposed that this difference could be accounted for by the generational differences between the Japanese American and Chinese American samples and the stage of minority identity development this entailed; the Japanese Americans tended to be third-, fourth-, or fifth-generation Americans, whereas most of the Chinese were first- or second-generation Americans. Asamen and Berry suggested that the Japanese Americans might be at a stage of their minority development where their self-concept and cultural identity were incompatible—a state of "dissonance." This hypothesis supports Weisman, Snadomsky, and Gannon's (1972) finding that even though foreign-born Chinese Americans tended to perceive more discrimination than did American-born Chinese Americans, the foreign-born Chinese Americans were more likely to have faith in the democratic system of the United States to eventually overcome such discrimination than were the American-born Chinese Americans.

In one of the few studies of the intergenerational impact of racism on Asian Americans, Nagata (1989, 1993) conducted a national survey and in-depth interviews of Sansei (third-generation Japanese Americans) whose parents were former internees to investigate the cross-generational impact of the internment of Japanese Americans during World War II. Nagata's study confirmed previous accounts that one of the major consequences of internment was silence, even within the family, about the experience of internment.

Some have proposed cultural explanations for this silence such as the Japanese sense of fatalism about that which is beyond one's control, exemplified in the Japanese saying *shi-ka-ta-ga-ni* ("it cannot be helped") or the Japanese concept of *ga-men* (which puts value on the ability to suppress one's emotions (Nagata, 1993). Other explanations for the silence include psychological factors such as shame or symptoms of posttraumatic stress (Nagata, 1993).

FUTURE DIRECTIONS FOR THEORY AND RESEARCH

As detailed throughout this chapter, prejudice and discrimination against Asian Americans in the United States continue to be an ongoing problem. Racism is a complex issue that has been examined along many dimensions—affective, attitudinal, and cognitive factors at the individual level; environmental, institutional, and social forces at the societal level; inter- and intragroup dynamics; and the economic, social, and psychological impacts of race-based discrimination. Because racism has been identified as a pernicious social problem, a large portion of the research has aimed (directly or indirectly) at eliminating the problem. This research tradition and its continuing efforts to clarify the problem of racism not only has been important in academic circles but also has been influential in shaping public policy and making contributions to the social ideals of the United States. Further research is needed in the field in general because, despite gradual societal change, the goal of eliminating racism remains elusive.

The sociopolitical climate created by the progress of the civil rights movement in the late 1960s and early 1970s supported a resurgence of interest in research on racism, and at that time many social scientists were optimistic that racist attitudes and discriminatory practices could be changed through governmental policies such as desegregation and affirmative action. However, according to Katz and Taylor (1988), controversy predominates current theories and research, especially on previously proposed solutions to racism. Katz and Taylor detailed three recent trends in the field: (a) the paradox of the coexistence of American *ideals* of equality and justice with the *actuality* of interracial prejudice and discrimination; (b) the contribution of larger numbers of ethnic minority researchers and theorists, who provide non-White perspectives that are crucial to the study of racism; and (c) the emergence of interest in racism research on ethnic minority groups other than African Americans such as Latino Americans, American Indians, and Asian Americans.

The last trend has particular significance to the present chapter. Because there exists an extensive body of research on racial prejudice, discrimination, and intergroup relations that was conceptualized and tested on Whites and African Americans (a formidable tradition that has not yet been achieved by research on racism toward other minority ethnic groups), most of the theories and findings presented in this chapter came out of that tradition. However, we do recognize the limitations of research concerned primarily with Black-White race relations or with the impact of racism on African Americans in that those findings might not generalize to Asian Americans. Although at the present time we tend to agree with Nakanishi (1988) that there needs to be a "convergence in race relations research" such that different minority groups, while remaining aware of their specific intergroup issues, can develop a common ground of minority-majority intergroup concerns, we also suggest that research focusing on racism and Asian Americans can provide valuable and unique contributions to the field.

Asian American racism research has the potential to inform the larger field of race relations research in that it could test the universalizability of current theories. There needs to be programmatic research into current models of racism as applied to Asian Americans. The theoretical constructs derived from Black-White research applied to Asian-White intergroup relations remain to be empirically tested. Although African Americans and Asian Americans share similar characteristics in that they have been victims of racism in the United States, it is likely that, given the markedly different histories of intergroup relations between White Americans and African Americans and Asian Americans, there will be significant issues for Asian Americans that cannot be understood by reference to theories previously developed to explain Black-White relations. Racism research on Asian Americans may allow the theoretical and empirical partitioning of historical or ethnic-specific factors versus other types of factors, which would greatly advance the field.

As suggested in this chapter, more is known about the details of racism against Asian Americans within the sociohistorical context of the United States, and the social and economic consequences of continued discrimination, than about the psychological impact of racism on Asian American individuals. Current and past research on the psychology of Asian Americans provides limited mention, if at all, of the role of racism on Asian American mental health. Much of the research that demonstrates an association between ethnic categories and mental health assumes that any found differences are due to "cultural" reasons and typically omit racism as an explanatory process.

We are at the stage in the study of Asian American psychological issues to begin to add more clarity to the constructs of race and ethnicity. As already mentioned, it typically is assumed that when ethnic differences are found (usually between an Asian American group and Whites), cultural factors are presumed to explain the findings. In the past, researchers have not tested specific hypotheses regarding cultural explanations. It is plausible that race-related factors might account for some of the variance in the dependent variable. Without extending our empirical investigations beyond race and ethnicity constructs to the specific sociocultural factors that underlie Asian American attitudes and behavior, we will fail to move the field beyond the existing knowledge base.

In studying ethnicity and racism with Asian Americans, we might be able to focus on factors other than those typically used in research on African Americans. For example, research could focus on clarifying whether foreign-accented English or Asian physical appearance alone (in the absence of a foreign accent) is sufficient to result in prejudice or discriminatory practices. Along a different line, further research could be done to explain the causes of found differences between second- and third-generation Japanese or between immigrant and native-born Asian American reactions to racism.

Promising new research and theories in the field include recent studies on generational differences within Asian American ethnic groups and further development of theories of immigrant ethnic identity formation. Although in the past "assimilation was viewed as the most logical . . . response to the dilemma imposed by racism" (Omi & Winant, 1994, p. 17), it is far from clear whether, in the case of Asian Americans, theories derived from European immigrant experiences in the United States are generalizable. Indeed, studies of "the resolution of tensions between the twin pressures of assimilation (dissolution of group identity) and cultural pluralism (preservation of group identity)" (p. 48) and the psychological impact of the pressures of such a tension on Asian American individuals remain to be done.

Future investigations on racism against Asian Americans are in a good position in that they can glean the best from the past research and learn from the conceptual and methodological difficulties that the pioneering research on African American-White race relations faced. Furthermore, because ethnic diversity in the United States is likely to continue, research on interminority relations, in addition to majority-minority relations, might help clarify and ultimately aid in promoting better group relations in the United States.

REFERENCES

Adorno, T. W., Frenkel-Brunswick, E., Levinson, D. J., & Sanford, R. M. (1950). *The authoritarian personality*. New York: Harper.

Allport, G. W. (1954). *The nature of prejudice*. Reading, MA: Addison-Wesley.

Aronson, E., & Gonzalez, A. (1988). Desegregation and Mexican Americans. In P. A. Katz & D. A. Taylor (Eds.), *Eliminating racism: Profiles in controversy* (pp. 301-314). New York: Plenum.

Asamen, J. K., & Berry, G. L. (1987). Self-concept, alienation, and perceived prejudice: Implications for counseling Asian Americans. *Journal of Multicultural Counseling and Development, 15*(4), 146-161.

Ashmore, R. D., & Del Boca, F. K. (1976). Psychological approaches to understanding intergroup conflicts. In P. A. Katz (Ed.), *Towards the elimination of racism* (pp. 73-123). New York: Pergamon.

Asian Week. (1991). *Asians in America: 1990 census classification by states*. San Francisco: Author.

Bierly, M. M. (1985). Prejudice toward contemporary outgroups as a generalized attitude. *Journal of Applied Social Psychology, 15*, 189-199.

Blaisdell, K. (1989). Historical and cultural aspects of Native Hawaiian health. *Social Process in Hawaii, 32*, 1-21.

Blake, R. R., & Mouton, J. S. (1979). Intergroup problem solving in organizations: From theory to practice. In W. G. Austin & S. Worchel (Eds.), *The social psychology of intergroup relations*. Pacific Grove, CA: Brooks/Cole.

Bobo, L. (1988). Group conflict, prejudice, and the paradox of contemporary racial attitudes. In P. A. Katz & D. A. Taylor (Eds.), *Eliminating racism: Profiles in controversy* (pp. 85-114). New York: Plenum.

Bobo, L. D., Johnson, J. H., Oliver, M. L., Sidanius, J., & Zubrinsky, C. (1992). *Public opinion before and after a spring of discontent: A preliminary report on the 1992 Los Angeles County social survey*. Occasional Working Paper Series, 3(1), Center for the Study of Urban Poverty, University of Caliornia, Los Angeles.

Bonacich, E. (1976). Advanced capitalism and Black/White relations in the United States: A split labor market interpretation. *American Sociological Review, 41,* 34-51.

Brewer, M. B., & Miller, N. (1988). Contact and cooperation: When do they work? In P. A. Katz & D. A. Taylor (Eds.), *Eliminating racism: Profiles in controversy* (pp. 315-326). New York: Plenum.

Brown, R. (1965). *Social psychology*. New York: Free Press.

Cabezas, A., Tam, T. M., Lowe, B. M., Wong, A., & Turner, K. O. (1989). Empirical study of barriers to upward mobility of Asian Americans in the San Francisco Bay area. In G. M. Nomura, R. Endo, S. H. Sumida, & R. C. Leong (Eds.), *Frontiers of Asian American Studies: Writing, research, and commentary*. Pullman: Washington State University Press.

Chan, S. (1991). *Asian Americans: An interpretive history*. Boston: Twayne.

Chance, J. E. (1985). *Faces, folklore and research hypotheses*. Presidential address presented at the annual convention of the Midwestern Psychological Association, Chicago.

Chesler, M. A. (1976). Contemporary sociological theories of racism. In P. A. Katz (Ed.), *Towards the elimination of racism* (pp. 21-71). New York: Pergamon.

Chung, R. C., & Okazaki, S. (1991). Counseling Americans of Southeast Asian descent: The impact of the refugee experience. In C. C. Lee & B. L. Richardson (Eds.), *Multicultural issues in counseling: New approaches to diversity* (pp. 107-126). Alexandria, VA: American Association for Counseling and Development.

Commission on Wartime Relocation and Internment of Civilians. (1982a). *Personal justice denied: Report of the Commission on Wartime Relocation and Internment of Civilians*. Washington, DC: Government Printing Office.

Commission on Wartime Relocation and Internment of Civilians. (1982b). *Personal justice denied: Part 2—Recommendations*. Washington, DC: Government Printing Office.

Cook, S. W. (1988). The 1954 social science statement and school desegregation: A reply to Gerard. In P. A. Katz & D. A. Taylor (Eds.), *Eliminating racism: Profiles in controversy* (pp. 237-256). New York: Plenum.

Crocker, J., & Major, B. (1989). Social stigma and self-esteem: The self-protective properties of stigma. *Psychological Review, 96,* 608-630.

Crocker, J., Thomson, L. J., McGraw, K. M., & Ingerman, C. (1987). Downward comparison, prejudice, and evaluations of others: Effects on self-esteem and threat. *Journal of Personality and Social Psychology, 52,* 907-916.

Daniels, R. (1988). *Asian America: Chinese and Japanese in the United States since 1850*. Seattle: University of Washington Press.

Daniels, R., & Kitano, H. H. L. (1970). *American racism: Exploration of the nature of prejudice*. Englewood Cliffs, NJ: Prentice Hall.

Dion, K. L., Earn, B. M., & Yee, P. H. (1978). The experience of being a victim of prejudice: An experimental approach. *International Journal of Psychology, 13,* 197-214.

Dollard, J., Doob, L. W., Miller, N. E., Mowrer, O. H., & Sears, R. R. (1939). *Frustration and aggression*. New Haven, CT: Yale University Press.

Fugita, S., & O'Brien, D. (1991). *Japanese American ethnicity: The persistence of community*. Seattle: University of Washington Press.

Gaertner, S. L., Mann, J., Murrell, A., & Dovidio, J. F. (1989). Reducing intergroup bias: The benefits of recategorization. *Journal of Personality and Social Psychology, 57,* 239-249.

Gerard, H. B. (1988). School desegregation: The social science role. In P. A. Katz & D. A. Taylor (Eds.), *Eliminating racism: Profiles in controversy* (pp. 225-236). New York: Plenum.

Gerard, H., & Miller, N. (1975). *School desegregation*. New York: Plenum.

Gottfried, A. W., & Gottfried, A. E. (1986). Home environment and children's development from infancy through the school years: Results of contemporary longitudinal investigations in North America. *Children's Environments Quarterly, 3,* 3-9.

Hechter, M. (1975). *Internal colonialism: The Celtic fringe in British national development, 1536-1966.* Berkeley: University of California Press.

Hirschman, C., & Wong, M. G. (1984). Socioeconomic gains of Asian-Americans, Blacks and Hispanics: 1960-1976. *American Journal of Sociology, 90,* 585-607.

Hirschman, C., & Wong, M. G. (1986). The extraordinary educational attainment of Asian-Americans: A search for historical evidence and explanations. *Social Forces, 65,* 1-27.

Hogg, M. A., & Abrams, D. (1988). *Social identifications.* New York: Routledge.

Johnson, J. H., Jones, C. K., Farrell, W. C., & Oliver, M. L. (1992). *The Los Angeles rebellion, 1992: A preliminary assessment from ground zero.* Occasional Working Paper Series, 2(7), Center for the Study of Urban Poverty, University of California, Los Angeles.

Johnson, J. H., & Oliver, M. L. (1989). Interethnic minority conflict in urban America: The effects of economic and social dislocations. *Urban Geography, 10,* 449-463.

Kame'eleihiwa, L. (1992). *Native land and foreign desire: Paeha La E Pono Ai?* Honolulu, HI: Bishop Museum Press.

Katz, P. A. (Ed.). (1976). *Towards the elimination of racism.* New York: Pergamon.

Katz, P. A., & Taylor, D. A. (Eds.). (1988). *Eliminating racism: Profiles in controversy.* New York: Plenum.

Kinder, D. R., & Sears, D. O. (1981). Prejudice and politics: Symbolic racism versus racial threats to the good life. *Journal of Personality and Social Psychology, 40,* 414-431.

Kitano, H. H. L. (1991). *Race relations.* Englewood Cliffs, NJ: Prentice Hall.

Kitano, H. H. L., & Daniels, R. (1988). *Asian Americans: Emerging minorities.* Englewood Cliffs, NJ: Prentice Hall.

Kuo, W. (1981). Colonized status of Asian-Americans. *Ethnic Groups, 3,* 227-251.

Langberg, M., & Farley, R. (1985). Residential segregation of Asian Americans in 1980. *Social Science Research, 70,* 71-75.

Leadership Education for Asian Pacifics. (1991). *Asian Pacific American experience in the United States: A brief chronological history—498-1989.* Los Angeles: Author.

LeVine, R. A., & White, M. I. (1986). *Human conditions: The cultural basis of educational development.* New York: Routledge.

Los Angeles County Commission in Human Relations. (1989). *Intergroup conflict in Los Angeles County schools: Report on a survey of hate crime.* Los Angeles: Author.

Matsui, R. T. (1987, November 11). *Anti-Asian violence* (House Subcommittee on Civil and Constitutional Rights). Washington, DC: Government Printing Office.

McQueen, M. (1991, May 17). Voters' responses to poll disclose huge chasm between social attitudes of Blacks and Whites. *The Wall Street Journal,* p. A16.

Messick, D. M., & Mackie, D. M. (1989). Intergroup relations. *Annual Review of Psychology, 40,* 45-81.

Myers, D. G. (1990). *Social psychology* (3rd ed.). New York: McGraw-Hill.

Nagata, D. K. (1989). Long term effects of the Japanese American internment camps: Impact on the children of internees. *Journal of the Asian American Psychological Association, 13,* 48-55.

Nagata, D. K. (1993). *Legacy of injustice: Exploring the cross-generational impact of the Japanese American internment* (Critical Issues in Social Justice). New York: Plenum.

Nakanishi, D. T. (1988). Convergence in race relations research. In P. A. Katz & D. A. Taylor (Eds.), *Eliminating racism: Profiles in controversy* (pp. 159-180). New York: Plenum.

Nikolinakos, M. (1973). Notes towards an economic theory of racism. *Race, 14,* 365-381.

O'Hare, W. P., & Felt, J. C. (1991). *Asian Americans: America's fastest growing minority group.* Washington, DC: Population Reference Bureau.

Okihiro, G. Y. (1991). *Cane fires: The anti-Japanese movement in Hawaii, 1865-1945.* Philadelphia: Temple University Press.

Omi, M., & Winant, H. (1994). *Racial formation in the United States: From the 1960s to the 1990s* (2nd ed.). New York: Routledge.

Ray, J. J. (1980). Authoritarianism in California 30 years later: With some cross-cultural comparisons. *Journal of Social Psychology, 111,* 9-17.

Ray, J. J., & Lovejoy, F. H. (1983). The behavioral validity of some recent measures of authoritarianism. *Journal of Social Psychology, 120,* 91-99.

Schlesinger, A., Jr. (1991). The American creed: From dilemma to decomposition. *New Perspectives Quarterly, 8*, 20-25.

Schmitt, E. (1992, November 20). Marines find racial disparity in officer programs. *The New York Times*, p. A8.

Sears, D. O. (1988). Symbolic racism. In P. A. Katz & D. A. Taylor (Eds.), *Eliminating racism: Profiles in controversy* (pp. 53-84). New York: Plenum.

Sherif, M. (1966). *In common predicament: Social psychology of intergroup conflict and cooperation.* Boston: Houghton Mifflin.

Siao, G. W. T. (1990, September 14). Steep rise in anti-Asian hate crimes in Los Angeles County. *Asian Week*, pp. 1, 5.

Stannard, D. (1989). *Before the horror: The population of Hawai'i on the eve of Western contact.* Honolulu, HI: Social Science Research Institute.

Stephan, W. G. (1978). School desegregation: An evaluation of predictions made in *Brown v. Board of Education. Psychological Bulletin, 85*, 217-238.

Stephan, W. G. (1986). The effects of school desegregation: An evaluation 30 years after *Brown.* In R. Kidd, L. Saxe, & M. Saks (Eds.), *Advances in applied social psychology* (pp. 181-206). Hillsdale, NJ: Lawrence Erlbaum.

Stephan, W. G. (1987). The contact hypothesis in intergroup relations. In C. Hendrick (Ed.), *Group processes and intergroup relations* (pp. 13-40). Newbury Park, CA: Sage.

Sue, D. W., & Sue, D. (1973). The neglected minority. *Personnel and Guidance Journal, 52*, 387-389.

Suzuki, B. (1977). Education and socialization of Asian Americans: A revisionist analysis of the "model minority" thesis. *Amerasia, 4*, 23-51.

Tajfel, H. (1982). Social psychology of intergroup relations. *Annual Review of Psychology, 33*, 1-39.

Tajfel, H., & Turner, J. C. (1979). An integrative theory of intergroup conflict. In W. G. Austin & S. Worchel (Eds.), *The social psychology of intergroup relations.* Pacific Grove, CA: Brooks/Cole.

Takaki, R. (1989). *Strangers from a different shore: A history of Asian Americans.* Boston: Little, Brown.

Takaki, R. (1990). *Iron cages: Race and culture in 19th century America.* New York: Oxford University Press.

Toupin, E. S. W. A. (1980). Counseling Asians: Psychotherapy in the context of racism and Asian-American history. *American Journal of Orthopsychiatry, 50*, 76-86.

Trask, H. (1990). Politics in the Pacific Islands: Imperialism and the native self-determination. *Amerasia, 161*, 1-19.

U.S. Bureau of the Census. (1990). *United States population estimates by age, sex, race, and Hispanic origin: 1980 to 1988* (Current Population Reports, Series P-25, No. 1045). Washington, DC: Government Printing Office.

U.S. Commission on Civil Rights. (1980). *The tarnished golden door: Civil rights issues in immigration.* Washington, DC: Government Printing Office.

U.S. Commission on Civil Rights. (1986). *Recent activities against citizens and residents of Asian descent.* Washington, DC: Government Printing Office.

U.S. Commission on Civil Rights. (1988). *The economic status of Americans of Asian descent: An exploratory investigation.* Washington, DC: Government Printing Office.

U.S. Commission on Civil Rights. (1992). *Civil rights issues facing Asian Americans in the 1990s.* Washington, DC: Government Printing Office.

Van Staden, F. J. (1987). White South Africans' attitudes toward the desegregation of public amenities. *Journal of Social Psychology, 127*, 163-173.

Wang, L. L. (1988). Meritocracy and diversity in higher education: Discrimination against Asian Americans in the post-Bakke era. *Urban Review, 20*, 189-209.

Weisman, S. S., Snadomsky, A. M., & Gannon, M. (1972). Chinese college students perceive their cultural identity. *Education, 92*, 116-118.

Wong, M. G. (1982). The cost of being Chinese, Japanese, and Filipino in the United States: 1960, 1970, 1976. *Pacific Sociological Review, 25*, 59-78.

Wong, M. G. (1991). *Rise in anti-Asian activities in the United States.* Paper presented at the annual meeting of the American Sociological Association, Cincinnati, OH.

Yinger, J. (1988). Examining racial discrimination with fair housing audits. In H. S. Bloom, D. S. Conray, & R. J. Light (Eds.), *Lessons from selected program and policy areas* (pp. 47-62). San Francisco: Jossey-Bass.

13

INTERNMENT AND
INTERGENERATIONAL RELATIONS

Donna K. Nagata

The majority of psychological research conducted with Asian American groups focuses on evaluations of their current functioning. These investigations are important in increasing our understanding of the experiences of these groups and in shaping effective clinical and community interventions. By contrast, there is little empirical research that assesses the potential intergenerational impact of historical events on Asian Americans (or, for that matter, on other ethnic minority groups) today. Current levels of functioning, however, might reflect the culmination of both contemporary forces affecting the quality of life for a given Asian American group and its members' historical experiences of racism, discrimination, and trauma. Explicit investigations of the enduring effects from the past can play a vital role in further increasing our knowledge of present-day Asian Americans.

A consideration of intergenerational dynamics is especially useful when conducting such research because experiences of trauma, whether racially based or not, can have consequences that endure beyond the life experiences of one generation. The effects of the Depression, for example, influenced not only those who lived through that time but also the interactions between those individuals and their sons and daughters born after the Depression (Elder, Caspi, & Ngyuen, 1986). Similarly, the children of Holocaust survivors have reported a variety of ways in which their parents' trauma affected their lives (Epstein, 1977; Halik, Rosenthal, & Pattison, 1990; Klein-Parker, 1988; Rose & Garske, 1987; Solkoff, 1992).

An intergenerational perspective also allows us to explore how the process of acculturation interacts with the long-term impact of critical historical events.

In the case of Asian American groups such as the Chinese Americans and Japanese Americans, who have been in the United States the longest, these events include a long history of racial discrimination encountered in this country (Daniels, 1978, 1988). Other historical traumas extend beyond the boundaries of the United States. Chinese Americans and Korean Americans, for example, might carry intergenerational legacies from Japan's invasion of their home countries years ago, and the traumas experienced by Southeast Asian Americans prior to immigration also might affect subsequent generations (Chambon, 1989; Mollica, Wyshak, & Lavelle, 1987). In each case, one can ask how these significant pasts have continued to shape Asian Americans and to what degree acculturation has modified these effects on successive generations.

Previous literature on intergenerational relations among Asian Americans offers primarily historical perspectives on migration patterns or studies of acculturation and ethnic identity among generations of Chinese and Japanese Americans (Connor, 1977; Daniels, 1988; Kitano & Daniels, 1988; Levine & Rhodes, 1981; Montero, 1980; Takaki, 1989; Weiss, 1970). The present chapter diverges from this emphasis by examining intergenerational relations within the context of a specific historical trauma: the World War II internment of Japanese Americans. The internment was unique within American history, and one cannot presume that its impact on Japanese American intergenerational relations will translate directly to other Asian American groups and their experienced traumas. Nonetheless, a study of the internment's intergenerational impact might have implications for research on the long-term effects of trauma among Asian Americans. In addition, incidents reflective of the type of prejudice and racism that underlay the internment continue to be directed toward Asian Americans more generally (Karnow & Yoshimura, 1992; U.S. Commission on Civil Rights, 1992). Hence, the research presented here is pertinent to groups other than Japanese Americans as well.

The chapter begins with a section detailing the historical background of the internment to highlight the significance of this event. Next, the rationale and methodology for the Sansei Research Project, a project designed to examine the effects of the internment on third-generation (Sansei) Japanese Americans whose parents were interned during the war, are described. The chapter concludes by discussing the significance of the project results for understanding Japanese Americans today and by raising additional areas in which historical events and intergenerational relations might be studied among other Asian American groups.

HISTORICAL BACKGROUND
OF THE INTERNMENT

The year 1992 marked the 50th anniversary of President Franklin D. Roosevelt's signing of Executive Order 9066, which led to the internment of close to 120,000 Japanese Americans in U.S. concentration camps during World War II. The date on which the president signed the order, February 19, is now known within Japanese American communities as a Day of Remembrance.

The internment stands as a powerful and traumatic event for many Japanese Americans. However, decades of anti-Asian prejudice and discrimination preceded World War II. As noted by Daniels (1993), "The wartime abuse of Japanese Americans . . . was merely a link in a chain of racism that stretched back to the earliest contacts between Asians and Whites on American soil" (p. 3). Japan's attack on Pearl Harbor dramatically heightened levels of racism and paranoia against Japanese Americans, and their removal from the West Coast of the United States was justified as a military necessity to protect the mainland from espionage and sabotage. All those of Japanese ancestry who lived along the West Coast, citizens and aliens alike, were considered potentially disloyal and ordered to "evacuate" their homes.

Although many of the interned were Issei (first-generation immigrants), most were American-born Nisei (second-generation Japanese). In fact, approximately two thirds of the interned Japanese Americans were U.S. citizens. No formal charges were brought against the internees, nor were they given the right to a trial. With often only a week's notice in which to sell their businesses, properties, and personal possessions before their removal, the Japanese Americans suffered tremendous losses. Professionals and salaried workers left thousands of dollars in uncollected bills, and farmers were forced to leave valuable crops and machinery (Commission on Wartime Relocation and Internment of Civilians [CWRIC], 1982). In fact, Okihiro and Drummond (1991) noted that a major force behind the internment came from leaders in Californian agriculture who wished to displace the successful Japanese American farmers and take over their lands.

The antagonism toward Japanese Americans following the bombing of Pearl Harbor led to drastic results on the mainland. Lieutenant General John L. De Witt, then commanding general in charge of West Coast security, stated,

> In the war in which we are now engaged, racial affinities are not severed by migration. The Japanese race is an enemy race, and while many second- and third-generation Japanese born on United States soil, possessed of United States citizenship, have become "Americanized," the racial strains are undiluted. (CWRIC, 1982, p. 82)

Attitudes such as De Witt's demonstrated the type of racism that placed Japanese Americans outside the moral community of the government and public sentiment (Nagata, 1990b). Both Germany and Italy were at war with the United States, yet neither German Americans nor Italian Americans were subjected to mass internment. By contrast, more than 90% of Japanese Americans living on the mainland were removed from the West Coast and rounded into concentration camps for up to 4 years (CWRIC, 1982). Ironically, although geographic proximity to the Pacific was cited as the major reason for the removal of the Japanese Americans from the mainland's West Coast, no mass internment took place in

Hawaii, which is much closer to Japan. Less than 1% of Hawaiian Japanese were interned (Ogawa & Fox, 1991). (Because the Japanese represented almost one third of the territory's population at that time and the U.S. military there depended on their services, mass internment in Hawaii was impractical [CWRIC, 1982].)

Most Japanese Americans endured two separate relocations, first to temporary assembly centers (frequently located in horse stalls at race tracks and fairgrounds) and later to one of the more permanent internment camps. The camps were situated in desolate areas of the interior such as deserts and swamplands. Temperatures ranged from over 100° in the summer to below freezing in the winter, and dust storms became a constant part of life in many sites. An average-sized camp held 10,000 internees within a single square mile of space. They lived in tarpapered barrack rooms that ranged from 20 by 8 feet for the smallest families to 20 by 24 feet for the largest. Mess halls served meals at designated times, and a single center for toileting and bathing was shared by 50 or more families (CWRIC, 1982; Daniels, 1988).

The cramped conditions imposed an artificially created communal lifestyle on the internees, reducing nearly all opportunities for privacy and breaking down the nuclear family role structures that had been central to their culture (Morishima, 1973). Parents were distressed to find their children spending more time with readily available peer groups than with their families. In addition, the Nisei's command of English put them in a position of power over their Issei parents because business within the camp bureaucracy was conducted in English (CWRIC, 1982).

Most Nisei were in their adolescence to early 20s at the time of the internment (Wilson & Hosokawa, 1980), and although the United States was their home country, citizenship failed to protect them from being interned. Older Nisei who already served in the U.S. military were discharged and sent to camps, and those who wanted a chance to prove their loyalty in combat were denied the opportunity until 1944, when the government acknowledged that the Japanese Americans posed no security threat and began to open enlistment into the armed forces. Even then, however, the Nisei were marginalized by being restricted to segregated military units (CWRIC, 1982).

There were other avenues for leaving camp aside from enlisting. Some Nisei left the camps to attend colleges in the Midwest and East, away from the military exclusion areas of the West. Beginning in 1943, others, who answered affirmatively to a government-required set of questions evaluating their loyalty, began receiving clearance to leave the camps for areas outside the restricted zones of the West Coast. With $25 and one-way transportation to begin a new life, these Nisei slowly started to relocate in cities such as Chicago, Denver, and New York (CWRIC, 1982; Sawada, 1986-1987; Thomas & Nishimoto, 1946). By 1944, small groups of internees were allowed to return to the previously excluded areas (Kashima, 1980). Most eventually returned to the West Coast, where the majority of Japanese Americans still reside. However, the patterns of resettlement initiated when the Nisei left the camps permanently changed the distribution of the Japanese American population, and Japanese American communities that did not exist before the war can now be found in areas of the Midwest and East (Daniels, 1993).

Resettlement was especially difficult for the Issei, and many remained in the camps through 1945, fearing racial violence and antagonism if they returned to their homes. Others had become dependent on the camp lifestyle or lacked the will to begin their lives again. Most never regained full employment after the war (CWRIC, 1982).

With the closing of the camps, however, Japanese Americans attempted to move on with their lives. School history books omitted discussion of the internment, and the injustice remained hidden from public view. It appeared that the past was over. However, the internment had not been forgotten by Japanese Americans. Slowly, over the late 1960s and 1970s, a movement emerged from within the Japanese American community to seek not only a government apology for the injustice of the internment but also monetary redress for surviving internees (Takezawa, 1995). In 1980, the Commission on Wartime Relocation and Internment of Civilians was established following the lobbying efforts of Japanese Americans. The mandate of the commission was to review the facts and circumstances surrounding Executive Order 9066 and the directives of the U.S. miltary requiring the relocation and detention of American citizens at that time and to make recommendations regarding appropriate remedies based on its findings (CWRIC, 1982). The commission launched a large-scale evaluation of the internment and its consequences and reviewed numerous government documents as well as the testimonies from more than 750 former internees, officials, scholars, and citizens.

During the testimonies from the 1980 CWRIC hearings, Japanese Americans began to come forward and, for the first time in more than 40 years, speak publicly about their past pain and trauma (CWRIC, 1982; "Testimonies to the Commission," 1981). Former internees revealed long-hidden stories of loss and suffering. The magnitude of economic losses alone was staggering. Taylor (1991) noted that although it is impossible to put a price on the total losses incurred, some have estimated that the amount of uncompensated losses suffered by Japanese Americans was between $1.2 billion and $3.1 billion. If a 3% interest rate were added to this, the figure would have ranged from $2.5 billion to $6.2 billion in 1986.

Aside from the economic losses, however, the CWRIC's (1982) final report noted that the "loss of liberty, and the stigma of the accusation of disloyalty, may leave more lasting scars" (p. 133). Former internees testified to a wide range of psychological effects stemming from their imprisonment. Some reported undeserved feelings of shame and humiliation similar to those reported by rape victims; somehow, they were to blame for their treatment (Hansen & Mitson, 1974). Others shared painful experiences of having lost loved ones in camp due to the inadequate health care and harsh living conditions. Still others described the anxiety of being away from family members sent to separate camps for prolonged periods of time. The press to become "super American," the press to deny their

Japanese heritage, and a lowered sense of self-esteem also were reported (CWRIC, 1982; Mass, 1991; Maykovitch, 1972). Many of the reactions paralleled the symptoms of posttraumatic stress disorder from trauma due to intentional human design (Loo, 1993).

In its final analysis, the commission concluded,

> The historical forces which shaped these decisions were race, prejudice, hysteria, and a failure of political leadership. Widespread ignorance of Japanese Americans contributed to a policy conceived in haste and executed in an atmosphere of fear and anger at Japan. A grave injustice was done to American citizens and resident aliens of Japanese ancestry. (CWRIC, 1982, p. 18)

The commission recommended that there be a national apology to include the following: that Congress pass a joint resolution to be signed by the president that recognized and apologized for the past injustice, that $20,000 be paid to each of the approximately 60,000 surviving internees to provide personal redress, and that funds be set aside to educate others about the internment and its effects (CWRIC, 1983). The commission's recommendations were taken to Congress, and in 1988, President Ronald Reagan signed the Civil Liberties Act, acknowledging the grave injustice done to Japanese Americans and granting $20,000 redress to each surviving internee.

EXAMINING THE CROSS-GENERATIONAL IMPACT OF THE INTERNMENT

Over the years, an increasing number of autobiographies, biographies, novels, and poetry have described the Japanese American experiences during and after the camps (Modell, 1973; Okubo, 1989; Sone, 1991; Tateishi, 1984; Thomas, 1952; Tsukamoto & Pinkerton, 1987; Uchida, 1989). These, combined with anthropological, sociological, and historical analyses (Daniels, 1972; Daniels, Taylor, & Kitano, 1991; Takezawa, 1995; Thomas & Nishimoto, 1946; Weglyn, 1976), have contributed to our understanding of the impact of the internment. Additional writings have discussed the psychological effects of the internment and resettlement years (Kashima, 1980; Kitano, 1969, 1991; Mass, 1991; Morishima, 1973). Most attention has been paid to the Nisei and, to a lesser degree, the Issei. Nearly all studies have been descriptive in nature.

A dearth of empirical data makes it difficult to assess the internment's immediate postwar effects on Japanese Americans. Testimonies from the CWRIC hearings and descriptive writings, however, have suggested that the trauma of internment was extensive enough to have had long-term effects on subsequent generations, including those third-generation Japanese Americans (Sansei) born after the war (CWRIC, 1982; Furutani, 1981). In addition, informal discussions with Sansei whose parents had been in camp during the war, and autobiographical accounts from Sansei writers (e.g., Mura, 1991), have indicated that their experiences were influenced by their parents' internment.

As noted earlier, extensive psychological and psychiatric literature already documents the variety of ways in which a parent's Holocaust trauma may affect the children of Holocaust survivors (see Solkoff, 1992, for a critical review of this literature). Areas of impact include family communication (Barocas & Barocas, 1979; Prince, 1985; Trachtenberg & Davis, 1978), perceptions of one's parents (Keinan, Mikulincer, & Rybnicki, 1988), issues of separation-individuation (Halik et al., 1990; Klein-Parker, 1988), and cultural identity (Halik et al., 1990; Heller, 1981). Although there are critical differences between the internment and the Holocaust, these findings have provided a useful framework for evaluating the effects of the internment. Heller (1981) found that children of Holocaust survivors showed a greater sensitivity to culture and ancestry than did peers who were not children of survivors and suggested a specific link between the intergenerational dynamics related to the Holocaust and the internment. He noted, "The responses of the Japanese to internment resemble quite closely the responses of survivor children to the Jewish Holocaust" (p. 259).

Miyoshi (1980) speculated early on about the importance of examining the internment from an intergenerational perspective and saw the Sansei as "heirs" to the ethnic values passed down from the Nisei. Based on interviews with a group of Sansei, Miyoshi observed a lack of communication between the third generation and their parents around the topic of internment and hypothesized that the camps represented a "symbol of an intergenerational ethnic and personal gap" that obstructed the Sansei's ability to develop a clear sense of identity. To bridge this gap, she employed family therapy to encourage greater dialogue between family members about the internment.

Miyoshi's (1980) work provided an important step in examining the issue of intergenerational relations and the internment. It appeared that additional research conducted with a larger and more broadly selected sample of Sansei would help to document the generalizability of her initial observations. Therefore, the Sansei Research Project was developed to explore the cross-generational impact of the wartime internment. The project included a national survey of nearly 750 third-generation Japanese Americans and more than 40 in-depth interviews.

Focusing on the Sansei Generation

A focus on the Sansei generation was considered useful for several reasons. First, the Sansei represent the first large postwar generation of Japanese Americans who did not directly experience the internment; most were born between 1945 and the 1960s. (Although there were Sansei who were interned as young children or were born in camps, they comprised a minority of that generation.) Second, it seemed particularly interesting to compare the Sansei generation to their Nisei parents because both shared the status of U.S. citizenship from birth, yet each had experienced their citizenship in very different societal contexts. By contrast, their immigrant grandparents, the Issei, were prohibited from becoming citizens until well after the war, in 1952 (Daniels, 1988). In addition, the Nisei and Sansei both are English speaking. This removed the barrier of language differences when examining the interactions between the generations. Finally, relatively little recent research has examined the Sansei experiences, yet such work is needed in documenting the psychology of Japanese Americans today.

Past studies that have been conducted on the Sansei frequently have evaluated their level of ethnic identity and acculturation in comparison to the Nisei and Issei. These investigations have suggested that, in many ways, the Sansei are more highly acculturated to the "White American mainstream culture" than are the Nisei, interact more with Caucasian Americans, and report less discrimination than does their parents' generation (Connor, 1977; Fugita & O'Brien, 1991; Hosokawa, 1978; Levine & Rhodes, 1981; Montero, 1980; O'Brien & Fugita, 1983; Yanagisako, 1985). Intermarriage rates are estimated to be 50% or higher (Kitano, Yeung, Chai, & Hatanaka, 1984). At the same time, findings indicate that many Sansei have retained aspects of their Japanese American culture including a more deferent and affiliative behavioral style, closer family ties, a greater sense of obligation and duty, and greater contact with ethnic organizations compared to their Caucasian American peers (Connor, 1977; Fugita & O'Brien, 1991). The Sansei, then, present a unique generation in which to explore not only the consequences of the internment trauma but also the ways in which those consequences might have interacted with the processes of acculturation over time.

THE SANSEI RESEARCH PROJECT

The Sansei Research Project was initiated in 1987 to explore the intergenerational effects of the internment among the postwar, third-generation sons and daughters of former internees. The following description of the project and its findings represents a condensation of information presented in other sources, and the reader is encouraged to refer to Nagata (1989, 1990a, 1993) for greater details. In particular, Nagata's (1993) book, *Legacy of Injustice: Exploring the Cross-Generational Impact of the Japanese American Internment,* offers a comprehensive presentation of the full project and its results.

Description of Sample and Procedures

The Sansei Research Project consisted of two parts: a large-scale national survey and a smaller sample of in-depth interviews. Both the survey and interviews explored the impact of the internment on the Sansei. Although the survey was constructed to quantitatively assess respondents' attitudes and perceptions and to allow for analyses of group characteristics, the interviews provided an in-depth qualitative exploration into the personal experiences of individual Sansei. Together, the survey and interview data provided complementary data on the questions of interest.

A total of 42 Sansei (22 females and 20 males) were interviewed by the author. They were contacted through the assistance of the Japanese American Citizens League (JACL), the largest national Japanese American organization. The numbers of interviewees from specific areas were as follows: California (17), Washington (6), Illinois (6), the East Coast (Massachusetts and New York, 7), and Hawaii (6). The average age was 39 years. Among the sample, 26 had both parents interned, 10 had one parent interned, and 6 had neither parent interned. Each interviewee participated in a semistructured interview focusing on demographic and background information as well as on questions regarding the impact of the internment on his or her life.

For the survey portion of the research, the names of 1,250 Sansei respondents were obtained through one of three methods. The majority of names came through the assistance of the JACL. Each individual was mailed a questionnaire along with a pre-stamped envelope in which to return their responses. Participation was entirely voluntary. An additional 78 surveys were mailed to directors of the Young Buddhist Association (YBA). Inclusion of the YBA respondents increased the possibility of reaching Sansei who were not JACL members. Finally, surveys were sent to individuals who requested to participate in the project after hearing about it from other Sansei, through a newspaper article describing the research, or through friends and relatives.

The use of the JACL and YBA as the primary contacts for obtaining the names of potential respondents resulted in a nonrandom sample. However, it was felt that use of telephone directories would be inefficient (it would be impossible to determine generational status from an individual's listing) and exclusive of Sansei females who had married non-Japanese and might not be listed with a Japanese surname. Given the high percentage of out-marriage within the Sansei generation, this presented a particular concern.

A total of 740 respondents returned questionnaires, representing a return rate of approximately 60%. Of these, 13 were received too late for inclusion and 134 were from Sansei who had directly experienced the internment. This latter group, Sansei who were themselves interned, also was excluded because the initial purpose of the Sansei Research Project was to examine the indirect effects of the camps. Their data are presented in a separate paper (Nagata, Trierweiler, & Talbot, 1997). The remaining sample of 596 included three groups of Sansei: those who had both parents interned (two-parent Sansei, $n = 323$), those who had only one parent interned (one-parent Sansei, $n = 168$), and those who had neither parent interned (no-camp Sansei, $n = 105$). Because most Nisei were in camps during the war, the majority of respondents fell into the two- and one-parent groups. However, Japanese Americans who lived outside the zones targeted for exclusion were not interned. This included the majority of those in Hawaii (as noted earlier) and those who lived east of the mainland exclusion areas. The responses of their children, the no-camp Sansei, provided a unique group against which the responses of the other Sansei groups could be compared to explore the effects of a parent's internment.

The greatest percentage of respondents came from California (44%), followed by the Midwest (18%), the Northwest (17%), the East (13%), and Hawaii (4%). As a group, the Sansei were highly educated. Fully 31% had completed college, and another 15% had completed postgraduate degrees. The average income level was between $25,000 and $35,000. Among the respondents, 46% reported being Protestant, 29% Buddhist, 5% Catholic, 17% members of "other religions," and 2% no religious affiliation. Initial analyses of variance revealed no significant differences among the two-parent, one-parent, and no-camp groups in terms of level of education or religious background.

Groups did differ with respect to age. The mean age of no-camp Sansei ($M = 36.48$ years) was significantly older than that of either the two-parent ($M = 31.79$ years) or one-parent ($M = 29.18$ years) group, and the mean age of the one-parent Sansei was significantly younger than that of either the two-parent or no-camp groups. It is unclear why the one-parent group tended to be younger, although analyses did show that the Sansei who had only a father interned were significantly younger than the other Sansei and that their parents also were younger than those of the other groups. A possible explanation for the older age of the no-camp group was the fact that this group contained the largest percentage of respondents from Hawaii. Although groups did not differ in their representation of respondents from California, the Northwest, Midwest, or East, the percentage of no-camp Sansei from Hawaii was 18% versus 3% for the two- and one-parent groups. The older age might have reflected the fact that, historically, the Japanese settled in Hawaii before coming to the mainland; therefore, the Hawaii sample would be more likely to include older Sansei. However, when respondents from Hawaii were omitted from age analyses, the significant difference remained. Subsequent analyses covaried out the effects of age when examining group differences.

The greater representation of Hawaiian respondents in the no-camp group also was problematic because the social and cultural environment for Japanese Americans in Hawaii differs so greatly from that on the U.S. mainland. (Relative to the mainland, Asian Americans constitute a significant portion of the Hawaiian population.) Hence, analyses also were conducted both with and without Hawaiian respondents.

The Impact of the Internment

Questions for both the survey and interviews explored the impact of the internment in a wide range of areas including family dynamics, levels of interest and knowledge about the internment, ethnic preference, confidence about one's status in the United States, and opinions about seeking monetary redress from the U.S. government for former internees. The major findings from these areas are presented here.

▩ *Family Communication*

Although previous researchers had observed a silence surrounding the internment years as a major consequence of that experience (CWRIC, 1982; Daniels, 1988; Kashima, 1980), the extent of this silence within families had not been evaluated. Survey data from the Sansei Research Project provided strong quantitative support for these earlier observations. The data indicated that although those who had one or both parents interned learned about the internment at a significantly earlier age and had more frequent and longer conversations with parents about that event than did the no-camp Sansei, nearly one-third also reported having had 10 or fewer such conversations with their parents in their lifetime. In addition, when these conversations did occur, they lasted an average of only 15 minutes. The two-parent, one-parent, and no-camp Sansei also did not differ significantly in the manner in which the internment was discussed within their families. When asked whether conversations tended to mention the internment as (a) an incidental topic in passing (e.g., "We knew her from camp"), (b) a reference point in time (e.g., "That was before/after camp"), or (c) a central topic of discussion (e.g., a parent talking about his or her experiences while in camp), only 30% of the entire sample reported that camp had been discussed as a central topic. Taken together, the data indicate a striking degree of family silence around the internment similar to the "shroud of silence" that has been reported in families of Holocaust survivors (Danieli, 1982, 1985).

Interview data provided rich descriptions of the minimal communication pattern between the Sansei and their Nisei parents. Virtually all interviewees who had at least one parent interned reported similar perceptions of their interactions, which they described as "left-handed conversations," "evasive," "superficial," "matter of fact," and "controlled." As one individual described it,

> A lot of times, you assume that your parents do not have a past when you're little and because you live in the present so much. The older I got, . . . I would ask more and more about their lives—how they got married and how they met. Through those discussions, . . . discussions of camp was conspicuously absent. . . . So, I really didn't learn about the camps through my parents. I got bits and pieces . . . [but] never a coherent full story. (quoted in Nagata, 1993, p. 82)

Despite the silence surrounding the internment, a great deal was communicated to the Sansei. They became more, rather than less, interested in what had happened but at the same time sensed a foreboding about the topic and knew not to ask many questions about it. Many worried that if they did ask for more information, their parents might break down. As one interviewee stated,

> It's like a secret or maybe more like a skeleton in the closet, like a relative in the family who's retarded or alcoholic. Everyone tiptoes around it, only discussing it when someone else brings it up, like a family scandal. (p. vii)

Another noted,

> My perception of them was that they did not speak honestly about the camp experience. Positive aspects were mentioned, if anything at all, but there always seemed to be something that was left out. My feeling was that there was much more to their experience than they wanted to reveal. Their words said one thing, while their hearts were holding something else deep inside. And, for me, it was as if there was a void in my personal history. (quoted in Nagata, 1993, p. 75)

Although the majority of Sansei reported their parents emphasizing only positive memories from the internment, several recalled times when old photographs, watching a film or television show about the camps, seeing certain foods, or visiting certain places triggered a parent's revelations about the harsher side of incarceration. Almost a third of the interviewees mentioned stories in which a mother or father expressed a strong dislike for a particular food. Corned beef and cabbage, apple butter, spam, and animal hearts were among the negative reminders of camp.

Why the level of silence between generations? Some have speculated that the Nisei felt too ashamed to discuss their internment, that an attitude of shame—of *hazukashi*—was widespread (Kashima, 1980). Weglyn (1976, as cited in Kashima, 1980) discussed the internment as creating "a psychic damage" in the Nisei that created "a deep consciousness of personal inferiority, a proclivity to non-communication and inarticulateness" (Weglyn, 1976, p. 273). The silence also might reflect an aspect of posttraumatic stress in response to the internment whereby thoughts and feelings associated with the original trauma are avoided (American Psychiatric Association, 1994). In addition, Japanese cultural influences contributed to the prevalence of silence. The phrase *shikata ganai,* which loosely translates into "it cannot be helped," indicates a sense of fatalism about forces that are beyond one's control (Kitano, 1969). *Gaman,* another Japanese concept, emphasizes the importance of internalizing or suppressing one's emotions (Kitano, 1969). Both of these cultural responses would make it unlikely for the Nisei to talk about the camp experiences with their children.

The Sansei's views regarding the role of Japanese culture in their parents' silence varied (Nagata, 1991a). Some interviewees admired the internalization of emotions as a sign of strength. Others saw the repression as unhealthy. In either case, these individuals contrasted the response of their parents' silence to their own self-perception that it would be difficult for them to repress their reactions to an experience of internment. This difference in response perhaps illustrates the fact that, compared to the Nisei, the Sansei are less bound to the Japanese culturally based norms of communication and find themselves more comfortable with a Westernized, verbally expressive style.

Several interviewees hypothesized that their parents did not discuss the camps so as to protect the Sansei from the burden of their experiences. This, in combination with the need for the Nisei to get on with their lives and not dwell on the past during the years of resettlement, minimized the likelihood of raising the topic of the camps. In this sense, the "social amnesia" that typified the Nisei's response reflected a group response to attain normalcy rather than an indication of each individual's psychological pathology (Kashima, 1980).

Although it is tempting to look to the Nisei to explain the lack of communication about the internment within families, it is important to recognize that the Sansei also have participated in the pattern of silence. Their perceptions that the camps were too traumatic to discuss, as well as respect for their parents' privacy and a fear of getting in touch with their own feelings about the internment, also contributed. As one interviewee noted,

> I realize that if I wish to know their personal feelings on the experience, I must ask direct, difficult questions of them. I find it hard to bring myself to do so. I guess it's partly due to their reticence but also because I have some deep personal anger myself that surfaces when the subject arises. I've always found that, for one who was not even interned myself, tears, frustration, and pain exists. (quoted in Nagata, 1993, pp. 83-84)

■ Interest in and Knowledge About the Internment

Most families did not openly discuss their camp experiences. Yet, the Sansei who had at least one parent in camp reported an increasing interest in the internment over time. Survey data and interviews indicated that although all respondents showed increasing levels of interest over their lives, the two- and one-parent Sansei reported significantly greater interest than did no-camp Sansei at the stages of elementary school, junior high, high school, and young adulthood. Most interviewees noted that they did not fully understand the injustice of the internment until high school. It was at this point that many chose to do their U.S. history papers on the camps. However, when asked to indicate their current level of interest on a scale of 1 to 7 (with 1 = *not interested* and 7 = *extremely interested*), there were no significant group differences. The relatively high level of interest ($M = 5.74$) reported by all groups most likely reflected the overall increase in consciousness about the internment stemming from the redress movement that was in process at the time of data collection.

Given the Sansei's generally higher degree of interest in the internment and the lack of parental communication about the topic, one might expect that the Sansei whose parents were interned would have sought out courses in Asian American studies to learn more about this part of their heritage. Survey data, however, revealed that Sansei who had at least one parent in camp were no more likely to take Asian American courses than were Sansei in the no-camp group. They also failed to demonstrate a dramatically greater level of factual knowledge about the internment than did the no-camp Sansei. All respondents answered 11 factual questions about the internment. (Although it is recognized that the particular questions sampled did not reflect a complete assessment of a respondent's level of internment knowledge, they did tap major areas of information related to that event.) The questions asked about (a) the date of the bombing of Pearl Harbor

(December 7, 1941), (b) the number of Japanese Americans who were interned (approximately 120,000), (c) the proportion of U.S. citizens who were incarcerated (about 66%), (d) the number of internment camps (10, plus credit for 6 Department of Justice/citizen isolation camps), (e) the names of the camps, (f) the locations of the camps, (g) the number of the executive order that allowed for the internment (Order 9066), (h) the name of the president who signed the executive order (Roosevelt), (i) the average length of time spent in camp (2 to 4 years), (j) the meaning of the acronym WRA (the War Relocation Authority, an organization formed to implement the internment process), and (k) whether or not Japanese in Hawaii underwent mass internment (they did not). (It should be noted that numerical answers were scored as correct within a liberal range. For example, answers ranging from 100,000 to 130,000 were scored as correct for the number of Japanese Americans interned.)

Group comparisons showed that Sansei who had at least one parent interned answered a significantly greater number of questions correctly than did the no-camp Sansei. However, two of the questions referred to identifying the names and locations of the 10 internment camps. Because the Sansei who had at least one parent in camp typically knew the names and locations of their own parents' camps, they had an advantage on these items. When these questions were removed, the differences in overall knowledge among the groups were minimal. In fact, many of the respondents, regardless of whether either of their parents had been in camp, were unable to correctly answer the historical questions. Half of the sample did not know how many Japanese Americans had been interned, 70% did not know what proportion of internees were American citizens, and 73% did not know how many camps were established.

This seemingly low level of knowledge might be due to the lack of family communication noted earlier. However, comments from interviewees also indicated that even though some Sansei had been exposed to this information, they were unable to recall it. Several individuals expressed puzzlement over the fact that they were very interested in the camps and had learned a great deal about the internment through readings or course work yet repeatedly forgot this information. Such an "amnesia" might reflect the Sansei's own repression of the internment trauma or the fact that it is the personal and emotional, rather than the factual, aspects of the internment that stand out most in their lives. The results are similar to those reported by Heller (1981), who found that children of Holocaust survivors were no more likely to have an awareness of Holocaust-related events than were their peers whose parents did not experience that trauma. This suggests that although dramatic events in a parent's life might have salience for the parent's children, they do not necessarily lead the offspring to seek and/or retain historical information about those events.

▓ Ethnic Preference, Out-Marriage, and Sense of Confidence

Through a principal components analysis of 27 individual attitude items from the survey, factors were developed to assess the Sansei's ethnic preference for

Japanese Americans and their sense of confidence in their status in the United States (see Nagata, 1990a, 1993). Ethnic preference items explored whether Sansei whose parents were interned might have retained a greater preference for contacts with fellow Japanese Americans due to the camp experiences. It was possible, for example, that these parents particularly encouraged ties within the Japanese American community as a result of their internment experiences. Items within the Ethnic Preference factor included statements such as "I feel more at ease with Japanese Americans than with Caucasians" and "All things being equal, I would prefer to go to a Japanese American for professional services over a Caucasian American." Support for the existence of greater in-group ethnic preference was found for the two-parent Sansei; the two-parent group had a significantly greater preference for Japanese Americans than did either the one-parent or no-camp Sansei. However, this elevated preference among the two-parent group for interacting with Japanese Americans in the broader social realm did not generalize to the Sansei's choice of marriage partners. Out-marriage rates (calculated in terms of both marrying non-Asian Americans and marrying non-Japanese Americans) did not differ among the groups. These results suggest the need to examine varied aspects of ethnic preference rather than presuming that behaviors such as out-marriage are the primary indicants of acculturative processes. In the present case, the two-parent Sansei simultaneously expressed a preference for Japanese Americans in some domains but not in others.

Why did the one-parent Sansei not also demonstrate significantly higher ethnic preference than that of the no-camp Sansei? One possibility is that having only one parent in camp resulted in less emphasis on maintaining in-group ties because the cross-generational effects of the internment were less intense. Two-parent Sansei were exposed to both a father and mother who might have held a greater in-group preference stemming from the internment, whereas one-parent Sansei would have had only one parent who underwent such circumstances.

One cannot assume, however, that having two interned parents necessarily resulted in greater consequences for Sansei than did having one interned parent, as is evident from the group comparisons on the Sense of Confidence factor. The Sense of Confidence factor evaluated whether having a parent interned increased the offspring's sense of vulnerability. Items under this factor included statements such as "I am confident that my rights as an American citizen would not be violated in this country" and "It is possible that Japanese Americans could be interned again in this country if war were declared against Japan." Although the two- and one-parent Sansei did not differ from each other, both expressed significantly less confidence in their status within the United States than did the no-camp group. Interview data provided insights regarding how the internment affected the Sansei's sense of confidence. In the words of one individual,

> It's affected my whole feeling about this country. I no longer stand up at baseball games and say the pledge of allegiance. . . . I'm real critical of this government. I feel I have very little patriotism in a way. I mean, I care about what happens to the country and I care about the people, but I don't feel this sense of, you

know, I love my country and I love my flag. . . . It's really because of what happened to my parents and grandparents. (quoted in Nagata, 1993, p. 115)

Similarly, another interviewee stated, "I think it has made me aware of the immense injustices that can occur in this society. It's made me cynical about government. . . . It's made me distrust power" (p. 130). The predicament described by one Sansei Vietnam veteran was especially poignant. After describing how the manager of his company kept calling him a "Jap," he stated,

> I don't understand where this was coming from. You know, my dad fought in the war. [The interviewee's father was a World War II Nisei veteran.] I fought in a war that nobody liked, . . . and here's this guy who thinks he's real American and he's taking this attitude. It really upset me. . . . What is it that this country has done by putting us in camps, by having my father go and actually fight the Japanese, which he is, and then draft me into a war? You know, all this stuff and you still have to put up with the prejudices! (p. 130)

Interviewees recognized the difficulty in separating the effects of the internment from the effects of growing up in a more general social environment characterized by a questioning of the government (e.g., the civil rights movement, Watergate, Vietnam). However, they clearly saw their parents' wartime experiences as a particularly strong force in shaping their lack of confidence. The internment is a reminder, noted one Sansei, that they are a visible minority group who never can truly assimilate into mainstream society.

▩ Pressure to Acculturate

It is perhaps ironic that although the Sansei viewed the internment as a reminder of their separateness from mainstream society, they also viewed an increased pressure to acculturate as one important consequence of the camps. Interviewees noted their parents' emphasis on blending into society, not "rocking the boat," and minimizing Japanese culture and language. Although many Nisei can speak and understand some level of Japanese, most Sansei today can do neither, and many identify the internment as a primary reason for this rapid loss.

At times, the goal of acculturation was expressed in what the Sansei perceived to be the Nisei's pressuring their children to achieve. Some interviewees saw this as their parents' way of ensuring their children's future security, a security many Nisei lost during the war. If one obtained a good education or job, then perhaps he or she would be less vulnerable to future discrimination. At the same time, the Sansei recognized that Japanese cultural values stressed the importance of educational achievement from before the internment and wondered to what degree their parents' experiences heightened an already existing cultural value.

Others pointed out that the effects of the internment actually undermined their attempts to achieve and interact with non-Japanese Americans. In their view, the internment lowered both their parents' and their own self-esteem, creating an "emotional inferiority." As one respondent stated, "There was something negative about being Japanese" (quoted in Nagata, 1993, p. 139). Several interviewees went so far as to attribute increased incidents of substance abuse within their communities to the Sansei's lowered self-esteem and identity problems stemming from the internment.

▧ Parental Health

Sansei also saw the internment as contributing to health problems and even premature deaths of their parents. Furutani (1981) hypothesized a connection between the trauma of the camps and earlier deaths among the Nisei, but no study has explored this issue. Although the Sansei Research Project survey did not ask respondents whether they attributed a parent's health problems to the internment, it did ask them to indicate whether a parent had died and, if so, the age at the time of death. Parents' ages at the times of death could then be compared between those Sansei who had at least one parent interned and those who did not. For mothers, there was no significant difference. However, more than twice as many of the previously interned Nisei fathers died before the age of 60 years compared to the noninterned fathers. This small sample of data clearly has limited generalizability. Nonetheless, it provided intriguing support for the possibility that the internment has had serious health effects on the Nisei generation. The occurrence of early parental death and illness, in turn, adversely affected the Sansei's lives.

▧ Positive Impacts

Not all impacts were negative. Some Sansei realized that they never would have been born without the internment because their parents met while in camp. All marveled at their parents' resilience and noted the positive effects of the Nisei's coping on their own lives. The Nisei have been important role models in this regard. Additional interview data indicated that there are Sansei who chose specific careers or educational institutions to fulfill the unfinished dreams of a parent whose life was disrupted by the camps. Here the pressure to achieve emerged from a personal sense of mission rather than from a need to assimilate. Several Sansei became lawyers to combat future legal and constitutional injustices, whereas others assumed roles as activists to help strengthen the Japanese American community. Even those Sansei whose careers had not been guided by a parent's internment frequently reported that the internment loomed as a significant force in lives, reminding them of the need to remain sensitive to human rights whenever possible.

▧ Redress Attitudes and Reactions

One way in which the Sansei expressed their concern for human rights was through their support for the redress movement. Whereas the Nisei played a primary role in the redress effort, the Sansei also were instrumental in resurrecting the internment from the past (Nakanishi, 1988). At the time of data collection, the outcome of the redress movement was unclear, and respondents were asked to indicate whether they supported seeking monetary compensation from the government. The majority (approximately 79%) of both those Sansei who had at least one parent interned and those whose parents were not interned supported seeking redress. Only 9% were opposed, whereas 12% were undecided. When asked why they supported redress, most interviewees cited both a desire to relieve the stigma long carried by their parents and grandparents and a general concern that the injustice be publicly recognized and redressed. Although they noted that no sum of money could repay their parents for what had happened, they saw the payments as symbolic of a much broader issue, that of communicating the seriousness of the government's error and of serving as a deterrent to future injustices.

The year following data collection for the Sansei Research Project, President Reagan signed into law the Civil Liberties Act of 1988. The act, as noted earlier, provided a one-time payment of $20,000 to each surviving internee and an official apology from the U.S. government. Although the original Sansei Research Project was completed before the passage of redress legislation, a smaller follow-up study was conducted in 1990. This second data set included questions on Sansei's reactions to the success of the redress effort. Among those who returned their surveys were 174 Sansei who had one or both parents interned during the war. They answered questions on a scale ranging from 1 to 5 (with 1 = *not at all* and 5 = *a great deal*) in rating the degree to which they felt the passage of redress had (a) increased their faith in the U.S. government, (b) reduced their negative feelings about the internment, (c) resulted in a feeling of personal relief, and (d) increased their parents' willingness to discuss the internment with them. Results indicated that, as a group, Sansei felt that redress did result in some degree of increased faith in the government ($M = 2.71$) and feeling of relief ($M = 2.57$). However, 17% of the sample did not feel that redress increased their faith in the government at all, and 28% felt *no* feelings of relief whatsoever. In addition, redress did not appear to necessarily reduce the Sansei's negative feelings about the internment itself ($M = 1.85$), with 47% of the respondents reporting no reduction in such feelings. These findings suggest that the Sansei's psychological reactions were multifaceted and that the success of redress, although highly significant, did not necessarily remove the negative legacies of the past.

At the same time, Takezawa (1995) observed that the redress movement enhanced the Sansei's ethnic pride and strengthened their empathy with other ethnic minorities outside of the Japanese American community. Within their own community, redress brought together all generations of Japanese Americans and increased the sense of community for many (Takezawa, 1995). Intergenerational relations between the Nisei and the Sansei also were positively affected. "Because of the movement, the Nisei and the Sansei began a true dialogue concerning the family and community history" (p. 173). Data from the Sansei follow-up study provide some support for this observation. Although respondents from that study did perceive redress as increasing their parents' willingness to discuss the internment somewhat ($M = 2.50$), 28% felt that there has been no such increase. However, it is possible that the dialogue between Nisei and Sansei occurred on a more general level, outside of the family, through community organizations, the media, and informal networks.

SIGNIFICANCE OF THE SANSEI
RESEARCH PROJECT FINDINGS

The results from the Sansei Research Project provide support for the existence of cross-generational internment effects. Although more than 50 years have passed since the incarceration of Japanese Americans, individuals whose parents were interned reported multiple ways in which that past event continues to affect their lives. Sansei reported both positive and negative consequences, suggesting the need to assess both the adaptive and maladaptive sequelae to racial traumas.

The findings help highlight the complexities of evaluating the effects of ethnicity and trauma across generations of Japanese Americans (Nagata, 1991a). In some instances (e.g., describing the impact of the internment on their sense of confidence in the United States), the Sansei saw a clear link between the internment and their present-day experiences. In others, however, it was difficult for them to decipher the degree to which preexisting Japanese cultural values played a role in their perceived internment effects. Was a parent's reluctance to discuss the internment an expression of gaman, shikata ganai, protectiveness, or a combination of some or all of these? From their perspective as third-generation Japanese Americans who grew up in a Westernized, Caucasian majority society, the Sansei expressed mixed reactions to the costs and benefits of maintaining Japanese cultural values in the United States. Similarly, Sansei wondered to what degree their parents' post-internment emphasis on achievement stemmed from preexisting cultural values or was accentuated by the trauma of the camps and discrimination. These examples point to the importance of investigating traumatic events within a larger cultural and historical context.

In interpreting the project results, there are methodological limitations that must be kept in mind (Nagata, 1993, 1995). Reliance on Japanese American community groups for sample selection increased the proportion of respondents who have retained ties with their ethnic community. (Interestingly, although most respondents were contacted through mailing lists of the JACL, 40% of the participants were not members of the JACL at the time of the study.) The voluntary nature of participation in the study also limits generalizability. We do not know how the opinions of those who did not return the survey might differ from those responses that were received.

Still, there is evidence that there are many Sansei who see the internment as a continuing force in their lives. In fact, more than 60% of the returned surveys included additional written comments following the 20 pages of questions. Many individuals thanked the researcher for investigating this issue and said that they experienced a sense of positive emotional release after completing their surveys. Others commented that before participating in the study, they thought that they were alone in wondering about these issues. They were surprised and pleased that someone else shared their concerns. Kidder and Fine (1986) pointed out the important role that social scientists can play by connecting personal stories to other personal stories, helping isolated individuals to see the connections between their experiences and the experiences of others. It would seem that this has been one important consequence of the Sansei Research Project. Future studies examining the intergenerational consequences of trauma among Asian Americans may well reveal similar instances in which the effects of the past have been perceived as individual traumas rather than as shared legacies. This might be especially so given the emphasis in most Asian American groups to keep emotional issues within the family rather than sharing them with others.

In looking to the experiences of other Asian American groups, additional questions arise. For example, although Chinese Americans were not interned, they too have historically suffered incidents of racism and violence in this country (Daniels, 1988). It would be interesting to assess the degree to which these events have affected the experiences of subsequent generations of Chinese Americans. For Filipino Americans, American colonialism and the presence of the U.S. military in the past have played a significant role in the Phillipines (Uba, 1994). What long-term intergenerational effects might be linked to these events? In addition, the horrors witnessed by Southeast Asian refugees have left both psychological and physical scars (e.g., Mollica, Wyshak, & Lavelle, 1987; Rozee & Van Boemel, 1989). How will the legacies of these traumas affect their children, and to what extent will their intergenerational dynamics parallel or diverge from findings for the children of Holocaust survivors?

Research is needed to refine our level of understanding about the relationship between significant group-related historical experiences and the diversity within and between Asian American groups. Among Southeast Asian refugees, for example, experiences might differ according to gender. Studies have revealed that some forms of the posttraumatic sequelae (Mattson, 1993; Rozee & Van Boemel, 1989) and levels of stress surrounding changes in intergenerational relations in the United States (Yee, 1992) might be unique to Southeast Asian women. Chung and Kagawa-Singer (1993) also found that various Southeast Asian groups might differ in their reported levels of distress 5 years after their migration to the United States. Another key issue concerns a recognition of how the developmental stage of the individual interacts with the observed intergenerational processes related to the past (Nagata, 1995). Participants in the Sansei Research Project, for example, revealed that their own reactions to their parents' lack of verbal communication about the internment changed from anger and frustration to respect and greater understanding over the course of time (Nagata, 1993).

Future studies also should examine possible regional differences within specific ethnic groups. East Coast respondents in the Sansei Research Project, for example, reported significantly lower levels of confidence in their rights than did either the California or Midwest Sansei. It would be useful to know how the sociocultural context in which Asian Americans live may moderate the relationships between the impact of historical events and current intergenerational processes. Finally, as pointed out by Uba (1994), there is diversity within Asian

American groups related to specific waves of immigration. Korean Americans who immigrated with the first wave in the early 1900s have had different experiences from Korean Americans who immigrated after the Immigration and Naturalization Act of 1965. Chinese Americans also may vary depending on waves of immigration. Some may be fifth- or sixth-generation Chinese Americans, whereas others may have arrived quite recently (Uba, 1994). These different immigration waves have important consequences for acculturation, intergenerational interactions, and experiences of significant historical events that must be considered as well.

It also is worth noting that the Sansei Research Project used a nonclinical sample. Given the low rate at which Asian Americans use mental health services (Leong, 1986; Sue & Morishima, 1982), it would be difficult to conduct the same study with a large clinical population of Sansei. However, professionals should bear in mind that themes related to the internment might emerge when conducting psychotherapy with Sansei clients who do enter into treatment (Nagata, 1991b; Tomine, 1997).

In conclusion, the presented research suggests that the internment continues to influence the lives of many of the sons and daughters of former internees. One can only speculate whether and how the effects of the internment will be passed on to the fourth (Yonsei) and fifth (Gosei) generations of Japanese Americans. Given the high percentage of out-marriage among the Sansei, we might expect the issue of the camps to fade over time. However, a closer look at current sociopolitical events suggests that the Sansei, out-married or not, might not soon forget the internment. Many U.S. citizens today see Japan once again as a threat, this time as an economic enemy. Japanese Americans and other Asian Americans, as well as Japanese nationals, are targets for "Japan bashing" and anti-Asian violence. These developments serve as grim reminders to the Sansei, their Nisei parents, and all generations of Japanese Americans that the issues of racism and anger that fueled the internment have not disappeared. History remains a part of their lives and the lives of other Asian Americans.

REFERENCES

American Psychiatric Association. (1994). *Diagnostic criteria from DSM-IV.* Washington, DC: Author.

Barocas, H. A., & Barocas, C. B. (1979). Wounds of the fathers: The next generation of Holocaust victims. *International Review of Psychoanalysis, 6,* 331-340.

Chambon, A. (1989). Refugee families' experiences: Three family themes—family disruption, violent trauma, and acculturation. *Journal of Strategic and Systemic Family Therapies, 8,* 3-13.

Chung, R. C., & Kagawa-Singer, M. (1993). Predictors of psychological distress among Southeast Asian refugees. *Social Science and Medicine, 36,* 631-639.

Commission on Wartime Relocation and Internment of Civilians. (1982). *Personal justice denied.* Washington, DC: Government Printing Office.

Commission on Wartime Relocation and Internment of Civilians. (1983). *Personal justice denied: Part 2—Recommendations.* Washington, DC: Government Printing Office.

Connor, J. (1977). *Acculturation and change in three generations of Japanese Americans.* San Francisco: R & E Associates.

Danieli, Y. (1982). Families of survivors and the Nazi Holocaust: Some short- and long-term effects. In C. D. Spielberger, I. G. Sarason, & N. Milgram (Eds.), *Stress and anxiety* (Vol. 8, pp. 405-423). Washington, DC: Hemisphere.

Danieli, Y. (1985). The treatment and prevention of long-term effects and intergenerational transmission of victimization: A lesson from Holocaust survivors and their children. In C. R. Figley (Ed.), *Trauma and its wake: The study and treatment of post-traumatic stress disorder* (pp. 295-313). New York: Brunner/Mazel.

Daniels, R. (1972). *Concentration camps U.S.A.: Japanese Americans and World War II.* New York: Holt, Rinehart & Winston.

Daniels, R. (Ed.). (1978). *Anti-Chinese violence in America.* New York: Arno.

Daniels, R. (1988). *Asian America: Chinese and Japanese in the United States since 1850.* Seattle: University of Washington Press.

Daniels, R. (1993). *Prisoners without trial: Japanese Americans in World War II.* New York: Hill & Wang.

Daniels, R., Taylor, S. C., & Kitano, H. H. L. (1991). *Japanese Americans: From relocation to redress* (rev. ed.). Seattle: University of Washington Press.

Elder, G. H., Jr., Caspi, A., & Ngyuen, T. (1986). Resourceful and vulnerable children: Family influence in hard times. In R. K. Silbereison, E. Eyferth, & G. Rudinger (Eds.), *Development as action in context: Problem behavior and normal youth development* (pp. 167-186). New York: Springer-Verlag.

Epstein, H. (1977). *Children of the Holocaust: Conversations with sons and daughters of survivors.* New York: Plenum.

Fugita, S. S., & O'Brien, D. J. (1991). *Japanese American ethnicity: The persistence of community.* Seattle: University of Washington Press.

Furutani, W. (1981). Testimony to the Commission on Wartime Relocation and Internment of Civilians. *Amerasia, 8,* 101-105.

Halik, V., Rosenthal, D. A., & Pattison, P. E. (1990). Intergenerational effects of the Holocaust: Patterns of engagement in the mother-daughter relationship. *Family Process, 29,* 325-339.

Hansen, A. A., & Mitson, B. E. (1974). *Voice long silent: An oral inquiry into the Japanese American evacuation.* Fullerton: California State University, Oral History Program.

Heller, D. (1981). Themes of culture and ancestry among children of concentration camp survivors. *Psychiatry, 45,* 247-261.

Hosokawa, F. (1978). *The Sansei: Social interaction and ethnic identity among the third generation Japanese.* San Francisco: R & E Associates.

Karnow, S., & Yoshimura, N. (1992). *Asian Americans in transition.* New York: The Asia Society.

Kashima, T. (1980). Japanese American internees return: 1945 to 1955: Readjustment and social amnesia. *Phylon, 41,* 107-115.

Keinan, G., Mikulincer, M., & Rybnicki, A. (1988). Perception of self and parents by second generation Holocaust survivors. *Behavioral Medicine, 14,* 6-12.

Kidder, L. H., & Fine, M. (1986). Making sense of injustice: Social explanations, social action, and the role of the social scientist. In E. Seidman & J. Rappaport (Eds.), *Redefining social problems* (pp. 49-63). New York: Plenum.

Kitano, H. H. L. (1969). *Japanese Americans: The evolution of a subculture.* Englewood Cliffs, NJ: Prentice Hall.

Kitano, H. H. L. (1991). The effects of evacuation on the Japanese American. In R. Daniels, S. C. Taylor, & H. H. L. Kitano (Eds.), *Japanese Americans: Relocation to redress* (rev. ed., pp. 151-158). Seattle: University of Washington Press.

Kitano, H. H. L., & Daniels, R. (1988). *Asian Americans: Emerging minorities.* Englewood Cliffs, NJ: Prentice Hall.

Kitano, H. H. L., Yeung, W. T., Chai, L., & Hatanaka, H. (1984). Asian-American interracial marriage. *Journal of Marriage and the Family, 2,* 179-190.

Klein-Parker, F. (1988). Dominant attitudes of adult children of Holocaust survivors towards their parents. In J. P. Wilson, Z. Harel, & B. Kahana (Eds.), *Human adaptation to extreme stress: From the Holocaust to Vietnam* (pp. 193-218). New York: Plenum.

Leong. F. T. L. (1986). Counseling and psychotherapy with Asian-Americans: Review of the literature. *Journal of Counseling Psychology, 33,* 196-206.

Levine, G. N., & Rhodes, C. (1981). *The Japanese American community.* New York: Praeger.

Loo, C. M. (1993). An integrative-sequential treatment model of posttraumatic stress disorder: A case study of the Japanese American internment and redress. *Clinical Psychology Review, 13,* 89-117.

Mass, A. (1991). Psychological effects of the camps on the Japanese Americans. In R. Daniels, S. C. Taylor, & H. H. L. Kitano (Eds.), *Japanese Americans: From relocation to redress* (rev. ed., pp. 159-162). Seattle: University of Washington Press.

Mattson, S. (1993). Mental health of Southeast Asian refugee women: An overview. *Health Care for Women International, 14,* 155-165.

Maykovitch, M. K. (1972). *Japanese American identity dilemma.* Tokyo: Waseda University Press.

Miyoshi, N. (1980, December 19-26). Identity crisis of the Sansei and the American concentration camp. *The Pacific Citizen,* pp. 41-42, 50, 55.

Modell, J. (1973). *The Kikuchi diary.* Urbana: University of Illinois Press.

Mollica, R., Wyshak, G., & Lavelle, J. (1987). The psychological impact of war trauma and torture on Southeast Asian refugees. *American Journal of Psychiatry, 144,* 1567-1571.

Montero, D. (1980). *Japanese Americans: Changing patterns of ethnic affiliation over three generations.* Boulder, CO: Westview.

Morishima, J. (1973). The evacuation: Impact on the family. In S. Sue & N. N. Wagner (Eds.), *Asian Americans: Psychological perspectives* (pp. 13-19). Palo Alto, CA: Science and Behavior Books.

Mura, D. (1991). *Turning Japanese: Memoirs of a Sansei.* New York: Atlantic Monthly.

Nagata, D. K. (1989). Long term effects of the Japanese American internment camps: Impact on the children of internees. *Journal of the Asian American Psychological Association, 13,* 48-55.

Nagata, D. K. (1990a). The Japanese American internment: Exploring the transgenerational consequences of traumatic stress. *Journal of Traumatic Stress, 3,* 47-69.

Nagata, D. K. (1990b). The Japanese American internment: Perceptions of moral community, fairness, and redress. *Journal of Social Issues, 46,* 133-146.

Nagata, D. K. (1991a, August). *Evaluating the effects of ethnicity and trauma across generations: The Japanese American internment.* Paper presented at the annual meeting of the American Psychological Association, San Francisco.

Nagata, D. K. (1991b). The transgenerational impact of the Japanese American internment: Clinical issues in working with the children of former internees. *Psychotherapy, 28,* 121-128.

Nagata, D. K. (1993). *Legacy of silence: Exploring the long-term effects of the Japanese American internment.* New York: Plenum.

Nagata, D. K. (1995). Studying the legacy of injustice: Psychological research on the Japanese American internment. In J. Fong (Ed.), *Proceedings of the Asian American Psychological Association annual convention* (pp. 67-73). Atascadero, CA: Rogers & Associates.

Nagata, D. K., Trierweiler, S. J., & Talbot, R. (1997). *Long-term effects of internment during early childhood among third generation Japanese Americans.* Unpublished manuscript, University of Michigan, Ann Arbor.

Nakanishi, D. T. (1988). Seeking convergence in race relations research: Japanese Americans and the resurrection of the internment. In P. A. Katz & D. A. Taylor (Eds.), *Eliminating racism: Profiles in controversy* (pp. 159-180). New York: Plenum.

O'Brien, D. J., & Fugita, S. S. (1983). Generational differences in Japanese Americans' perceptions and feelings about social relationships between themselves and Caucasian Americans. In W. C. McCready (Ed.), *Culture, ethnicity, and identity: Current issues in research* (pp. 223-240). New York: Academic Press.

Ogawa, D. M., & Fox, E. C., Jr. (1991). Japanese American internment and relocation: The Hawaii experience. In R. Daniels, S. C. Taylor, & H. H. L. Kitano (Eds.), *Japanese Americans: From relocation to redress* (rev. ed., pp. 135-138). Seattle: University of Washington Press.

Okihiro, G. Y., & Drummond, D. (1991). The concentration camps and Japanese economic losses in California agriculture. In R. Daniels, S. C. Taylor, & H. H. L. Kitano (Eds.), *Japanese Americans: From relocation to redress* (rev. ed., pp. 168-175). Seattle: University of Washington Press.

Okubo, M. (1989). *Citizen 13660.* Seattle: University of Washington Press.

Prince, R. M. (1985). Second generation effects of historical trauma. *Psychoanalytic Review, 72,* 9-29.

Rose, S. L., & Garske, J. (1987). Family environment, adjustment, and coping among children of Holocaust survivors. *American Journal of Orthopsychiatry, 57,* 332-344.

Rozee, P. D., & Van Boemel, G. (1989). The psychological effects of war trauma and abuse on older Cambodian women. *Women and Therapy, 8,* 23-50.

Sawada, M. (1986-1987). After the camps: Seabrook Farms, New Jersey, and the resettlement of Japanese Americans, 1944-1947. *Amerasia, 13,* 117-136.

Solkoff, N. (1992). Children of survivors of the Nazi Holocaust: A critical review of the literature. *American Journal of Orthopsychiatry, 62,* 342-358.

Sone, M. (1991). *Nisei daughter.* Seattle: University of Washington Press.

Sue, S., & Morishima, J. K. (1982). *The mental health of Asian Americans.* San Francisco: Jossey-Bass.

Takaki, R. (1989). *Strangers from a different shore: A history of Asian Americans.* Boston: Little, Brown.

Takezawa, Y. I. (1995). *Breaking the silence: Redress and Japanese American ethnicity.* Ithaca, NY: Cornell University Press.

Tateishi, J. (1984). *And justice for all: An oral history of the Japanese American detention camps.* New York: Random House.

Taylor, S. C. (1991). Evacuation and economic loss: Questions and perspectives. In R. Daniels, S. C. Taylor, & H. H. L. Kitano (Eds.), *Japanese Americans: From relocation to redress* (rev. ed., pp. 163-167). Seattle: University of Washington Press.

Testimonies to the Commission on Wartime Relocation and Internment of Civilians. (1981). *Amerasia, 8,* 58-105.

Thomas, D. S. (1952). *The salvage.* Berkeley: University of California Press.

Thomas, D. S., & Nishimoto, R. S. (1946). *The spoilage.* Berkeley: University of California Press.

Tomine, S. I. (1997). Counseling Japanese Americans: From internment to reparation. In C. C. Lee & B. L. Richardson (Eds.), *Multicultural issues in counseling: New approaches to diversity* (2nd ed., pp. 189-206). Alexandria, VA: American Counseling Association.

Trachtenberg, M., & Davis, M. (1978). Breaking silences: Serving children of Holocaust survivors. *Journal of Jewish Communal Services, 54,* 293-302.

Tsukamoto, M., & Pinkerton, E. (1987). *We the people: A story of internment in America.* Elk Grove, CA: Laguna.

Uba, L. (1994). *Asian Americans: Personality patterns, identity, and mental health.* New York: Guilford.

Uchida, Y. (1989). *Desert exile: The uprooting of a Japanese American family.* Seattle: University of Washington Press.

U.S. Commission on Civil Rights. (1992). *Civil rights issues facing Asian Americans in the 1990s.* Washington, DC: Author.

Weglyn, M. (1976). *The untold story of America's concentration camps.* New York: William Morrow.

Weiss, M. S. (1970). Selective acculturation and the dating process: The pattern of Chinese-Caucasian interracial dating. *Journal of Marriage and the Family, 32,* 273-278.

Wilson, R. A., & Hosokawa, B. (1980). *East to America: A history of the Japanese in the United States.* New York: William Morrow.

Yanagisako, S. J. (1985). *Transforming the past: Tradition and kinship among Japanese Americans.* Stanford, CA: Stanford University Press.

Yee, B. (1992). Elders in Southeast Asian families. *Generations, 16,* 24-27.

14

PSYCHOPATHOLOGY

Kevin M. Chun
Karen L. Eastman
Grace C. S. Wang
Stanley S. Sue

Analyses of psychopathology among Asian Americans usually involve a series of questions that increase in complexity. For example, one can start with a basic question—What are the rates of mental disorders among Asian Americans?—and generate a whole set of more complex questions: Are Asian Americans at increased risk for mental illness? Does culture affect how Asian Americans experience stressors and psychopathology? Do Asian Americans exhibit unique patterns of symptom expression? How are rates of mental disorders determined, and are assessment and diagnostic procedures valid for Asian Americans?

This chapter addresses these questions by reviewing the current state of research on Asian Americans, which, in many respects, remains quite limited. For heuristic purposes, we propose a multicomponent model for the analysis of psychopathology among Asian Americans. The components of this model include (a) Vulnerability (biopsychosocial considerations that increase or decrease risk for psychopathology, (b) Experience (the cognitive and emotional organization of psychopathology), (c) Manifestation (symptom expression of psychopathology), and (d) Prevalence (the extent of psychopathology in the population). In positing a Vulnerability-Experience-Manifestation-Prevalence model, we have

AUTHORS' NOTE: The writing of this chapter was supported by National Institute of Mental Health Grant R01 MH44331 to the National Research Center on Asian American Mental Health.

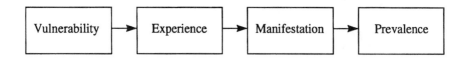

Figure 14.1. Conceptual Model for the Analysis of Psychopathology

delineated four common components of psychopathology to examine the importance of cultural and minority group factors in each component. Nevertheless, the components in our model are logically linked, as depicted in Figure 14.1, and can be used to conceptualize psychopathology for all populations.

Vulnerability encompasses those person and environmental factors that contribute to the development of psychopathology. According to the diathesis-stress model (Meehl, 1962; Rosenthal, 1970), certain environmental stressors may activate an inherent predisposition or diathesis to illness. This model has particular relevance for Southeast Asian refugees given their repeated exposure to catastrophic environmental stressors such as premigration war trauma. Furthermore, many Southeast Asian refugees have experienced multiple life changes in their native lands, during migration, and on resettlement in the United States that might compound their risk for psychopathology. Past research shows that undesirable life changes are correlated with anxiety, depression, and physical symptoms (Sarason, Johnson, & Siegel, 1978). Research also has demonstrated that genetic factors may contribute to certain psychiatric disorders such as panic disorder (Crowe, Noyes, Pauls, & Slymen, 1983; Torgersen, 1983), unipolar and bipolar mood disorders (Goodwin & Guze, 1984), and schizophrenia (Kendler, 1983, 1988). Is it possible that Asian Americans possess unique genetic or biological risk factors for psychopathology? Research is far from conclusive, but investigators have found significant psychobiological differences between Asians and Whites in their reactivity to alcohol (Akutsu, Sue, Zane, & Nakamura, 1989) and psychopharmacological agents (Lin, Lau et al., 1988; Lin, Poland, Nuccio et al., 1989; Lin, Poland, & Lesser, 1986) that eventually might help clarify the role of psychobiology in the etiology of mental illness among Asians.

A preexisting vulnerability coupled with environmental stressors may lead to the *Experience* of mental illness. Kleinman (1988) asserted that individuals conceptualize the nature and causes of psychopathology in terms of culturally embedded "explanatory models" of mental illness. In support of this notion, research illustrates that Asian Americans may organize and perceive mental health in a culturally distinct manner. Asian cultures hold unique conceptualizations, nomenclature, and coping responses that often challenge Western perspectives of mental health. Such cultural differences are especially noteworthy for recently arrived Asian Americans who organize their concepts of mental health around traditional folk beliefs, as will be seen later in this chapter.

Manifestation is closely linked to Experience and constitutes the expression and course of psychopathology. It is widely recognized that symptom presentations for particular disorders often vary across ethnic groups. For example, Kitano (1969) found that Japanese schizophrenics exhibited more withdrawal symptoms than acting out behaviors. Kitano attributed this finding to the Japanese culture, which reinforces internal or intrapersonal means of resolving conflicts. In addition, the literature on depressive symptomatology among Asian Americans illustrates that Asians tend to underreport psychological problems and overendorse bodily complaints compared to other ethnic groups. Finally, studies also indicate that Asian Americans may exhibit symptoms that are associated with culture-specific syndromes such as *koros* as witnessed in the Chinese and Southeast Asian cultures and *hwabyung* as witnessed in the Korean culture. Such syndromes provide the most compelling examples of cultural variability in symptom expression.

Lastly, *Prevalence* focuses on the actual reported rates of psychopathology among Asian Americans. Determining the prevalence of psychopathology among Asian Americans is a formidable task given that large-scale epidemiological studies have not been conducted in this ethnic population. Prevalence estimates based on use of mental health services have been misleadingly low because Asian Americans tend to underutilize such services. Furthermore, numerous assessment and diagnostic instruments that are used in prevalence studies emphasize Western health concepts and, therefore, might lack construct validity for Asian Americans. The development and theoretical basis of culture-specific instruments and their contribution to the assessment and diagnosis of Asian Americans are examined in this chapter.

In summary, the components of the Vulnerability-Experience-Manifestation-Prevalence model are logically linked. Vulnerability factors may contribute to the development of psychopathology, whereas the cognitive and emotional responses to these factors comprise the experience of mental illness. In turn, experience affects how psychopathology is manifested, and the manifestation of disorders forms the basis for prevalence estimates. As will be seen throughout this chapter, cultural factors and/or minority group status are intimately involved in all of these processes for Asian Americans.

Before discussing the research literature, two caveats are in order. First, research on overseas Asians is included in this chapter despite the psychological, sociopolitical, and economic differences they might have with their Asian American counterparts. In many respects, however, these two groups are culturally similar, and the abundant studies on overseas Asians have made major conceptual contributions to the study of Asian American health. Second, heterogeneity exists among Asian American groups. It is difficult to appreciate this heterogeneity because many Asian American groups are overlooked in research, and findings from one group often are generalized to the entire population.

VULNERABILITY

Are Asian Americans at increased risk for psychopathology? Past research strongly suggests that this is indeed the case for certain segments of the Asian American population. However, it is difficult to determine the extent to which biological and environmental vulnerability factors contribute to mental illness for Asians. Investigating biological vulnerabilities is especially difficult given the inherent complexity of the research; thus, it remains a matter of conjecture whether Asian Americans are more biologically predisposed to certain mental disorders than are other ethnic groups. Nevertheless, investigations on the response to alcohol and psychotropic medications demonstrate that significant psychobiological differences exist between Asians and Caucasians. For example, in regard to alcohol intake, Lin, Poland, Smith, Strickland, and Mendoza (1991) noted that approximately half of all East Asians, such as the Chinese and Japanese, lack the active form of the aldehyde dehydrogenase, which may contribute to the high incidence of "flushing" (e.g., facial flushing, palpitation, tachycardia, dysphoria, nausea, vomiting) among Asians. Furthermore, these researchers also stated that 85% to 90% of Asians possess an atypical alcohol dehydrogenase isozyme that has the capacity to convert alcohol into acetaldehyde, a highly toxic subtance that contributes to flushing when it is accumulated. Finally, psychopharmacological studies have shown that Asians, when compared to Caucasians, require lower dosages for optimal clinical response to haloperidol (Lin et al., 1989), alprazolam (Lin et al., 1988), and tricyclic antidepressants (Lin et al., 1986). Lin and colleagues (1989) suggested that such findings might stem from ethnic differences in neurological receptor mediated responses between Asians and Caucasians. Still, these studies do not indicate whether Asians possess culturally distinct biological vulnerabilities to mental illness.

Research on newborn infants further highlights ethnic differences in the psychobiology of Asians and Caucasians. Freedman (1975) compared 24 Chinese American newborns to 24 Caucasian American newborns according to five categories: (a) temperament, (b) sensory development, (c) autonomic and central nervous system maturity, (d) motor development, and (e) social interest and response. Although a substantial overlap among all infants was found along these five categories, the two groups significantly differed on items measuring temperament and on those that appeared to assess excitability/imperturbability. The Chinese American newborns tended to be less changeable and perturbable, habituated more quickly, and calmed themselves more readily when upset compared to the Caucasian newborns. Although these findings are inconclusive, they suggest that important psychobiological differences exist between Asians and Caucasians, especially considering that these findings were evident at such an early age.

Unlike the lack of research on biological vulnerabilities, there are numerous studies that link environmental stressors to increased risk for psychopathology among Asian Americans. This is especially the case for the growing influx of Asian immigrants and Southeast Asian refugees who encounter multiple environmental stressors in the United States such as culture conflicts, language problems, strained financial resources, prejudice and discrimination, and lack of familiar and adequate social support. Furthermore, many of the Southeast Asian refugees have been repeatedly traumatized prior to their entry into the United States, as will be discussed later in the chapter.

Past research illustrates that immigrant status increases the risk for adjustment problems among Asian Americans. Ying (1988) found that foreign birth coupled with a limited period of residence in the United States was associated with a higher degree of depressive symptoms for Chinese Americans, although this relationship was not significant when social class was controlled. Using the Omnibus Personality Inventory, Sue and Zane (1985) likewise reported adjustment difficulties for a sample of recently immigrated Chinese students who spent 6 years or less in the United States. These researchers stated that the immigrant Chinese students in their study were less autonomous and extroverted and more anxious than Chinese students who had lived longer in the United States. Interestingly, however, the academic achievement levels of the foreign-born students exceeded those of the general student body. Therefore, Sue and Zane cautioned that academic performance should not be used as an indicator of psychological well-being or adjustment for newly arrived Chinese college students. In another study, Abe and Zane (1990) found significant differences between Caucasian American and foreign-born Asian American college students on a measure of psychological adjustment. Results from this study demonstrated that foreign-born Asian Americans reported greater levels of interpersonal distress than did their White counterparts, even after controlling for demographic differences and the influences of social desirability, self-consciousness, extraversion, and other-directedness (i.e., being attuned to the desires and needs of others). These results are especially interesting given that the foreign-born Asian American sample had resided in the United States for an average of 10 years. Abe and Zane proposed that the various stressors that many foreign-born Asian Americans face, such as language barriers and loss of social support networks, might have long-term negative effects on psychological adjustment.

Kuo and Tsai (1986) presented several interesting findings in their study of Asian immigrants who resettled in Seattle, Washington. These researchers found that the Koreans, the most recently arrived immigrants, exhibited twice the rate of depression compared to the Chinese, Japanese, and Filipino groups under investigation. For the overall sample, immigrants who possessed accurate information about living in the United States prior to immigration reported fewer financial worries and adjustment difficulties, such as problems with the English language, homesickness, and lifestyle changes, than did those without such information. Immigrants who moved at an earlier age also experienced fewer adjustment difficulties. In regard to social support, immigrants who reported having numerous friends who were available for frank discussions, or "available" relatives in one's residential area, exhibited fewer depressive symptoms than did those who lacked such an extensive social network. Finally, Kuo and Tsai found that immigrants with "hardy" personalities reported less stressful life events, financial worries, adjustment difficulties, and symptoms of depression than did those who lacked hardy traits. Thus, hardy Asian immigrants, or those who felt a sense of control over their life events, maintained a strong commitment to their life activities, and perceived change as an exciting opportunity for personal development, were more likely to display positive adjustment to their new American lifestyles.

Studies also have consistently shown that Southeast Asian refugees constitute a high-risk group for mental disorders. Adjustment difficulties in Southeast Asian refugees have been linked to repeated exposure to catastrophic environmental stressors such as torture, combat, witnessing the death of family members and relatives, and forcible detainment in harsh refugee camp conditions. In one particular study, Southeast Asian refugees who had experienced multiple premigration traumas were significantly at risk for experiencing psychosocial dysfunction or impaired daily functioning (Chun, 1991).

The extent of traumatization in the Southeast Asian refugee community has been widely documented. Gong-Guy (1987), in a statewide mental health needs assessment, reported that 55% of Southeast Asian refugees experienced separations from or deaths of family members, with 30% experiencing multiple separations or losses. For the Cambodian sample alone, nearly two thirds of the surveyed adults endured the loss of family members. Cambodian women were particularly traumatized; more than one in five experienced the death of a husband. Many of these women described incidences of unspeakable trauma in which they witnessed their husbands and children being shot, tortured, or starved to death or instances in which they were wounded or victimized themselves. Mollica, Wyshak, and Lavelle (1987) also reported episodes of repeated traumatization in their Southeast Asian refugee patient sample. These researchers found that the Southeast Asians in their study had experienced an average of 10 traumatic episodes that were characterized by various atrocities such as deprivation of food and water, torture, physical injury from war, sexual abuse, and solitary confinement.

Elevated rates of mental disorders have coincided with multiple traumatic episodes for Southeast Asian refugees. Kinzie and colleagues (1990) reported that 70% of their overall Southeast Asian refugee patient sample met *DSM-III-R* criteria for a current diagnosis of posttraumatic stress disorder (PTSD) and 5% met criteria for a past diagnosis (American Psychiatric Association, 1987). Furthermore, 82% suffered from depression, the most common non-PTSD diagnosis, and approximately 16% had schizophrenia. The elevated incidence of PTSD among these highly traumatized Southeast Asian refugees was even more alarming when group differences were analyzed. In this case, PTSD was diagnosed in 95% of the Mien sample (a highland tribe from Laos) and in 92% of the Cambodian sample. The clinical significance of these findings is underscored by the fact that most of these PTSD sufferers had experienced their traumatic events 10 to 15 years prior to assessment. Such prolonged effects of trauma on psychological functioning also were evidenced in a follow-up study of Cambodian adolescents who had survived Pol Pot's concentration camps (Kinzie, Sack, Angell, Clarke, & Ben, 1989). In this study, 48% of the adolescents suffered from PTSD and 41% experienced depression approximately 10 years after their traumatization.

Similar results were found by Mollica, Wyshak, and Lavelle (1987). About 50% of their Southeast Asian refugee patients fulfilled *DSM-III* criteria for PTSD, and 71% suffered from major affective disorder. Certain groups had even higher prevalence rates. The Hmong/Laotian group exhibited the highest rates at 92%

for PTSD and 85% for major affective disorder, whereas 57% and 81% of the Cambodians suffered from PTSD and major affective disorder, respectively.

In a point prevalence study of adult Hmong refugees, a rural and agrarian people from Laos, Westermeyer (1988) found that 43% met *DSM-III* criteria for various Axis I diagnoses such as adjustment disorder, major depression, and paranoia. Westermeyer emphasized that despite the relatively small sample ($N = 97$) that was investigated, the high rate of Axis I diagnoses exhibited by these refugees—twice the expected rate for the general U.S. population—underscored the degree of psychopathology that is likely to occur in Southeast Asian refugee groups.

In addition to premigration trauma, certain postmigration status variables also have been associated with increased susceptibility for adjustment difficulties among Southeast Asian refugees. Older age has been associated with more symptoms of depression for Hmong refugees (Westermeyer, Neider, & Callies, 1989), and being a divorced or widowed female head of household has been linked to increased susceptibility for psychological and physical complaints (Lin, Tazuma, & Masuda, 1979). Other postmigration variables that might predispose Southeast Asians to adjustment difficulties include limited English proficiency (Nicassio, Solomon, Guest, & McCullough, 1986), a 10- to 12-month length of stay in the host country (Beiser, 1988), and low income and less education (Nicassio & Pate, 1984). In support of these findings, Tran (1989) found that low income, a poor educational background, and limited English-speaking skills were negatively associated with psychological well-being in Vietnamese refugees. Finally, researchers also have discovered a significant relationship between yearnings to return to one's native land and mental health problems. In a study by Westermeyer et al. (1989), Hmong refugees who maintained the wish to return to Asia had a higher probability of exhibiting psychopathology. However, Abe, Zane, and Chun (1994) found that preservation of cultural identity and affiliation with one's ethnic community in the United States acted as protective factors against posttraumatic stress for Southeast Asian refugees. These researchers also found that trauma-related anger played a significant role in adjustment; refugees without PTSD expressed less anger than did their counterparts who suffered from this disorder.

Asian American Vietnam war veterans represent another high-risk group due to their exposure to adverse environmental stressors that compounded the trauma of combat. Many of these veterans encountered racism by fellow U.S. soldiers, faced combat experiences that challenged traditional cultural norms, and identified with a wartime enemy who, in many respects, could be regarded as a fellow Asian (Chun & Abueg, 1989). A Japanese American marine corporal described his experience in a military training class:

> I was used as an example of a gook. You go to class and they say you'll be fighting the VC [Viet Cong] or the NVA [North Vietnamese Army]. But then the person who was giving the class will see me and he'll say, "He looks just like that, right there." (quoted in Hamada, Chembtob, Sautner, & Sato, 1988)

Population estimates from the National Vietnam Veteran Readjustment Study (Kulka et al., 1988) indicate that approximately 34,100 of the 3.1 million men and women who served in the Vietnam war zone were of either Asian American or Pacific Islander descent. Although the prevalence rate of mental illness among Asian American Vietnam veterans is speculative, one study (Matsuoka & Hamada, 1991) reported PTSD rates of 0% for Japanese Americans to 40% for various Pacific Islander groups (e.g., Samoans, Tongans, Guamanians). Although these reported rates remain somewhat speculative due to acknowledged methodological difficulties, they highlight the variable risk status of different Asian American veteran groups.

In respect to the preceding findings, there currently is no conclusive evidence that Asian Americans are more biologically vulnerable to certain mental disorders than are other ethnic groups. However, this does not imply that significant psychobiological differences between Asians and Caucasians do not exist. Research provides strong evidence that Asians and Caucasians differ significantly in their psychobiological reactions to both alcohol and psychotropic medications. Studies of newborn infants also suggest that important psychobiological differences exist between Asians and Caucasians, as evidenced in early developmental differences in temperament and excitability/imperturbability. The role of biology in the development of mental illness among Asian Americans requires further exploration nonetheless.

Studies have uncovered numerous environmental stressors that place Asian immigrants and refugees at increased risk for psychopathology. Such stressors include culture conflicts, language difficulties, lack of social supports, and financial strain that might contribute to the elevated rates of depression and anxiety disorders that have been reported in these communities. Still, Kuo and Tsai (1986) found that Asian immigrants with hardy personality traits are less susceptible to adjustment difficulties than are those without such traits. Settling in the United States poses yet additional environmental stressors to Southeast Asian refugees, many of whom already have faced the trauma of war and political upheaval in their native lands. This traumatized group exhibits elevated rates of PTSD and depression that are even more alarming when group differences and sociodemographics are analyzed. In this case, women in highly traumatized groups, such as the Cambodians and Hmong, are especially vulnerable to psychopathology. Lastly, research also suggests that Asian American Vietnam veterans are at increased risk for mental illness due to their repeated exposure to combat trauma and racial victimization. Because this special group of veterans tends to avoid mental health services for both cultural and sociopolitical reasons, many continue to suffer in silence and have truly become the forgotten warriors of a devastating war.

EXPERIENCE

Does culture affect how Asian Americans experience stressors and psychopathology? Marsella (1988) offered a definition of culture that provides some insight to this question. Marsella defined *culture* as shared learned behavior which is transmitted from one generation to another for purposes of individual and societal growth, adjustment, and adaptation; culture is represented externally as artifacts, roles, and institutions, and it is represented internally as values, beliefs, attitudes, epistemology, consciousness, and biological functioning. (pp. 8-9)

In this context, culture may be regarded as the basis from which Asian Americans experience mental illness; it plays an important role in shaping traditional health beliefs, coping strategies, representations of the self, and terminology that meaningfully describes physical and emotional states.

The influence of culture on traditional Asian health beliefs is most evident in the Chinese term for psychology itself, which is composed of two characters depicting "heart" and "logic" or "thought." In this sense, the Chinese culture ascribes to the notion that thought is intimately tied to the heart, which is the seat of emotional and physical health. Ying (1990) found support for this cultural construct among immigrant Chinese women who framed the experience of mental illness within this dynamic soma and psyche concept. When asked to conceptualize the problems of a depressed Asian woman in a fictitious scenario, Ying's participants responded by describing the causes and consequences of depression both in psychological (e.g., low/unstable mood) and physiological (e.g., heart problems) terms.

Research also suggests that the Asian American experience of mental illness might reflect Western beliefs of stress and adjustment as well. Loo, Tong, and True (1989) found that mental health beliefs among Chinese residents of San Francisco's Chinatown were more Westernized than expected. In this case, 30% of Loo et al.'s community sample believed that mental disorders were caused by pressures and problems (e.g., overstressed, overworked, pressure at work), whereas 20% attributed them to personality (e.g., too sensitive), 8% to neglect (e.g., lack of love), and 5% to a combination of these causes. Interestingly, only 7% held the more traditional Asian belief that mental disorders were caused by genetic or organic factors. Loo et al. suggested that the participants in their study endorsed more Western-oriented health beliefs because they were more acculturated compared to the samples in previous studies. This is substantiated by the fact that 40% of Loo et al.'s sample had lived in the United States for more than 10 years and 30% had lived in this country for more than 20 years. By contrast, Ying's (1990) participants had resided in the United States for an average of only 2.7 years.

The coping strategies of Asian Americans also might differ from those of other ethnic groups due in part to cultural differences in the conceptualization of mental and physical illness. For instance, the immigrant Chinese women in Ying's (1990) study were more likely to seek professional help (e.g., psychologist, medical doctor, government support) if they conceptualized depressive symptoms in predominantly physiological terms. Conversely, those who emphasized the psychological aspects of depression were more inclined to seek nonprofessional help (e.g., advice from family, husband, friend, or elderly) or rely on their own resources (e.g., no treatment, pleasant activities, social activities, financial improvement, eating nutritious food, comfort self). Along similar lines, Cheung (1987) found that Chinese psychiatric outpatients who reported both physical and psychological symptoms were the quickest to seek professional help. When patients described their problems in purely psychological terms, however, they sought professional help after engaging in self-help strategies. Lastly, patients with purely somatic presentations, representing only a fraction of the entire sample, exhibited a delay in reaching mental health services but were more likely to seek professional help promptly.

Loo et al. (1989) found that Chinatown residents reported varied and complex means of dealing with problems, which argues against cultural homogeneity in the way in which Asian Americans cope. Coping strategies for participants in this particular study ranged from acceptance of fate (e.g., "Fate can't be changed. Whatever happens to me, I would take as a way it's supposed to be") to determination (e.g., "Try to be logical"). However, one-fourth of the participants reported using multiple means of coping that were sequential or dependent on the nature of the problem or consequences of the initially attempted solution. For instance, one participant stated, "I try my best to face and solve [my problems], and I get advice from friends. If it's too hard to solve, I try to forget it."

Cultural representations of the self also may affect how Asian Americans experience mental illness or adjustment problems. Markus and Kitayama (1991) posited that representations of the self and others can influence and even determine the nature of one's experience. Furthermore, they asserted that "self-construals" can be broadly conceptualized in terms of independence versus interdependence depending on the normative tasks of one's culture. One may hypothesize that Asian cultures tend to place a high value on group harmony, thereby reinforcing self-construals of interdependence. This is reflected in the Japanese word for self, *jibun,* which refers to "one's share of the shared life space" (Hamaguchi, 1985). Such representations of the self, which foster group cohesion, might conceivably affect the experience of mental illness for Asian Americans. For instance, Asian Americans might be particularly concerned with conflicts of interdependence such as interpersonal tension, social isolation, and group disharmony. This was evidenced in Ying's (1990) sample of immigrant Chinese women, who consistently conceptualized depression as a catalyst to interpersonal conflict. This finding was especially interesting considering that these women projected this concern onto a fictitious scenario in which interpersonal relationships were not even mentioned. Ying hypothesized that this projection reflected the importance of interpersonal harmony both as a precursor to and as a consequence of positive mental health in the Chinese culture.

Research also suggests that Asians with interdependent representations of the self might attribute interpersonal problems to situational rather than dispositional causes. Okazaki and Zane (1990) found that Asian Americans rated interpersonal problems of overinvolvement (e.g., "I feel too responsible for solving others' problems") and negative assertion (e.g., "I have difficulty letting other people know what I want") as less personally involving (i.e., less personal investment in the problem) and less internally caused than did Caucasians. Furthermore, there was a consistent acculturation effect such that foreign-born Asians rated these interpersonal problems even less personally involving and internally caused than did American-born Asians. Based on these findings, Okazaki and Zane proposed that Asians are more other-directed and situationally oriented than Caucasians; thus, Asians tend to place less emphasis on internal attributions and personal involvement in interpersonal conflict.

Finally, culture may influence how Asians describe and express their emotional and psychological states. Russell (1991) illustrated that emotional and psychological terminology found in Asian cultures often lacks semantic equivalents in Western psychiatric nomenclature. For example, Russell mentioned that the Chinese culture does not possess an exact translation for Western notions of depression, guilt, and anxiety. Furthermore, Cheng (1977) noted that two Chinese words that are similar to "anxiety" are better translated as "tension" and "worry." Tseng and Hsu (1969) stated that "depressed mood," as construed in the West, does not have a cultural equivalent in colloquial Mandarin spoken in Taiwan.

Russell (1991) further mentioned that preliterate societies that speak languages that are least similar to English show the greatest cultural variability in the categorization of emotional states. This has important implications for understanding and treating psychopathology among Southeast Asian refugees such as the Hmong, whose culture is without an indigenous written language. Thus, psychiatric concepts that are rooted in the Western culture, such as depression and anxiety, might fail to capture the psychosocial experience of these preliterate Southeast Asian peoples.

The preceding studies demonstrate that culture may influence numerous aspects of the Asian American experience of mental illness. For the Chinese, the traditional belief in the intertwining soma and psyche relationship may lead to both psychological and physiological conceptualizations of mental illness. Furthermore, such conceptualizations may determine the coping strategies among Asians. Research suggests that those who conceptualize psychopathology in terms of both psychological and physiological causes are the best candidates for seeking professional help. Also, interdependence conflicts such as interpersonal tension, social isolation, and group disharmony might be particularly salient for many Asians who maintain culturally proscribed interdependent representations of the self. Research also suggests that Asians with interdependent self-representations might attribute interpersonal problems according to situational rather than dispositional factors. Still, studies demonstrate that the Asian experience of psychopathology is heterogeneous. Experience appears to vary with acculturation such that mental health beliefs among recently arrived Asians might be more embedded in their native culture compared to those who have resided in the United States for a longer duration. Finally, psychologists and other mental health professionals must be mindful of the fact that psychiatric nomenclature that frequently is used in the West might fail to capture the psychosocial experience for certain segments of the Asian American population, especially for those who come from preliterate societies such as the Hmong refugees.

MANIFESTATION

Do Asian Americans exhibit unique patterns of symptom expression? Research provides strong evidence that Asians do exhibit culturally distinct symptom patterns. This is most evident in various culture-specific syndromes such as *koro* and *hwabyung*. *Koro,* which has been evidenced primarily in the Southeast Asian and Chinese cultures, usually is associated with anxiety symptoms stemming from the fear of genital retraction and often is accompanied by the belief that complete retraction of the genitals into the abdomen will lead to death (Bernstein & Gaw, 1990; Westermeyer, 1989). According to Pang (1990), *hwabyung,* or "fire-illness"— *hwa* meaning both "fire" and "anger" and *byung* meaning "illness"—is predominantly found in the Korean culture. Furthermore, Koreans ascribe this disorder to multiple causes such as lasting anger, disappointments, sadness, miseries, hostility, grudges, and unfulfilled dreams and expectations. *Hwabyung* is manifested in a broad range of physical symptoms ranging from abdominal pain to poor eyesight.

These culture-specific syndromes, which may be regarded as indigenous expressions of distress, are intimately connected to the Asian experience of stress and mental illness, as mentioned previously. For instance, the traditional mind-body concept is evidenced in both *koros* and *hwabyung* such that stress or psychological distress is likewise accompanied by disturbances in somatic functioning. Further evidence for culturally influenced symptom patterns among Asians also can be seen for Western psychiatric syndromes such as depression.

In a study of Asian and Caucasian American college students, ethnic differences were found for items that discriminated between depressed and nondepressed respondents using the Zung Self-Rating Depression Scale (SDS) (Marsella, Kinzie, & Gordon, 1973). Gastrointestinal symptoms such as poor appetite, indigestion, and suffering from gas and belches differentiated depressives from nondepressives for the Chinese and Japanese but not for the Caucasians. However, "the urge to eat when not hungry" discriminated depressives from nondepressives only for the Caucasians. In another study examining depressive symptomatology among college students, Chang (1985) reported that overseas Chinese were more likely to indicate trouble with constipation and feeling restless than were Black and Caucasian Americans.

Depressive symptom patterns also have been investigated in other Asian clinical populations. Cheung, Lau, and Waldmann (1981) studied depressive symptoms among Hong Kong Chinese medical outpatients who initially sought services at a private clinic for general medical complaints. Upon intake, these patients were diagnosed as depressed or nondepressed using a translated Chinese language version of the Hamilton Rating Scale for Depression (HRSD). The most common presenting problems of the depressed group were sleep disturbance, tiredness, headache, menopausal symptoms for the women, loss of appetite, abdominal pain, palpitation, bodily weakness, fearfulness, and epigastric pain. More strikingly, however, none of the depressed patients came to the clinic with initial complaints of sadness, unhappiness, or depressed mood. Still, Cheung and colleagues found that the depressed and nondepressed groups differed significantly on all HRSD items with the exception of the "suspicious of others" item. Fully 82% of the depressed group and only 30% of the nondepressed group acknowledged "feeling sadness" on the HRSD. The most frequently endorsed items for the depressed group were "feeling tired and fatigued," "pains and aches," and gastro-intestinal or cardiovascular symptoms. Tension, nervousness, agitation, and restlessness also were endorsed by a majority of the depressed group.

Kinzie et al. (1982) developed and validated the 15-item Vietnamese language Depression Rating Scale, which provided information on both the universal and culture-variant aspects of depressive symptomatology. Results showed that Vietnamese normals and psychiatric outpatients reported symptoms common to Western psychiatric conceptualizations of depression such as poor appetite, various aches and pains, hopelessness, poor concentration, and exhaustion. Mood items such as "low-spirited" and "sad and bothered" also were readily endorsed. However, within-culture symptom patterns were noticed as well. The Vietnamese respondents reported a pervasive sense of suffering and anxiety surrounding their somatic symptoms. In addition, depression often was accompanied by feelings of shame and dishonor, a strong sense of desperation, fear of "going crazy," and feelings of demoralization associated with the inability to fulfill familial or ancestral obligations.

Unlike the preceding studies, a multination, multicenter, psychiatric epidemiological study conducted by the World Health Organization did not report significant differences in depressive symptoms between Asians and other ethnic groups (Sartorius, Jablensky, Gulbinat, & Ernberg, 1980). One of the centers that participated in this study included 222 Japanese psychiatric outpatients in Nagasaki and Tokyo, Japan. Data from the Schedule for Standardized Assessment of Depressive Disorders (SADD) indicated that patients from each of the study sites (including India, Switzerland, Iran, and Canada) exhibited similar depressive symptoms such as sadness, joylessness, anxiety, tension, lack of energy, loss of interest, loss of ability to concentrate, and ideas of insufficiency, inadequacy, or worthlessness. Although there was a lack of symptomatic variation across the centers, the investigators acknowledged that the SADD might not have adequately measured culture-specific depressive patterns.

Factor analytic studies have been another method of examining symptom patterns in Asians. Principal component factor analysis combined with varimax rotation was applied to the Center for Epidemiologic Studies of Depression scale (CES-D) in Kuo's (1984) study of Asians in Seattle, Ying's (1988) study of Chinese in San Francisco, and Lin's (1989) study of residents in Tienjin, China. Although the reported CES-D factor structures and item indicators for these studies were quite similar to those found in Radloff's (1977) original CES-D study, there also were several important differences. Radloff originally obtained four interpretable factors for the CES-D using predominantly Caucasian communities in the United States. These factors were (1) depressed affect, (2) positive affect, (3) somatic and retarded activity, and (4) interpersonal problems (e.g., unfriendly, disliked, talk less, lonely). However, in Kuo's (1984) study, the four factors that accounted for a total of 53% of the variance were (1) depressed affect and somatic complaints, (2) positive affect, (3) interpersonal problems, and (4) pessimism. Ying (1988) reported three factors that accounted for 43.2% of the variance and that were nearly identical to those found in Radloff's (1977) and Kuo's (1984) studies: (1) depressed affect and somatic complaints, (2) positive affect, and (3) interpersonal problems. Thus, the depressed affect and somatic complaints items emerged as one single factor in both Kuo's (1984) and Ying's (1988) studies. Lin (1989) failed to replicate this latter finding; however, he identified three factors that accounted for 47% of the variance for a sample of mainland Chinese. These factors consisted of (1) somatic-retarded activity, (2) interpersonal problems, and (3) depressed affect or affective mood. Thus, Lin's sample yielded two separate factors for depressed affect and somatic complaints, as originally reported for the Caucasian American sample in Radloff's (1977) study.

The discrepancies in these factor analytic findings were unexpected because it was assumed that the Seattle and San Francisco Chinese, whom presumably were more Americanized than the mainland Chinese, would respond more similarly to Radloff's (1977) sample than would their overseas counterparts. This might be explained by differences in the translation of the CES-D or other methodological procedures. Furthermore, these unexpected findings might be attributed to the fact that acculturation involves other variables such as cultural attitudes, lifestyle practices, and English language proficiency in addition to place of birth or residency. Nevertheless, the CES-D factor analytic results for the two Asian American samples were consistent; depressed affect and somatic complaints emerged as one factor.

Factor analytic studies also have been performed for Zung's SDS. Chang (1985) reported that a mixture of affective and somatic complaints accounted for most of the variance in a Black college student sample, whereas existential (e.g., "loss of interest in life," "feeling that the future is hopeless") and cognitive (e.g., "mind is not alert," "thoughts are confused") concerns contributed to the most variance for Caucasian students. However, the factor that contributed to the most variance for overseas Chinese students was characterized by somatic complaints. Chang noted, however, that the Chinese did not have quantitatively less affective complaints; rather, the affective components were not "grouped" with the somatic symptoms.

These findings were similar to those of Marsella et al.'s (1973) earlier factor analysis of the SDS. In Marsella and colleagues' study, the Japanese, Chinese, and Caucasians all evidenced similar patterns of existential complaints. However, cognitive complaints were somewhat independent for the Japanese and Chinese, whereas cognitive complaints usually were associated with other areas of functioning (e.g., existential complaints) for the Caucasians. For the Chinese, there also appeared to be a clear pattern of depression associated with somatic complaints, whereas the other groups manifested somatic symptoms with other disturbances. Finally, interpersonal complaints proved to be the best indicator of depression mainly for the Japanese.

Factor analytic studies of the CES-D and Zung's SDS demonstrate the centrality of somatic concerns among Asians. The differences in sample populations (e.g., students, community samples, treated cases), instrumentation, and methodology among these studies only serve to strengthen the argument that Asians and Asian Americans manifest depression in ways that are different from other comparison groups.

Cultural differences in symptom expression have been the focus of studies on somatization among Asians. *Somatization* refers to an expression of distress that is manifested as general or vague physical complaints. This might involve general aches and pains in the extremities or head, weakness throughout the body, nausea or upset stomach, or numbness and tingling. Westermeyer, Bouafuely, Neider, and Callies (1989) found several correlates to somatization among Hmong refugees. These included older age, a limited formal education, unemployment, and English nonfluency.

Several theories have been offered to explain the high incidence of somatization among Asians. As suggested previously, traditional health beliefs may lead to the expression of somatic symptoms. Thus, a problem, be it physiological, social, or affective in origin, may be expressed in both physical and psychological domains as specified by the soma and psyche conceptualization of health. It also has been suggested that the shame and stigma that are attached to psychological distress in the Asian culture might inhibit Asians from reporting mental health problems (Sue & Sue, 1987; Tsai, Teng, & Sue, 1980). Mechanic (1980) proposed that reporting physical symptoms might be more "culturally neutral," whereas reporting psychological symptoms is more dependent on social acceptability. Thus, somatization allows Asians to "save face" in the event of psychological distress. Lin (1989) argued that the high rate of somatic complaints among the Chinese reflects cultural rather than cognitive preferences, and given appropriate structured inquiry, the Chinese can express cognitive symptoms. For instance, Lin explained that the open-ended probing of most diagnostic or descriptive instruments might elicit a high number of somatic complaints among the Chinese. Nevertheless, Beiser & Fleming (1986) found no relationship between reports of depressive symptoms and somatization among Southeast Asian refugees. This latter finding disputes the notion that somatization is a substitute for psychosocial distress. Thus, Asians possess the capacity to express themselves in psychological terms, although somatic complaints might predominate their symptom presentation. This was clearly evidenced in Cheung's (1982) sample of Hong Kong Chinese who endorsed psychological symptoms equally as, if not more so, than physiologically based symptoms. According to Rumbaut (1985), researchers often assume that somatization among Asians stems from their tendency to deny or suppress emotions, which only serves to perpetuate cultural stereotypes of Asians. Rumbaut stated,

> Instead of illuminating our understanding of affective processes, the "somatization" concept seems to us to function more as a superficial and prejudicial mode

of dismissing complex psychocultural realities and of discrediting the experience of human suffering of different social classes. While the expression of emotional pain may be socially stigmatized or culturally proscribed in particular situations, the emotional experience of human suffering—certainly as reflected in the [Southeast Asian] refugee experience we have studied—emerges as transcultural and universal. (p. 476)

In sum, the research illustrates that Asians and Asian Americans may exhibit different symptom patterns than do other ethnic groups. This is most evident in studies of various culture-specific syndromes such as koros (as documented in the Chinese and Southeast Asian cultures) and hwabyung (as documented in the Korean culture). Studies of symptom expression for Western constructs of mental health also reveal significant cultural differences. This is especially the case for depression; bodily symptoms that include gastrointestinal problems, headaches, palpitations, and physical weakness may predominate the symptom presentation of depressed Asians. Still, Asians experience emotional distress and have the capacity to express psychological difficulties, although such somatic complaints might be more readily apparent. There are cultural factors that may, nonetheless, contribute to somatization such as cultural stigma and traditional health beliefs. Finally, Rumbaut (1985) contended that the concept of somatization should be reconsidered because it perpetuates Asian stereotypes and often dismisses the notion that emotional suffering transverses cultural boundaries.

PREVALENCE

How are rates of mental disorders determined, and are assessment and diagnostic procedures valid for Asian Americans? Currently, the prevalence of psychopathology in the Asian American population is unknown because of the lack of large-scale studies. Although estimates from the Epidemiologic Catchment Area Study indicated that nearly 20% of the American population either had experienced a mental disorder within the past 6 months or currently were experiencing one, prevalence rates for the Asian American community were not established because of inadequate sampling (Meyers et al., 1984). Researchers have, nonetheless, estimated the rates of mental illness among Asian Americans using treated and untreated case methods. Furthermore, culturally sensitive assessment and diagnostic instruments have been developed that have made important contributions to prevalence studies, as will be discussed later in this section. First, estimated rates of mental illness among Asians, as determined by treated and untreated cases, are examined.

Treated Cases

Researchers have estimated prevalence by examining the number of Asian Americans who have sought services for their mental health needs. Although this treated case method is inadequate because Asian Americans tend to underutilize mental health services, it provides an initial step to gaining a better understanding of the extent of mental disorders among Asian Americans.

Findings from early treated case studies suggested that proportionally far fewer Asian Americans were suffering from mental illnesses compared to other ethnic groups. For instance, Kitano (1969) found that Japanese and Chinese Americans were admitted to California state hospitals from 1960 to 1965 less often than were Caucasian Americans relative to their proportions in the state population. Based on admission rates per 100,000, Japanese rates ranged from 40 to 60, whereas Chinese rates ranged from 70 to 90 each year during the 1960-1965 period. Meanwhile, the Caucasian rates during this period ranged from 150 to 180 per 100,000. Similarly, results from a study conducted by the state of Hawaii (1970) showed that the Chinese, Hawaiians, Japanese, and Filipinos displayed lower hospital admission rates for mental disturbances than did Caucasians during the 1969-1970 period. In that study, Caucasians comprised 48.5% of first admissions to state hospitals, although they accounted for only 39.2% of the population in Hawaii. This was compared to the Japanese (15% of first admissions, 28.3% of the population), Filipinos (8% of first admissions, 12.4% of the population), Hawaiians (0.6% of first admissions, 9.3% of the population), and Chinese (1.5% of first admissions, 6.8% of the population).

Sue and Sue (1974) also reported low utilization rates of mental health services among Asian American college students. For example, Sue and Sue found that only 4% of all students who used a campus psychiatric clinic were Chinese or Japanese American, yet both ethnic groups together comprised approximately 8% of the total student population. Such low utilization rates suggested that the Asian American students were relatively well adjusted compared to their non-Asian counterparts. However, Sue and Sue found that those Asian American students who were treated by the university clinic had higher Minnesota Multiphasic Personality Inventory scale scores and more psychotic profiles than did non-Asian American clients. They consequently argued that the most severely disturbed Asian American clients were more likely to use mental health services than were those with milder problems.

Sue and McKinney (1975) found similar results in a 3-year comprehensive study of Asian American patients who were treated at 17 community mental health centers in the Seattle area. These researchers discovered that only 0.7% of the patients were Asian Americans, although this ethnic group represented approximately 2.4% of the population served by these centers. Congruent with Sue and Sue's (1974) findings, Sue and McKinney (1975) reported that those Asian Americans who sought services were more severely disturbed. Thus, those who used services received a higher proportion of psychotic diagnoses than did Caucasian American patients, even when demographic differences such as age and educational level were controlled.

The preceding research studies illustrate that Asian Americans are more severely impaired despite their underutilization of mental health services. This supports the assertion by Sue and colleagues (Sue & Morishima, 1982; Sue & Sue,

1987) that only the most severely disturbed Asian American clients tend to seek treatment. This also was evidenced by Brown, Stein, Huang, and Harris (1973), who found that Chinese American inpatients at a community mental health center exhibited more serious psychotic behaviors than did Caucasian inpatients, although the two groups did not differ on psychiatric diagnosis and were matched on sex, age, and economic and legal admission status. More recently, records for all adult inpatient and outpatient clients seen in the Los Angeles County mental health system from 1983 to 1988 revealed that a greater proportion of Asian American clients received psychotic diagnoses than did Caucasian American clients (Flaskerud & Hu, 1992). In addition, Asian Americans were diagnosed with major affective disorders more often than were African or Latino Americans, and a greater number of Asian Americans than Caucasian Americans were diagnosed with schizophrenia. Finally, in another study that focused on Chinese and Caucasian American outpatients who used Los Angeles County mental health services, Eastman (1991) found that proportionally more Chinese Americans than Caucasian Americans were diagnosed with major depression.

Untreated Cases

Prevalence rates of psychopathology also can be estimated by examining untreated community samples rather than treated client populations. Researchers following this method assess psychopathology by using self-report measures, interviews, or rating instruments, often through face-to-face or telephone contact with community residents. A few untreated case studies have suggested that the rates of psychopathology in the Asian American community might be as high as, or even higher than, those in other ethnic communities.

From their interviews of adult residents in a large Chinatown community, Loo et al. (1989) found that more than one-third of their sample admitted to symptoms of emotional tension. Feelings of depression also were common among the residents, with 4 out of 10 complaining of a "sinking feeling like being depressed." In addition, a quarter of the residents admitted to having "periods of days, weeks, or months when [they] couldn't take care of things because [they] couldn't get going." In regard to feelings of loneliness, more than half of the respondents wished that there was someone they could really talk to. Furthermore, loneliness was surprisingly more prevalent among younger adults than among the elderly. Finally, Loo and colleagues reported that 35% of the respondents endorsed four or more items on the Langner Scale, whereas 20% acknowledged seven or more items. Such endorsement rates on the Langner Scale traditionally have been considered to be indications of psychiatric impairment. The two most frequently endorsed Langner Scale items included "a memory that's not all right" (40%) and "worrying a lot" (42%). Loo and colleagues concluded that the former result might have been related to the predominant elderly representation in the Chinatown community and the latter to the combination of disadvantaged status and age. Although this sample was not representative of the general Chinese American population, this study points to the levels of distress in a particular ethnic Chinese enclave.

Several studies have examined the rates of depression among Asian Americans using the CES-D. Surveying Asian Americans living in Seattle, Kuo (1984) found that Chinese, Japanese, Filipino, and Korean American immigrants reported slightly more depressive symptoms, on average, than did Caucasian respondents in other studies. Also using the CES-D, Hurh and Kim (1990) similarly found that Korean immigrants residing in Chicago had higher scores for depression than did Caucasians. High rates of depression were once again revealed in a telephone survey of Chinese Americans in San Francisco. Using the CES-D, Ying (1988) conducted a telephone survey among Chinese Americans in the San Francisco area and found them to be significantly more depressed than the Chinese Americans in Kuo's study. Still, it is difficult to compare the CES-D findings among these studies given their differences in methodological and sampling procedures.

In a review of the literature on the mental health of various ethnic minority groups, Vega and Rumbaut (1991) remarked that knowledge of Asian Americans is much less developed than for African Americans and Latinos and that no national-level epidemiological surveys have been conducted with this ethnic population. Nevertheless, tentative conclusions can be derived from the treated and untreated case studies presented here. First, there is no indication that Asian Americans have lower rates of mental disturbance than those of Caucasians, especially when rates of depression are considered. Second, there are important within-group differences (e.g., between Koreans and Chinese) in the prevalence of disorders among Asian Americans.

The validity of diagnostic and assessment procedures is a central issue in studying the rate and distribution of mental disorders among Asian Americans. If case-finding strategies or assessment procedures are inappropriate or culturally biased, then it is difficult, if not impossible, to accurately estimate the prevalence of disorders. Although reasonable efforts have been made by investigators to consider the issue of cultural bias in assessment, it is difficult to determine the actual extent to which cultural factors affect assessment findings.

Past case illustrations indicate that Asian American clients might be overdiagnosed (i.e., inappropriately defined as psychiatric cases) when cultural influences on symptom presentation are overlooked. Westermeyer (1987) illustrated a case of overdiagnosis of a 48-year-old Chinese woman who was given antipsychotic and antidepressant medication for psychotic depression. According to Westermeyer, a decisive factor in her diagnosis lay in her belief that her deceased mother, whom she had seen in her dreams, had returned to bring her into the next world. Later, it was recognized that this symptom was not indicative of a delusional disorder but instead was congruent with her cultural beliefs. The patient's condition improved once her antipsychotic medication was discontinued and the dosage of her antidepressants was reduced.

By contrast, behaviors that appear to be normative to the Asian culture might, in fact, indicate mental illness on closer inspection. For example, Westermeyer (1987) presented a clinical case involving a 26-year-old Vietnamese refugee who spoke in a philosophical manner and wore religious garb on admission to a psychiatric clinic. The attending psychiatric resident's diagnosis revealed minor anxiety symptoms but no serious psychopathology. However, information from the patient's ethnic peers revealed that the patient wore odd clothing and held bizarre religious notions that were inconsistent with their cultural norms. Further evaluation showed that the patient viewed himself as a reincarnation of Buddha, Christ, and Mohammed who had been sent to save the world. In addition, organic testing indicated that the patient suffered from brain damage.

Language barriers pose additional challenges in the assessment of Asian Americans. As mentioned previously, researchers have argued that many non-Western languages do not possess cultural equivalents for numerous Western psychological constructs. Interpreters often cannot overcome such language barriers and, even worse, might further compound the difficulties in assessing Asian American clients. As Sue and Sue (1987) mentioned, the inclusion of interpreters expands the therapeutic process to a triadic situation, thus increasing the risk for miscommunication and inaccurate diagnoses. Marcos (1979) also found that the attitudes and personal beliefs of the interpreters might distort their translations. In this case, an interpreter might minimize pathology or avoid culturally sensitive issues such as sexual relations and death, especially if the interpreter is related to the client.

Given these difficulties in the assessment and diagnosis of Asian Americans, what can be done to improve measurement strategies? Sue and Sue (1987) provided a conceptual overview of measurement strategies that have been used with ethnic minority groups. The first strategy, point research, entails the application of measures of one culture with members in a different culture. In this case, scores on the measures are compared between cultures and are interpreted according to the norms of the culture from which the instrument was developed. For example, the Hopkins Symptom Checklist, which was developed in the West, was translated for use with Southeast Asian refugees (Mollica, Wyshak, de Marneffe, Khuon, and Lavelle (1987). Clearly, there are potential problems in using this point research approach. One must be cautious in using emic (or culturally specific) assessment instruments in an etic (or cross-cultural) manner. By using a culturally specific assessment tool in another culture, one is assuming that all cultures share the same construct that is to be measured. The inherent difficulties of point research are illustrated in a study by Takeuchi, Kuo, Kim, and Leaf (1989), who found that 54 scale items on the Symptom Checklist (SCL) did not correspond to the SCL's five hypothesized factors (anxiety, depression, interpersonal sensitivity, obsessive-compulsive, and somatization) among four ethnic groups that resided in Hawaii. Among the different groups, Caucasians appeared to have the best fit between empirical and hypothesized factors on the SCL, followed by the Japanese, Filipinos, and Native Hawaiians. Kinzie and his colleagues (1982) similarly showed that the Beck Depression Inventory exhibited low reliability and validity among the Vietnamese. These studies illustrate that the validity and reliability of point research findings often are open to question.

The second assessment strategy, linear research, involves a series of studies that are used to systematically test hypotheses related to the construct under investigation. Similar to the point research strategy, a measure is developed in one culture and then applied to another culture. However, in linear research, several studies using the measure are conducted to provide additional points of reference from which to compare groups. The construct of interest can then be considered etic in nature (or suitable for cross-cultural comparison) if the hypotheses in each study are supported. A multimethod approach is another strategy that is related to the linear model in that several tests are conducted but with multiple measures to test a particular construct. Consistent differences across measures in support of hypotheses provide strong evidence that real cross-cultural differences exist. However, incongruence between findings across measures leads to problematic construct validity.

Finally, in a parallel assessment approach, a combined etic-emic strategy is followed such that an etic construct is identified and then an emic measure is developed to test the validity and reliability of the construct in each culture. Cross-cultural comparisons are made based on the emically defined construct. This approach offers a comparative evaluation of a construct across cultures without restriction from any single cultural frame of reference. An illustration of the parallel approach is found in a study by Kinzie (1982) describing the development of the Vietnamese Depression Inventory. In short, Kinzie and colleagues (1982) collaborated with four bilingual Vietnamese mental health workers to develop a measure of depression for Vietnamese patients using Vietnamese words that described feelings or behaviors associated with depression. After a series of validity and reliability procedures were conducted, it was found that differences between Vietnamese and Western reports of depression were attributed to culturally distinct constructs. Adoption of research strategies with parallel approaches is difficult to conduct, but these strategies are ultimately the most valuable because they enable us to accurately assess psychopathology for different cultural groups.

The preceding studies show that our knowledge of the nature and extent of psychopathology among the Asian American population is growing but still quite limited. Nevertheless, data from treated and untreated case methods indicate that Asian Americans do not have lower rates of mental disturbance than Caucasians. Furthermore, there are significant within-group differences in prevalence rates among Asian Americans. Many of our current diagnostic and assessment procedures that are used in prevalence studies have been validated using Caucasian populations, which might contribute to cultural bias toward Asian Americans. Culture-specific instruments, as applied in parallel research, might help resolve this dilemma by using the native language and emic constructs of a particular culture to assess its psychocultural experience.

CONCLUDING COMMENTS

The proposed Vulnerability-Experience-Manifestation-Prevalence model highlights the role of culture and minority group status in these primary components of psychopathology. However, there are numerous questions that are left unanswered. For example, in regard to Vulnerability, future research could address questions such as "What is the role of psychobiology in mental illness for Asian Americans?" Studies also could further examine the process of adjustment among traumatized Southeast Asian refugees. In this case, the impact of PTSD on the functioning of the Southeast Asian family remains unclear. One can only speculate on the magnitude of problems that Southeast Asian families experience given that multiple family members often suffer from the debilitating effects of PTSD.

In regard to Experience, future research could investigate how the organization and perception of adjustment problems affects the outcome of psychotherapy for Asian clients. For example, one can hypothesize that outcome is more favorable for Asian clients if they hold similar notions of the causes and nature of adjustment problems as their therapists. Moreover, such incidences of "cognitive match" might be more likely if both the therapist and client share the same ethnic background or cultural beliefs. These issues currently are being investigated in a study conducted by the National Research Center on Asian American Mental Health.

Questions also remain regarding the Manifestation of psychopathology among Asian Americans. The cultural mechanisms in symptom expression could be further explored. For instance, studies could resolve the conflicting findings on the relationship between acculturation and somatization. This could be achieved by first developing a comprehensive index of acculturation that evaluates acculturation on a global level to include demographic background, cultural attitudes, and traditional practices. Such a global measure of acculturation could then be used to identify those who are more likely to somaticize their distress. Past research on symptom expression and help-seeking behavior suggests that this has important implications for developing treatment services that are responsive to Asian clients who may be more inclined to first seek medical help for underlying psychopathological conditions.

Finally, large-scale studies that use culturally sensitive measures are needed to determine the Prevalence of mental disorders among Asian Americans. Toward this end, current measures used in the study of psychopathology need to be assessed for their validity in various ethnic groups. Multimethod approaches need to be used, and where constructs are found to be invalid, emic measures might need to be developed in accordance with the parallel assessment approach. One recent development might have major implications for understanding the prevalence of psychopathology in the Asian American population. The National Research Center on Asian American Mental Health has been awarded a National Institute of Mental Health research grant to conduct a 5-year, large-scale study of the prevalence of mental disorders among Chinese Americans. The intention of this study is to ascertain the rate and distribution of mental disorders and identify correlates (e.g., immigrant status, stressors, resources) to mental health. It is hoped that insights into processes that affect mental health will be gained, not only for Chinese Americans but also for Asian Americans in general.

Recommendations

Several conceptual and methodological recommendations might advance these future studies of psychopathology among Asian Americans. First, on a conceptual level, existing models of psychopathology should be evaluated to determine whether they are valid for Asian Americans. For example, research indicates that the stress-coping model of mental illness may be applied to Asian American populations such as Southeast Asian refugees whose adjustment has been linked to both coping resources, such as social and financial supports, and exposure to environmental stressors. Second, if such models prove to be valid, then their individual elements should be analyzed to determine whether they are fundamentally different for Asian Americans. Using the stress-coping model as an example once again, one might argue that there are important cultural differences within this model, although its overall theoretical scheme applies to Asian Americans. For instance, Asian Americans might initiate unique coping strategies because they perceive stress in a culturally distinct manner. This was evidenced in the Experience section of this chapter, which illustrated that Asians may perceive or organize stress on a primarily somatic basis, which in turn influences their help-seeking behavior. Third, such instances of cultural variability should be organized to formulate a new model of psychopathology that builds on the theories of existing models. The stress-coping model might therefore develop into a more complex model that accounts for the influence of cultural attitudes, beliefs, problem perception, and even traditional health practices that are embedded in Asian cultures.

This conceptual scheme integrates the multimethod and parallel assessment approaches mentioned earlier. For instance, the overall stress-coping model may be considered etic in nature, but cultural differences might exist within its individual elements. Using the parallel assessment approach, an emic measure can then be developed that better identifies and measures the construct within the Asian American population. The integration of emic elements thus contributes to the relevance and validity of the overall model.

These conceptual issues in the study of Asian American psychopathology can be examined using a two-stage methodological strategy. In the first stage, a microanalysis of a heterogeneous Asian American sample can be performed. This would entail gathering data on indigenous conceptualizations and expressions of psychopathology from a small cross section of Asian American groups through a series of in-depth interviews. This would allow researchers to identify important cultural constructs of mental health and to estimate group differences or heterogeneity across Asian American populations. The second stage would involve the evaluation of the data gathered from the first stage on a macro level using a larger sample. However, practical constraints would prevent in-depth analysis of a larger sample; thus, the best possible instruments must be selected from existing measures, or new measures might have to be developed based on the microanalytic data from the first stage. Finally, the selected measures can then be applied in an epidemiological study throughout the Asian American population that will identify and describe those factors that might contribute to or prevent psychopathology.

REFERENCES

Abe, J. S., & Zane, N. W. S. (1990). Psychological maladjustment among Asian and White American college students: Controlling for confounds. *Journal of Counseling Psychology, 37,* 437-444.

Abe, J. S., Zane, N. W. S., & Chun, K. M. (1994). Differential responses to trauma: Migration-related discriminants of post-traumatic stress disorder among Southeast Asian refugees. *Journal of Community Psychology, 22,* 121-135.

Akutsu, P. D., Sue, S., Zane, N. W., & Nakamura, C. Y. (1989). Ethnic differences in alcohol consumption among Asians and Caucasians in the United States: An investigation of cultural and physiological factors. *Journal of Studies on Alcohol, 50,* 261-267.

American Psychiatric Association. (1987). *Diagnostic and statistical manual of mental disorders* (3rd ed., rev.). Washington, DC: Author.

Beiser, M. (1988). Influences of time, ethnicity, and attachment on depression in Southeast Asian refugees. *American Journal of Psychiatry, 145,* 46-51.

Beiser, M., & Fleming, J. A. (1986). Measuring psychiatric disorder among Southeast Asian refugees. *Psychological Medicine, 16,* 627-639.

Bernstein, R. L., & Gaw, A. C. (1990). Koro: Proposed classification for DSM-IV. *American Journal of Psychiatry, 147,* 1670-1674.

Brown, T. R., Stein, K. M., Huang, K., & Harris, D. E. (1973). Mental illness and the role of mental health facilities in Chinatown. In S. Sue & N. Wagner (Eds.), *Asian Americans: Psychological perspectives* (pp. 212-231). Palo Alto, CA: Science and Behavior Books.

Chang, W. C. (1985). A cross-cultural study of depressive symptomatology. *Culture, Medicine, and Psychiatry, 9,* 295-317.

Cheng, T. (1977). *A phenomenological study of emotional experience: A search for cultural differences and similarities in the construction of emotion by a Hong Kong Chinese sample.* Unpublished master's thesis, University of Hong Kong.

Cheung, F. M. (1982). Psychological symptoms among Chinese in urban Hong Kong. *Social Science and Medicine, 16,* 1334-1339.

Cheung, F. M. (1987). Conceptualization of psychiatric illness and help-seeking behavior among Chinese. *Culture, Medicine, and Psychiatry, 11,* 97-106.

Cheung, F. M., Lau, B. W., & Waldmann, E. (1981). Somatization among Chinese depressives in general practice. *International Journal of Psychiatry in Medicine, 10,* 361-374.

Chun, K. M. (1991, August). *Predictors of adjustment among Southeast Asian refugees.* Paper presented at the annual convention of the Asian American Psychological Association, San Francisco.

Chun, K. M., & Abueg, F. R. (1989, May). *An Ericksonian conceptualization of cultural factors in the adjustment of an Asian American Vietnam veteran.* Paper presented at the 18th annual Western Psychology Conference, Santa Clara, CA.

Crowe, R. R., Noyes, R., Jr., Pauls, D. L., & Slymen, D. (1983). A family study of panic disorder. *Archives of General Psychiatry, 40,* 1065-1069.

Eastman, K. L. (1991, August). *Social and demographic variations between depressed Chinese Americans and Caucasians.* Paper presented at the annual convention of the Asian American Psychological Association, San Francisco.

Flaskerud, J. H., & Hu, L. (1992). Relationship of ethnicity to psychiatric diagnosis. *Journal of Nervous and Mental Disease, 180,* 296-303.

Freedman, D. G. (1975). Culture, inbreeding, and behavior: With some thoughts on inter-ethnic communication. In L. Levi (Ed.), *Society, stress and disease,* Vol. 2: *Childhood and adolescence.* Oxford, UK: Oxford University Press.

Gong-Guy, E. (1987). *The California Southeast Asian mental health needs assessment* (Contract No. 85-76282A-2). Sacramento: California State Department of Mental Health.

Goodwin, D. W., & Guze, S. B. (1984). *Psychiatric diagnosis* (3rd ed.). New York: Oxford University Press.

Hamada, R. S., Chemtob, C. C., Sautner, B., & Sato, R. (1988). Ethnic identity and Vietnam: A Japanese-American Vietnam veteran with PTSD. *Hawaii Medical Journal, 47,* 100-109.

Hamaguchi, E. (1985). A contextual model of the Japanese: Toward a methodological innovation in Japan studies. *Journal of Japanese Studies, 11,* 289-321.

Hurh, W. M., & Kim, K. C. (1990). Correlates of Korean immigrants' mental health. *Journal of Nervous and Mental Disease, 178,* 703-711.

Kendler, K. S. (1983). A current perspective on twin studies of schizophrenia. *American Journal of Psychiatry, 140,* 1413-1425.

Kendler, K. S. (1988). Familial aggregation of schizophrenia and schizophrenic spectrum disorders. *Archives of General Psychiatry, 45,* 377-383.

Kinzie, J., Boehnlein, J. K., Leung, P. K., Moore, L. J., Riley, C., & Smith, D. (1990). The prevalence of posttraumatic stress disorder and its clinical significance among Southeast Asian refugees. *American Journal of Psychiatry, 147,* 913-917.

Kinzie, J., Manson, S. M., Vinh, D. T., Tolan, N. G., Anh, B., & Pho, T. N. (1982). Development and validation of a Vietnamese-language depression rating scale. *American Journal of Psychiatry, 139,* 1276-1281.

Kinzie, J., Sack, W., Angell, R., Clarke, G., & Ben, R. (1989). A three-year follow-up of Cambodian young people traumatized as children. *Journal of the American Academy of Child and Adolescent Psychiatry, 28,* 501-504.

Kitano, H. H. (1969). Japanese-American mental illness. In S. Plog & R. Edgerton (Eds.), *Changing perspectives in mental illness* (pp. 256-284). New York: Holt, Rinehart & Winston.

Kleinman, A. (1988). *Rethinking psychiatry: From cultural category to personal experience.* New York: Free Press.

Kulka, R. A., Schlenger, W. E., Fairbank, J. A., Hough, R. L., Jordan, B. K., Marmar, C. R., & Weiss, D. S. (1988). *Contractual report of findings from the National Vietnam Veterans Readjustment Study,* Vol. 1: *Executive summary, description of findings, and technical appendices.* Research Triangle Park, NC: Research Triangle Institute.

Kuo, W. H. (1984). Prevalence of depression among Asian-Americans. *Journal of Nervous and Mental Disease, 172,* 449-457.

Kuo, W. H., & Tsai, Y. M. (1986). Social networking, hardiness, and immigrants' mental health. *Journal of Health and Social Behavior, 27,* 133-149.

Lin, K. M., Lau, J. K., Smith, R., Phillips, P., Antal, E., & Poland, R. E. (1988). Comparison of alprazolam plasma levels in normal Asian and Caucasian male volunteers. *Psychopharmacology, 96,* 365-369.

Lin, K. M., Poland, R. E., & Lesser, I. M. (1986). Ethnicity and psychopharmacology. *Culture, Medicine, and Psychiatry, 10,* 151-165.

Lin, K. M., Poland, R. E., Nuccio, I., Matsuda, K., Hathue, N., Su, T., & Fu, P. (1989). A longitudinal assessment of haloperidol doses and serum concentrations in Asian and Caucasian schizophrenic patients. *American Journal of Psychiatry, 146,* 1307-1311.

Lin, K. M., Poland, R. E., Smith, M. W., Strickland, T. L., & Mendoza, R. (1991). Pharmacokinetic and other related factors affecting psychotropic responses in Asians. *Psychopharmacology Bulletin, 27,* 427-439.

Lin, K. M., Tazuma, L., & Masuda, M. (1979). Adaptational problems of Vietnamese refugees: I. Health and mental health status. *Archives of General Psychiatry, 36,* 955-961.

Lin, N. (1989). Measuring depressive symptomatology in China. *Journal of Nervous and Mental Disease, 177*(3), 121-131.

Loo, C., Tong, B., & True, R. (1989). A bitter bean: Mental health status and attitudes in Chinatown. *Journal of Community Psychology, 17,* 283-296.

Marcos, L. R. (1979). Effects of interpreters on the evaluation of psychopathology in non-English-speaking patients. *American Journal of Psychiatry, 136,* 171-174.

Markus, H. R., & Kitayama, S. (1991). Culture and the self: Implications for cognition, emotion, and motivation. *Psychological Bulletin, 98,* 224-253.

Marsella, A. (1988). Cross-cultural research on severe mental disorders: Issues and findings. *Acta Psychiatrica Scandinavica, 78*(344), 7-22.

Marsella, A. J., Kinzie, J., & Gordon, P. (1973). Ethnic variations in the expression of depression. *Journal of Cross-Cultural Psychology, 4,* 435-458.

Matsuoka, J., & Hamada, R. (1991). The wartime and postwar experiences of Asian-Pacific American veterans. *Journal of Applied Social Sciences, 16,* 23-36.

Mechanic, D. (1980). The experience and reporting of common physical complaints. *Journal of Health and Social Behavior, 1,* 146-155.

Meehl, P. E. (1962). Schizotaxia, schizotypia, schizophrenia. *American Psychologist, 17,* 827-838.

Meyers, J. K., Weissman, M. M., Tischler, G. L., Holzer, C. E., Leaf, P. J., Orvaschel, H., Anthony, J. C., Boyd, J. H., Burke, J. D., Kramer, M., & Stoltzman, R. (1984). Six-month prevalence of psychiatric disorders in three communities. *Archives of General Psychiatry, 41,* 959-967.

Mollica, R., Wyshak, G., de Marneffe, D., Khuon, F., & Lavelle, J. (1987). Indochinese versions of the Hopkins Symptom Checklist-25: A screening instrument for the psychiatric care of refugees. *American Journal of Psychiatry, 144,* 497-500.

Mollica, R., Wyshak, G., & Lavelle, J. (1987). The psychosocial impact of war trauma and torture on Southeast Asian refugees. *American Journal of Psychiatry, 144,* 1567-1572.

Nicassio, P. M., & Pate, J. K. (1984). An analysis of problems of resettlement of the Indochinese refugees in the United States. *Social Psychiatry, 19,* 135-141.

Nicassio, P. M., Solomon, G. S., Guest, S. S., & McCullough, J. E. (1986). Emigration stress and language proficiency as correlates of depression in a sample of Southeast Asian refugees. *International Journal of Social Psychiatry, 32*(1), 2-28.

Okazaki, S., & Zane, N. (1990, April). *Conceptualization of mental health problems among Asian Americans.* Paper presented at the annual convention of the Western Psychological Association, Los Angeles.

Pang, K. Y. C. (1990). Hwabyung: The construction of a Korean popular illness among Korean elderly immigrant women in the United States. *Culture, Medicine, and Psychiatry, 14,* 495-512.

Radloff, L. (1977). The CES-D scale: A self-report depression scale for research in the general population. *Applied Psychological Measurement, 1,* 385-401.

Rosenthal, D. (1970). *Genetic theory and abnormal behavior.* New York: McGraw-Hill.

Rumbaut, R. (1985). Mental health and the refugee experience: A comparative study of Southeast Asian refugees. In T. C. Owan (Ed.), *Southeast Asian mental health: Treatment, prevention, services, training, and research* (pp. 433-486). Washington, DC: National Institute of Mental Health.

Russell, J. A. (1991). Culture and the categorization of emotions. *Psychological Bulletin, 110,* 426-450.

Sarason, I. G., Johnson, J. H., & Siegel, J. M. (1978). Assessing the impact of life changes: Development of the Life Experience Survey. *Journal of Consulting and Clinical Psychology, 46,* 932-946.

Sartorius, N., Jablensky, A., Gulbinat, W., & Ernberg, G. (1980). WHO collaborative study: Assessment of depressive disorders. *Psychological Medicine, 10,* 743-749.

State of Hawaii. (1970). *Statistical report of the Department of Health.* Honolulu, HI: Department of Health.

Sue, D., & Sue, S. (1987). Cultural factors in the clinical assessment of Asian Americans. *Journal of Consulting and Clinical Psychology, 55,* 479-487.

Sue, S., & McKinney, H. (1975). Asian-Americans in the community mental health care system. *American Journal of Orthopsychiatry, 45,* 111-118.

Sue, S., & Morishima, J. (1982). *The mental health of Asian Americans.* San Francisco: Jossey-Bass.

Sue, S., & Sue, D. W. (1974). MMPI comparisons between Asian American and non-Asian students utilizing a student health psychiatric clinic. *Journal of Counseling Psychology, 21,* 423-427.

Sue, S., & Zane, N. W. S. (1985). Academic achievement and socioemotional adjustment among Chinese university students. *Journal of Counseling Psychology, 32,* 570-579.

Takeuchi, D. T., Kuo, H. S., Kim, K., & Leaf, P. J. (1989). Psychiatric symptom dimensions among Asian Americans and Native Hawaiians: An analysis of the Symptom Checklist. *Journal of Community Psychology, 17,* 319-329.

Torgersen, S. (1983). Genetic factors in anxiety disorders. *Archives of General Psychiatry, 40,* 1085-1089.

Tran, T. V. (1989). Ethnic community supports and psychological well-being of Vietnamese refugees. *International Migration Review, 21,* 833-845.

Tsai, M., Teng, L. N., & Sue, S. (1980). Mental health status of Chinese in the United States. In A. Kleinman & T. Y. Lin (Eds.), *Normal and abnormal behavior in Chinese culture* (pp. 291-310). Boston: D. Reidel.

Tseng, W., & Hsu, J. (1969). Chinese culture, personality formation, and mental illness. *International Journal of Social Psychiatry, 16,* 5-14.

Vega, W. A., & Rumbaut, R. G. (1991). Ethnic minorities and mental health. *Annual Review of Sociology, 17,* 351-383.

Westermeyer, J. (1987). Cultural factors in clinical assessment. *Journal of Consulting and Clinical Psychology, 55,* 471-478.

Westermeyer, J. (1988). DSM-III psychiatric disorders among Hmong refugees in the United States: A point prevalence study. *American Journal of Psychiatry, 145,* 197-202.

Westermeyer, J. (1989). A case of koro in a refugee family: Association with depression and folie a deux. *Journal of Clinical Psychiatry, 50,* 181-183.

Westermeyer, J., Bouafuely, M., Neider, J., & Callies, A. (1989). Somatization among refugees: An epidemiologic study. *Psychosomatics, 30*(1), 34-43.

Westermeyer, J., Neider, J., & Callies, A. (1989). Psychosocial adjustment of Hmong refugees during their first decade in the United States: A longitudinal study. *Journal of Nervous and Mental Disease, 177*(3), 132-139.

Ying, Y. (1988). Depressive symptomatology among Chinese-Americans as measured by the CES-D. *Journal of Clinical Psychology, 44,* 739-746.

Ying, Y. (1990). Explanatory models of major depression and implications for help-seeking among immigrant Chinese-American women. *Culture, Medicine, and Psychiatry, 14,* 393-408.

15

MENTAL HEALTH SERVICES AND TREATMENT

JEAN LAU CHIN

In general, the literature on mental health services and treatment for Asian Americans has been sparse. With the rapid growth of the Asian population in the United States (which doubled between 1980 and 1990) and the growing diversity within the Asian American population, the challenges of providing relevant and effective mental health services and treatment to Asian Americans are significant. Much of the early empirical work was on Chinese and Japanese American populations, primarily from California or Hawaii. More recent work has focused on Southeast Asians as the new Asian Americans. Several reviews of the literature exist in describing mental health services to Asian Americans; this chapter reviews the literature since 1986 (Leong, 1986; Sue & Morishima, 1982).

A predominant perception is that Asian Americans experience few mental health problems, have little need for mental health services, and have sufficient resources; this perception continues despite substantial unmet needs and gaps in services (Wong, 1977). Several trends can be identified in the clinical literature on mental health treatment with Asian Americans and other ethnic minorities.

As Comas-Diaz (1992) pointed out, the ethnic minority literature began with a reactive approach to "mainstream research," moved to an inquisitive approach of consciousness raising, and currently is involved in a revisionist approach. Work with Asian Americans parallels this direction, with an early emphasis in the literature on comparing Asian Americans to Whites on some psychological dimension or service utilization criteria (Arkoff, 1959; Meredith, 1966), that is, reactive. Unfortunately, these early approaches served to reinforce the perception of different as pathological. Consequently, Asian Americans often were labeled as more pathological and as poor candidates for psychotherapy. As the ethnic consciousness of Asian Americans was raised, the literature began to reflect the unique characteristics of Asian culture and to question the relevance of "standard" approaches for Asian American clients. This resulted in advocacy for cultural sensitivity, bilingual/bicultural mental health providers, and the development of cross-cultural training skills (Sue, 1981). Implications for treatment often emphasized the acquisition of culture-specific knowledge, raised questions of ethnic match, and emphasized the development of therapist sensitivity (Shon & Ja, 1982; Toupin, 1980).

Currently, there is an emphasis on revising existing approaches and/or developing new approaches to be more responsive to the differences found among Asian American clients. Consistent with the women's movement in psychotherapy, this has meant an increased emphasis on empowerment of Asian American clients within psychotherapy. As clinicians and researchers move beyond cultural sensitivity, this has meant a search for theoretical models that reflect cultural differences and examination of specific variables important to effective treatment with Asian American clients. It also has meant a questioning of the ethnocentric bias and the use of "classical" perspectives as universal. This emphasis reflects a movement away from traditional Western standards as the model for comparing relevance when working with ethnic minority populations.

It is this perspective that guides this review of the literature in mental health services and treatment with Asian Americans. Although commonality exists among different Asian American groups, there also is considerable diversity by country of origin, generations in the United States, language, ethnic group, and the like that must be factored into the provision of mental health services and treatment. The historical and cultural context of each ethnic group together with individual and family experience will significantly influence differences in clinical presentation and practice.

EVALUATION OF MENTAL HEALTH SERVICES AND PSYCHOTHERAPY

Although the methods for the evaluation of psychotherapy have been controversial in general, still other considerations emerge when we consider those used in the evaluation of psychotherapy with Asian Americans. Specifically, the use of empirical data (i.e., research) over clinical case studies as the more relevant method has been questioned. As Strupp (1986) pointed out, practitioners remained skeptical that researchers had much to contribute to their professional practice, and there remained prevalent the view that the clinical literature was richer, more insightful, more relevant, and more useful to the practicing therapist than were the growing number of research publications.

Second, the evaluation of therapeutic outcomes, the subject of many research studies, could not be separated from process variables that stress the quality and function of the interpersonal systems in which the patient participates. From an

Asian American perspective, these process variables, which define the client and therapist relationship from a Western perspective, raise questions of their validity for effectiveness of psychotherapy when the client is operating from dominant values, worldviews, and perspectives that are different. Are we introducing other artifacts, intrinsic to research methodology, when we evaluate psychotherapy effectiveness among Asian Americans using methods validated within a Western-dominated perspective? Do we miss those process variables crucial to defining cultural empathy when we try to operationalize therapeutic outcomes within a static empirical framework? Should we use comparative models that presume Western culture as the standard for utilization, outcome, and process in psychotherapy with Asian Americans?

These questions have had an impact on the literature in several ways. Empirical studies of treatment with Asian Americans have been sparse compared to case study approaches that emphasize identifying special needs or problems of providing psychotherapy with Asian Americans (Nishio & Bilmes, 1987). Much of the literature consists of treatment strategies and recommendations for working with Asian Americans (see Leong, 1986, for a review) and advocates for sensitivity to specific cultural attitudes and knowledge.

ENTRY TO SERVICES: HELP-SEEKING BEHAVIORS

Because of a holistic emphasis within Asian cultures, there often is a belief among Asians that the health of the body and mind are inseparable. Consequently, help-seeking behaviors among Asian clients often take the form of somatization and emphasis on medication (Cheung & Lau, 1982; Lorenzo & Adler, 1984; Moon & Tashima, 1982).

Second, Asian clients frequently expect advice and information from a therapist and tend to view the therapist as an authority figure (Leong, 1986; Yuen & Tinsley, 1981). Sometimes this is related to social class, and other times it is related to expectations of authority figures and family elders to be advice givers.

Third, the concept of psychotherapy is unfamiliar and/or unacceptable to many Asian American clients. For immigrants and refugees, solutions to life problems often are sought through friends, family, and/or religious leaders rather than through psychotherapists (Moon & Tashima, 1982; Nishio & Bilmes, 1987). Shame and stigma often are associated with mental illness (Kinzie & Mason, 1983).

Ying (1990) explored explanatory models of major depression among recently immigrated Chinese American women. Those who provided a psychological conceptualization tended to turn to family and friends for help, whereas those who held a physical conceptualization were more likely to seek out medical services.

Despite these commonalities observed about help-seeking behaviors among Asian American clients, few have systematically studied differences in immigration history, educational levels, and socioeconomic status as defining differences in help-seeking behaviors.

UTILIZATION OF MENTAL HEALTH SERVICES

In general, utilization rates for mental health services for Asian Americans have been lower than those for Whites. Kitano (1969) found that hospital admissions rates for mental disturbance were many times lower for Japanese and Chinese Americans compared to those for Caucasian Americans during each of the years from 1960 to 1965. This also has been corroborated in Hawaii for Chinese, Hawaiian, Japanese, and Filipino Americans. In addition, this has been shown to be the case for outpatient services within community mental health centers (Brown et al., 1973; Sue & McKinney, 1975; Sue & Sue, 1974). However, Berk and Hirata (1973) pointed out that admissions to state mental hospitals in California doubled for the general population while it increased sevenfold for Chinese Americans between 1855 and 1955.

As pointed out by Sue and Morishima (1982), utilization is a poor indicator of degree of mental disturbance in Asian American populations. Confounded in many of the studies is the tendency to use "standardized" measures for assessing psychopathology and degree of disturbance and to use Caucasians as matched controls.

Sue and Morishima (1982) summarized some factors that contribute to underutilization. These include cultural factors of stigma and shame, use and availability of alternative resources (e.g., general practitioners and medical clinics, counseling over psychiatric services, herbalists, family), cost considerations, location and knowledge of facilities, hours of operation, belief systems about mental health, and responsiveness of services. Whereas some studies have found no evidence of differential treatment by ethnicity (Kinzie & Tseng, 1978; Sue & McKinney, 1975), others have questioned whether qualitative variables would show equality and responsiveness of treatment (Sue, 1977).

Wu and Windle (1980) correlated utilization of mental health services by Asian Americans in community mental health centers with the presence of Asian American staff. Although Asian Americans were not disaggregated, ethnic similarity correlated with utilization.

DIAGNOSIS AND ASSESSMENT

Leong's (1986) review of diagnosis and assessment of Asian Americans concluded that culture influences (a) symptom expression, (b) cultural biases on the part of therapists, (c) problems with the use of interpreters, and (d) problems with the use of clinical and personality tests. Whereas diagnosis and assessment presumes a standard against which pathology is determined, culture will alter that standard for both client expression of symptoms and bias of those interpreting them. In Asian American clients, several common themes are apparent.

Symptom Expression: Somatization

There is a marked predominance of somatization in the presentation of depression among Asian clients and a tendency to replace psychological symptoms with somatic ones (Cheung, Lau, & Waldmann, 1980; Gaw, 1982; Kleinman & Sung, 1979). Specifically, Kleinman (1986) showed that headaches, dizziness, and lack of energy form a symptom cluster among Chinese in both Taiwan and China. However, there has been some controversy over the interpretation of these symptoms. Kleinman stressed the cultural relativity of psychiatric diagnosis. He used "culture-bound syndromes" to describe those disorders found only in particular cultures and as reflecting cultural idioms of distress. Somatization, an instance of a cultural idiom of distress, is viewed as the expression of personal social distress through an idiom of bodily complaints and medical help seeking (Lin, Carter, & Kleinman, 1985). Mollica and Lavelle (1988), however, viewed these phenomena as Asian patients "hiding" their depression behind somatic chief complaints and the dominance of somatization over psychological insights.

Acculturation

Given the prevalence of immigrants and refugees among Asian Americans, much of the literature emphasizes the acculturation process as dominant in the diagnosis of psychological problems among Asian Americans. This has been described as due to increased stress resulting from the refugee experience among Southeast Asians (Williams, 1985) and the higher marginality and anxiety and the lower modernity experienced by immigrants (Smither & Rodriguez-Giegling, 1979).

Posttraumatic Stress Disorder

Anxiety and depression, correlated with the refugee experience, have been found with greater prevalence among Vietnamese (Lin, Masuda, & Tazuma, 1982) and Hmong (Westermeyer, Vang, & Neider, 1983a) clients. Given the prevalence of war trauma experiences among Southeast Asian refugees, major depression and posttraumatic stress disorder (PTSD) have been found to be more prevalent (Kinzie, Fredrickson, Fleck, & Karls, 1984; Lin & Shen, 1991; Mollica, Wyshak, & Lavelle, 1987; Moore & Boehnlein, 1991). Mollica, Wyshak, and Lavelle (1987) identified the prevalence of nightmares and insomnia as an expression of PTSD among many Southeast Asians due to premigration trauma of war, escape, torture, and refugee camp experiences.

Without diminishing the importance of acculturation and premigration trauma experiences as stressors among Asian Americans, these approaches have resulted in an underdiagnosis of other psychopathology and overuse of these diagnoses among Asian American immigrants/refugees. Often left undifferentiated is the confounding of the normal developmental experience of immigrants with psychopathology. Finally, this emphasis appears to reflect the bias of those who conceptualize the immigrant/refugee experience as unidirectional, that is, toward Westernization, Americanization, and "nonacculturation" as pathological.

Use of Clinical Tests

The use of clinical tests adds yet another confounding variable to the diagnosis and assessment of Asian American clients. Tests that have been developed and normed on White samples might not be predictive or valid with other ethnic groups. Many versions of standardized questionnaires and assessment instruments have been translated into Asian languages; these have been used for diagnostic and comparative purposes to determine prevalence of disorders and symptoms among Asian Americans. Tests that have been translated include the Minnesota Multiphasic Personality Inventory (MMPI) (Butcher & Clark, 1979), the Hopkins Symptom Checklist (Mollica, Wyshak, de Marneffe, Khuon, & Lavelle, 1987), and the Wechsler Intelligence Scales for Children–Revised (WISC-R) and Wechsler Adult Intelligence Scales–Revised (WAIS-R). Used as clinical instruments, they need to be complemented by examiner caution and recognition of cultural bias. Used as research instruments, they have questionable validity unless cultural bias and relevance are acknowledged. It is commonly recognized that the use of interpreters often results in content and process distortions. When used during the administration of psychological tests, it adds yet another confounding variable.

Kleinman (1988) described the complexity of developing culturally meaningful translations of assessment instruments. He felt that questionnaires ought to operationalize symptom clusters to identify locally salient illness experiences or else they will fail to validly register cultural differences in the symptomatology of mental illness. Most psychiatric assessment instruments are developed in a vernacular that is difficult to translate into other languages.

Chin (1983) critiqued the importance of language and cultural variables in the diagnostic assessment of Asian Americans. Bilingual background contributes many confounding variables that cannot be eliminated with simple translation of English psychological tests for Asian clients. The use of typologies, common in personality studies, also has resulted in reinforcing stereotypical views of Asian personality traits. Yet, many studies of Asians are premised on diagnostic comparisons between Asians and Whites using translated tests and/or typologies that might not be culturally relevant (Arkoff, 1959; Butcher & Clark, 1979; Meredith, 1966; Vernon, 1982). As a result, Asian Americans tend to be viewed as less verbal, having more personality problems, more neurotic, more anxious and introverted, and less dominant than Whites. In using these comparative models, the studies generally interpret Asian traits as less favorable and more pathological. Chin (1983) argued for diagnostic assessment to evaluate behaviors based on how they reflect the adaptive potential and lifestyle goals of a client in the context of different cultural values.

PSYCHOTHERAPY AND COUNSELING

The early literature on psychotherapy and counseling with Asian Americans focused on broad questions of relevance and effectiveness. Given cultural differences, how relevant (i.e., how responsive) is psychotherapy as a method for Asian Americans? How do different theoretical models fit the Asian American client? The literature here generally contrasted Asian culture with Western culture and examined how these differences influenced the relevance of psychotherapy for Asian American clients. The second question was as follows: How effective is psychotherapy (i.e., does it work) with Asian American clients? The literature here described what went on within the psychotherapy and counseling process and critiqued what must occur to make it effective with Asian American clients. What must therapists do differently?

Several differences characterize the experience of Asian Americans in psychotherapy. First, differences in values, practice, and beliefs exist between the Asian and Western cultures. Second, Asian Americans are characterized by their ethnic minority status, that is, difference from predominant culture and race. Language and acculturation differences add yet further dimensions of difference to the experience of immigrants and refugees among Asian American populations. Each of these differences has been examined in terms of relevance and effectiveness. Many have criticized the low utilization rates as due to a lack of responsiveness by clinicians to the special needs of Asian American clients (Kim, 1978; Sue, 1977).

Impact of Cultural Differences on Therapeutic Content

What comes up in psychotherapy with Asian Americans, and how do we interpret this content? The many differences between the Asian and Western cultures have led many to question the relevance and effectiveness of psychotherapy when the therapist operates from a Western framework. Consequently, the literature has documented cultural differences within the Asian culture (Lum, 1980; Shon & Ja, 1982) that must be attended to in the practice of psychotherapy. Some cultural beliefs and values emphasized within the Asian culture, which will emerge as therapeutic content, include filial piety, extended family networks, harmony, cooperation, and shame. The identification of these differences has generally come from descriptive clinical data. Few empirical studies, if any, have systematically examined these variables among different Asian American groups. Although it has been suggested that variations will occur because of differences in ethnicity, number of generations a group or individual has been in the United States, and individual differences.

Some have questioned the relevance of psychotherapy for Asian Americans due to the contextual influence of racism (Toupin, 1980; Weil, 1983). How this biases selection of clients toward White, middle-class norms has been challenged. In particular, Asian Americans have been viewed as less verbal, less introspective, and more passive. Tong (1983) challenged these stereotypical images viewed as common among Chinese Americans as reflective of a racist ideology. In particular, he challenged whether not being like "Caucasians who behave in a more spontaneous and assertive manner" is reflective of psychopathology; rather, he viewed it as reflective of a Western and racist approach to understanding Asians. He used a historical analysis of Chinese immigration to identify the aggressive, seafaring spirit of the Toisanese Chinese, which challenged the view of the passive, self-effacing Asian.

Relevance of Theoretical Models

Some existing models of psychotherapy have been questioned as to their relevance for Asian Americans based on cultural difference. Some have questioned the overall relevance of theoretical models of psychotherapy given their base in Western models of philosophy and cultural norms, whereas others have supported modifications of existing theoretical models to achieve cultural relevance and therapeutic effectiveness.

Kim (1985) proposed a strategic-structural family therapy framework as a viable model because of its cultural fit; that is, an approach that focuses on external stress, direct problem-solving techniques, active problem management, and external resolution can be more effective with Asian American families. Tung (1991), on the other hand, supported the usefulness of a psychodynamic model if modifications are made to take into consideration the interdependent nature of the Chinese self. Typically, the emphasis on insight, introspection, and free association is viewed as inconsistent with Asian values. Chin (1994) supported the notion that a psychodynamic approach is relevant to Asian American clients if changes and refinements of the theory are made to reflect the different perspectives related to race, worldviews, authority, and bicultural identity and are used to interpret therapeutic content and understand the formation of the therapeutic relationship.

Another approach has been to examine Asian philosophy and to compare its elements with principles of psychotherapy and psychopathology. Tseng (1973) examined the concept of personality in Confucian thought and used this to assess psychopathology within a developmental and cultural context. Thus, the emphasis on order from the inside of oneself toward the outside world, on harmony with one's environment, on the regulation of emotions, on interdependence, and on achieving personal maturity in the later part of life—common within Confucian thought—has major implications for therapeutic interpretations and interventions with Asian American clients.

Watts (1961) analyzed methods and objectives common to both Western psychotherapy and many Eastern philosophies including Buddhism, Vedanta, Yoga, and Taoism. He concluded that the concerns of both are to bring about changes of consciousness and changes in our feelings about our own existence and our relation to human society and the natural world. As such, he pointed to the misconception about Eastern philosophies to alter consciousness as "depersonalization." Rather, he viewed this as a form of regression to a primitive or infantile type of awareness not unlike the concept of "regression in the service of the ego" in Freudian terms.

Hirai (1988) described Zen meditation, a form of discipline and training employed in Zen Buddhism, and its therapeutic effects on the human mind. In particular, he found changes in electroencephalographic patterns evident during Zen meditation as reflective of altered states of consciousness. He suggested that these changes lead to enlightenment consistent with the ultimate goal of psychotherapy. Seitz, Olson, Locke, and Quam (1990) also drew parallels between the effective management of energy in Asian martial arts and therapeutic goals of mental health professions. Consequently, understanding the importance of managing energy within our bodies and interpersonal relationships as a continuum between mind and body should be an important dimension of culturally relevant psychotherapeutic practice.

Emphasis on Cross-Cultural Understanding

Emphasis on cross-cultural understanding has been viewed as a prerequisite for working with Asian American clients (Kitano, 1989; Shon & Ja, 1982; Sue & Morishima, 1982; Sue & Sue, 1985). Many have emphasized the importance of cultural sensitivity; knowledge of the culture; recognition of differences in values, beliefs, and worldviews; and development of cross-cultural skills as essential ingredients for achieving empathy and forming a therapeutic alliance. Baczynsky (1991) pointed to the feminist orientation of Southeast Asian women refugees and drew on her own identification with their experience of survival as a bond for working cross-culturally. Root (1990) described the phenomenological experience of biracial individuals and provided a model for movement toward a positive, stable self-image.

Influence of Acculturation in Psychotherapy

Given the more recent migration of Asian Americans to the United States, acculturation has been a common treatment variable studied in the literature. The degree of acculturation to Western culture (Connor, 1974; Fong, 1973; Long, 1980; Sue & Morishima, 1982) and the experiencing of cultural conflict (Fong, 1973; Kitano & Sue, 1973; Kuo, 1976) by clients are two variables generally correlated with clients' ability to use psychotherapy. As Southeast Asian refugees have migrated in greater numbers, there has been descriptive information about Southeast Asians and the culture (Nishio & Bilmes, 1987; Williams, 1985) and about the plight of the refugee experience (Baczynsky, 1991) as it relates to the practice of psychotherapy.

It has been generally agreed that there is greater stress experienced by immigrants and refugees in adjusting to a new lifestyle and culture within the United States, which will correlate with greater prevalence of mental health problems. However, the emphasis on acculturation often results in a therapeutic approach that emphasizes education about the American culture and adjustment to the lifestyle in the United States. Needing more attention is the establishment of bicultural identity for Asian immigrants and refugees and how these influence psychotherapy.

Influence of Language in Psychotherapy

Many investigators have identified language as an important client variable when working with Asian Americans (see Leong, 1986, for a review). This has been a function not only because of the need for interpreters with non-English-speaking clients but also because nonstandard English dialects may create a negative bias on the part of therapists, which poses barriers to communication. This dimension has not been studied systematically in the literature. The use of interpreters clearly distorts the therapeutic relationship and introduces yet another dimension to the therapist-client dyad. It is not always clear how accurate interpreters are in translating what the therapist says. Moreover, their presence in the situation introduces a triadic relationship to psychotherapy. Thus, the literature generally supports the need for bilingual/bicultural therapists.

McGill (1987) focused on the logic and grammar of the Japanese language as reflective of other-centeredness, indirection, indecision, and apology, which becomes the foundation for Japanese relationships. He used these dimensions to illustrate the centrality of interdependency (*amae*) and public and private selves (*omote/ura*) within the Japanese culture, and he drew implications for how they influence presenting complaints, therapeutic relationships, and psychotherapy. Specifically, destructive acts toward the self or society within the Japanese culture might be correlated with culturally accepted ways of seeking dependency. Moreover, language nuances important to culture might have important implications for interpreting behavior in psychotherapy.

Psychopharmacology and Psychotherapy

The use of psychopharmacology with Asian American clients has shown that differences in dosage requirements and side effect profiles are significant (Lin, Okamoto, Yamamoto, & Chien, 1986). Neuroleptic studies with Asians have reported their greater likelihood of developing acute extrapyramidal side effects as compared to Whites on comparable doses of haloperidol (Binder & Levy, 1981; Potkin, Shen, & Pardes, 1984). In addition, Asians appear to require lower doses of these drugs to achieve therapeutic effects (Ananth & Lin, 1982; Lin & Finder, 1983; Yamamoto, Fund, Lo, & Reece, 1979).

Impact of Culture on the Therapist-Client Dyad

Culture also has been described as influencing the therapist-client dyad with Asian American clients. It provides a context of cultural differences (Hong, 1993) that influence how the therapist and client perceive the relationship (Atkinson, Maruyama, & Matsui, 1978), the achievement of empathy and the forming of a therapeutic alliance (Ham, 1993), the different worldviews that clients bring to psychotherapy (Sue, 1978), and the identity issues brought by biracial clients to the therapeutic relationship (Root, 1990).

In general, Asian Americans are likely to enter treatment reluctantly, be more reliant on authoritative aspects of the relationship, be unfamiliar with the treatment process, and somatize their symptoms. These descriptions about Asian Americans have led to some common prescriptions about how to engage Asian Americans in treatment or intervene when they are in treatment. Prescriptions have emphasized supportive and concrete approaches with Chinese immigrants (Lorenzo & Adler, 1984), vocational counseling and retraining with Hmong refugees (Westermeyer, Vang, & Neider, 1983b), use of family and extended family networks as support systems (Gaw, 1979; Lee, 1982), and use of advice giving and directive approaches (Hong, 1989; Sue & Morishima, 1982).

As the literature has focused on differences between the Asian and Western cultures, it has established the notion of difference and diversity as important ingredients to the therapist-client dyad. Consequently, researchers have begun to examine more specific treatment process variables to achieve cultural relevance and therapeutic effectiveness with Asian American clients.

Sue and Zane (1987) argued that the emphasis on cultural knowledge and culture-specific techniques in psychotherapy with ethnic minorities often is distal to effective psychotherapy because it does not necessarily result in positive outcomes. They argued for a reformulation that stresses therapist-client matches based on more proximal variables, for example, matches between client beliefs and therapist understanding, rather than more distal ones (e.g., ethnicity of therapist and client). They emphasized credibility (i.e., perception of the therapist as an effective and trustworthy helper) and giving (i.e., client's perception that something was received from the therapeutic encounter) as important proximal variables when working with ethnic minority clients.

Chin (1990, 1993b) identified some transference issues that are relevant to working with Asian Americans. The importance of benevolence and respect associated with authority, self-identity associated with biculturalism, and racism associated with power will influence the development of the transference relationship. Consequently, Chin argued that additional concepts are needed to reflect their important transference dimensions when working with Asian American clients.

Yamamoto and Chang (1987) identified Asian forms of empathy as involving sympathy and related behaviors of compassion, generosity, and kindheartedness, whereas Western forms of empathy involve identification with the other person and an awareness of the other's feelings.

SERVICE DELIVERY SYSTEMS

Service delivery systems for Asian Americans arose from the demands of Asian communities, and their designs were driven by clinical experience. Whereas mental health services and treatment often are synonymous with psychotherapy and counseling, there is a range of services necessary to ensure a relevant and effective service delivery system. Although hospitalization and inpatient services are distinct services, other services such as case management, social services, outreach, home visiting, consultation, and liaison services are interrelated with psychotherapy and counseling in a complex manner, especially within community mental health systems.

In the delivery of mental health services to immigrant and low-income Asian American populations, psychotherapy and counseling services often cannot be isolated from the full array of support services. Mental health professionals often must perform these services to (a) gain credibility, (b) establish a therapeutic alliance, (c) respond to the immediate need or crisis, (d) respond to the perceived problem, and (e) otherwise provide effective psychotherapy and counseling. This emphasis on concrete services has been well documented in the literature (Leong, 1986; Sue & Morishima, 1982). Lorenzo and Adler (1984) recommended the adaptation of Western modalities of psychotherapy, insight into culturally relevant issues, drawing on community support systems, emphasizing concrete outcomes, and client education and outreach for Asian Americans seen within a community setting.

As a result, mental health services with Asian Americans, especially immigrants and refugees, often take place within the public and/or community mental health sector. Some "mainstream agencies" have developed specific mental health services for Asian Americans through community mental health centers and hospitals. These often have been driven by an inability of the mainstream agencies to deliver services to non-English-speaking clients. The Indochinese Psychiatry Clinic in Boston (Mollica & Lavelle, 1988) and the Asian Psychiatric Unit of San Francisco General Hospital (Lu, 1981) are examples. "Ethnic-specific services" also have been developed within community-based settings to interface with the mainstream system. These include many community-based agencies that began by responding to the social service needs of non-English-speaking Asian Americans (see Sue & Morishima, 1982, for a review). These needs included interpreter services, transportation/escort services, eligibility applications, advocacy, and English as a second language classes. As mental health problems emerged, the absence of bilingual services within the mainstream system drove the development of these ethnic-specific services to fill the gap. Some examples include the South Cove Community Health Center in Boston (Chin, 1991); the Richmond Area Maxi-Center (Wong, 1981) in San Francisco; the Northeast Community Mental Health Center in San Francisco; Asian Community Mental Health Services in Oakland, California; Asian Counseling and Referral Services in Seattle, Washington; and the Asian/Pacific Counseling and Treatment Center in Los Angeles. For Southeast Asians, these ethnic-specific services often developed through mutual assistance agencies and voluntary agencies organized for a range of purposes including fraternal, social, and recreational ones. Many have provided services including educational, support, job training, cultural orientation, and refugee resettlement (see Bui, 1983, for a review).

Indigenous to these examples is the fact that the services were developed to be ethnic specific and responsive to the unique cultural and language characteristics of the Asian American populations they served. Common to the development of parallel and ethnic-specific services is the emphasis on concrete services, principles of consumer empowerment, and community-based networks. Given the growing numbers of Asian immigrants and refugees over the past decade, these ethnic-specific services have continued to prosper. As mental health service needs become less driven by language barriers, the challenges faced in the next decade are whether and how the need for bicultural services will remain a priority.

TRAINING

Professional training itself can contribute a source of bias when working with Asian American clients (Leong, 1986). Because models of training also are rooted in Western frameworks and cultural norms, the universality of training approaches has been challenged (Sue, 1981). The development of training models sensitive to Asian American cultural background and experiences has been described by many (Kushida, Montenegro, Chikahisa, & Morales, 1976; Lee, 1980; Root, Ho, & Sue, 1986; Wong, Kim, Sue, & Tanaka, 1981). These generally emphasize bilingual/bicultural services and availability of Asian professional role models.

Several factors are important in looking at the responsiveness of training models for Asian Americans. First, does the standard of practice bias practitioners toward Western norms? Second, how does the program evaluate cultural sensitivity and promote cultural competence? Third, does the training program provide a critical mass of Asian American professionals for students? Chin (1991) spoke to the need for revisiting clinical training if it is to be responsive to the needs of Asian Americans. The diversity among Asian American groups, the relative small numbers, and the geographic dispersion among Asian American groups make for particular challenges in developing a critical mass to be responsive. Although the need for bilingual/bicultural providers is acute, few training programs justify significant resources to recruit bilingual Asian students. Frameworks for clinical practice with Asian American clients still refer to ethnic content and modifications of existing theories and practice. As a result, they bias toward Western norms as a reference group rather than responding to the diversity of ethnic communities in the United States.

FUTURE OF MENTAL HEALTH SERVICES

The future of mental health services needs to move from viewing Asian Americans as a population for whom modifications need to be made to service delivery models whose concepts define specific principles for working with diverse groups of Asian Americans. Some approaches already exist in the literature.

Sue (1988) evaluated research findings over the past two decades and pointed to the mixed findings that fail to demonstrate that ethnic minorities achieve differential treatment outcomes when matched by ethnicity. He argued that the issue has been misconceptualized; failure to differentiate between ethnic match and cultural match has prolonged failure to resolve the question. Sue defined ethnic or racial match as a moral/ethical issue involving the shortage of ethnic therapists and the resulting lack of freedom of choice in selection of therapists. This is differentiated from cultural match, which is more an empirical issue defining treatment effectiveness and outcome. Although ethnic match has not been shown to consistently improve treatment outcomes, research has been devoted to ethnic match rather than cultural match variables because of the difficulties in defining culture. Sue argued for the study of actual behaviors in therapy to yield insight into how cultural matches and mismatches are reflected in treatment. This approach would define the complexity of the problem, provide an analysis of the advantages and disadvantages of cultural match and mismatch variables, and take into consideration individual differences as important mediators.

Tyler, Sussewell, and Williams-McCoy (1985) presented an ethnic validity model as an alternative framework to practice psychotherapy within and across ethnic groups. The model addresses the convergence (i.e., some ways of living are valid across cultural contexts), divergence (i.e., some are different), and conflict among different ethnic worldviews and their consequent emergence in cross-ethnic patterns of interactions. It criticizes an ethnocentric approach and emphasizes that there are a variety of ways of living (of being human), each of which offers strengths and limitations. The model acknowledges the salience of ethnic variables and the racial/ethnic social context.

Hansen and Falicov (1983) looked at cultural dimensions using family therapy and defined those cultural aspects of families that influence the practice of psychotherapy. Cultural dimensions are defined as involving the historical continuity and psychological identity that affect the thinking, feeling, and behavior of family members. The authors approached cultural dimension as different from a focus on specific ethnicities that permeate family life, as taken by the McGoldrick, Pearce, and Giordano (1982) approach. Rather, Hansen and Falicov (1983) defined cultural issues as sets of common adaptive behaviors and experiences derived from membership in a variety of different contexts including ecological, philosophical, religious, national, ethnic, family organization, social class, occupation, migratory patterns, stages of acculturation, or shared values derived from partaking in similar historical moments.

Kleinman (1988) questioned psychiatry from an anthropological perspective. As such, it has been Western dominated and has regarded cross-cultural research as marginal, although more than 80% of the world's people inhabit non-Western societies. From this perspective, his research placed vulnerability for mental illness within a social context, that is, lack of social support, poverty, unemployment, and forced acculturation as risk factors. His description of culture-bound syndromes pointed to the importance of cultural contexts in defining the manifestation of psychopathology. Specifically, Kleinman described psychotherapy as merely one indigenous form of symbolic healing, that is, a therapy based on words, myth, and ritual use of symbols. Ethnographic accounts of healing rituals cross-culturally point to the universality of a tripartite process: (a) an underlying causal agent is announced (i.e., recognizing the problem); (b) the symbolic form that causes or materializes pathology is manipulated via therapeutic rituals (i.e., working through); and (c) the causal agent, on the plane of the interpretive system's core symbols, is removed (i.e., termination).

Cross, Bazron, Dennis, and Isaacs (1989) approached this issue from a systemic perspective. They developed the principle of cultural competence as the capacity to function effectively and to acknowledge and incorporate the importance of culture at all levels. It implies the acceptance and respect for difference, continuing self-assessment regarding culture, and careful attention to the dynamics of difference. The authors defined a developmental model for implementation and evaluation of culturally competent service delivery systems and advocated for its use at all levels of a service delivery system (i.e., policy making, administrative, practitioner, and consumer).

Chin (1993a) argued for a psychology of difference that examines and evaluates underlying assumptive frameworks, which define ways in which therapists and clients understand one another within the therapeutic relationship. She pointed to troublesome concepts commonly used in the literature that hinder the evolution of clinical practice to be culturally relevant and therapeutically effective for a culturally diverse population. Concepts such as mainstreaming and acculturation bias researchers and practitioners toward frameworks that are rooted in Western perspectives and standards. As such, they are likely to result in interpretations of behaviors in psychotherapy as pathological and inferior when they differ.

What these approaches have in common is that they go beyond defining Asian Americans as a population and toward defining specific variables for culturally competent clinical practice. They also go beyond comparing Asian Americans to Westerners as the valid methodology for evaluating cultural responsiveness and studying treatment effectiveness. Finally, they move away from minority status toward ethnically valid models of practice that substantiate principles of difference and diversity.

Emerging Issues

As differences between Asian and Western cultures are accepted as valid variables for differential practice and research, several overriding issues emerge as important to the future of mental health treatment with Asian Americans.

We need ethnic validity models to validate the experience of Asian Americans as essential to defining clinical practice. We need to start from the worldviews of Asian American clients. How do Asian philosophies add or contribute to the practice of psychotherapy with Asian Americans? What do they tell us about development, pathology, and adaptation patterns among Asian Americans, and how does this influence clinical practice and psychotherapy? Core concepts of power and authority need to be examined from different cultural perspectives. For example, power from an ethnic minority perspective is intricately tied to racism, whereas this is not true when applied to the White majority. Similarly, authority from an Asian perspective is tied to benevolence and respect, unlike the emphasis on punishment and transgression from a Western perspective.

We need to differentiate Asian American culture as distinct from but related to Asian cultures as its origin. Contextual influences of racism, political and social history, and evolution of Asian Americans as a group in the United States will have a bearing on how they present in treatment. In this regard, race, gender, and class need to be examined variables along with culture as influencing treatment outcomes. Bicultural models of development need to be stressed over the acculturation process. Difference frameworks, which validate ethnic minorities as having a different experience, need to be examined.

We need to focus on diversity frameworks and on how they influence treatment practice and outcomes. What variables are important for whom, and when do these achieve therapeutic outcomes? This is in contrast to ethnocentric frameworks, which examine questions of ideal fit (e.g., Which Asian American clients do well in psychotherapy?). In this regard, we need to view clinical practice from client perspectives (e.g., client empowerment would be emphasized over therapeutic compliance).

We need to examine process variables that influence the nature of the therapeutic relationship and the therapist-client dyad. What client-therapist perceptions and behaviors contribute to empathy? How do different cultural values, beliefs, and behaviors influence transference reactions and therapeutic alliance? How do language and semantic meanings related to culture influence therapist interpretation and client behavior? What factors facilitate psychotherapy for which Asian American clients?

REFERENCES

Ananth, J., & Lin, K. M. (1982). Physical and ethnic variables in dosage for Asians [letter to the editor]. *American Journal of Psychiatry, 139,* 539-540.

Arkoff, A. (1959). Need patterns in two generations of Japanese Americans in Hawaii. *Journal of Social Psychology, 50,* 75-79.

Atkinson, D. R., Maruyama, M., & Matsui, S. (1978). Effects of counselor race and counseling approach on Asian Americans' perceptions of counselor credibility and utility. *Journal of Counseling Psychology, 25,* 76-85.

Baczynsky, W. (1991). Refugees as feminists. In M. Bricker-Jenkins, N. R. Hooyman, & N. Gottlieb (Eds.), *Feminist social work practice in clinical settings.* Newbury Park, CA: Sage.

Berk, B. B., & Hirata, L. C. (1973). Mental illness among the Chinese: Myth or reality? *Journal of Social Issues, 29,* 149-166.

Binder, R. L., & Levy, R. (1981). Extrapyramidal reaction in Asians. *American Journal of Psychiatry, 138,* 1243-1244.

Brown et al. (1973). Mental illness and the role of mental health facilities in Chinatown. In S. Sue & N. Wagner (Eds.), *Asian Americans: Psychological perspectives.* Palo Alto, CA: Science and Behavior Books.

Bui, D. (1983). The Indochinese mutual assistance associations. In Social Work With Southeast Asian Refugees (Ed.), *Bridging cultures: Southeast Asian refugees in America.* Los Angeles: Special Service for Groups.

Butcher, J. N., & Clark, L. A. (1979). Recent trends in cross-cultural MMPI research and application. In J. N. Butcher (Ed.), *New developments in the use of the MMPI.* Minneapolis: University of Minnesota Press.

Cheung, F. M., & Lau, W. K. (1982). Situational variations of help-seeking behavior among Chinese patients. *Comprehensive Psychiatry, 23,* 252-262.

Cheung, F. M., Lau, W. K., & Waldmann, E. (1980). Somatization among Chinese depressives in general practice. *International Journal of Psychiatric Medicine, 10,* 361-374.

Chin, J. L. (1983). Diagnostic considerations in working with Asian Americans. *American Journal of Orthopsychiatry, 53,* 100-109.

Chin, J. L. (1990). Transference and countertransference issues as related to gender and ethnicity with Asian Americans. *The Clinical Psychologist, 43*(5), 65-69.

Chin, J. L. (1991). The South Cove Community Health Center: An approach to community-based training. In H. F. Myers, P. Wohlford, L. P. Guzman, & R. J. Echemendia (Eds.), *Ethnic minority perspectives on clinical training and services in psychology.* Washington, DC: American Psychological Association.

Chin, J. L. (1993a). Toward a psychology of difference: Psychotherapy for a culturally diverse population. In J. L. Chin, V. De La Cancela, & Y. Jenkins (Eds.), *Diversity in psychotherapy: The politics of race, ethnicity, and gender.* Westport, CT: Praeger.

Chin, J. L. (1993b). Transference. In J. L. Chin, J. H. Liem, M. D. Ham, & G. K. Hong (Eds.), *Transference and empathy in Asian American psychotherapy: Cultural values and treatment needs.* Westport, CT: Praeger.

Chin, J. L. (1994). Psychodynamic approaches. In L. Comas-Diaz & B. Greene (Eds.), *Women of color and mental health.* New York: Guilford.

Comas-Diaz, L. (1992). The future of psychotherapy with ethnic minorities. *Psychotherapy, 29,*(1), 88-94.

Connor, J. W. (1974). Acculturation and family continuities in three generations of Japanese Americans. *Journal of Marriage and the Family, 36,* 159-165.

Cross, T. L., Bazron, F. J., Dennis, K. W., & Isaacs, M. R. (1989). *Towards a culturally competent system of care.* Washington, DC: CASSP Technical Assistance Center.

Fong, S. L. M. (1973). Assimilation and changing social roles of Chinese Americans. *Journal of Social Issues, 29*(2), 115-127.

Gaw, A. (1979). *Cross-cultural psychiatry.* Boston: Littleton.

Gaw, A. (1982). *Cross-cultural psychiatry.* Boston: John Wright.

Ham, M. D. (1993). Empathy. In J. L. Chin, J. H. Liem, M. D. Ham, & G. K. Hong (Eds.), *Transference and empathy in Asian American psychotherapy: Cultural values and treatment needs.* Westport, CT: Praeger.

Hansen, J. C., & Falicov, C. J. (1983). *Cultural perspectives in family therapy.* Rockville, MD: Aspen Systems.

Hirai, T. (1988). *Zen meditation and psychotherapy.* New York: Japan Publications.

Hong, G. K. (1989). Application of cultural and environmental issues in family therapy with immigrant Chinese Americans. *Journal of Strategic and Systemic Therapies, 8,* 14-21.

Hong, G. K. (1993). Contextual factors in psychotherapy with Asian Americans. In J. L. Chin, J. H. Liem, M. D. Ham, & G. K. Hong (Eds.), *Transference and empathy in Asian American psychotherapy: Cultural values and treatment needs.* Westport, CT: Praeger.

Kim, B. C. C. (1978). *The Asian Americans: Changing patterns, changing needs.* Urbana, IL: Association of Korean Christian Scholars in North America.

Kim, S. C. (1985). Family therapy for Asian Americans: A strategic-structural framework. *Psychotherapy, 22,* 342-348.

Kinzie, J. D., Fredrickson, R. B., Fleck, J., & Karls, W. (1984). Post-traumatic stress disorder among survivors of Cambodian concentration camps. *American Journal of Psychiatry, 141,* 649-650.

Kinzie, J. D., & Mason, S. (1983). Five years' experience with Indochinese refugee psychiatric patients. *Journal of Operational Psychiatry, 14*(2), 105-111.

Kinzie, J. D., & Tseng, W. S. (1978). Cultural aspects of psychiatric clinic utilization: A cross-cultural study in Hawaii. *International Journal of Social Psychiatry, 24,* 177-188.

Kitano, H. H. L. (1969). Japanese American mental illness. In S. Plog & R. Edgerton (Eds.), *Changing perspectives in mental illness.* New York: Holt, Rinehart & Winston.

Kitano, H. H. (1989). A model for counseling Asian Americans. In P. B. Pedersen, J. G. Draguns, W. J. Lonnder, & J. E. Trimble (Eds.), *Counseling across cultures.* Honolulu: University of Hawaii Press.

Kitano, H. H. L., & Sue, S. (1973). The model minorities. *Journal of Social Issues, 29*(2), 1-9.

Kleinman, A. (1986). *Social origins of distress and disease: Depression, neurasthenia and pain in modern China.* New Haven, CT: Yale University Press.

Kleinman, A. (1988). *Rethinking psychiatry: From cultural category to personal experience.* New York: Free Press.

Kleinman, A. M., & Sung, L. H. (1979). Why do indigenous practitioners successfully heal? *Social Science and Medicine, 138,* 7-126.

Kuo, W. (1976). Theories of migration and mental health: An empirical testing on Chinese Americans. *Social Sciences and Medicine, 10,* 297-306.

Kushida, A. H., Montenegro, M., Chikahisa, P., & Morales, R. (1976). A training program for Asian and Pacific Islander Americans. *Social Casework, 57,* 185-194.

Lee, E. (1980). Mental health services for the Asian-Americans: Problems and alternatives. In U.S. Commission on Civil Rights (Ed.), *Civil rights of Asian and Pacific-Americans: Myths and realities.* Washington, DC: Government Printing Office.

Lee, E. (1982). A social systems approach to assessment and treatment for Chinese American families. In M. McGoldrick, J. K. Pearce, & J. Giordano (Eds.), *Ethnicity and family therapy.* New York: Guilford.

Leong, F. T. (1986). Counseling and psychotherapy with Asian Americans: Review of the literature. *Journal of Counseling Psychology, 33,* 196-206.

Lin, E. H., Carter, W. B., & Kleinman, A. M. (1985). An exploration of somatization among Asian refugees and immigrants in primary care. *American Journal of Public Health, 75,* 1080-1084.

Lin, K. M., & Finder, E. (1983). Neuroleptic dosage for Asians. *American Journal of Psychiatry, 140,* 490-491.

Lin, K. M., Masuda, M., & Tazuma, L. (1982). Adaptational problems of Vietnamese refugees. Part III: Case studies in clinic and field—Adaptive and maladaptive. *Psychiatric Journal of the University of Ottawa, 7,* 173-183.

Lin, K., Okamoto, T., Yamamoto, J., & Chien, C. (1986). Psychotropic dosage in Asian patients. *P/AAMHRC Research Review, 5*(1/2), 1-3.

Lin, K. M., & Shen, W. W. (1991). Pharmacotherapy for Southeast Asian psychiatric patients. *Journal of Nervous and Mental Disorders, 179,* 346-350.

Long, P. B. (1980). The issue of family reunification facing Indochinese refugees in the U.S. In U.S. Commission on Civil Rights (Ed.), *Civil rights issues of Asian and Pacific Americans: Myths and realities.* Washington, DC: Government Printing Office.

Lorenzo, M. K., & Adler, D. A. (1984, December). Mental health services for Chinese in a community health center. *Social Casework,* pp. 600-609.

Lu, F. G. (1981). *The Asian and Pacific American In-Patient Psychiatric Program at San Francisco General Hospital.* Paper presented at the conference on Innovations in the Mental Health Care of Asian Americans, New York.

Lum, R. G. (1980). Impact of mental illness on Chinese families. *Dissertation Abstracts International, 41,* 656B.

McGill, D. (1987). Language, cultural psychology, and family therapy: Japanese examples from an international perspective. *Contemporary Family Therapy, 9,* 283-293.

McGoldrick, M., Pearce, J., & Giordano, J. (Eds.). (1982). *Ethnicity and family therapy.* New York: Guilford.

Meredith, G. M. (1966). *Amae* and acculturation among Japanese American college students in Hawaii. *Journal of Social Psychology, 70,* 171-180.

Mollica, R. F., & Lavelle, J. (1988). Southeast Asian refugees. In L. Comas-Diaz & E. E. H. Griffith (Eds.), *Clinical guidelines in cross-cultural mental health.* New York: John Wiley.

Mollica, R. F., Wyshak, G., de Marneffe, D., Khuon, F., & Lavelle, J. (1987). Indochinese version of the Hopkins Symptom Checklist-25: A screening instrument for the psychiatric care of refugees. *American Journal of Psychiatry, 144,* 497-500.

Mollica, R. F., Wyshak, G., & Lavelle, J. (1987). The psychosocial impact of war trauma and torture on the Southeast Asian refugee. *American Journal of Psychiatry, 144,* 1567-1572.

Moon, A., & Tashima, N. (1982). *Help seeking behavior and attitudes of Southeast Asian refugees.* San Francisco: Pacific Asian Mental Health Research Project.

Moore, L. J., & Boehnlein, J. K. (1991). Treating psychiatric disorders among Mien refugees from highland Laos. *Social Science Medicine, 32,* 1029-1036.

Nishio, K., & Bilmes, M. (1987). Psychotherapy with Southeast Asian American clients. *Professional Psychology: Research and Practice, 18,* 342-346.

Potkin, S. F., Shen, Y., & Pardes, H. (1984). Haloperidol concentrations elevated in Chinese patients. *Psychiatric Research, 12,* 167-172.

Root, M. P. P. (1990). Resolving "other" status: Identity development of biracial individuals. *Women and Therapy, 9*(1), 185-205.

Root, M., Ho, C., & Sue, S. (1986). Issues in the training of counselors for Asian Americans. In H. P. Lefley & P. B. Pedersen (Eds.), *Cross-cultural training for mental health professionals.* Springfield, IL: Charles C Thomas.

Seitz, F. C., Olson, G. D., Locke, B., & Quam, R. (1990). The martial arts and mental health: The challenge of managing energy. *Perceptual and Motor Skills, 70,* 459-464.

Shon, S. P., & Ja, D. Y. (1982). Asian families. In M. McGoldrick, J. K. Pearce, & J. Giordano (Eds.), *Ethnicity and family therapy.* New York: Guilford.

Smither, R., & Rodriguez-Giegling, M. (1979). Marginality, modernity, and anxiety in Indochinese refugees. *Journal of Cross-Cultural Psychology, 10,* 469-478.

Strupp, H. H. (1986). Psychotherapy: Research, practice, and public policy (how to avoid dead ends). *American Psychologist, 41,* 120-130.

Sue, D. W. (1978). World views and counseling. *Personnel and Guidance Journal, 56,* 583-592.

Sue, D. W. (1981). *Counseling the culturally different: Theory and practice.* New York: John Wiley.

Sue, D. W., & Sue, D. (1985). Asian Americans and Pacific Islanders. In P. Pedersen (Ed.), *Handbook of cross-cultural counseling and therapy.* Westport, CT: Greenwood.

Sue, S. (1977). Community mental health services to minority groups: Some optimism, some pessimism. *American Psychologist, 32,* 616-624.

Sue, S. (1988). Psychotherapeutic services for ethnic minorities: Two decades of research findings. *American Psychologist, 43,* 301-308.

Sue, S., & McKinney, H. (1975). Asian Americans in the community mental health care system. *American Journal of Orthopsychiatry, 45,* 111-118.

Sue, S., & Morishima, J. K. (1982). *The mental health of Asian Americans.* San Francisco: Jossey-Bass.

Sue, S., & Sue, D. W. (1974). MMPI comparisons between Asian American and non-Asian students utilizing a student health psychiatric clinic. *Journal of Counseling Psychology, 21,* 423-427.

Sue, S., & Zane, N. (1987). The role of culture and cultural techniques in psychotherapy: A critique and reformulation. *American Psychologist, 42,* 37-45.

Tong, B. R. (1983). On the confusion of psychopathology with culture: Iatrogenesis in the treatment of Chinese Americans. In R. F. Morgan (Ed.), *The iatrogenics handbook: A critical look at research and practice in the helping professions.* Toronto: IPI Publishing.

Toupin, E. A. (1980). Counseling Asians: Psychotherapy in the context of racism and Asian American history. *American Journal of Orthopsychiatry, 50,* 76-86.

Tseng, W. (1973). The concept of personality in Confucian thought. *Psychiatry, 36,* 191-202.

Tung, M. (1991). Insight-oriented psychotherapy and the Chinese patient. *American Journal of Orthopsychiatry, 61,* 186-194.

Tyler, F. B., Sussewell, D. R., & Williams-McCoy, J. (1985). Ethnic validity in psychotherapy. *Psychotherapy, 22,* 311-320.

Vernon, P. E. (1982). *The abilities and achievements of Orientals in North America.* New York: Academic Press.

Watts, A. W. (1961). *Psychotherapy: East and West.* New York: Ballantine Books.

Weil, M. (1983). Southeast Asians and service delivery: Issues in service provision and institutional racism. In Social Work With Southeast Asian Refugees (Ed.), *Bridging cultures: Southeast Asian refugees in America.* Los Angeles: Special Service for Groups.

Westermeyer, J., Vang, T. F., & Neider, J. (1983a). A comparison of refugees using and not using a psychiatric service: An analysis of DSM-III criteria and self-rating scales in cross-cultural context. *Journal of Operational Psychiatry, 14,* 36-41.

Westermeyer, J., Vang, T. F., & Neider, J. (1983b). Refugees who do and do not seek psychiatric care: An analysis of pre-migratory and post-migratory characteristics. *Journal of Nervous and Mental Disease, 171,* 86-91.

Williams, C. L. (1985). The Southeast Asian refugees community mental health. *Journal of Community Psychology, 13,* 258-269.

Wong, H. Z. (1977). *Community mental health services and manpower and training concerns of Asian Americans.* Washington, DC: President's Commission on Mental Health.

Wong, H. Z. (1981). Contextual factors for the development of the national Asian American psychology training center. *Journal of Community Psychology, 9,* 289-292.

Wong, H. Z., Kim, S. C., Sue, S., & Tanaka, M. (1981). The training of ethnic minority clinical-community psychologists: The case of Asian Americans. *Journal of Community Psychology, 9,* 287-288.

Wu, I. H., & Windle, C. (1980). Ethnic specificity in the relationship of minority use and staffing of community mental health centers. *Community Mental Health Journal, 16,* 156-168.

Yamamoto, J., & Chang, C. (1987, August). *Empathy for the family and the individual in the social context.* Paper presented at the interactive forum on Transference and Empathy in Psychotherapy With Asian Americans, Boston.

Yamamoto, J., Fund, D., Lo, S., & Reece, S. (1979). Psychopharmacology for Asian Americans and Pacific Islanders. *Psychopharmacology Bulletin, 15,* 29-31.

Ying, Y. W. (1990). Explanatory models of major depression and implications for help-seeking among immigrant Chinese-American women. *Cult-Med-Psychiatry, 14,* 393-408.

Yuen, R. K. W., & Tinsley, H. E. A. (1981). International and American students' expectations about counseling. *Journal of Counseling Psychology, 28,* 66-69.

16

FAMILY VIOLENCE

JOYCE L. LUM

> *I sat down and remembered a saying Old Aunt used to tell me whenever I complained that I had been wrongly accused: "Don't strike a flea on a tiger's head." Don't settle one trouble only to make a bigger one. So I decided to say nothing, do nothing. I made myself blind. I made myself deaf. I let myself become just like Hulan and Jiaguo, that time they said nothing when Wen Fu slapped me.*

—A. Tan, *The Kitchen God's Wife* (1991, p. 260)

Many observers of Asian cultures have noted how interpersonal harmony within Asian groups is an extremely important value. To preserve this harmony, the individuals' needs often are suppressed for the benefit of the group/community and communication is indirect so as not to offend another. Ideally, the leader and group members are sensitive to others' needs that are indirectly expressed, so that the overall well-being of the group thrives. These dynamics illustrate the high value placed on collective peace. Given these strong values on interpersonal harmony, one might expect very little physical violence within Asian American families. In reviewing the evidence, however, the results suggest that family violence among Asian Americans is both an ignored and a significant problem. This chapter focuses primarily on understanding the physical abuse of wives, although a brief discussion is given to other forms of family violence, such as child abuse and sexual abuse, that sometimes occur in conjunction with spousal abuse.

PHYSICAL ABUSE OF WIVES

Defining the prevalence of family violence for Asian Americans is a difficult task for a number of reasons. The growing literature on family violence has examined violence primarily in the context of the Euro-American population. Early studies made little or no references to race/ethnicity. Several researchers have noted the paucity of information on family violence among ethnic minority populations in general (Abraham, in press; Kanuha, 1994; O'Keefe, 1994; Root, 1996) and among Asian Americans in particular (Ho, 1990; Huisman, 1996; Song, 1996; Sorenson, 1996). Recent studies that included race/ethnicity as an intervening variable have focused on African Americans and Euro-Americans (Kesner, Julian, & McKenry, 1997; Lockhart, 1985; see also Kanuha, 1994, for a review of earlier studies). Asian Americans have been either collapsed with other racial groups (e.g., Kratcoski, 1987, simply divides race into categories of White and non-White) or excluded. Five recent studies that examined racial variables have done so in terms of Euro-Americans, African Americans, and Hispanic Americans without referencing Asian American and American Indian populations (Fagen, Stewart, & Hansen, 1983; Gondolf, Fisher, & McFerron, 1988; Neff, Holamon, & Schluter, 1995; O'Keefe, 1994; Sorenson, Upchurch, & Shen, 1996).

One of the difficulties when including Asian Americans in research is accounting for the diversity of groups that fall under the rubric of "Asian Americans." The term *Asian American* or *Asian/Pacific Islander American* is applied to more than 25 groups including Chinese, Filipino, Japanese, South Asian (also known as Asian Indian), Korean, Vietnamese, Cambodian, Hawaiian, Lao, Thai, Hmong, Samoan, and Guamanian (Uba, 1994). Based on the 1990 census (Uba, 1994), the Asian American subgroups that comprise more than 10% of the Asian American population are the Chinese (22.6%), Filipinos (19.3%), Japanese (11.7%), South Asians (11.2%), and Koreans (11.0%). Except for the Japanese Americans with only 33% being foreign born, the majority of Asian Americans are foreign born (56% of Chinese, 64% of Filipinos, 57% of South Asians, 71% of Koreans, 92% of Vietnamese, and 80% of Cambodians). With so many different cultural subgroups, the task of measuring family violence in a culturally sensitive manner that overcomes barriers of language and cultural norms regarding family privacy, history, and so forth becomes very complicated.

Given some of the difficulties of research among these diverse groups, it is not surprising that of the published studies examining Asian American families in the United States, only one to date has attempted a systematic survey of Asian American women to assess the prevalence of family violence in the United States (Root, 1996). Using organizational directories and a snowball approach to gain interviews with 150 immigrant Korean women in Chicago, Song (1996) found a high proportion (60%) of Korean women sampled to report being battered. Of those battered, 70% reported that the physical abuse resulted in bruises, 57% said that they were hit with a closed fist, and 29% reported that the emotional/mental distress required medical attention. Of the battered women, more than a third reported the frequency of abuse to be at least once a month (37%), and

78% reported greater frequency and severity of abuse within the first 3 to 5 years of residency in the United States as compared to subsequent years in this country. More of these women preferred to allow time to solve the problem of abuse (42%), keep the problem in the family (35%), or pray (27%) rather than to talk to friends and relatives (12%) or seek professional help (5%).

Four other empirical studies have focused on the experience of Asian Americans in abusive relationships and the special needs of these individuals. Given the differing needs of Asian Americans, Ho (1990) employed focus groups for Chinese, Vietnamese, Cambodians, and Laotians to explore domestic violence attitudes among their communities in Seattle, Washington. Ho found tolerance for men's domination over their partners present in all the focus groups, although the degree of tolerance varied. The Chinese women expressed a clear disregard for physical abuse, yet they informally estimated that between 20% and 30% of families experienced some form of family violence. The Vietnamese men and women expressed acceptance in regard to men's wishes being important, and the Laotian and Cambodian women were described as being the most subservient to their husbands. Abraham (in press) surveyed several South Asian women's organizations and conducted interviews with South Asian women who had experienced abuse to examine the role of such organizations in ending violence in families. She found that these women's organizations were instrumental in assisting South Asian women end violence in their lives. Dasgupta and Warrier (1996) interviewed several South Asian American women who had been victims of physical abuse to further elucidate the experiences of South Asian women. Huisman (1996) interviewed several service providers and community activists to examine the unique needs of abused Asian American women. Her study found that the needs of Asian American women, particularly those of recent immigrants and refugees, differed from the needs of the general population of women who have suffered abuse.

In contrast to the paucity of empirical information for Asian Americans, many anecdotal references exist concerning family violence. Several studies have included participants' and observers' comments that physical violence is pervasive and tolerated to varying degrees among Asian American families. These observations have been made with regard to Cambodian (Frye & D'Avanzo, 1994; Ho, 1990), Chinese (Chin, 1994; Ho, 1990), Filipino (Cimmarusti, 1996), Korean (Song, 1996; Yim, 1978), Laotian (Ho, 1990), South Asian (Abraham, in press; Dasgupta & Warrier, 1996), Vietnamese (Ho, 1990; Kibria, 1993), and Hmong (Norton & Manson, 1992) communities. Because these reports were based on unsystematically measured observations, one cannot generalize such experiences to the entire Asian American population. These anecdotal accounts, however, serve to point out the possibility that domestic violence problems have been underestimated in Asian American communities.

Given the lack of more direct empirical work to validate the existence of Asian American family violence, perhaps the most persuasive evidence is in the response that shelters and other women's organizations have had from abused Asian American women. Abraham (in press) found that in the 1985-1993 period, approximately 1,071 South Asian women in abusive relationships sought help from women's organizations. In Rimonte's (1989) discussion on domestic violence, she reported that 3,000 women were helped by a center designed specifically to serve Asian Americans in Los Angeles from 1978 to 1985. The races/ethnicities of those served included Korean, Southeast Asian, Chinese, Filipino, Japanese, South Asian, Thai, and Samoan Americans.

In addition, evidence shows that as resources have been allocated to support Asian American women, Asian American women have responded. When the New York Asian Women's Center began its telephone line for abused Asian women in 1985, people questioned whether Asian women would use such a service (Hays, 1993). However, in the first 6 weeks of the service, the center reported receiving more than 55 calls. Dasgupta and Warrier (1996) noted that following the 1985 establishment of Manavi, the first South Asian women's group to focus on preventing violence against women in New Jersey, the group assisted more than 500 women seeking help over the next 5 years. Presently, urban areas with larger Asian American populations, such as Los Angeles, San Francisco, New York, and Boston, have organizations with hotlines specifically designed for Asian women who are victims of family violence. One such agency in San Francisco reported having to turn away nearly 75% of women's requests to stay at its shelter (Furiya, 1993). This agency sheltered approximately 300 women and their children in the 1988-1993 period. In addition, there are several ethnic group women's organizations across the nation (e.g., Manavi) that are geared to help abused women from their specific ethnic groups. Abraham (in press) cited six such organizations for South Asian women as making progress in turning family violence from a private matter into a community concern.

These numbers of Asian American women who have accessed outside help are impressive, especially when one considers the evidence that shelters and organizations usually are the last resort that Asian American women use. The South Asian women in Dasgupta and Warrier's (1996) study sought help from a women's shelter after an average of 8.5 years of abuse. Likewise, only a small percentage of the Korean women in Song's (1996) study left their homes after battering incidents; only 13.3% reported leaving their homes, and 3.3% reported staying elsewhere (not necessarily at shelters). Instead, most of the women's responses to the battering incidents were kept within their homes; for example, 28.9% fought back physically, 57.8% fought back verbally, 21.1% stared at the batterers, and 8.9% tried to ignore the battering or did nothing. Most of these abused women (70%) reported not knowing about formal services that could help them.

There is some controversy over whether family violence is greater in home countries or in the United States for Asian Americans. Song (1996) suggested that violence is higher in the United States due to the stresses of immigration and adjustment. However, the evidence from recent studies is that family violence exists in home countries as well. In their study assessing attitudes toward legal interventions in cases of domestic violence, Choi and Edleson (1995) noted that growing public concern and media publicity have highlighted the issue of wife assaults in Singapore in recent years, and they named four organizations that have established special programs to help victims of family violence. In a systematic national study of Korea, Kim and Cho (1992) undertook a three-stage, stratified random sample of 707 women and 609 men. They found that 37.5% of women reported being battered by their partners in the past year. In Japan, Yoshihama and Sorenson's (1994) survey of 796 women found that a significantly large number (58.7%) of women reported having experienced physical abuse by their intimate partners and that 59.4% reported sexual abuse. A recent study that included both an ethnographic and a quantitative approach to assess family violence in rural Bangladesh found that 19% of the 1,300 randomly sampled women reported being beaten in the past year (Schuler, Hashemi, Riley, & Akhter, 1996). The ethnographic study focused on a select few villages and found that nearly twice as many women (38%) reported being beaten in the past year.

Although it is difficult to compare prevalence rates across cultures and countries given differing methodologies and cultural norms toward research and individual rights, the importance of noting these recent studies is to highlight the growing concern over family violence that happens in Asian families. The paucity of studies on other Asian groups might indicate that, among other factors, family violence is not perceived as a significant problem to investigate, and it definitely underscores how inadequate the current knowledge base is.

Several factors may contribute to the perception that family violence is not a significant problem. First, researchers have ignored minority experiences in general and with respect to Asian Americans in particular. The two national surveys by Straus, Gelles, and Steinmetz (1980) and Straus and Gelles (1986), which established domestic violence as a significant social concern for American families, did not include participants who did not speak or read English, eliminating a significant proportion of the Asian immigrant population. Given that most Asian Americans are foreign born (based on 1990 census data [Uba, 1994]), these studies omitted a potentially large portion of Asian Americans. In addition, Asian Americans might be neglected in research because of particularly complex issues created by diversity among Asian American subgroups that were noted earlier. Finally, many have observed that Asian Americans tend to underutilize the mental health organizations and other resources accessed by the mainstream population (Uba, 1994). This underutilization might have given a misleading impression that Asian Americans do not have similar needs for such resources when, in fact, they do (Uba, 1994).

A related issue is that the cultural dynamics discourage Asian Americans from revealing potentially "shameful" information regarding their families. Several studies have observed a reluctance to share the dysfunctions within families with outsiders despite the great distress experienced. Norton and Manson (1992) noted that of the Southeast Asian women dealing with family violence and seeking help at a mental health clinic, *none* presented family violence as an issue in her initial disclosure of problems, even though family violence later emerged as a significant contributor to the woman's depressive state. A study that compared child sexual abuse among minorities in San Francisco found that Asian American primary caretakers were half as likely as Hispanic, European, or African American caretakers to spontaneously report child sexual abuse to authorities (Rao, DiClemente, & Ponton, 1992). Song (1996) reported that the majority of abused Korean women believed that seeking help from formal sources would shame them in front of their neighbors and relatives.

The sense of shame can be pervasive, and combined with the more traditional sense of the married woman belonging to her husband's family, some victims have reported that when their families are aware of the abuse, the families have chosen not to see it or have taken more protective action. Huisman's (1996) interviews with 18 participants who have worked with Asian American women in abusive relationships in both social service and legal fields found that although sometimes the victim's extended family acted to protect the victim, more often the victim's extended family was observed to maintain the status quo and sometimes even contributed to the violence. According to one study participant, "Many of the women live in extended families where it is the in-laws or the kin family that is actually contributing to the abuse or is encouraging it—for example, 'You have to teach her a lesson' " (quoted in Huisman, 1996).

Dasgupta and Warrier (1996) discussed the problem of tolerating violence on the larger scale of the community turning a blind eye to the needs of women despite the many indicators of family violence being a problem. Sometimes even in the face of collected data on domestic violence, researchers have chosen not to include information on family violence. For example, Nah (1993) interviewed 90 Korean families with the purpose of examining perceived problems among Korean immigrants. Nah noted that when they discussed their personal problems, additional problems such as child rearing, mental illness, domestic violence, and legal and financial worries emerged. In the statistical table reporting problem types and response percentages, however, data were shown for each of the listed additional problems (child rearing, mental illness, legal and financial worries) except for domestic violence. A cursory glance at the table would not inform the reader that family violence was an issue. Uba's (1994) exhaustive literature review of Asian American mental health issues mentioned physical punishment of children and discussed Ho's (1990) study in terms of finding greater tolerance among Southeast Asian women for meeting their husbands' sexual demands. However, the analysis failed to cite the focus of Ho's study—domestic violence— as an issue. In both cases, the issue of family violence, namely wife abuse, became invisible.

The desire to make family violence invisible is in many ways to be expected. Family violence reveals an ugly side of our immediate/extended families and communities. This is difficult and unpleasant to face, especially if there is uncertainty over what can be done to stop such violence. The cultural value of accepting one's fate might inadvertently lead to an acceptance of violence. In addition, there might be unspoken fears on both individual and community levels about bringing what has been a private family matter into the public, thereby violating cultural norms concerning face and shame. It may be believed that discussing family violence openly might mislead those outside the Asian American community to mistakenly assume that all Asian American families are violent. This erroneous view might enhance negative stereotypes and racist thinking concerning Asian Americans. Making family violence invisible is a solution, a way of saving face and avoiding outsiders' criticisms. However, the cost of this invisibility is enormous. Before addressing more completely the costs of keeping family violence invisible, two other aspects of family violence are addressed: sexual abuse and child abuse.

SEXUAL ABUSE

Traditional Asian cultural values place a premium on sexual chastity before marriage and faithfulness to a woman's husband after marriage (Chan & Leong, 1994). This value might be reflected in the results of several studies that have showed that a lower percentage of Asian American college students report being sexually active in comparison to their non-Asian peers (Cochran, Mays, & Leung, 1991; Huang & Uba, 1992; Jessor, Costa, Jessor, & Donovan, 1983). At this point in time, studies focusing on incidence and prevalence rates of sexual abuse in Asian American families do not exist; however, the existing research suggests that sexual abuse in the form of incest might not be as prevalent in the Asian American population as in the general U.S. population.

Ima and Hohm (1991) reviewed 158 child abuse cases that a California state agency had referred to an Asian/Pacific Islander social service organization due to the families' limited English or to culturally related concerns. These cases were comprised of Cambodian, Hmong, Korean, Laotian, Filipino, and Vietnamese families. Among the distribution of the types of maltreatment, the researchers found sexual abuse reports for these children to be significantly lower as compared to the general population (4.9% vs. 27.8%). The reports of sexual abuse were found only among the Filipino and Vietnamese groups. Although the findings of this study are limited in terms of Asian American subgroups sampled and thus are not representative of other unsampled and/or more acculturated groups of Asian Americans, they provide some indication that sexual abuse of children is not as prevalent in the Asian American communities as in the general population. Hall, Windover, and Maramba's (in press) article on Asian American sexual aggression concluded that the rates of perpetration of sexual aggression and sexual victimization are lower for Asian Americans than for other racial groups. Their findings were based on national arrest rate reports and a national survey of university students conducted by Koss, Gidycz, and Wisniewski (1987). Although the scope of Hall et al.'s (in press) review tended to focus on the college population and did not purport to investigate sexual abuse within families, their finding of lower sexual aggression might indeed reflect a lower prevalence of sexual abuse within Asian American families.

When child sexual abuse does occur in Asian American families, several differences have been observed when comparing rates of sexual abuse in other ethnic groups. The Rao et al. (1992) study used data collected from the San Francisco General Hospital to compare similarities and differences in child sexual abuse among American minorities. The Asian Americans in their sample were comprised of Filipino (30%), Vietnamese (16%), Pacific Islander (16%), Chinese (12%), Fiji Indian (6%), Cambodian (6%), Laotian (1%), Thai (1%), multi-Asian (4%), and other Asian Americans (7%). The authors found that these Asian Americans were distinct from African Americans, Hispanic, and Euro-Americans in several significant ways. For the Asian Americans, on averge, the age of the abused child was older, the abuse was less severe (less physical intrusiveness), the victim and perpetrator were more likely to be immigrants, the victim was more likely to have both parents living at home, the perpetrator was more likely to be a male relative, the victim was less likely to show anger and more likely to express suicidal ideation, and the mothers was less likely to believe reports of sexual abuse or to talk to authorities regarding the abuse as compared to African Americans, Hispanic Americans, and Euro-Americans. Some indicators suggest that married immigrant Asian American women are at higher risk for sexual abuse because they feel that they have fewer sexual rights than do their husbands. Ho's (1990) study on domestic violence found that Cambodian and Laotian women did not feel that they had the right to reject their husbands' sexual wishes, lest they be suspected of having affairs. The Vietnamese women felt that rejection of their husbands' sexual wishes was possible only if they had good excuses and that they had to tolerate their husbands' extramarital affairs. The Vietnamese men expressed a sense of "ownership" of their wives.

The only empirical work to investigate the prevalence of sexual abuse in Asian families is the Yoshihama and Sorenson (1994) study surveying women in Japan. They found that 59.4% of women reported experiencing one or more acts they considered sexually abusive from their intimate partners such as forced sex. One fourth of those women reporting sexual abuse stated that their partners used physical violence as well. Although Song's (1996) study did not extensively survey sexual abuse, it found that 36.7% of the physically abused Korean women also reported experiencing forced sex by their partners. These higher percentages of self-reported sexual abuse among Asian Americans differ from Koss et al.'s (1987) data, perhaps because both the Song (1996) and Yoshihama and Sorenson (1994) studies surveyed women who were older (mean ages = 43.5 and 36.2 years, respectively) and mostly married, in contrast to a younger (mean age = 21.4 years) and mostly single (85%) sample that Koss et al. (1987) surveyed. Perhaps the discrepant findings between Koss et al.'s study and the Song (1996) and Yoshihama and Sorenson (1994) studies are due to different attitudes and roles that Asian women are expected to fulfill at various stages of life. The expectations of sexual chastity before marriage and subordination to their husbands after marriage possibly place married Asian women at higher risk of becoming victims of sexual aggression as compared to college-aged, single Asian women. These interspousal dynamics might not be as prevalent among Asians and Asian

Americans who have acculturated the value of women having equal sexual rights as men.

PHYSICAL ABUSE OF CHILDREN

As with sexual abuse, there is little empirical literature that focuses on Asian American child abuse, although there has been some discussion about the cultural differences in what is perceived as useful to children. Ima and Hohm (1991) noted that some folk medicinal practices such as "coining" or "cupping," a vigorous rubbing of coins or cupping of skin that leaves bruises, are thought to be helpful by Southeast Asian parents yet conflict with laws requiring those who work with children to report suspected child abuse, as the bruises might indicate. The number of reported cases of child abuse among Asian Americans is lower (Ima & Hohm, 1991). The Ima and Hohm (1991) study that examined referred cases of child abuse among limited English-speaking Asian American families in San Diego noted that there were proportionally fewer reported cases of child maltreatment among the Asian American population compared to other ethnic groups in San Diego County.

There are some indicators that, given the types of maltreatment (physical abuse, sexual abuse, emotional abuse, and neglect), Asian American children are more at risk of experiencing physical abuse than of experiencing sexual abuse, emotional abuse, or neglect. In examining the distribution of maltreatment, Ima and Hohm (1991) found the distribution of physical abuse to be far greater than that of sexual abuse (53% vs. 5%). This distribution of physical abuse was significantly higher in comparison to that of the general U.S. population, where physical abuse is reported in 28% of the child abuse cases and sexual abuse is reported in 12% of the cases (Ima & Hohm, 1991). The other study to note a higher degree of tolerance for physical punishment among Asian Americans is Ho's (1990) study with Southeast Asian Americans. Ho found that physical punishment of children was a common and openly accepted form of discipline among the Laotian, Cambodian, and Vietnamese focus groups. The study's Chinese participants gave mixed reactions to physical punishment, with some concluding that physical punishment was acceptable and others concluding that it was not.

A few have commented on a high tolerance for physical punishment within some Asian cultures as a form of social control (Ima & Hohm, 1991; Kibria, 1993; Rimonte, 1989; Uba, 1994). A study by Kim and Ko (1990) supported these observations. In a survey of 1,142 Korean children between the ages of 9 and 11 years in Korea, the authors found that only 34% reported not being physically assaulted, 58% reported being mildly battered, and 8% reported being severely battered. Of those who reported not being physically assaulted, 24% reported that someone else in their family had been physically abused. Kim and Ko found that more severe forms of physical abuse occurred in situations where the fathers were unemployed and the mothers were employed, where the children lived apart from their biological parents (e.g., with stepparents, widowed fathers, or grandparents), and where the families occupied lower socioeconomic backgrounds.

CONSEQUENCES OF FAMILY VIOLENCE

The consequences of family violence may be both subtle and severe. On a concrete level, a violent encounter may leave physical injuries that range from bruises to fractures and internal injuries (including injuries that result in miscarriages) that require hospitalization. Focus group members from African American, Asian American, Euro-American, and Latino backgrounds reported dealing with hearing loss, broken bones, cuts, bruises, brain injury, and miscarriages as a result of physical violence (Sorenson, 1996). The extreme consequence of family violence is the death of family members. Data from the early 1980s suggested that among the general population in the United States, slightly more than half of the women who were murdered were killed by their male partners (Browne & Williams, 1993). Statistics show that women murder their male partners as well, although that scenario is less likely. Browne (1993), Walker (1989), and Wilbanks (1983), among others, suggested that in most such cases, women have murdered their partners in retaliation for abuse.

Less concrete, but perhaps just as distressing, are the personal and psychological experiences and reactions to being abused. Survivors of family violence have been found to have significantly increased levels of anxiety, depression, and somatic complaints relative to those of nonvictims (Jaffe, Wolfe, Wilson, & Zak, 1986). Browne (1993) suggested that, for the general population, the effects of severe violence by a partner are psychic numbing, depression, anxiety, hypervigilance, insomnia, constricted affect, and flashbacks to an abusive event. Browne indicated that these symptoms correspond to the symptomatology of the posttraumatic stress disorder (PTSD) diagnosis. The application of such a diagnosis is useful with survivors of abuse because it validates the impact that traumatic external events have on an individual's psyche. This diagnosis also is important for treatment implications because those with PTSD often fail to fully respond to medication and instead require direct intervention that focuses on the trauma experienced (Browne, 1993; Dutton, 1992; Fairbanks & Nicholson, 1987). This lack of a full response to antidepressant medication was observed among Southeast Asian women who were being treated for depression that was linked to family violence (Norton & Manson, 1992). Over a long period of abuse, survivors of abuse have been found to respond to others with fear, have memory loss of traumatic episodes, shut down their affective responses, feel highly anxious, and be hypervigilant (Browne, 1993; Dutton, 1992).

Depression is commonly experienced by survivors of abuse (Heise, Pitanguy, & Germain, 1994). This connection between depression and family violence among Asians is supported by a study of Chinese women in Hong Kong. Tang (1997) found that the women who were physically abused and the children who witnessed abuse had higher levels of depression, anxiety, and distress than did nonabused women and children. This study also found that children who were abused by fathers had higher levels of depression and aggression than did non-abused children. The outcome of such personal despair and distress can be lethal. Higher levels of suicidality were found among Asian American children who had experienced incest (Rao et al., 1992). Among the general population, victims of physical abuse have been observed to have elevated levels of suicidal ideation and suicide attempts along with depression (Browne, 1993; Hilberman & Munson, 1977-1978). In addition to the personal distress of the victims, there are costs to communities and society as a whole (Heise et al., 1994). These include the social well-being and economic costs of having families stigmatized and withdrawing from the rest of the community, of increasing the economic or psychological reliance on others, and of increasing financial needs for police, legal, penal, health, welfare, and shelter services (Heise et al., 1994). In addition, the children who witnessed abuse, as well as those who were physically abused, have been found to be at elevated levels of risk for emotional and behavioral problems that interfere with school and family goals (Jaffe et al., 1986; Wolfe, Jaffe, Wilson, & Zak, 1985), and these problems also may tax community resources.

Without intervention, the short-term consequences are to permit violence to escalate, perhaps to the point of homicide (Fontanarosa, 1995) or suicide (Chin, 1994). The long-term consequence of not intervening with families appears to be that violence will continue to affect future generations. A study that focused on 181 families across three generations in the United States found both child and marital violence in the first generation to be predictive of child abuse potential and relationship aggression in the second generation, which, in turn, was pre-dictive of aggression in the third generation (Doumas, Margolin, & John, 1994). Ignoring the problem allows it to exist. If the problem cannot be acknowledged, then interventions cannot be implemented in a meaningful way. Both preventative and direct responsive measures are important in stopping family violence from continuing to diminish the quality of families and communities.

ASIAN AMERICAN ISSUES IN FAMILY VIOLENCE

The importance of discussing family violence specifically for Asian Americans is that several factors may contribute to a different experience of family violence as compared to the general population. Asian American families often share a set of different cultural and environmental circumstances that need to be con-sidered when making therapeutic interventions. This section addresses these fac-tors, which include immigration, the psychological/cultural dynamic for Asian Americans, cultural values, and issues concerning culturally sensitive therapeutic interventions.

Family violence for an immigrant family presents unique concerns. Immi-gration and its accompanying challenge of adjusting to a different, and sometimes even hostile, social environment are immensely stressful events. The optimism of moving to a "land of opportunity" might soon collide with the reality of downward mobility in the United States. In Song's (1996) study, 58% of the Korean men who were abusive had taken jobs in the United States that were at a lower employment level than those they held prior to immigration, as compared to 17% of the nonabusive Korean men who had taken jobs at a lower employment level. Traditional Asian culture emphasizes honoring a hierarchical structure, working hard to enhance one's status, and avoiding the loss of face. During this transitional period, more traditional Asian men might feel that preserving one's identity in terms of status and position of power is essential, and the loss of such status might contribute to exercising power in destructive ways within the family.

When violence has occurred, the language barrier for immigrants might further compound the social isolation that violent families experience. Not being able to read magazines or understand television programs that deal with family violence amid the general population can limit immigrants' knowledge about abuse and lessen the available resources on which to draw. Even if they are able to read and understand English, the ability to carry on a conversation in English might be limited, and this could prevent them from contacting anonymous hotlines or other sources of outside help. Lack of familiarity with transportation systems and location of services can further impede access to help. Given the stigma of being abused, talking about such problems to those they know in their communities might only isolate these immigrants, especially if relatives or friends are less understanding and criticize the women for "causing" the abuse. Language barriers notwithstanding, women's alternative choices might be confined by economics. Limited economic resources might particularly jeopardize immigrant women who have no other relatives, friends, or means of support in the United States that could enable them to leave abusive partners. Those women whose entire economic support lies with their abusive partners might be completely defenseless in times of crisis (DasGupta, 1993). The totality of these various factors can leave immigrants in violent families feeling extremely isolated and helpless. This sense of isolation might even redouble wives' efforts to cope with the abuse, especially if they do not see alternative choices.

For immigrants, culturally appropriate avenues for dealing with family problems, such as using an uncle or a respected elder to intervene with an abusive spouse, might not exist in the United States. This makes it difficult for an immigrant woman to get help and further isolates her. This was the case of M, a Vietnamese woman seeking help. M reported that she felt isolated when she tried to talk to her abusive husband's brothers, who lived nearby, and they did not do anything. Because M had left her family back in Vietnam and did not have much contact with them, she did not feel that she could talk to her family about the abuse and felt that the family members were too far away to do anything anyway. She coped by withdrawing from both her husband and her children.

Apart from issues of immigration, the psychological experience of family violence might differ significantly for Asian Americans due to different psychological and cultural factors. Traditional Asian cultures have been organized along collectivistic orientations that require a greater degree of cohesion and conformity among members (Triandis, 1995). Markus and Kitayama (1991) discussed this similar idea in terms of construals of the self that differ among cultures. In their conceptualization, many social groups, including traditional Asian cultures, have a collectivistic or "interdependent" sense of self (as opposed to the individual self). This collectivistic (interdependent) self is less differentiated from intimate others, defines experiences in terms of group/other awareness, and prizes maintaining connections with others despite costs to one's self. By contrast, the individualistic or "independent" sense of self establishes identity apart from intimate others, defines experiences based on a self-awareness, and seeks fulfillment of the self's needs. These different construals of the self subsequently affect how one experiences emotions and behaves (Markus & Kitayama, 1991).

Using the collectivistic/individualistic frame can be helpful in understanding the psychological layer of the effects of abuse for Asian Americans. Given the focus on others, an Asian American woman with a strong collectivistic self would be very concerned and centered on the state of her family and partner and might not examine costs to herself. Despite anger at being hit by her partner, she might instead concentrate on her partner's needs in day-to-day situations, trying to fulfill them. She might be sensitive to the racism he faces at work and, consequently, might feel and behave in ways that are protective of him because in so doing she also is protecting her collective self that extends to her family. Because the collectivistic self is less differentiated from intimate others, talking about her partner's episodic explosions to an outsider might be experienced as though she were revealing something defective about herself. Hence, bringing up the subject of his abuse would be avoided. This dynamic has been addressed elsewhere in the literature in terms of shame (Rimonte, 1989). An Asian American with a highly developed collective sense of self might not consider leaving an abusive relationship because, in addition to economic reasons, such an act would be psychologically tearing herself apart. To be separated or alone would be extremely psychologically painful; it could be experienced as cutting off herself (as well as her partner) from a group cultural life that is vitally important. This may be especially true for an Asian American living in a predominantly non-Asian community who already feels culturally alienated. Instead, she might endure the blame and even internalize intense shame for "causing" such explosions of anger to keep a vitally important connection with her partner and sense of self.

In a research project in which White and South Asian British women were interviewed, Hanmer (1996) found that women from both cultural backgrounds were concerned about family and shared similar ways of understanding violence. However, the White women often escaped physical and sexual violence by leaving their abusive partners and living with other men, whereas the South Asian women did not. This difference in behavior might be explained in terms of the contrasting senses of self. The more individualistic cultural view of self would allow women to pursue other relationships to meet their individual needs, whereas the more collectivistic cultural view of self would promote the preservation of their present families. The social milieu of collectivism/individualism sustains these different psychological experiences. There often is a stricter moral code to ensure group cohesion among collectivistic groups (Hanmer, 1996; Triandis, 1995). For example, in Asian communities, divorce carries a stronger stigma (Huisman, 1996). In DasGupta's (1993) work with South Asian women, she noted that the stigma is so strong that many educated, professionally employed South Asian women in abusive marriages will not think about separation, divorce, or remarriage because of their fear of socially dishonoring their parents and husbands.

Both respect for hierarchy and distinct gender roles are cultural values that affect an Asian woman's response. Traditional hierarchical structure in Asian cultures accords older individuals more status over younger ones and men more status over women (Chan & Leong, 1994). Traditional gender roles designate the men to provide economically for their families, whereas the women attend to the social and physical needs of their husbands and children. This hierarchical structure, along with distinct gender roles, organizes family life in most Asian cultures and allots women a lesser status. Disruptions in family life often are socially perceived as the wives' failure. This hierarchical structure combined with a collectivistic sensibility results in women feeling helpless and shameful and, consequently, being silent about abuse. Suffering quietly through violence is a way of keeping the collective peace and harmony. Although the literature on domestic violence suggests that all women in abusive relationships can feel isolated and stigmatized by violent intimate partners, the social context of being an Asian American and the particular circumstances of being an immigrant, along with the Asian cultural and moral values that prioritize familial duties over individual needs, can combine and serve to extremely intensify these feelings of shame and isolation for Asian American women.

Given these cultural values and others that promote loyalty, duty, self-effacement, and obligation to a woman's family, family violence survivors might not directly address the violence in their homes but instead have somatic and other physical complaints. Seeking outside help for ailments such as headaches, fevers, insomnia, and so forth can be more socially and psychologically acceptable (Chan & Leong, 1994) than addressing the issue of family violence.

THERAPEUTIC CONSIDERATIONS

More than likely, the survivor of family violence, not the abuser, will be the one to seek help. Given the hardships the client probably already has endured, the precipitating event to seeking professional help may be of huge crisis proportions for the client. However, cultural norms of self-effacement and inhibition of emotional reactions in public may cause an Asian American client to appear less outwardly distressed compared to non-Asian women in similar situations, an important consideration when making an initial assessment.

Initially when starting therapeutic work with a client, an assessment of the lethality of her situation is critical. Hattendorf and Tollerud (1997) suggested examining the current presence and history of abuse, her present needs and fears, her resources of ego and self (such as her ability to calm herself, be aware of her needs, tolerate strong emotions, or tolerate aloneness), and imagery related to her trauma. If the therapist determines that the client is in danger, Hattendorf and Tollerud recommended devising a safety plan with her because such a measure affirms the seriousness of her concerns and empowers her to protect herself without criticism. For an Asian American woman, this plan should include knowing where she would feel the most comfortable staying if she needed to leave home, considering which relatives and/or friends would provide emotional support, providing emergency shelter phone numbers, discussing what going into a shelter would be like, and thinking ahead how this might affect her children as well as other ways in which to best protect the children. Shelters that are geared to meet the needs of ethnic minority women (e.g., familiar food, culturally aware counselors, ability to speak their language) are critical in providing the necessary support for ethnic minority women during a traumatic time (DasGupta, 1993); leaving home for an unknown experience can be frightening. If such a shelter is not available, then preparing the client for the resources that exist can aid in her making an uncomfortable change.

If the situation is not lethal, then the therapist may concentrate on both providing psychoeducational information on abusive relationships and developing a therapeutic relationship with the client. The psychoeducational components might include giving important information such as the definition of violence,[1] the cycle of abuse, the legal recourse one has,[2] and the fact that family violence is against the law. For Asians, this can be an important educational piece to end family violence given the cultural respect for law and hierarchy, especially when working with an abuser (Ho, 1990). Another psychoeducational component might include making links between somatic complaints and depression to the stresses stemming from family violence. This can be a useful strategy to connect culturally legitimate concerns over physical health to the psychological stresses that result from family violence. Norton and Manson (1992) found that accompanying the cessation of violence in cases involving Southeast Asian women were reports that the headaches and depressive symptoms had disappeared.

Creating a steady, therapeutic relationship with the client is desirable so that the therapist becomes a reliable resource to use in times of family chaos. Conveying understanding and appreciation for the tremendous obstacles the client has overcome in seeking help might aid in establishing rapport with the client. Another way in which to build a supportive relationship is to show understanding and empathy for her position and the difficulties she faces in protecting herself. The client might be sensitive to criticism, especially if no one in her immediate environment has been supportive of her. Therefore, it might be crucial for the therapist to validate the client's experiences and show respect for her needs and decisions by not judging her (DasGupta, 1993). The therapist may seek to empower the client by reflecting on her feelings about events, looking at consequences of her (and others') actions, and exploring alternative courses of action.

It is helpful to assess whether a client has a strong collective or independent sense of self. Working to establish the woman's self as an independent self may assist more-acculturated Asian Americans. However, a different approach might be more effective for less-acculturated Asian American women and women with a strong collective sense of self. When working with a woman with a strong sense of collective self, a therapist might need to support the client's collective self by identifying it and defining what a healthy collective self is: A healthy collective self protects and cares for everyone's welfare, and physical violence violates this collective self. It is healthy for the collective group/self (including for the abusive partner) to stop abusive behavior. From a collectivistic view, to accept a partner's abuse not only injures the abused but also hurts the abuser. When an abuser hits his partner, he is hurting the one who nurtures him, which results in less care and more anxiety and trauma for the group as a whole. Working with a survivor with a strong sense of collective self might mean exploring how the abusive partner, the children, and one's self will survive and be healthier if limits to the abuse are held and the abuser ends his violent behavior. The survivor might need to talk about her fears that her partner might not be able to live on his own if she were to leave or act to protect herself. In addition, the therapist might work with the survivor to decrease her feelings of stigmatization caused by her situation. A survivor should understand that she is not a social failure, that she is not the only one to experience violence in an intimate relationship, that her partner's abusive behavior is not acceptable, and that her partner needs to find constructive ways in which to communicate with his family.

Another therapeutic issue for a woman with a strong sense of collective self might be her fear that she would not survive the loneliness of separation, a critical area of psychological need. Paying attention to ways in which a client can expand her social support system might assist her in offsetting the loneliness and sense of isolation that she might encounter as she takes steps to end a violent relationship. If possible, support from the client's community (e.g., elders, respected teachers, and clergy who are sensitive to family violence issues) might be elicited to intervene with the abusive partner (Ho, 1990) or provide the needed social acceptance and support. An ethnographic study of a Vietnamese community revealed that social support for the survivor and social pressure and stigma placed on the abuser were effective in stopping marital violence (Kibria, 1993). In cases where the abusive partner is not interested or invested in changing his violent behavior, however, the abuse survivor might need to realistically appraise her situation. Helping a woman to accept that she cannot change her partner's behavior despite her best efforts might be the most difficult issue given that the Asian American woman might be dutifully persisting in her efforts to please or change him so as not to be a social "failure." Affirming her success in surviving and making heroic efforts to please him despite the continued abuse, affirming her right to protect herself, and offering the alternative of leaving the abusive situation actually might be a relief for someone who has exhausted her existing coping mechanisms.

Hines (1994) believed that if the decision is made to leave the relationship and one's partner is not accepting of the change, then the following self-protective measures should be considered: leaving when the partner is not at home to avoid an explosive confrontation, taking the children to ensure their safety, contacting the police immediately to provide extra surveillance, and getting a protection order that makes it a legal violation for an abusive partner to be near his partner (although this order might not actually protect a woman from an abuser who ignores and violates the order). The order can be obtained prior to leaving and be served to the abusive partner once the survivor has left. Making copies of important papers and legal documents (e.g., legal certificates, marriage license, wills, property deeds, credit card numbers), as well as having copies of keys and leaving these copies in a safe place (e.g., safe deposit box, trusted friend, post office box), will give one access to needed information (Hines, 1994).

There may be many different solutions for ending violence in relationships. Ideally, when the survivor wants to remain with her partner, the abusive partner also wants to keep the relationship intact and ends his violent behavior by using his resources of family, friends, clergy, counselors, and other professional services. His therapeutic work is to understand how he affects those within his collective self, to develop empathy for his partner and children, to feel powerful without needing to act violently, and to acknowledge what frustrates him without resorting to violence or inflicting emotional abuse on another. As mentioned previously in regard to using cultural respect for law and hierarchy, letting an abusive partner know that family violence is against the law can be helpful in setting clear boundaries of acceptable behavior (Ho, 1990).

CASE STUDY

To protect client confidentiality, the following case study is a composite of several Asian American clients who have sought professional support due to family violence. Any identifying information has been removed.

S initially presented herself in counseling because of a violent episode with her husband. S was a college-educated, 27-year-old Japanese American woman who was married to an older Japanese American man. She recalled that she thought she felt very emotionally close to her husband early in their relationship and felt that they had good relationship overall, especially because he seemed to provide her with a sense of material security and appeared to need and appreciate her. However, she became frightened and sought help when she told him that she feared she might be pregnant and he tore into her, yelling at her and physically throwing her against a wall. Although he had hit her twice previously in a fit of rage, she never had told anyone because she felt she had contributed to his anger by ignoring him.

Later, S revealed that they had many ongoing conflicts in their marriage and that she felt very angry at him for not understanding her needs—that he failed to anticipate her needs, yet she was constantly working to give him what she thought he wanted. She did not want to leave him because of her fears about the economic and social consequences of being on her own. She sometimes expressed her anger in both suicidal and homicidal ideation.

As a result of the violence, we explored S's surprise, hurt, sense of betrayal, and anger at her husband. Over the course of therapy, we worked to help S recognize her own needs in the absence of her husband's ability to recognize them, her expectation that he understand her needs without her telling him, and her disappointment that he often did not act in caring ways. At the same time, S expressed her conflicting wishes to be connected to him given how she saw him needing her and how empty she felt without him. She also was worried about what others would think of her if she left him. Her family's initial reactions led her to believe that she would not be able to remarry or regain a respectable life. Eventually, her husband decided to leave her, which prompted both suicidal and homicidal thoughts. At that point, her therapy focused on dealing with her grief and feelings of helplessness over not being able to keep her marriage intact and not acting on her suicidal/homicidal thoughts. In her difficult situation, S found that she was able to let go of the debilitating sense of shame that isolated her and kept her from establishing new relationships. She dealt with her fears of being judged by allowing her parents and a few supportive friends to know increasingly more about her past difficult marital relationship, including the abuse, as they responded with more concern for her. Over time, she regained confidence in herself and made use of others' support to move on to more healthful relationships.

SUMMARY AND CONCLUSION

The Asian cultural values of loyalty, hierarchy, collectivism, obligation, loss of face, and so forth all uphold the Asian American family unit. These values have kept Asian American families working successfully together despite tremendous difficulties that include making huge adjustments to living within a new culture, combating racism, and pursuing a strong family life that considers each other's welfare. Even so, when a problem arises that is perceived as shameful, these same values that hold the family unit together might also prevent the family from seeking outside help.

Family violence is neither the Asian American cultural ideal nor the norm. Perhaps in an effort to keep the peace within the Asian American family and community, however, we have not wholeheartedly examined this difficult area. Ignoring the problem of family violence allows violence to exist to the detriment of all. As this chapter has outlined, there are both clear and undefined needs within Asian American communities to deal with the issue of family violence. Clearly, the existing evidence reveals that family violence is a significant concern. The extent, nature, and course of family violence in Asian American communities are less well understood. In this chapter, I have presented several cultural and therapeutic considerations when working with Asian Americans; nonetheless, more researched data and discussions on culturally sensitive therapeutic work are needed to further our knowledge regarding effective ways in which to end family violence within Asian American communities. Perhaps if we can extend the sense of collective self to see and hear our hurting families, we can justify the intrusion into family life, risk knowing that violence exists within some of our families, and begin to build our community resources by educating teachers, clergy, and other community helpers about family violence. These are necessary measures so that when family violence occurs, it is accepted as a community problem and community understanding and support are given to end the violence. Our Asian American communities can be proud of many accomplishments and achievements obtained in the United States, and we can further our successes by freeing all families from violence.

NOTES

1. This includes, but is not limited to, slapping, pinching, kicking, choking, hitting, and committing other verbally, emotionally, and sexually abusive acts.

2. It might be helpful for immigrants to know that the 1994 Violence Against Women Act permits undocumented abused women to obtain legal permanent resident status by self-petitioning or by suspension of deportation (Huisman, 1996; Orloff & Kelly, 1995).

REFERENCES

Abraham, M. (1995). Ethnicity, gender, and marital violence: South Asian women's organizations in the United States. *Gender & Society, 9,* 450-468.

Abraham, M. (in press). Speaking the unspeakable: Marital violence against South Asian immigrant women in the United States. *Indian Journal of Gender Studies.*

Browne, A. (1993). Violence against women by male partners: Prevalence, outcomes, and policy implications. *American Psychologist, 48,* 1077-1087.

Browne, A., & Williams, K. R. (1993). Gender intimacy and lethal violence: Trends from 1976-1987. *Gender & Society, 7,* 78-98.

Chan, S., & Leong, C. W. (1994). Chinese families in transition: Cultural conflicts and adjustment problems. *Journal of Social Distress and the Homeless, 3,* 263-281.

Chin, K. (1994). Out-of-town brides: International marriage and wife abuse among Chinese immigrants. *Journal of Comparative Family Studies, 25,* 53-69.

Choi, A., & Edleson, J. (1995). Advocating legal intervention in wife assaults: Results from a national survey of Singapore. *Journal of Interpersonal Violence, 10,* 243-258.

Cimmarusti, R. A. (1996). Exploring aspects of Filipino-American families. *Journal of Marital and Family Therapy, 22,* 205-217.

Cochran, S. D., Mays, V. M., & Leung, L. (1991). Sexual practices of heterosexual Asian-American young adults: Implications for risk of HIV infection. *Archives of Sexual Behavior, 20,* 381-391.

DasGupta, K. (1993). Asian Indian women: Guidelines for community intervention in the event of abuse. *Family Violence and Sexual Assault Bulletin, 9,* 25-29.

Dasgupta, S. D., & Warrier, S. (1996). In the footsteps of "Arundhati": Asian Indian women's experience of domestic violence in the United States. *Violence Against Women, 2,* 238-259.

Doumas, D., Margolin, G., & John, R. S. (1994). The intergenerational transmission of aggression across three generations. *Journal of Family Violence, 9,* 157-175.

Dutton, M. A. (1992). Assessment and treatment of PTSD among battered women. In D. Foy (Ed.), *Treating PTSD: Procedure for combat veterans, battered women, adult and child sexual assaults.* New York: Guilford.

Fagen, J., Stewart, D., & Hansen, K. (1983). Violent men or violent husbands? Background factors and situational correlates. In D. Finkelhor, R. Gelles, G. Hotaling, & M. Straus (Eds.), *The dark side of families: Current family violence research* (pp. 49-69). Beverly Hills, CA: Sage.

Fairbanks, J. A., & Nicholson, R. A. (1987). Theoretical and empirical issues in the treatment of posttraumatic stress disorder. *Journal of Clinical Psychology, 43,* 44-45.

Fontanarosa, P. B. (1995). The unrelenting epidemic of violence in America: Truth and conse-quences. *Journal of the American Medical Association, 273,* 1792-1793.

Frye, B. A., & D'Avanzo, C. D. (1994). Cultural themes in family stress and violence among Cambodian refugee women in the inner city. *Advances in Nursing Science, 16,* 64-77.

Furiya, L. (1993, October 22). Asian women's shelter fills a need in community. *Asian Week,* pp. 1, 20.

Gondolf, E. W., Fisher, E., & McFerron, J. R. (1988). Racial differences among shelter residents: A comparison of Anglo, Black, and Hispanic battered women. *Journal of Family Violence, 76,* 39-51.

Hall, G. C. N., Windover, A. K., & Maramba, G. G. (in press). Sexual aggression among Asian Americans. *Cultural Diversity and Mental Health.*

Hanmer, J. (1996). Women and violence: Commonalities and diversities. In B. Fawcett, B. Featherstone, J. Hearn, & C. Toft (Eds.), *Violence and gender relations: Theories and interventions* (pp. 7-21). London: Sage.

Hattendorf, J., & Tollerud, T. R. (1997). Domestic violence: Counseling strategies that minimize the impact of secondary victimization. *Perspectives in Psychiatric Care, 33,* 14-24.

Hays, C. L. (1993, December 6). Enduring violence in a new home. *The New York Times.*

Heise, L. L., Pitanguy, J., & Germain, A. (1994). *Violence against women: The hidden health burden.* Washington: World Bank.

Hilberman, E., & Munson, K. (1977-1978). Sixty battered women. *Victimology: An Interna-tional Journal, 2,* 460-470.

Hines, S. (1994, Spring). Getting out. *Mothering,* pp. 104-107.

Ho, C. K. (1990). An analysis of domestic violence in Asian American communities: A multicultural approach to counseling. In L. Brown & M. P. P. Root (Eds.), *Diversity and complexity in feminist therapy* (pp. 129-150). New York: Haworth.

Huang, K., & Uba, L. (1992). Premarital sexual behavior among Chinese college students in the United States. *Archives of Sexual Behavior, 21,* 227-240.

Huisman, K. A. (1996). Wife battering in Asian American communities. *Violence Against Women, 2,* 260-283.

Ima, K., & Hohm, C. F. (1991). Child maltreatment among Asian and Pacific Islander refugees and immigrants: The San Diego case. *Journal of Interpersonal Violence, 6,* 267-285.

Jaffe, P., Wolfe, D., Wilson, S., and Zak, L. (1986). Similarities in behavioral and social maladjustment among child victims and witnesses to family violence. *American Journal of Orthopsychiatry, 56,* 142-146.

Jessor, R., Costa, F., Jessor, L., & Donovan, J. E. (1983). Time of first intercourse: A prospective study. *Journal of Personality and Social Psychology, 44,* 608-626.

Kanuha, V. (1994). Women of color in battering relationships. In L. Comas-Diaz & B. Greene (Eds.), *Women of color* (pp. 428-454). New York: Guilford.

Kesner, J. E., Julian, T., & McKenry, P. C. (1997). Application of attachment theory to male violence toward female intimates. *Journal of Family Violence, 13,* 211-228.

Kibria, N. (1993). *Family tightrope: The changing lives of Vietnamese Americans.* Princeton, NJ: Princeton University Press.

Kim, K., & Cho, Y. (1992). Epidemiological survey of spousal abuse in Korea. In E. C. Viano (Ed.), *Intimate violence: Interdisciplinary perspectives.* Washington, DC: Hemisphere.

Kim, K., & Ko, B. (1990). An incidence survey of battered children in two elementary schools of Seoul. *Child Abuse and Neglect, 14,* 273-276.

Koss, M. P., Gidycz, C. A., & Wisniewski, N. (1987). The scope of rape: Incidence and prevalence of sexual aggression and victimization in a national sample of higher education students. *Journal of Consulting and Clinical Psychology, 55,* 162-170.

Kratcoski, P. C. (1987). Families who kill. *Marriage and Family Review, 12,* 47-70.

Lockhart, L. L. (1985). Methodological issues in comparative racial analyses: The case of wife abuse. *Social Work Research and Abstracts, 21,* 35-41.

Markus, H. R., & Kitayama, S. (1991). Culture and the self: Implications for cognition, emotion, and motivation. *Psychological Review, 98,* 224-253.

Nah, K. (1993). Perceived problems and service delivery for Korean immigrants. *Social Work, 38,* 289-296.

Neff, J. A., Holamon, B., & Schluter, T. D. (1995). Spousal violence among Anglos, Blacks, and Mexican Americans: The role of demographic variables, psychosocial predictors, and alcohol consumption. *Journal of Family Violence, 10,* 1-21.

Norton, I. M., & Manson, S. M. (1992). An association between domestic violence and depression among Southeast Asian refugee women. *Journal of Nervous and Mental Disease, 180,* 729-730.

O'Keefe, M. (1994). Racial/ethnic differences among battered women and their children. *Journal of Child and Family Studies, 3,* 283-305.

Orloff, L. E., & Kelly, N. (1995). A look at the Violence Against Women Act and gender-related asylum. *Violence Against Women, 1,* 380-400.

Rao, K., DiClemente, R. J., & Ponton, L. E. (1992). Child sexual abuse of Asians compared with other populations. *Journal of American Academy of Child and Adolescent Psychiatry, 31,* 880-886.

Rimonte, N. (1989). Domestic violence among Pacific Asians. In Asian Women United of California (Ed.), *Making waves: An anthology of writings by and about Asian American women* (pp. 327-336). Boston: Beacon.

Root, M. P. (1996). Women of color and traumatic stress in "domestic captivity": Gender and race as disempowering statuses. In A. J. Marsella, M. J. Friedman, E. T. Gerrity, & R. M. Scurfield (Eds.), *Ethnocultural aspects of posttraumatic stress disorder: Issues, research, clinical applications* (pp. 363-387). Washington, DC: American Psychological Association.

Schuler, S. R., Hashemi, S. M., Riley, A. P., & Akhter, S. (1996). Credit programs, patriarchy and men's violence against women in rural Bangladesh. *Social Science and Medicine, 43,* 1729-1742.

Song, Y. I. (1996). *Battered women in Korean immigrant families.* New York: Garland.

Sorenson, S. B. (1996). Violence against women: Examining ethnic differences and commonalities. *Evaluation Review, 20,* 123-145.

Sorenson, S. B., Upchurch, D. M., & Shen, H. (1996). Violence and injury in marital arguments: Risk patterns and gender differences. *American Journal of Public Health, 86,* 35-40.

Straus, M. A., & Gelles, R. J. (1986). Societal change in family violence from 1975 to 1985 as revealed by two national surveys. *Journal of Marriage and the Family, 48,* 465-479.

Straus, M. A., Gelles, R. J., & Steinmetz, S., (1980). *Behind closed doors: Violence in the American family.* Garden City, NJ: Anchor.

Tan, A. (1991). *The kitchen god's wife.* New York: Putnam.

Tang, C. S. (1997). Psychological impact of wife abuse: Experiences of Chinese women and their children. *Journal of Interpersonal Violence, 12,* 466-478.

Triandis, H. C. (1995). *Individualism and collectivism.* Boulder, CO: Westview.

Uba, L. (1994). *Asian Americans: Personality patterns, identity, and mental health.* New York: Guilford.

Walker, L. E. A. (1989). Psychology and violence against women. *American Psychologist, 44,* 685-702.

Wilbanks, W. (1983). The female homicide offender in Dade County, Florida. *Criminal Justice Review, 8.*

Wolfe, D. A., Jaffe, P., Wilson, S. K., & Zak, L. (1985). Children of battered women: The relation of child behavior to family violence and maternal stress. *Journal of Consulting and Clinical Psychology, 53,* 657-665.

Yim, S. B. (1978). Korean battered wives: A sociological and psychological analysis of conjugal violence in Korean immigrant families. In H. H. Sunoo & D. S. Sunoo (Eds.), *Korean women: In a struggle for humanization* (pp. 171-189). Memphis, TN: Association of Korean Christian Scholars.

Yoshihama, M., & Sorenson, S. B. (1994). Physical, sexual, and emotional abuse by male intimates: Experiences of women in Japan. *Violence and Victims, 9,* 63-77.

17

ADDICTIVE BEHAVIORS

Nolan W. S. Zane
Jeannie Huh-Kim

Drug use and other addictive behaviors such as gambling have become a major focus of social concern in the United States. This concern reflects the growing reality that accessing legal or illicit sources for maintaining these maladaptive habits is not difficult, even for the very young. There is the popular notion that an addictive behavior such as substance abuse becomes problematic only when someone has an addiction. Contrary to this belief, an addictive behavior such as psychoactive substance abuse can involve a pattern of maladaptive use that has not as yet progressed to the stage of full-blown dependence or physical addiction. For example, according to the 4th edition of *Diagnostic and Statistical Manual of Mental Disorders* (DSM-IV) (American Psychiatric Association, 1994), a person still can have a substance problem if he or she either (a) persistently uses a substance despite social, occupation, psychological, or physical problems or (b) continues to use a substance in physically dangerous situations.

Despite consistent efforts by federal, state, and local agencies to control and inhibit substance use and abuse, a great number of Americans continue to use a drug of some type or another. Alcohol is the most widely used of all the psychoactive drugs. In 1988, 25% of those between 12 and 17 years of age had consumed an alcoholic beverage during the previous month, as had 65% of those between 18 and 25 years of age (Bootzin, Acocella, & Alloy, 1993). In 1987, the average annual alcohol consumption of adults in the United States was 2.3 gallons

AUTHORS' NOTE: This chapter was supported in part by the National Research Center on Asian American Mental Health (NIMH No. R01 MH44331).

of distilled spirits, 3.4 gallons of wine, and 34.4 gallons of beer (U.S. Bureau of the Census, 1990). Moreover, the National Institute on Alcohol Abuse estimated that there are now nearly 13 million alcoholics and alcohol abusers in the United States (Kaplan & Sadock, 1991). As for tobacco use, 3 out of 10 American adults are habitual smokers (Toneatto, Sobell, Sobell, & Leo, 1991). This makes nicotine dependence the most common form of drug dependence in the United States. Heroin is the most widely used type of illegal narcotic drug. In the early 1970s, heroin use increased each year. In 1972 and 1973, it was estimated that there were 600,000 narcotic addicts in the United States. Since then, the percentage of heroin users in the country seems to have remained constant. The popularity of cocaine soared in the 1970s, peaked in the mid-1980s at 5.8 million users, and declined to 2.9 million users by 1988 (National Institute on Drug Abuse, 1989). The use of marijuana also is fairly common. More than 1 out of 2 Americans between 18 and 25 years of age have tried marijuana, and many have become frequent users (National Institute on Drug Abuse, 1989). Marijuana use among the young increased dramatically in the 1970s, peaked in 1979 and 1980, and has been declining slowly since then. However, it still is America's most popular illicit drug. In many cases, drugs are not used individually. Often users like to combine the effects of several drugs, with the most common combination involving the use of marijuana and alcohol.

The negative consequences of addictive behavioral problems to a person's physical health and mental health have been well documented, but what often is overlooked is the cost incurred by society in general. For example, it is estimated that alcohol-related problems cost the American economy more than $116 billion in 1983 (National Council on Alcoholism, 1986). Most of this economic loss is concentrated in three areas: decreased work productivity, health problems, and motor vehicle accidents. The largest portion of this loss—about $70 billion—is due to decreased work productivity. Workers with drinking problems are slower and less efficient, lose time on the job, make hasty decisions, cause accidents, and lower the morale of their coworkers. Furthermore, they are more likely to become prematurely disabled and to die young (Bootzin, Acocella, & Alloy, 1993). In terms of medical costs, $15.9 billion was spent in 1981 on medical treatment and support services for alcoholics. In one case, it was estimated that alcoholic employees cost their companies the equivalent of 25% of their salaries (Alcoholism Council of Greater New York, 1987). Approximately half of all occupied beds in American hospitals are filled by people with ailments linked to alcohol consumption (U.S. Department of Health and Human Services, 1981). Finally, $10 billion is lost annually in alcohol-related motor vehicle accidents. Alcohol is implicated in as many as half of all car accidents, and it is involved in more than half of the accidents in which there are fatalities.

Little has been written about the prevalence of addictive disorders such as gambling and alcohol and drug abuse among Asian Americans. What little that is known about this ethnic population is from two sources: research based on either treated or untreated cases. The former involves estimating prevalence based on samples of individuals who are in clinical treatment for their addictive problems. The latter involves surveys on noninstitutionalized populations. In the following sections, research on alcohol and other drug use, smoking, and gambling is presented and discussed.

ALCOHOL AND OTHER DRUG USE

The untreated cases research on the prevalence and extent of alcohol and other drug problems among Asian American populations tends to cluster into four domains. First, a number of studies have focused on adolescent populations. It is important to distinguish this research from that conducted on Asian adults because the drug use patterns among the younger and predominantly American-born Asian populations can differ greatly from those among the older adult and predominantly immigrant populations. Second, a large number of studies have surveyed various Asian groups in Hawaii. These studies have revealed interesting inter-Asian differences in drug use, but, as discussed later, the generality of these findings to mainland Asian populations might be limited. Third, a number of investigations have examined Asian drug use in West Coast populations. Finally, cross-national studies have been conducted on Asian populations in the United States and/or East Asia. The subsequent sections review the studies from each of these four major sources of information.

Drug Use Among Asian American Youths

A number of studies on substance use have focused on adolescent populations. Maddahian, Newcomb, and Bentler (1985) examined patterns of drug use for 847 adolescents from four different ethnic backgrounds over a 5-year period. A total of 65 Asian students participated in this study (7.7% of total sample). In Year 1, Asian adolescents showed the highest rate of single alcohol use, which diminished over time. Asians were the largest group that had tried only alcohol and no other substance. In Year 5, Asians had the highest percentage of nonusers (29.2%) among the ethnic groups. Nakagawa and Watanabe (1973) surveyed Asian students in junior and senior high schools on personal drug use (excluding marijuana and alcohol) in Seattle, Washington. Among the 339 males and 367 females surveyed, 12% of the males and 17% of the females were classified as "users." By ethnic group, 49% of "other Asians," 45% of Filipinos, 29% of Japanese, and 22% of Chinese had some experience with "hard" drugs such as amphetamines, barbiturates, psychedelics, cocaine, and heroin (in descending order of frequency of use).

Kandel, Single, and Kessler (1976) conducted a study of drug use in New York City high schools and sampled 7,530 students. They found that Asian Americans had the lowest level of overall drug use when compared to American Indians, African Americans, Hispanics, and Whites. To obtain baseline epidemiological data on drug use, Porter, Vieira, Kaplan, Heesch, and Colyar (1973) surveyed the majority of students in the 6th through 12th grades in Anchorage, Alaska.

Of the 15,634 students surveyed, 0.6% were Asian American. Although Asian American students had the lowest percentage (26.0%) of users (i.e., those who had used one or more of the drugs on the list at least once) when compared to Native Alaskans (43.5%), Whites (35.7%), and African Americans (32.2%), they reported the highest use among those students who had used only alcohol or tobacco or both (52.0%). In terms of nonusers, Asian Americans ranked second (22.0%) after Native Alaskans (21.8%). Strimbu et al. (1973) surveyed college students in a large southeastern state. In a sample of 20,547 respondents, 1% of the respondents were classified as Asian Americans. Asian Americans ranked lowest on tobacco and alcohol use and ranked second lowest on the use of marijuana and strong stimulants when compared to the American Indian, African American, and White samples.

A study that was conducted throughout the state of New York surveyed a large representative sample of 27,335 students in the 7th through 12th grades (Barnes & Welte, 1986). Asian Americans had the highest percentage of abstainers (55%), followed by African Americans (41%), Hispanics (37%), American Indians (27%), and Whites (24%). Heavy drinking was reported in 18% of American Indians, 16% of Whites, and only 6% of Asians. However, Asian American students who did drink consumed the largest amount of alcohol per day when compared to the other ethnic groups (1.46 ounces of absolute alcohol vs. 0.76 ounces for White drinkers, 0.86 ounces for Hispanic drinkers, and 1.29 ounces for American Indian drinkers). The same pattern of high levels of abstinence but with high levels of consumption among Asian American adolescent drinkers was reported in an earlier national survey (Rachal et al., 1975). In a survey of males and females 16 through 22 years of age with the San Diego Job Corps, Morgan, Wingard, and Felice (1984) found that a smaller percentage of Indochinese males and females reported drinking when compared to White, African American, and Hispanic youths.

In 1980, the Department of Health and the Department of Education in Hawaii initiated several Risk Reduction Projects designed to prevent or delay the onset of alcohol, cigarette, and marijuana use among students in the 7th through 12th grades. The Risk Reduction Projects found that the frequency of heavy beer use (weekly or daily) was fairly evenly distributed among the White, Japanese, and Filipino youth groups. However, for those Native Hawaiian youths who drank, heavy drinking was more than twice as likely as moderate or infrequent drinking (Ahern, 1989).

Drug Use in Hawaii

The state of Hawaii has a diverse ethnic composition among its population including substantial numbers of Native Hawaiians, Japanese, Filipinos, Chinese, and Whites as well as smaller numbers of Koreans, Samoans, Portuguese, and persons of mixed ancestry. In Hawaii, the existence of ethnocultural and socioeconomic diversity, coupled with a relatively high incidence of alcohol consumption, provides a favorable environment for conducting alcohol research, especially as it relates to different ethnic groups. Hawaii is racially and culturally diverse. The most salient feature of Hawaii's population is its ethnic diversity. The largest ethnic groups are Whites, Japanese, Native Hawaiians (part Hawaiians and full-blooded Hawaiians combined), and Filipinos. Hawaii is a major consumer of alcoholic beverages. Stinson (1984) found that per capita consumption of ethanol in Hawaii had increased strikingly and consistently since 1970.

Lemert (1964) was the first to systematically examine ethnic group differences in alcohol use in Hawaii. On the basis of questionnaires and interviews, Lemert obtained data on alcohol use, drinking habits, beverage preferences, and drinking problems from 480 workers on several large sugar plantations on the island of Hawaii in 1959 and 1960. He found that Whites led all other ethnic groups in the proportion of current drinkers (97.1%). Filipinos ranked next (90.1%), followed by Japanese (85.3%), Puerto Ricans (77.8%), and Hawaiians (50.0%). It is questionable that the study was even representative of Hawaiian plantation workers. Lemert indicated that more than 50% of the workers in his sample were Mormon, which was far greater than expected for any random sampling of Hawaiian plantation workers.

The following studies conducted in Hawaii have tended to find lower rates of alcohol consumption for Asian American populations when compared to those for Whites. Wilson, McClearn, and Johnson (1978) studied data obtained from 2,418 respondents from four different ethnic groups in Hawaii. They employed a sampling plan based on the 1970 census. There were more than 600 respondents in each group with the exception of the Hapa-Haole sample (mixed-race individuals with one White and one Asian parent), in which there were 443 respondents. Asian ethnic groups (Chinese, 18%; Japanese, 17%; Hapa-Haole, 7%) were more likely to be abstainers than were Whites (4%). Overall, females (17%) were nearly twice as likely as males (9%) to indicate that they never drank. In a sample of 3,714, Schwitters, Johnson, McClearn, and Wilson (1982) also reported a greater percentage of abstainers among Asians (Chinese, 17.1%; Filipinos, 31.0%; Japanese, 16.7%; Hawaiians, 11.1%; Hapa-Haole, 7.0%) compared to Whites (4.3%). In addition, the Whites in the study were characterized as being much heavier drinkers than their Asian counterparts. Kotani (1982) also reported a lower percentage of heavy drinkers in Asian American populations (Hawaiian, 19.4%; Japanese, 11.4%; Filipinos, 8.8%; Chinese, 2.2%) than in Whites (40.6%).

A statewide epidemiological survey was conducted in Hawaii in 1984 (Murakami, 1989). It sampled 2,503 individuals age 18 years or older including Whites (28.5%), Japanese (21.6%), Filipinos (11.4%), and Native Hawaiians (18.9%). A structured interview was conducted with each respondent to elicit information on individual alcohol consumption, problems related to drinking, and drug use. The following definitions for extent of drinking were used: *Nondrinkers* reportedly drank less than 1.0 ounce of alcohol in a year and included former drinkers and abstainers, *light drinkers* drank between 1.0 and 76.6 ounces of alcohol in a year, *moderate drinkers* drank between 76.7 and 361.0 ounces of alcohol in a year, and *heavy drinkers* drank more than 361.0 ounces of alcohol in a year. The findings indicated that in the Hawaiian population, 44.4% were nondrinkers, 26.7% were light drinkers, 19.8% were moderate drinkers, and 9.1% were heavy drinkers. Native Hawaiians consumed less alcohol than did Whites but consumed more than did other ethnic groups such as the Japanese and Filipinos. Drinking prevalence rates for Native Hawaiians and Whites consistently exceeded those of the Japanese and Filipinos as well as the statewide rates in the light, moderate, and heavy drinker classifications. As expected, the Japanese and Filipino groups had higher percentages of nondrinkers than did the Native Hawaiian and White groups, whereas the reverse was found in the light drinker classification. These findings are supported by previous studies conducted in Hawaii. The rates for males were higher than those for females in the moderate and heavy classifications. Although more than 50% of the males within each ethnic group were nondrinkers or light drinkers, a fairly large proportion of moderate and heavy drinkers were found, especially within the Native Hawaiian and White groups. At least 67% of the females within each of the ethnic groups were either nondrinkers or light drinkers. The percentage of females who drank heavily was higher for the White (9.1%) and Native Hawaiian (8.2%) groups than for the other two ethnic groups.

Attitudes toward help seeking for alcohol and drug problems also were assessed. Close to two thirds of the Whites (65%) would definitely seek professional help, whereas fewer Japanese (53%), Native Hawaiians (51%), and Filipinos (42%) would use professional services. A higher percentage of Native Hawaiians, Japanese, and Filipinos reported barriers than did Whites. Personal shame and embarrassment appeared to be a major barrier with more Japanese (26.9%), Native Hawaiians (24.2%), and Filipinos (23.5%) than Whites (19.1%) identifying this as a problem in help seeking.

In one of the most comprehensive studies on Asian ethnic differences in drinking in Hawaii (Marchand, Kolonel, & Yoshizawa, 1989), interview data were collected over a 5-year period (1975-1980) from a representative sample of 50,000 Hawaiian residents from the five major ethnic groups (Whites, Japanese, Chinese, Filipinos, and Native Hawaiians). Native Hawaiians had the highest consumption of beer, and Whites had the highest consumption of wine and spirits. Overall, total ethanol intake was similar for these two ethnic groups and was considerably higher than that for the other three Asian groups. This pattern of ethnic differences was observed when either daily or lifetime use of alcohol was analyzed, and the pattern was rather consistent among the genders and among different age groups. Native Hawaiians who drank tended to consume more ethanol than did drinkers in the other Asian groups. In both genders, Whites reported the highest ethanol consumption, followed closely by Native Hawaiians. Japanese, Filipinos, and Chinese had markedly lower ethanol intakes. For example, compared to Whites, the Chinese had an ethanol intake 3.5 times lower for males and 13.3 times lower for females. Ethanol intake was greater for males than for females and was greater for middle-aged groups than for younger and older groups. The percentage of drinkers in each gender/ethnic group reflected a similar pattern of alcohol use, with Whites most likely and Chinese and Filipinos least likely to be alcohol users. Weekly drinking patterns were very similar across ethnic groups and did not suggest that binge or regular drinking was more likely for any particular group. Some of the differences in ethnic drinking rates could be attributed to differences in beer consumption. Native Hawaiians reported drinking more beer than did the other races in a very consistent fashion across genders and age groups. Beer consumption also was greater among White males than among Asian males. There were some interesting interactions between age and ethnic group in consumption. For example, most of the differences in beer consumption between Japanese and White males occurred in the younger age groups; after 40 years of age, Japanese males reported drinking as much beer as did White males. Chinese respondents had the lowest level of beer consumption among males. Among females, beer consumption was much lower overall than among males, and most of the beer drinking by females occurred among Native Hawaiians and Whites. Wine and hard liquor were most consumed by Whites of both genders, with a trend toward increasing consumption with increasing age. A similar trend was discernible for hard liquor consumption among males of the other ethnic groups and among Native Hawaiian and Chinese females.

The overall prevalence rates for alcohol found in this study were low compared to those found by others in Hawaii (Murakami, 1989). This was due partly to the fact that the survey questionnaire identified only regular alcohol drinkers. Thus, the "abstainer" group included some "rare" and "occasional" drinkers. In an effort to examine health problems associated with drinking, alcohol consumption was correlated with the ethnic-specific cancer incidence rates. The results indicated that the alcohol intake patterns in Hawaii helped explain the ethnic variation in the incidence of oropharyngeal cancer. However, alcohol intake patterns do not adequately account for the ethnic variation in rate of esophageal cancer.

Due to the great cultural diversity of the state population, drug use studies in Hawaii have been especially effective in examining the ethnic variation that exists among different Asian groups in alcohol use. The research indicates that there is great variability in estimates of the prevalence of alcohol users, abusers, and alcoholics across ethnic groups in Hawaii (Ahern, 1989). Nonetheless, in terms of the overall use of alcohol, the accumulated evidence seems to indicate that Whites and Native Hawaiians do not differ significantly from each other but that these two groups had significantly higher drinking rates than did the Japanese, Chinese, and Filipinos. In most estimates of drinking prevalence and alcohol abuse, the Chinese and Filipinos had the lowest rates. These studies also found that females used alcohol far less than did males and that these gender differences tended be very consistent across the various ethnic groups. Some researchers have suggested that Asian groups from Hawaii might be quite different from their mainland counterparts in terms of their nonminority status, acculturation, English language proficiency, community cohesiveness, social-political identification, and so forth (Kitano & Daniels, 1988; Sue & Morishima, 1982). Nevertheless, the Hawaiian research has been valuable in alerting policymakers, care providers, and researchers to the important variation that can exist among different Asian American populations with respect to drug use and abuse.

Asian Drug Use in the Continental United States

The best national information on drinking frequency for Asian Americans is the data collected by the 1977 National Health Interview Survey (HIS) conducted by the National Center for Health Statistics. The HIS consists of continuous sampling and interviewing of 41,000 households annually nationwide. In 1977, data on the health practices of Asian and Pacific Islander (API) Americans were obtained on a one-third subsample of persons age 20 years or over. The results showed that 32% of the 256 API Americans in the subsample never drank alcoholic beverages or liquor, 52% drank occasionally, 9% drank once or twice a week, and 8% drank three or more times a week. These rates were significantly lower than the rates found for Whites or other ethnic minority groups.

Studies in the continental United States have tended to focus on Asian American populations residing on the West Coast. Most of these studies have been reviewed elsewhere (Zane & Kim, 1994). In general, they have found that Asian Americans have higher rates of abstinence and lower rates of drug use than do other ethnic groups. However, important variations among different Asian groups have been found. For example, Klatsky, Siegelaub, Landy, and Friedman (1983) collected data from 59,766 individuals who had multiphasic health examinations at Kaiser-Permanente Medical Care Program from 1978 to 1980. In examining ethnic patterns of alcohol use, they found that Asian men reported much less drinking than did White, Black, and Hispanic men. Similarly, Asian women reported much less drinking than did women from other ethnic groups. Among the Asians, Chinese men reported the least drinking, whereas Japanese men reported the most alcohol use. Among women, Filipinos reported the least drinking, whereas Japanese women reported drinking more than the other Asian ethnic groups. For each Asian ethnic group, there was a higher percentage of abstainers among foreign-born Asians (Chinese, 38.8%; Japanese, 29.4%; Filipinos, 39.9%) than among their American-born counterparts (Chinese, 24.8%; Japanese, 17.8%; Filipinos, 12.6%). This finding points to the importance of not only differentiating among Asian ethnic subgroups but also considering Asian within-group variation on acculturation-based variables such as foreign-born status and other dimensions (e.g., ethnic identity, refugee vs. immigrant status, cultural values) when examining alcohol and other drug use patterns. In an earlier study based on the Kaiser-Permanente Medical Care Program data collected from 1964 and 1968, Klatsky, Friedman, Siegelaub, and Gerard (1977) reported the proportions of drinkers and nondrinkers among persons of White, African American, and Asian groups. The majority (57%) of those classified as Asian were Chinese. The data showed that from 15 to 79 years of age, 37% of the 1,744 Asian men and 58% of the 1,989 Asian women in the sample were nondrinkers compared to 16% of the White men, 25% of the White women, 24% of the African American men, and 42% of the African American women.

In a comparison study examining the consequences of drinking, Yu, Liu, Xia, and Zhang (1989) examined national death rates for chronic liver disease and cirrhosis specified as alcoholic. They found that compared to White and Black Americans, the Chinese had the lowest death rates per 100,000 (1.2 per 100,000 age-adjusted death rate).

It is now clear that Asian groups can differ in alcohol and drug use patterns. The most extensive examination of intergroup Asian variation in drug use was conducted by Kitano and his colleagues. Their study sampled 1,103 Asians including 298 Chinese, 295 Japanese, 280 Koreans, and 230 Filipinos (Kitano & Chi, 1985). The prevalence of heavy drinkers was highest among the Japanese (25.4%), followed by the Filipinos (19.6%), Koreans (14.6%), and Chinese (0.4%). On the other hand, they found the highest percentage of moderate drinkers to be among the Chinese (48.3%), followed by the Japanese (41.7%), Filipinos (29.1%), and Koreans (23.6%). The Koreans had the highest percentage of abstainers (61.8%), followed by the Filipinos (51.3%), Chinese (41.3%), and Japanese (32.9%). Those who drank tended to be men under 45 years of age, those of higher socioeconomic status (i.e., more often college graduates in professional occupations), and those living in large cities. As expected, those who drank endorsed more permissive attitudes toward alcohol use and reported socializing with friends who were more tolerant of drinking.

Using the same data set, Sue and his colleagues (1985) studied gender differences in the drinking patterns of the Chinese, Japanese, and Korean respondents. The Korean males and females had the highest percentage of abstainers (males, 55.5%; females, 80.8%), followed by the Chinese (males, 47.7%; females, 73.8%) and Japanese (males, 36.4%; females, 63.3%). The percentage of heavy drinkers ranged from 29.8% in the Japanese to 13.6% in the Koreans and 8.4% in the Chinese. Surprisingly, a substantial number of Japanese females (11.7%) reported that they were heavy drinkers, whereas less than 1% of Korean and Chinese females reported this pattern of alcohol consumption. Kitano, Chi, Rhee, Law, and Lubben (1992) conducted additional analyses of the Japanese subsample and found that Japanese born in Japan were more likely to engage in heavy drinking (51.5%) than were Japanese born in America (17.3%). Kitano and colleagues also reported that there was a tendency for more drinking in third- and fourth-generation Japanese Americans, which the researchers attributed to the impact of acculturation. Sue, Kitano, Hatanaka, and Yeung (1985) also found that a larger percentage of foreign-born Chinese were heavy drinkers than were their American-born counterparts (9.5% vs. 0.0%). However, the opposite pattern was found in a college sample (Sue, Zane, & Ito, 1979) and by Klatsky and his colleagues (1983) in that American-born Chinese were found to drink more. These differences in drinking patterns between foreign-born and American-born Asians might be due to age, regional, and temporal differences in the samples between the Kitano and Chi (1985) and other studies. Nevertheless, the results again underscore the importance of examining within-group variation in Asian substance use.

In another follow-up study, Lubben, Chi, and Kitano (1989) examined the data from the Korean American subsample of the original Los Angeles study (Kitano & Chi, 1985). Korean immigrants were predominantly Christians, and most indicated a strong devotion to the organized church. This strong religious affiliation tended to differentiate the Koreans from the other Asian immigrant groups. Substantial gender differences were found. All but one of the heavy drinkers were male, and more than three quarters (75.2%) of the females were abstainers. The stereotype of Koreans as either abstainers or light drinkers was strongly supported by the data. In addition to gender, several other characteristics distinguished the Korean drinkers from abstainers. Those who attended regular weekly religious services also were more likely to be abstainers. Respondents were more likely to drink alcohol if their parents also drank. Surprisingly, parental opposition to drinking was highly associated with a respondent being a drinker. It appeared that social support sources involving both the family and the church had significant influence on Korean drinking behavior. Three social activities also were significantly related to drinking. Relative to abstainers, drinkers more often participated in sports; went to bars, taverns, and/or nightclubs; and played indoor games (e.g., cards).

Cross-National Studies on Asian Drug Use

The Asian American population still is predominantly an immigrant population with more than 70% of the Asians born outside of the United States. East Asian countries are the primary source of this immigration. Consequently, the drug use prevalence rates found in these countries must be considered as a major influence of substance use patterns in Asian American communities in the United States.

Yu et al. (1989) reviewed epidemiological data collected on alcohol use among Chinese individuals from several different localities including the United States, Taiwan, and China. The investigators believed that the generalization that the Chinese are nondrinkers needed to be reexamined in light of the more recent findings. Using the translated version of the Diagnostic Interview Schedule-III, they interviewed a random sample of 3,098 individuals in Shanghai. In terms of the frequency of drinking, the study found that 60% of the Shanghainese men and 93% of the women had abstained from drinking. In terms of drinking pattern, 29% of the men and 7% of the women drank occasionally, and 11% of the men and 1% of the women drank sometimes. Only 1.7% of the Chinese had drunk daily for a month or more during their lifetimes. Of these individuals, only 26.4% were found to be problem drinkers in that they met the DSM-III criteria for alcohol abuse or dependence. As in other studies, the large majority of the problem drinkers were men. An examination of the elderly, those age 50 years or over, indicated that lifetime abstention rates for alcohol decrease with increasing age. In the 50- to 64-year-old age group, 59% of the Chinese elderly had abstained from alcohol compared to only 45% of those age 80 years or over. Gender differences in abstention rates also were less pronounced for the older Chinese, as 51% of the older Chinese men and 57% of the older Chinese women had abstained from alcohol.

The Shanghai study findings suggested that alcohol abuse and dependence rates were fairly low for the Chinese, but a study conducted on Chinese in Taiwan found some important differences. Yeh and Hwu (1984) surveyed 5,005 community participants to examine the prevalence of alcohol abuse in Taiwan. They found that the lifetime prevalence for males was 6.4% compared to 0.4% for females. Lifetime prevalence for alcohol dependence was 2.8% for males and 0.1% for females. These rates are much higher than those reported from the Shanghai study.

In a collaborative study of alcohol consumption patterns between the United States and Japan, an extensive epidemiological survey was conducted sampling four groups: Japanese in Japan, Japanese Americans in Hawaii, Japanese Americans in California, and Whites in California (National Institute on Alcohol Abuse and Alcoholism & National Institute on Alcoholism in Japan, 1991). In all the study sites, the proportion of current drinkers (those who drank alcohol within the past year) was somewhat higher than rates found for the general adult population of the United States. Japanese men (91%) had the highest proportion of current drinkers, followed by White men (85%), Japanese American men in California (84%), and Japanese American men in Hawaii (80%). In general, women drank less and the pattern of ethnic variation differed from that found for men. White women had the highest proportion of current drinkers (81%), followed by Japanese women in California (75%), Japanese females in Hawaii (68%), and Japanese women (61%).

With regard to frequency of drinking alcoholic beverages, the data showed that patterns of alcohol use varied across the different locations. A majority of Japanese men in Japan (62%) reported drinking at least three times a week; only 7% of this group indicated that they drank less than once a month. Almost half of the White male drinkers (44%) reported drinking three or more times a week, whereas 13% indicated that they drank less often than once a month. The findings for White men in California were very similar to the national rates (National Institute on Drug Abuse, 1990). However, Japanese Americans used alcohol less frequently. Less than one third of the Japanese American males in Hawaii (32%) and California (29%) reported drinking as often as three times a week, whereas close to one fourth (20% and 26%, respectively) reported drinking less often than once a month. Different drinking patterns were found for the women. White women in California (32%) had the highest proportion of individuals drinking three or more times a week. These women drank more than either Japanese in Japan or Japanese Americans, and their consumption was higher than the national sample of White women (21%). Japanese women in Japan had the next highest proportion of frequent drinkers (21%), whereas the Japanese American women had the lowest proportion of frequent drinkers (9% for both Hawaii and California).

Using the data from the collaborative study, Kitano et al. (1992) compared the drinking practices and norms of Japanese in Japan and Japanese Americans living in Hawaii and California. Their purpose was to explore possible national and regional differences in normative drinking practices based on age and gender. In their reanalysis of the data, they found that the highest percentage of male heavy drinkers was in Japan (32.4%) relative to Hawaii (29.0%) and California (12.9%). On the other hand, the highest percentage of male abstainers was in Hawaii (20.8%) relative to California (18.5%) and Japan (9.4%). Among women, Hawaii (9.1%) had the highest proportion of the heavy consumers of alcohol relative to California (4.2%) and Japan (3.8%). California (26.6%) had the highest frequency of light/moderate users relative to Japan (20.3%) and Hawaii (14.0%). For female abstainers, California (26.5%) had the highest percentage of abstainers, whereas Japan had the lowest percentage (9.4%). The findings suggested that Japan appeared to have the most permissive norms for male drinking, followed by California and Hawaii, whereas the greatest tolerance of female drinking was observed in California, followed by Hawaii and Japan. In general, all three localities were much more tolerant of male drinking than of female drinking. Overall, the respondents from California and Hawaii appeared to be similar in drinking norms, whereas the respondents in the Japanese sample often differed from their American counterparts.

The researchers accounted for the similarities between California and Hawaii and the differences between the Japanese and the American sites by enculturation and acculturation. Most of the Japanese Americans included in the study were children and grandchildren of immigrants who left for Hawaii and California in the early part of the 20th century, so that they have not been influenced by the recent sociological changes that Japan has undergone (enculturation). Instead, the Japanese Americans have been more affected by acculturation experiences as a result of living in the United States. Chafetz (1964) noted that prior to World War II, alcoholic beverages were consumed in Japan, but the incidence of alcoholism was rare. Since World War II, there have been numerous changes in Japanese society including the impact of the American occupation, rapid urbanization and industrialization, and a questioning of traditional values. In modern Japan, when one has been drinking, a person's behavior is attributed primarily to the effects of alcohol and not the person. For example, one can express anger at one's boss while drunk, a behavior that would be unthinkable and unacceptable when the person is in a sober state. There also is an emphasis on males joining one another after work for the comaraderie of drinking. Business executives also have generous expense accounts for entertaining customers with dinner and drinks. It appears that these changes have altered attitudes toward drinking and drinking practices such that a rise in the annual per capita alcohol consumption rate, from 1.4 to 4.6 liters, has been observed between 1951 and 1970 in Japan (Nakuda, 1972). By comparison, Hawaii and Santa Clara show the "effects of local styles and the influence of acculturation" (Kitano et al., 1992).

Drug Use Estimates Based on Treated Cases Data

Another source of epidemiological information comes from institutionalized patient data and prevalence rates of drug abuse based on treated cases. One study (Ball & Lau, 1966) showed that the Chinese were overrepresented among addict populations between 1935 and 1964. Although the Chinese constituted less than two tenths of 1% of the U.S. male population at that time, Chinese narcotic addicts constituted 3% of the 32,209 male addicts treated at the U.S. Public Health Service hospital in Kentucky. However, the investigators concluded that opium addiction among Chinese Americans appeared to be a pattern of the past associated with the early immigrant Chinese male laborers who came to the United States in the 1890s.

More recent data from drug abuse treatment populations provide another source of current data on Asian American populations. Asian Americans in San Francisco comprised 3.3% of all admissions for drug abuse treatment in the 1981-1982 period. Rather than reflecting low prevalence, this finding more often has been interpreted as an underutilization of services because of the great discrepancy between utilization rates and the proportion of Asians in the local population. In San Francisco, Asian Americans constitute 21.6% of the city's population. Asian Inc. (1978), using a key informant needs assessment approach, indicated that the prevalence of Chinese American and Filipino American drug use was lower than that of the general population. A California study in the 1970s revealed that of the approximately 1,000 Asian inmates in that state's correctional institutions, roughly 90% were there for drug-related crimes (Trimble, Padilla, & Bell, 1987).

In an analysis of drinking patterns, Chin, Lai, and Rouse (1991) sampled 70 Chinese male alcoholics in New York City. On the basis of judgments made by the treatment staff, 75% of the patients were diagnosed as alcohol dependent and 19% were assessed as alcohol abusers. Except for 1 patient, none of the patients was involved with other drugs. Most were employed and relatively old. They also had little contact with the criminal justice system. Only 4% had ever been imprisoned, and on the basis of self- and family reports, few were known for violent behaviors. Because few of them had driver's licenses or access to automobiles, driving while intoxicated (DWI) convictions were uncommon.

More than half of the sample drank only hard liquor, usually whiskey or brandy. A small number (17%) were beer drinkers, and none drank wine. On a typical drinking day, 57% of the sample had nine drinks or more. Most of the respondents reported drinking more than half a bottle of whiskey or brandy each day. Typically, they drank slowly but continuously, beginning at lunch or dinner and continuing throughout the remainder of the day. Most preferred to drink alone; only 16% reported drinking with others. Few (15%) patronized bars on a regular basis. These results were similar to the drinking patterns of Chinese alcoholics in Los Angeles (Chi, Lubben, & Kitano, 1989) and San Francisco (Chu, 1972).

The use of data from treated cases to estimate prevalence is fraught with difficulties, sampling bias, and interpretation problems. Along with others, Sue and Nakamura (1984) noted that one of the problems with the treated cases method is that the demand for treatment (i.e., seeking and/or receiving treatment) is not equivalent to the need for treatment (i.e., those in the population who should receive treatment). Moreover, there is convergent evidence that Asian Americans consistently have underutilized drug abuse and mental health treatment programs relative to their respective proportions in the local populations (Sue, Zane, & Young, 1994; Uba, 1994). For Asian Americans, help-seeking behavior is influenced by many factors including one's cultural values, the shame or stigma attached to seeking treatment, the perceptions of the effectiveness of treatment, and the availability of alternative resources (Sue & Morishima, 1982).

Although studies concerning alcohol use and other drug use in the Asian American population are scarce and often use unrepresentative samples, certain conclusions can be reached. First, it would appear that Asian Americans are less likely than other groups to seek treatment for alcoholism. Second, Asian Americans tend to use alcohol less than other ethnic or racial groups. Native Hawaiians are the exception to this pattern in that their alcohol drinking rates are comparable to Whites in Hawaii. Third, a greater percentage of Asian males drink and are more likely to drink heavily compared to Asian females. Fourth, among the Asian American population on the mainland United States, Japanese Americans tend to be most likely to use alcohol and Chinese Americans the least likely. Fifth, the frequency and amount of drinking are increasing in Asians both living in the United States and living overseas. Sixth, it is important to consider generational status, degree of acculturation, specific ethnic group, place of birth, and gender when analyzing patterns of alcohol use in Asian Americans.

A number of culturally based explanations have been offered to account for the differences in alcohol consumption among the different Asian groups. Singer (1972) observed a dual belief about the use of alcohol in Chinese culture. On the one hand, alcohol is attributed to certain negative effects on a person: (a) impairment of intellect, (b) impairment of morals, (c) predisposition to physical illness, (d) sexual impairment, (e) shortening of life span, (f) increased risk of suicide, and (g) increased risk of criminal behavior. On the other hand, alcohol is believed to have beneficial effects if used in moderation: (a) relief of rheumatism, (b) increase in blood circulation, (c) increase in blood production, (d) improvement of mental well-being, (e) relief of exhaustion, (f) improvement of digestion, (g) improvement of complexion, (h) improvement of appetite, and (i) expulsion of intestinal gas. Traditionally, drinking alcohol is sanctioned in defined social situations including banquets, family meals, and ceremonial occasions. Unlike modern and Western societies, in which social drinking is institutionalized and drinking excessively is used as a way of coping with life's stresses, alcohol consumption in Chinese folk society appears to be sanctioned primarily for ceremonial or medicinal purposes. Excessive drinking, secret drinking, drinking alone, and intoxication are highly disapproved by the Chinese. In addition, there is an absence of drinking-centered institutions and social groups in Chinese culture, which prevents people from drinking regularly and to the point of intoxication. Based on these observations, Singer concluded that there should be low rates of alcoholism among the Chinese.

Chu (1972) concurred that although Chinese American use of alcohol is common, the incidence of alcoholism is relatively rare due to norms related to moderation. He studied the drinking patterns of 41 low socioeconomic status, single Chinese males in San Francisco. The results indicated that 60% of the sample were abstainers, whereas only 7% were considered heavy drinkers. He found that there was a strong consensus that drunken behavior was inappropriate under any circumstances.

Koreans have been called the "Irish of the Orient" in part because of a purported proclivity toward alcohol use (Park et al., 1994). In modern Korean culture, importance is placed on males socializing together, drinking heavily, and competing with their friends and colleagues in rounds of drinking. However, the research on Korean Americans has found low rates of drinking. One explanation centers on the role of the Korean American churches in the United States. These churches serve an important function as sources of personal, social, and economic security for new Korean immigrants. The churches also practice strong prohibitions against alcohol use. It is possible that Korean males might greatly curtail their alcohol intake in America in contrast to the larger amounts usually consumed in Korea.

SMOKING AND TOBACCO USE

Since the 1960s, the public has become increasingly aware of the health risks associated with smoking. Long-term smoking has been linked to serious medical problems including lung cancer, emphysema, cancer of the larynx and esophagus, and a number of cardiovascular diseases (Jaffe, 1985). Cigarette smoking is responsible in some way for one of every six deaths in the United States, killing about 1,000 people each day (Cimons, 1992; U.S. Department of Health and Human Services, 1989). Similar to alcohol, the economic costs associated with cigarette smoking are substantial. Each year, smokers compile more than 80 million days lost at work and 145 million extra days of disability. Health costs associated with cigarettes exceed $30 billion annually in the United States (Davison & Neale, 1994). The prevalence of habitual smoking has decreased significantly since 1965 among the general American adult population (Cimons, 1992; U.S. Department of Health and Human Services, 1989), but the prevalence remains higher among Asian Americans, particularly among the immigrant populations. Smoking among youths has not declined as significantly as has that of adults, and the use of smokeless tobacco has increased in recent years (Chassin, Presson, Sherman, McLaughlin, & Gioia, 1985). The research also indicates that if both parents and an older sibling smoke, then a youngster is four times as likely to smoke as when none of the other family members smoke (Davison & Neale, 1994).

Important differences exist in the prevalence of smoking among various racial and ethnic groups in the United States. De Moor, Elder, Young, Wildey, and Molgaard (1989) studied the prevalence of overall or "generic" tobacco use (i.e., cigarettes, chewing tobacco, or snuff) among Hispanic, White, African American, and Asian American youths in the 4th, 7th, 10th, and 12th grades in San Diego. The sample consisted of 3,068 (61.6%) Whites, 969 (19.5%) Hispanics, 553 (11.1%) APIs, and 390 (7.8%) African Americans. Overall, the prevalence of regular use (i.e., those who used tobacco at least once a month) was highest among Whites (25.8%), followed by Hispanics (19.7%), African Americans (17.6%), and Asians (12.6%). Asians had the lowest prevalence of regular users at each grade level and the lowest lifetime prevalence (i.e., those who used tobacco at least once in their lifetimes) at each grade level except the 10th grade. Of the lifetime users, Whites had the highest proportion of regular users (36.5%), followed by Hispanics (31.1%), African Americans (26.3%), and Asians (24.1%). Drug use involving marijuana, alcohol, or other drugs was found to be the most important predictor of tobacco use in each of the ethnic groups. Gender differences among the Asians were large relative to those found for Whites. At each grade level except the 10th grade, a greater percentage of Asian males were regular users (e.g., in the 12th grade, 18.8% male regular users vs. 8.3% female regular users), whereas the gender differences were less substantial for Whites (e.g., in the 12th grade, 31.9% male regular users vs. 31.2% female regular users). The investigators also examined the effect of exposure to adult tobacco use in the home on the tobacco use of the students. Youths who reported being exposed to tobacco use in the home had a significantly higher probability of regular tobacco use than did those who reported no exposure at home. The ratio of regular tobacco use among those exposed to in-home use relative to those not exposed was found to be the highest for Asians, which suggested that the exposure effects were greatest for this particular ethnic minority group.

Landrine, Richardson, Klonoff, and Flay (1994) hypothesized that although peer smoking may be the best predictor of smoking among White adolescents, this might not be the case across different ethnic groups, which could have serious implications for smoking prevention interventions. They examined the rates and predictors of adolescent cigarette smoking among 4,375 9th-grade students from Los Angeles and San Diego counties. The sample consisted of 1,293 White, 514 Black, 1,798 Latino, and 759 Asian American adolescents. Overall, they found that White adolescents smoked more than did minority youths. Whites had the highest frequency of smoking, followed by Hispanics, Asians, and African Americans. There were few ethnic minority differences, and the only significant difference in smoking rate was found between Hispanics and African Americans. Among the nonsmokers, 57.8% of the Asians had never smoked compared to 49.6% of the Whites, 59.5% of the African Americans, and 48.9% of the Hispanics. Asians had the lowest proportion of participants who smoked monthly (34.7%), but they also had the second highest rate of individuals who smoked weekly or daily (7.5%), exceeded only by Whites (9.7%). In terms of predictors of smoking, for Asians, not attending school was the single best predictor, accounting for 17.3% of the variance. Other predictors included smoking by peers (9.6% of the variance) and drinking by significant adults (4.5% of the variance), whereas drug context at school, poor grades, self-care habits, risk taking, and smoking by the mother accounted for minimal variance. This study was one of the first to examine the significant predictors of smoking for Asian Americans. However, as in earlier research, this study did not investigate important inter-Asian variation related to different Asian ethnic subgroups or level of acculturation.

In one of the few studies to examine a specific Asian ethnic group, Wiecha (1996) surveyed Vietnamese, African American, Hispanic, and White adolescents in Massachusetts. Tobacco use among Vietnamese adolescents was of particular concern because studies of Vietnamese adult men have shown that this group's smoking rates are higher than those found in the general U.S. population. Estimates of smoking prevalence range from 35% to 57%. Southeast Asian men have been designated as a high-risk group by the Public Health Service because of the extent of the smoking problem among Vietnamese and other Southeast Asian men. Of the 2,816 respondents from two public middle schools and two public high schools, 8.1% were Vietnamese, 9.4% African American, 19.4% Hispanic, 57.5% White, and 5.6% other races/ethnicities. The results revealed that the prevalence of cigarette smoking among Vietnamese males (27.9%) was similar to that among White males (28.3%) and was higher than that among Hispanic (19.7%) and African American (18.9%) males. Vietnamese adolescent females had a very low proportion of smokers (3.7%). In general, Vietnamese males were less likely to smoke in middle school than were other students but were more likely to report smoking in high school than were non-Vietnamese students. The point estimate for current smoking for older (i.e., age 16 years or older) Vietnamese males (37.7%) exceeded the smoking rates of all other male subgroups in the study and was equivalent to the rate for older White girls (38.0%). In addition, older age, male gender, peer smoking, and carrying of a weapon were risk factors for current cigarette smoking for this group. One of the important social influences identified for the Vietnamese adolescents involved family members who smoked. In particular, 44.2% of the Vietnamese students had fathers who smoked, whereas only 8.1% had mothers who smoked.

Among adults, ethnic differences in the prevalence of smoking also vary by gender. According to the 1985 Health Interview Survey, African American, Asian American, and Hispanic men have surpassed White men in the prevalence of smoking. However, among women, smoking prevalence is highest among African Americans, followed by Whites, Hispanics, and Asians (Martin, Cummings, & Coates, 1990). One study examined ethnic differences in smoking behavior and attitudes among White, African American, Hispanic, and Asian American medical patients who were smokers (Martin et al., 1990). All patients who had smoked a cigarette within the past 7 days were asked to participate in the study. A total of 2,972 patients completed the baseline questionnaire including 1,840 Whites, 675 African Americans, 189 Hispanics, and 131 Asians. The small number of Asians surveyed was due in part to the exclusion of those patients who could not read English or who could not understand and respond to the questions. This process could have excluded a significant number of Asians who were foreign born, particularly the recent immigrants and refugees who likely would have been heavier smokers. The results indicated that Asian smokers were significantly different from the other three ethnic groups in terms of the influence of family and friends on their smoking. They reported less parental smoking, less spousal smoking, and more pressure to quit smoking from both family and friends. The investigators suggested that this might be due, in part, to the greater number of children in the homes of Asian patients. Moreover, Asian smokers frequently cited keeping their children from being exposed to smoking as the reason for quitting. Contrary to previous findings examining gender differences, Asian women smoked slightly more cigarettes per day than did Asian men. However, given the exclusion of non-English-speaking respondents, the sample of Asians probably was not representative of the surrounding Asian American population. Asians comprised only 4.6% of the study's sample, whereas they constituted 14.1% of the population in the four cities from which the sample was collected.

In sum, the research suggests that gender and acculturation have important influences on the smoking rates of Asian Americans. Studies have shown that Asian Americans tend to smoke less than Whites and other ethnic minority groups, but these differences can be primarily attributed to the low smoking rates of Asian American women. Asian American men, especially those who are less acculturated, have smoking rates similar to those found for Whites. For example, Vietnamese male youths had rates similar to those found for White male youths, but Vietnamese female youths had the lowest smoking rate. Moreover, the smoking rate of the Vietnamese male youths exceeded rates found for both Hispanic and African American male youths.

GAMBLING

Like alcoholism and drug dependence, compulsive gambling is a progressive impulse disorder. Gambling has increased substantially in the past decade, and the problems associated with gambling have had profound social and economic consequences for the United States. Gambling expenditures have escalated greatly since 1974. In that year, approximately 61% of the U.S. population gambled (Lesieur & Rosenthal, 1991). At that time, it was estimated that Americans legally wagered $17.35 billion (Commission on the Review of the National Policy Toward Gambling, 1976). In 1988, $210 billion was legally wagered (Christiansen, 1989), and by 1992, the money wagered legally had increased to $330 billion (Volberg, 1996). This represents a 19-fold increase in less than 20 years. Gambling is now legal in some form in 48 of the 50 states. Current estimates are that the large majority of the U.S. population gambles. A 1989 Gallup poll found that 81% of the general population had gambled, with 71% doing so in the past year and 31% doing so weekly (Hugick, 1989). Despite the substantial increase in gambling in recent years, gambling has received relatively less public scrutiny than has alcohol, smoking, and other drug use. Accordingly, a detailed discussion of pathological gambling is presented here, followed by an analysis of the research on gambling among Asian Americans.

Recent prevalence studies have been conducted through telephone surveys involving primarily adult samples (Culleton & Lang, 1985; Sommers, 1988; Volberg & Steadman, 1988, 1989). From this research, the rate of problematic gambling has been estimated to range from 0.1% to 6.3%, depending on the particular location, the prevalence time frame (e.g., current vs. lifetime), the type of gambling involvement (e.g., problem vs. probable pathological), and the methodology. For example, Sommers (1988) conducted a telephone survey in the Delaware Valley and found that 4.12% of respondents were potentially pathological gamblers and 3.37% were probable pathological gamblers. Volberg (1996) reported that 2.9% of a California sample were classified as problem gamblers and 1.2% as probable pathological gamblers. In one of the most frequently cited prevalence studies, Volberg and Steadman (1988) conducted a telephone survey among the adult population in New York. This study found that 2.8% of the respondents were classified as problem gamblers and an additional 1.4% were classified as probable pathological gamblers, according to their scores on the South Oaks Gambling Screen (SOGS). As in the Volberg and Steadman study, most of the prevalence studies have differentiated between pathological and problem gamblers based on scores on the SOGS, in which the latter group's gambling behavior is frequent but the problems associated with the gambling are less numerous and less severe relative to those of the former group (Lesieur & Blume, 1987).

Pathological gambling is a diagnosable mental disorder and is defined in the DSM-IV as a problem of impulse control characterized by "persistent and recurrent maladaptive gambling behavior that disrupts personal, family, and vocational pursuits" (American Psychiatric Association, 1994, p. 615). Pathological gamblers often encounter family, job, financial, and legal difficulties as a result of their addiction. In the family, excessive gambling is associated with increased stress, a pattern of lies and deception on the part of the gambling spouse, increased risk of divorce, and other forms of family dysfunction (Lesieur, 1984; Lorenz & Shuttlesworth, 1983; Wanda & Foxman, 1971). On the job, pathological gamblers are more likely to be less productive and to embezzle when employed by others, and they have high rates of business failure when self-employed (Lesieur, 1984; Livingston, 1974). The evidence consistently shows that pathological gambling is associated with financial difficulties and illegal activities to support an increasingly expensive addiction (Custer, 1982; Lesieur, 1979). Estimates of the prevalence of the disorder in the United States range from 1.1 million (Custer & Milt, 1985) to 9.0 million (Gam-Anon Publishing, n.d.).

Although the type of gambling engaged in depends in large measure on what is available, the preferred forms of gambling seem to be sports betting, cards, casino gambling, and horse racing. Significant problems also are encountered among those favoring the lottery, stock market, bingo, pull tabs, and bar games as well as those betting on games of skill (e.g., golf, bowling, pool). In males, the disorder typically begins early in adolescence (Custer & Milt, 1985; Lesieur &

Rosenthal, 1991). Although a few are "hooked" with their first bet, for most, it is more insidious. There may be gradual dependence or years of social gambling, followed by an abrupt onset of pathological gambling. The latter may be precipitated by greater accessibility and exposure to gambling or by some psychologically significant loss or life stressor.

Approximately one third of the pathological gamblers are female (Lesieur, 1988; Lesieur & Blume, 1991), and the natural history of the disorder is somewhat different for the two genders. Women typically start gambling later in life, often after adult roles have been established. They are more apt to be depressed and to gamble less for the action or excitement than for the escape. Winning big is less important, as is the need to impress. They typically play less competitive forms of gambling in which luck is more valued than skill, and they play alone. Female gamblers are underrepresented in treatment programs and make up only 2% to 4% of the population of Gamblers Anonymous. This is largely a function of the greater stigma for women. There is a high possibility of multiple addictions. They may be simultaneous or sequential. Various studies of pathological gamblers in treatment have revealed that approximately 50% have histories of alcohol or drug abuse or dependence (Lesieur, 1988; Linden, Pope, & Jonas, 1986; Ramirez, McCormick, Russo, & Taber, 1984). According to several surveys of pathological gamblers in treatment or Gamblers Anonymous (Ciarrocchi & Richardson, 1989; Custer & Custer, 1978; Lesieur, 1988), 18% to 43% had a parent who was alcoholic or had a significant alcohol or drug problem, and 20% to 28% had a parent who was a probable pathological gambler.

There typically are four phases or stages in the career of the pathological gambler: winning, losing, desperation, and hopelessness. Compulsive gambling generally progresses in a pattern, with predictable crises and accelerated efforts to recoup losses. The personality traits and social characteristics of both male and female compulsive gamblers include above-average intelligence and education; a need for challenge, stimulation, and risk taking; and competitiveness (Peck, 1986). In the early stages of the disorder, the gambler tends to win and often continues to win because initial luck is replaced by skillful playing and astute betting strategies. During the winning phase, confidence builds along with excitement and the sense that the gambler is exceptional. At this point, the big win occurs; the amount won may exceed a year's salary. The gambler's story almost always includes a big win that sets off the compulsion (Custer & Custer, 1978).

The big win typically introduces the next phase—losing. In the losing phase, the gambler is betting compulsively and "chasing"—betting more and more to get back the money lost. Skilled gamblers know that chasing is a loser's or a novice player's strategy, but the gambler cannot stop himself or herself. The gambler, now betting poorly and more heavily, incurs more and more losses. After income and savings are depleted, the gambler borrows. The irrational belief that he or she will soon win and repay the debt has become a part of the gambler's self-concept and sense of value. Most compulsive gamblers report that the initial experience of borrowing brings a feeling akin to that of the big win. Now the pathological gambler begins to borrow heavily as losses mount—with predictable consequences. The gambler conceals losses and manipulates family members and friends as he or she tries to pay off pressing debts. When legal financial resources are exhausted, compulsive gamblers might turn to loan sharks and bookies. Divorce, imprisonment, and job loss become increasing threats. With fear of exposure and financial ruin, the compulsive better might become paranoid. Some confess their problem to family members and receive partial or temporary help in the form of a financial "bailout." The bailout only defers an acceptance of responsibility. For the pathological gambler, the reprieve is like the big win or an initial loan (Peck, 1986). After the bailout and repeated failures to keep promises to stop gambling, the third and final phase—desperation—sets in. Gambling continues with an "all-consuming intensity and apparent disregard for family, friends, and employment" (Moran, 1970). Eating and sleeping disturbances ensue, and symptoms at this stage include depression, irritability, hypersensitivity, and restlessness.

Anecdotal accounts strongly suggest that Asian Americans may gamble more than other ethnic groups (e.g., Kim, 1996). For example, Lesieur (1989) noted, "Folk wisdom has it that Chinese Americans are heavy gamblers, yet there is no research on problem gambling among members of this ethnic group to my knowledge." In the only study that examined ethnic differences in gambling, Asians gambled the most frequently. Lesieur et al. (1991) studied gambling and pathological gambling among students from six colleges and universities in five states in the northeastern area of the United States. Of the 1,771 students surveyed, 4% of the sample were Asian Americans. Results indicated that Asians had by far the highest rate of gambling (12.5%) compared to African Americans, Whites, and American Indians (rates of 4% to 5%).

METHODOLOGICAL AND CONCEPTUAL PROBLEMS

The research conducted on addictive problems among Asian Americans has been informative in that previously little research, if any, had been conducted on this population. However, there are some important limitations that must be considered when interpreting this information. Many of the studies have (a) focused on the larger and more acculturated Asian Pacific groups such as Chinese and Japanese, (b) used primarily student samples, (c) rarely examined the Asian American groups who might be at greatest risk for addictive problems (e.g., refugees, recent immigrants, adolescents), (d) relied on disproportionately small sample sizes, (e) seldom controlled for socioeconomic and other demographic differences that might be confounded with ethnicity, (f) failed to use bilingual measures, (g) administered translated measures without evaluating conceptual equivalence, and (h) not accounted for cultural differences that might affect self-report or self-disclosure with respect to addiction problems that often carry with them great social stigmas. Although a number of these problems can be observed in certain studies, the most frequent limitations have involved the lack of attention to inter-

and intragroup diversity among Asian Americans, the use of self-report measures, and the infrequent use of culturally based variables to explain ethnic differences in addictive behaviors.

Any examination of Asian American addictive problems must address the wide range of diversity among different Asian American groups. As in other areas of social science research, previous research has assumed or treated Asian Americans as one aggregated, single population entity. Often the intergroup diversity among Asian Americans has gone unrecognized or underappreciated. More than 20 API groups have been identified by the U.S. Bureau of the Census. The diverse nature of these populations is evident on a number of demographic characteristics such as birthplace, age, family income, and educational attainment and achievement. Concomitant with this intergroup diversity are important within-group differences in terms of acculturation level, ethnic identity, primary language dialect, country of origin, and the like. Some of these variables might be important predictors of addictive behaviors for a particular Asian American population. A related problem is the need to reappraise the measurement of acculturation and cultural identity variables. These variables constitute one of the most important domains of individual differences within Asian American groups. Previous research has assumed that acculturation and cultural identity development reflect a bipolar model. This model posits that as people become more acculturated or identified with Western culture, they become less acculturated or identified with their particular Asian American culture. However, studies on acculturation (Hurh & Kim, 1984) and cultural identity (Oetting & Beauvais, 1990-1991) have found that for ethnic minority populations, identification or association with a particular culture may occur independently of identification or association with another culture.

Almost all of the measures used in addictive behavior research on Asian Americans rely on the self-report of the respondent. A number of problems can occur when using self-report measures with certain Asian American populations. First, many Asian Americans whose primary language is not English might have difficulty in responding to items that have very little context in terms of time, place, and person. Second, there often is substantial social stigma and shame associated with having personal problems such as substance abuse or gambling that impair a person's ability to fulfill role responsibilities and obligations to the family or community. Consequently, self-report responses may vary greatly depending on the public or private nature of the measure's administration. Many self-report measures need to be administered under fairly public conditions because many Asian Americans who are non-English speaking require bilingual interviewers who can translate the questionnaire. In these cases, the public nature of the administration might seriously compromise open self-disclosure of sensitive, personal issues associated with addiction problems.

Too often, addictive behavioral research on Asian Americans has been focused at a descriptive level in which ethnic differences are examined. The distinction between ethnic and cultural differences is an important one to make because it appears that the latter constitute the more proximal determinants of addictive behaviors. Ethnic differences refer to variations on those personal-social charac-teristics (e.g., social class) that an individual tends to have simply by being a mem-ber of a certain ethnic group. Cultural differences, on the other hand, imply certain differences in attitudes, values, and perceptual constructs as a result of different cultural experiences. Whereas the former simply involve group mem-bership, the latter constitute a host of sociopsychological variables that are linked to different cultural lifestyles and perspectives. Ethnicity implies cultural differ-ences, but often these sociopsychological variables have not been directly assessed in addictive behavior research. At a minimum, research on cultural differences must achieve two empirical tasks. First, a study must demonstrate that differences exist on a sociocultural variable. Second, there must be some evidence that there is a functional link or relationship between these differences and the behavior of interest, in this case, an addictive behavior. For example, studies on substance abuse either have simply described ethnic differences in drug consumption or have examined cultural differences but not linked these differences to differential substance use.

As in other areas of social science, etiological research on addictive behaviors has suffered from a lack of causal specificity. As Cullen (1984) noted, social science research addresses two general issues: (a) the identification and examination of social and/or personal conditions that motivate, predispose, or increase a person's vulnerability to develop some type of disorder or social deviance and (b) the identification and examination of conditions that account for the *specific* form of the disorder or deviance. Researchers have tended to assume a one-to-one correspondence between etiological factors and a specific type of disorder (e.g., gambling, alcohol abuse) when, in reality, this relationship does not exist, leading to the "fallacy of etiological specificity" (Cassell, 1975). Rather, these conditions often cause all types of disorders reflecting an indeterminate relationship between the cause and a particular disorder. This *problem of indeterminacy* can be seen in the research on stress.

Stress has been an integral concept in understanding how social factors con-tribute to psychological problems. The stress construct has become one of the unifying themes for many sociological and psychiatric epidemiological studies that, over time, have led to a voluminous number of empirical articles (Thoits, 1995). Despite the immense activity that has been generated to identify specific circumstances under which stress predisposes people to develop psychological problems, it is clear that much of this work has been attempts that addressed only the first issue posed in the preceding paragraph; that is, the research has found that although stress is associated with a particular type of mental health or social problem, it also is associated with a wide range of other problem be-haviors. In other words, it has a universal negative effect on an individual's functioning (Aneshensal, Rutter, & Lachenbruch, 1991; Horwitz, White, & Howell-White, 1996; Umberson, Chen, House, & Hopkins, 1996). Most stud-ies on stress cannot address the second question because most designs have pre-maturely assumed etiological specificity and have not concurrently assessed other disorders with which stress might be associated. As a consequence, the second issue has been virtually lost from most discussions about stress and the problem behavior. Similarly, in addictive behavior research, it is unclear whether factors found to be related to one addictive problem, such as gambling, also are, in general, factors that are related to any mental health problem or at least to other difficulties involving problems of internal control (e.g., substance abuse). For example, Lopez-Ibor and Carrasco (1995) found that the prevalence of pathological gambling is higher among first-degree relatives (e.g., parents, siblings) of pathological gamblers (20%). However, they also found that 25% to 50% of all pathological gamblers had first-degree relatives who abused alcohol.

It would be more informative if future research on addictive behaviors placed a more concerted effort on the second issue by examining variables (called "structuring variables") that shape the specific behavioral and psychological responses to stress (Cullen, 1984). More specifically, the research should employ designs that can distinguish between the *nonspecific* factors that predispose or make a person vulnerable to developing pathology and the *structuring* factors that shape gambling behavior and gambling problems. This approach might be especially important in the study of cultural factors. It is highly possible that the cultural context in which addictive behaviors develop may serve to structure the specific form that the addiction takes. In other words, cultural variables might be some of the most important structuring factors for a particular addictive disorder. In this way, we can attain a better understanding of how culture actually affects a person's addiction and its subsequent effects on functioning.

REFERENCES

Ahern, F. M. (1989). Alcohol use and abuse among four ethnic groups in Hawaii: Native Hawaiians, Japanese, Filipinos, and Caucasians. In National Institute on Alcohol Abuse and Alcoholism (Ed.), *Alcohol use among U.S. ethnic minorities* (NIAAA Research Monograph 18, DHHS Publication No. [ADM] 89-1435, pp. 315-328). Rockville, MD: NIAAA.

Alcoholism Council of Greater New York. (1987). *Some facts of the alcoholism industry.* New York: Author.

American Psychiatric Association. (1994). *Diagnostic and statistical manual of mental disorders* (4th ed.). Washington, DC: Author.

Aneshensal, C. S., Rutter, C. M., & Lachenbruch, P. A. (1991). Social structure, stress, and mental health: Competing conceptual and analytic models. *American Sociological Review, 56,* 166-178.

Asian Inc. (1978). *Assessment of alcohol use service needs among Asian Americans in San Francisco.* Unpublished manuscript, Asian Inc., San Francisco.

Ball, J. C., & Lau, M. P. (1966). The Chinese narcotic addict in the United States. *Social Forces, 45,* 68-72.

Barnes, G. M., & Welte, J. W. (1986). Patterns and predictors of alcohol use among 7-12th grade students in New York State. *Journal of Studies on Alcohol, 47*(1), 53-62.

Bootzin, R. B., Acocella, J. R., & Alloy, L. B. (1993). *Abnormal psychology: Current perspectives.* New York: McGraw-Hill.

Cassell, J. (1975). Social science in epidemiology: Psychosocial processes and "stress" theoretical formulation. In E. Struening & M. Guttentag (Eds.), *Handbook of Evaluation* (pp. 537-549). Beverly Hills, CA: Sage.

Chafetz, M. E. (1964). Consumption of alcohol in the Far and Middle East. *New England Journal of Medicine, 271,* 297-301.

Chassin, L., Presson, C., Sherman, S. J., McLaughlin, L., & Gioia, D. (1985). Psychosocial correlates of adolescent smokeless tobacco use. *Addictive Behaviors, 10,* 431-435.

Chi, I., Lubben, J. E., & Kitano, H. H. L. (1989). Differences in drinking behavior among three Asian-American groups. *Journal of Studies on Alcohol, 50*(1), 15-23.

Chin, K., Lai, T., & Rouse, M. (1991). Social adjustment and alcoholism among Chinese immigrants in New York City. *International Journal of the Addictions, 25,* 709-730.

Christiansen, E. M. (1989). 1988 gross annual wager. *Gaming and Wagering Business, 10,* 8.

Chu, G. (1972). Drinking patterns and attitudes of rooming-house Chinese in San Francisco. *Quarterly Journal of Studies on Alcohol, 6,* 58-68.

Ciarrocchi, J., & Richardson, R. (1989). Profile of compulsive gamblers in treatment: Update and comparisons. *Journal of Gambling Behavior, 5,* 53-65.

Cimons, M. (1992, May 22). Record number of Americans stop smoking. *Los Angeles Times,* p. A4.

Commission on the Review of the National Policy Toward Gambling. (1976). *Gambling in America.* Washington, DC: Government Printing Office.

Cullen, F. T. (1984). *Rethinking crime and deviance theory: The emergence of a structuring tradition.* Totowa, NJ: Rowman & Allanheld.

Culleton, R. P., & Lang, M. H. (1985). *The prevalence rate of pathological gambling in the Delaware Valley in 1984.* Camden, NJ: Rutgers University Press.

Custer, R. L. (1982). An overview of compulsive gambling. In P. A. Carone, S. N. Yoles, & L. Krinsky (Eds.), *Addictive disorders update: Alcoholism, drug abuse, gambling* (pp. 107-124). New York: Human Sciences Press.

Custer, R., & Custer, L. (1978). Characteristics of the recovering compulsive gambler: A survey of 150 members of Gamblers Anonymous. Paper presented at the Annual Conference on Gambling, Reno, NV.

Custer, R. L., & Milt, H. (1985). *When luck runs out.* New York: Facts on File Publications.

Davison, G. C., & Neale, J. M. (1994). *Abnormal psychology* (6th ed.). New York: John Wiley.

De Moor, C., Elder, J. P., Young, R.L., Wildey, M. B., & Molgaard, C. A. (1989). Generic tobacco use among four ethnic groups in a school age population. *Journal of Drug Education, 19,* 257-270.

Gam-Anon Publishing. (n.d.). *Gamblers Anonymous* (3rd ed., pamphlet). Los Angeles: Author.

Horwitz, A. V., White, H. R., & Howell-White, S. (1996). The use of multiple outcomes in stress research: A case study of gender differences in responses to marital dissolution. *Journal of Health and Social Behavior, 37,* 278-291.

Hugick, L. (1989). Gambling on the rise: Lotteries lead the way. *Gallup Reports,* No. 285, pp. 32-39.

Hurh, W. M., & Kim, K. C. (1984). *Korean immigrants in America: A structural analysis of ethnic confinement and adhesive adaptation.* Rutherford, NJ: Fairleigh Dickinson University Press.

Jaffe, J. H. (1985). Drug addiction and drug abuse. In Goodman and Gilman (Eds.), *The pharmacological basis of therapeutic behavior.* New York: Macmillan.

Kandel, D., Single, E., & Kessler, R. C. (1976). The epidemiology of drug use among New York State high school students: Distribution, trends, and change in rates of use. *American Journal of Public Health, 66,* 43-53.

Kaplan, H. I., & Sadock, B. J. (1991). *Synopsis of psychiatry: Behavioral sciences, clinical psychiatry* (6th ed.). Baltimore, MD: Williams & Wilkins.

Kim, Y. (1996). Leaving Las Vegas. *A Magazine, 42,* 39-43, 83-84.

Kitano, H. L., & Chi, I. (1985). Asian Americans and alcohol: The Chinese, Japanese, Koreans, and Filipinos in Los Angeles. In D. Spiegler, D. Tate, S. Aitken, & C. Christian (Eds.), *Alcohol use among U.S. ethnic minorities* (pp. 373-382). Rockville, MD: National Institute on Alcohol Abuse and Alcoholism.

Kitano, H. H. L., Chi, I., Rhee, S., Law, C. K., & Lubben, J. E. (1992). Norms and alcohol consumption: Japanese in Japan, Hawaii and California. *Journal of Studies on Alcohol, 53*(1), 33-39.

Kitano, H. H. L., & Daniels, R. (1988). *Asian Americans: Emerging minorities.* Englewood Cliffs, NJ: Prentice Hall.

Klatsky, A. L., Friedman, G., Siegelaub, A. B., & Gerard, M. J. (1977). Alcohol consumption among White, Black, or Oriental men and women. *American Journal of Epidemiology, 105,* 311-323.

Klatsky, A. L., Siegelaub, A. V., Landy, C., & Friedman, G. D. (1983). Racial patterns of alcoholic beverage use. *Alcoholism: Clinical and Experimental Research, 7,* 372-377.

Kotani, R. (1982). AJA's and alcohol abuse. *Hawaii Herald, 3*(13), 4.

Landrine, H., Richardson, J. L., Klonoff, E. A., & Flay, B. (1994). Cultural diversity in the predictors of adolescent cigarette smoking and the relative influence of peers. *Journal of Behavioral Medicine, 17,* 331-346.

Lemert, E. M. (1964). Forms and pathology of drinking in three Polynesian societies. *American Anthropologist, 66,* 361-374.

Lesieur, H. R. (1979). The compulsive gambler's spiral of options and involvement. *Psychiatry, 42,* 79-87.

Lesieur, H. R. (1984). *The chase: Career of the compulsive gambler.* Cambridge, MA: Schenkman Books.

Lesieur, H. R. (1988). The female pathological gambler. In W. R. Eadington (Ed.), *Gambling studies: Proceedings of the 7th International Conference on Gambling and Risk Taking* (pp. 230-258). Reno: University of Nevada.

Lesieur, H. R. (1989). Current research into pathological gambling and gaps in the literature. In H. J. Shaffer, S. A. Stein, B. Gambino, & T. N. Cummings (Eds.), *Compulsive gambling: Theory, research, and practice* (pp. 225-248). Lexington, MA: Lexington Books.

Lesieur, H. R., & Blume, S. B. (1987). The South Oaks Gambling Screen (SOGS): A new instrument for the identification of pathological gamblers. *American Journal of Psychiatry, 144,* 1184-1188.

Lesieur, H. R., & Blume, S. B. (1991). Evaluation of patients treated for pathological gambling in a combined alcohol, substance abuse and pathological gambling treatment unit using the Addiction Severity Index. *British Journal of Addiction, 86,* 1017-1028.

Lesieur, H. R., Cross, J., Frank, M., Welch, M., White, C. M., Rubenstein, G., Moseley, K., & Mark, M. (1991). Gambling and pathological gambling among university students. *Addictive Behaviors, 16,* 517-527.

Lesieur, H. R., & Rosenthal, R. J. (1991). Pathological gambling: A review of the literature (prepared for the American Psychiatric Association Task Force on DSM-IV Committee on Disorders of Impulse Control not elsewhere classified). *Journal of Gambling Studies, 7,* 5-39.

Linden, R. D., Pope, H. G., & Jonas, J. M. (1986). Pathological gambling and major affective disorder: Preliminary findings. *Journal of Clinical Psychiatry, 47,* 201-203.

Livingston, J. (1974). *Compulsive gamblers: Observations on actions and abstinence.* New York: Harper Torchbooks.

Lopez-Ibor, J. J., & Carrasco, J. L. (1995). Pathological gambling. In E. Hollander & D. J. Stein (Eds.), *Impulsivity and aggression* (pp. 137-149). Chichester, UK: Wiley.

Lorenz, V. C., & Shuttlesworth, D. E. (1983). The impact of pathological gambling on the spouse of the gambler. *Journal of Community Psychology, 11,* 67-76.

Lubben, J. E., Chi, I., & Kitano, H. H. L. (1989). The relative influence of selected social factors on Korean drinking behavior in Los Angeles. *Advances in Alcohol and Substance Abuse, 8*(1), 1-17.

Maddahian, E., Newcomb, M. D., & Bentler, P. M. (1985). Single and multiple patterns of adolescent substance use: Longitudinal comparisons of four ethnic groups. *Journal of Drug Education, 15,* 311-326.

Marchand, L. L., Kolonel, L. N., & Yoshizawa, C. N. (1989). Alcohol consumption patterns among the five major ethnic groups in Hawaii: Correlations with incidence of esophageal and oropharyngeal cancer. In National Institute on Alcohol Abuse and Alcoholism (Ed.), *Alcohol use among U.S. ethnic minorities* (NIAAA Research Monograph 18, DHHS Publication No. [ADM] 89-1435, pp. 355-371). Rockville, MD: NIAAA.

Martin, R. V., Cummings, S. R., & Coates, T. J. (1990). Ethnicity and smoking: Differences in White, Black, Hispanic, and Asian medical patients who smoke. *American Journal of Preventive Medicine, 6*(4), 194-199.

Moran, E. (1970). Varieties of pathological gambling. *British Journal of Psychiatry, 116,* 593-597.

Morgan, M. C., Wingard, D. L., & Felice, M. E. (1984). Subcultural differences in alcohol use among youth. *Journal of Adolescent Health Care, 5,* 191-195.

Murakami, S. R. (1989). An epidemiological survey of alcohol, drug, and mental health problems in Hawaii: A comparison of four ethnic groups. In National Institute on Alcohol Abuse and Alcoholism (Ed.), *Alcohol use among U.S. ethnic minorities* (NIAAA Research Monograph 18, DHHS Publication No. [ADM] 89-1435, pp. 343-353). Rockville, MD: NIAAA.

Nakagawa, B., & Watanabe, R. (1973). *A study of the use of drugs among Asian American youths of Seattle.* Seattle, WA: Demonstration Project for Asian Americans.

Nakuda, A. (1972). Urbanization and consumption of alcoholic beverages. *Journal of Human Ergology, 1,* 29-44.

National Council on Alcoholism. (1986). *Facts on alcoholism.* New York: Author.

National Institute on Alcohol Abuse and Alcoholism & National Institute on Alcoholism in Japan. (1991). *Alcohol consumption patterns and related problems in the United States and Japan: Summary report of a joint United States-Japan alcohol epidemiological project.* Washington, DC: Government Printing Office.

National Institute on Drug Abuse. (1989). *1988 National Household Survey on Drug Abuse.* Rockville, MD: Author.

National Institute on Drug Abuse. (1990). *National Household Survey on Drug Abuse: Population estimates 1988.* Rockville, MD: Author.

Oetting, E. R., & Beauvais, F. (1990-1991). Orthogonal cultural identification theory: The cultural identification of minority adolescents. *International Journal of the Addictions, 25,* 655-685.

Park, J. Y., Huang, Y., Nagoshi, C. T., Schwitters, S. Y., Johnson, R. C., Ching, C. A., & Bowman, K. S. (1994). The flushing response and alcohol use among Koreans and Taiwanese. *Journal of Studies on Alcohol, 45,* 481-485.

Peck, C. P. (1986). A public mental health issue: Risk-taking behavior and compulsive gambling. *American Psychologist, 41,* 461-465.

Porter, M. R., Vieira, T. A., Kaplan, G. J., Heesch, J. R., & Colyar, A. V. (1973). Drug use in Anchorage, Alaska: A survey of 15,634 students in Grades 6 through 12—1971. *Journal of the American Medical Association, 223,* 657-664.

Rachal, J. V., Williams, J. R., Brehm, M. L., Cavanaugh, G., Moore, R. P., & Echerman, W. C. (1975). *A national survey of adolescent drinking behavior, attitudes and correlates: Final report.* Springfield, VA: National Technical Information Service.

Ramirez, L. F., McCormick, R. A., Russo, A. M., & Taber, J. L. (1984). Patterns of substance abuse in pathological gamblers undergoing treatment. *Addictive Behaviors, 8,* 425-428.

Schwitters, S. Y., Johnson, R. C., McClearn, G. E., & Wilson, J. R. (1982). Alcohol use and the flushing response in different racial-ethnic groups. *Journal of Studies on Alcohol, 43,* 1259-1262.

Singer, K. (1972). Drinking patterns and alcoholism in the Chinese. *British Journal of Addiction, 67*(1), 3-14.

Sommers, I. (1988). Pathological gambling: Estimating prevalence and group characteristics. *International Journal of Addictions, 23,* 477-490.

Stinson, F. S. (1984). *Use of alcohol by Native Hawaiians.* Unpublished manuscript, CSR Inc., Washington, DC.

Strimbu, J. L., Schoenfeldt, L. F., & Sims, O. S., Jr. (1973). Drug usage in college students as a function of racial classification and minority group status. *Research in Higher Education, 1,* 263-272.

Sue, S., Kitano, H. H. L., Hatanaka, H., & Yeung, W. T. (1985). Alcohol consumption among Chinese in the United States. In L. A. Bennett & G. M. Ames (Eds.), *The American experience with alcohol.* New York: Plenum.

Sue, S., & Morishima, J. K. (1982). *The mental health of Asian Americans.* San Francisco: Jossey-Bass.

Sue, S., & Nakamura, C. (1984). An integrative model of physiological and social/psychological factors in alcohol consumption among Chinese and Japanese Americans. *Journal of Drug Issues, 14,* 349-364.

Sue, S., Zane, N., & Ito, J. (1979). Alcohol drinking patterns among Asian and Caucasian Americans. *Journal of Cross-Cultural Psychology, 10,* 41-56.

Sue, S., Zane, N., & Young, K. (1994). Research on psychotherapy with culturally diverse populations. In A. Bergin & S. Garfield (Eds.), *Handbook of psychotherapy and behavior change* (4th ed.). New York: John Wiley.

Thoits, P. A. (1995). Identity-relevant events and psychological symptoms: A cautionary tale. *Journal of Health and Social Behavior, 36,* 72-82.

Toneatto, T., Sobell, L. C., Sobell, M. B., & Leo, G. I. (1991). Psychoactive substance use disorder (alcohol). In M. Hersen & S. M. Turner (Eds.), *Adult psychopathology and diagnosis* (2nd ed., pp. 84-109). New York: John Wiley.

Trimble, J. E., Padilla, A., & Bell, C. S. (1987). *Drug abuse among ethnic minorities.* Rockville, MD: National Institute on Drug Abuse.

Uba, L. (1994). *Asian Americans: Personality patterns, identity, and mental health.* New York: Guilford.

Umberson, D., Chen, M. D., House, J. S., & Hopkins, K. (1996). The effect of social relationships on psychological well-being: Are men and women really so different? *American Sociological Review, 61,* 837-857.

U.S. Bureau of the Census. (1990). *Statistical abstract of the United States* (110th ed.). Washington, DC: Government Printing Office.

U.S. Department of Health and Human Services. (1981). *The fourth special report to the United States Congress on alcohol and health.* Washington, DC: Alcohol, Drug Abuse, and Mental Health Administration.

U.S. Department of Health and Human Services. (1989). *Reducing the health consequences of smoking: 25 years of progress* (DHHS Publication No. CDC 89-84-11). Washington, DC: Author.

Volberg, R. A. (1996). Prevalence studies of problem gambling in the United States. *Journal of Gambling Studies, 12,* 111-128.

Volberg, R. A., & Steadman, H. J. (1988). Refining prevalence estimates of pathological gambling. *American Journal of Psychiatry, 145,* 502-505.

Volberg, R. A., & Steadman, H. J. (1989). Prevalence estimates of pathological gambling in New Jersey and Maryland. *American Journal of Psychiatry, 146,* 1618-1619.

Wanda, G., & Foxman, J. (1971). *Games compulsive gamblers, wives and families play.* Downey, CA: Gam-Anon Publishing.

Wiecha, J. M. (1996). Differences in patterns of tobacco use in Vietnamese, African-American, Hispanic, and Caucasian adolescents in Worcester, Massachusetts. *American Journal of Preventive Medicine, 12,* 29-37.

Wilson, J. R., McClearn, G. E., & Johnson, R. C. (1978). Ethnic variation in use and effects of alcohol. *Drug and Alcohol Dependence, 3,* 147-151.

Yeh, E., & Hwu, H. (1984). *Alcohol abuse and dependence in a Chinese metropolis: Findings from an epidemiologic study in Taipei City.* Paper presented at the Third Pacific Congress of Psychiatry, Seoul, Korea.

Yu, E. S. H., Liu, W. T., Xia, Z., & Zhang, M. (1989). Alcohol use, abuse, and alcoholism among Chinese Americans: A review of the epidemiological data. In National Institute on Alcohol Abuse and Alcoholism (Ed.), *Alcohol use among U.S. ethnic minorities* (NIAAA Research Monograph 18, DHHS Publication No. [ADM] 89-1435, pp. 329-341). Rockville, MD: NIAAA.

Zane, N., & Kim, J. (1994). Substance use and abuse among Asian Americans. In N. Zane, D. Takeuchi, & K. Young (Eds.), *Confronting critical health issues of Asian and Pacific Islander Americans.* Thousand Oaks, CA: Sage.

NAME INDEX

SUBJECT INDEX

Absenteeism, 339

Abuse. *See* Family violence

Academic achievement
  career development and vocational behaviors, 375, 384-385
  conclusions, 354-355
  curricular and extracurricular activities, 339
  degrees, higher education, 349-353
  desegregation of schools, 422-423
  elementary/secondary schools, 327-333
  enrollment in higher education institutions, 345-349
  expectations, educational, 91-92
  faculty and administration in higher education, 353-354
  families, 90-93
  graduate and professional schools admissions, 340-345
  heterogeneity, intragroup, 60, 152, 333
  high school graduation and college admissions test scores, 333-340
  model minority stereotype, 18, 152-154, 325-326
  parental attitudes about schooling, 141-142
  parsing research questions, 22-23
  policy implications, 355
  psychopathology, 463
  racism, 412-413
  statistics on, 26
  student population, 14

Acculturation process
  Acculturation Rating Scale for Mexican Americans, 56
  developmental states influencing, 53
  elderly population, 184-186
  ethnic groups, distinguishing among, 54-57, 64-65
  ethnic identity contrasted with, 291-292
  families, 84, 123
  heterogeneity, intragroup, 86
  identity, the Asian American, 291-292, 306-310
  immigration, 433-434
  independent model, 309-310
  internment during World War II, Japanese, 448-449
  interracial dating and intermarriage, 250-251
  label, Asian American, 62
  lifestyle habits, 123
  linear model, 307-309
  parent-child relationships, 140
  psychopathology, 489
  psychotherapy, 493-494
  research methods in Asian American psychology, 310-313
  selective, 198
  Vietnamese Americans, 185, 196

Acetaldehyde, 460

Acquiescent response, 40

Active coping, 190

Adaptation, issues of

ABOUT THE EDITORS
AND CONTRIBUTORS

EDITORS

Lee C. Lee, Ph.D., is Professor of Developmental Psychology and Asian Studies at Cornell University. She currently is Director of Graduate Studies in the Graduate Field of Human Development. She was the Founding Director of the Asian American Studies Program at Cornell. Her research is in the areas of psychosocial well-being of Asian American children and youths and in various aspects of the socialization of children. Her interest in differentiating ethnicity and culture takes her around the world to study Chinese children in different countries.

Nolan W. S. Zane, Ph.D., is Associate Professor in the Graduate School of Education and the Department of Asian American Studies at the University of California, Santa Barbara. He also is Research Faculty of the National Research Center on Asian American Mental Health and serves as the leader of the center's research program on treatment process and outcomes. His research interests include the development and evaluation of culturally responsive treatments for Asian and other ethnic minority clients, change mechanisms in treatment, program evaluation of substance abuse and mental health programs, and the cultural determinants of addictive behaviors among Asian Americans. His current research focuses on cultural differences in the role of loss of face in interpersonal relationships with a special focus on client-care provider interactions.

CONTRIBUTORS

Jean Lau Chin, Ed.D., is President of CEO Services in Newton, Massachusetts, and Assistant Professor in the Department of Community Health at Tufts University. She was Executive Director of the South Cove Community Health Center

583

in Boston for 9 years. She has been active in policy and advocacy related to community health and mental health through her participation on many national boards and federal planning committees.

Kevin M. Chun, Ph.D., is Assistant Professor in the Department of Psychology at the University of San Francisco. His research interests include the psychological adjustment of traumatized Asian American populations, with particular attention to Southeast Asian refugees and cultural conflict issues among Asian American families.

Karen L. Eastman, Ph.D., is Postdoctoral Fellow in the Neuropsychiatric Institute at the University of California, Los Angeles. She conducts research on the referability of child and adolescent problems for mental health services and on the relationship between parenting styles and child outcomes.

Angela Ebreo, A.M., is Postdoctoral Fellow in the Department of Behavioral Science, College of Medicine, University of Kentucky. Her research interests include cultural differences in social support and health maintenance, ethnic minority identity, and culturally sensitive research methodology.

Diane C. Fujino, Ph.D., is Assistant Professor in the Department of Asian American Studies at the University of California, Santa Barbara. Her research and teaching interests include examining the intersection of race, class, and gender in interracial relationships, discrimination and coping among women of color, and grassroots political activism among Asian American women.

Jayjia Hsia, Ph.D., is retired. She was a Senior Research Scientist at the Educational Testing Service, where her research focused on the academic and professional progress of Asian Americans.

Larke N. Huang, Ph.D., is Consulting Psychologist with the National Technical Assistance Center for Children's Mental Health Services at the Georgetown University Center for Child Health and Mental Health Policy. Her research and teaching interests focus on acculturation influences on mental health and on developmental issues for ethnic and racially diverse youths.

Jeannie Huh-Kim, Ph.D., is Clinical Assistant Professor at the California School of Professional Psychology in Los Angeles. Her current research interests include value conflicts in families, psychological distress among adolescents, ethnic identity development, acculturation and immigration issues, addictive behaviors, and Asian American mental health issues.

Harry H. L. Kitano, Ph.D., is Professor in the Department of Social Welfare and the Department of Sociology at the University of California, Los Angeles. His research focuses on race relations, racism, ethnic identity, intergenerational issues,

Asian American mental health, and the Japanese American relocation and redress experience.

Frederick T. L. Leong, Ph.D., is Associate Professor of Psychology at Ohio State University. His major research interests are in career development of ethnic minorities, cross-cultural psychotherapy, Asian American psychology, and organizational behavior.

Angela Lew, Ph.D., is Staff Psychologist at Madison Center and Hospital in South Bend, Indiana. She has authored articles on adolescents, depression, and Asian American identity issues.

Nancy Linn, M.A., M.S., is a doctoral student in quantitative psychology at the University of Illinois, Urbana-Champaign. Her research focuses on time-series analysis, multivariate statistics, cultural/ethnic self-identification, and environmental psychology.

Joyce L. Lum, Ph.D., is Senior Staff Psychologist at the University of Oregon's Counseling Center. Her clinical and research interests focus on women's issues, communication in relationships, multiracial issues, and forms of emotional expression among Asian Americans.

Winnie S. Mak, M.A., is a doctoral student in clinical psychology at the Counseling/Clinical/School Psychology Program of the University of California, Santa Barbara. Her research interests include cultural value differences, symptomatology of mental disorders among Asian Americans, and culturally sensitive psychological assessment.

Osvaldo F. Morera, Ph.D., is Postdoctoral Fellow at the Survey Research Laboratory at the University of Illinois, Chicago. He has investigated factors related to smoking cessation and various aspects of decision making.

Donna K. Nagata, Ph.D., is Associate Professor of Psychology at the University of Michigan. Her research interests focus on Asian American mental health, interpersonal interaction, family processes, and the long-term psychosocial effects of the World War II internment on Japanese Americans.

Samuel S. Peng, Ph.D., is Acting Director of the Statistical Standards and Service Group of the National Center for Education Statistics in the U.S. Department of Education. He has conducted research addressing issues relating to disadvantaged children, minority students, and mathematics and science education.

Maria P. P. Root, Ph.D., is Associate Professor of American Ethnic Studies at the University of Washington. Her research and clinical interests include multiracial identity, interracial families, Asian American women, and Asian American mental health.

Jane Takahashi Sato, Ph.D., was a Postdoctoral Fellow in the Asian American Studies program at the University of California, Los Angeles. Her research interests focus on cross-cultural issues among Asian poplulations in Hawaii.

David Sue, Ph.D., is Professor of Psychology at Western Washington University. His research centers on issues of multicultural counseling, the Asian American personality, and assertiveness training.

Derald W. Sue, Ph.D., is Professor of Psychology at the California School of Professional Psychology and California State University, Hayward, and is President Elect of the Society for the Psychological Study of Ethnic Minority Issues. He has published extensively on multicultural counseling and therapy and on identity development issues.

Stanley S. Sue, Ph.D., is Professor of Psychology and Psychiatry at the University of California, Davis, Director of the National Research Center on Asian American Mental Health, and Director of the Asian American Studies Program. His research has been devoted to ethnic/cultural influences on mental health services, psychological adjustment of culturally diverse groups, and Asian American mental health issues.

David T. Takeuchi, Ph.D., is Associate Professor of Psychiatry at the University of California, Los Angeles. His research interests focus on the investigation of social and cultural factors associated with psychological distress, help seeking, and service utilization.

Jeffrey S. Tanaka, Ph.D., was Associate Professor of Educational Psychology and Psychology at the University of Illinois, Urbana-Champaign, until the time of his death in November 1992. His areas of research included multivariate statistics and structural equation modeling with latent variables.

K. Victor Ujimoto, Ph.D., is Professor of Applied Sociology at the University of Guelph. He has published articles on Japanese Canadians, multiculturalism, aging ethnic minorities, and the role of information technology in gerontological research.

Grace C. S. Wang, Ph.D., is Staff Psychologist in Counseling and Psychological Services at Stanford University. Her research and clinical interests include Asian American mental health, eating disorders, domestic violence, issues in therapist training, and the development of leadership and cross-cultural competence skills.

Paul T. P. Wong, Ph.D., C. Psych., is Professor and Director of the Graduate Program in Counseling Psychology at Trinity Western University. His research interests include stress and coping, cross-cultural counseling, the role of personal meaning in mental health, and successful aging.

Barbara W. K. Yee, Ph.D., is Associate Professor in the Department of Health Promotion and Gerontology at the University of Texas Medical Branch. Her research interests focus on coping, adjustment, intergenerational stress, and health beliefs among middle-aged and elderly Southeast Asian refugees and their families.

Kathleen Young, Ph.D., is a recent graduate of the University of California, Los Angeles. Her research interests include help-seeking strategies and mental health service utilization among Asian Americans, psychotherapy with culturally diverse populations, and Asian and Pacific Islander mental health.

Ginny Zhan, Ph.D., is Assistant Professor of Psychology at West Liberty State College. Her research examines the relationship between Chinese children and their parents, in particular, Chinese adolescents' perceptions of their parents.